PENTECOSTALISM

PENTECOSTALISM

Origins and Developments Worldwide

WALTER J. HOLLENWEGER

HENDRICKSON PUBLISHERS

Copyright 1997 by Hendrickson Publishers, Inc.
P. O. Box 3473
Peabody, Massachusetts 01961-3473
All rights reserved.
Printed in the United States of America

First Printing—October 1997

ISBN 0-943575-36-2

Library of Congress Cataloging-in-Publication Data

Hollenweger, Walter J., 1927–
    Pentecostalism: origins and developments worldwide / Walter J.
Hollenweger.
    Includes bibliographical references and index.
    ISBN 0–943575–36–2 (cloth)
    1. Pentecostalism—History.   I. Title
BR1644.H65   1997
270.8'.2—dc21   97–35885
                                                        CIP

Dedication

To my friends and teachers in the Pentecostal Movement who taught me to love the Bible

and to my teachers and friends in the Presbyterian Church who taught me to understand it.

To my friends and scholars in the Pentecostal Movement who taught me to criticize and understand Pentecostalism's weaknesses and blind spots

and to the friends and scholars in the universal Church who showed me Pentecostalism's strengths and potentials.

To the ex-Pentecostals who were wounded and broken by Pentecostalism and who couldn't help but respond by fighting their former friends and to the new converts to Pentecostalism who found an inspiring spirituality and new life in Pentecostalism.

All these are included in my prayers which accompany this book.

Table of Contents

CHAPTER**ONE**

Introduction

Little did I know when I started Pentecostal research almost forty years ago that at the end of my academic career I would return to this very topic. In fact my wife, who has followed my theological pilgrimage patiently and critically—thank God for a critical and questioning wife—asked me: "Why do you invest so much work in this book? Your academic career is completed."

If one's wife asks such a question, one had better have a convincing answer. My answer was: The main reason is not the stupendous growth of Pentecostalism/Charismatism/Independentism from zero to almost 500 million in less than a century, a growth which is unique in church history not excluding the early centuries of the church. The main reason is that Pentecostalism "has come to a crossroads."[1] From its own ranks there comes the challenge for a critical historiography, for social and political analysis, for a more differentiated treatment of the work of the Spirit, for a spirituality which does not blend out critical thinking, for a new appraisal of pre-Christian cultures in their own Third World sister churches, for ecumenical openness and dialogue. This story must be told, all the more as this is not understood by Pentecostals as a concession to the world or the ecumenical movement but as a more thorough reading of their own past. The details are worked out in this volume. It is difficult to predict which way the major Pentecostal churches, the Charismatic Renewal Movement, and the Pentecostal or Pentecostal-like "non-white indigenous churches" (Barrett) in the Third World will go. It is my hope and my prayer that this volume will perhaps help Pentecostals

---

[1] Faupel, "Whither?" 9–27, quote, 10. See also Robeck, "Where?" 1.

and non-Pentecostals to a more genuine understanding of what it means to be a Pentecostal.

Compared to the earlier volume, *The Pentecostals*, this is a thoroughly theological book, but it tells theology in the form of histories. This seems to me to be a form of scholarly treatment which is more appropriate to the contextual spiritualities of Pentecostalism than propositional, so-called universal statements and discussion, because it places Pentecostal convictions and practices in their different cultural contexts. This is already visible in the complex analysis of the five historical roots. Graphically this can be presented as follows:

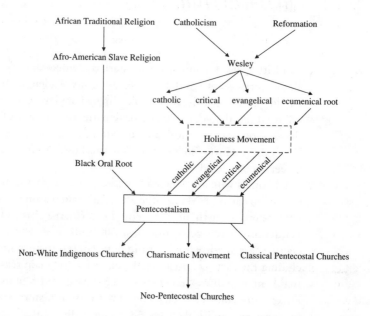

I am not the only one who has discovered the significance of our topic for religion, politics and the future of our world. Harvey Cox, famous for his *The Secular City*, in contrast to the general ignorance on the subject in academia, writes: "A religious movement that already encompasses nearly half a billion people and is multiplying geometrically should not be dismissed so easily." Cox cites eminent sociologists as projecting that "by early in the next century, Pentecostals in all their variegated manifestations will outnumber both Catholics and Protestants." However, "its real growth area is not in America, not on television and not among white people"[2] but in the Third World, because it represents a certain "down-to-earth this-worldliness Christian secularity."[3]

---

[2] Cox, "Why," 3–8, 47, quote, 8. On Cox see Hollenweger, *Wie*, 142–45 and *ITh* 2, 35f, 39, 123; *ITh* 3, 164, 176–78.

[3] Cox, "Reflections," 29–34, quote 31. For Cox's pertinent critique mainly on North American Pentecostalism, see ch. 16, pp. 213f.

That makes it attractive. Is this why a prestigious Presbyterian Church, the Riverside Church, New York, has appointed of all people a black Pentecostal, Professor James A. Forbes[4] from Union Theological Seminary, as pastor, without asking him to give up his Pentecostal affiliation? I suppose it will take some time before European universities and cathedrals will look for help from Pentecostals. But who knows?

"Pentecostal spirituality is the future," says Werner Hoerschelmann,[5] one of the "Hauptpastoren" of the Lutheran Church in Hamburg. For many years, Hans-Jürgen Becken, a German specialist of the African Independent Churches, points not only to the growth but also to the theological and medical contribution of these churches. From an encounter with them he expects not only help in "solving the apparent crisis of our Western Health services but also a change of heart of the individual, be he or she medical doctor or patient."[6] John A. Mackay, the grand old man of Presbyterianism and ecumenism, one-time president of Princeton Theological Seminary, has said that "the true hope of ecumenism is the charismatic renewal,"[7] for "uncouth life is better than aesthetic death."[8] That Pentecostalism and ecumenism must find a way of working together much more intensely seems clear to any informed observer. This will require repentance on both sides, and organizational, financial and theological commitment. After all, the World Council of Churches actively sought the cooperation of the Orthodox Churches (a very much smaller segment of Christianity) and did this—rightly so, I think—at great political and financial risk. So why not with the Pentecostals?

It seems that the World Council of Churches is slowly moving in this direction. On the question "Whither World Council of Churches?" its general secretary, Konrad Raiser, had this to say: "The present growth of Christianity is almost entirely due to Pentecostal and evangelical churches . . . This means for the World Council of Churches that it has to open itself to these new manifestations of Christian existence, Christian church, and Christian witness."[9]

From the Pentecostal side the problem has also been recognized as will be seen in section V (pp. 334–88). As the Pentecostal ecumenist Cecil M. Robeck, Jr. says: "Ultimately, the Twentieth Century will be evaluated by church historians as the century in which the Holy Spirit birthed and nurtured two great movements: one of them formally known as the Ecumenical Movement, the other one, hardly acknowledging itself as ecumenical, the Pentecostal/Charismatic Movement. These two movements have had much in common, but have rarely acknowledged the hand or Spirit of God as being present in

---

[4] Stout, "Forbes," 34.
[5] Hoerschelmann, "Machtfaktor," 67–70, quote 67.
[6] Becken, "Afrikanisches," 166.
[7] John A. Mackay in an interview, quoted in Curlee/Curlee, *Springtime,* 79.
[8] Mackay, *Ecumenics,* 198.
[9] Raiser, "Interview," 5.

the other." And Dale T. Irvin adds that Pentecostals have yet to act on the ecumenical theology of their founder, William J. Seymour.[10]

Critical discussion with Non-Pentecostals can be seen in the growing interest of Pentecostal theologians in the work of Jürgen Moltmann. They discuss with him in writing and face to face. The *Journal of Pentecostal Theology* has dedicated a whole issue to Moltmann's *The Spirit of Life*. Pentecostal theologians seem to be well informed on the whole work of Moltmann, at least as far as it has appeared in English. Some read his books also in German. They welcome his overcoming of the Filioque (chapter 17, pp. 218–22), his emphasis on pneumatology, his attempt to include experience in theological reflection. However, they regret that he seems to be unaware of the growing scholarly literature of charismatics and Pentecostals.[11] Moltmann defends himself against this reproach. He declares himself as a German theologian, influenced by Luther, Melanchton, Kant, Hegel, and Barth.[12] For these reasons specific questions of the Pentecostals did not find an echo in his opus. This is of course true. Only, it also shows the narrowness of what we call scholarly theology. Moltmann says against the reproach of the Pentecostals, that he "was unfortunately never 'the World Council of Churches' theologian.' "[13] In spite of this he has always been very alert on the ecumenical development. If such a theologian must confess his ignorance on such an important issue, how would his colleagues fare? This is unfortunate and will have to change in the future if European theology is not to become the ideology of some "Western European tribes."

One of the most difficult but also most promising areas of ecumenical cooperation is prayer—prayer in public. Public prayer is very difficult because one has to find a balance between exhibitionism on the one side and religious trivialities on the other. The cultural and psychological differences between a Latin American and a German praying, between a Pentecostal and a Lutheran praying, are enormous. Nevertheless, I believe there are ways of praying together, not least the Lord's Prayer.

For many years I have tried to formulate prayers in which religious and non-religious people, people of the high-voltage religion of the Pentecostals and of the low-tension religion of the main-line churches can join. I have inserted some of these in this volume.[14]

---

[10] Robeck, in his review of Jerry L. Sandidge, *Roman Catholic/Pentecostal Dialogue* in *Pneuma* 11/2, 1989, 135–37, quote 135. Irvin, "One Bond," 53.

[11] Stibbe, "Appraisal," 5–16; Kuzmič, "War-Time Reading," 17–24, esp. 23; Macchia, "Response," 25–33, esp. 33; Chan, "Asian," 35–40; Sepúlveda, "Perspective," 41–49; Lapoorta, "African," 51–58.

[12] Moltmann, "Response," 59–70, esp. 60.

[13] Ibid., 61.

[14] Prayers on pp. 40 (earthworm), 80 (caterpillar), 180 (mosquito), 199–200 (turtle), 216–217 (cow), 286–87 (singing bird), 387–88 (frog), 400 (ostrich).

Dear God,
My father says that I am too small.
My mother says that I am slow.
My teacher says that I am a dreamer.
My boss says that the others are better.
My colleagues say that I lack solidarity.
My lieutenant says that I am a coward.
My pastor says that I am a sinner.
My wife says that others earn more.
My children say that I am old-fashioned.
And you, my God, what do you say?
You say that you made me in your likeness.

This book contains many quotations. They are important, at any rate more important than my interpretation, for I intend to document the state of discussion at a decisive moment of Pentecostal/Charismatic history. These quotations are almost without exception drawn from scholarly articles. I could almost entirely omit propaganda, polemics, and devotional literature. I am looking for readers of the kind which I have described in the dedication: Pentecostal/Charismatics and their opponents but also those who long for the renewal of the Church. Where I use formulations which might hurt a reader, I ask for forgiveness in advance. My intention is not to hurt, but to challenge. Writing a theological book on such a controversial topic can only be done in the hope of mercy, both from God and the readers.

This book is not a translation from the German. I tried to write it in English. I am grateful to Joan Pearce, my former secretary from Birmingham, for helping me. Other people too have generously helped me. Professors Robeck and Spittler, both Assemblies of God ministers from Fuller Theological Seminary, Pasadena, have graciously supplied me with information and have frequently discussed the content of this book. William Faupel, Professor at Asbury Theological Seminary, Wilmore, Kentucky, and one of my former doctoral students, has supplied me regularly with news from the Society for Pentecostal Studies. Other Pentecostal researchers have sent me articles and books and kept me informed on important trends. Credit is given to them wherever I have used their material. Finally, I want to thank the publisher for his patience and encouragement.

Krattigen, Switzerland
September 28, 1997
Seventy-five years after the death of the black founder of the
Charismatic/Pentecostal movement, William J. Seymour

CHAPTER TWO

Saints in Birmingham

The following story tries to cover all aspects of Charismatic/Pentecostal spirituality in order to give an introduction to this type of religion. The main character (Mr. Chips) is of course fictional[1] but the events either are documented or have been observed by me. The "memorial service" at the end of the story was—at the time of writing—wishful thinking. In the meantime great progress has been made.[2] The story started as a lecture at the consultation between the Charismatic Movement and the World Council of Churches at Bossey[3] and has since been reprinted several times.

As Mr. Chips approached the city center the taxi driver pointed out the Rotunda, an elegant thirty-story building which towered over the shopping center. The traffic came to a halt and the taxi stopped. Chips saw the blue lights of police cars and ambulances and heard their familiar siren. A police loudspeaker announced: "This is an emergency. Will all taxi drivers please come to the Rotunda. They are urgently needed." The taxi driver said, "Sorry!" and leaned back to open the cab door. Before Chips realized what was happening he found himself standing on the pavement in the cold. Luckily he had just enough time to grab his suitcase.

Bombs in Birmingham

He was sorry that he had never learned to curse properly. Now, he thought, he could have used a few strong words—but after all he was a well-educated man and a grammar school teacher. He started to walk towards New Street Station, but a

---

[1] For the fictional person of Mr. Chips see James Hilton, *Goodbye, Mr. Chips*.
[2] See ch. 9, pp. 106–16.
[3] See ch. 27, pp. 377–82. For earlier publ. see Hollenweger, "Saints."

police cordon blocked the way. A police constable ordered everyone to leave the area immediately because a bomb had gone off in a very crowded pub. When he looked round, Chips could see the broken windows. He walked away but did not know where to go. It was obviously going to be impossible to find a taxi as they were all too busy assisting the ambulances to carry the many injured to hospital. He tried telephoning his friend Shirley Delattre, a French nun, to explain his predicament. He found a phone box and looked for Shirley's number, but a big bang shook the booth. Chips covered his ears with both hands. As he jumped outside the booth he could see that another bomb had exploded on the other side of the street. He could hear the cries and moans of the wounded. Half the street was littered with debris, and Chips could hardly believe his eyes when he saw bruised and bleeding arms and legs lying among the scattered furniture, bricks and broken glass. He ran across the road and helped a woman to get out of the ruins of the bombed building.

"Just like during the war, just like during the war," he thought. "And we have learned nothing." Although the woman was only slightly injured, her face was gruesomely cut by the broken glass and she was covered in blood. Chips gave her his handkerchief. Now the police and the ambulance men who had been working at clearing the pub where the first explosion had occurred came running over to search for further victims. A constable said politely but firmly to Chips, "Please move along. There could be another bomb in store for us." Chips looked at him. "Of course. If only I knew where to go."

Somehow he found another taxi, and the driver told him that he had heard on local radio that over two hundred people had been wounded and twenty had been killed. "It's always these bloody Irish," he added, and shook his head.

"Just in time, just in time," said Shirley Delattre, when Chips arrived at her home. "Tonight you are coming with me to an evening of spirituality at the home of Mr. Hellberg, a well-known orthopedic surgeon." "Wait a minute . . . " Chips grumbled. "No, there is no time for waiting, you can explain everything on the way." Before Chips realized what was happening, he was in Shirley Delattre's French "Ugly Duckling" and off they went.

He cleared his throat and said, "You heavenly charismatics, you don't care a thing about the world. As long as you have your religious parties, nothing else matters. The world could go to pieces or starve to death. . . . "

"Oh, I see," the French nun smiled at him. "You know, my friend, when you come to the Hellberg's you will see for yourself that now is the time to pray and that prayer is more important than mourning and complaining."

Mrs. Hellberg received them personally at the front door and introduced them to the other guests who had already arrived and who were sitting or standing in the big living room. Shirley Delattre told Chips about Mr. Hellberg: He was regarded very highly for his professional skill, although he was looked on as a little bit odd. For instance it was said that he had introduced himself at an official banquet as a carpenter. A carpenter he was, so he said, because he repaired bones. He replaced them, put them together again just as a cabinet maker would repair a precious antique cupboard. In their house the Hellbergs had an old French medicine cabinet made in Napoleon's time. Chips would have loved to have seen it, but he did not have the courage to ask. After all, he had been invited to an "evening of spirituality."

When Jesus Comes . . .

For the moment, however, the atmosphere did not look spiritual to him. People were laughing and talking, and what did he see over there—the manager of the local bank had a whiskey in his hand. Chips greeted him with a nod of the head. Ah, yes, the Hellberg's eldest son was pouring out drinks for everyone. There was white wine, red wine, whiskey, beer, and orange juice. Suddenly a young woman smiled at him and said with a marked Irish accent, "Good evening, Mr. Chips. Don't you recognize me?"

Chips could not place her, until it dawned on him that this was the young woman who cleaned his classroom every evening. In her trousers, headscarf and apron, she looked very different. Now for the first time he could see her shining red hair and her brilliant eyes.

"My sister is with me," she said, and smiled teasingly. "She has never seen a real live grammar school teacher. Moira, come over here!" Moira came across and greeted Mr. Chips. "So this is what a grammar school teacher looks like," she said. Embarrassed, Chips laughed uncomfortably and thought, "And this is what a real Irish revolutionary bride looks like." But, being an Englishman, he hid his thoughts.

Instead he said, "Nice to meet you. What are you actually doing here?"

"For the past year we have come regularly to these prayer meetings," she replied. "When we first came to England, we were lost. The weather and the people seemed so cold. The manager of the bank over there—I clean his bank every Friday—invited us here. He is an Anglican, but I am a Catholic. I wanted to ask our priest if we should go, then he decided to come with us and was astonished to find out that the hosts, the Hellbergs, are Catholics too. English Catholics of course. And what's more, we found quite a number of sisters and monks from different orders here as well. I like it here."

Nobody seemed to have heard about the bombs in the city center. Everybody was happy—Irish and English, Catholics and Protestants.

Mrs. Hellberg lifted her guitar down from the wall and began to sing some short simple songs which Mr. Chips had never heard before. "Spirit of the living God" was one; another was the story of a man—

> Who sat alone beside the highway begging.
> His eyes were blind, the light he could not see.
> He clutched his rags and shivered in the shadows.
> Then Jesus came and bade his darkness flee.
> When Jesus comes the tempter's power is broken,
> When Jesus comes the tears are wiped away.
> He takes the gloom and fills the life with glory
> For all is changed when Jesus comes to stay.[4]

---

[4] Oswald J. Smith, "Then Jesus Came," 35.

Everyone joined in the chorus, "When Jesus comes . . . " The two Irish women had unpacked their guitars and were also playing, whilst a young black man accompanied the singing with an original ostinato bass on his trombone.

The Hippie from Athens

Then Mrs. Hellberg began to recite a kind of litany. It sounded very Catholic to Mr. Chips' ears, and yet it was not Catholic in the way that he expected it to be. The invocation of the saints began with the "bridegroom of poverty, our brother Francis, follower of Jesus and friend of creation." It included Gandhi, "apostle of non-violence, reproach to the churches"; "Good Pope John, friend of the poor, who longed for the unity of all people"; Athenagoras, "patriarch of love" and Simon Kimbangu, "prophet and prisoner of hope"; the "peace-makers," Dag Hammerskjold and Albert Luthuli, Gautama Buddha, "mask of Christ" and "fountain of compassion"; John of Patmos, "visionary and apostle, resister to the World Beast"; Dante, Bunyan, and Isaac Watts, "visionaries and poets, pilgrims of the inner light"; Mary Magdalene, "faithful harlot, first witness of new life"; Bach, Mozart, and Beethoven, "who speak the soul's language"; Darwin and Teilhard de Chardin, "students of the earth, voyagers in the past and in the future"; Einstein, Marx, and Freud, "children of the synagogue"; Menno Simmons and George Fox, "explorers of the gospel, generals in the warfare of the Lamb," and many others whom Chips did not know. Also included were the innocent victims of Coventry, Dresden, and Hiroshima and the more recent ones in Londonderry, Belfast, and Birmingham. ("So, had they heard of the bombs?" Chips asked himself.) Socrates was called "the hippie of Athens," much to the astonishment of Mr. Chips who was after all an educated man.[5]

Mrs. Hellberg continued, remembering the "unwed mother, blessed Mary, wellspring of our liberation." The litany culminated in the praise of "our hero and leader, Jesus the manual laborer, root of our dignity, the prophet who resisted the Establishment, the Liberator, the king because first a servant, the poet who gave us a new language, Jesus, the Son of God, bright cornerstone of our unity in a new Spirit."

Chips was profoundly astonished by this intercultural theology. The prayer meeting went on. Without embarrassment they prayed for personal matters, for sickness, children, their work, the school (here Chips sighed slightly), the churches, their boys in the British Army and their boys in the Irish Republican Army. Again and again they prayed for the Holy Spirit.

"Come, Holy Spirit!" they sang.

A man, whom Chips did not know, prayed in tongues. Chips turned his head in order to hear better, but he could not understand a word. After the message in tongues—silence. One of the Irish girls interpreted. "How could she?" Chips asked himself. Her English was simple and almost without fault,

---

[5] This liturgy in Brown–York, *Covenant*. Discussion in *ITh* 1, 96ff.

something which Chips noticed with satisfaction. At least these prayer meetings were good for the culture of the English language.

Chips kept his eyes open. Something tickled his nose. The Catholic priest sitting on the floor next to him was slowly smoking his pipe. "Well," thought Chips, "is this a party or a prayer meeting?"

Party or Prayer Meeting?

Mrs. Hellberg began to lead the small community in a chorus and then asked: "Does anyone want to read a Bible passage or ask a question?"

Chips would have liked to put his question, "Party or Prayer Meeting?" but now a woman, a late-comer he had so far not observed, stood up. She tried to talk but she couldn't because her words were smothered by waves of violent weeping. Chips was very embarrassed but he was obviously the only one who was. At last the woman began to speak.

"I have just lost my brother and my husband," she said. "Blown to pieces by an Irish bomb." Silence. "I am a Protestant and I would like to ask a Catholic and a Protestant to pray together with me so that the bitterness in my heart does not take root. Please help me to believe in God and to love his children." She sank to her knees and broke down.

The Catholic priest came forward. "Which of the Protestants is going to pray with me?" he asked. Shirley Delattre nudged Chips, but he did not want to be part of this public group-therapy scene. "No," he whispered. Fortunately Mr. Thoroughgood, a teacher whom he knew by name, volunteered. What they prayed, Chips immediately forgot, because he just could not understand how on earth a Catholic and a Protestant could pray together in this situation for peace and reconciliation.[6]

They must be suffering from a mild form of religious madness, he told himself. Then they all sang the Lord's Prayer together and most of the guests left for home.

Chips wanted to leave and to say good-night to Mr. Hellberg, but he could not find him. Mrs. Hellberg explained that her husband had been called out to a patient during the meeting, but that he was now in the kitchen drinking coffee. Chips knocked at the door and went in. Mr. Hellberg was sitting at the kitchen table, his head buried in his hands. The coffee in his cup was cold. Chips would have liked to make his excuses and leave, but the doctor said, "Come in. Come and sit down. My coffee is cold. Let's make a fresh pot."

Chips said nothing and sat down.

"Something is very wrong with little Peter," the doctor continued, speaking his thoughts aloud. "Something is very wrong and I have failed. True 'when Jesus comes the tempter's power is broken.' I have done my job and I

---

[6]On the significance of the charismatic movement for the conflict in Ireland, see McCarthy, "Charismatic Renewal." Idem, *Significance;* Kerr, *Power to Love.* Flynn, *Irish Experience.*

have prayed too. But Peter's leg is not right. And why was it injured in the first place? Peter is not a politician, just a schoolboy. Why should he have been wounded? Now he will never be able to walk normally. Who has done a shoddy job here, Jesus or I, or both?"

Chips felt very uncomfortable. He had never expected to hear the famous doctor talk like this. Mrs. Hellberg came in and joined them at the table in silence, for there was nothing to say. Embarrassed, Chips put his hand into his pocket and pulled out a tract which somebody had given him that evening. He read:

> If you will turn your faith loose tonight you can take heaven home with you.
> If there is going to be any healing for that body in that heaven, there is healing down here now.[7]

Such nonsense, Chips thought, and he decided to put the tract back in his pocket.

Then he realized that the doctor was still looking at him and waiting for an answer. "I cannot answer your question," Chips said abruptly. "But one thing I can tell you. What you have said to me tonight is more important for me than the whole evening of spirituality. I too have my difficulties, but that a famous doctor like you has his doubts, that has been a visitation of the Holy Spirit for me."

On his way home Mr. Chips sang quietly to himself, "When Jesus comes the tempter's power is broken." But he was slightly irritated by the song. Was it not a little bit too simple?

The Memorial Service

The following Sunday a great remembrance and memorial service was held in the Cathedral under the auspices of the Birmingham Council of Churches. In order not to offend either the Protestants or the Catholics, it was decided that John Adegoke, a leader of a black Christian church, should preside. At least half the nave was filled with black people who had come to mourn and pray with the white congregation.

A long procession filed into the church: first a large black choir, followed by the choir and the canons of the Cathedral; then the Chancellor of the University; behind him the Catholic Archbishop and the Anglican Bishop; following them the chief shop stewards at British Leyland and the Conservative Mayor of the city; and finally John Adegoke, Senior Apostle of the Cherubim and Seraphim Society.

A young Negro opened the service with a song. He sang accompanied by a battery of drums and the cathedral organ.

> "When the Holy Ghost fills you
> you can smile
> When you feel like the baptist . . . "

---

[7] From a tract of the "Apostolic Faith" (Portland, Oregon).

and here he interrupted his singing and commented: "You know, brothers and sisters, John the Baptist, the one who had to eat locusts and wild honey. When you feel like the Baptist . . . " And most of the congregation—although not the two bishops—joined him: "You can smile."

"When your heart is full of mourning
you can smile."

The black choir, dressed in long bright gowns took up the theme. "You can smile." The drummers took up the rhythm, first very softly: "You can, you can, yes, you can smile." The choir joined in with full harmony and strong syncopation. And the drummers made their sticks dance on their drums. "You can smile."

The soloist sang the next stanza:

"When they throw bombs at you"

And here he was not able to sing "You can smile." Only the drummer beat out the rhythm and the congregation remained silent.

"When they stare at you because you are black
you can smile."

"Hallelujah, you can smile." The choir began to move and, with short, rhythmical steps, they danced up the aisle into the church nave. Many in the congregation stood up and shouted and sang repeatedly,

"Yes, Lord, you can smile."
"When the National Front throws stones at you
you can smile.
When the Black Power people call you a coward
you can smile."

John Adegoke stood up. "In the name of the Father, and of the Son, and of the Holy Spirit." The choirs and the congregation responded, "Amen."

"Here in the cathedral of Birmingham we all meet as brothers and sisters, members of the body of Christ. We greet the Anglican Bishop, the Roman Catholic Archbishop. We greet Catholic and Protestant Christians."

"And now with angels and archangels and all the glorious company of heaven, the saints of the past from Europe and Africa, including those saints who died this week, we laud and magnify thee."

"Amen," sang the choirs again.

"Let them rest in peace," said the Senior Apostle.

The black choir sang another hymn. It was one of those famous spirituals about the final liberation of all people. Superficially it was a hymn about heaven. "I'm going to lay down my heavy load." Chips knew the spiritual well. It came from Michael Tippett's oratorio "A Child of Our Time." His wife had sung it to him many times.

"What, brothers and sisters, shall we lay down?" asked one of the singers. And in full harmony the choir and congregation replied, "I'm going to lay down my heavy load."

An elderly Negro woman sang the next stanza. She did not only sing with her mouth, which she could open unbelievably wide. Everything about her sang—the well-upholstered hips, the thick legs, the strong arms. Even the large, swaying breasts sang the rhythm of the hymn:

> "I know my robe's going to fit me well.
> I've tried it on at the gates of hell."

And again the congregation joined in: "I'm going to lay down my heavy load."

Chips couldn't help but think of the civil war which was tearing his country apart, a war between Catholics and Protestants, between Irish and English, between the left and the right. Unbidden a prayer rose in him: "Thy Kingdom Come."

When the hymn ended, John Adegoke greeted the few German Lutherans who were also among the congregation. "You know, Martin Luther, the great hero of faith, is their church father," he explained, for he had learned something about Luther in the Theology Course which the University of Birmingham had started for black church leaders. To Chips' great astonishment, the congregation—first the black and then the white—broke out into the hymn: "We shall overcome . . . "

Chips wondered whether they were not confusing Martin Luther with Martin Luther King. Perhaps the two were one and the same person to them. It seems that the dimension of time does not exist for the black Christians. Nearness to them is neither temporal nor spatial. That which moves them is near.

"Yes, good people," the Catholic Archbishop took up the theme, "we shall wonder, wonder and marvel, when we overcome, when we all triumph over our own egoism, when all the saints are marching into the city of golden streets . . . " He had hardly finished when the trombone began to play—it was the same trombonist whom Chips had seen at the Hellbergs. The trombone played: "Oh, when the Saints . . . " The music now came from all sides in any number of variations. "Oh, when the saints, oh, when the saints, oh, when the saints come marching in." And the choir and some members of the congregation stood up and danced and marched through the church.

Then the Catholic Archbishop said aloud, "Amen" and everything was quiet again.

"Friends," it was now the turn of the Anglican Bishop to preach. "Friends," he said, "when the saints march into the new Jerusalem, do you think there will be Catholic saints, Lutheran saints, Anglican saints, Pentecostal saints?"

"No, no," the black Christians shouted and the white Christians looked around. The Anglican Bishop was very surprised—bishops are always surprised when the people of God answer their rhetorical questions—but he continued. "Will there be black saints and white saints, Irish saints and English saints?"

And the congregation shouted again "No, no," and this time a number of the English and Irish joined in.

"No," the preacher continued. "No, there will only be saints. Saints who have dedicated their lives to Christ. But some of us will marvel. In heaven we will marvel even more than down here. You see, in heaven it will become clear, very clear indeed, what we worship. Whether we worship Jesus, the manual worker, Jesus our savior, or whether we worship our own fears and our own prejudices. Yes, it will become clear whether we worship our own race, our money, our church, our culture, and our tradition, or whether we worship Jesus. I wouldn't be a bit surprised if, on the Day of Judgment, all white people stand confronted by a black Jesus . . . " The preacher paused. There was dead silence in the church.

The Bishop continued. "Yes, I wouldn't be surprised in the least if all white people stand confronted by a black Jesus, and all black people by a white Jesus. Amen."

John Adegoke thanked the two preachers and added, "I wouldn't be a bit surprised if, on the last Judgment Day, all Irish stand confronted by an English Jesus, and all English by an Irish Jesus. Let us pray."

The prayer was a silent prayer. Nobody said a word. Only a few sighs were to be heard and some weeping. After the prayer the Cathedral choir sang one of its beautiful traditional hymns.

"Let us confess our sins," said John Adegoke. The Mayor, the chief shop steward from British Leyland and a black lady came forward. They prayed in turn, and in the intervals the choir sang "Lord have mercy."

> "We first sought to win elections
> and not the good of the people."

> "Lord have mercy"

> "We first sought to coerce people into trade unions
> and did not seek the good of the people"

> "Lord have mercy"

> "We thought that first and foremost our people want money
> and we did not realize that what they wanted was honesty."

> "Lord have mercy"

> "We behaved like the churches.
> We believed that we, the vicars of the Unions,
> we believed that we, the pundits of the parties,
> knew best what was good for the people."

> "Lord have mercy"

"And now that our country is in ruins
our youngsters laugh at us
our neighbors shake their heads
We come humbly to thee, O Lord, and beseech thee,
to help us to become human,
human in our industrial negotiations,
human in our political tactics."

"Lord have mercy."

After a long silence, the Chancellor of the University made the final announcements. He said, "Let me ask you a question which puzzles me. Although I am a Christian, I do not understand why it is that we can mourn together but not act together. Why is it that we can sing together but not celebrate the Eucharist together? Will you promise me that you will think about this? It is a simple question of a layman."

With this "benediction" the congregation was dismissed and Chips reflected: A simple question of a layman, certainly, but the most important question.

That was the beginning of a thorough process of re-thinking by the Christians in Birmingham. They pooled their spiritual and intellectual resources—and occasionally even their financial resources—and demonstrated that Christians are different.

I

THE BLACK ORAL ROOT

CHAPTER THREE

The Beginnings

A Black Church Founder:
William Joseph Seymour (1870–1922)

Two worldwide Christian movements were founded by non-Europeans. One is the global Pentecostal Movement, the other is Christianity. The former's founder was a black ecumenist from the United States, the latter's a story-telling Rabbi who belonged to the oral culture of the Middle East.

Both movements owe their initial growth to the oral structures of their origins. The reason for Pentecostalism's breathtaking growth does not lie in a particular Pentecostal doctrine. Doctrinally, Pentecostalism is not a consistent whole, still less if one subsumes under Pentecostalism the non-white indigenous churches and the Charismatic Movement. There are trinitarian and non-trinitarian, infant and adult baptizing Pentecostals, and many other variations. There are even Pentecostal denominations which accepted state subsidies (e.g., Norway, certain Eastern European countries under the communist regimes and certain African countries). The reason for this growth lies in its black root which can be described like this

- orality of liturgy;
- narrativity of theology and witness;
- maximum participation at the levels of reflection, prayer and decision-making and therefore a form of community that is reconciliatory;
- inclusion of dreams and visions in personal and public forms of worship; these function as a kind of icon for the individual and the community;
- an understanding of the body/mind relationship that is informed by experiences of correspondence

between body and mind, the most striking applications of this insight being the ministry of healing by prayer and liturgical dance.

In Europe and North America, Pentecostalism is fast developing into an evangelical middle class religion. Many of the elements that were vital for its rise and expansion into the third world are disappearing. They are being replaced by efficient fund-raising structures, a streamlined ecclesiastical bureaucracy, and a Pentecostal conceptual theology. In Europe and North America this theology follows the evangelical traditions, to which is added the belief in the baptism of the Spirit, usually but not always characterized by the "initial sign" of speaking in tongues.

Things were different, however, at the beginning, during the Azusa Street[1] revival in Los Angeles under the black leader William Joseph Seymour. His story was told for the first time by Douglas Nelson.[2] James Cone is right when he states: "The histories are going to have to be rewritten after reading Nelson."[3]

Who was William Joseph Seymour? He was born the son of former slaves from Centerville, Louisiana. He taught himself to read and write and was for a time a student in Charles Fox Parham's Bible School in Topeka, Kansas. Parham (1873–1929), often described as a pioneer of Pentecostalism, was also a sympathizer of the Ku Klux Klan—he therefore excluded Seymour from his Bible classes. Seymour was allowed only to listen outside the classroom through the half-open door. Nevertheless, Seymour accepted Parham's doctrine of the baptism of the Spirit and began to teach it in a Holiness church in Los Angeles.

---

[1] This chapter is kept short because Cecil M. Robeck is preparing a meticulous history of the Azusa Street revival, in which he will use a detailed file containing the names of all documented visitors and/or members of the Azusa Street meetings, along with a documented history of every meeting in spring and summer 1906, thus giving a minute reconstruction of the revival's religious and sociological development: Cecil M. Robeck, *The Azusa Street Revival* (in preparation). A foretaste is Robeck, "Azusa," 31–36 (with a list of international visitors to Azusa) and in Robeck "Origins," 166–80 (contra Robeck: Goff, "History," 186–91. Lapoorta, "South Africa," 25–33. Horn, "Experience," 117–40. Lovett, "Black Origins." Faupel, "Durham," 85–96. DuPree, *Biographical,* reviewed by David D. Daniels, *Pneuma,* 13 (1, 1991), 86–88.

[2] Sources: Nelson, *For Such a Time as This.* For a thorough review of this important dissertation including its weaknesses see van der Laan, C., *EPTA Bulletin* 4/1, 1985, 13–16. Older literature in *The Pentecostals,* 22–24. See also MacRobert, "Black Roots," 73–84; idem, *Racism;* idem, *Black Pentecostalism;* Hollenweger, "Bonhoeffer," 192–201; Synan, "Seymour," 778–81; Tinney, "Seymour," 33–34; idem, "Blackness," 27–36; Robeck, "Seymour," 72–95; idem, "Taking Stock," 35–60, in particular, 11–14; Brooks, *Azusa Street Revival.* Nelson–Gerloff, "Seymour," 908–9; Irvin, "One Bond," 25–53. Important are the first issues of Seymour's *Apostolic Faith* (Los Angeles, 1906–8), reprinted in Corum, *Like as of Fire;* idem, *God's Glorious Outpouring* (two documentary videos available from CTL Productions, P.O. Box 1428, Whittier, CA 90609). Van der Laan, C., "Portret," 7–11.

[3] Quoted by Clemmons, "True Koinonia," 46–56, quote 52.

Seymour and his black brothers and sisters suffered bitterly. During Seymour's adult life-time 3436 black persons were known to have been lynched, averaging two a week. Innumerable brutalities took place around him, many of them instigated by Christians. In spite of constant humiliation, he developed a spirituality that in 1906 led to a revival in Los Angeles which most Pentecostal historians believe to be the cradle of Pentecostalism. The roots of Seymour's spirituality lay in his past. He affirmed his black heritage by introducing Negro spirituals and Negro music into his liturgy at a time when this music was considered inferior and unfit for Christian worship. At the same time he steadfastly lived out his understanding of Pentecost. For him Pentecost meant more than speaking in tongues. It meant loving in the face of hate—overcoming the hatred of a whole nation by demonstrating that Pentecost is something very different from the success-oriented American way of life.

In the Los Angeles revival white bishops and black workers, men and women, Asians and Mexicans, white professors and black laundry women were equals (this in 1906!). No wonder the religious and secular press reported the extraordinary events in detail. As they could not understand the revolutionary nature of this Pentecostal spirituality, they took refuge in ridicule, scoffing: "What good can come from a self-appointed Negro prophet?"

The mainline churches also criticized the emerging Pentecostal movement, despising the Pentecostals because of their lowly black origins.[4] Social pressure soon prompted the emerging Pentecostal church bureaucracy to tame the Los Angeles revival[5] by segregating Pentecostal churches into black and white organizations just as most of the other churches had done. This segregation, however, did not hinder the Pentecostal denominations from developing on a worldwide scale. Today, Pentecostalism is strongest in those countries of the Third World where an oral mode of communication is almost the only way to spread the Gospel.

Parham or Seymour?

Most Pentecostal historians mention Parham[6] and Seymour as co-founders of the movement. Who was Charles Fox Parham? The most thorough answer is given us in a well-documented biography by James R. Goff.[7] Goff makes clear—and it has not been disputed by knowledgeable researchers—that Parham "invented" the doctrine of "initial evidence." Goff thus states his

---

[4] "The amazing argument that Pentecostalism should be repudiated on the basis of the Los Angeles connection was probably an allusion to the black origins" (Van der Laan, C., "Proceedings," 36–41, quote 39).

[5] Detailed and documented reported by Gerloff, *Plea*, 67ff. (reviewed by Peter Hocken in *Pneuma* 15/1, 1993, 117–19).

[6] One of the first to "re-evaluate" Parham was Kendrick, *Promise Fulfilled*, 52ff.

[7] Goff, *Fields* (reviewed by Augustus Cerillo, Jr., in *Pneuma* 15/1. 1993, 77–88). See also Goff, "Parham," 660–61.

main thesis as follows: "It is Parham alone who formulated the distinguishing ideological formula of tongues as initial evidence for Holy Spirit baptism. That discovery, in effect, created the Pentecostal movement."[8]

Goff describes in detail how Parham developed the "initial evidence" doctrine. In fact, all authentic glossolalia was for Parham xenolalia (that is the ability to speak an identifiable human language without ever having learned it); and xenolalia was to become for him both the "seal" of a missionary's call to a particular mission field and the divine enabling gift to carry out this call. Goff shows convincingly, in other words, that glossolalia did not "fall from heaven" (as it is often described in Pentecostal books). "There can be little doubt that Parham was consciously motivating his students toward this mission tongues concept."[9]

Goff illuminates further details of Parham's life which have not been taken seriously enough in the past; for example, Parham's strict and life-long opposition to medicine and vaccination,[10] his pacifism during World War I, his sympathy for socialism, and his doctrine of "conditional immortality" (i.e., the "destruction of the wicked").[11]

On the homosexuality charge, Goff comes to the conclusion that "in the final analysis the Parham scandal remains a mystery."[12] Too many questions remain open. Where did the rumors come from? Voliva of Zion City was of course highly motivated to destroy Parham—he was his arch-rival. But he could not have invented the charges, although he "produced" evidence which nobody else could confirm. Why was Parham arrested and then the charges dropped, and why can court records not be found? It seems to me that, until further evidence is presented, Parham should be considered as having been "not guilty as charged." Furthermore, the Parham story (and other similar stories) might sometime stimulate Pentecostals to theologically re-examine their approach to homosexuality, especially in the light of newer theological and medical evidence.

In the light of later racial separation in Pentecostalism, Parham's racial ideology and praxis are important. He propagated Anglo-Israel theories and Zionism. I quote verbatim from Parham: "The Old Testament distinction of the peoples of the earth remain almost the same today. The Hebrews, Jews, and the various descendants of the ten tribes—The Anglo-Saxons, High Germans, Danes (Dan), Swedes, Hindoos, Japanese and the Hindoo-Japanese of Hawaii, and these possess all the spiritual power of the world. The

---

[8] Goff, *Fields*, 164.

[9] Goff, *Fields*, 75.

[10] "The devil tried to make us believe that we could be a physician and a Christian too," Parham, Charles F., *Voice*, 18–19; Goff, *Fields*, 28. Parham, Charles F., *Voice*, 46f; Goff, *Fields*, 41. *Apostolic Faith* (Topeka) 1 (13.9.1899), 7; Goff, *Fields*, 43. *Kansas City Times* (1901); Goff, *Fields*, 83.

[11] *Apostolic Faith* (Baxter), Special ed. (25.12.1910), 5 and 2 (2.8.1962), 2; Goff, *Fields*, 153.

[12] Goff, *Fields*, 141.

Gentiles—French, Spanish, Italian, Greek, Russian, and Turkish. These are formalistic, and so are their descendants in all parts of the world. Heathen are mostly heathen still—the Negro, Malay, Mongolian and Indian."[13]

Parham's hierarchy of races, with the Anglo-Saxons on top as master-race, fits well with the attitudes current in the southern US of his time. In fact some Christian leaders were much more racist than he (e.g. Carother), but others rejected all racist theories and attitudes (e.g. J. A. Dowie and parts of the Holiness Movement).

For Parham, to allow W. J. Seymour to follow his Bible studies in an adjoining room through the half-open door was already a great concession. Goff calls this a "benign paternalistic" approach. However, when Seymour no longer accepted Parham's authority without question, the benign paternalism turned into hostility. Parham said that Seymour was "possessed with a spirit of leadership." Now the black Pentecostals were "spook-driven" and "hypnotized."[14] "The paternalistic racism which he had practiced prior to Azusa Street gave way to a harsher, more blatant racism."[15]

Finally, Goff's claim that Parham and Parham alone is the founder of Pentecostalism—because he formulated the doctrine of the "initial evidence" for the first time—must be examined.

I do not want to disagree with Goff on facts (although I suppose there are others who would make the same claim of primacy for Tomlinson).[16] His conclusions, however, are another matter. Goff dismisses W. J. Seymour as the pioneer of Pentecostalism because his ecumenical, race- and class-transcending understanding of Pentecost was by and large unsuccessful in the United States. Therefore the only candidate left is the racist Charles F. Parham. With this kind of argumentation one can of course prove that Jesus Christ is not the founder of Christianity, because the Christian church very soon gave up important aspects of Christ's example and teaching. More ironically, however, if one applies Goff's criteria to Parham himself, he too fails badly. His understanding of glossolalia as missionary xenolalia did not survive much longer than Seymour's interracial understanding of Pentecost. Even the "initial sign" is now questioned. Russell Spittler, an American Assemblies of God pastor, New Testament scholar and director of the David Du Plessis Center at Fuller Theological Seminary, says: "Glossolalia is a human phenomenon, not limited to Christianity nor even to religious behavior . . . The belief that *distinguishes* the movement can only wrongly be thought of as describing the *essence* of Pentecostalism."[17]

---

[13] *Topeka State Journal* 9.1.1901, 6; see also 6.1.1901, 2 and 21.1.1901, 7; Goff, *Fields,* 102.

[14] Parham, Sarah E., *Life,* 163; Goff, *Fields,* 130.

[15] Goff, *Fields,* 132.

[16] E.g., Conn, *Like a Mighty Army.* But Harold Hunter (like Conn, from the Church of God [Cleveland]) dismisses the claim: Hunter, "Spirit-Baptism," 1–17.

[17] Spittler, "Glossolalia," 340. See ch. 17, p. 222.

Parham's pacifism, his doctrine on the "destruction of the wicked," his animosity to medicine, his Anglo-Israel theories, his sympathy with the Ku Klux Klan—all this has been contradicted by Pentecostalism. What is more, American Pentecostalism is not the only kind of Pentecostalism. Take away Seymour's understanding of Pentecost and all the statistical hallelujahs of Pentecostalism are silenced, because there is hardly a Pentecostal movement in the world that is not built on Seymour's oral black modes of communication. Furthermore, Pentecostalism has not yet come to its maturity. It could very well be that it offers the key to overcoming racism in the world today, as some of the more enlightened Pentecostals are now discovering that Pentecost is more than Parham's narrow ideology.

It seems that by now the Assemblies of God have cast their lot with Seymour as founder of the movement. They write: "The Azusa Street revival witnessed the breakdown of barriers which normally divide people from one another: race, class, gender, wealth, language, education, church affiliation and culture . . . The mission had an integrated leadership and congregation—and although it was decades before the civil rights movement, had an amazing lack of discrimination. This did not please all who observed—including Charles Parham, the spiritual father of William J. Seymour. Racially prejudiced himself, Parham came to Azusa Street and denounced the mingling of races and thereafter his ministry declined. God will not bless such hostility toward anyone for whom Christ died."[18]

In the final analysis the choice between Parham and Seymour is not an historical but a theological one. Where does one see the decisive contribution of Pentecost: in the religious experience of speaking in tongues as seen by Parham, or in the reconciling Pentecostal experience of Pentecost as seen by Seymour (which of course includes glossolalia and gives it an important role)?

In my opinion Goff made the wrong theological decision. But that hardly diminishes the importance of his book. By giving all the details of Parham's life fairly and squarely, he makes it possible for the critical reader to come to a conclusion which is diametrically the opposite of his own.

Finally, Azusa fits in with a much larger and older Christian tradition, namely that of a congregation where everybody is a potential contributor to the liturgy. This can be demonstrated in the arrangement of the benches in Azusa: all seats are on the same level; there is no elevated front-platform (where everything happens). See the following comparison between the Azusa Street Church and a rural Kimbanguist church (chapter 6, p. 24).

Other churches emerging in the midst of persecution are the Waldensian churches in the Piemont and the Camisards in the Cevennes (France) (chapter 25, p. 338). Both have architectural arrangements very similar to that of Azusa

---

[18] "Being the People God Called," *PE*, 29.9.1991, 3–7, 20–21 (quote 6). This is an official report of the "Spiritual Life" committee of the Assemblies of God. See also Robeck, "Social Concern," 97–106.

Street. The oral participatory style was not restricted to Pentecostals or to blacks, but can be observed in many other churches of the persecution.

Azusa Street

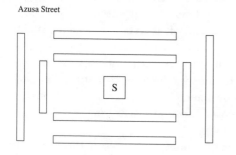

Rural Kimbanguist Church

S = Seymour who acts as enabler and leader but not as the only or even as the most important "performer."

A rural Kimbanguist "church" consists of sticks which mark the "sanctuary" as long as the saints gather for worship. This is the church of a pilgrim congregation in the times of persecution. After the service the sticks are taken out. For each service the "church" is rebuilt. In the middle there is an area for the leader who acts very much like Seymour. No benches!

CHAPTER FOUR

A Kite Flies Against the Wind: Black Power and Black Pentecostalism in the USA[1]

The United States "must choose between democracy and repression, between the republic and a police state; for America cannot keep down thirty million people who are moving up, without destroying the entire nation in the process."[2] This was not written by a critical leftist theologian, but by

A Black Pentecostal Evangelist: Arthur Brazier[3]

In an exact and detailed report, written in the late 1960s, he describes one of the slum quarters of Chicago, the so-called Woodlawn. This is not an idyllic park lawn but a slum area, where 60,000 black people vegetate on two square miles, in

---

[1] This chapter started as a chapter in my *Pentecost Between Black and White*. It appears here in a revised, updated, and annotated version. Documents, literature and sources on Black Pentecostals in Hollenweger, *Black Pentecostal Concept*. Cf. too, *The Pentecostals*, 22–24, 469f. Lovett, "Black Holiness-Pentecostals," 76–84. idem, "Black Theology," 84–86. idem, "Black Origins," (Lovett's pioneering works are a mine of seminal thinking and information). Jones, C.E.., *Black Holiness* (bibliography).

[2] Brazier, *Black Self-Determination*, 5.

[3] Cf. Brazier's "Origin," 3, as well as his official request to the executive board of his church (Pentecostal Assemblies of the World; lit., documents, sources, *Handbuch* 02a.02.139; Hollenweger, *Black Pentecostal Concept* 59–67; Reed, "Assemblies," 700–701) for "guidance in regard to taking part in demonstrations presently being conducted in Albany, Georgia. He read a telegram from the Reverend Abernathy and Reverend Martin Luther King asking either the support of our Bishops or his [Elder Brazier's] presence in the demonstrations. After due deliberation and counsel, we recommend that Elder Brazier be left to the discretion of his own conscience." (1963 *Minute Book of the Pentecostal Assemblies of the World*, n.p., 1963, 63; Hollenweger, *Black Pentecostal Concept*, 67.)

indescribable conditions of hygiene; where garbage is either not, or only partly, collected; where rats and vermin reign; and where the children learn so little in their over-crowded classes that on leaving school they only swell the army of unemployed and drug-addicts.

Brazier protests against this state of affairs. He wants to destroy the myth of the intellectual and moral supremacy of the whites. America, he says, was built on the backs of the blacks. The blacks planted the cotton; but they walked around in rags. The blacks built the railways; but they were not allowed to ride on them. A black doctor discovered blood plasma; but he died because nobody was ready to give him a blood transfusion.[4]

This situation cannot be changed by the violence of arms; only by the violence of non-violence. We black people, he writes, are also for law and order; but not for that law which the white wants to force upon us, which brands as criminals the demonstrators who publicize this appalling injustice, while those responsible are left in peace. We do not understand as law the practice of the police by which a suspect can be shot down as a criminal—making the policeman judge, juror, and hangman in one person. Certainly, Brazier concedes, the majority of the police do not misuse their power. But there are too many who do.

How does the "violence of non-violence" which Brazier advocates work in practice? Brazier's program is one of self-determination for the people of Woodlawn, carried out through the Woodlawn Organization. This organization is at first subsidized by white churches, but it is organized and directed by the blacks of the slum area. Its founding principle is that it is up to the blacks themselves to do something about the up-grading of their houses. Otherwise they will never learn to organize, to think and to cooperate. Under the direction of Brazier and other black Pentecostals, Woodlawn Organization sets up control-stations where those who feel that they have been cheated in the shops can check the prices, quality, and weight of the goods they have bought. Offending shop-keepers are taken to task and in the case of repeat offenders, their names are published. House owners who make their money in Woodlawn by overcharging on rents, but who themselves live in the villas of the suburbs, are informed of the miserable state of the houses they rent out—of the plague of rats and woodworm. But that hardly helps. So then the press and television are invited in to photograph the defunct toilets, the houses where heating systems have ceased to function, the houses where plaster is falling down, where doors and windows are cracked and roofs leak. This is uncomfortable for the owners, but seldom alters their ways. Generally Woodlawn has to go a step further—to organize a rent strike, in which the rents are paid to an account of Woodlawn Organization instead of to the banks of the owners. If the lazy house owners then go to court, all their misbehavior is exposed.

---

[4]Brazier, *Black Self-Determination*, 12.

Similar programs are invented for improving the miserable schools, which are under white direction. In order to put an end to looting and shooting—against which the police are almost powerless—two youth organizations ("Rangers" and "Disciples") have been trained and are used to maintain order.

Theologically these different activities are seen within the framework of a Pauline doctrine of charisms. In addition to the charisms which are known in the history of Pentecostalism, such as speaking in tongues, prophecy, religious dancing, and praying for the sick, they practice the gifts of demonstrating, organizing, and publicizing. These are considered as another kind of prophecy. I have known black Pentecostal churches in which these activities were explicitly mentioned in a list of gifts of the Spirit.[5] These gifts do not usurp the place of others, as in the many political church groups in Europe where political analysis replaces prayer and song (not to speak of dancing and speaking in tongues). Instead, they become part of a new unity between prayer and politics, social action and song.

The Black Pentecostals Awake

In this battle against injustice, the church is ahead of the world—this is how Brazier summarizes his book. Yet Brazier's example is not unique. During a research tour in 1970 of the most important black Pentecostal churches in the USA (whose adherents number in the millions[6]), I discovered similar programs. Dietrich Bonhoeffer[7] has already drawn attention to these black American "step-children of church history." Yet their oral theology (handed down just as the New Testament was handed down [according to form criticism] before it attained written form), their missionary work in the West Indies, their elementary social and political reflection—all of these are still ignored, and even misunderstood as evidences of a form of the faith growing towards fully-fledged European literary Christianity, both by white Pentecostals and by the main-line churches. There are important exceptions to this oversight and misinterpretation, however, not so much in the standard works on social ethics, or in the histories of theological thought, but in certain other works. Take for example the thoughtful study of worship by the Roman Catholic liturgiologist Lothar Zenetti, who has dedicated his book *Hot Melodies*[8] to a black Pentecostal church (Temple Church of God in Christ), in whose midst he experienced the power of the living Holy Spirit and the "new song"; or the travel report by the late Ernst Benz, professor at the University of Marburg,

---

[5] The House of the Lord (Hollenweger, *Black Pentecostal Concept*, 57ff.).

[6] At least 1.5 million, at the most 5 million, depending whether or not one is prepared to accept the statistics of the Church of God in Christ (3.7 million; 02a.02.075; *Black Pentecostal Concept*, 27) and those of the House of Prayer for All People (*Handbuch*, 02a.02.097; *Black Pentecostal Concept*, 43ff). Barrett gives 3.4 million ("Statistics," 817).

[7] Bonhoeffer, "Bericht," I, 97.

[8] Zenetti, *Heisse*, 7.

who, in his book *The Holy Ghost in America*[9] describes his first encounter with black Pentecostals as a "surprising discovery of something absolutely new"; or the masterly *Religious History of the American People* by S. E. Ahlstrom,[10] which gives some recognition to black Pentecostalism; or finally, works by my doctoral researchers Roswith Gerloff[11] and Ian MacRobert.[12]

An increasing awareness of the values inherent in black culture can be observed among the black Pentecostals.[13] One of their churches, the Church of the Living God,[14] has expressed this awareness in an interesting exegesis of the Bible—claiming that most of the Bible saints, including Jesus, belong to the black race. As Jesus is descended from David and Abraham (both belonging to the black race), Jesus himself belongs to the black race. At the same time, however, Jesus did not have an earthly father; thus he belongs to all men and not just to the blacks: he represents the whole of humanity.

Concerning social issues Bishop F. D. Washington, from the Church of God in Christ, deplores the church's "mental block" which is responsible for a false understanding of evangelism because it attempts to promote the church building or organization when, as he states:

> Whether we like to admit it or not, the church (as a building or denomination) has the poorest appeal of all to sinners. Its rating is exactly zero, because most sinners do not go to church. Yet the fantastic fact remains that the person of Jesus Christ—when He is presented right—has the greatest single appeal to the human heart in this world.[15]

It is only logical that this black Pentecostal leader was greatly attracted by the concept of evangelism as presented in the studies by the World Council of Churches.[16] "How can one join this World Council of Churches?" he asked abruptly and unexpectedly. It is furthermore understandable that the strike of sanitation workers in Memphis under the leadership of Dr. Martin Luther King had its headquarters in the big Mason[17] Temple of the above-mentioned Church of God in Christ. The murder of Martin Luther King hit the black

---

[9] Benz, *Amerika*.

[10] Ahlstrom, *History*, 1059f. See also Piepkorn, *Religious Bodies* (esp. vol. III: *Holiness and Pentecostal*).

[11] Gerloff, *Plea*.

[12] MacRobert, *Racism* (for further publications on the topic by MacRobert see short titles list).

[13] Cf. Jones, O. T., "Crisis," and the works by Lovett (see short titles list).

[14] *Handbuch*, 02a.02.082; Hollenweger, *Black Pentecostal Concept*, 34–40. Jones, C. E., "Living God," 211.

[15] Bishop F. D. Washington at the 62nd Convocation of the Church of God in Christ 1969 (*Holy Convocation*, ed. J. O. Patterson, n.p., 1969).

[16] Wieser, *Planning for Mission*. Hollenweger, *Church for Others*. Idem, *Kirche*. Further developed in *ITh*, 3 vols.

[17] C. H. Mason (1866–1961) was the almost legendary founder of the Church of God in Christ (biography and lit., *Handbuch*, 07.907.001; Clemmons, "Mason," 585–88, lit. See also Baer, "Socio-Religious."

Pentecostals in a very personal way, but has so far not destroyed their hope in the power of non-violence.

That hope, in turn, means that black Pentecostals cannot agree with a purely "spiritual" evangelism. In an interview regarding Billy Graham, the black Pentecostal evangelist George M. Perry said: "We believe in the content of the Graham message, but we can't go along with its suburban, middle class, white orientation that has nothing to say to the poor nor to the black people." In short, the mass evangelism practiced by the Reverend Billy Graham and other preachers—Perry concluded—never had and never will have any relevance to the black community.[18]

"A theology developing out of any oppressive situation such as the black scene in America must begin with the socio-cultural factors that act upon one's humanity for good or evil," says the black Pentecostal theologian Leonard Lovett. He adds:

> The avoidance of local problems of socio-economic injustices and discriminations in changing society on the part of early White Pentecostals led to what Fidler refers to as a "fatalistic Premillennialism which allowed White Pentecostals to relegate the close range problems to 'when Jesus comes,'" while in foreign areas they could "rush the rapture" with a distant paternalistic application of Christian love and concern.[19]

Another issue which might be even more disturbing for the white Pentecostal denominations is the discovery by some researchers not only of the Afro-American, but also of some of the original African roots of the Pentecostal revival. But why should this frighten us? As God chose the despised children of Israel to bring blessings to the whole world, he chose again black slaves (including that which was good in their pagan past) to bring blessings to their white masters, and to the church universal. After all, Christianity was not born in Europe![20] One practical manifestation of those blessings is that

> black Pentecostals have won seats on city councils and in state legislatures and have been appointed to minor cabinet positions in the executive branch of the federal government. Robert L. Harris, a Church of God in Christ pastor, became the first black state legislator in Utah history when he defeated a white Mormon candidate. J. O. Patterson, Jr., the son of the late leader of the Church of God in Christ, is the first African-American candidate from Shelby County, Tennessee, to be elected to the Tennessee state senate since Reconstruction. Samuel Jackson, a Church of God in Christ member, served as assistant secretary of Housing and Urban Development during the 1970s.[21]

---

[18] Dugan, "Mass Evangelism."

[19] Fidler, "History," quoted in Lovett, "Perspectives."

[20] Full discussion in my *Handbuch*, 02a.02.049. Sources: Herskovits, *Myth*, DuBois, *Souls*, idem, *Negro Church*, von Hornbostel, "African Negro Music," idem, "American Negro Songs," Tiérsot, "La musique," Ley, *Spirituals*.

[21] Lincoln–Mamiya, *Black Church*, 84, quoted in Baer–Singer, *African-American Religion*, 176f.

Revolutionary Past of White Pentecostals

It is clear that this new orientation of black Pentecostals is watched by the established white Pentecostal churches of the USA with amazement. However, as we have seen, they know that they themselves trace back their history to a revival in a black church in Los Angeles. The Pentecostal movement began in the same milieu in which the spiritual, jazz, and blues emerged. Yet while black music has gained recognition as a contribution by the Negroes to universal culture, the black influence on the Pentecostal movement, which has today over 400 million adherents, has been forgotten—and this in spite of the fact that the Pentecostals regard W. J. Seymour as one of their pioneers. "That the one outstanding personality in bringing about the Pentecostal revival in Los Angeles was a Negro is a fact of extreme importance to Pentecostals of all races" states the Pentecostal historian Vinson Synan.[22] I agree with this evaluation. "Even more significant is the fact that this inter-racial accord took place among the very groups that have traditionally been most at odds, the poor whites and the poor blacks."[23] Even more astonishing, white Pentecostals received their ordination from the hands of black Pentecostal bishops.[24] A Pentecostal eye-witness, Frank Bartleman, proudly relates that in the revival in Los Angeles "the 'color line' was washed away in the blood."[25] Another Pentecostal pioneer, the Anglican clergyman Alexander A. Boddy, described the revival in Los Angeles as "something very extraordinary" because "white pastors from the South were eagerly prepared to go to Los Angeles to the Negroes, to have fellowship with them and to receive through their prayers and intercessions the blessings of the Spirit. And it was still more wonderful that these white pastors went back to the South and reported to the members of their congregations that they had prayed in one Spirit and received the same blessings as they,"[26] a tradition which is followed up by Michael Harper: "To deny a colored person the same human rights as a white one, or treat a person differently because of the color of his skin, is a sin against God. A prophetic ministry should seek to bring conviction of this sin to those who indulge in it."[27]

No explanation has been offered as to why the Negro churches have not become part of the organization of the Pentecostal Fellowship of North America.[28] The reason for this development lies on the one hand in the loud criticism against Pentecostalism voiced by the mainline churches, which tried to discredit Pentecostals by pointing to their lowly beginnings in a Negro church; and on the other hand in the laws of the southern states, which have

---

[22] Synan, *Holiness–Pentecostal.*
[23] Ibid., 165.
[24] Sources in Synan, *Holiness–Pentecostal,* 80, 137.
[25] Bartleman, *What Really Happened at Azusa Street?* 29.
[26] Boddy, "Ueber Land und Meer."
[27] Harper, "Question," 2–3.
[28] Synan, *Holiness–Pentecostal,* 180.

prohibited racially mixed meetings. It would therefore be unfair to blame the white Pentecostals alone for this development. They have simply adapted themselves to what was considered at that time to be American Protestantism.

Black Pentecostals are not satisfied that some white Pentecostals in America still see social and political commitment as a task for the individual Christian and not for the churches as a whole,[29] nor with their tardy and generalized appeals for Christian love.[30] For black Pentecostals the "Pentecostal problem" is the "cleavage of the races," which must be solved before the movement can "shake the world."[31] The appeal by R. C. Cunningham for "conversion," "not coercion"[32] will fall on deaf ears as long as it continues to be uttered only to those below and not equally loudly to those above.

One can understand the pastor of the Assemblies of God in Alabama who stated: "I felt that the greatest indictment against the church of the Lord Jesus in our country is our stand (or lack of one) on racial problems."[33] And the historian of the Pentecostals Assemblies of the World, Morris E. Golder, compares the Baptist Martin Luther King and his liberating ministry ("almost single-handedly he challenged the mores of the South") with the high-flung statements of the Pentecostals on the power of the Holy Spirit. Golder says:

> If the white [Pentecostal] brethren would have stood firm against prejudice and racial injustice, having the most powerful authority (the Holy Spirit) and the most powerful message (the Gospel of Jesus Christ), they could have been the instruments of God for the destruction of this hideous ideology. But instead of fighting against it, they submitted to its influence and have been affected by it even until now.[34]

And Lovett concludes:

> Black Pentecostalism affirms with dogmatic insistence that liberation is always a consequence of the presence of the Spirit. Authentic liberation can never occur apart from genuine Pentecostal encounter, and likewise, authentic Pentecostal encounter cannot occur unless liberation becomes the consequence. It is another way of saying *no man can experience the fullness of the Spirit and be a bona fide racist"* (italics mine).[35]

I wonder what white Pentecostals and theologians have to say to this pneumatology!

---

[29] Cf. a report of a speech by former Congressman W. H. Judd, "Political Action," 23.

[30] Assemblies of God, *Our Mission in Today's World*, 85. But see the very different tone in ch. 3, p. 23 and ch. 15, pp. 193f.

[31] Editorial in *International Outlook* (Los Angeles), Oct./Dec. 1963, 15; quoted in Synan, *Holiness-Pentecostal*, 179.

[32] Cunningham, "Social Concern," 5.

[33] Assemblies of God, *Our Mission in Today's World*, 133.

[34] Golder, *History of the Pentecostal Assemblies of the World*, 80.

[35] Lovett, "Perspectives"; also in his unpublished dissertation, "Black Holiness-Pentecostals," 165; quoted in Volf, "Materiality," 447–67, quote, 462, note 97.

The Songs of the Blacks

We have noted that the Pentecostal movement arose in the same milieu which incubated and birthed the now-famous music and songs of the blacks. Opinions vary concerning the origin and function of the Negro spiritual. It is either considered as a misinterpreted hymn of white Christians,[36] as a "confession of faith" of the black church,[37] as the "clearest exponent of the Negro's real self,"[38] as an oral document of events in the history of the American Negro,[39] as a protest against social injustice,[40] as an adaptation of African songs,[41] as songs originating in the camp meetings of the white revival movement,[42] as the products of black bards like "singing Johnson" and "Ma White,"[43] or as a blending of American and European melodies with African rhythm.[44] Whatever the history of the spiritual,[45] it is itself at the root of at least four musical trends today: 1. The different styles of jazz including the blues. 2. The music found in white Pentecostal churches, which is rooted in black music but which has been greatly changed and adapted to the white ear, particularly in the USA, where some of the earliest hymn writers were black Pentecostals.[46] 3. The spontaneous gospel music which is more contemporary, and related mainly to the Pentecostals and to some black Baptist churches. The gospel song is indigenous to the local community and reflects the current living conditions of the congregation, in contrast to the more traditional spiritual. 4. Attempts to adapt it to European and American traditional church music.[47] Yet there is great controversy as to whether the spiritual has a place in a non-black church service, a controversy which becomes even sharper when the spirituals are translated into French or German or when they are sung in English by a non-English congregation.[48]

---

[36] Jackson, G. P., "Spirituals," 8.8–12.

[37] Läuchli, "Negro Spirituals," 446ff.

[38] Odum, "Religious Folk Songs," 265–365.

[39] Fisher, *Negro Slave Songs.*

[40] Lovell, "Social Implications," 634–43. See also his monumental *Black Song.* Also: Spencer, *Protest and Praise.*

[41] Krehbiel, *Afro-American Folk Songs.* DuBois, *Negro Church.*

[42] Washington, Booker T., *The Story of the Negro.*

[43] Johnson, *Books of American Negro Spirituals.*

[44] Von Hornbostel, "American Negro Music," 30–62. Idem, "American Negro Songs," 748–53.

[45] More literature in *Handbuch,* 02a.02.049ff.; in Hollenweger, *Black Pentecostal Concept,* 9–10, and in idem, "Spirituals."

[46] E.g., G. T. Haywood ("Jesus, the Son of God," "I See a Crimson Stream of Blood"; literature in Robeck, "Haywood," 349–50). T. Harris ("All That Thrills My Soul is Jesus," "He's Coming Soon," "More Abundantly," "By His Stripes We are Healed," "Pentecost in My Soul," "Jesus Loves the Little Children"); Wilson, E. A., "Harris," 347–48.

[47] Examples: Michael Tippet, *Oratorio "A Child of Our Time,"* and Dvorak's String Quartet, F major, op. 96 ("Sometimes I feel like a motherless child").

[48] E.g., Rutenborn, "Theologie," 65–69. Hanft, "Theologie," 160–68. Kern,

Whether or not one accepts M. M. Fisher's interpretation of the spiritual as a means of communicating historical data in an oral culture, to save the black past from being forgotten, it is certain the spiritual is a powerful means of communication which has "preached" and communicated the gospel in black American communities more powerfully than any book or sermon. And it is this element of black spirituality that was taken up by the Pentecostal revival in those parts of the world where that revival was really successful; e.g. Latin America, Zaïre, Italy, Indonesia, Korea, and Russia. Where Pentecostals work in a pre- or post-literary society, they do not think along systematic and logical lines, but in parables and associations. Their main medium of communication is not the book or the newspaper but the proverb, the chorus, the joke, the testimony, the miracle story, or the television and radio program.

These songs are not, as James H. Cone pointed out, unpolitical and otherworldly. "Contrary to popular opinion," says Cone,

> the spirituals are not evidence that black people reconciled themselves with human slavery. On the contrary, they are black freedom songs which emphasize black liberation as consistent with divine revelation. For this reason, it is most appropriate for black people to sing them in this 'new' age of Black Power. And if some people still regard spirituals as inconsistent with Black Power and Black Theology, that is because they have been misguided and the songs misinterpreted. There is little evidence that black slaves accepted their servitude because they believed God willed their slavery. The opposite is the case. The spirituals speak of God's liberation of black people, his will to set right the oppression of black slaves despite the overwhelming power of white masters. For blacks believed that there is an omnipotent, omnipresent, and omniscient power at work in the world, and that he is on the side of the oppressed and the downtrodden. As evidence they pointed to the blind man who received his sight, the lame who walked, and Lazarus who was received into God's kingdom while the rich man was rejected. And if "de God dat lived in Moses' time is jes' the same today," then God will vindicate the suffering of the righteous blacks and punish the unrighteous whites for their wrongdoings.[49]

Starting from M. M. Fisher's fundamental analysis, Cone says:

> The divine liberation of the oppressed from slavery is the central theological concept in the black spirituals. These songs show that black slaves did not believe that human servitude was reconcilable with their African past and their knowledge of the Christian gospel. They did not believe that God created Africans to be the slaves of Europeans. Accordingly they sang of a God who was involved in history—*their* history—making right what whites have made wrong. . . .
>
> Because black people believed that they were God's children, they affirmed their somebodiness, refusing to reconcile their servitude with divine revelation.[50]

"Jazz"; Koch, "Variationen," 77f.

[49] Cone, "Black Spirituals," 54–69, quote 60. See also idem, *Spirituals and the Blues.*

[50] Cone, "Black Spirituals," 59.

The black man's church

was his school, his forum, his political arena, his social club, his art gallery, his conservatory of music. It was lyceum and gymnasium as well as sanctum sanctorum. His religion was his fellowship with man, his audience with God. It was the peculiar sustaining force which gave him the strength to endure when endurance gave no promise, and the courage to be creative in the face of his own dehumanization.[51]

It is by now clear that the Christians of the Third World will outnumber those of Europe and America in the year 2000.[52] Christianity started as a Third World movement somewhere in a forgotten corner of the Roman Empire; it now returns to its non-western beginnings—within a decade the majority, or at least a very considerable part, of Christians will identify most strongly with the spontaneous non-literary type of Pentecostal spirituality. It seems therefore that the spiritual and liturgical methods of the black Pentecostal and Pentecostal-like communities in the USA will play a strategic role in the future, as they belong phenomenologically to non-literary humanity, although they are living in the literary culture of America. That is why in future they may have to play an important role in the "translation" from one culture into the other, in both the theological and the political realm.

Movements of Social Transformation

From the foregoing we can see that black Pentecostalism and Black Power are not opposites, as some might wrongly suppose. A European observer might be inclined to consider black Pentecostalism as a religious mechanism of adaptation and Black Power as a political protest movement. This is not the case—at least not in this antithetic formulation. In a comparative study Luther P. Gerlach and Virginia Hine describe both as "movements of social transformation."[53] In Pentecostalism they include not only black and white Pentecostals, but also the mushrooming and increasingly important charismatic groups within the main-line churches, particularly among Roman Catholic intellectuals. This burgeoning "main-line" movement has destroyed the generally accepted theory that Pentecostal spirituality is bound to the milieu of the spiritually and materially poor. At the meetings of the charismatics one found initially not the uneducated but the intellectuals, not the uncritical but the critical exegetes, not frustrated puritans but normal Christians. Still today,

---

[51] C. E. Lincoln, preface to Washington, J. R., *Black Sects and Cults*, ix–x.

[52] See Barrett, *WChE*. Idem, *Schism and Renewal*. Idem, "AD 2000," 39–54. Criticizing Barrett's view: Osobo, "Fascinating," 64–69. Mitchell, "Towards the Sociology of Religious Independency," 2–21. Barrett's statistics in the seventies have proved to be accurate. His critiques were wrong because they did not consider the missionary and innovative power of the independent and Pentecostal churches. Whether Barrett's predictions for the year 2000 will be as accurate we do not know. However, the trend is clear.

[53] Gerlach–Hine, *People, Power, Change.*

these people not only speak in tongues and pray together; they eat, smoke, and drink together. Luther P. Gerlach has observed that people with a higher education are attaining the Pentecostal experience of baptism in the Spirit more readily than students with an inferior education, and that speaking in tongues is less frequent among Pentecostal Mexicans than among white, middle-class Americans. The attempts to describe speaking in tongues as a pathological or half-pathological phenomenon of marginal people have been disproved (insofar as it is possible to give objective criteria) by competent psychological and sociological studies.[54]

In their comparison between Black Power and Pentecostalism these two American anthropologists, who belong neither to Black Power nor to the Pentecostal movement, came to the conclusion that Black Power cannot be seen as a contrast to the black Pentecostal movement. Both movements are religious *and* revolutionary, and it is difficult to draw a dividing line between the two.

Pentecostalism is revolutionary because it offers alternatives to "literary" theology and thus defrosts the "frozen thinking" within literary forms of worship and committee-debate and gives the same chances to all—including the "oral" people. It allows for a process of democratization of language through a dismantling of the privileges of abstract, rational and propositional systems—which, as is shown by the growth of the charismatic movement within the historical churches, is even experienced as beneficial by the intellectuals. Such examples of political alphabetization are found not only in the black Pentecostal churches in the USA, but also in the Russian, South African, Swedish and Latin American Pentecostal movements. Our socio-political search has entirely by-passed—and here the World Council of Churches must explicitly be mentioned among the culprits—this political and religious awaking, sometimes with a light undertone of regret for these religiously slightly doped believers.

Likewise Gerlach affirms that Black Power is a religious movement. He points to the conversion of Malcolm X to Islam, from which emerged the Black Muslim identity. The religious language of the rest of the Black Power movement is also remarkable. Devotees talk of "transfiguration into blackness" and "baptism into blackness," and see in Black Power *expressis verbis* a religion, into which one is initiated by an experience of commitment—a kind of conversion, which is articulated in the framework of a liturgy.

---

[54] The literature on glossolalia is legion. One of the first was the South African psychiatrist L. M. Vivier-van Eetveldt. Others were G. J. Jennings, V. H. Hine, W. J. Samarin, D. Christie-Murray, M. T. Kelsey, W. E. Mills, C. C. Williams, R. P. Spittler (Spittler also mentions the European research from the beginning of this century which did not subsume "glossolalia" under "pathology," e.g., Lombard and Mosimann). Robert Mapes Anderson (in his otherwise excellent *Vision of the Disinherited*) disregards newer research on glossolalia and therefore comes down on the side of the old, but out-dated, deprivation theory. For full bibliography see short titles list. See also ch. 26, pp. 358–62.

It belongs furthermore to the essence of this cultural revolution that it develops fluid organizational forms, which our linear thinking can only understand with difficulty. It is led in a polycephalous way—i.e., by several heads—and finds its adherents through normal communication in everyday life, in the lower class particularly among relatives, in the upper class among circles of friends. The executives in this polycephalous arrangement change frequently, and the different groups change their status in the whole framework of the movement from week to week. Only this polycephalous organization makes it possible for a minority to withstand a majority. The unity of the movement is not assured by normal headquarters but by "traveling evangelists" (in the charismatic movement as well as in the Black Power movement) and through common code words and songs. It is easy, says Gerlach, to find out if a Black Power group is led by communists. As soon as there are clear hierarchical structures and traceable executive centers, then we are dealing with a communist organization. And that is exactly why the very few communist-led Black Power groups are not revolutionary but reactionary, because they do not liberate black people from white tutelage, but replace one infantilizing structure with another.

Likewise the transition from the charismatic *movement* to a Pentecostal *church* is recognizable by the emerging linear structure of dependence and direction. Such a transition from the polycephalous charismatic movement to a centrally organized church (whether along presbyterian, congregational, or episcopal lines) can often be observed in individual cases. At the same time, a new protest is kindled against the manipulative "thinking from above," which either leads to the formation of a new charismatic/pentecostal revival (outside the organization in question) or calls the organization back to its initial polycephalous form.

In dealing with the attitude of these movements to opposition, Gerlach draws a further parallel. *A kite flies against the wind.* A revolutionary movement like Black Power or the Pentecostal movement can only rise against the wind of opposition. That is why Black Power emerged in many towns only with the help of police action. In the same way many charismatic movements could only form themselves in the main-line churches with the help of the opposition of the ecclesiastical hierarchy to speaking in tongues.[55]

Such a polycephalous revolutionary movement, says Gerlach, can be effectively counteracted only by "overkill," i.e. by a rigorous control of all the media of communication, including the mail and the telephone, and by arresting and eliminating all suspicious and sympathetic fellow-travelers, including those who are wrongly thought to be in sympathy with the movement. This method was used in earlier times in the Roman Catholic Church, in certain

---

[55] A similar observation has been made by G. Balandier on the rise of Kimbanguism in Zaïre (ch. 6): "We have to see that the organized repression by the Belgian authorities has really established the new Church. . . . " (Balandier, *Sociologie actuelle,* 434f.).

fascist states, and in Russia. Yet in the United States—and one would like to add, in the Christian church—such a method is unthinkable. Therefore, Gerlach concludes, what ecclesiastical intervention *is* brought to bear against charismatic revolutionaries, and what state intervention comes against Black Power, represents exactly that amount of wind which those movements need in order to rise and fly. It produces exactly the opposite of what is intended.

Tolerance and Conviction

Gerlach's analysis is fascinating. But does it fit all situations? It seems to me that the revolutionary quality of such movements depends on two conditions which are logically exclusive of each other. Firstly, they must have an almost axiomatic emotional and existential basis which cannot be shaken either by argument or further investigation; or—if one prefers—they must rest on a religious conviction. But secondly, they must allow question and criticism by fact and argument, in order to prevent this religious conviction from becoming an ideological prison.

For the first thesis there are enough examples in the present day. Looked at objectively and rationally, the Red Chinese were defeated by Chiang Kai Shek when they started their long march. Similarly, the escalation of the bombardment of North Vietnam should have led to the capitulation of the North Vietnamese. However, in both instances the "logical" consequence did not result. Why not? Gerlach answers (according to his conviction as an agnostic) that religious commitment has such a power that it changes realities. From this Gerlach draws a conclusion which is extremely relevant to the whole debate on development and hunger, namely that political and economic tinkering with the treatment of symptoms has to be replaced by the acknowledgment of these culturally revolutionary groups as catalysts of transformation.

For the second thesis Mao Tse Tung and the Pentecostal movement again provide striking examples. The undifferentiated and unquestioned ideologies which prohibit tolerance and lay taboos on important questions destroy, by this very act, the original charismatic and revolutionary outbreak. What we then face is the well-known keeping of the letter of the law—whether Protestant, Catholic, Pentecostal or communist—by which people compensate for the sacrifices they have had to make by compelling others to make the same sacrifices *(Ersatz-Lust)*.[56] Black Power and Pentecostalism have broken up institutionalized hypocrisy by taking literally that which was affirmed officially but not practiced (in the church: the priesthood of all believers; in the state: equal rights for black and white). Yet these movements become victims of institutionalized hypocrisy at the moment when they create a closed ideology of this revolutionary act. It seems that utter commitment and conviction does not allow for the "luxury of tolerance." Either a person is ready to risk

---

[56] Mitscherlich, *Die Unfähigkeit*, 122.

everything for a recognizable goal, but then is not prepared to be diverted from this goal by arguments or by facts; or he is a critical, liberal and tolerant person, but then lacks that utter commitment which alone acts as a catalyst of transformation.

One may well ask: Can only fanatics be evangelists? Church history seems to answer this question in the affirmative. Neither the biblical prophets, nor the New Testament evangelists, nor the Reformers, nor the theologians, evangelists, and missionaries of today, all of whom are faithful to an utter commitment, have been tolerant—with some notable exceptions. In light of this fact, the Pentecostals have sometimes said that the tolerance of many of today's Christians has its roots in their religious insecurity.

The Holy Spirit is a "Gentleman"

In spite of all this, I am not prepared to accept that there is a definite conflict between utter conviction and genuine tolerance. The Holy Spirit is a "gentleman," the Pentecostals rightly say.[57] If we have to use all our energies in order to suppress all critical arguments, then we lack the necessary energy which we need for more differentiated tasks. To combine tolerance with utter conviction, however, demands one's whole life and energy. In this sense lived tolerance can be understood as a concretization of the doctrine of justification by grace alone: If we really believe that we are *sola gratia* Christians, theologians, pastors, church bureaucrats, evangelists, or politicians, then we will always have to reckon with the possibility that we might be wrong—and yet justified by God—and secondly that the one whom we want to convince will be justified by God *sola gratia*, even if he is wrong.

In relation to Black Power and to the Pentecostal movement, this would mean we have to acknowledge equal rights to non-literary theology. Only in the encounter between "literary" and "oral" cultures can we find out how far our "literary" theology (i.e., our critical analytical methods) relates to pre-and post-rationality, and what the relationship is between "the logic of the guts" and "the logic of the brain." Then we can ask: How does the dance speak to us and how does the thesis provide a variation on a theme? Or in an image: what is the reason that it is only the many colors of the rainbow in the spectrum which can create that bright light which allows us to see reality? If God has given us a head, "heart and reins" that we might know the world, he surely will not allow us to let one of these ways of perception wither. On the contrary, we have to investigate how the head can learn from the heart-beat and the heart from critical thinking.

These are not the questions of a specialist. In answering (or refusing to answer) these questions, we decide whether the church, as a universal, really catholic church, has a future, because the number of those Christians and theologians—if we are prepared to call them by this name—who look for and

---

[57] The Holy Spirit is a woman, say the feminists, because "Ruach" is female.

practice an oral theology as an alternative or complement to a rational and logical system of terms, is greatly increasing. This topic has been developed in depth in the three volumes of my intercultural theology and in many plays for musicians, dancers and actors in Germany and Switzerland. In these plays, there is no need for the artists to be committed Christians, because the biblical texts—and in the case of the Bonhoeffer Requiem the texts of Bonhoeffer—find their way into the hearts of both spectators and actors.[58]

One thing is sure: the ecumenical problem of the immediate future is not the relationship between Catholic and Protestant, but between "oral" and "literary" theology.

The relationship between oral and literary, between black and white, is also an unsolved intra-Pentecostal problem. The white Pentecostal Cecil M. Robeck, Jr., bluntly states: "Most of the major Pentecostal denominations in the U.S. are highly segregated. *Racism is a rampant problem in American Pentecostalism.* . . . White Pentecostals have supported the Republican party and the so-called 'religious right' while Black Pentecostals have tended to support the Democratic party and have refused to be co-opted by the 'religious right.' "[59]

Samuel Solivan criticizes the failure of Pentecostalism in relation to race:

> We have opted for an easy "I love you in the Lord" approach to the problems of racism and bigotry. Our denominational structures, or district organizations, our national assemblies are controlled and defined by a small number of people and their friends who all if not the great majority look and think alike. We have institutionalized our prejudice, and our racism. We have justified, sanctified, and have baptized it and we have fooled ourselves into believing that the Spirit has led us. A spirit has, but which one? Not everything that claims to be of the Spirit of God is His Spirit.[60]

The "Miracle of Memphis"

In the fall of 1994 the old Pentecostal Fellowship of North America (in which only white churches were represented) was dissolved.[61] A new organization was founded, in which black and white Pentecostal churches were equal members (but without the Oneness Churches).[62] It was called "Pentecostal/ Charismatic Churches of North America." With explicit reference to the founder of Pentecostalism, William Joseph Seymour, who saw in the integration of black

---

[58] The topic is further developed in ch. 9, pp. 106–16, in Hollenweger, "Theology," and idem, "Music," 276–86. On my plays and musicals see Heuberger, "Hollenweger als Dichter und Liturgiker," 61–72. For a list of these plays see ch. 21, note 29, p. 283.

[59] Robeck, "Taking Stock," 35–60, quotes 46f., emphasis mine.

[60] Solivan, "Cultural Glossolalia," 25. See also, Butler, "Walls."

[61] Synan, "Miracle," n.p.; Robeck, "Memphis," 36–73; Maempa, "Interracial," 24–26.

[62] Reed, "Oneness," 644–51.

and white people in his church an essential characteristic of the work of the Holy Spirit, the race-war between black and white Pentecostals was ended.[63] A symbol of this was that a white Assemblies of God pastor spontaneously washed the feet of black bishop Ithniel Clemmons[64]—a gesture whose significance cannot be underestimated and which would have been impossible a few years ago.

The choice of Memphis for the event is no accident. That is the place where Martin Luther King, Jr., was shot. Without the confession of guilt, "our participation in the sin of racism by our silence, denial and blindness"[65] reconciliation would not have been possible. Whether this reconciliation is as "epochal" as some observers think will only be seen when the religious reconciliation is transformed into political reality.[66]

Prayer of the Earthworm

Dear God,
sometimes I feel like an earthworm.
I crawl on my belly and eat earth from morning till evening and dirt from evening till morning.
And people walk by and say: Ha, it's only an earthworm and they hurt me and trample on me with their shoes. And sometimes a magpie walks up and down, all majestic in black and white, and he pecks at me and I have to slip away into the earth.
Why do I have to be an earthworm?
Why can I not be a flamingo, or a mighty roaring lion, or at least a butterfly?
Why am I just an earthworm?

Dear God, you did not ask me whether I wanted to be an earthworm.
My parents did not ask me whether I wanted to be an earthworm, or whether I wanted to be at all.
And so I am what I am, an earthworm
'til that moment when you God, whisper into my ear:
Earthworm, you are important! Without you there is no life, no plants, no vegetables, no animals, no people, no university, no government, no science and art and no magpies in all their academic glory.
What can I say to this, dear God?
I know what I say: I say, thank you, dear God, thank you indeed.
I am important.
But, dear God, I wonder whether you couldn't tell that to the magpies too.
Thank you.

---

[63] Point 10 of the "Racial Reconciliation Manifesto" ("lay aside our warring"), *PE* 4205, 11.12.1994, 25.

[64] See the photography in *Ministries Today* 13/1, Jan./Feb. 1995, 36.

[65] Point 4 of the "Racial Reconciliation Manifesto" *PE* 4205, 11.12.1994, 25. *Ministries Today* 13/1 Jan./Feb. 1995, 38.

[66] Critical voices on "Memphis" in *Pneuma* 18/1, Spring 1996 (contributions by Clemmons, Lovett, Gaxiola-Gaxiola, Solivan, Amos, Robeck, and Macchia).

CHAPTER **FIVE**

South Africa

Dangerous Memories: Integrated Beginnings

In South Africa, Pentecostalism started as an integrated church and developed—as in the USA—into a segregated church. The roots and origins have been described in detail in *The Pentecostals*.[1] There one may also find a description of the connection between Pentecostalism and the black Zionist churches.[2]

The first Pentecostal services, although not initiated by blacks, were conducted in a black church in Doornfontein.[3] John G. Lake (1870–1935)[4] and Thomas Hezmalhalch (1845–1934),[5] the early Pentecostal missionaries to South Africa, had both worshipped in Seymour's church and were already acquainted with the non-racial commitment and practice of Seymour at the Azusa Street Mission. Although there is a theory that Lake advocated segregation in social life,[6] he initially supported non-racialism in the church.[7]

---

[1] *The Pentecostals*, 111–75. Other sources are: Hayes, *Black Charismatic Anglicans*. Robinson, *To the Ends of the Earth*. Merwe Burger, *Die Geloofsgeskiedenis*. Horn–Louw. *Eén Kudde*. Watt, *From Africa's Soil*. de Wet, *Apostolic Faith Mission in South Africa*. Horn, "Experience," 117–40. idem, "South African Pentecostals and Apartheid," 157–68. Saayman, "Some Reflections," 40–56 (richly documented).

[2] The rest of this chapter mostly follows Horn verbatim ("Experience," 128–30).

[3] Merwe Burger, *Die Geloofsgeskiedenis*, 167.

[4] Zeigler, "Lake," 531.

[5] Warner, "Hezmalhalch," 389.

[6] While Kamphausen accepts my theory that Zionism is a fruit of the Pentecostal missionary, he states that Zionism has paralyzed Ethiopianism and robbed it of its political substance. He quotes from a letter from Lake to the President of the Transvaal, Louis Botha: "We have worked mostly among the Ethiopians with the intention to bring them under white control. . . . We have found that when the Ethiopians are really saved, they give up their Ethiopianism and accept with joy white control and government from us." (Letter from Lake to Louis Botha, 27.9.1909,

After Lake had moved from the black church in Doornfontein to a white Zionist church ("White Zionist" does not refer to Zionism in South Africa, but to the Catholic Apostolic Church from Zion, Ill.)[8] in the center of Johannesburg, he openly resisted whites who wanted to exclude the later well-known black Pentecostal leader, Elias Letaba, from the church, and he kissed him in the sight of the whole congregation.

However, the executive, which consisted only of whites, soon gave in to the pressure of the racist white community. As early as November 1908, the executive decided "that the baptism of natives shall in future take place *after* the baptism of the white people."[9] Early in 1909 the executive decided that baptism of "whites, coloreds and natives shall be separate."[10]

The Apostolic Faith Mission, the movement started by Lake, reflected all the racial taboos of South African society. In 1910 Lake could still write to the Upper Room Mission that although the Afrikaners have, like the Southerners, a strong prejudice against blacks, there are many white workers whose hearts "God has caused to love the natives."[11] In 1944, however, the executive stated that the Mission stood for segregation. "The fact that the native, Indian or colored is saved does not render him European."[12]

After the Second World War, when the Nationalist Party gained power in South Africa, the Apostolic Faith Mission consistently supported the government and its apartheid policy. In 1955, when prime minister J. Strydom enlarged the Senate to obtain the required majority in both Houses of Parliament to remove the so-called colored voters from the electoral roll, G. R. Wessels, vice-president of the Apostolic Faith Mission, was one of the senators while remaining an ordained minister. Thus the Apostolic Faith Mission became a direct partner of the Government in its implementation of apartheid.

Secretary for Native Affairs, vol. 92, No. 36606, 1909, Gov. Arch. Pretoria; Kamphausen, *Anfänge*, 464. Kamphausen quotes the letter in his own German translation. I have translated the letter back into English).

It is certain that this document mirrors the opinion of the then missionaries and also of today's leaders of the Apostolic Faith Church. But that does not mean that the Zionists agree with it. Why did they all split from the Apostolic Faith Church? Whether Zionism is apolitical is still another question, since we find among their first prophets such political leaders as Elias Mahlangu (1881–1960) who joined the African National Congress (Sundkler, *Zulu Zion,* 61). Or, to give an example from a different quarter, an evangelist who sounds as apolitical as Nicholas Bhengu told me: "There is no point in telling the Europeans the truth. They only hear what they want to hear. I am too old to change anything. However, things cannot continue as they are." How right he was!

[7] Merwe Burger, *Die Geloofsgeskiedenis,* 149f; Burton, *Pastor,* 55f.

[8] *The Pentecostals,* 116ff.

[9] Burton, *Pastor,* 52. Minute Book of the Apostolic Faith Mission, 6.11.1908, Sundkler, *Zulu Zion,* 54.

[10] Merwe Burger, *Die Geloofsgeskiedenis,* 175.

[11] Ibid. See also Lindsay, *John Lake,* 22. Sundkler, *Zulu Zion,* 54.

[12] Merwe Burger, *Die Geloofsgeskiedenis,* 422f.

It is therefore not surprising that white South African Pentecostals reject the idea that the Pentecostal Movement was founded by a black minister, along with the broader notion that the black experience has had an impact on the beliefs and practices of the movement. Like many white Pentecostals, F. P. Möller traces the origin of the movement back to Parham.[13] Although he recognizes the part played by Seymour, he dismisses the whole controversy around the leadership of Seymour and the black/white relationship: "Later Seymour was replaced by more able people and the different races ceased to worship together."[14]

Burger, an historian of the Apostolic Faith Mission, sees Parham as the dogmatic father of the movement. He describes my own thesis (as well as Lovett's and MacRobert's) which states that Pentecostalism was born in a Negro church, as a "warped, one-sided conclusion." He calls the subsequent segregation of the Pentecostal Movement a "natural and spontaneous racial segregation." He also states that when Seymour had fulfilled his function "stronger men with more initiative and stronger leadership potential" took over.[15] Burger ascribes segregation in the Apostolic Faith Mission to the fact that the Afrikaners understood the history, nature, and attitude of race relations in South Africa better than did the American missionaries.[16]

It would be unfair to ascribe the black/white split in the South African Pentecostal Movement to apartheid. It has been shown that the white South African Pentecostals did not differ from the rest of the movement. Neither can the interpretations by Burger and Möller be seen as unique to South Africa. However, in South Africa, with its legalized apartheid, the distortion of history has prevented Pentecostals from breaking the racial barriers and becoming a unique witness of the unifying power of the Spirit. The major breakthrough in the fight against apartheid came from a Dutch Reformed Prime Minister negotiating with the leader of the African National Congress and not from the Spirit-filled Pentecostal leaders? The observation by Mac-Robert concerning the American and British Pentecostals (at least in the past) is also applicable to South Africa:

> Many white Pentecostals I have spoken to—both British and American—are profoundly embarrassed by the black origins of the movement and are quick to refute the leading role played by Seymour. They would rather rehabilitate Parham—even if he was homosexual, at least he was white—or deny the existence of human leadership, than accept a black man as their founder.[17]

---

[13] See also F. P. Möller's remarks on my chapter on South Africa, *The Pentecostals,* 121, 124f., 145f., 148, 155, 171, 173.

[14] Möller, *Diskussie oor die Charismata,* 18.

[15] Merwe Burger, *Die Geloofsgeskiedenis,* 80.

[16] Ibid., 175.

[17] MacRobert, "Black Roots," 89.

Recapturing the Past in Overcoming Racism

This section is again based on J. N. Horn. Mostly I quote him verbatim, since I want to give prominence to a new way of doing Pentecostal theology which sees in the "black connection" not an embarrassment but a promise. In my opinion this relates both to the origins of the movement and to its implantation in Africa, as for example in the form of Kimbanguism,[18] and Zionism.[19]

As we have seen, the Pentecostal Movement changed from a fully integrated movement often under black leadership in its early years, into several segregated communities. However, the most shameful aspect of this history is not merely that the movement eventually organized itself into racial assemblies and churches, but that some of its white leaders were later involved in racist activities, while many others tacitly accepted the racism of church and society.[20]

At least two early Pentecostals, Charles Parham and Aimee McPherson,[21] had close ties with the Ku Klux Klan in the 1920s.[22] Parham contributed articles to a racist, anti-Semitic periodical and often preached to the Klansmen, whom he referred to as "those splendid men," and whose aims he interpreted as "high ideals for the betterment of mankind."[23]

Anderson divides Parham's life into three periods, the pre-Pentecostal period in which his racism was clearly apparent, the initial dynamic phase of the Pentecostal Movement in which his racism was held in abeyance, and finally the post-revival period during which those racial hostilities matured. Anderson suggests that the Pentecostal experience might have been the reason for the moderate approach of Parham and other white Pentecostals during the movement's initial phase.[24]

---

[18] See ch. 6, pp. 54–80.

[19] See *The Pentecostals*, 149–75.

[20] This tacit acceptance was broken in the "Declaration of Solidarity with the Relevant Pentecostal Witness from South Africa" at the "Conference on Charismatic and Pentecostal Research" in Kappel a. A., Switzerland, July 1991. It states: "We regret that we did not speak out courageously and consistently against apartheid and the political oppression and economic exploitation that this immoral system has caused for our brothers and sisters in South Africa. We also acknowledge our uncritical attitude in accepting the information disseminated by the media without independently verifying the facts about the ongoing struggle of the Church in the South African situation. Therefore we repent . . . " Published with an introduction by Murray W. Dempster in *Transformation* 9/1. January/March 1992, 32f. and in *EPTA Bulletin* 10/1. 1991, 34f. The declaration was signed by a number of well-known Pentecostal scholars.

[21] Although Robeck mentions that McPherson encouraged Black evangelist Emma Cotton, Robeck, "McPherson," 568–71. On the McPherson controversy see *The Pentecostals*, 487–88.

[22] Anderson, Robert Mapes, *Vision of the Disinherited*, 190.

[23] Ibid.

[24] Ibid.

C. de Wet, a Pentecostal missiologist from South Africa, tries to explain the return of Pentecostal believers to racism from a pneumatological perspective. He suggests that during times of dramatic outpourings of the Spirit and consequent revivals, the color line is swept away.[25] Or, putting it more theologically, the indwelling Spirit, who fills the Christian, takes away all racism. Once the revival is over, however, and the initial enthusiasm makes way for organization and dogmas, all the old prejudices come back.

If de Wet's hypothesis is to be taken seriously by Pentecostals, it will have an important outcome. It will mean that the Pentecostal doctrine of the baptism of the Holy Spirit will have to be investigated in light of the "original sin" of Pentecostals, i.e., racism. In this light we may see that Spirit baptism is not a "once and for all" experience. Certainly, the racial experiences of the Pentecostal fathers indicate that Spirit-filled Christians can lose the fullness of the Spirit. The question often asked by black Pentecostals needs more attention: "Can a white racist be filled with the Spirit?"

By accepting the possibility that believers can lose the fullness of the Spirit, Pentecostals will bring their pneumatology in line with their soteriology, which accepts that believers can lose their salvation. Pentecostal history reminds us that non–racialism was one of the clearest signs of the baptism in the Spirit. This does not mean that Pentecostals should necessarily reject their doctrine of tongues (or other gifts) as the initial evidence of the baptism. But it will ask Pentecostals not to rely merely on the "initial evidence," but to expect of those who claim to have had a Pentecostal or charismatic experience that they rid themselves of racism.

The statement by the Assemblies of God in the twenties that "there might be true Christians in the Klan" and similar statements by South African Pentecostals concerning the right-wing political movements need to be questioned.[26]

More positively: If there is any substance of truth in de Wet's hypothesis, then the Pentecostal message has the challenging latent potential of overcoming racism. Thus, despite the negative history of Pentecostalism in this area, its positive beginning gives hope for the future. If the South African Pentecostal movement can experience a real "outpouring of the Spirit," it can (and will) serve as an example to the world. The Pentecostal movement can then serve as a catalyst for a new society, an instrument of hope in "our broken land."

The "color line" can once again be "washed away in the blood." When the Spirit comes, proud white racists kneel before black ministers for prayer, white ministers are ordained by black prophets,[27] and Christians see one another as children of God, rendering skin pigmentation irrelevant.

---

[25] de Wet, *Apostolic Faith Mission in South Africa*, 181f.

[26] Anderson, Robert Mapes, *Vision of the Disinherited*, 191.

[27] Horn, "Experience," 122. Clemmons, "Mason," 585–88.

Is it far-fetched to dream of white ministers coming from Krugersdorp to Soweto to receive the baptism in the Spirit? And is a non-racial congregation under the leadership of a black minister possible in South Africa? If the Holy Spirit is really moving, it is not an eschatological dream, but a Pentecostal possibility.

Not only the early history of the classical Pentecostal movement, but also the history of the charismatic movement has underlined the potential of the Pentecostal experience in bringing people from a diversity of backgrounds together. In the heyday of the charismatic movement in America, Catholics, Orthodox Christians, Protestants (and even Pentecostals!) gathered in their thousands to praise the Lord and to have fellowship.[28] J. Buck, commenting on the third Holy Spirit conference in Jerusalem, points to the fellowship between the Orthodox priest, Fr. Bartholomew, and a Roman Catholic, Fr. Orsini.[29] In South Africa, the South African Renewal Conference in 1980 had the same impact. In an editorial on this event, Crompton comments:

> More hundreds than we can estimate came into an experience of the Holy Spirit and thousands had their attitudes fundamentally changed towards one another: English to Afrikaans [sic], Afrikaans [sic] to English, Black to White, White to Black, Colored to African and both to Indian, Protestant to Catholic and vice versa, Pentecostal to mainline.[30]

Unfortunately, this "flow of the Spirit," like the first Pentecostal revival, did not produce lasting inter-racial results. There are literally thousands of Spirit-filled Pentecostals and charismatics in South Africa who fail to understand the discrepancy between racism and a Spirit-filled life.

The early Pentecostal movement showed us an alternative to the way we currently deal with the race problem. Discovering the roots and history of their own movement will allow South African Pentecostals to face the challenge of the Spirit to break through the strong barriers of racism, racial superiority complexes and racial hatred.

Re-Evaluation of Black Roots

As we have seen, the humble beginnings of the movement in a black church under black leadership are an embarrassment for many white Pentecostals. The reaction of Charles Parham in his post-Pentecostal period is still typical of many Pentecostals and charismatics:

> There was a beautiful outpouring of the Spirit in Los Angeles . . . Then they pulled off all the stunts common in old camp meetings among colored folk . . . That is the way they worshipped God, but what makes my soul sick, and make[s]

---

[28] Buck, "Logos," 40f.

[29] Ibid.

[30] Crompton, "Tide Has Turned," 1–13. See also Poewe, "Links and Parallels," 141–58.

me sick at my stomach is to see white people imitating unintelligent, crude negroism . . . and laying it on the Holy Ghost.[31]

However, this black heritage does not have to be an embarrassment, but rather can be a liberating experience for white South African Pentecostals. The long controversy between Pentecostal and mainline churches over liturgical practices is just one area where black history can be valuable for Pentecostals. MacRobert points out that the Afro-American heritage of Seymour and his compatriots was the main influence that gave the Pentecostals their unique liturgy. Seymour affirmed his black heritage by introducing Negro spirituals and Negro music into his liturgy at a time when this music was considered inferior and unfit for Christian worship, for "he had drunk from the 'invisible institution' of black folk Christianity" with its themes of freedom, equality and community.[32]

For many years, Pentecostal liturgy came under fierce attack in South Africa. As late as 1984 some of the larger Reformed churches reacted strongly against the South African Broadcasting Corporation when it invited Pentecostals to take part. The "unacceptable liturgy" of the Pentecostals and the "disorder" in the services were the main reasons for the opposition.

If the African influence in such liturgy is taken into account, this criticism can be seen as opting for "superior Western values" in the church. To broadcast Pentecostal liturgies can have significant symbolic meaning as an expression of the African roots of all South African Pentecostals. Pentecostals have always refused to be impressed by the Western Protestant criticism of their liturgy. Apart from the traditional defenses—"Scripture ordains freedom," "the Bible instructs us to praise the Lord" etc.—Pentecostals in South Africa can add one more very legitimate defense: Pentecostal liturgy in South Africa is an expression of our rich African heritage and a valuable expression of faith for the people of Africa, both white and black.[33]

Blackness as an experience and a God-given reality can also find liberation in Pentecostal history. In a world where blackness has often been portrayed as at worst a curse, or at best something second-class, black Pentecostals can rejoice in the fact that God chose to use a black man to kindle the Pentecostal fire.

Pentecostals believe that the Pentecostal revival was an act of God, an outpouring of the Spirit. If this Pentecostal Movement is of the Spirit, then it is also of the Spirit that a black man stood at its beginning. In South Africa's apartheid this fact alone must liberate white Pentecostals from their paternalism and from their tendency to expect so little from blacks.

---

[31] Quoted in Anderson, Robert Mapes, *Vision of the Disinherited,* 190.

[32] Hollenweger, "Intercultural," 526–56; MacRobert, *Black Pentecostalism* (bibl.).

[33] This has enormous consequences for Pentecostal mission, see ch. 22, pp. 288–306 on mission and ch. 6, pp. 54–80 on Simon Kimbangu.

The fear of black leadership in South Africa is not confined to the political arena. In white Pentecostal circles this fear has been the major stumbling-block in the way of unification attempts between the black and white sections of more than one Pentecostal denomination.[34] So far I followed Nico Horn, a colored South African Pentecostal.

A Relevant Pentecostal Witness

For three decades I have advocated the thesis that Pentecostalism owes a great part of its substance to William J. Seymour and his African heritage. I have been maligned and ridiculed for taking this position, but now it is winning ground, and the consequences of its acceptance are obvious.

What are these consequences for South Africa? Among others, they include a political awareness which pleases neither the theologians of liberation (because it rejects violence) nor the more conservative theologians (because it is revolutionary). Revolutionary it is, because it starts to question the traditional South African Pentecostal theology. F. P. Möller for instance wrote in 1988: "In the event of a revolution, or armed revolt, the church must not be implicated. She must always be in a position where she can minister to people of all conflicting groups,"[35] to which de Wet replied:

> Presently the church is not ministering to "people of all conflicting groups." The Apostolic Faith Mission has chaplains ministering to the government's troops. When a pastor of the Apostolic Faith Mission in Africa, Frank Chikane, tried to minister to the "other" groups, he was defrocked for "being involved in politics."[36] If Möller's statement is to be taken at face value, and the Apostolic Faith Mission wants to minister to "people of all conflicting groups," it will have to appoint chaplains also to the forces opposing the government. If not, the chaplains serving the armed forces of the government must be withdrawn.[37]

Japie Lapoorta, another Black South African Pentecostal, shows convincingly that the Apostolic Faith Mission was heavily involved in the politics of Apartheid; for instance, when they adopted a resolution in April 1947 to acknowledge December 16th, Dingaansdag (the commemoration of the day when the Boers made a vow to God and killed a large number of Zulus at Blood River) as a religious holiday of the same importance as Christmas or Good Friday.[38] The involvement of G. R. Wessels in the Nationalist Party has already been documented,[39] as has the fact that Nationalist leaders and ministers were frequently invited to Apostolic Faith Mission Workers' Conferences. On the

---

[34] Horn–Louw, *Eén Kudde*, 78. I am not sure on what Horn bases his statement. For the education of Seymour see Nelson, *For Such a Time as This.*

[35] Möller, *Church and Politics*, 39f.

[36] On Frank Chikane see Chikane, *No Life of My Own.*

[37] De Wet, *Apostolic Faith Mission in South Africa.*

[38] Lapoorta, "South Africa," 28. Horn–Louw, *Eén Kudde,* quoted in Lapoorta, "South Africa," 28.

[39] Lapoorta, "South Africa," 28.

other hand, P. L. le Roux, president of the Apostolic Faith Mission from 1913 to 1943, "fought a long battle against Afrikaner nationalism, nazism and other right wing movements."[40] He held, for example, that "The remembrance of white military victories and occupation of the land caused racism and anti-Semitism, which is not of God, but of the spirit of the time and of the Anti-Christ."[41]

On the other hand the Apostolic Faith Mission is—as far as I know—the only Pentecostal denomination which has an official Secretary for Ecumenical Affairs (who was very prominent at the Roman Catholic/Pentecostal dialogue).[42] Ultimately of more significance than this officially sanctioned Office for Ecumenical Affairs may be the work of Pastor Frank Chikane. Because of his outspoken criticism of the South African system of Apartheid, he has on several occasions been detained by the police, imprisoned, and tortured. Throughout his troubles, he attempted to serve as a minister with the Apostolic Faith Mission. In 1981, however, he was placed on suspension by the denomination, and asked to return his credentials for actions which the church labeled "political." Although Chikane returned his credentials, he remained a member in good standing of the Apostolic Faith Mission by holding membership in his father's congregation. In 1990 his suspension was lifted; today, he once again appears on the clergy rolls of the Apostolic Faith Mission.

From 1983 onward Chikane was General Secretary of the Institute for Contextual Theology. Among the programs which he oversaw, one of the most ecumenically significant was the writing of the now famous *Kairos Document*. Later, together with 132 "Concerned Evangelicals," he signed the document *Evangelical Witness in South Africa*, a re-writing of the *Kairos Document* in evangelical language.[43] It was against these documents that R. P. Möller wrote his book *Church and Politics*, already quoted. In particular Möller said that it breathed "the spirit of revolution and confrontation" and used "the Bible and theological utterances" to promote Marxist ideology. Indeed, so convinced was Möller of the "Marxist-Communist" sympathies of some of his Pentecostal sisters and brothers that he argued that the "Marxist-Communist onslaught against South Africa . . . clothes itself with a religious cloak . . . It is even prepared to pose as 'Pentecostal.' "[44]

Shortly after the publication of the *Kairos Document*, Frank Chikane was elected to replace Archbishop Desmond Tutu as Secretary General of the South African Council of Churches. This is extraordinary since the Apostolic Faith Mission is not part of the Council. It is said that this denomination is

---

[40] Horn, "South African Pentecostals and Apartheid," 160.

[41] Le Roux, "Die Gees," 6–7; quoted in Horn, "South African Pentecostals and Apartheid," 160.

[42] Robeck, "Pentecostals and Ecumenism," 20. See also Hollenweger, "Koinonia," 154–57.

[43] This section is heavily based on Robeck, loc. cit., *Kairos Document, Evangelical Witness*. See also Robeck, "Taking Stock," 35–60, in particular 48f.

[44] Möller, *Church and Politics*, 20.

now about to consider a request for official observer status.[45] The most important contribution by Frank Chikane was, however, the writing of *A Relevant Pentecostal Witness*.[46] This document should be read and studied by every Pentecostal and Charismatic because it shows the political, social, and theological potential of Pentecostal experience.[47] It starts with a reminder of the black roots of Pentecostalism and bemoans the "silence of Pentecostals": "Our silence is a willful support of an ideology that is irreconcilable with the Holy Scriptures and with our Christian Faith. . . . It is ironic that severe discipline is placed upon those who falter and commit sins which we as Pentecostals emphasize, yet those who are guilty of many of the apartheid sins can even find sanctuary behind our pulpits." Then follows a discussion of holiness, life of morality, goodwill, honesty, sober habits, meekness, obedience to the Word of God and respect for law and order.

> What is not understood, however, is that these virtues are normally easily attainable in an affluent middle class society. Those who have to struggle with inferior housing, and inferior jobs, have neither the luxury nor the inclination to indulge in feelings of goodwill, meekness and obedience to their white "masters". Consequently we are faced with the situation where a believer from an oppressed community, in order to receive the Spirit baptism, has to make a greater stride towards holiness than a believer from an affluent white community.

> As Pentecostals we have failed to see that the maintenance of white affluence is done at the expense of black poverty and oppression. We have failed to acknowledge that the social conditions in the oppressed communities are a direct result of the social conditions in the affluent white communities. We do not deny that those aspects of morality and holiness which Pentecostals point out are important. However, in our situation they are ineffective when they are not seen as being intrinsically linked with the corruptness of white affluence. . . . In South Africa the Body of Christ is not united but politically and economically divided."

The document adds, "The early Christians did not appease the ruling government so that life could be made easy." And Japie Lapoorta says bluntly: "Non-racialism is a gift of the Spirit just like tongues." Finally, the black Pentecostals in South Africa ask over and over again: Can one be Spirit-filled and racist?

This question surely went through Frank Chikane's mind when he was tortured by an elder of his own Pentecostal denomination (who was a policeman). Who is Spirit-filled here: the torturer, the tortured, both, or neither? It is high time that Pentecostal theologians and exegetes address this kind of question.

---

[45] Robeck, "Pentecostals and Ecumenism," 20.

[46] Originally published under the title "The Road to Damascus: Kairos and Conversion"; commonly quoted as *A Relevant Pentecostal Witness*.

[47] See in particular Lapoorta's interpretation, "South Africa," 28.

As to the call for full integration, the question must be allowed: What does integration mean? Does it include the many independent Pentecostal Zionist churches in South Africa? And does it mean—for instance in matters of liturgy and theology—the capitulation of black identity to the white tradition? It cannot mean this. This has been tried for over a hundred years and has failed. Does it mean the capitulation of white culture to the black tradition? This has never been tried, and it is not at all clear that it would work. Does it mean a compromise between the two? What would such a compromise look like? Would it mean integrated congregations, or more or less segregated congregations in an integrated denomination? It certainly could mean integration in theological education, if it were made clear from the beginning that theological education does not indoctrinate, but rather develops several theological and cultural models of being a Christian. It could also mean holding occasional (or even regular) integrated meetings, while maintaining culturally and racially segregated congregations. This is a tricky question; one which we will explore further in chapter 9.

J. N. Horn seems to be aware of the structural difficulties of an integrated church when—in another context—he discusses the leadership patterns of the church and asks tentatively whether or not an apostolic (or in modern ecclesiological terminology an "episcopal") leadership might not be at least as spiritual as a polity led by democratically elected leaders.[48] But then, persons of "apostolic stature" are not particularly numerous in the Christian church. Not everyone claiming apostolic authority is a Don Helder Câmara, or a Martin Luther King, a Beyers Naude or a Frank Chikane. In fact—with one exception, namely Câmara—none of those mentioned had the title of "bishop" or "apostle" conferred on him. Certainly there are real apostles and bishops in the Christian church. Unfortunately—or perhaps fortunately, who knows?—they are seldom recognized as such. That there are many *so-called* apostles and bishops in the Christian churches—both big and small—is too commonly known to need documentation.[49]

uMoya—A Black Pentecostal Pneumatology

Another option might be to resolutely explore the possibilities of a black pneumatology based on the Zulu concept and experience of uMoya, the Spirit in Zulu culture.[50] Such an attempt is made by the Pentecostal theologian Allan Anderson.[51] He reminds us of the fact that Christian theology has not entered Africa in a vacuum. Just as the Hellenistic theologians accepted certain connotations of Greek culture with the Greek term *pneuma;* just as the Latin theologians accepted certain dualistic connotations of the Latin-Hellenistic

---

[48] Horn, "Apostolic Leadership."
[49] See Donald Gee quoted in *The Pentecostals*, 193.
[50] See the extensive discussion in *The Pentecostals*, 149ff.
[51] Anderson, *Moya*.

culture with the term *spiritus* (with far-reaching consequences for European theology—which has forgotten the original meaning of *ruach jahwe*, the Hebrew term);[52] just as the French theologians hear in the word *esprit* and the German theologians in the word *Geist* some of the intellectual and "spirited" cultural background of these words; so Anderson tries to use the term *Moya* in order to discover the Holy Spirit in an African context with its understandings of power, spirit, world, and the ancestor cult. It will be interesting to see how his fellow Pentecostals in Africa and elsewhere will react.

He underlines the phenomenological and historical parallels between Pentecostalism and African religion, and is particularly interested in what he calls the Spirit-type churches (which I call independent African Pentecostal or Zionist churches). He includes in his overview also Kimbanguism from Zaire, Aladura churches from Nigeria and similar churches from Ghana. The most important conclusion of this thesis, which was submitted to the University of South Africa—beside his clear acknowledgment of a historical continuum between African religion and Pentecostalism[53]—is his statement: "The Holy Spirit has sanctified for his use religious expressions which are found in traditional Africa!"[54]

On the other hand, I did not find any trace of such reflections in the otherwise interesting story of the Assemblies of God in Southern Africa by Peter Watt—and this, in spite of his emphasis on the fact that the majority of the adherents of the Assemblies of God are black. He is very clear on "ecclesiastical colonialism" by foreign missionaries[55] and pleads for ecumenical openness.[56] On the other hand there is a very clear political commitment expressed in an official statement already in 1989 (!):

> We are against unjust exploitation, racial discrimination . . . Biblical justice would best be expressed in the principle of one person, one vote. We believe that it is a real matter of urgency that a National Convention be convened. This must include the leaders of significance in South Africa, whether these be presently detained, banned, imprisoned, in exile, or functioning under the present system.[57]

Certainly that is not the expression of a "pie-in-the-sky" apolitical spirituality.

A discussion between Peter Watt, Allan Anderson, J. Nico Horn, Japie Lapoorta, Frank Chikane, and others might produce a fruitful South African theological and political agenda, or in African terms, an African pneumatol-

---

[52] On this in detail *ITh* 3.

[53] Anderson, *Moya*, 126–29.

[54] Ibid., 123. An important paper on this issue was delivered at the Brighton conference by Daneel, "African"; also in *International Review of Mission*, 82/326, April, 1993, 143–66.

[55] Watt, *From Africa's Soil*, 197f.

[56] Ibid., 151–64.

[57] Ibid., 182f.

ogy. A recently published book by Allan Anderson, *Bazalwane,*[58] will be important for this discussion because of its rich historical material on African Pentecostals in South Africa (including Zionists and other independent Pentecostal churches) and because the author sees not only a historical but also a theological link between these different types of Pentecostalism in South Africa.

This theological link is identified by a Canadian anthropologist, Karla Poewe. She observes that in South Africa, as anywhere else,

> written liberation theologies were popular among students, professors, and especially, politically radical Christians of the South African Council of Churches. They were oppositional theologies whose adherents talked revolution, but worked within the formal sectors of society which they opposed. While liberationist practices were often rejected by members of the various independent churches, even by their well-educated followers, written liberation theologies were understood by them and were seen to have served a specific and important function.[59]

"Black theologians talk black and do white," says Kenosi Mofokeng, who heads the Association of African Spiritual Churches.[60] The reason is that written theologies of liberation

> grew out of the experiences of Catholic priests, often well educated Americans, or other scholars who worked with the poor. They did not grow out of the experiences of the poor themselves, but out of how priests and scholars who encountered the poor imagined the poor to experience their poverty. Consequently, they are first and foremost theologies which registered the culture shock of those who worked with the poor.[61]

Unfortunately this type of liberation theology has at times developed into an ideology where all evil is seen in "the system," and where to kill and mutilate blacks and whites alike who happen to disagree with one's revolutionary ideology is seen as necessary, in the interest of the struggle for freedom.

As an outsider to this struggle I do not feel that I can or should pass a judgment on this. One thing however is sure: The liberationists have so far not shown enough respect for the religion of those whom they want to liberate. Theirs is very often still a colonialist model.[62]

---

[58] On this book see ch. 20, pp. 266f.

[59] Poewe, "Theologies of Black South Africans," 43–65, quote 46.

[60] Ibid., 46.

[61] Ibid., 47. See also Poewe-Hexham/Hexham, "Apartheid," 78–83. Responses by J. N. Horn and Wynand J. de Kock in the same volume.

[62] More on African theology in ch. 6, pp. 70–80.

CHAPTER **SIX**

Pentecost of N'Kamba: Simon Kimbangu and His Church[1]

Neither in the strictly dogmatical nor in the historical sense does the *Eglise de Jésus-Christ sur la terre d'après le prophète Simon Kimbangu* (EJCSK) belong to the Pentecostal movement. Their idiosyncratic practice of Spirit baptism,[2] for example, is unknown among Pentecostals. In contrast to other independent churches in Africa,[3] the Kimbanguist Church did not emerge from Pentecostal missionary work. But on the other hand there are remarkable parallels between Pentecostals and Kimbanguists: healing through prayer; spontaneous worship within the framework of unwritten, but nevertheless efficient, liturgies; the congregation as a brotherly, all-embracing community; the hierarchical leadership of the church; and speaking in tongues, trembling,[4] and visions. Above all both Kimbanguists and Pentecostals believe that the Holy Spirit can be experienced, and that evil spirits are best counteracted by the power of the Spirit.[5] When at the Central Committee of the World Council of Churches in Canterbury (1969) the

---

[1] This chapter started as a chapter in my *Pentecost Between Black and White*. It has been thoroughly revised, updated, and annotated.

[2] See below p. 70.

[3] E.g., in South Africa, cf. *The Pentecostals*, 120–22, 149–75 and Oshun, "Perspective," 105–14; *EPTA Bulletin* 4/2, 1985, 73f.

[4] See the oldest report (Nfinanangani–Nzungu, "Kimbangu," 15–42). The document was found in the archives of the Service Colonial des Affaires Indigènes et de la Main d'Oeuvre, Léopoldville (today Kinshasa). It mentions Kimbangu's speaking in tongues twice: "I spoke in a strange tongue" ("Kimbangu," 24); "He spoke in a new tongue" ("Kimbangu," 35). Trembling and speaking in tongues are discouraged today.

[5] This aspect particularly has been treated by E. Bazola in his sociological analysis. Bazola, "Kimbanguisme," 144–52.

Brazilian Pentecostal church *Brasil para Cristo*[6] was admitted to the World Council together with the Kimbanguist Church, the Brazilian Pentecostal leader Manoel de Melo named the chief spiritual of the Kimbanguists, Joseph Diangienda, a Pentecostal, while the latter accepted de Melo as a Kimbanguist.

There is another reason for including this chapter in a book on Pentecostalism's promises and problems. The EJCSK is one of the best documented and researched churches of a Pentecostal type in the Third World. Its history and theology contain in a nutshell almost all the problems and promises of such churches.

Pentecostal Movement and Kimbanguists in Zaïre[7]

Susan Asch gives *grosso modo* the following statistics: 12 million Catholics, 9 million in the Eglise du Christ au Zaïre,[8] and three million Kimbanguists,[9] out of a population of 28 million. The number of Pentecostals in this picture is almost negligible, perhaps 130,000. The following statistics are available:

- *Communauté Assemblées de Dieu à l'Est du Zaïre* (*Handbuch*, 01.18.003): 21 congregations, 30,613 members (*WChH* 1968, 64); Barrett (*WChE*, 762) gives for the same church 220 congregations, 4,409 members, 10,780 adherents (ex Assemblies of God, UK).
- *Communauté Assemblées de Dieu au Zaïre* (*Handbuch*, 01.18.004): 51 pastors and congregations, 50,000 adherents (*WChH* 1968, 64); Barrett (*WChE*, 762): 270 congregations, 16,019 members, 50,000 adherents (ex Assemblies of God, USA)
- *Communauté Evangélique de Pentecôte au Shaba:* Barrett (*WChE*, 763) 120 congregations, 18,014 members, 50,000 adherents (related to Zaïrian Evangelistic Mission).
- *Communauté Pentecôtiste au Zaïre:* Barrett (*WChE*, 763) 600 congregations, 54,371 members, 180,000 adherents (ex Zaïrian Evangelistic Mission).
- *Eglise de Dieu:* Barrett (*WChE*, 762) 29 congregations, 6,163 members, 10,000 adherents (ex Church of God, Cleveland).
- *Communauté des Eglises de Grace au Zaïre:* Barrett (*WChE*, 762) 152 congregations, 5,538 members, 20,000 adherents. Together less than one of the splinter churches of the "official" EJCSK. Obviously, Pentecostalism in Zaïre is not represented by the many Pentecostal mission churches but by Kimbanguism in all its forms. Barrett rightly

---

[6] *The Pentecostals*, 99–108.

[7] Zaïre is the African name for the former Belgian Congo.

[8] This is the name of the former Protestant Council of Churches into which most protestant missionary churches were forced by government decree. In the statistics below all the churches with the prefix "communauté" are members of the Eglise du Christ au Zaïre.

[9] Asch, *Kimbangu*, 91.

mentions the different organizations of Kimbanguism under the heading "Pentecostalism."[10] It is of course a Pentecostalism *sui generis*.

The history in Zaïre of the British and North American Assemblies of God,[11] the British Congo Evangelistic Mission (today Zaïrian Evangelistic Mission, ZEM)[12] and French Assemblées de Dieu[13]—including the remarkable school and hospital work of the Norwegian[14] and Swedish[15] Pentecostals—has not yet been written. We know little or nothing about their relationships (or non-relationships) to Kimbanguism.

It seems that the different Pentecostal missions have had hardly any contact with each other, possibly because each works in a different part of this large country. Marie-Louise Martin mentions 46 Protestant missionary societies and churches in Zaïre—many of them evangelical.[16] One must look at the protest against the fragmentation of the church in Zaïre in light of this background. Young people lay the blame for this at the feet of "the treacherous and merchandising missionaries."[17]

One would have hoped that there would be cooperation at least between Pentecostals and Kimbanguists in Zaïre, and one can see a few encouraging signs here. While it is true that the rejection of black Pentecostal churches in South Africa in the past[18] finds its parallel in the rejection of the Kimbanguists by the American Assemblies of God,[19] at present—and this is a new develop-

---

[10] Barrett, *WChE*, 762f.

[11] Wilson, E. A. G., *Making Many Rich*, 161–70. Carmichael, "Congo," 19f.

[12] Steiner, L., *Mit folgenden Zeichen*, 98. Burton, "Kongo." 19ff; idem, *Man;* idem, *Working;* idem, *Village;* idem, *Pastor;* idem, *Missionary;* idem, *Signs;* idem, *Mafundijyo*. Moorhead, *Congo Forest*. Gee, *Flesh*, 63–67 (also in Gee, *Wind and Flame*, passim); Frodsham, *With Signs Following*, 165–75; Hodgson, *Out of the Darkness*.

[13] Giraud, "Congo," 35/7–8: 22–23; 35/11: 24–25. Vernaud, "Congo," 37/6: 23–24; 37/7–8: 20–21; 36/10: 21–22.

[14] Andresen, "Literaturmisjon," 189–92. Bårdli, "Skolearbeidet," 176–88. Børresen, "1955–1960," 165–69. Orlien, "Sykehuset i nay Kaziba," 169–75.

[15] Stenholm, "Svenska,"quoted by Blomquist, *Svenska pingstväckelsen*, 264.

[16] Martin, M.-L., *Kirche ohne Weisse*, 56f.

[17] Mukuan, "Dupl. minutes." Cf. also, *Service oecuménique de Presse* 38/15, 10.6.1971, 2 (WCC, Geneva, only in the French edition) and *Ecumenical Press Service* 39/2, 20.1.1972.

[18] *The Pentecostals*, 126–39; above ch. 5, pp. 41–43.

[19] "The village of Banza Mateke, seventy-five miles northeast of Matadi, Belgian Congo, has become the center of a nationalistic religious movement which is causing some concern among the Congo missionaries. The 'Nguza' movement is extremely nationalistic, having vowed to 'drive all whites into the ocean'. It has within its creed a mixture of spirit worship, materialism, and elements of Christianity. Their Christ is a Congolese, Simoni Kimbangi (sic), who lived a good life and died a Romanist. They maintain that 'Jesus Christ is the white man's Savior. Ours is Simoni Kimbangi, and he will soon rise from the dead and lead us to victory'. The Ngunza preachers pray 'in the name of the Father and Simone, and the Holy Ghost'. It is not unusual for thousands to come to this village bringing their sick to the Ngunza preacher Gabriel Mabwaka, for prayer, hoping for some miracle to relieve their suffering. The

ment—the voices of those Pentecostals who see in the Kimbanguists their brothers and sisters are increasing. Christian Krust, a German pentecostal, reports from the Fourth Assembly of the World Council of Churches at Uppsala in 1968 as follows:

> Hitherto I had known nothing of the existence of such a church [namely the Kimbanguist church]. But when, after greeting and introducing ourselves, we knelt down and prayed together, the two [Kimbanguist] brethren from the Congo joined in prayer. It is true that I understand French only partially and it was not possible for me to follow the exact wording of their prayer but the way in which they prayed and spoke with God, that made a tremendous impression on me and the others in the prayer-room: These brothers are specially inspired by the Holy Spirit! They spoke with such dignity and serenity that it warmed one's heart. In the subsequent informal discussion the impression was deepened that those two brothers [Jean-Claude L. Luntadila, Philip Nanga] were firmly rooted in faith, that they were true members of the body of Christ, born again and baptized with the Holy Spirit.[20]

One can only hope that the Assemblies of God will change their unfavorable judgment of the Kimbanguists (a "false Christ" religion) in the light of the reports by European Pentecostals.

My assessment is based on confidential documents and correspondence in the archives of the World Council of Churches,[21] on personal acquaintance with Kimbanguists and a visit to Zaïre, and above all on the seminal works by Asch and Ustorf.[22]

---

ritual includes elements of witchcraft and perverted prayer. It will take real prayer in the name of our Lord Jesus Christ to overcome this 'false Christ' religion." *PE* 2401,15.5.1960, 10. Against these reproaches see pp. 69f.

[20] Krust, "Kimbanguistenkirche," 147–48. Cf. also Steiner, L., "Kimbanguistenkirche."

[21] Partly summarized in a document which was written together by the WCC and the Kimbanguists, "The Kimbanguist Church in the Congo," printed: *Ecumenical Review* 19/1, Jan. 1967, 29–36. Some of the more important of these documents are quoted and summarized by Niederberger, "Kimbangu-Kirche," 215–19.

[22] In addition to the literature mentioned in the notes, one would have to mention: Béguin–Martin, "Kimbanguisme," 5–37; Casebow, *Kimbanguisme.* "Le Kimbanguisme," *Courrier hebdomadaire* 8.1.1960. Dialungana, *Kisikulusa;* Diangienda, "Kimbanguisme," 16–17; idem, "Coup"; Lasserre, "L'Eglise," 45–52; Lerrigo, "Prophet Movement in the Congo," 270–77; Luzolo, *Mvand'avelela;* Martin, M.-L., "Prophetism in the Congo," 154–63. Idem, *Prophetic Christianity in the Congo;* Masembo, *Le Prophétisme kongo.* Mwene-Batende, *Etude sociologique;* Ntontolo, *Mouvements prophétiques;* Ryckmans, *Les mouvements prophétique du kongo;* Doutreloux, "Prophétisme"; Lanternari, *Movimenti,* 11ff. Bibliography in Mitchell–Turner, *Bibliography.* Follow-up in *Journal of Religion in Africa 1,* 1968, 173–210. Chassard, "Essai de bibliographie," 43–49.

Besides the work of Susanne Asch, the most important research is by Werner Ustorf, *Afrikanische Initiative.* In his *Christianized Africa—De-Christianized Europe?* Ustorf summarized in a less critical form his insights (34, 43f, 49–57, 60–70, 73f, 99). For solid research on Kimbanguism, Ustorf's *Afrikanische Initiative* is indispensable.

Marie-Louise Martin also had access to documents relevant to the origin of the church, and was able to interview eyewitnesses.[23] That enabled her to recognize many stories and reports as legends and to discard them. Some of these legends appeared in 1961 in a small liturgy,[24] allegedly published by Kimbanguist pastors with the approval of their spiritual head. Though this booklet has often been used as a source by researchers,[25] it is without doubt a forgery; for one thing, the Kimbanguists did not use printed liturgies.[26]

Werner Ustorf, however, has serious doubts whether Marie-Louise Martin's description presents anything more than the streamlined "orthodox" view of Kimbanguism as it is presented today by its urban leadership. He has attempted a thorough reconstruction of the life and death of Simon Kimbangu on the basis of hitherto unknown or forgotten documents (among them two letters by Simon Kimbangu).

Simon Kimbangu

The Kimbanguists make fun of the European pneumatology which says that the Holy Spirit is a bird; for the Kimbanguists the Spirit manifests itself in a man, Simon Kimbangu.[27] A very interesting pneumatology! However, once this man had died, his sons became the incarnation of divine power and guidance.

Who was Simon Kimbangu? He was born in 1889 at N'Kamba (Thysville, Lower Zaïre). Kuyela, his father, and Lwezi, his mother, died early. He was educated by his aunt, Kinzembo. As a young man he became a Christian. He had his theological education from the Baptists, and in July 1915 was baptized in the river that passes by Ngombe-Lutete, together with his wife Mvilu Marie and the man who later became his assistant, Mikala Mandombe. He tried to become a catechist with the Baptist Missionary Society, but was refused because he was only "village trained" and could only read "stumblingly."[28]

---

[23] Among the documents, hitherto unknown, particularly important are: reports of the secretaries of Simon Kimbangu, Nfinangani and Nzungu, which were confiscated by the Belgian colonial administration 17.6.1921 (see above, note 4); a report by the Belgian administration (so-called "documents secrets belge") which fell into the hands of the Kimbanguists in 1960; a number of letters and reports by missionaries of the British Baptist Missionary Society (in their London archives) and others.

[24] *Nkanda Bisamu bia Simon Kimbangu*. French subtitle: *Office du prophète Simon Kimbangu*, 1961.

[25] Chomé, *Kimbangu*; Raymaekers in his introduction to the document mentioned in note 4.

[26] Martin, M.-L., *Kirche ohne Weisse*, 48; English translation: *Kimbangu*, 40.

[27] Asch, *Kimbangu*, 165.

[28] Casebow on the 23d April 1958 from Ngombe Lutete in the Circular Letter no. 2 to the Baptists Missionary Headquarters (Baptist Missionary Society Archive, Casebow Papers; Ustorf, *Afrikanische Initiative*, 122, 154. Martin, M.-L., *Kirche ohne Weisse*, 70). Today's Kimbanguist leaders say Kimbangu was a catechist with the Baptists.

In 1918 he tried his hand as a worker in the Huileries du Congo Belge, and later as a kind of street seller in Kinshasa, for which he needed a "permis de séjour."[29] The street trading was a failure. He "returned to N'Kamba and tried to make ends meet as a farmer and a carpenter. Nevertheless the family suffered greatly."[30]

Already in 1915/16 he had received a first vocation: "I had a dream from God who told me: 'I have heard your prayer. People think that one needs "de l'esprit"[31] for doing my work, but I will give you in abundance.' "[32]

One night in the year 1918, when many were dying of flu because the medical help promised by the missions did not arrive, Kimbangu heard a voice saying: "I am Christ, my servants are unfaithful, I have chosen you to witness and convert your brothers . . . Take care of my sheep."[33] Simon answered: "I do not know this kind of work, Lord. There are others better educated than me, they will take care of the flock."[34] Night after night the audition was repeated, and Simon's wife heard Simon answering.

On the morning of the 6th of April, 1921 (today celebrated as the foundation-day of the church) Simon went to the market. Then he felt compelled against his will to go into the neighboring village of Ngombe-Kinsukke, to enter the hut of Nkiantondo, a sick woman, and to lay his hands on her head and heal her in the name of Christ. The woman was healed. Soon other healings followed. Marie-Louise Martin sums up this period:

> The most important point made by Kimbanguist narrators is: "Should the same not happen in the Congo as happened in Palestine? Has the time of miracles passed? Did Christ not ordain his disciples to preach *and* heal? If we recall the stories in the Acts of the Apostles, did they not do it in the power of the Holy Ghost?"[35]

"As far as the followers of Kimbangu were concerned, nothing less than a new Pentecost had come. The Holy Spirit had evidently descended on Simon Kimbangu and had given him authority to heal and to preach."[36] This conviction is so great that the trinitarian formula "in the name of the Father, the Son and the Holy Ghost" is often supplemented by the words "which has come upon Simon Kimbangu," or "which has spoken to us through Simon Kimbangu." That does not mean, as has been stated,[37] that Simon Kimbangu replaces the

---

[29] *Ordonnance* of 10.8.1920, quoted by Feci, "Kimbangu," 9, according to the *Progrès colonial* of 16.6.1921 and 23.6.1921, quoted in Asch, *Kimbangu*, 21.

[30] Sources in Ustorf, *Afrikanische Initiative*, 125.

[31] "De l'esprit" in the French sense means "intelligence."

[32] Nfinangani–Nzungu, "Kimbangu," § 2.

[33] Choffat, "Kimbanguiste," 4.

[34] Desanti, "Golden Anniversary," 7–19 (with excellent photographs).

[35] From an unpublished draft of Martin, M.-L., *Kirche ohne Weisse*.

[36] Martin, M.-L., *Kirche ohne Weisse*, 74; English; *Kimbangu*, 47 (my translation).

[37] Buana-Kibongi, "Kimbanguisme," 75–81. This formulation is very similar to Montanus'. Tertullian's use of the term "Spirit," "when describing Montanus seems to have been his way of equating the *words* of Montanus with the teachings of the Spirit, not their *persons*." Robeck, *Prophecy*, 260, note 27. On the famous comparison

Holy Spirit in the eyes of his followers, but it does mean that they consider him to be an instrument (or perhaps an incarnation) of the Holy Spirit.

This becomes more understandable if one realizes the plight in which the population found itself at this time. Colonialism, with its oppression and its contagious diseases, had reduced the population of the Bakongo by two-thirds. In the face of epidemics European medicine was powerless. It is therefore understandable that Kimbangu's healings were considered a gift from God.[38]

Now the masses flocked together. Without wanting it, Kimbangu became the founder of a large and enthusiastic movement which shook the whole country. With the Bible in his hands he asked his countrymen to stamp out all witchcraft and to abstain from heathen dances and from polygamy. Surprised by the great success, he chose five African helpers. But the missionaries and the then Belgian colonial government became very suspicious.[39] Churches and workshops were deserted, for which Kimbangu was made responsible. However, one could call this—as Ustorf does—an "apocalyptically-based movement of non-cooperation which spoiled the smooth running of colonial economy."[40] Kimbangu was unjustly accused of hatred of the Europeans[41] and of seducing people into laziness and refusing to pay their taxes.[42]

---

of man "as a lyre" see Robeck, *Prophecy*, 287, note 29. Robeck is a Pentecostal patristic scholar who writes about prophecy in Carthage as somebody who knows the problem and promise of continuing revelation and prophecy today. See also Robeck, "Canon." I owe this comparative reflection to Dr. Robeck.

[38] Asch, *Kimbangu*, 17, 19, quoting van Wing, "Kimbanguisme," 563–618, quote 565.

[39] Choffat ("Kimbanguiste," 32, note 34) quotes some such voices from *La Voix du Rédempteur*, Aug . 1921 and Dec. 1921; likewise Bertsche, "Kimbanguism," 18) quotes Dunfoneny, *Congo*, 2/4, 1924, 380–88.

[40] Ustorf, *Afrikanische Initiative*, 194.

[41] This is contradicted by a prayer of Simon Kimbangu which has been kept: "Bless all the races of the earth, the big and the small ones, women and men, white and black" (published in the Kimbanguist document *Mise au points*, 1957, quoted by Martin, M.-L., *Kirche ohne Weisse*, 77.) Cf. Gilis, *Kimbangu, fondateur de l'église*, 39, and furthermore by a declaration which appeared in the periodical *Kimbanguisme* (no. 1, May 1960): "Our religion remains open to all races" (quoted by Decapmaeker, "Kimbanguisme," 64). In spite of the hard and unjust treatment, which the Kimbanguists experienced from the whites, it was a Kimbanguist (Charles Kosolokele) who during the riots in 1960 used all his influence in order to get the whites free (Martin, M.-L., *Kirche ohne Weisse*, 171. Hoskyns, *Congo*, 90). On the other hand it is true that, according to Bazola, the Kimbanguists have occasionally *criticized* the missionaries. But from this one cannot easily deduce that they hated the whites. See e.g.: "The catholic and protestant missionaries have brought us the Gospel and the doctrine of Jesus Christ, only begotten Son of God, who died on the cross for the salvation of all men, who, by the sin of Adam, have violated the divine ideal which had become impossible to attain because of their degenerated nature" (Wikisi–Yowani–Luntadila–Diata, *Mise au point*, quoted by Bazola, "Kimbanguisme," 133). "The missionaries have falsified the message of the Gospel in hiding some doctrine, namely the one of the Holy Spirit" (Bazola, "Kimbanguisme," 148).

[42] Cf. the obligation to pay taxes in the Kimbanguist ethics, below p. 67.

In the Name of Law and Order . . .

The Belgian civil servant Morel was asked to open an investigation of the Kimbanguist revival. When Morel arrived at N'Kamba the prophet and his five disciples felt the Spirit upon them, and they spoke in tongues and sang throughout the whole night.[43]

Morel came to the conclusion:

Kimbangu wants to found a religion which reflects the mentality of the Africans, a religion, which contains the fundamentals of protestantism, mixed up with practices of witchcraft . . . Everybody can see that the European religions have been petrified by abstractions and do not correspond to the mentality of the Africans who are longing for tangible facts and protection from demons. The religion of Kimbangu suits them because it is supported by tangible facts.[44]

And Marie-Louise Martin adds: "How right Morel was, but the time to view this insight positively had not yet come!"[45] for Morel continues: "Therefore it is necessary to fight Kimbangu. His tendency is pan-African. Natives will say: 'We have found a God of the blacks, the religion which suits the African' . . . Law and Order demands that Kimbanguism be stopped quietly but immediately."[46]

When the colonial government decided to arrest Kimbangu, he fled from N'Kamba; but in September 1921, of his own free will, he presented himself before his persecutors. Before that, he admonished his followers to accept sufferings courageously, never to use the sword, and never to repay the evil done by the Europeans by doing evil to them. Although no white man was ever injured, Kimbangu was arrested in September 1921 after only five months of public ministry. In a pseudo-process—the Belgian writer Chomé called it a "judicial monstrosity"[47]—the military commander Rossi sentenced him to 120 lashes,[48]

---

[43] Nfinangani–Nzungu, *Kimbangu*, note 4.

[44] The Morel Reports in Ryckmans, *Les mouvements prophétiques du kongo*, 47 and in Ustorf, *Afrikanische Initiative*, 375, note 4. The reports of the colonial administration were extremely racist and superficial. They accused Kimbangu of "superstition" (Rapport de l'administration du Congo Belge, 1922, quoted in Asch, *Kimbangu*, 28) or of mental illness (same report 1921, Asch, *Kimbangu*, 25).

[45] Martin, M.-L., *Kirche ohne Weisse*, 87f.; English, *Kimbangu*, 57 (my translation).

[46] Ryckmans, *Les mouvements prophétiques du kongo*. Indeed it is possible that Kimbangu had been in contact with the ideas of some black Baptists whose ideas one can summarize like this: a) the black civilization is at the root of European civilization; b) blacks must break their chains and become again pioneers of humanity; c) Christ himself was black; d) he calls the blacks to create their own religion based on their own traditions. For connections between black Baptists and Kimbangu, see Asch, *Kimbangu*, 21f. On a visit to Kinshasa the Kimbanguists told me that two of them had tried to visit the aging Morel in order to tell him that they had forgiven him. Although they had flown to Brussels for this visit, Morel did not receive them.

[47] Chomé, *Kimbangu*, 72.

[48] A later lashing, when he was delivered to prison, is described by one of colonial agents as follows: "First discipline. My Kibangu [sic] has earned his lashes, he shall

followed by capital punishment. However the Belgian King, Albert I, commuted capital punishment to life imprisonment, partly because of intercessions by some missionaries.[49] Kimbangu was deported to Katanga where he was imprisoned for thirty years. He died in the prison of Elisabethville (today Lubumbashi) on the 12th October 1951. J. van Wing (whose report was also obviously used by the Assemblies of God) stated that on his death-bed Kimbangu had agreed to become a Catholic, but this statement is categorically denied by the sisters who had looked after Kimbangu in prison, and by one of his warders.

The Benedictine François Xavier Nsenkoto affirms that Kimbangu converted to the Catholic Church shortly before his death and he, Nsenkoto baptized him.[50] This is strongly denied by Sinda[51] and the neo-Kimbanguist leaders.[52] Ustorf, who discusses the whole material carefully and in detail, had corresponded with Nsenkoto and published also two (disputed) letters by Kimbangu from prison. Nevertheless he tends to agree with Nsenkoto. Gilis says rightly: "Whether he died a catholic or a Kimbanguist, what does it matter. He died in peace."[53]

Ustorf, who discusses the emerging prophetic awareness in Kimbangu in the social and historical context of the time can explain a certain sobering in prison (cf. Mt 11:3) and interprets Kimbangu's mission adequately when he writes: "Kimbangu tried less to find a meaning in the Bible or to find a text geared to his situation. He was looking much more—as Pentecostals do in general—for parallels to his social and personal history in the Bible which would uncover its meaning. Clearly he discovered other texts in the Bible than the missionaries."[54] Note that this is a kind of hermeneutics which we find also among the early disciples of Jesus.[55]

---

have them, this is clear. The Kimbanguists smiled. They thought the whip would break in the air. Kibangu and his epidermis are holy, untouchable. A miracle was going to happen. Emotion. Silence. Whack! My prophet cries like mad. His . . . well, you understand, was sensitive like that of anyone. Whack! He is writhing and grimacing. That was the end. Kibangu understood that he was not a prophet and the other prisoners understood too. That heals many a thing, the whip." (Statement by Enauts, quoted in Chalux [pseudonym], *Congo Belge,* 409).

[49] The difficult situation of the protestant missionaries who "were caught in a cross-fire between the administration, the Roman Catholic and many African Protestant Christians" (Irvine, "Birth," 23–76) is discussed by Ustorf, *Afrikanische Initiative;* Irvine, "Birth"; and Fehderau, "Prophetic Christianity," 157–78.

[50] Nsenkoto, *La Croix du Congo,* 25/46, 17.11.1975, 1f. quoted in Ustorf, *Afrikanische Initiative,* 457f. Similar van Wing ("Kimbanguisme" note 39) and Ngindu, "Colloque," 631–45.

[51] Sinda, *Le messianisme congolais,* 85.

[52] Martin, M.-L., *Kirche ohne Weisse,* 97; English: *Kimbangu,* 64.

[53] Gilis, *Kimbangu, fondateur de l'église,* 109.

[54] Ustorf, *Afrikanische Initiative,* 184.

[55] Weber, H.-R., "Bibel," 97–107.

Sufferings

Much suffering down here.
Sickness makes us suffer.
Tears are flowing.
Come to our aid!
Holy Ghost, come, o come!
Come to our aid![56]

Many hymns tell of the sufferings of this time when Kimbangu accepted his imprisonment without putting up any resistance. Before entering prison, Kimbangu had admonished his followers not to exercise any opposition, leaving them nothing but the Bible and the suggestion that they should join the Protestant missions. The Kimbanguists were now faced with a cruel persecution which lasted almost forty years. About 37,000 persons were deported, and most of them died in exile.[57] One had only to be accused of being a Kimbanguist, or to utter the name Simon Kimbangu, in order to be deported without trial. During a meal in Kinshasa at which a drama group played the "Passion of Kimbangu," a Kimbanguist told me that he was arrested at four o'clock in the morning because the police found in his house a newspaper article on Kimbangu. He was put into a concentration camp[58] where each morning a number of Kimbanguists were beaten up and killed—just for fun. However, deportation did not break the spirit of witness of these Christians. Proof of this is in their hymns:

God has created Heaven and Earth.
Nobody is more powerful than He.
One of these days he is going to end all palaver.
Come quickly, let us pray![59]

In the former Belgian and French Congo, Gabon, Angola, and Rwanda, Kimbanguist congregations emerged, but mostly in secret. As the leaders were regularly arrested, some of these groups degenerated and began endless quarrels with each other. The latest arrests took place in 1957 (according to Ustorf 1959). Then followed the episode—famous in the history of the Kimbanguist church—in the sports stadium of King Baudouin, today Stadion St. Raphael. Joseph Diangienda recounted the event to Marie-Louise Martin as follows: While he stayed in the car and prayed,

> a delegation of Kimbanguists went with a letter to the Belgian Governor-General, Pétillon. The letter, signed by six hundred leading Kimbanguists who were

---

[56] Bolamba, *Diaconie,* 19; Asch, *Kimbangu,* 23. The Kimbanguist hymns were collected by the Belgian police, see Boka–Raymaekers, *Chants.*

[57] Only 2685 survived. Asch, *Kimbangu,* 40, quoting a document by Luntadila, Nov. 1971, 3 (archives EJCSK, General Secretariat). Also Desanti, "Golden Anniversary," 18.

[58] Such concentration camps are documented in Asch, *Kimbangu,* 33.

[59] Boka–Raymaekers, *Chants,* no. 3.

known for their irreproachable conduct read as follows: "We are suffering too much. Wherever we assemble for prayer your soldiers arrest us. We do not want to make such trouble for the police. We will all assemble in the stadium of King Baudouin—unarmed—and there you can massacre us if you want." The alternative solution—not expressed in the letter—"or give us religious liberty."

The delegation went to M. Pétillon while the Kimbanguists began to assemble in the Stadium Baudouin to prepare themselves for arrest and death. The governor was in a very tricky situation. "Do you believe that the government has the right to wipe out a whole section of the population without reason?" he asked the delegates. They answered: "Well, does the government not have this right? Why then does it have the right to deport 37,000 families?" Pétillon hesitated. He wanted to avoid a decision. What would Brussels say if he were to order the police to shoot at the unarmed crowd? What would the world press say? On the other hand, what would the *colons*, the white settlers, say if he were to concede religious freedom to the Kimbanguists? But the delegation insisted on a clear yes or no. Finally the governor did the only reasonable thing. He conceded tolerance, saying: "I grant you tolerance but without the guarantee of the government. For this I am not authorized. Yet I do not arrest you."[60]

"We were overjoyed,"[61] ends Luntadila, the general secretary of the Church, in his report on the incident. The negotiations still took some time. At Christmas, 1959—after almost forty years wandering in the wilderness—the Kimbanguist Church was recognized by the Belgian government and put on the same level as the Catholic and Protestant missions. On June 30th, 1960, the Congo shook off the colonial yoke. Those deported Kimbanguists who had survived could return.

The Kimbanguist Church Today

The Actual Doctrine on Simon Kimbangu

An examination of all the passages in Kimbanguist literature which relate to Kimbangu show him as the "envoy of Our Lord Jesus Christ"[62]; as

---

[60] Martin, M.-L., *Kirche ohne Weisse*, 151–53; English: *Kimbangu*, 105 (my translation); Asch, *Kimbangu*, 38f. The Kimbanguists had already acted in a similar way earlier: 1923 when several catechists were arrested (Balandier, *Sociologie actuelle*, 443) and 1964 in Stanleyville (Choffat, "Kimbanguiste," note 34, 12). Ustorf (*Afrikanische Initiative*) considers the story to be a legend. In general he considers Marie-Louise Martin's *Kirche ohne Weisse* (English: *Kimbangu*) to be an uncritical adaptation of the "official church history" by the now leading Kimbanguist hierarchy. But Asch gives good documentation. Ustorf expressed his criticism of the "official history" also in the review of Diangienda's *L'histoire du Kimbanguisme* in *Zeitschrift für Mission* 11/4, 1985, 248–50.

[61] Luntadila, *L'Essor*.

[62] *Catéchisme* 11.7.1957, question 1: Qui est Tata (respectful title which means father addressed to every adult man) Simon Kimbangu? Answer: "Tata Kimbangu est l'envoyé de Notre Seigneur Jésus-Christ." In the Kikonga catechism (1958) the corresponding passage reads as follows: "O Tata Simon Kimbangu inani? O Tata

"prophet"[63] and "example"[64]; as the one through whom "the people of the Congo know that God and Jesus remembered us"[65]; and in one instance as the comforter promised in John 14:12–18.[66] The statements on the second coming of Kimbangu[67] and his pre-existence,[68] which a European theologian could misunderstand as Christological ideas, are interpreted by Marie-Louise Martin in the context of an African understanding, which—similar to that of the Orthodox church—assumes the living and the deceased Christians to be one single community. The title "God" is explicitly rejected for Kimbangu.[69] The most understandable term for a European reader is probably that of an intercessor;[70] i.e., Simon Kimbangu has a position in the Kimbanguist Church

---

Simon Kimbangu i Ntumwa Nfumu' eto Yesu Klisto" (Both catechisms quoted in full by Raymaekers, *Zaïre*, 737–40.

[63] Dialangana, *Zolanga*, no. 3; quoted by MacGaffey, "Beloved City," 138.

[64] Dialangana, *Tanganinia*, 22ff.: "Tata has exactly walked in the foot-prints of our Lord Jesus Christ. We must follow him, because our Lord has chosen him to show us the way." Quoted by Martin, M.-L., *Kirche ohne Weisse*, 205; English: *Kimbangu*, 145.

[65] Dialangana, *Zolanga*, no. 4.7: "Because Simon Kimbangu obeyed the voice of Jesus, all things promised were fulfilled in him, the work of Jesus was revealed, and the names of God the Father and the Lord Jesus were glorified. Since the coming of the missionaries it had never happened that the dead arose, the lame walked, and the blind saw, or that people of their own free will threw away their fetishes, or wanted to pray to God. And only then did we the people of Kongo know that God and Jesus remembered us. The grief and suffering of our fathers were heard by God the Father, and the tears of us the black people are wiped away in Kongo" (quoted by MacGaffey, "Beloved City," 139).

[66] *Catechisme*, 11.7.1957, question 2: "Comment le savons-nous que Tata Simon Kimbangu est l'envoyé de Notre Seigneur Jésus-Christ? Jésus-Christ lui–même nous a promis de demander à son père de nous envoyer un autre Consolateur pour réaliser plus que lui. Lisez Jean 14.12–18." Kikongo: "Bweyi tuzayidi vo tata Kimbangu Simon i Ntumwa Klisto? Kadi Yandi Mfumu eto Yesu Klisto kibeni watusila nsila vo sikatulombela kwa Se katufidisila onsadisi wa nkaka yni sikavanga mavangu masundidi (Womai 14:12–18)," quoted by Raymaekers, *Zaïre*, 737–40.

[67] The catechisms of 1957 (answer 13) speaks of Kimbangu, who "est mort et résuscité et demeure avec nous en tout esprit." Question 11: "Tata Simon kimbangu saura-t-il revoir encore? Quelle est la conclusion de tout cela? Certes, il reviendra, car tout ce qui a commencé doit avoir sa réalisation! Jean 16.19–33" (quoted by Raymaekers, *Zaïre*).

[68] *Catéchisme*, 1957, Question 20: "A quel moment Tata Simon Kimbangu a-t-il commencé? Il demeurait avec Dieu dès le commencement (Jean 1.1)," quoted by Raymaekers, *Zaïre*, and Gilis, *Kimbangu, fondateur d'église*, 104. *Le Catéchisme concernant le prophète Simon Kimbangu* (N'Kamba 1970) likewise (1.4, quoted by Wainwright, "Reflections," 22f.

[69] *Catéchisme*, 1957, Question 19 and hymn no. 5 in collection of hymns mentioned in note 56 above, also quoted by Bazola, "Kimbanguisme," 132f.

[70] Calendar of the Kimbanguist church 1969: Simon Kimbangu "intercedes for the needs of the believers with Jesus, so that he might have mercy." (Martin, M.-L., *Kirche ohne Weisse*, 208). Likewise in their magazine *Kimbanguisme* (2.9. 1960) in an article by Victor Fwakwanzo: "Oh prophète, vous qui aves répondu à la voix de Dieu, vous qui avez vécu tant de peines pour le salut de tous les hommes sans distinction de couleur ni de race, veus qui avez vécu une vie misérable ici–bas, vous qui prêchez l'amour du prochain, vous qui avez été maltraité pour avoir prêché la doctrine divine,

similar to that of the saints in the Catholic church. That may be due to Catholic influence. "Yet more important is the fact that in Africa one does not approach the highest authority directly; modesty forbids it. One turns to a go-between . . ."[71]

The Hereditary Princes

The Kimbanguist church is today led by a kind of hereditary hierarchy, embodied in the sons of Kimbangu. Joseph Diangienda for instance is *Tata mfumu'a nlogon*, translated by the Kimbanguists as *chief spiritual*. This title means in fact a kind of sacred supreme head or king. This hereditary religious hierarchy is often criticized by Christian theologians as being contrary to the principles of a Christian church. In this connection Marie-Louise Martin says: "We need not only educated leaders, but also charismatic leaders, in whom—as in Joseph Diangienda—something of the *exousia*, of the authority of Christ shines through. The lack of such leaders in Africa [and in Europe?] is responsible for many a crisis in the church. Africa does not live by ideas, formulas and sound creeds but by incarnations of Christian faith in the widest sense."[72] In my opinion Martin does not here quite explain why this charismatic quality has to be hereditary—despite all the profound insights expressed in her statement. The problem will come up again, in all its ambiguity, in the next generation of leaders.

Schools, Mission, and Social Work

When the Kimbanguist children were forbidden to attend the missionary schools, the Kimbanguists had to build their own schools and dispensaries. By 1968, the Kimbanguist school system taught 96,000 pupils in state-subsidized schools and many hundreds of thousands of children and young people in schools which at that time had not been recognized. Today, the system is under the leadership of F. M'Vuendy,[73] a Kimbanguist who earned his doctorate at the Sorbonne. M'Vuendy has also become "le nouveau commissaire d'état à l'einseignement primaire et secondaire"—a kind of Minister of Education in the Government.[74]

In addition there are schools for women, workshops for apprentices and cooperatives for farmers, as well as Kibbutzim (collective farms). The Kimbanguists also build their own bridges, electricity plants and factories. A Kimbanguist evangelist has begun missionary work among the pygmies, and shows them how to plant manioc and corn and how to raise chickens. Thus

---

vous qui avez vécu une vie semblable à celle de notre Seigneur Jésus-Christ, nous vous implorons que ceux qui vous ont fait souffrir soient pardonnés, car ils ne savaient pas que vous êtes l'envoyé de Dieu." Lasserre, "L'église," 26.

[71] Martin, M.-L., *Kirche ohne Weisse*, 208; English: *Kimbangu*, 147 (my translation).

[72] Martin, M.-L., *Kirche ohne Weisse*, 215f; English: *Kimbangu*, 152 (my translation).

[73] M'Vuendy, *Kimbanguisme*.

[74] Asch, *Kimbangu*, 76, 81.

the pygmies are first given help with their economic needs in the transition from a hunting culture to an elementary agricultural culture.

In and with this social work the Kimbanguists proclaim the Gospel. They even began a mission among the blacks in the United States, with whom they expressed their solidarity. In one of their catechisms we read:

Know this, that we the black race are the most dishonored of all races whom God created on this earth. We could not finish telling the torments imposed upon us by the white man, especially the government white men. Think how we were transported by the peoples of Europe, how many blacks were put in ships like sardines at sea, with never a hand extended to save them. At other times a small number managed to arrive in America and other countries of the white man, but even those few fell into unlimited suffering.[75]

Ethics and Political Position[76]

According to the church order of March 6th, 1960, the Kimbanguists follow these ethical rules:

- to respect the authorities (Rom. 13:1–3)
- to love each other, including one's enemies (Mt. 5:43–45)
- to abstain from strong drinks
- to abstain from tobacco and above all from drugs
- to abstain from dancing or even assisting at dances (immoral dances)
- not to swim or sleep naked
- to act with charity towards those who need it, irrespective of race or color (Rom. 12:9–21)
- to abstain from witchcraft
- to pay taxes (Mt. 22:17–21)
- to avoid all backbiting against a neighbor
- to avoid all calumny against a neighbor
- every member to confess his faults to a selected body
- Kimbanguism is a church of the Holy Spirit. Therefore all the Kimbanguist Christians have to behave according to the Holy Spirit.
- the EJCSK does not prohibit any food, except pork and monkey
- the church has the right to exclude a member who does not want to follow these rules.[77]

The Church "condemns all use of violence in trying to settle problems among men."[78] In spite of this, the Kimbanguists sign on for military service.

---

[75] Dialangana, *Zolanga* no. 3.1; quoted MacGaffey, "Beloved City," 136.

[76] Cf. on this Sinda, *Le messianisme congolais.* Hollenweger, *Marxist and Kimbanguist Mission;* idem, *ITh* 1 (index). Banda-Mwaka, "Kimbanguisme," 3–53. Cf. also the "message to all Christians" of the EJCSK, published in *Zeichen der Zeit* 3/193, 112.

[77] Quoted by Martin, M.-L., *Kirche ohne Weisse,* 186; English: *Kimbangu,* 132 has a different version. A similar church order quoted by Raymaekers, *Zaïre,* 695, from the year 1959.

[78] Diangienda, "Eglise et politique," 41.

They reject capitalism and communism alike.[79] This statement has been questioned by most knowledgeable observers; they point to the extreme loyalty of the Kimbanguist leadership to the Mobutu regime[80] which can only be understood (but perhaps not justified) as the reaction of a persecuted minority to finding, at last, a respectable place in society.

Worship

In the Kimbanguist service the hymns,[81] which have sometimes been created during the times of persecution, are as important as the sermon. The first historian of the Kimbanguists called their singers "chantres."[82] Often the singing is accompanied by flute orchestra. Occasionally a brass band plays. Men and women share alike in the proclamation of the word. The *chief spiritual,* Joseph Diangienda, does not preach. He prays; for—he says—praying is more important for a religious head or bishop, than preaching. Kimbanguists meet daily in small groups for a short house-meeting. At twelve o'clock they pray again. Wednesday afternoon and evening they hold short prayer-meetings. Every Saturday they meet in small prayer-groups in houses and pray throughout the night. On Sundays they celebrate their main service which—above all in Kinshasa—is extended once a month to a big festival service. At the festival service they bring their offerings according to the African custom: money, produce and other gifts. Without ever having read Bonhoeffer, the Kimbanguists admit no strict division between sacred and profane. The social get-together and profane singing, music-making, palavering, and gift-giving have as much religious character as the "religious" singing, praying, music-making, offertory and stylized dancing.[83]

The Catholicity of the Kimbanguists[84]

With endurance and patience, the Kimbanguists have tried to enter into dialogue with the European churches. For this purpose, they sought entry to

---

[79] "Un fidèle de l'EJCSK ne peut accepter de propager ou d'adhérer à une idéologie, doctrine ou théorie sur laquelle se fonde un sytème politique, économique et social qui tend à expliquer l'évolution historique du monde en écartant l'intervention divine" (Diangienda, "Eglise et politique," 40). Cf. also Diangienda, "L'EJCSK face aux problèmes politiques, économiques, sociaux tel qu'ils se posent au Congo, en Afrique et dans le monde" (dupl.; quoted by Bertsche, "Kimbanguism," 27), where a plea is made for a free medical service, free schooling for all citizens, and other things.

[80] Asch, *Kimbangu*, 109, 130–33, 74–78.

[81] On this in detail Raymaekers, *Zaïre*, 675–756. and Masson, "Chants kimbanguistes," 82–90.

[82] In the report, mentioned note 4, p. 35.

[83] One would be tempted to describe the rhythmical stylized steps of this ceremony as a dance. But dancing is highly controversial (both sacred and secular) in the Kimbanguist church, cf. above, p. 67, Raymaekers, *Zaïre*, 587f and Asch, *Kimbangu*, 143.

[84] Cf. Niederberger, "Kimbangu-Kirche," 215–22. Italiaander, "Prophet," 31–44. Martin, M.-L., "Afrikanische Gestalt," 16–29. Central Committee of the WCC,

the World Council of Churches. In the view of the Kimbanguists, a Zaïrian church is not a church in the full sense of the word, for the church is either universal or it is not a church at all.[85] As the Kimbanguist church cannot be universal on its own, it considers the World Council of Churches to be an instrument through which it can participate in the catholicity of the whole church—an ecclesiological insight which many European churches lack. However, considerable opposition was mounted against the entry of the Kimbanguists into the World Council of Churches.

This came from two quarters: On the one hand it was feared—and rightly so!—that the reception of the Kimbanguists into the World Council would relativize European and American missionary work in Africa. On the other, the Kimbanguists were not trusted theologically. They were asked to submit their confession of faith—something which had never been asked from a European or American Church. But the Kimbanguist church did not have a confession of faith. Their theology is embodied in their hymns and liturgy. "I do not have the spirit for reading," said Simon Kimbangu. "Nevertheless I have considerable intelligence for religion."[86] In order to please the World Council of Churches the Kimbanguists wrote a normal evangelical confession, which was recognized in Geneva as plagiarism. The submission by one of the World Council of Churches executives in Geneva—which stated that under these conditions neither the apostles nor our Lord Jesus Christ would ever have had a chance of being received into the World Council of Churches—remained unanswered. As the negotiations dragged on for several years, Joseph Diangienda wrote an important letter to the General Secretary of the World Council of Churches on July 15th, 1969.[87]

Three points from that letter:

1. The Kimbanguist Church does not seek entry into the World Council of Churches for material advantage. She has developed independent of foreign money and she will continue to do so.

2. The reason for the Kimbanguist church's application is a spiritual one. It is high time that Christians take seriously the problems of world peace, of justice, of help to those without any rights. This is something the Kimbanguist church cannot do by herself. This task has to be undertaken by the world-wide church.[88]

Minutes and Reports of the 23rd Meeting, CC 1969 (Canterbury), 11. *La Documentation catholique*, no. 1547, Sept. 1969, 830: "L'Eglise Kimbanguiste admise au C.O.E."

[85] That can already be seen in the name of the church: Eglise de Jésus-Christ *sur la terre* par le prophète Simon Kimbangu. "Sur la terre" can be understood as a translation of "kat'holen ten gen" (catholic). The knowledge of languages and the multi-language services among the Kimbanguists (Kikongo, Lingala, Tchiluba, French) underline the ecumenicity of the church (Heimer, "Kimbanguists," 16–17).

[86] Quoted in the report of Kimbangu's secretaries, quoted above note 4 (p. 21).

[87] Letter of 15.7.1969, archive of the General Secretariat of the WCC.

[88] The Brazilian Pentecostal leader M. de Melo had argued similarly: *The*

3. But if the World Council of Churches comes to the conclusion that the entry of Kimbanguists would "pollute" the purity of the ecumenical institution then we have to accept this with regret. But we would still like to let you know that we remain your friends.

The Kimbanguist Church was received into the World Council of Churches in 1969.

An African Theology

The African elements in the Kimbanguist church have already been pointed out. The question is, however, whether or not the Kimbanguist church will develop a theory; that is, a theological articulation of its practice. Perhaps this might happen in their doctrine of the sacraments. Until recently the church did not celebrate the Lord's Supper, being of the opinion that the sacraments do not belong to one denomination—even if that be the Kimbanguists. In principle the Kimbanguists argue that there are no denominational (i.e., sectarian) sacraments but only catholic (i.e., ecumenical) sacraments. "For us," declared Joseph Diangienda to Dominique Desanti, "communion will be more ecumenical than it is for the Catholics or the Western Protestants."[89] A denominational Communion contradicts the intention of the Sacrament, which is a non-rational expression of the communion of all Christians transcending rational articulation. In the opinion of the Kimbanguists it is therefore necessary that Communion be dealt with at least within the framework of all the churches in Zaïre. In spite of this the first Communion of the Kimbanguists celebrated on 6th April 1971 was not held as an open Communion.[90] Three hundred and fifty thousand Kimbanguists took part in a celebration which lasted for one and a half days. Instead of imported wine and bread they used "honey-water; a bread made with potatoes, maize and bananas prepared in a traditional way, the banana acting as leaven."[91] At the moment—as in Zwingli's days—it will be celebrated only three times a year (Easter, the memorial day of the death of Kimbangu, and Christmas).

So far the church does not practice baptism by water. Instead they practice spirit baptism (by a handshake, followed by the raising up of the candidate, who kneels before the pastor). This spirit baptism is not administered to Christians who come to the Kimbanguists from other churches. As they have already been baptized, they are simply prayed for. For children there is a ceremony of blessing.

Pentecostals, 99–110. De Melo, "Participation," 245–48.

[89] Diangienda, in an interview with Desanti, "Golden Anniversary," 18.

[90] Whether that is meant as a transitory solution or as an adaptation to the general denominational policy of the Christian churches (negative influence of ecumenical fellowship!) remains to be seen.

[91] Martin, M.-L., "Congolese Church Celebrates," quoting an undated press release by Luntadila ("Réflexions sur la Sainte Cène").

Marie-Louise Martin

The pastors of the church are mostly honorary and earn their own living. The problem of theological education for present and future pastors is therefore quite acute. The late Marie-Louise Martin tackled this problem in spite of great difficulties and at great personal sacrifice. It seems that she succeeded in educating a score of African theologians without alienating them, by their education, from their social[92] and religious[93] milieu.

One evaluation of the church which I want to mention is that by Geoffrey Wainwright. He measures the Kimbanguists with the yardstick of a rather strictly definable protestant orthodoxy. Not everything in the doctrine and practice of the Kimbanguists corresponds with these assumptions. In spite of this Wainwright comes to the conclusion that "within Kimbanguism an African conception of Christ . . . may be struggling to find theological expression, and that in a potentially orthodox way." He concedes, however, that already in New Testament times the concepts of Christ (Christ, Lord, Savior, Son of God, Son of Man) "came from their previous multiple background charged with associations not entirely appropriate to Jesus without transformation."[94] Wainwright does not seem to consider the possibility that the so-called orthodox position might perhaps not be as biblical as is generally assumed.

Marie-Louise Martin judges the chances for an "African theology" much more positively: "What faces us in the independent churches of Africa in general and in the Kimbanguist Church in particular is that for which missiologists in Europe have been asking for so long: the beginnings of a Christian theology in African garb."[95] H. W. Fehderau concludes pointedly: "There has been much talk of making our mission churches indigenous; the Kimbanguist church *is* indigenous."[96] And James E. Bertsche compares the mission-based churches with the Kimbanguists:

> Against a background of a partially subsidized and largely institutionalized mission program, there is the challenge of Kimbanguism's dynamic grass-roots lay movement. Spreading along arteries of communication, across tribal lines and language barriers, its shock troops have been its enthusiastic, unsalaried laymen. . . . By comparison with the effervescence of this lay movement, the average mission-established church program must appear quite routine and unexciting indeed to the Kimbanguist.[97]

From this Marie-Louise Martin draws the following conclusion:

---

[92] Education takes place partly in evening courses.
[93] Education takes place within the framework of Kimbanguist spirituality.
[94] Wainwright, "Reflections," 18–35. Cf. also, van Wing, "Kimbanguisme," 618.
[95] Martin, M.-L., *Kirche ohne Weisse*, 203; English: *Kimbangu*, 175 (my translation).
[96] Fehderau, "Prophetic Christianity," 178.
[97] Bertsche, "Kimbanguism," 32.

Until now in most African theological faculties and seminaries one has taught theology according to the European pattern. Even the courses were—and still are—in keeping with this pattern. Of course one has translated the dogmas into African languages, and the German, French and English hymns have also been translated into the languages of the Basotho, the Zulu, the Bavenda, the Bakongo and many other people, together with the Western revival or reformation melodies, and even the harmoniums. But have these translations brought the Gospel to them? There is something more needed than just translation if we are really to communicate the Gospel. The Gospel and the church must no longer appear in Western garments. Such new clothing can only be tailored by an African Church, tested through sufferings and proud of its mission. I believe that this is the case in the Kimbanguist existential interpretation of salvation-history, their hierarchy, their symbols, their rites, their African or Africanized music and images. That is a promising beginning. We can only hope that when the Kimbanguist church has its own university-trained theologians they will not betray their heritage and speak in Western jargon. We theologians from the West have only a small part to play in this development by explaining the historical background of the biblical texts, pointing out the *Formgeschichte*, the literary forms of biblical tradition, which have many similarities with African forms of passing on tradition. Perhaps we can also be of help when the Africans use our own terminology and do not understand it. We might also assist them in telling them how other churches have developed in other parts of the world, with special emphasis on the Early Church, the church fathers and the old African churches in Egypt, Nubia and Ethiopia, as far as we know their development. This gives us an opportunity to show where—as the case may be—wrong developments took place and why certain churches have accepted certain rites and forms. Thus we can further ecumenical understanding. Perhaps we can also assist in solving the burning ethical questions in the new Africa on the basis of a biblical theology by pointing out the dangers of a new legalism. And finally it will be our task to point again and again to the cross of Christ, which is the crisis of all human undertaking, of all human desires, ideas, symbols and theologies, but where pardon, resurrection and the new creation is promised.

I do not believe that we can do much more. We have to leave as much as possible to the Africans and be patient even when their expression, their terms, their forms, their organizations and their structures appear to us to be imperfect or even totally wrong. We have to overcome our fear of a possible syncretism [chapter 11, pp. 132–41], which does not mean that we close our eyes to its dangers. But it means that we trust the Holy Spirit, as Paul did, to lead the African brothers into all truth. If we adopt this attitude the day might come when Africa will produce a new formulation of the message of Jesus Christ, which might be significant for the West too and might give to the ecumenical dialogue a new dimension.

The Gospel is a Gospel of salvation. That is exactly what Africa has perhaps understood better than the West, where we understand the word "salvation" too often as the "salvation of the soul." Salvation means in Africa that which "shalom" meant for the Hebrews: Salvation and healing—not only from infirmity, but salvation in the widest sense, "a new earth and above all, a new heaven," social justice, peace, following from this no discrimination, no bitter poverty side by side with overwhelming riches; brotherhood, order in freedom, development of all one's potentials, but in such a way that the community is served, which is more important for Africans than individual fulfillment. Salvation includes healing; a new life in a new earth, free of hatred, passion, lies, corruption, oppression; and holiness as an expression of our thankfulness and the freedom which God has given in his love to all men.[98] That will be a true eschatology.[99]

Other African Theologies

Since Marie-Louise Martin wrote her book, others have developed African theologies, but mostly as ideas and not—so far as I can see—in an African theological education program. One might mention, among others,[100] Kwesi Dickson, and above all, E. Fasholé-Luke. Dickson, an African professor in the University of Ghana, describes the plight of African theological education in unflattering terms (quoting Fasholé-Luke[101]):

> African theologians continue to mouth the theological platitudes they have picked up in universities, theological seminaries and colleges abroad, or parade their erudition by quoting the latest theological ideas in Europe and North America. In consequence theological education in Africa has generally had the effect of producing theologians who are more at home in Western theological thought even if such thought pertains only to a certain level of their consciousness. True, one cannot ignore what has gone on before, even if it has come out of other contexts. Nevertheless, it cannot be seriously argued that in the interests of uniformity of theological expression, and as a symbol of the oneness of the Church, the theological insights emanating from the West should be considered normative also outside the West.

He goes on to regret the fact that all theological expression is tied to English, French or Portuguese, and therefore—since these languages are foreign languages in almost all African countries—remains a foreign affair. Thus, he says, the Church suffers under a devastating and unbiblical division of labor: here the producers of theology, the clergy; there the mere consumers, the laity. No wonder that some of the better-trained lay people are no longer interested in this kind of theology, since they are mainly considered as sources of income, and not as theological partners and experts in applied theology. This is a situation of course which we in the West already know only too well.

---

[98] On such an understanding of salvation see the papers of the ecumenical study on "Structures of a missionary congregation." Wieser, *Planning for Mission*; Hollenweger, *Church for Others*; idem, *Kirche*. See also ch. 19 on soteriology, pp. 246–57.

[99] Martin, M.-L., *Kirche ohne Weisse*, 248–50; English: *Kimbangu*, 175–77 (my translation).

[100] Pobee, *Exploring Afro-Christology*. Parrat, *Reader in African Christian Theology*. Berinyuu, *Pastoral Care*. Lartey, *Pastoral Counseling*.

[101] E. Fasholé-Luke, in Anderson and Stransky (eds.), *Mission Trends* no. 3, 137; quoted in Dickson, *Theology*, 4.

Dickson draws attention to the different approach in the independent churches (such as the Kimbanguist church), and states in no uncertain terms: "No serious study of Christian theology in Africa can with any justification ignore these churches and their life and thought."[102] "And thought," he adds! African theology may not be systematic, he says; but the systematic form, the propositional articulation of a chain of arguments, is not obligatory for its presentation. So, one wonders, what are the alternatives?

One may justly consider Dickson's theology as such an alternative. Outwardly, it looks like a systematic presentation; but its inner dynamic is different. To be sure it is coherent and clear, but its coherence is more that of a New Testament Gospel or a radio feature than that of a systematic treatise. This becomes evident when one considers that the first item he treats under "Towards a Theological Expression" is music. Then in the chapter on "The Theology of the Cross in Context," he deals at length with European/American commercialized funeral customs (as an example of avoiding the reality of death), which he contrasts with the public mourning in African society (as an example of what Mitscherlich calls *Trauerarbeit* ["mourning-work"]).[103] He looks for new christological titles like Christ "the Ancestor," "the greatest of ancestors who never ceases to be one of the 'living-dead.' "[104]

It is clear that Dickson would have failed had he presented his book for a doctoral degree at a British, Swiss or German university. That is of course not a verdict on Dickson's book but on our own lack of flexibility. It is perhaps not without significance that one of the most important books of European theology, namely Karl Barth's *Commentary on the Epistle to the Romans*, would have suffered the same fate had he not chosen to bypass the academic establishment. Why is it that we are not able to recognize the seminal thinking of such works within the structure of our educational tradition?

To this one must add the plight of scholarly theology in Europe and America. We are drilled in all methods of critical exegesis and critical thinking, but our church members still discuss whether or not Adam and Eve, Noah and Methuselah, were historical persons. They still discuss whether or not God could have created the universe in seven days. The whole theological establishment looks like a huge, expensive, but futile hobby. Theology has "become cut off from the community for whose life its results might be significant."[105] Since my topic here is not European theological education I leave it with these remarks. But when one thinks that we export this "hobby" to the Third World as the latest achievement in scholarship then one finds Dickson's verdict even mild.

As another example of African theology I take the important book *Christianity in Independent Africa*, edited by E. Fasholé-Luke. Almost fifty scholars—African and European, Catholic, Protestant and Independent—present

---

[102] Dickson, *Theology*, 10.
[103] Mitscherlich, *Die Unfähigkeit*.
[104] Dickson, *Theology*, 198.
[105] Wink, *Bible in Human Transformation*, 10. More on this in ch. 23, pp. 307–25.

here the condensed result of years of joint critical research. It is a book which questions, sometimes with humor, sometimes with painful accuracy, not only our own missionary and theological past (this, it seems, we are now almost forgiven by the Africans), but, even more, our thoughtless present-day European theological isolation.

We are told by R. Elliot Kendall that 36,000 missionaries are now working in Africa.[106] While the older missionary societies reduce the number of their missionaries, the new faith missions increase the number of theirs. There are now more missionaries working in Africa than before independence, yet they are less significant in the leadership of the churches.[107] There are for example an estimated 36,750,000 Roman Catholics in Africa. These are served by 3,700 African and 10,900 white priests (1973). Adrian Hastings describes strikingly what "africanization" means in this context. "300 dioceses means 300 bishops, 300 vicars general, 300 priests to administer the cathedral parish, 600 or more to teach in seminaries, 300 directors of diocesan catechesis, 300 chaplains for secondary schools, a hundred or so for national ecclesiastical administration, another hundred to study, two or three hundred more sick or old. How many are left for regular rural pastoral work?"[108] The answer to that anomalous situation is not "the need for more priests, more sisters and brothers, and more money" from abroad. "It is illusory to hope for a really 'local' Church in Africa unless we are prepared to question even the system itself," says the former director of the Centre for Black and White Christian Partnership in Birmingham, Patrick A. Kalilombe.[109]

One of the facts which put the system in question is that, in order to survive, the older churches tend to become more and more like the independent churches.[110] These independent churches are not merely marginal sects but a newly emerging social and political force, as we have seen in this chapter. Turner describes a visit to the Celestial Church of Christ in Ibadan in 1973. "I found myself in conversation before and after the service with four people—the first two worked in administrative offices of the University of Ibadan, the third was a lecturer there, and the fourth (who earlier had been observed leading a Bible class in his white robe and bare feet) proved to be the Deputy Vice-Chancellor of the University."[111] Similarly, "top politicians, ministers of state or members of Parliament" frequently consult the prophets of the Aladura churches (a group of Independent churches) in Nigeria.[112]

---

[106] Kendall, "Missionary Factor," 16.

[107] Tasie–Gray, "Introduction," 7.

[108] Hastings, "Ministry," 38. Cf. also Hastings, *History of African Christianity*.

[109] Kalilombe, "Local Churches," 89.

[110] Tasie–Gray, "Introduction," 4. Setiloane, "Traditional," 404 (quoting Sundkler, *African Studies*, 20.4.1961, 203).

[111] Turner, "Patterns," 50. I have visited the same church and was impressed by its vitality, openness, and innovative spirit (e.g., in church architecture).

[112] Omoyajowo, "Aladura Churches," 99.

It is, however, for another even more important reason that the spirituality of these churches is becoming politically significant. "The political significance of a church depends on the nature of its contacts with women, rural illiterates, urban unemployed, and other less privileged sections and minorities."[113] The great festivals of the Kimbanguist and other churches, which regularly bring together thousands of worshippers, "have an immensely significant potential as communication foci in a situation where other media tend to be either under strict surveillance or primarily concerned with the interest of the highly educated."[114]

In this communication process women are crucial. The revival in the Bukoba church "meant that women, who had always been quiet in public, began speaking in meetings and at small gatherings."[115] It is just here that the traditional churches have proved very "unpolitical," because of their poor record in the matter of "female clerical leadership."[116]

Politics in Africa cannot be divorced from religion. "Virtually no African ruler has been able to adopt a purely secular stance."[117] In principle it is possible to conceive of a basis for nations other than religion. "In practice only religion is strong enough to sustain them."[118] "Scratch the prominent layman politician and you discover that his public bold face and animal courage are against the background of his secret endless groveling before masters of the supernatural forces in traditional society."[119]

The interdependence of politics and religion has both its dangers and promises. A critical and prophetic religious ministry is only slowly emerging, but it *is* emerging, for instance in South Africa (chapter 5, pp. 48–51), or in Rwanda, where racial riots "brought an African state, founded on a moral cause, into the innermost circle of political hell reserved for South Africa."[120] Dr. Fasholé-Luke, Head of the Department of Theology at the University of Sierra Leone, writes[121] that Christians in the independent states of Africa seem to believe that oppression is confined to South Africa and to white colonialism, but fail to see the oppression of blacks by blacks in their own countries.

In the more theological field Desmond Tutu complains that "African theology has failed to produce a sufficiently sharp cutting edge." The South African archbishop and Nobel Peace Prize Winner adds:

> Why should we feel embarrassed if our theology is not systematic? Why should we feel that something is amiss if our theology is too dramatic for verbalization but can be expressed only adequately in the joyous song and the scintillating

---

[113] Tasie–Gray, "Introduction," 7.
[114] Ibid., 12.
[115] Swantz, "Changing Role," 145.
[116] Steady, "Role of Women," 156.
[117] Tasie–Gray, "Introduction," 8.
[118] Mushete, "Authenticity and Christianity in Zaïre," 238.
[119] Ayandele, "Appendix," 612.
[120] Linden, "Rwanda," 250.
[121] Fasholé-Luke, "Introduction," 358.

movement of Africa's dance in the liturgy . . . Let African theology enthuse about the awesomeness of the transcendent when others are embarrassed to speak about the King, high and lifted up, whose train fills the temple.[122]

Even an organization like the World Council of Churches finds it difficult to match words with deeds. Gabriel Setiloane[123] describes his disappointment when a World Council publication crossed out the section on the ancestors in one of his meditations. The ancestors are present everywhere in Africa and not only for the poorly educated. Simon Barrington-Ward, Anglican bishop in Conventry, and Michael Singleton[124] deserve high praise for introducing this fascinating but controversial topic. For them belief in ancestral spirits is not just a remnant of the African past but a way of dealing with a complex technological and pluralistic situation, a way of putting a shattered world together, and a bridge between Europe and Africa—an idea which has already been put forward by the French sociologist Roger Bastide.[125]

This excursus into African theology suffices to show that Kimbanguist theology is not just a kind of local or exotic theology. The questions which Kimbanguism raises are questions central to Africa (*and* Europe), although it is debatable whether they have yet found adequate answers.

Kimbanguism of the Kimbanguists and "Official Kimbanguism"

The Kimbanguist church has experienced tremendous growth. From a small minority church it has grown to a church of the masses with three (or perhaps even more) million adherents. This growth happened—at least in the initial stage—without money from outside. With their own hands—but with some help from the government—they have built their churches and their schools. One might say: well, missions have done just the same. True, but here is a church which, out of her poverty, out of the midst of her celebration and prayer, has opened herself to the social problems of her country without asking for crumbs from the rich tables of Europeans and Americans.

The wildfire development of Kimbanguism not only implies great opportunities but also many dangers. Many questions remain open, as Dominique Desanti, who describes himself as a "non-believing, yet profoundly interested observer,"[126] has put it.

It might be argued, in the first place, that the strict morality and austere puritanism of Kimbanguism is running counter to present-day trends. The young people in the town, who are constantly faced with such a totally different style of life, may well prefer a more tolerant form of religion. Perhaps there's

---

[122] Tutu, "Whither African Theology?" 368f.
[123] Setiloane, "Traditional," 406.
[124] Barrington-Ward, "Centre Cannot Hold," 455–70. Singleton, "Direction," 471–78.
[125] Bastide, *Les religions africaines au Brésil*, 515 (*The Pentecostals*, 97).
[126] Desanti, "Golden Anniversary," 15 (only in the French version of this article).

danger that the hierarchical organization of the clergy, who are picked by the spiritual leader with no right of appeal, might tend to dampen the mystical ardor which was the strength of the early communities. Will the Church find herself forced into a certain conformity by accepting Government subsidies for schools and clinics? Finally, isn't it possible that the introduction of the Holy Communion[127] will put an end to one of the most original aspects of this religion, namely direct communication with God through invocation and mysticism?

These are questions which faced the early Christians almost two thousand years ago; questions with which the Waldensians, the Anabaptists, the churches of the Reformation, and in our century the Pentecostals had to wrestle, and which they all tried to solve in their own way; questions which focus once again on the ecumenical significance of Kimbanguism. They expected the kingdom of God. What came was the (Kimbanguist) church. That is how Paul Raymaekers paraphrases the situation. He concludes: "But the new church and the new society in Zaïre would not have come without this faith in a kingdom which is beyond the churches and society."[128]

On another level, questions arise which are similar to those known in the European and American churches. They are highlighted by Werner Ustorf and Susan Asch.[129] Werner Ustorf shows certain parts of the "official version" of Kimbanguist history to be legendary. After all, the documents issued by the present leadership in Kinshasa reflect the history of their church from the orthodox (Kimbanguist) point of view. In historical terms, their documents reflect church history written from the point of view of the victors. But the Kimbanguist history also includes victims who so far have been silenced. Those are the Kimbanguists who cling to the old rural tradition of Simon Kimbangu. They are condemned by the Kimbanguist leadership as heretical—thus since 1966 at least 17 factions (some of them rather strong) have separated from the EJCSK; for instance "Le Salut en Jésus-Christ par le Témoin Simon Kimbangu, Eglise Congolaise."[130] This church was prohibited on June 9th 1966 because of "danger to public order." Their founder, Bamba, was executed on June 2nd 1966 after a trumped-up and illegal trial in the center of Kinshasa before 300,000 spectators. The reason for the assassination of Bamba and three other high-ranking ministers in the Republic of the Congo was the formation of a "Committee for Returning to Legality," which tried to end the bloody regime of General Mobutu without the shedding of blood. However, the plot was betrayed.[131]

The transition from an oppressed movement to an established church has produced problems for the Kimbanguists similar to those experienced by the early church as it moved from persecuted minority to state church status. Now,

[127] On the introduction of Communion see above, p. 70.
[128] Raymaekers, "Kimbanguisme," 7–14.
[129] Asch, *Kimbangu*, 51.
[130] On this church and its leader see ibid., 37, 68, 64, 67.
[131] Ustorf, *Afrikanische Initiative*, 222.

as then, these problems will have to be dealt with on at least two levels. Firstly, almost certainly the Kimbanguist Church will have to write its history in dialogue with and in opposition to those rural Kimbanguists who do not see a continuum between Simon Kimbangu and today's leadership of the EJCSK. What will happen if the documentary basis of the "official" church history is shaken? What will happen if the diversity of opinions as to the "right interpretation" of Kimbanguist history forces the Kimbanguists to write their history in dialogue with their own dissenters? What will happen if *all* documents are made available? Many of the more rural Kimbanguists are probably closer to the tradition and values of Simon Kimbangu than to those of the present leaders in Kinshasa, who have rejected Kimbangu's own teachings as "heretical." Some of these rural Kimbanguists have remained with the "official" church, others have formed their own Kimbanguist or quasi-Kimbanguist organizations. The battle-cry "Back to Kimbangu; back to the times of revival" might create similar stimuli and confusions as the cry "Back to Luther," "the Church Fathers," "the early Pentecostal revival" or even "the New Testament." One would expect a serious questioning of ecclesiastical authority in the Kimbanguist church. If one of the dissident bodies should decide to apply for membership in the World Council of Churches, both the World Council and the Kimbanguist leadership would be in trouble.[132]

Secondly, the problem of authority in the church is not solved. The system of hereditary princes will certainly be challenged, in relation to the direction of the church and in relation to the right interpretation of the life and message of Simon Kimbangu. As the case of Bamba and those of other dissenters shows, the story of Kimbangu can be interpreted in different ways. A situation could arise in which the Kimbanguist church would be forced to go back to its tradition of opposition through suffering.

Susan Asch comes to conclusions similar to those of Werner Ustorf. She speaks of the Kimbanguism of the Kimbanguists (with its rural tradition) in distinction from the official Kimbanguism of the church's Kinshasa leaders. The irony is that the "official" Kimbanguism is a minority.[133]

This situation is of course not peculiar to Kimbanguism. Probably official Catholicism is a tiny minority in the world-wide Catholic Church, and the same applies probably more or less to all big churches, as well as to political parties. It is certain that the leadership of the British Conservative Party is rather a small minority in the party; the same is true for the French socialists and many other organizations.

There are two churches in the Kimbanguist church in another sense, as well. When I visited the Kimbanguists I observed that when they spoke in an African language they spoke unashamedly of Kimbangu, on whose presence and help they were counting. But when they spoke in French a kind of flawless Barthianism was produced. That is not just a question of language. To the

---

[132] Ibid., 51.
[133] Asch, *Kimbangu*, 95, 299.

outsider the Kimbanguists presented the image of an orthodox Protestant church, an image provoked into life by endless discussions in the World Council of Churches (and elsewhere), during which the Kimbanguists have had to prove that they are not heretics. But among their own African rural constituency they speak from the heart.

This double face of Kimbanguism is confirmed by an alarming discovery made by Susan Asch.[134] She shows that most of the prestige development projects of Kimbanguism are—because of imported methods and personnel—a failure. This is true no more in Kimbanguism than in other churches, but nevertheless it is disturbing. Asch says that most of Kimbanguism's teaching corpus is foreign (Haitian and Egyptian).[135] I am not able to judge Susan Asch's evaluation, but some of the facts which she presents seem to suggest that the Kimbanguist Church has received too much finance from development agencies, and that this money has been unhealthy for the very development projects being funded. If this is true, then we have a situation similar to that facing other development projects in Africa.

However, I do not want to end the chapter on this somber note. Whatever the organizational and political draw-backs of Kimbanguism, its spiritual and practical vitality impresses any observer. The Kimbanguists will have to sort out their difficulties with their own insights and spiritual strength. No ex–patriate can do this for them.

Prayer of the Caterpillar

Dear God,
Sometimes I feel like a caterpillar, I eat grass and leaves and leaves and grass.
Sometimes a bird flies over me and I am afraid. Or a hen comes along and cackles and scratches the earth with her foot, and I have to hide again.
Why must I be a caterpillar, dear God,
why can I not jump like an ibex, fly like an eagle, swim like a fish.
Why can I only creep like a caterpillar.
I have not made myself, and you did not ask me whether I wanted to be a caterpillar, nor whether I wanted to be at all. Nor did my parents consult me and ask for my consent.
And that's why I am what I am, a poor creepy caterpillar from A to Z.
Until that day when I am closed in a little chamber and the door falls into the lock, and I am longing, longing, longing in the dark, and things move and I get changed and I break out of the chamber
and I fly into the sunshine of an eternal Sunday morning.
And then I am happy having been a caterpillar because you, my God, you give a new life to this caterpillar, the life of a beautiful butterfly.

---

[134] Ibid., 117, 183, 185, 187, 190, 256.
[135] Ibid., 204.

CHAPTER SEVEN

Mexico: Flowers and Songs. A Mexican Contribution to Doing Theology[1]

Intercultural Theology—A Two-Way System

Is a theological dialogue possible between the churches of Third World and the theological systems of Europe and America? If there is any meaning in the ecumenical slogans "Unity of Mankind, Unity of the Church"[2] or "Mission in Six Continents,"[3] then such a dialogue must be possible. But up to now the Third World has made a theological appearance only when it has made use of European/American concepts. Our theological partners from the Third World, who think differently from us, either never make themselves heard in their own terms, or else lose interest in this theological debate. It becomes a luxury which they can afford only with subsidies from abroad. The rules of this theological game are ours even when the game

---

[1] This chapter started in Spanish (Concepto Latinoamericano III: "Flores y Cantos:" Un Concepto Mexicano, *Concept*, Special Issue 32, Oct. 1970, Geneva: World Council of Churches). A summary appeared later in *Int. Review of Mission* (60/238, April 1971, 232–44) and in my *Pentecost Between Black and White*. It is published here in a revised, updated, and annotated version. In addition to the sources quoted in the following notes one may consult: Gaxiola-Gaxiola, "Inicios del Pentecostalismo en Mexico," 25–48. Idem, "Pentecostal Ministry," 57–63. Idem, *The Serpent and the Dove*. Goodman, "Apostolics of Yucatan." Idem, "Shaman," *Pneuma* 13/2, 1991, contains original articles from Latin American Pentecostals and an excellent bibliography (193–97). Since this is primarily a chapter in which the oral root (in some cases pre-Christian) of Pentecostalism is discussed, I do not enter into a detailed history of Pentecostalism in Mexico.

[2] Theme of the "Commission for Faith and Order," 1971, at Louvain. Cf. the study document "Unity." Also J. Robert Nelson, "Unity of the Church."

[3] Orchard, *Witness in Six Continents*.

is played in Nairobi or Mexico. This is the main reason for the alarming fact that most of the Christian churches in the Third World are not members of the World Council of Churches, and most are also disregarded in the fields of systematic theology, church history, and missiology. Comb the theological literature of the past twenty years or the reports of the various committees of the World Council of Churches for theological contributions from the Third World, and the result is lamentable. Philip Potter of the West Indies, former General Secretary of the World Council of Churches, explains that it is easy to see why (for example) African delegates at the Fifth Assembly of the Lutheran World Federation in Evian, 1970, simply imitated traditional European theology:

> What opportunity had they to think about the faith in their own way? If they hadn't been "good boys" they would never have become church leaders. . . . We have seldom been allowed to think for ourselves. For long enough we have put up with a kind of theological imperialism. I call this racism. Unless we non-Westerners stick rigidly to the precise formulae of Western scholasticism, we are not considered theologians, or bright enough to communicate the Gospel.[4]

The Mexican Pentecostal bishop, Manuel Gaxiola-Gaxiola, joins in this critique in his dissertation on Mexican Pentecostalism. He describes Mexico as being "so far from God and so close to the United States"[5] and speaks of "an unnecessary meddling by the United States in the internal affairs of the Latin Americas [Monroe doctrine],"[6] and "the American intervention in favour of Victoriano Huerto, the bloodiest villain of the Mexican Revolution, and, of course the large American investments, which require diplomatic protection and pressure."[7] This situation "has not yet convinced everybody that becoming Protestant does not equal becoming American, which is one of the greatest obstacles to the conversion of many."[8] "The new proletarian in Mexico is super efficient and super cheap. The man finds work outside the modern factories, but he knows he is being employed because he is the lowest paid man doing that work, but once the transnational company he works for finds another man in another country who is willing to work for less, the factory will move to that country."[9]

When the Silenced Begin to Speak

It is high time to look for non-Western categories for thinking theologically and presenting theology. The Division of World Mission and Evangelism of the World Council of Churches has been working on such experiments—and

---

[4]Philip Potter in an interview on the "so-called crisis of Mission." "Zur sogenannten Grundlagenkrise der Mission."

[5]Gaxiola-Gaxiola, *Mexican*, 49. See also his "Inicios del Pentecostalismo en Mexico."

[6]Gaxiola, *Mexican*, 48.

[7]Ibid., 49.

[8]Ibid., 256.

[9]Ibid., 301.

they are certainly experiments! The different road the World Council is seeking can be found only in dialogue with those people in the Third World who cannot and will not accept our modes of communication.

The historical background to such conversations in Mexico is interesting. The purpose of what the World Council of Churches is doing was described at a press conference in Mexico as the revolutionary movement "which Christian faith not merely permits but positively requires," whereby

> men without a voice, men who have been reduced to silence by our intellectual concepts and racial prejudices should be allowed to speak for themselves. It means that the dialogue must not have a built-in advantage for the Westerner. This is the revolution we seek. This, too, is what Paolo Freire is after. The rulers of Brazil feared this revolution more than they feared any armed uprising. That is why they jailed the former minister of education, Freire, for men who are aware of their dignity and significance are more dangerous than armed slaves.[10]

To Enable Others to Develop a Face

A thousand years ago Mexico had already developed one of the most advanced programs of education, and a fascinating philosophy. To formulate their philosophy, however, they did not create a system comparable with the system of an Aristotle, a Thomas Aquinas, or a Hegel. Miguel León-Portilla, the expert on ancient Mexican (Nahuatl) civilization, rightly points out that the quality of a philosophy, theology or theory of education cannot be judged by whether or not it creates a system.[11] While there may be philosophers and theologians "who still consider the construction of a coherent logical system to be the only form of philosophical thought"[12] this is a mistaken attitude which if accepted would require us to exclude from discussion even such famous Western philosophers as Augustine, Pascal, Kierkegaard, Unamuno, Ortega and Bergson, not to mention Luther and the Bible.

The non-systematic philosophy of the ancient Mexicans did not prevent them from creating a compulsory educational program which gave children in the humblest circumstances an equal opportunity of education with the nobility and royalty.[13] The key figure in this education was the *tlamantini:* the wise man, or "he who knows things,"[14] or "the one who makes others develop a face, a personality." Of this figure, León-Portilla tells us "He puts them, as it were, before a mirror and makes them discover themselves."[15] Under his

---

[10] Boletin de Cencos A. C. Nr. 4164, Mexico, 13.5.1970. Freire, *Pedagogy.*

[11] León-Portilla, *La filosofía náhuatl,* XV.

[12] Ibid., XVI.

[13] Soustelle, *La vie quotidienne,* 203; León-Portilla, *La filosofía náhuatl,* 224.

[14] Códice Matritense de la Real Academia (textos en náhuatl de los indígenos informantes de Sahagún), ed. facs de Pasy y Troncoso, Madrid, VIII, 1936, 118r, 118v; León-Portilla, *Aztec Thought and Culture* (English translation of *La filosofía náhuatl*), 63f. On the grammar of the old Mexican language: Garibay, *Llave de Náhuatl.*

[15] Te-ix–tomani, ibid.; León-Portilla, *Aztec Thought,* 13; idem, *La filosofía náhuatl,* 68.

influence people "humanize their will." "The good *tlamantini*—like a good doctor—submits himself to practical criticism of his methods and is ready to experiment. A bad *tlamantini*—like a bad doctor—keeps his tradition to himself. Like the lizard, he likes the dark corners; he deals in secret magic potions and in this way destroys men's faces, men's personality."[16]

The educational medium among these ancient Mexicans was not the manual or the textbook, but poetry. On this earth no one can declare the truth, said the *tlamantini*, except perhaps through "flowers and songs."[17] If they wanted to be precise they did not call for sharper definitions, but described what they meant by referring to two of its most remarkable features *(difrasismo)*. For example, they described a woman as "skirt and blouse," a city as "water and hill" and the transcendence of God as "night and wind."[18] Like a hunter, the *tlamantini* was chasing songs; he "steals flowers and songs,"[19] "butterflies of song."[20]

This approach refused to express the inexpressible. Hence the skepticism and agnosticism of the Nahuas. Can we say anything certain about the future, about life after death, or even about life's meaning?[21] This skepticism found final expression in the question: Does man possess any truth?[22] What was in question here was not man's sincerity; it was the much more radical question of whether man could possess truth at all. Both the nature of truth and the world of goods, we have to "consider as lent to us, oh friends."[23]

Enter the "True Faith"

With the arrival of the Spaniards, the songs died away, the flowers were trampled under foot, the quetzal-feathers torn out. The philosophy of the Mexicans was despised as superstition, even though on the basis of their educational program of "flowers and songs" the Mexicans had developed a mathematics, an astronomy and an architecture which still move us to admiration today. The books of the Nahuatl people were burned, their temples

---

[16] Itech netlacaneco, ibid.; León-Portilla, *Aztec Thought*, 15; idem, *La filosofia náhuatl*, 70.

[17] Ibid. 118/19; León-Portilla, *Aztec Thought*, 27, 73; idem, *La filosofia náhuatl*, 84. in xochitl in cuiatl; Peñafiel, *Cantares Mexicanos*, 13r; León-Portilla, *Aztec Thought*, 76; idem, *La filosofia náhuatl*, 153.

[18] In cuéitl in huipilli—in atl in tépetl—yohualli ehécatl. León-Portilla, *Aztec Thought*, 102; idem, *La filosophia náhuatl*, 178.

[19] Peñafiel, *Cantares Mexicanos*; León-Portilla, *Aztec Thought*, 181; idem, *La filosophia náhuatl*, 320.

[20] Peñafiel, *Cantares Mexicanos*, 11v; León-Portilla, *Aztec Thought* 182; idem, *La filosophia náhuatl*, 321.

[21] Peñafiel, *Cantares Mexicanos*, 17r; León-Portilla, *Aztec Thought*, 7; *La filosophia náhuatl*, 60.

[22] ¿Cuix oc nell'n tlaca? Peñafiel, *Cantares Mexicanos*, 10v; León-Portilla, *Aztec Thought*, 7, *La filosophia náhuatl*, 61.

[23] Ma oc netlataneuh o nican in antocnihuam. Peñafiel, *Cantares Mexicanos*, 17r; León-Portilla, *Aztec Thought*, 124; idem, *La filosophia náhuatl*, 203.

plundered, their language suppressed, their teachers and priests put to death. Las Casas, a Catholic missionary and defender of the Indians, estimated that 12 million Indians died in 38 years, mostly as slaves in the mines.[24]

The last testimony of the Nahuas is found in the contemporary record[25] of the discussion which some of the *tlamatinime* had with the newly arrived Spanish missionaries. The missionaries urged them earnestly to abhor, to despise, to curse and spit on the gods they had worshipped. The Mexicans answered courteously that they were fully aware of the difficulties and dangers the Spaniards had had to endure in crossing the ocean:

> *Our Lords, our very esteemed Lords:*
> *great hardships have you endured to reach this land. . . .* [26]
> *You said*
> *that we know not*
> *the Lord of the Close Vicinity*[27]
> *to Whom the heavens and the earth belong.*
> *You said*
> *that our gods are not true gods.*
> *New words are these*
> *that you speak;*
> *because of them we are disturbed,*
> *because of them we are troubled.*[28]

How could the missionaries say such offensive things? The Mexicans had known God for centuries, insofar as God can be known by anyone. What the missionaries wanted them to believe they did not believe to be true, even if to say this offended the missionaries. Then, simply and impressively, the Mexicans responded:

> *Allow us then to die,*
> *let us perish now,*
> *since our gods are already dead.*[29]

A Heretic Defends the Indians

From about 1509 Catholic legal experts held it to be necessary, before embarking on war, to justify this step to the heathen peoples of Latin America and to call upon these peoples to surrender voluntarily.

This official proclamation (known as the *requerimiento*) was obligatory from the year 1513 . . . The country's inhabitants were informed that there was only one

---

[24] Biermann, *Las Casas*, 59.

[25] Lehmann, *Sterbende Götter*. The excellent source-book contains the text in the original Náhuatl and in an Old Spanish translation from José Maria Pou y Marti, *El libre perdido*.

[26] Lehmann, *Sterbende Götter*, 93.

[27] In tloque navaque (name of God).

[28] Lehmann, *Sterbende Götter*, 102.

[29] Ibid.

God and that His representative was the Pope in Rome and furthermore that the latter had given their territories to the kings of Spain. The people were then required to accept and submit to the Christian faith. Willful refusal to do so would bring on them war, all kinds of misfortune, the enslavement of them all together with their wives and children, since they would be rebels against their rightful lord. Since no one, of course, submitted voluntarily, the slaughter began.[30]

Those who did submit were nevertheless enslaved. One of the few to challenge these practices was the Dominican, Fray Bartolomé de las Casas. Briefly and sharply he branded as unjust all the wars fought by the Spaniards.[31] "The supposedly glorious feats of Spanish heroes are gross iniquities. Spain will still have to pay for this to the last farthing. She has failed in the task entrusted to her and proved herself unfit to derive the least material benefit from these colonial lands."[32] Accordingly Fray Bartolomé refused absolution to the departing soldiers.[33] Furthermore, he insisted that the Emperor Charles V should restore all the property he had unjustly seized.[34] We are not surprised to learn that Spaniards reviled Las Casas as a heretic, and a Lutheran antichrist.[35]

The controversy came to a head in the disputation between Las Casas and Juan Ginés de Sepúlveda in 1550–1557. Sepúlveda gave four reasons to justify war against the heathen:

1. Because of the heinous character of their sins, particularly their idolatry and sins against nature, they deserved to be punished.

2. Because of their primitive condition, they had a duty to serve the more advanced Spaniards, and if they refused, should be compelled by war to do so.

3. Because the way to the preaching of the Gospel could only be prepared by conquest.

4. Because the innocent human beings destined for sacrifice must be freed, and cannibalism wiped out.[36]

Las Casas' reply to the first point was that the sins of the heathen did not come within the competence of the church. "For what have I to do with judging outsiders? . . . God judges those outside," said St. Paul (1 Cor. 5:12f). To the second point he replied that the Indians were not merely uncouth barbarians. He answered the third point by reminding Sepúlveda that Christ, in sending his disciples, counseled them that they must be ready to lay down their

[30] Biermann, *Las Casas*, 55.
[31] In the tract "Sobre los indios hechos esclavos." Las Casas, *Opúsculos*, 257–90 (quoted Obras V); quoted in Biermann, *Las Casas*, 53.
[32] In Doce Dudas (Obras V, 478–536); Biermann, *Las Casas*, 71.
[33] Biermann, *Las Casas*, 18.
[34] In the Representación (Obras V, 123–33); Biermann, *Las Casas*, 26, note 99.
[35] Ximénez, *Historia*, I, 346; Biermann, *Las Casas*, 32.
[36] Biermann, *Las Casas*, 43.

lives for His sake. To his opponent's final point, Las Casas answered that war brought in its train enormities, hatred, fear, and falsehood; thus the evils of war far outweighed any possible benefits to be gained in protecting the innocent.[37]

Ruins

Las Casas was not heeded. All that is left, therefore, of the Mexican educational system, language, art, and architecture is—ruins. It is not unfair to say that Mexico's present widespread illiteracy and economic dependence were created by Europeans, and have been maintained by Americans. The invasion and conquest of Mexico was the beginning of a long martyrdom. It is still going on before our very eyes. The *mestizos* and the Indians, "out of a sense of the profoundest spiritual shame, hardly dare to raise their heads. The problem of the peasant is not simply that he has only a few coins in his purse. It is something more, which reduces him to something less than a man," says Oscar Maldonado, a Mexican Roman Catholic priest.[38]

Yet in a fragmentary way the ancient Mexican tradition lives on. Even the remains of the sculptures, temples and books compel the admiration of the visitor to the Anthropological Museum in Mexico.[39] But the ruins that are left are not only those of stone. There are remnants of the Mexican tradition which are discovered, for example, when priests and nuns join with the *campesinos* in excavating the buried humanity of the ancient Mexicans. The peasants can once again recover "their face." But we also meet this ancient Mexican tradition in the Mexican Pentecostal movement. These Pentecostals are developing their own social and economic life—perhaps even their own theology—independently of foreign missionaries.[40]

Iglesia Cristiana Independiente Pentecostés

One of the churches of these Pentecostals is the Iglesia Cristiana Independiente Pentecostés with 150,000 members.[41] Its founder was Andrés

---

[37] Las Casas, *Apologia,* preserved as Manuscript at the Bibliothèque Nationale, Paris, Nuevos Fondos Latinos 12, 926. Biermann, *Las Casas,* 43.

[38] Maldonado, "Mexicanos," 20–25.

[39] Cf. e.g., Bernal, *Cien obras.*

[40] Exact statistics on Mexican Pentecostalism are difficult to assess. Cf. *Handbuch,* 02b.22. The best is probably Barrett, *WChE,* 487, which gives for 1980 550,000 Protestants and 1,500,000 Mexican Independents (most of them Pentecostals). Further statistics in Gaxiola, *Mexican,* 227, and in Müller, "Mexiko," 692, where he mentions over 4 million protestants (1990); but he does not break down this figure into protestants and Pentecostals resp. independents. For the whole of Latin America about 25% of the population will be *evangélicos,* the majority Pentecostals (2000; Zanuso, *Iglesias,* 267; Gaxiola-Gaxiola, "Latin American," 107, 129, quote 107. In Brazil there are more people in Assemblies of God churches than catholics in Catholic Churches (14.4 million as over against 12.6 million), hence the nervous statements of catholic bishops and the pope (Robeck, "Southern," 101–6, quotes, 102).

[41] Barrett, *WChE,* 491. Amerlinck y Assereto, *Ixmiquilpan,* 88.

Ornelas Martínez (died 1958),[42] a miner from San Juan de Los Lagos in the Mexican state of Jalisco. Shortly after the First World War Ornelas emigrated to Miami (Arizona) where somebody gave him a Spanish edition of the Book of Proverbs. The book at first sight did not interest him. On his return to his native village,[43] he began reading it out of boredom, and found it interesting. But the last pages in the book were missing, so he ordered the whole "Book of Proverbs" from the address in Los Angeles printed at the bottom of the title page. He received some tracts, the book of Proverbs, and a New Testament. The study of the New Testament captivated him so much that when others were sleeping at night he went into the countryside to pray, confess his sins, and ask God that he might use him for something worthwhile. In December 1920[44] he traveled again to Miami in search of a complete Bible. Overhearing a fellow-miner uttering the word "Bible" he asked him: "Do you have a Bible? Can you show it to me?" He could hardly wait for the end of the shift in order to see the Bible. The colleague took him to his pastor who gave Andrés Ornelas a Bible. (This Bible is kept today at the headquarters of the Iglesia Cristiana Independiente Pentecostés, Pachuco).

In May 1921 Ornelas returned to Mexico, and went first to the services of the Methodists in Pachuco (Hgo). There he met Raymundo Nieto, who introduced him to the Pentecostal baptism of the Spirit and baptized him in October 1922 in a river.[45] By June 1922 the two had already founded a Pentecostal congregation in Pachuco which is considered today as the mother church of the Iglesia Cristiana Independiente Pentecostés.[46] By their fearless testimony, healing of the sick, and practical Christianity, they won a number of followers. However, that was also the time when the government favored Protestantism because of its antipathy to the Catholic Church.[47] In 1927 Raymundo was no longer "considered to be in a position to continue his pastorate" (as Ramírez puts it).[48] Ornelas became the pastor of the Pachuco church.

By amalgamation with other churches, among them one which had been founded by the Swedish Pentecostal missionary Axel Anderson (Filadelfia Church, renamed Saron Church) in Mexico City, the organization grew

---

[42] The important diaries of Andrés Ornelas Martínez are at the headquarters of the Iglesia Cristiana Independiente Pentecostés in Pachuco (Hgo). There one finds also the autobiography of the founder (now out of print). Lit. on Martínez and his church: Amerlinck y Assereto, *Ixmiquilpan*, 88f. Crouch, *World Outlook*, 33–35. Ornelas, "Libertad." Espinosa, "Datos." Idem, "Cinco." Tschuy, "Lateinamerika," 1–4. Ramírez, *Bodas de Oro.*

[43] Ramírez indicates El Saus de los Ibarras as the native village of Andrés Ornelas (*Bodas de Oro*, 19).

[44] That is the earliest biographical date for Andrés Ornelas Martínez which I could find (Ramírez, *Bodas de Oro*, 24).

[45] Ramírez, *Bodas de Oro*, 31.

[46] Ibid., 30.

[47] Amerlinck y Assereto, *Ixmiquilpan*, 88.

[48] Ramírez, *Bodas de Oro*, 39.

steadily. In 1941 Ornelas disassociated himself from foreign missionaries. In 1953 he was successful in pulling together two hundred congregations into one organization. "It was an historic act when he threw away the yoke of the bad foreigners and their Mexican paladines," states the official journal of the church in a short historical account.[49] In 1955 the church amalgamated with the important Iglesia Evangélica Independiente. The united church is called today—after further amalgamations—Iglesia Cristiana Independiente Pentecostés. Very early they sent their missionaries to Colombia and Puerto Rico.[50] They were also instrumental in founding a bank, El Banco del Fondo Común.[51] Ramírez proudly relates in the preface to his history of the church: "The movement is genuinely indigenous. It does not receive subsidies from any foreign country or mission."[52]

Ixmiquilpan

"The Mesquital region of the state of Hidalgo in Mexico is one of the driest and poorest places of the country. Prairie-like valleys are framed by yellow mountains. During the day the sun burns mercilessly and at night it can become very cold, as the valleys are 6,000 feet above sea-level."[53]

The industrialization which invaded Mexico City, Monterrey, and Guadalajara in the fifties has not yet reached the region of Mesquital, where agriculture and a small cottage industry give a very meagre income, and where in 1960 more than half of the population still spoke the Indian Otomí language. Those Indians can be divided again into half who speak Otomí exclusively and half who, beside the Indian language, have mastered some Spanish.[54] More than a third are illiterate.

The effects of the political and social revolution which conquered the big cities between 1910 and 1917 reached the country of the Otomí much later. Far into the thirties one could find hardly any Protestants here. Those who dared to confess the new faith were either driven away or killed.

That is why in 1936 a young Indian by the name of Venancio Hernández[55] had to leave his native valley and the hacienda where he and his ancestors had worked since the arrival of the Spaniards. After having taught himself to read and write, he managed somehow to acquire a Bible. He began to read it, at first very skeptically because he knew that the great Mexican revolution was very

---

[49] Espinosa, "Datos."

[50] Ramírez, *Bodas de Oro*, 96f.

[51] Ibid., 84.

[52] Ibid., 13.

[53] Tschuy, "Lateinamerika," 1.

[54] Amerlinck y Assereto, *Ixmiquilpan*, indicates 337,061 inhabitants in the region of Mesquital (1960). Of these 81,562 speak Otomí and 17,113 only Otomí. In the region of Ixmiquilpan (24,871 inhabitants) 13,927 are bilingual and 5,763 speak only Otomí. Hence the significance of services in Otomí (Ibid., 12).

[55] See Hernández, "Hombres nuevos."

consciously anti-ecclesiastical if not anti-religious. As an Indian he knew too how the religion of the conquerors had been thrust on the native population, often by brute force, and how the hierarchy of the church had sided, during the early nineteenth century's war of independence, with the Spaniards and the foreign king.

Yet the Bible which Venancio Hernández now read appeared to him to be entirely different. The Christ which it described was not half hidden by the Virgin Mary or the Saints. He was neither a poor and feeble child nor a thorn-crowned, weeping, dying, or even dead son of God. On the contrary: he spoke with authority, he showed courage, and he feared neither the mighty ones of this world nor the indignation of the people who had expected another Messiah. Such a personality would have fitted the Mexican revolution well! More: this Christ talked with individual people about their sin, their *lostness;* and he revealed God to them through his love for man, and through his sacrificial death, by which he reconciled man with God. One had only to accept this gift . . . ! Why had no one brought this message to Venancio Hernández? The Virgin Mary, the Saints, the places of pilgrimage and the indulgences: none of that was necessary if this book were true. And it *was* true, for Venancio acquired an inner confidence hitherto unknown to him. Here was a message which finally gave the right spiritual guidance to his revolutionary thinking, and to his search for social and political justice.[56]

Venancio Hernández did not want to, and could not, remain silent. During the siesta he read to the other farm workers from the wonderful book. They believed and were converted, changed their old habits, and soon, under the tree where they assembled, were transformed into a small congregation.

The owner of the hacienda was informed that some of his Indian farm workers had become Protestants. He summoned Venancio Hernández and his friends before him and prohibited them to have any further religious meetings. The Indians did not answer, but common prayer and Bible reading went on. The owner of the hacienda, the local priest, and other Indians gathered to drive the small congregation out of their valley under threat of death.

Under the leadership of Venancio they wandered into the next valley, to the village of Ixmiquilpan,[57] where the main road from Mexico City to Guadalajara passes. Outside the village, on a little hill on which the army had installed a small observation post, the small group settled down. Taking advantage of

---

[56] After his conversion he did not give up his fight against the exploiting rich but he realized that the 300 shots of ammunition and his brother's pistol (of best German quality as he mentions explicitly) was too feeble for his battle. He needed better and more efficient weapons. And these are not peace in the heart and an individualistic religion, as one might expect, but the demonstration in praxis (and not just the proclamation) of models of an alternative society. See his letter to his brother Silvester in Ramírez, *Bodas de Oro*, 25f.

[57] According to Ramírez two years before the arrival of Hernández (in the year 1936) Prudencio Esquivel had already founded a small Pentecostal group in Ixmiquilpan. (*Bodas de Oro*, 125; pagination is wrong, wrongly printed 117).

the military post gave them a certain protection. Hernández knew that the small congregation had to stick together if it were not to risk sudden disbandment. At this time, the system of land reform limited estate ownership to five hundred hectares, thus one of the big land owners of Ixmiquilpan had to sell part of his land. Venancio and his followers approached him and managed to get a favorable contract. They bought a good piece of land with irrigation rights. As they possessed very little cash, the former owner allowed them to repay the purchase price by installments.[58] The small evangelical community of Christians had impressed him and, in spite of pressure from other quarters, he gave them a chance. "God has been with us!" said Venancio ponderingly, when recalling those pioneer days.[59]

A Pentecostal Cooperative

The newly acquired farm land was under collective ownership, but the land on which the small stone houses and family gardens were now gradually being built were privately owned. Up to this time the Indians had lived only in Cactus huts; now they organized themselves into agricultural cooperatives, and built a cooperative textile factory which they continue to modernize. Compared with Europe and America, their tools and machines are modest. The outstanding fact, however, is that the Indians have created this local economy themselves. They are not dependent on foreign finance and expertise—even in the form of missionaries—since this handicraft production is based on traditional skills. These Indians are unusually gifted, both intellectually and manually: With precision and expertise such an Indian will install a projector together with a generator (in order to produce the necessary electricity), not forgetting to check carefully all the contacts. He is also able to service and repair his versatile agricultural tractor himself.

Through the years, their church had to weather heavy persecution from the local Catholic clergy. "Sometimes the priest said we were not good people, even that we were of the devil," they recalled later to Maria Amerlinck (a Catholic anthropologist who has made a careful anthropological study of the Pentecostal church at Ixmiquilpan).[60] "In fact," Amerlinck comments, "persecution had not been initiated by the priests, but by some of the richer people of Ixmiquilpan who could count on the local political structure and who disliked the acquiring of land by the Indians. Yet with the help of regional[61] and national political forces and with some economic help from outside the difficulties were overcome."[62] Pentecostals considered it their duty not to

---

[58] According to Amerlinck y Assereto, the Pentecostals bought 10,000 m² of land and 75 houses between 1948 and 1956 (*Ixmiquilpan*, 96).

[59] Tschuy, "Lateinamerika," 1–3. According to Amerlinck y Assereto, the foundation of the congregation of Ixmiquilpan goes back to the years 1938 to 1940.

[60] Amerlinck y Assereto, *Ixmiquilpan*, 87.

[61] A loan from the Instituto Lingüístico de Verano (Ibid., 98).

[62] Ibid., 87f. On the persecutions: Lascári, "Josefina Láscari." *Mensajero Pente-*

respond to persecution with vengeance. "By praying and reading the Bible they searched for the will of God and instead of exercising vengeance they offered pardon. The murderers recognized their wickedness, repented and became members of the church."[63]

When the governor of their state needed workers for building roads, they made the following offer: "We know," they said, "that you want to build roads in our region but that you lack workers. We will provide three hundred men daily free of charge if you provide machines and technical know-how. That is how we are going to show to you that we 'cristianos' are useful citizens." This demonstration proved better than any theoretical statement that they were not—as their persecutors accused—sectarian, but responsible members of society. During the road-building they composed new songs in the soft restrained style of the Otomí. Today these songs form part of their liturgy, and remind them of the time of persecution and how it was overcome.[64]

Dangers from Outside

The church is no longer threatened by the Catholics. Indeed the latter are ready to learn from Venancio, who has, for example, been made a member of the Advisory Theological Commission of the Catholic Church of Mexico. Today the church is threatened by a different "true faith." I was personally present at a service in Ixmiquilpan at which an American missionary was the preacher. At the beginning of the service three young Indians came forward with their guitars, knelt down and quietly prayed. Then they played and sang with a cultured restraint and manner which was extremely moving. Even the members of the congregation did not sing at the top of their voices, as one usually finds in Pentecostal circles. But then came the missionary's sermon! His words went back and forth across the Indian congregation like a steamroller. The Indians gently lowered their heads but even so I thought it scarcely possible for them to sustain this flood of oratory without injury. But four centuries have developed in them a capacity to remain dignified and noble even in humiliation. When the appeal for conversion was issued, many of them came to the front, covered their face with their *rebozos* and quietly wept. Before the end of the service the missionary and his entourage quit the chapel.

In the house of the chief a large table was spread with a dozen varied Mexican dishes, lovingly and skillfully prepared, together with fruits and drinks. The missionary talked incessantly—in English, which the Otomí do not understand—while the chief stood at the door with his wife and served

---

costés 2/62, March 1961, 20 (Victoriano Montiel, Ixmiquilpan) Raymundo Ramírez, "Hilario Aragón," quoted in *Mensajero Pentecostés* 2/72, Jan. 1972, 24f. ("en una turba de fanaticos, el cura y el cdte municipal son los autores intellectuales del crimen"). Ramírez, *Bodas de Oro*, 128–33, passim.

[63] Tschuy, "Lateinamerika," 5.

[64] Ramírez, *Bodas de Oro*, 80.

the guests. When the food had disappeared, everyone rose. "Excuse me," said the Indian chief, "I have a sick friend and I would like you to pray for him." "Of course," answered the missionary. "Let us pray." And in his booming voice he rattled off a prayer: "Lord, you can heal even from afar. Make our unfortunate friend well. Amen. But now we have to be going." And with that, he went. But Venancio was sorry for him. How could the missionary be blamed for being a *gringo?*

Conversion and Development

The secret of Venancio's congregation lies in its theological and economic independence. I cannot find out exactly when Venancio united his congregation with the Iglesia Cristiana Independiente Pentecostés, whose headquarters are in the nearby Pachuco. He is head pastor, and has under him about forty *obreros,* lay preachers who each, in addition to their work as farmers and craftsmen, serve congregations of about a hundred people.[65]

The upward social movement of the members of the church is phenomenal. "There is a close link between evangelism and the search for education,"[66] says Amerlinck. Giving their testimony,[67] participating in the life of the congregation, financing the church themselves,[68] "develops" the latent gifts in these Indians to their full potential. For them "giving" (money, animals, vegetables, even drinks) to the church is not "alms-giving," because God is not a beggar *(limosnero).* She sums up her assessment as follows: "Under these circumstances religious conversion is the only way out of the narrow confines of traditionalism . . . The Indians need this new ideology as a means of rationalization which enables them to understand their relationship to the changing world around them and gives a definite dignity to the individual person."[69]

While in the Catholic church in Ixmiquilpan most of the priests are foreigners,[70] the Pentecostals have exclusively native ministers (who almost without exception earn their living in secular work). Before their conversion most of them were employed as farm workers on a day-to-day basis. Today

---

[65] Amerlinck y Assereto, *Ixmiquilpan* (23, 89) gives the following statistics:

	Catholics	Pentecostals	Others
1940	18,338	57	
1950	20,912	245	
1960	23,657	1,069	145 (*)

(*) no information, no religion, 8 other denominations and religions.

[66] Ibid., 112.

[67] Ibid., 122.

[68] Ibid., 123.

[69] Ibid., 4–5.

[70] Two Italian, one American priest, six American lady missionaries, no Mexican in Amerlinck y Assereto's list (*Ixmiquilpan,* 23).

most of them are farm owners, masons, owners of small shops and mills, truck drivers, and mechanics.[71]

The Pentecostal pastors do not consider their ministry as a purely religious ministry which would distinguish and separate them from the rest of the population. They do not see themselves as paid specialists of religion, but very much more as "economic evangelists" of a kind, or "evangelistic development advisers." They earn their living because their example and the way in which they build their own houses is part of their proclamation. They feel themselves to be superior to the Catholic priests and are very proud of their special ministry of evangelism. They criticize the priests openly—and, if opportunity arises, also the Catholic hierarchy[72]—because they work solely as priests and lay themselves open to the reproach that they exercise their ministry for money.[73] Discussing the question of a full-time, paid pastoral ministry, they say: "What would our colleagues at work say? As a full-time ministry we would become estranged from them."[74] Hernández summarizes the theology of their *lived fellowship* in these words: "The community believes in the salvation of the hands by work, of the mind by learning to read, of the body by divine healing[75] and of the soul by new birth."[76]

There is no doubt that the Otomí have created an example of development policy which by its very simplicity is fascinating. Within this system they have explicitly included the women[77]—a revolutionary act in their society. Here and there, but very reluctantly, there are also beginnings of a dialogue with European theology and churches.[78] The attempt is not without dangers—Maria Amerlinck draws attention to growing paternalism, particularly among the leaders in Pachuco.[79] Their theological and economic independence is impressive, and was a matter of life and death in the pioneering phase of the church; but will it last in the more complex economic situation of the future? And what

---

[71] Amerlinck y Assereto gives an exact list from a pattern of 83 family fathers: occupation before conversion, occupation after conversion; accommodation before and after conversion etc. While almost all of them had been farm workers before conversion, Amerlinck y Assereto found after conversion: 18 farm owners, 23 masons (almost a monopoly of the Pentecostals!), 3 shop owners (one owns a Nixtemal mill), 2 employees at a petrol station, 1 mechanic, 1 apprentice mechanic, 4 "promotores de asuntos indígenas," and only 8 farm workers and 2 women servants. (*Ixmiquilpan*, 104ff.).

[72] *Mensajero Pentecostés* 2/61, May 1961, 20: "El Cardenal José 'Efrain' Rivera" (quoted from *Rototemas* 6.12.1958): "Para nadie es un secreto que Garibi Rivera representa el sector mas sectario, intransingente y obstruso de la iglesia en Mexico."

[73] Amerlinck y Assereto, *Ixmiquilpan*, 129.

[74] Ibid., 130.

[75] That is how the doctrine of the American healing evangelists is taken up, such as Oral Roberts, "Fe contra," 9–11, Osborn, T.L., "Preguntas," 6–8; idem, "Hoy," 3–7.

[76] Tschuy, "Lateinamerika," 4.

[77] Special women's meetings (cf. e.g., *Mensajero Pentecostés* 2/51, Aug. 1961, 5–7).

[78] Niemöller, "Nochebuena" (Niemoeller's sermon in Mexico and mention of "El hombre que se enfrentó a Hitler" by Pedro Gringoire, Mexico 1938).

[79] Keller, "La Biblia."

will the Otomí do if they are restricted by political and economic power structures which cannot easily be overcome by their method of self-help? It is also possible that in a wider sphere their intelligence, charm and theological understanding will produce solutions which we Europeans have not yet discovered. But in order to give any solution the necessary scope, their buried humanity and culture must be excavated in a broader, ecumenical field. I was involved in an attempt at such an "ecumenical excavation expedition."

Excavating the Ruins

In order to avoid wreaking destruction by our excavation, we had to find someone in Mexico who could talk both with intellectuals and with people with little or no formal education. This was particularly important since our efforts were not to be restricted to the Indians, but to cover all sections of the Mexican people, and be a joint discovery made with their participation. We worked on the assumption that it was both possible and desirable to initiate a theological dialogue between intellectuals and illiterate people; Mexican Indians, European Mexicans and half-breeds; Jesuit college lecturers and Adventist roadworkers; journalists and Pentecostal preachers; middle class Methodists and Indian Mormons. The invitation to the "discussions" had to be conveyed personally so as not to miss the illiterate. Miss Maria Antonieta Hernández, then a lecturer in Christian Education in the Comunidad Teológica of Mexico, was the right person for this job. Her unmistakable Mexican appearance overcame any mistrust on the part of the Indians and *campesinos*, Pentecostals and Mormons. As an Anglican she had access to both Protestants and Catholics. Through her flair for the "flowers and songs" mode of communication she aroused the curiosity of journalists and television people. What were the results of the excavation? Since detailed reports of the six seminars held in the spring of 1970 in Monterrey, Mexico, Merida, Amecameca and Guadalajara have been published in Spanish, I confine myself to summarizing some of the main points that were discussed.[80]

The "Flowers and Songs" Method

A theological discussion on the basis of fictional or biblical stories, making use of films and pictures, seemed to most participants the obvious approach. The showing of the film "Parable"—a silent film depicting the passion and resurrection of Christ using the medium of a clown's martyrdom—provoked objections from some Methodist and Baptist intellectuals. Christ could not be presented in the symbol of a clown, they believed. "Why not?" demanded a colored worker (a Pentecostal preacher). "This film shows the circus of life in which we are all performers whether we like it or not. We dance just like puppets, to the pattern decided by those who manipulate the strings. *Gracias*

---

[80] Available in Spanish in *Concept* mentioned above, note 1.

a Dios, Christ came, put himself in our place that we might be set free, that we might be people with a face."

In the discussion of the four different versions of the story of Peter's confession (Mark 8:27–33; Matthew 16:13–23; Luke 8:18–22; John 6:66–71), two groups came to the following conclusion:

> It is hardly possible to formulate a modern confession of faith in conceptual terms. Confessing the faith today presupposes an on-going exchange, mutual correction and relation to constantly changing situations. We can, however, see four elements which must be there in any confession of faith:
>
> • A confession of faith today requires various confessions. This variety can sometimes even include mutually contradictory confessions. We could not agree whether this pluralism had to be confined to various biblical positions or could be extended to include new positions not represented in the Bible.
> • Confessing the faith *(martyria)* involves the element of suffering.
> • Every confession of faith must be related to the history of Jesus of Nazareth.
> • The test as to whether a confession of faith is biblical or merely a human invention is ecumenical discussion crossing racial, confessional, social, national and sexual boundaries.

The Human and the Holy

The participants then considered the story of the "Guardian Angel," by Gerardo Murillo,[81] which tells of a rather uncouth but kind-hearted woman who takes into her care a young girl whose mother has been wrongly imprisoned for some months. By her courage and persistence she secures the mother's release. The discussion started from the question: In what sense was this woman a "guardian angel"? In answering this question some took the traditional line and separated the action of the Holy Spirit (or of the angel) from purely human sympathy, while others maintained that the woman, being of divine origin as a human person, was in fact an instrument of the Holy Spirit in spite of her crude language and penchant for alcohol.

This finding made necessary further discussion of the relationship between the Lukan and Pauline pneumatologies in the New Testament. During this fascinating discussion one of the *campesinos* formulated the following pneumatology: "Training in the Bible and the liturgy is not a condition for the work of the Holy Spirit in a human being. The Holy Spirit has been given to the whole of mankind." To the objection that the Holy Spirit only works in those who are obedient to Him, one *campesina* said this: "That's not true. Mary Magdalene, for example, who approached Jesus with a desire to win him, put on a very revealing robe and covered Jesus with a very seductive perfume. Of course she wasn't ready to receive the gift of Jesus. But Jesus looked on her and gave all he had to give." Astonishingly it was a Catholic who put forward this evangelical interpretation.

---

[81] Murillo, "Un ángel mexicano," 46–51.

Non-Christian Religions

In connection with the story of the Ethiopian eunuch (Acts 8:26–40), the question was raised whether baptism was essential to salvation. The information that the critical verse 37 is absent from certain manuscripts stirred up no fundamentalist feelings as sometimes happens in Europe. Neither when the two-source theory was mentioned (only as a hypothesis), nor during detailed discussion of form-criticism of Peter's confession, did anyone ask the anguished question which inevitably arises in Europe: "What is there left to believe?" The facts were noted, but the question which mattered more for these people was: What is the relevance of these facts?

In discussing the story of the Ethiopian eunuch, a Jesuit explained that Philip's interpretation of the Isaiah passage (Isa 53:7–8) in Acts 8:32–33 conflicts with that of the exegetes of his day. The question therefore arose as to the authority of Philip's exegesis, interpreting the Isaiah passage as referring to Jesus. Are there not events and texts which have today to be interpreted in terms of Jesus, in opposition to both Christian and non-Christian tradition? "There are disciples of Jesus Christ outside the Church. The external sign of being a Christian is not therefore baptism, nor abstinence from alcohol and nicotine, nor the pictures of saints in our homes, but the discovery that Jesus Christ is greater than our theological and political ideas, indeed, greater than our faith."[82]

Some Indian Mormons "excavated" the buried concerns of their forefathers within the traditional Mormon fiction-history, with its insistence on the appearance of Christ on the American continent before the arrival of Columbus. What they were primarily concerned with was not the historical accuracy of this statement but its function, namely the expression of the faith that even the ancient Mexicans had received a revelation from God. They also wanted to know, therefore, whether the Christian revelation had been made once and for all or whether there was still revelation today. When this was affirmed—with the qualification that present-day revelation must be considered in relation to its source and be corrected in ecumenical discussion—the decisive question was put: Is this process of correction a mutual one? What they were obviously concerned to do was to excavate the buried testimonies of their past and to see them afresh in the light of the revelation of Christ. God's ways here too are strange: this illuminating suggestion came from Mormon Indians, of all people!

An evangelical reader may well ask: Where in all this is the center of the gospel, justification by faith? It was already formulated above in the story of Mary Magdalene, in the insight that being a Christian transcends the traditional expressions of Christian faith. Perhaps it was also there in the view of one group about the theology of the Yahwist, which concluded with the wish:

---

[82] Later I developed this problem in a three-act play "The Adventure of Faith," Verlag Metanoia, Kindhausen, Switzerland.

"We need today prophets like the Yahwist to make it clear to the Church that it lives solely by God's mercy and not on the basis of its faith and Christian achievements."

Mexico is usually regarded as a secularized country. Theological and religious topics are seldom taken up by the mass media. It was all the more surprising therefore to find the Monterrey television devoting an hour's program to this kind of interpretation of the Bible, and the press reporting it as an "active, practical school of Christian renewal." This dialogue was described as a "faithful exegesis of Holy Scripture," unlike the methods of indoctrination and polemics.[83]

Outlook

Since I have visited the Mexican Pentecostals, Manuel Gaxiola-Gaxiola has written his dissertation. He mentions several problems which have emerged in the meantime (not specially with the Iglesia Cristiana Independiente Pentecostés but more with the Pentecostal churches in Mexico City). Here the Pentecostals must learn—according to Gaxiola—that "confessions framed in one context do not remain the same when that context changes."[84] That means that the Pentecostal minister must be able to speak on several levels simultaneously. He must be bilingual; that is, he must know the oral language of the roots of Pentecostalism, but he must also be able to converse and understand the written language of concepts and definitions. Thus a well educated ministry *without a middle class image* is emerging.[85]

On the other hand the ecumenical climate is—in spite of the Pentecostal/Vatican dialogue[86]—not satisfactory. A leading Archbishop has even said that the "sects" are more injurious than AIDS.[87] The Catholic church does not seem to learn that something fundamental must change if they want to stop the drain of 8,000 persons who break with the traditional system daily.[88] Here again it is regrettable that the Latin American Pentecostals and Catholics were not involved in the Catholic/Pentecostal dialogue. It seems, however, that this will change very quickly.

---

[83] *Tribuna de Monterrey*, 2.3.1970, 5; *El Provenir* (Monterrey), 2.3.1970, 5.
[84] Gaxiola-Gaxiola, *Mexican*, 290.
[85] Ibid., 318.
[86] See chapter 13, pp. 165–80.
[87] Gaxiola-Gaxiola, *Mexican*, 270.
[88] Ibid., 276. More information on Mexican Pentecostalism in Gill, *Contextualised*, and in Hollenweger, *El Pentecostalismo*, 83–117.

CHAPTER**EIGHT**

Korea: The Oral Shamanist Culture in Pentecostal Transformation[1]

An Old Culture

Dr. Boo-Woong Yoo is a Presbyterian pastor from Korea. His church sent him to Kenya as a theological teacher. At the same time, he was asked to write his theological dissertation on Korean Pentecostalism, for which he traveled regularly to Birmingham. His topic is as extraordinary as his method and his working energy.

First he had to gather the numerous Korean documents on his topic. He found them in several archives in Korea and in the United States. He studied them in Birmingham and in a rather remote seminary at the foot of Mount Kilimanjaro where he taught theology. He told me how he wrote chapter after chapter, packed his manuscripts into a land-rover and traveled several days to Nairobi where he typed them on two electric word processors, one in English, the other in Korean (for the original documents). Word processors were not available in his African college.

In his introduction, Yoo emphasizes that Korea has a very old culture. The written history of Korea goes back to the first millennium B.C.—a time when our forefathers had no written culture, and many still walked about in bearskins. The oral tradition goes even further back, to the year 2332 B.C., 1000 years before King David, and 3400 years before William the

---

[1] This chapter is heavily based on Yoo, *Korean Pentecostalism* and Yoo, "Response to Korean Shamanism."

Conqueror. The modern history of Korea starts with the Yi Dynasty (A.D. 1392) which unified the disparate Korean kingdoms.

Since Korea has for a long time been influenced by China, it is not astonishing that the first main religions of Korea were Buddhism, and later Confucianism. However, very early on these two religions were penetrated by Korean Shamanism. Christianity also, in its Catholic, Protestant and Pentecostal versions, has borrowed much from Korean shamanism.[2]

It was only in the sixteenth century that the first Catholic missionaries arrived in Korea. However, Catholicism did not spread at the same rate as Protestantism has in the twentieth century. One of the reasons for this may be that Protestantism (under the influence of Pentecostal Minjung theology) is financially and theologically more independent than Catholicism.

Protestantism in Korea started only about a hundred years ago—a very short time compared with the many thousands of years of Korean history. The first Protestant missionaries concentrated their work among the poor, the peasants, and later, when industrialization came, among the workers. One of these first missionaries was H. Appenzeller, a Swiss-born American, who had been taught the German Heidelberg Catechism by his mother.

Since the year 1910 (the first year of the Japanese occupation, which lasted until 1945) Protestantism has doubled every ten years (see chart). All churches contribute to this growth, but the Pentecostals have made a particularly strong contribution.

Growth of Korean Protestantism 1960–83

1960	1,250,000
1970	2,200,000
1980	7,000,000
1983	8,500,000[3]

Yoo divides the history of Korean Pentecostalism into three typical streams: (1) fundamentalist Pentecostalism (from 1900 onward), (2) mystical Pentecostalism (in the thirties) and (3) Pentecostalism which takes its roots from the Minjung tradition (1970ff.)

---

[2] On the Pentecostal pastor as a "shaman" see *The Pentecostals*, 474ff. The famous Korean Pentecostal pastor Paul Yonggi Cho (born 1936) could be considered a Pentecostal Shaman par excellence, although his Western biographers avoid this term (D. J. Wilson, "Cho"; Kennedy, *Dream*). But see Villafañe, *The Liberating Spirit*, 208, and Cho, *Fourth Dimension*, 90, 96, 100, where a very much more inclusive view of the Spirit of God is presented. Mark R. Mullins describes Paul Yonggi Cho's theology "as a synthesis of Korean shamanism, Robert Shuller's 'positive thinking', and the pragmatism of the Church Growth School of Missiology associated with Fuller Theological Seminary's School of World Mission." See the excellent article, Mullins, "Empire," 87–102, esp. 92.

[3] Source: *Studies on Pentecostalism in Korea* (Seoul: Korean Christian Academy Press, 1983, 300f. [Korean]); Yoo, *Korean Pentecostalism*, 3.

Fundamentalist Pentecostalism

The first Pentecostalism was a popular movement which worked through the shamanist forms of religion (characterized by the healing of the sick, visions, ecstasies, the priesthood of women, and lack of theological education). These forms were adapted in a Pentecostal way. These early Pentecostals took the biblical text at its face value and experienced deep revivals which can be compared to the revivals of early Pentecostalism in Europe and America.

In contrast to those revivals, the Korean revivals did not lead to separate churches, but remained more or less within the mainline churches as charismatic-ecumenical revival movements. They thus influenced these churches deeply. It is this influence which makes early Korean Pentecostalism important—more important at any rate than the later Korean Pentecostal churches.

This influence has also had its drawbacks. Critical thinking has in the past been neglected in favor of religious experience; eternal salvation has been considered more important than changes in society. But both "weaknesses" are understandable. The people who were touched by these early revivals had no access to higher education. And, since Korea was at that time occupied and oppressed by Japan, ordinary people had no opportunity to "change society." However, the resistance to Japanese occupation among the ordinary people was clearly felt.

The fact that today many Korean theologians (Pentecostals and others) do post-graduate studies in America and Europe shows that change has been rapid.

Mystical Pentecostalism

The second Pentecostalism started with the mystical tradition of Korea. Its most important representative is Yong-do Yi. Yi proclaimed a dualistic doctrine: the spiritual, the religious, the immaterial is good; the material, the worldly is bad. He himself took his doctrine very seriously. He gave his clothes to a beggar, sold his house, and used the proceeds of the sale to finance the studies of a young theologian. His central concept was that of "dying daily."

He was a poet, and wrote hymns on the passion of Christ:

The crown of thorns my Lord once wore.
Come and put these on me.
I see now my Golgotha is approaching
Whip me. Hasten me.
Let me declare my completion.
You shall know where I come from,
When you drink my blood and eat my flesh.
O Lord, grant me the day when I may say,
"It is finished."[4]

---

[4] Pyun, *Diary.* Yoo, *Korean Pentecostalism,* 119.

Those knowledgeable in devotional literature will recognize in these lines Catholic or even Buddhist themes. An influence from Catholicism on Yi is unlikely, in light of his attacks on the mainline churches which rejected this outspoken passion mysticism. Yi's community has died out—except for a small remnant—but his influence on Korean spirituality should not be underestimated.

Minjung Pentecostalism

The third Pentecostal movement has much in common with the so-called Minjung theology, which tries to interpret the Bible *with* the people (ochlos). In Minjung, theology is no longer something which is imported from abroad. The people of Korea also have knowledge; not everything must be taught to them by American or European theologians. It is no longer acceptable that the people learn the culture of the oppressor, of the intellectual and economic élite. How can those who are the prisoners of the culture of oppression (those theologians who are trained in a Western way) know what the people feel? In contrast to the Latin American theology of liberation, Minjung sees the police who persecute the Christians as also part of the people. They too are oppressed; the torturers also need to hear the Gospel, many times by those they are torturing. Finally Yoo and his friends ask: Why is there not one writer of the Latin American theology of liberation who is representative of the oppressed people of Latin America, of the American Indians, of the blacks? Only the descendants of the Spanish and Portuguese invaders write a theology of liberation. For Yoo that means that the Latin American theology of liberation has yet far to go in order to become a theology of liberation.[5]

In relation to the Korean Minjung theology Yoo suggests critically: Perhaps the official printed Minjung theology is again a theology which an élite wrote *for* the people. For him a contrast and a complement to the printed Minjung theology is the *lived* Minjung theology of the independent indigenous Pentecostal churches, and of those churches which have been influenced by this tradition. In these churches the whole people of God does theology, not only the scholars. It does theology in songs and prayers, in testimonies and Bible studies. This is a daring thought, which will not be acceptable everywhere in Korea, Europe, or America. However, Yoo teaches theology in Africa. He must have realized there that the thought-patterns of Western theology fail to work in an Asian context.

---

[5] When I wrote a review of Yoo's book for a Swiss periodical, it was rejected because the Catholics did not like his criticism of the (mainly Catholic) theology of liberation. It is always the same story: Third World theologians may be as revolutionary as they like as long as they are revolutionary in our way, but if they think theologically for themselves they are not welcome!

This lived Minjung theology, writes Yoo, has learned something very important from Korean Shamanism by giving a voice to the women,[6] and to the so-called lay-people, the cultural proletariat of Korea.

Yoo has produced a new and original study. He has also described the various American "church growth evangelists" who have worked in Korea. My impression, however, is that because of the enormous language barriers the Americans say one thing and the Koreans understand something else. For once the difficult Korean language, which cannot easily be learned by Westerners, is an advantage. It protects the expertise of the people from being paralyzed by foreign experts on evangelism.

Yoo's presentation is also remarkable: Korean Pentecostalism is not presented as a product of Western Pentecostal missionaries. That is why Korean Pentecostalism is very different. All founding pioneers are Koreans, who are deeply rooted in Korean popular culture and integrate this culture selectively into their spirituality.

Accurate statistics are notoriously difficult to come by in a country where new churches are founded every year, and people become Christians by the thousands. According to Yoo, of the 8,500,000 Protestants and 1,160,000 Catholics (1983 figures—population of Korea: 37,500,000), two thirds are influenced by Pentecostalism. There are, however, only about 1,100,000 adherents of Pentecostal churches in the strict sense. It is difficult to assess the accuracy of these statistics because it is not clear how many adherents of the "non-white indigenous churches" in Barrett's statistics belong to independent Pentecostal churches (see chart).

Christians in Korea (1985)

Non-white indigenous churches	4,801,600	12.8% of population
Protestants	4,025,500	10.8% of population
Catholics	1,160,000	3.1% of population
Sects	110,000	0.3% of population
Anglicans	110,000	0.3% of population
Orthodox	43,000	0.3% of population[7]

For 1985, Barrett gives 11,000,000 Christians; that does not agree entirely with Yoo's numbers for 1983. Perhaps the difference between Yoo and Barrett can be explained as follows: Yoo is a Korean theologian. He includes the non-white indigenous Korean churches (which do not belong to any of the Western churches) with the Protestants, and does not count them as a special category. The Anglican Barrett on the other hand distinguishes between the

---

[6] One remembers the protest against Chung, Hyun Kyung at Canberra (see chapter 27, pp. 382–84). Chung, *Struggle*. She is another uncomfortable Korean theological thinker; on a Pentecostal approach to ancestors see chapter 20, pp. 266–67.

[7] Source: Barrett, *WChE*, 440ff.

Western-based mission-churches and the financially and theologically independent Korean churches. It is certain that Korean Protestantism will become more and more independent, both financially and theologically. This is already to be seen in their important missionary work in Asia and Africa. Only Catholics and Anglicans will remain dependent on the West. Once again it becomes clear that even simple statistics are theological judgments: Including all Korean Christians (except the Catholics) with the Protestants presents a *Korean picture* of the Protestant Church. Distinguishing between Korean independent churches and Western-based Protestants is the *view from outside.*

Further development is difficult to assess. At the moment the churches are still growing very rapidly. The influence of Shamanism, Minjung and Pentecostalism, and revival spirituality will not wane. In the future we shall see a strong theologically- and organizationally-independent Korean church emerge.

The Korean interpretation of Pentecostalism by Yoo got a very mixed reception. Robeck for instance writes:

> North American Pentecostals who align with the concerns of the Pentecostal Fellowship of North America will find this study to be a frustrating one . . . This is no history of North American Pentecostal missions. This is no history of the founding and formation of Korean Pentecostal denominations along the lines of their Pentecostal Fellowship of North America counterparts. This is no history of such churches as Full Gospel Central Church. On the whole, it is an overview of renewal movements in which the Holy Spirit has been acknowledged as playing a major role.[8]

A Korean reviewer says: "I question whether Minjung theology can be related to the Pentecostal movement of Christianity in Korea."[9] Yoo is criticized in Korea because he did not follow the neat categories of the Minjung intellectuals. He is rejected by American Pentecostals because they "will have some difficulty recognizing themselves here."[10] But what if Korean Pentecostalism is a different kind of Pentecostalism (more related to the other churches, less denomination-centered), and if it is not only permissible but necessary to interpret and criticize it with the categories of a Shamanistic culture of several thousand years? I wonder sometimes how one would have to write the history of American Pentecostalism if one took as a starting point history and theological categories imposed from outside the US; for instance, from Korea.

On the other hand Mark R. Mullins, Associate Professor at Meiji Gakuin University, Tokyo, seems to agree with Yoo on the influence of shamanism on

---

[8] Cecil M. Robeck, in a review of Yoo's *Korean Pentecostalism*, *Pneuma* 12/1, 1990, 61.

[9] Review by Wi Jo Kang in *Missiology* 21/1, Jan. 1993, 593. The Korean book by Jae Bum Lee *(History)* is not accessible to me.

[10] Robeck, Cecil M. Jr., *Pneuma*, 12/1, 1990, 62.

Pentecostalism. Yoo sees in shamanism "a faith for the masses." Because it is oral, it articulates *Han* (a kind of collective feeling of defeat, resignation and nothingness; but also of the tenacity and will for life which comes from the weak), and makes it concrete in healings, visions, and spirit experiences.[11] "Although Pentecostal church leaders would deny the influence of 'pagan religion' most scholars agree that shamanism has been the central force shaping the development of Korean Pentecostalism."[12]

[11] Yoo, "Response to Korean Shamanism," and Yoo, *Korean Pentecostalism*, 223ff.

[12] Mullins, "Empire," 92. Mullins is supported by Grayson, *Early Buddhism and Christianity in Korea*, 205, Lee, Jae Bum, *Korean*, 279–86, and Suh, "Forty Years of Korean Protestant Churches: 1945–1985." Mullins also discusses, in his well-documented article, the following authors: Syn-Duk, Choi, "A comparative study of two new religious movements in the Republic of Korea: the Unification Church and the Full Gospel Central Church"; Byron H. Earhardt, "The New Religions of Korea: A Preliminary Interpretation," *Transactions of the Korea Branch of the Royal Asiatic Society* 49, 1974; Byong-Suh Kim, "The Explosive Growth of the Korean Church Today: A Sociological Analysis," *Int. Review of Mission* 74/293, 1985, 61–74.

CHAPTER**NINE**

England: Interaction Between Black and White in Theological Education[1]

The Story of the "Black School"

Apartheid in spite of good laws on racial discrimination

"How is it," the Dean of the Faculty of Arts in the University of Birmingham asked, "that we have hardly any black students in our university? That is to say, we have quite a number of black students from Africa, and even from the United States, but where are our British-born blacks? I don't believe that they couldn't cope with higher education. There must be other reasons." A remarkable observation indeed in a country in which racism is outlawed; in which, to give just one example, somebody who advertises a house for sale "to white purchasers only" would be prosecuted. The reason for the lack of black British-born students at the university lies in the fact that English schools have been structured for English pupils, so that blacks cannot identify either with their curriculum or with their staff. Black themes, black culture are absent. When I brought these facts to the notice of my colleagues in the Faculty of Arts and asked for the introduction of black studies at the university, so that we might get teachers who have at least an idea of black theology, black history, black language and black music, I received benign smiles from some and raised eyebrows from others: "What is this 'black theology'? There is

---

[1] This chapter started as an article in *Theology* (Hollenweger, "Interaction"). It has been revised, updated, and annotated. See also Thompson ("Popular Religiosity in Britain"), who puts the black experience in Britain in a wider context.

only *one* theology. Some day you are going to ask for a Chair of Black Music and Literature."

To tell the truth, that is exactly what I had in mind. But I dared not express this adventurous idea. I must add, however, that at least the theologians knew that such a thing as "black theology" exists. But the faculty was unmoved by my remarks. Instead of a black theologian they appointed a forensic graphologist—as if that were the most pressing academic need in our university!

The results of this educational policy have been catastrophic. I do not pretend that the riots and burning streets, the petrol bombs, and the dead and wounded which Birmingham has seen in the 1980s[2] are the direct outcome of our educational policy, but much of it could certainly have been avoided had we had more black teachers, policemen, civil servants, politicians, social workers and university students. The English will pay dearly for the fact that they have not taken a leaf out of the American book. Over twenty years ago the Americans had to wrestle with similar problems, and decided to work for a massive improvement in black education.

In this context, it is no wonder that the Anglican and Methodist churches have hardly any black clergy (in spite of the fact that they have many black members).[3] If one points to this anomaly it is said: "Blacks do not apply for these posts; and those who do apply are not qualified." Even if one considers this as just an excuse, it is at least a good excuse. However, it would be better to go to the root cause than just to make excuses. That is exactly the task which the Centre for Black and White Christian Partnership in Birmingham has taken on.

The Beginning[4]

At the start the Centre was mainly directed towards the training of worker pastors from the 750 black congregations in England, which are organized in over 100 black denominations. These churches are of very differing traditions: Methodist, Adventist, Pentecostal, and those which so far have not existed in Europe—black independent churches from West Africa and the Caribbean. Some of these churches are very large in their countries of origin, and twenty percent of the black population of Britain belong to them. That makes the church the most important, if not the only relevant, form of organization for blacks in Britain, a fact of which white Christians, politicians, and local councils were almost totally unaware.

It is quite remarkable that the British mission societies, which are famous for their pioneering ecumenical and missiological work in the Third World, have almost totally missed the opportunity for a renewing intercultural

---

[2] On this see Hollenweger, "L'expérience," 186–92.
[3] Wilkinson, *Church in Black and White.*
[4] See the report by one of its first directors: Mazibuko, *Education.*

dialogue in their own country. The Labor Party also, which could not criticize South African apartheid enough, are unable to recognize the cultural, political and spiritual leadership potential of these churches in their own country. It took two foreign "missionaries" to see this—a German pastor and a Swiss university professor. On the basis of the research work of the former, Roswith Gerloff,[5] contacts were made with black church leaders. In spite of the fact that many of them had only a few years' schooling, what they wanted was a theological educational program at a university level.

Almost all the black church leaders are worker-pastors. During the week they work in factories, or as bus drivers, railwaymen or bookkeepers, unless they are unemployed—as is often the case. On weekends they are pastors or bishops, and many of them wear beautiful liturgical gowns and episcopal mitres, to which in comparison the vestments of a Roman Catholic cardinal pale. To create a theological program at a university level for these worker-pastors was quite a challenge. We had to invent a course of studies which both made sense for the blacks and was acceptable to the university. The school was organized as a series of weekend courses, taught by teachers from the university and the Selly Oak Colleges. The educational method is that of Paolo Freire: the language, thought categories, and experiences of the course participants form the basis for the teaching.

Later, in reading the reports of the theologians from Korea, I recognized in their oral language the same method, which rejects the conceptual (literary) language of the West and the cultural (literary) language of China. Yet it must be said that this method does not fit easily into our European scholarly tradition.[6]

The Curriculum

The courses in the black program appear at first glance to be rather traditional: Mission, Old Testament, New Testament, Christian Doctrine. In the mission course students start with the history and experience of black churches; with the experience of slavery, the experience of the church as "the place and means of survival," the mission of black churches in white England. In the biblical courses, they start with the astonishing biblical knowledge of the participants, with the biblical vocabulary known to them, but also with the differing interpretations on fasting, foot-washing, visions, and speaking in tongues, which emerge clearly for instance between the African and the Caribbean students. They are then able to show that not only are opinions on these and other forms of spirituality divided at the present time, but the New Testament itself already contains records of a plurality of spiritualities and theologies. Thus the participants see historical-critical research not as something

---

[5] See her exhaustive study: Gerloff, *Plea*. Also by the same author "Education." There is more literature by the same author in the Short Titles List, pp. 426–27.
[6] Vongbock, *Minjung Theology*.

which they have to learn in order to pass examinations, but as an important tool for dealing with the differences in the black Christian community.

The course on Christian doctrine is developed in a similar way. Among the participants there are those representing at least half a dozen different doctrinal traditions. These can be explained on the one hand by different Western traditions to which the black churches have been exposed, and on the other hand by different cultural influences (African, Caribbean, North American). It is particularly important to isolate and interpret the African religious symbols and forms of language which stem from their common African pre-Christian roots, and which have been "saved through slavery" by the oral tradition of mothers and grandmothers. Worship, prayer, singing and witnessing are as important in this school as lectures and examinations.

I suggested to my colleagues at the university that they make a practice of starting their lessons with prayer and singing; that they include a supper shared by students, teachers and guests; and that they conclude the weekend course with a worship service either in a black or a white church. When I suggested that all these activities be considered as basic didactical elements, they smiled at me. I was reminded that Birmingham is a totally secular university in which prayer, worship, banquets, singing and dancing are not part of the educational program. I defended my proposal by pointing to the facts that blacks do not speak about God without also speaking to God; that a critical analysis of biblical texts without dance, singing and witnessing is inconceivable to them; and that to engage in a fierce debate on white oppression without subsequent reconciling intercultural celebration is not Christian to them. The result of these deliberations was that all these elements were included in the course under the cover of "cultural concessions." In the meantime the white students asked me why they could not be educated in a similar way, since the black students passed the rigid examinations of the university, and some of them even produced interesting master's dissertations.[7]

One experience is particularly revealing for understanding the theology which is taught in this school. One of the lecturers, a New Testament scholar, was also an Anglican clergyman. For many years he had had difficulties with his received tradition. He explained to me once why he could not possibly believe in God. His reasons did not make much sense to me because they belonged to the English tradition of rationalism and positivism. One day he startled his bishop by asking to be relieved of his ordination vow. He made public his reasons for this step.

Think of the confusion that produced among the Christians in Birmingham. Some of the evangelicals who otherwise are not very interested in the black Churches argued fiercely with them. "And this creature, who does not

---

[7] E.g., Foster, *Black Women;* Pemberton, *A Study of Caribbean Religions;* Simmonds, *"A Portrayal of Identity";* Tomlin, *Black Preaching Style.* Publication of some or all is planned in IC.

even believe in God (not to speak of the fact that he is not born again), this creature teaches you New Testament!" "Well, let us examine the situation," answered the blacks. So they met with their teacher and said to him:

1. "You said on the radio that you did not believe in God. We knew this all the time. From now on things can only improve since you have confessed in public."

2. "We know that faith is a gift from God which we receive by grace alone. It is obvious that so far you have not received this grace. However, you are an excellent teacher in New Testament exegesis. That is why we come to the university. As to faith, we know that this cannot be taught, it is received by grace alone. But as to the craft of proper and skillful interpretation of the New Testament, you are our teacher. We do not think that you are disqualified as our teacher because you do not believe in God."

3. "You may be assured that we pray for you that the gift of faith may be given to you one day."

This is the theology of pastors who are considered theologically uneducated!

Roswith Gerloff, for many years the director of the Centre, summarized her experience in a biblical image:

The friends of the lame man in the Gospel broke through the roof because they were convinced that this man needed help and that Jesus was in the house. We too have broken through the roof, we have protected underprivileged people because we are convinced of their spiritual and intellectual potential and because we know that Christ has something to say to our academic and ecclesiastical institutions. It was not confidence in the goodness of these institutions which prompted us to act in this way. It was confidence in the Christ who calls these institutions to repentance. In this process something like conversions were possible, conversions of so-called uncritical students to clear thinking and conversions of so-called unspiritual scholars to an experience of faith.[8]

The Experiment and Its Assessment

There are ways of communication other than those of propositional philosophical and theological discourse. There are ways of education other than those predominant in our universities. These forms are not inferior, they are different. It is necessary to digress from the path of tradition if we want to progress. Of course this was disputed. In our case protest did not come in the first instance from the university but from the churches. They saw the strengthening of black leadership potential as an unecumenical act. They would have liked us to condition our black students to return to the white churches. Since the blacks had chosen the opposite path and had established their own structures, the white churches reacted to the Centre with much

---

[8] From an earlier, unpublished draft of Gerloff's "Education."

antipathy. This is the worst form of apartheid, we were told by Methodist headquarters. Pauline Webb, one of the foremost fighters against racism in the world-wide ecumenical context, discovered how difficult it is to accept in her own country that blacks do their own thing.

The introduction of black competence in church and university jeopardizes white privileges. It calls into question our pecking order. When the theologically competent handling of an "unbelieving teacher" (see example above) is seen in its theological significance and is in fact theologically more significant than the discussion of received theological traditions, then our privileges are called into question. And that can be very threatening. However, a theological school—if it is truly theological—has always been dangerous.

That has also been the experience of the Minjung theologians in Korea. They gave up the conceptual language of the oppressors and opted instead for the oral language of the common people, the *ochlos* of the Gospel of Mark, the Minjung of Korea. This was both a cultural and a political decision. Many of them have lost their academic status as a result of this choice. It does not mean they choose a cultural class struggle; the Minjung theologians reject class theories. They look for a dialogue with their oppressors (for instance the policemen who torture them) analogous to that of Jesus and the Roman colonial administrators. They are skeptical of the Latin American theology of liberation and ask the obvious question: Are these theologians really theologians of the people or is their theology rather a theology written by an élite for the people?[9]

For Birmingham this means that dialogue between the police, the church and the university authorities is as important as dialogue between whites and the black grass roots. Only one condition has to be met—the dialogue has to be conducted in an oral language, so that the oppressors, the educated people, cannot claim all advantages for their side. If this condition is met then both black and white, the so-called educated and so-called uneducated, will enter into a dialogue with a theological and humane promise.

This insight has been articulated for many years for the Western churches by Theophil Vogt.[10] On the basis of long experience, he describes the theological fruit of group Bible study which is orientated to lived religion, and in which the people of God are the subject of hermeneutics. Theoretically this insight is already present in the Reformers and in Karl Barth, who started his *Church Dogmatics* with the sentence, "theology is a function of the Church." However, it is not sufficient merely to put such a sentence at the beginning of a dogmatic. We need methods which make it possible for the people of God to enter into this theological process. If theologians call on the so-called outsiders, the oppressors and the oppressed, the "literary" and the "oral" people, for the production of their theology, and theologians cease to believe in a "division of labor" into the producers (the university theologians) and the consumers

---

[9] See chapter 8, pp. 99–105.
[10] Vogt, *Bibelarbeit*, 149.

(the people of God), then a new and radical theology emerges. Since literary people are always also oral people (but not vice versa), it is important that our study of the Bible be conducted in an oral medium. Vogt sees in this use of the oral medium a chance for "the discrepancy between a growing specialization of the academic theologian and an ever-growing theological illiteracy of the people of God to be bridged." He regrets, however, that the fruits of these Bible studies are so far almost completely ignored by the academic establishment.

The reason for this might be that Vogt's Bible-study method combines insights from historical-critical exegesis with those of group therapy and Theme-Centered Interaction (TCI). He manages to keep the tension alive between the "foreignness" of the text and the nearness of its message by giving equal weight to both, to the exegetical and the TCI aspects. How such a combination can become fruitful is now demonstrated by looking at the black school in the context of TCI.

The Black School in the Context of TCI[11]

At first glance it becomes clear that the four components of TCI are present in the educational adventure of the Centre for Black and White Christian Partnership and that a balance is sought between [1] the person (I), [2] the group interaction (we), [3] the topic (it), and [4] the context (the globe).

The Person: "I"

In university education the "I" is probably the most neglected of the four ingredients. It is thought to be unscholarly to consider the "I" in academic research. That not only leads to an elimination of the "I" but it also gives the alpha-person (usually the teacher) an unacceptably privileged position—even more so when this happens unconsciously. In science it has been understood for some time how heavily the "I" influences research results. This is no less true for human than for natural sciences.[12] The "I" is in part responsible for the questions we ask, the priorities of our research, and therefore the results of our research. In the case of our school the inclusion of the "I" was a question of "to be or not to be."

I mention as an example a lecture in which a New Testament scholar explained to the students why Matthew had added the words "and fasting" in the sentence "this kind [of demon] never comes out except by prayer and fasting" (Matt 17:21), in contrast to Mark (Mark 9:29), who does not add "and fasting." Matthew, argued the teacher, adds these words because in his congregation, in his tradition, fasting was well known. That which one does is handed down (in our case we are not sure whether this was a tradition handed down from Jesus, or an addition influenced by the practice in Matthew's congregation). The students wrote in their notebooks: "That which is done is

---

[11] Farau–Cohn, *Gelebte Geschichte der Psychotherapie.*
[12] Kuhn, *The Structure of Scientific Revolutions.*

reflected in the liturgy and the theology of a congregation. That which is not done is likely to be forgotten."

Out of the blue, and apparently out of context, a student asked the teacher (disturbance!): "Have you ever fasted in your life?" This question seemed to the teacher irrelevant, so he repeated: "This is a problem of text-tradition. That which is done is retained . . . " However, the student was not to be side-tracked. "But have you ever fasted?" he asked again. The teacher gave up his fixation on the "it" and replied frankly: "No." "But I have," said the student. "You see, I belong to a tradition in which experiences of fasting are made [he had learned to use abstract terminology in order to say simple things]. And I can tell you, it is a beautiful and important thing."

Thus the ban was broken and the "topic" (namely fasting) was allowed to speak for itself apart from its literary fixed form. Similar things happened in interpreting healing stories in the New Testament, and in studying the reports of visions and auditions.

The Group Interaction: "We"

Group interaction generally appears in university education in the form of a seminar. Since we manage to create homogenous seminar groups through a seemingly objective process of selection (on the European continent we even manage to separate Protestant and Catholic students for their theological education!), we either have to introduce artificial conflicts into the seminar in order to make it interesting, or the seminar becomes just a lecture presented by several readers.

A seminar in the Centre for Black and White Christian Partnership is different. There are white and black students, young and old, men and women, academically trained and students with only a few years elementary school, all adherents of many different churches. It must be ensured that interaction is not dominated by one group alone; say, the academically trained or the religiously articulate. In the interest of a proper interaction, a continuous process of translation from one "language" into the other is necessary. This is only possible with the help of the students. Furthermore, it is important that the teacher learns the new "languages" from his students. Thus he is at the same time a teacher and a student. A hasty harmonization has to be avoided, for instance, when Sabbatarians defend the Saturday as a divinely ordained day of rest, or when others consider this sabbatarian biblical hermeneutic as an outmoded religion of the law.

The Topic: "It"

The curriculum of the school is *grosso modo* the Bible and the function (the mission) of black Churches and cultures in England. In order to understand these, the students have to be introduced to their own history, the African background, slave-trade and slavery, Caribbean culture, migration to England, and so on. They know this history as a family memory from their grandfathers and grandmothers, and as daily experience in England. Many of the students know that they themselves are the indirect results of the rape of their great-grandmothers by white overseers and governors. One of them, who knows his genealogy in detail, irritated the English participants by pointing out that he was a relative to the Queen. (Sometimes a royal duke was active in increasing the slave population—in particular after the abolition of slave trade.)

However, the participants can not usually integrate this topic into a wider world and church history. If they were ever taught history, it was always taught without reference to their own family and group experience, their own passion story. This means that history has to be retold, but in such a way that the individual and collective fragments of memories receive their legitimate place in this historical view.

The Context: "The Globe"

The context of the school is the university and British society. A total integration of black education into the university is logically not possible as long as the university functions as a context for expressing and arguing for white privilege. Indeed, the black school is a foreign body in the corpus of the university; but perhaps it is also a hope for the future, once we realize the shortcomings of our Western education.

In spite of this logical impossibility, the school does function within the university framework of rules and regulations, essays and examinations. This is only possible because teachers and examiners are pragmatic English men and women who—at least for the time being—are prepared to suspend their "academic prejudices."

A further insight of TCI is the connection between mind and body. "The human person is a psycho-biological unity and is thus part of the universe."[13] If that is correct, then teaching and learning have to be related to this psycho-biological unity and not just to the cognitive faculties of humankind. That is why the teaching is not only carried on by lectures and seminars, but also by prayer (integration of the cosmos), worship (integration of the *oikoumene*), dramas (in particular by *ad hoc* sketches in which problems and solutions are presented by the participants), and above all dance, about which we white teachers understand very little. Dance is a mode of expression which also contains cognitive elements. Watching others dancing, one can learn much about oneself and the others. By dancing oneself, one can learn much about the "I," the "We," and the "It." Furthermore, dancing is a mode of expression which favors the gifts in which these students are more developed than the teachers.

A Look Into the Future

Black churches are found not just in England, but in Holland, France, Germany, and Italy.[14] This makes the introduction of significant black ele-

---

[13] Cohn, "Das Modell der themenzentrierten Interaktion," 357.
[14] Ter Haar, "Strangers," 1–31. Gerloff, "Lebendige Bibel," 411–14.

ments into European academic learning all the more important; if an interaction between black and white culture is successful, that would be the beginning of a cross-cultural education, and of an intercultural theology. That we were successful in securing black teachers for the school bodes well for such education (although one teacher had to be brought in from South Africa, as we could find nobody suitable in the indigenous black population!).

The Birmingham project is not the first school of this kind, for similar attempts are under way in the United States of America and in South Africa, but it was the first of its kind in Europe. Hence it has been a test of the intercultural competence and ability of European scholarship. Of course much has been written about this kind of education on a theoretical level—one thinks of Illich and Freire; but so far no sustained program has been attempted in Europe. This experiment shows the viability of a workers' university (about which much has been said but little done) that does not force students to give up the scholarly competence of their working-class culture.

It is my considered opinion that the experiment will either run out of funds or it will be ignored. It is able to carry on now only thanks to subsidies from Switzerland and Germany. The British Government contributes little or nothing, and the churches are reluctant to help in a significant way, not least because the school strengthens the possibility of an attractive and sustainable alternative to the European churches. After having received their certificates, if the blacks returned to the arms of the traditional churches, then the experiment would be justified from the point of view of the British churches. But so far this has not been the intention of the blacks. On the contrary, the school strengthens their self-awareness, and enhances their ability to articulate their own spirituality, a fact which will also bear political fruit in the future. It is commonly accepted that the blacks are to be admired so long as they do their own thing in South Africa or in Zimbabwe. If, however, they intend to contribute their black competence to an educational system which is very resistant to "alien" cultures, people become rather nervous.

It has to be admitted that a racially divided church is not ideal. But before we can talk about ecumenical unity between black and white, black Christians must become sure of themselves. They must discover their "I" and articulate it in relation to the "We" and the "It." At a later date one might work out a more explicit interaction between black and white churches. However, this will not happen according to our rules and our priorities, but rather according to rules and priorities worked out together. In this sense the Centre for Black and White Christian Partnership is not only a school for underprivileged black worker-pastors, but also a parable depicting the promises and problems of an interaction between black and white competence.

One thing is sure, at least for theology, but very likely also for medicine, psychology, pedagogy and economics: the model of interaction is not a luxury in which we may indulge when we have nothing else to do. It is part of the very essence of education.

In her seminal *Plea for British Black Theologies*, Roswith Gerloff shows convincingly that most of the black churches in Britain are of a Pentecostal type. John Wilkinson, in his analysis of blacks in the Anglican churches,[15] shows that black Anglican spirituality has much in common with the black Pentecostal tradition (although not so much with Pentecostal theology).

The story of the Centre for Black and White Christian Partnership is important for Pentecostal educators *and* mainline academic institutions.[16] It shows what can happen both to Pentecostals and to university teachers when they begin to do theology together.

In general it is feared that such an ecumenical adventure will either result in Pentecostals losing their fire or—equally undesirable—academic establishments lowering their standards. These fears are understandable, but the Birmingham experiment and subsequent experiments in Germany and Switzerland show that such a fear is ill-founded. It is possible to combine the black oral root with the critical root of Western European education, and come to both a more relevant and a more critical theology.

---

[15] Wilkinson, *Church in Black and White.*

[16] Roswith Gerloff now heads a similar program at the University of Leeds (England). Also, the integration of black Pentecostal churches into British and European ecumenical agencies is an exciting new development, but it will also create problems for the smooth running of these ecumenical organizations.

CHAPTER**TEN**

Chile: Methodism's Past in Pentecostalism's Present[1]

The purpose of this chapter is to prepare the reader for chapter 12, where it will be argued that much of what today we call "Pentecostalism" is based on Wesley. As an example I use the story of the early Methodist mission to Chile, concentrating on the revival under Willis Hoover, the blending of Wesleyan and Chilean popular cultures, the clash which arose between the Chileans and the Americans, and the subsequent establishment of the first theologically and financially self-sufficient Protestant church in the Third World: the Pentecostal Church in Chile.

In the following interpretive section, I shall ask why the common roots of American and Chilean Methodists were not discovered at the time, and why these commonalities are still now accepted only with great reluctance. The answer is that the conflict in our story was not a theological but a cultural clash. This fact, in turn, has repercussions for our ecumenical and educational activities.

---

[1] This chapter started as a lecture at the World Methodist Historical Society in Birmingham (1978). It was published in *Epworth Review* 6/2, May 1979, 35–47 (but with significant deletions mainly on early positive testimonies on Hoover) and integrally in *Methodist History* 20/4, July 1982, 169–82. Spanish in *Spiritus* 1/1, 1985, 31–46 (Mexico). It has been revised and updated.

Sources: Methodist Files, Methodist Letter-books, Presbyterian Microfilms, referred to hereafter, are located in the Interchurch Center, New York. Detailed material in my *Handbuch*, 02b.08 (60 pages documents and interpretation). Also: Ossa, *Lo ajeno*. Idem, *Espiritualidad popular*. Irma Palma, *En tierra extraña*.

The Story

A Self-Supporting Methodist Mission

The mission work of the Methodists in Chile started, in the late 1880s, with William Taylor and his self-supporting mission. Because Taylor disagreed with the mission board's policy, which he felt provided too much financial support and so undermined the new converts' sense of responsibility, he was unwilling to place his mission under the board's control. In turn, the bishops of the Methodist Episcopal Church felt that they could not ordain Taylor's missionaries, and that they could not allow them to retain their conference connection in the United States. Thus, Taylor's hopes to finance his missionary enterprise through missionary schools and colleges were frustrated, and the work was taken over by the Methodist Church of the United States in 1897.[2]

Nevertheless the short attempt at a self-supporting church is in my opinion at the root both of the difficulties of the Methodist Episcopal Church in Chile in 1909 and of the emergence of an indigenous Methodist Church (later the Iglesia Metodista Pentecostal).

As Taylor's missionaries had—up to 1897—no official church backing, they tended to be drawn from the less cultured, revivalist fringe of the Methodist Church in the United States. No wonder that a Presbyterian, Florence Smith, stated bluntly that the Chilean Presbyterian Mission "is far and away ahead of the Methodist Episcopal Church in education, culture, sound judgment and worldly wisdom." But she also had to admit: on the other hand,

> we do lack warmth of spiritual life and love, or is it that we do not know how to express the warmth and love we feel? Mr. Hoover, the Methodist Episcopal missionary in charge of the work here, is a man of one idea. He is not too cultured to call the Chileans brothers. He is narrow, even bigoted, but I believe he can truly say: "This one thing I do" and "I count all but loss that I may win the Chileans to Christ." He is inordinately proud of the remarkable success of their work—to us offensively so! There is a great deal of froth and bombast and other defects it is easy to point out, but the fact remains, the poor have the Gospel preached to them.[3]

The "froth and bombast" produced interesting results. Between 1893 and 1897 the Methodist church in Chile more than doubled in size; between 1897 and 1903 it doubled again, and from 1903 to 1907 it doubled a third time. In 1906 Chilean Methodists numbered more than 4,000 (see chart).

The most important of these "bigoted" and "inordinately proud" but successful missionaries was Willis Hoover. He was born in 1858 in Freeport,

---

[2] Barclay, *History of Methodist Missions, III,* 792. Lalive d'Epinay, *Haven of the Masses,* 5. Bundy, "Taylor[a]," 197–210; "Taylor[b]," 3–21.

[3] Florence Smith's letter to Speer written from Valparaiso, dated 22.1.1906 (Presbyterian Microfilms); quoted in Kessler, *Study,* 105.

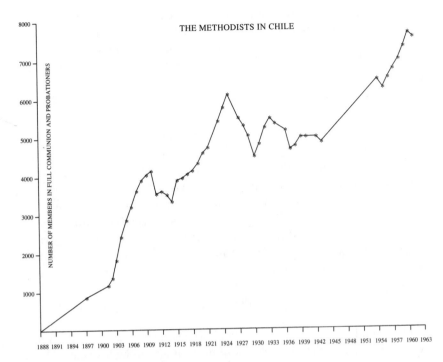

THE METHODISTS IN CHILE

Illinois.[4] He studied medicine in Chicago, but the work of a doctor did not satisfy him. In 1889 he offered himself to William Taylor's self-supporting mission. He then learned to speak Spanish well, and became pastor at the church in Iquique. In 1902 he replaced E. E. Wilson as pastor of the church in Valparaiso. There, he began to feel that the members had rather vague ideas on the vital Methodist teaching of sanctification. During a series of studies on the Acts of the Apostles for the Sunday School teachers, one of them asked what prevented their church from being like the apostolic church. Hoover replied that the only impediment to this lay in themselves.[5]

In 1906 a terrible earthquake destroyed both their old church and a building under construction which was to have become their new church. Renewed efforts were necessary in order to build a third church. It was dedicated on March 7th, 1909.[6] Built largely by the gifts of the congregation itself, it seated 1,000 people. An important principle had been established which became decisive for future developments; namely, that of large-scale lay participation both in financial and spiritual ministry.

---

[4] Methodist Files; Kessler, *Study*, 108. Jones, C. E., "Hoover."
[5] Hoover, *Historia*, 11. This remark shows that Hoover took Arminianism to its logical conclusion, and also that even at that time he had decidedly opted for Luke's pneumatology. On this see Schweizer, "pneuma" and *The Pentecostals*, 336–41.
[6] *Actas de la conferencia misionera occidental de Sud América de la Iglesia Metodista Episcopal*, Temuco 19–23 de febrero 1909; Kessler, *Study*, 110.

The younger and "better-educated" missionaries, however, who were now arriving from the United States, disapproved of Hoover's old-time revivalism, his self-assuredness, his friendship with the Chileans, and his protest against using the missionaries' finance committee "for dealing behind the nationals' backs."[7]

Methodist Past Revived[8]

In 1907 Mrs. Hoover received a pamphlet on "the baptism of the Holy Ghost and fire"[9] written by Minnie Abrams, who had been a student at Chicago Training School[10] at the same time as Mrs. Hoover. The tract describes a Pentecostal revival in the girls' home run by a Brahman lady, Pandita Ramabai, in Mukti.[11] Visions, trances, and speaking in tongues were features of the revival. Most important was Miss Abrams' contention that the baptism of the Holy Ghost and fire was something additional to the experience of justification and sanctification known among the Methodists.[12] Hoover tried to find out more about the early Pentecostal revival, and corresponded with, among others, T. B. Barratt, the controversial Methodist evangelist in Oslo[13] who was later to become the "Pentecostal apostle" for the whole of Europe.[14]

On a Sunday night in February 1909, when Hoover was at the meeting of the annual conference in Temuco, one of the brothers of the Valparaiso church

---

[7] Information given to Kessler by Merayne Copplestone, New York (*Study*, 110). See also Campbell, Buell, letter to Stuntz, 31.10.1910, in which he complains that Hoover's church felt that they were "more holy than the others." Kessler, *Study*, 110.

[8] Lalive states that the "birth of Chilean Pentecostalism is still too little known" (Lalive d'Epinay, *Haven of the Masses*, 7). Yet the source situation is very good. The Chilean Pentecostal leaders have—in good Methodist tradition—kept the records of the past. Part of this material, plus the files of the Methodist Church in New York, have been used by Kessler. In addition there are *Chile Pentecostal* and other religious periodicals in Chile, and Vergara, *Protestantismo*. Less important for historical research are the major sociological works: Lalive d'Epinay, *Haven of the Masses;* Willems, *New Faith;* Martin, David, *Tongues*. Older literature extensively in my *Handbuch*, 02b.08.

[9] Abrams, " Mukti"; idem, *Fire*.

[10] Frodsham, *With Signs Following*, 175.

[11] The religious revival sometimes took ecstatic and strange forms. The religious press was jubilant about the "heavenly fire in India." The careful biography of Ramabai by Sengupta *(Pandita Ramabai)* gives some cautious information on the revival, emphasizes the social work of Pandita Ramabai, but plays down the theological and cultural problems of the revival. Today the Ramabai Mukti Mission states that they are totally ignorant of the Pentecostal revival (Letter G. Fletcher, Superintendent Ramabai Mukti Mission, 21.3.1963 to the author). Extensive bibliography and discussion in *Handbuch*, 03.07.013. Bixler puts the record straight ("Ramabai"). See also, McGee, "Abrams," 7.

[12] Hoover, *Historia*, 14.

[13] Barratt's answer to Hoover in ibid., 95–98.

[14] Bloch-Hoell, *The Pentecostal Movement*, 75ff.

called the members of the official board to occupy the front seats at the beginning of the service. Reading the second chapter of Joel, from the 12th verse and onward, he said: "You and I are responsible for the condition of this church and we must repent and get right with God [even] if it takes all night." After a season of prayer at the altar he dismissed the congregation, asking the official board to remain with him all night, with any others who might desire to remain with them. Twenty or thirty remained. During the night one saw a brazier of coals within the altar. Others felt the hand of the Lord on their head as they prayed at the altar; such was the blessing received that they asked this man to appoint another all night meeting, which he did, naming the following Saturday.[15]

Upon his return Hoover was asked what should be done about the vigil planned for the following Saturday. His reply was that it should take place. This was another turning point in the course of events. First the Chileans had taken responsibility for their church building, now they took responsibility for the content of their worship life and the direction of church life as a whole—the cause both of the subsequent revival and the difficulties with the American missionaries.

The vigil became a regular feature in the church. But "the overwhelming flood came on the 4th of July, 1909, which was Sunday. Saturday night was an all night prayer, during which four vain young ladies (three of whom were in the choir) fell to the floor under the power of the Spirit. One of them, after lying a long time, arose and with remarkable power began to exhort, saying, 'The Lord is coming soon and commands us to get ready.' The effect produced was indescribable."[16]

When Hoover was questioned about the girls lying on the floor, "Llama Ud, eso humano?" he replied calmly, "No." "But what is it then?" he was asked again. "Divino," he said.[17]

The emphasis at this early stage was on renewal of life by the Holy Spirit. Sins were confessed in public, debts repaid, hardened wrongdoers converted, and people who had been estranged from each other reconciled.[18]

An English girl, Nellie (or Elena) Laidlaw, was an important link between Valparaiso and Santiago. She had been a drunkard and a prostitute, but

---

[15] Frodsham, *With Signs Following*, 176f.

[16] Ibid., 177f.

[17] Hoover, *Historia*, 30.

[18] *El Cristiano* 5.7.1909; Hoover, *Historia*, 26f.; Kessler, *Study*, 116. Even Buell Campbell who was the first permanent pastor of the Methodist church in Valparaiso after Hoover, and who was very critical of his predecessor, admitted that these early meetings had "many elements of good" (Campbell, letter to Stuntz, 25.7.1910; Kessler, *Study*, 114). One brother left a vigil to give back some goods that had been entrusted to him at the time of the earthquake in 1906, but which he had not returned. At the next vigil, while he was praying, he was overcome by a bout of gentle laughter (Hoover, *Historia*, 20). Victor Pavéz Toro (*El Cristiano*, 21.6. and 2.8.1909; Kessler, *Study*, 116), Rice (*Actas*; Kessler, *Study*, 116), Tulio Moran, a Presbyterian from Concepción, were convinced at that stage of the genuineness of the work.

professed conversion, and became one of the chief prophetesses in Valparaiso.[19] Her most controversial activity was to walk about the congregation with closed eyes, suddenly single somebody out, and order them to kneel down. Nellie then revealed what was in their heart, called them to repentance and laid her hands on them in order to give them the Spirit.[20] Even if Hoover had wished, he could not have intervened, as he had told his congregation that the pastor was nothing more than the humblest member, and that they all had merely to follow the leading of the Spirit. How this leading of the Spirit was to be made operational either in shamanistic,[21] Episcopal,[22] or group-dynamic congregational forms—this the Pentecostals had still to learn.

Law and Order

In early September, 1909, Nellie Laidlaw visited her sister in Santiago. On September 12th, she went to one of the two Methodist churches in Santiago, wanting to speak, but was refused by Robinson, the pastor. So Nellie went out into the courtyard, where she gave her revelations.[23] Later some of her followers went inside again to remonstrate with Robinson. In the argument which followed, Robinson pushed a man away, but lost his footing and fell off of the platform, cutting his head open.[24]

Reports based on hearsay and stating that "Robinson was struck a blow on the head"[25] were sent to New York. These and other even worse allegations are today irreconcilably contradicted by the best evidence available in Santiago.[26]

In the evening Nellie Laidlaw again wanted to speak in the church. Rice, the minister, asked her to keep quiet. When she failed to do so, he brought the waiting policeman into the meeting and told him to arrest her. At this Nellie's supporters became furious and shielded the girl so as to prevent her from being taken. The policeman called for reinforcements. These cleared the hall and took Nellie to the police station, where she spent the night.[27]

---

[19] On Nellie Laidlaw in detail (and documented): Kessler, *Study*, 117ff.; see also Lalive d'Epinay, *Haven of the Masses*, 9ff.

[20] Hoover, *Historia*, 35.

[21] On the Pentecostal minister as a "modern shaman" see *The Pentecostals*, 474ff.

[22] Chilean Pentecostal churches are episcopal, so are most black Pentecostal churches in the USA and many Third World Pentecostal churches.

[23] *El Cristiano* 20.9.1909; Hoover, *Historia*, 36.

[24] *El Mercurio*, 13.9.1909; Kessler, *Study*, 117.

[25] Neely, Bishop, letter, 16.10.1909. (Methodist Letter-book, vol. 156, 109). Neely quoted a report by *El Heraldo Evangélico*, the Presbyterian paper in Chile, which in turn had relied on other reports; Kessler, *Study*, 120.

[26] Kessler carefully examines the available documentary evidence and gives priority in his report (on which I base my summary) to eyewitnesses.

[27] *El Cristiano* 20.9.1909. Nellie Laidlaw's further life was a tragic one. She became a drug addict and died unrepentant. (Stuntz, letter to Sampson Rogers, 10.5.1910 [Methodist Letter-book, vol. 156, 19]), Kessler, *Study*, 121. But ten years later her antagonist, Rice, was expelled from the Methodist mission for disciplinary reasons (Lalive d'Epinay, *Haven of the Masses*, 12).

September 12th, 1909, is an important date in Chilean church history. On this day the Methodists secured law and order, but lost the people's heart. The Pentecostals celebrate September 12th as their reformation anniversary. The third reformation, as Lalive calls it—the first being the reformation of Luther, Zwingli and Calvin, the second the reformation of Wesley.

The meetings in Valparaiso went on in a rather noisy way, which disturbed the neighborhood and led to an official investigation by the municipality.[28] Then a journalist started reporting on the meetings. To arouse the interest of his readers he filed a criminal charge against Hoover for, among other things, giving his congregation a pernicious drink called "the blood of the lamb," which made them lie for hours on the ground in a stupefied state.[29] Rice felt justified in intervening. Together with Robinson and the American consul he visited the judge in Valparaiso on October 4th, and found that an order had been written to close the Methodist church there on the grounds that it was a public nuisance.[30] The municipality required Hoover to sign a document undertaking that he would close the meetings at ten o'clock at night, but did not otherwise interfere with his work. The criminal charge was soon dismissed as being absurd, but Rice cabled to New York: "Hoover criminally prosecuted . . ."[31] Under the impression that Hoover was under arrest, Stuntz cabled the finance committee[32] to send Hoover on furlough at once, if they thought this was necessary.[33] The scene was set for a great heresy trial.

The Heresy Trial

The place was Valparaiso and the date was February 10th, 1910. A commission under the chairmanship of Robert Elphick presented the findings of its examination of Hoover's doctrine and practice to the Annual Conference. Apart from the charges connected with the excesses which have already been discussed, and which Hoover by this time had largely eliminated, the commission found Hoover guilty of teaching false doctrines.[34]

A resolution was reached[35] which rejected the false doctrine that the baptism of the Holy Spirit is accompanied by tears, visions, miracles, healings,

---

[28] Hoover, *Historia*, 51.

[29] *El Mercurio* 2.10.1909; Hoover, *Historia*, 38f.

[30] Campbell, letter to Stuntz, 25.7.1910; Kessler, *Study*, 123.

[31] Stuntz, letter to Bristol, 7.10.1909 (Methodist Letter-book, vol. 155, 251).

[32] I.e., the committee in Chile which was composed entirely of missionaries.

[33] Stuntz, letter to Neely, 19.10.1909 (Methodist Letter-book, vol. 155, 259); Kessler, *Study*, 123. Although Godsil Arms defended Hoover (Hoover, *Historia*, 55).

[34] On the sources: The conference minutes deleted almost all mention of Hoover being repudiated because a deal was made at the last minute that Hoover should go on furlough and the case be hushed up, an agreement which in the end did not materialize. Most of the deliberations, however, were published in *El Cristiano* (14.2.1910, of which Rice was the editor), much to the chagrin of Hoover but to the advantage of today's historian; Kessler is very detailed on this.

[35] Formally directed against Nellie Laidlaw, but in essence aiming at the new revival.

and other manifestations. It declared "that such doctrines are anti-methodist, contrary to Scripture and irrational."[36]

As the trial took place in public, the Chilean church members were able to follow the proceedings themselves. In their eyes it was not only Hoover but their own Chilean revival that was on trial. At stake was not only a vital doctrinal issue[37] but an even more important cultural issue. "Irrational perhaps," the Chileans responded to the charges leveled against them, "but certainly not anti-methodist and contrary to Scripture."

It was not Hoover but the awakened Chileans who finally realized that the break with the American missionaries was inevitable. Hoover was asked to go on furlough, but the Chileans asked him to stay and stick it out together with them. He stayed, losing his status in and income from the Methodist Church. The Chileans lost their church buildings, for which they had paid themselves, out of their poverty, but they gained what is very probably the first theologically and financially independent Protestant church in the Third World. In this sense September 12th, 1909 can be considered as the anniversary of the Third Reformation.

"The considered opinion even of those Methodists most able to appreciate the good points in the Pentecostal revival in Chile, was that the movement was doomed to become a struggling sect which would probably collapse within a few years."[38] How wrong they were. It took the Methodists not seven years to double their membership again as in the years previous to the schism with the Pentecostals, but seventy years, whilst in the same period the Pentecostal churches have reached approximately one million members.

The Methodist Church cut itself off from what it considered to be anti-methodist and irrational; by doing this, it also cut itself off from the very soil in which a Methodist Church in Chile could grow.

The Interpretations

The Iglesia Metodista Pentecostal in Chile states categorically that it is a faithful Methodist church.[39] They have said: "The difference between the

---

[36] Hoover, *Historia*, 62f.: "Resolución: Por cuanto ciertas doctrinas falsa, tales como la enseñanza que el bautismo del Espíritu Santo es acompañado por el don de lágrimas y visiones, milagres de sanidad, y otras manifestaciones, han sido diseminadas en varias partes de esta conferencia, y representadas como las doctrinas de la Iglesia Metodista Episcopal, nosotros por la presente declaramos que aquellas doctrinas son antimetodistas, contrarias a las Escrituras e irracionales, y nuestros miembros están avisados que no deben aceptarlas como las enseñanzas de nuestra Iglesia." Speaking in tongues is not even mentioned!

[37] Kessler, *Study*, 128.

[38] Stuntz, letter to Robinson, 7.7.1910 (Methodist Letter-book, vol. 156, 101); Kessler, *Study*, 130.

[39] The Iglesia Metodista Pentecostal grew out of the Methodist Episcopal Church "no por ningún desacuerdo que tuviera con los principios o doctrinas, sino que sigue el mismo régimen" (Iglesia Metodista Pentecostal, "Introducción," *Himnos*), quoted in Vergara, *Protestantismo*, 123.

Methodists and us does not lie in a different doctrine. It is just that they have merely the Methodist doctrines, while we experience them."

In fact the Iglesia Metodista Pentecostal has not developed what is sometimes called "a typical Pentecostal doctrine," if by that is meant a Pentecostal doctrine of the type held by the Assemblies of God. They do not teach the "initial sign," that is to say, that speaking in tongues is the outward sign of the baptism of the Spirit. Other signs and gifts can just as well fulfill this function. They practice infant baptism, continue the Methodist class system and the Methodist episcopal order, use Methodist literature and liturgical agendas freely, and print the twenty-five articles of the Methodist Episcopal Church without alteration in their hymn books. Moreover, they have strong objections to the USA-based missionaries of the Assemblies of God in Chile, both on doctrinal grounds and in defense of their own cultural, political and organizational independence.[40]

The Cultural Question

The Chilean Pentecostal movement interprets its own beginnings as follows: "The brethren were possessed by dancing and spiritual visions, they spoke in tongues of angels, prophesying about the great spiritual revival. The Holy Spirit seized them in the streets. The authorities took them into the prisons as criminals, but the brethren danced in the prisons, speaking in tongues and prophesying to these same officials."[41] W. C. Hoover describes:

Laughing, weeping, shouting, singing, foreign tongues, visions and ecstasies during which the individual fell to the ground and felt himself caught up into another place, to heaven, to Paradise, in splendid fields with various kinds of experiences: conversations with God, the angels or the devil. Those who experienced these things profited greatly and generally were changed by them and filled with praises, the spirit of prayer and love.[42]

For the yellow press (El Chileno) it was the "work of a hoaxer or madman." "Shouting, fainting fits, and blows" were considered "tragi–comical scenes." It was therefore necessary that "the Law intervene."[43]

The Christian and Missionary Alliance described the revival as an excess of religious fanaticism with "gesticulaciones grotescas."

They prayed so loudly, that one could hear the cries as far as a block away. The meetings lasted until midnight and sometimes even into the small hours of the

---

[40] Hollenweger, "Latinamerika." See on this chapter 17, pp. 222–24.

[41] *Chile Pentecostal*, Sept. 1954; quoted by Vergara, *Protestantismo*, 111. On the function of dance, see Hollenweger, "Danced." See also Robeck, "Taking Stock," 35–60, esp. 50.

[42] Hoover, *Historia*, 33.

[43] Ibid., 39.

morning. . . Some cried like cocks, others danced, others thought they were playing a string instrument, others again fell to the floor crying and shouting; their bodies became without feeling; others confessed their sins and the whole thing ended as a real scandal.[44]

For the Methodists, as we have seen already, the revival was simply "antimethodist, contrary to Scripture and irrational."

There is not much theology in any of these interpretations. In fact the Methodist periodical, *El Cristiano*, rejected an article by Hoover which consisted entirely of quotations from Wesley in defense of the revival.[45] If not theological, what then was the motivation for the strong statements made by those on both sides?

The Pentecostals had found that the manifestations allowed them to participate in worship with their own gifts. They could become liturgically and theologically active on the level of and with the means of their own culture. As these means resembled so very much the records of the Methodist and biblical past there was only one interpretation possible. If it was the Holy Spirit then, it must be the same Holy Spirit today.

The Methodists and the Christian and Missionary Alliance were unable to join in worship on that level. Yet these manifestations came dangerously near to the records of their origin. The upsurge of the past, with all the religious prestige of treasured church history, was a most dangerous threat to a present which pretended to be a continuation of that past, but which was in fact culturally discontinuous.

What else was there left for the Methodists to do, other than to state that the Chilean revival was not part of their tradition? It was so threatening that it had to be declared foreign and irrational—as if previous Methodist revivals had been particularly blessed by rationality, and as if in Scripture "rationality" was presented as a touchstone for truth.

The Missiological Question

What is the Western tradition of Christianity going to do when our converts develop a type of Christianity which is not only different from ours, but strikingly resembles a stage of our own past? We do not, of course, object to historical research, but we are afraid when history comes alive again. What is the Western tradition going to do if this new type of Christianity not only becomes a vital part of the Christian church, but seems to become the most important part of Third World Christianity?[46]

So far we have invited these Christians into the ecumenical fellowship with some (not striking) success. We have convinced ourselves that these Christians are theologically not well informed, that they are evangelically

---

[44] Oyarzún, *Reminiscensias*, 50–52; quoted by Vergara, *Protestantismo*, 112f.
[45] Lalive d'Epinay, *Haven of the Masses*, 9.
[46] On the problem of this cultural clash see Lalive d'Epinay, "Chile."

narrow, and not interested in the wider church. Thus we have "explained" why the greater part of Christianity in the Third World is not related to any ecumenical agency. We must provide *some* explanation, considering how the World Council of Churches has set itself up as representative of Third World Christianity. The Third World Christians are *not* in the World Council of Churches. Why not?

Listen to the story of one of the leaders of the Iglesia Metodista Pentecostal, Alfredo Ramírez Ramírez, who took part in the Uppsala Full Assembly of the World Council of Churches (1968). I listened to the report which he gave to his colleagues on his return to Santiago. Firstly Ramírez was greatly astonished that in Uppsala sermons were *read:* "As I said, the sermon was read, which seems to be customary [to them]. They do not preach as we do. We speak freely in our sermons with the aid of the Lord, with full spiritual freedom, in accordance with the inspiration of the Holy Spirit, because he alone knows the needs of every heart." But he was greatly impressed by the singing in one of the services.

> The whole service was unforgettable. So was the band consisting of 120 wind instruments which played the hymns so divinely that I was on the point of being inspired to dance by the Spirit of the Lord. Yes, dear brethren, I was on the point of doing so. But I asked myself, "What would these brethren think, who do not believe in the manifestations of the Holy Spirit?" Perhaps some of them would have been scandalized if they had seen me dance to the Lamb of God. Thanks be to God that He did not carry out this spiritual manifestation in me.[47]

This last remark shows that although the Chilean Pentecostals understand their liturgical dancing to be inspired by the Spirit, it does not happen entirely outside their control. In fact, it is beautifully controlled and integrated into their services. The nearest parallel I can find is that of a really skillful pianist who has mastered the technique of keyboard playing. The skill is a matter of many years of practice and exercise; the way in which he uses it is a matter of the inspiration of the moment. This flair for dancing is something which the Chileans have inherited from generations of dancers; the way in which they use it is a matter of the inspiration of the moment.

But what about his other remark: "Perhaps some of them would have been scandalized . . . "? It made me profoundly sad when I learned from him that he did not feel free to bring his contribution to that worship service.[48] Perhaps he was right. Perhaps some would have been scandalized. But why should we be more scandalized when the Chileans bring their liturgy into the ecumenical movement than when we introduce our liturgy to Chile? Indeed they are unhappy about our kinds of liturgy. This uneasiness is—in my opinion—really responsible for the very tenuous relationship between Third World Pentecostals (and other indigenous churches) and the historical churches. The

---

[47] Ramírez-Ramírez, "I Could Have Danced."
[48] On the function of Pentecostal liturgy see chapter 21, pp. 273–77.

theological reasons which are given are mostly based on mutual misunderstandings and secondary rationalizations.

This is not a plea for the introduction of dancing into our Western liturgies, but I am concerned that we are not really catholic, not really ecumenical. A really catholic and ecumenical movement would find ways of bridging this cultural gap. Some Western Christians may be able to join in a Third World Pentecostal liturgy. All the better for them. But that is not even necessary. What is necessary is a free space of tolerance—allowing these other Christians to remain true to themselves when they meet us. Without such a space of tolerance—a bridge over the troubled waters of cultural difference—the church will never become catholic and acknowledge the fruit of its own missionary work.

The Theological Question

I am not going to answer the question of whether the Chilean Pentecostals were "anti-methodist" or not. This is a question I want to leave the Methodists to answer. However, I would like to offer some observations on the basis of which we can answer that question.

(1) A comparison between the descriptions of the revival in Chile and Wesley's revival, and a comparison of the theological interpretations of these revivals, is a very crude approach to our question. It should be clear by now that any theological statement and any religious experience is culturally conditioned and can therefore not be judged on its own. We have to evaluate both on the basis of their *function* in a given context. There are theological statements and religious experiences which fulfill a theologically justifiable function in a specific context. There are those which do not fulfill such a purpose.

(2) This would imply that Christianity, including Christian theology and Christian religious experiences, is not phenomenologically and conceptually the same everywhere and always. In order to see this, one has only to study the history of mission or church history in general—that is, if one has not already learned it from good Old and New Testament theologies. If Christianity is not the same everywhere and always, and if, furthermore, different stages of church history are today preserved side by side; if, in other words, the chronological contemporaries are not cultural contemporaries; then we have to come to terms with having "the pasts of Christianity" present in our churches. If cultures from different countries co-exist in one and the same place; if, in other words, local co-habitants are not cultural co-habitants, then we have to come to terms with having different cultures present in one place. That is why we are faced with the quest for an "intercultural theology."

(3) If such an outspoken Pentecostalist as Oral Roberts[49] can become a Methodist minister *without changing his theology*, then it is difficult to accuse

---

[49] Roberts, Oral, *The Call;* Robinson, *Oral; The Pentecostals*, 363–65; Chappell, "Roberts," 759f.

the Chileans of being "anti-methodist." In studying carefully the Swiss and German Methodist publications between 1900 and 1910, it has appeared to me that the vocabulary and the concepts of the Chilean Pentecostals are often more Methodist than those of their Methodist opponents.[50]

A Quest for an Intercultural Theology

If, as we have suggested, the Iglesia Metodista Pentecostal and the Methodist Episcopal Church are simply two cultural variations of the same Methodist tradition, then the obvious questions are: *First,* is it possible, and in fact desirable, for the two churches to grow together again? *Second,* how do culturally incongruous churches discuss theology and come to a common evaluation of the advantage (or disadvantage) or the desirability (or undesirability) of specific inculturations of Christianity?

In an article which was translated by the Basel Mission,[51] two Chilean researchers have come to a positive evaluation of the cultural form of Chilean Pentecostalism. From their point of view, the Chilean Pentecostal church and the Methodist Episcopal church are not "simply variations of the same Methodist tradition" (as I have written), but indigenous Chilean Pentecostalism is a valid[52] expression of indigenous popular religion—and the Methodist church is not.

Since a re-unification of the two churches seems unlikely (although not quite impossible) the question of ecumenical cooperation becomes more important.[53] This is also the conviction of Juan Sepúlveda, a Chilean Pentecostal. It is not surprising, he writes, "that both Latin American and world ecumenism are increasingly . . . thinking about the possibility of a massive incorporation of Pentecostalism in the ecumenical task."[54] He also rejects the notion of Pentecostalism as a representative of the old order. Because of its character as "popular religion," he suggests, Pentecostalism is not a "survival of tradition." Its message has not opposed projects of modernization.

> Rather, they have devoted their efforts, from the standpoint of their "new faith," to promote a new religious experience, which has arisen through the work in small rural schools and among people who have become enthusiastic about the movement towards popular religiosity. Neither is Pentecostalism an easy problem for social science critics to understand. The depth of its religious experience

---

[50] In particular *Evangelist* and *Schweizer Evangelist*. See chapter 12, pp. 144–45.
[51] Palma–Villela, "Volksreligion," 24–32.
[52] The authors write "the only expression of popular religion," Palma–Villela, "Volksreligion," 25. The Chilean Pentecostal Juan Sepúlveda ("Struggle") confirms the aspect of "popular religion" which he calls "Pentecostalismo criollo" but his approach is more analytical and somewhat more critical. More on this in chapters 16 (pp. 204–16) and 17 (pp. 218–27).
[53] On Pentecostalism and ecumenism in Chile, see chapters 27 (pp. 367–71) and 27 (pp. 384–87). *Handbuch,* 02b.08.054d and *The Pentecostals,* 438ff.
[54] Sepúlveda, "Pentecostalism."

has not shown any evidence of interest in historical criticism of society. This has given critics the impression that Pentecostalism is a new instrument of the prevailing ideology of domination, thus curtailing people's possibility of expressing their criticism. Social scientists' opinion of Pentecostalism is shown among others in the following expressions: opium, domination via religion, religious proclamation of social conformism, "refuge of the masses." To this is added the evident effort from abroad to guide this religious tendency through the dramatic display of professional preachers of the so-called "electronic church."[55]

In conclusion, Sepúlveda quotes Professor Edenio Valle from Brazil, who sees in this type of popular religion a psychological mode of opposition:

> The individual group that appeals to this code reveals non-acceptance of the official codes propounded or imposed by those who exercise power. They show that the accepted language is considered by them as foreign, therefore alienating in relation to the individual or collective experiences, particularly those that are suppressed.

This democratization of language "exercises a protective function. That is to say, the oppressed are able to tell the oppressor their own feelings in such a way that the answer given is concealed."[56] In other words, we have here a process similar to that expressed in the hymns and spirituals of the oppressed slaves in the USA (chapter 4, pp. 32–34). Sepúlveda sees in the indigeneity of Chilean Pentecostalism the reason for its extraordinary growth. Its churches have outnumbered all other Protestant churches by a factor of 300.[57] It had moved from a persecuted sect to an official church. Some sections of Pentecostalism have indeed supported the Pinochet regime;[58] but others are participating in prophetic actions "criticizing the authorities in the light of the promises of God."[59]

---

[55] Sepúlveda, "Pentecostalism," 81.
[56] Valle, "Psicologia"; Sepúlveda, "Pentecostalism," 88.
[57] *Handbook*, of the WCC gives for 1985 the following statistics of member churches: Lutherans 2000; Methodists 6000; Iglesia Pentecostal de Chile 90,000; Misión Iglesia Pentecostal 12,000 (*Handbook*, 264–66). *CC*, 1988, 11, does not even mention the Methodists. Barrett estimates for 1980 over 1.8 million Chilean indigenous (= Pentecostals) in a population of about 11 million. (Barrett, *WChE*, 226ff.).
[58] "Declaración de apoyo a la Junta de Govierno de las iglesias evangélicas" no. 2, in *Posición Evangélica* (Santiago), 1975; Sepúlveda, "Struggle," 312.
[59] Sepúlveda, "Struggle," 315. "The majority of the churches that are members of the 'Confraternidad Cristiana de Iglesias,' an ecumenical organization that has maintained, since 1982, a critical posture toward the military regime, are Pentecostals." Sepúlveda, "Struggle," 315, note 10.
   More literature on Chilean Pentecostals: Sampedro, *Pentecostalismo; História del avivamiento;* Schick–Talbert, *La Iglesia Metodista Pentecostal;* Alvarez, *História;* Cook, William, "Interview"; Godoy, "Ochenta"; Tennekes, *El movimiento;* idem, "Mouvement Pentecôtiste"; Valencia, *En tierra extraña;* Vidal, M. and Ana, *El pentecostal.* The important article by Samuel Palma Manriquez, general secretary of SEPADE (Evangelical Source for Development, Chile) and professor of Sociology at the University of Santiago de Chile ("Religion of the People and Evangelism"), could

All of this makes ecumenical cooperation imperative. The plain fact, however, is that up to now we have not had a language which enabled us to carry out a theological debate with theologians from churches outside of our culture, who use a language of religious experiences from outside of our analytical tradition.

It seems to me that there are only two ways open. Either they learn our language and our way of doing theology or we learn their way. The first has been tried for almost a hundred years. We call it theological education; *de facto* it is a process of epistemological brain-washing and cultural imperialism. Even the many forms of "theologies of liberation" are still structured and built in our way, although they are directed against the political and economic (but not the cultural) power base of Europe and America. As the first way has proved dysfunctional in training an indigenous pastorate in Latin America and Africa, we might consider following the second way. This is where the attempts at "narrative theologies"[60] become academically necessary, because they at least would give theology the possibility of becoming universal. Either theology is universal and intercultural or it does not deserve the title of an academic discipline.

---

not be integrated in this chapter. It confirms many of my own observations: the religion of the poor in the form of Pentecostalism is self-sufficient and self-sustaining, in contrast to the so-called historical churches (p. 365); it has an ambiguous relationship toward indigenous culture and society at large; a younger generation of Pentecostals is well educated and is struggling with a new interpretation of Pentecostalism, trying to fill the gap between their experience and their traditional ideology. A mine of information on the social, political, theological, and ecumenical development of Chilean Pentecostalism is the periodical *Evangelio y Sociedad* (Passy 032, Provincia—Santiago, Casilla 238 Correo 3, Chile).

[60] As an example see chapter 2, pp. 6–15.

CHAPTER ELEVEN

A Plea for a Theologically Responsible Syncretism

Christianity is a Syncretism Par Excellence[1]

Before we pursue the historical roots of Pentecostalism in Wesley and in his catholic mentors, a pressing theological problem has to be addressed. Reading through section I of this book the question might be raised more than once: Is all this not just a form of Christian syncretism—the acceptance of shamanistic forms of religion in Korea (chapter 8, pp. 99–105), the black and African roots in Pentecostalism (chapter 3, pp. 18–24), the attempts to integrate popular religion in Chilean Pentecostalism (chapter 10, pp. 117–31), the Africanization of Christianity in Zaïre (chapter 6, pp. 55–58), and in South Africa (chapter 5, pp. 54–80), the excavation of old Mexican cultural elements in Mexico (chapter 7, pp. 81–98)? And indeed there is no question that these are forms of syncretism. However, so are all forms of Christianity, also and in particular Western Christianity. The question is not "syncretism yes or no," but what kind of syncretism. Already the Bible is an example of theologically responsible syncretism. Remember the example of the exile.[2] The Israelites came to Babylon with the theology of the Yahwist. They brought a nomadic religion which quickly became dysfunctional.

---

[1] Cf. the chapter "Syncretism" in Boff's seminal work *Church, Charism and Power*, 92ff. Also the leader of the Musama Christo Disco Church in London notices that the question is not "syncretism yes or no," but what kind of syncretism. See the excellent lecture by this African Pentecostal leader at a WCC Conference (Jehu-Appiah, "Overview").

[2] Told in detail in Hollenweger, *Conflict*.

In order to understand this situation one can imagine three parties: The first was the "party of the old-time religion." Those of this party said: "If it was good enough for father Abraham, it's good enough for us. We know that the world is an oasis, that's how it is written in our holy books. Yahweh has led us out of Egypt. What the Babylonians say is darkest paganism."

The second was the party of philobabylonian Jews. They said: "Perhaps once upon a time Yahweh saved us from Egypt, but now he is vanquished. The temple is destroyed. The aristocracy has been led into captivity. We have saved only a few remnants of our old documents. The ten commandments? The Babylonians have them too and in an up-dated version! Babylon is the victorious cultural and military power; their science explains the world."

The third party was a minority. It is documented by Ezekiel, some authors of the psalms and above all the priestly code (P). They said: "We do not quarrel with the Babylonians on the origin and shape of the world. Perhaps they are right. Only, they should be a little more consistent and a little more critical, for there is no evidence of a goddess of chaos, as they pretend. The water which surrounds the world is not a goddess but simply a material substance. Sun and moon are not gods, they are lanterns *(oroth)*. Blood is not the blood of a god as the Babylonians say. All these are biological and physical phenomena. Things they are, not gods; and they function according to God's law. They are made by him but are not identical with him." In fact, these insights are the basis of our natural sciences, for as long as the moon is a god one cannot walk on him. As long as water is a goddess, one cannot submit it to electrolysis. These are things, and therefore open to man's investigation and manipulation. Whether this approach to nature also has its drawbacks is another question.

It is clear that the Jews would have disappeared in Babylon if only the two first parties had existed. We owe it to the third party that the biblical tradition could continue. It is an example of a theologically responsible syncretism.

We find more such syncretisms in the Bible. The temple, for instance, was built according to Canaanitic plans, by Canaanitic craftsmen and architects. Only where the idol had stood in a Canaanitic temple, there was the ark and the tablets of the commandments, the signs of the covenant of God with his people.

If we turn to the New Testament we find the same kind of syncretism. Matthew was audacious enough to state that the magis (not kings) found their way to the cradle of Jesus on the basis of their pagan astrology, while the Bible-reading scribes in Jerusalem tried to kill little Jesus. Matthew should perhaps have been glad that he did not have to submit his Gospel to a theological commission for approval: he would have failed.

We shall see later that Paul, too, does not shy away from syncretism. His famous 13th chapter in I Corinthians is a collage of contemporary popular religious sayings (as one can find out by consulting any critical commentary). He even manages not to mention Christ in the whole chapter. It becomes Christian only through its inclusion in 1 Corinthians. The "popular ring" in this passage is perhaps the reason why so many couples choose it as a text for their wedding.

The same applies to our modern churches, whether Catholic, Protestant, or Pentecostal: they are examples of syncretism. For example, since Thomas Aquinas we have accepted the methodology of a pagan philosopher (Aristotle). This is particularly true of the evangelicals who say that all statements in the Bible must be harmonizable in order to be true. The presupposition that logical consistency is a sign of the truth is certainly not a biblical but an Aristotelian philosophical insight. At our universities and Bible schools we function according to the laws of coherence and logic. Otherwise we would not fit into this culture. However, this becomes fatal if we think that our forms of thinking are the thing itself. If we forget that there are cultures, e.g., the Chinese, the Hebrew, or the Old Mexican (chapter 7, pp. 81–98), who do not operate according to Aristotle, we take our forms of thinking for the truth. In more recent times even some mathematicians and physicists have discovered that the laws of logic and coherence, the law of incontradictability, are only true in a limited way.[3] Similarly, we discover in daily life that somebody can be inconsistent but reliable—ask any married man or woman. There are persons, indeed who are totally consistent—they function like a computer— yet they have proved to be unreliable. So it is with the Bible: it, too, is reliable but not consistent.

It is also well known that our rites and festivals (Christmas, Easter), and even the names of our days (Sunday, Monday, etc.), do not come from the New Testament, but from our Celtic and Germanic forefathers. So too with the form of our sermons, and with our church buildings, which are often built on the foundation of pagan temples. Our Christian rites and festivals carry with them a great heritage from our pagan past. Think of our marriage ceremonies and funerals—they too go back to pagan patterns. The New Testament Christians did not conduct funerals. They did not dream of such things. "Let the dead bury their dead," they said. Christ disturbed every single funeral where he was present by raising the corpses. From this I do not draw the conclusion that pastors have to resurrect the dead instead of burying them. This kind of Christian adaptation to new situations, this theologically responsible syncretism, is necessary. We no longer expect the parousia around the corner as the early Christians did. Therefore other forms of witness are demanded from us.

Religion is the Business of the Future

Twenty years ago we were promised a totally secularized future. The contrary is now the case. We are flooded by one religious wave after the other. "We cannot be unbelievers . . . In order to carry through atheism one would

---

[3] This epistemological problem is discussed in detail in the chapter "The End of Natural Science" in *ITh* 3, 286ff.

need a deep religious commitment."[4] No theological discussion can do away with this fact. Religion is part of humankind. That is why religion has to be dealt with in the same way as other givennesses of creation, such as trade and commerce, eros and friendship.

Think of the confusion we create in people who have had religious or parapsychological experiences. Theologians believe they are competent in matters of ecology and economics, in politics and psychology. And it is right that they make a contribution in these matters, although greater modesty would be appropriate. But it is not right to refuse cooperation in the field where we should be experts—in the field of religions. This kind of refusal is not the fault of the pastors, but of our theological education. There the topic of *lived religion,* especially of popular religion, is taboo. But to forbid discussion of this sort is to misunderstand Karl Barth, who said that if he wrote his dogmatics again he would do it in dialogue with the great world-religions. Of course he would still come to a christologically centered theology, but his dialogue partners would include not only Augustine, Luther, and the Bible; but also Buddha, Mohammed, the Indian religions, and the re-emerging popular religions.

The reason why pastors fail in this area is that we cannot articulate our own religious experiences. It is not true that the clergy is unbelieving. But it is true that they are the prisoners of a bourgeois—so-called scholarly—culture, where one can talk in public about everything, even the most intimate things, but not about one's own religious experience. This is why people think we are unbelievers. No wonder that religion seeks a place outside the churches, that it creates its own organizations everywhere.

Those who have religious dreams do not go to the pastor but to the psychiatrist or to self-appointed gurus from overseas. Those who yearn for religious experience, for direction in their life and for fellowship, go to the charismatic prayer groups, to a bible study group or to a Yoga class. They make a pilgrimage to Taizé, to an Indian Ashram, to a Philippine ghost healer or to the German Kirchentag. But they couldn't care less about the parish around the corner. "Amongst all my patients under the age of forty, there is not one whose final problem is not a religious one," says Carl Gustav Jung.[5] That was also true for the formerly communist countries. Even before Gorbachev there were more Christians in the Soviet Union than members of the Communist Party. And that, after almost a century of communist propaganda. In China the church has tripled since the missionaries had to leave.

One thing is sure: religion will not die out. The question is only, in whose service will it be? Will it serve the thirst for self-realization, for inner peace of the modern Westerner? Today Westerners have houses, cars, and clothes in abundance. Now they are seeking inspiration in drugs, in exotic tastes, in extraordinary images and sounds, in re-birthings into a former existence, in

---

[4] Lange, *Predigen,* 83.
[5] Jung, "Psychotherapie," 362.

therapies and new and exciting feelings. The one who can "sell" feelings does the business. It is no longer a disgrace to lose possessions, but it is a disgrace not to have tried out the newest fashion in religion. Harvey Cox calls this "spiritual gluttony."[6] In the past one made journeys to Africa. Today one makes trips into transcendence. After the commercialization of sex, we are now watching the commercialization of religion (chapter 18, pp. 229–33). With religion one can earn a lot of money, and not only in America. The clients deliver both capital and raw-material. Today, the data banks of the electronic church are sold and hired to political organizations and commercial mail-order enterprises.

Certainly, the churches do protest against this religious weed, against this banalization of the Holy, this commercialization of religion—and with reason. But without success. The pastors are unable to fight against the religious multinationals. For in this matter it is true as in everything else: The best critique of the false is the praxis of the true.

The question is: faced with this religious boom, what should the church do? The easiest and financially most profitable way out would be to turn the church into a highly organized religious industrial complex, with its super-markets in every town. There one could buy according to taste, religious experiences, therapies, meditations and—why not?—ecstatic experiences and short-lived fellowship. Then the functions would be clear, the books well-kept, and the status of the church in society unquestioned. This direct capitulation before religious market forces is of course a theologically irresponsible syncretism. But equally irresponsible is a stubborn opposition: whosoever wants religion must buy it in the packaging, in the quality and at the prices which we alone offer. Such a position is only possible where the churches have a monopoly in the religious market. And this time is definitely over.

More important than the market argument is the biblical. By the isolationist position mentioned, we would forgo our critical and prophetic task for a theologically responsible syncretism. It is my opinion that we should accept the challenge, but in such a way that it remains clear that God is something different from our experience of God, and that transcendence is something different from a trip into transcendence.

The models for such a syncretism are the biblical authors; but not that we must say: In the New Testament there are no funerals, no military chaplains, no Sunday Schools, no infant baptism, no Christmas trees, no doctrine of the trinity, no church bells, ergo it is all false. Rather, that we must ask: How did the biblical authors deal with the religious context of their time?

The same is true for our dialogue with medicine, the sciences, the popular religions and even patriotism. The biblical authors only rarely denied the relative truth of the other world views around them. But they converted them, and dethroned them from their absolute status (this would

---

[6] Cox, *Turning East*, 133.

apply today to medicine, economics, and science). They recognized them as things created by God; things are not gods. They realized that all these things are part of God's creation. That is a missiologically important insight. A missionary who refuses to speak in Chinese, Yoruba, or Telugu is not a missionary, but a European propagandist. In other words, there needs to be not only one syncretism but many, depending on the partners with whom we speak. After all, we have four Gospels, which emerged in different cultures and situations. These different syncretisms do not have so much a common content as a common method, which we will now examine through a concrete example.

The Epistle to the Colossians: An Example of a Theologically Responsible Syncretism[7]

I quote the hymn in Col. 1:15–20 without the interpretations and corrections of the author of Colossians:

He is the image (eikon) of the invisible God,
the first-born (prototokos) of creation
for in him everything was created in heaven
and on earth, the visible and the invisible.

Through him and for him everything is created.
He is before all—
everything has in him its coherence.
He is the head of the body.

He is the beginning (arche), the first-born of the dead;
for in him all the fullness (pleroma) wanted to live,
and to reconcile everything through him and for him,
making peace on earth and in heaven.

This is a quotation from the "New Age Hymnal" of the Church at Colossae. We can understand that this hymn was sung in the Colossian church in honor of a godhead which is present in the whole cosmos ("he is the head of the body"). For the Colossian Christians this is certainly Christ, although Christ is never mentioned in the hymn. The lack of such reference suggests that this was once a non-Christian hymn.

The hymn is sung by people for whom the world, the body of the cosmos, is torn asunder. The streams of harmony are disturbed. The cosmos is in uproar with itself and must be reconciled; even the very existence of the cosmos is in question. The battle of the natural elements against each other issues in catastrophes, and threatens to lead to a general collapse of the whole world. People are the victims of this shaky world; they experience themselves as prisoners of a nature which is in turmoil.

---

[7] I used the commentaries by Schweizer and Lähnemann (see Short Titles List). Cf. also *1Th* 2, 158ff.

We know the New Age literature of this time. It is full of gripping complaints on the sorrowful existence of man. One can do nothing about this condition. The famous psalm of the Naassenes[8]—a pagan hymn—complains:

> *The soul is like the timid game*
> *ever hunted over the earth by stern death*
> *proving his power ceaselessly in the long chase.*
> *If today in realm of light, then tomorrow sunk in sorrow.*
> *Father, look down and bless this sore afflicted being,*
> *as she wanders far from home, aimless across the earth and grieving.*
> *Wants to flee the bitter chaos, but she knows not any way out.*

The people were longing for the salvation of the world, for deliverance from the cosmic forces which tortured them. The Colossian Christians replied: Our Christ has overcome these powers, pacified the cosmos, killed death. He is arch-principle, he is preserver of the cosmos, regent and prince of its incalculable forces. "Everything finds in him its coherence" (Col 1:17). He is the boss, the head of this cosmic body.

That then is the situation in Colossae. How does the author of the epistle to the Colossians react? For brevity's sake I call him Paul. What does Paul do with this text?

First he accepts the mythical and for him foreign language—very different to many of today's theologians. He tries to answer in the language of the Colossians, and deals with this popular New Age religion in the "hymn book" of the Colossians. At the same time, however, he essentially corrects this popular religion by his interpretations and changes, as well as through the interpretations which he adds at the end of the hymn. Three examples:

The Colossians sang: Christ is the head of the cosmic body. Paul corrects and writes: Certainly, Christ is the head of the body. But "the body" is not—as you think—the world. The body is people. The body is you, the Colossians. The body is the church (he adds "tes ekklesias"). Through you, you Colossians, Christ exercises his headship—an unexpected statement given the small number of Christians in Colossae: they were members of a small sect, and relatively unimportant in the Roman Empire.

The Colossians sang: Christ has reconciled cosmos and forces, people and powers through his resurrection. Paul adds: Certainly he is the first-born of the dead, and has reconciled us. He reconciled us through "his death in his body of flesh" (1:22). This is a massive formulation: the assertion that the first-born of all creation, the image of the invisible God, is the very same one who died a lamentable death on a cross at a given time, at a given place. He is not just a principle, a cosmic power which operates in the world. He is also an historical person.

---

[8] The *Psalm of the Naassenes* is a contemporary hymn "directly suited to performance in the theater." Translated here by A. S. Worrell from the German version by Harnack, *Lehrbuch*, 257: Apocrypha 2, 436. For an English translation of this psalm see Hippolytus 5.10.2 (*Ante-Nicene Fathers* [reprint; Peabody: Hendrickson, 1994]).

The Colossians sang: The chaos in the cosmos must be overcome. Something must happen to this world. Paul answers: Certainly, our world is sick and must be healed; however, healing does not happen through mysterious cosmic powers, but through people who follow the one who died on a cross; that is, through reconciled and reconciling people.

What does Paul do here? He accepts the syncretism of the Colossians and transforms it into a theologically responsible syncretism. He socializes their syncretism, changing references to powers into references to people. The abstractions of the New Age syncretism are made concrete: Paul deals in detail with that which is under the lordship of Christ. Already his concrete list makes clear that the thrones and lordships, the powers and radiations—the laws of economics and technology, but also the rays of the stars, of crystals, and so forth—may no longer play the same role which they have traditionally played in Colossae. The rule of this Lord over everything includes under it the lives of those to whom the epistle is written. This is why Paul can no longer speak ahistorically. In fact, he must speak even of himself. The power of Christ which penetrates the whole world is not a mysterious cosmic power, but the power of the word and life of the apostle who fulfills his ministry in the shadow of the cross. And that ministry entails perspiring and freezing, being hungry and thirsty, being beaten and ridiculed, as he walks the roads of the Roman Empire.

The theologically responsible syncretism anchors the Colossian New Age syncretism not in a myth, but in the fact of the cross. Of course Paul knows that the Gospel means also deliverance from cosmic powers. But the mythical poetry is replaced by the factual event of the cross.

A Modern Example: Syncretism with the Culture of Economism (Capitalism)

The following is based on the work of a lecturer on economics at the University of Cambridge, who under my supervision wrote a doctoral dissertation on the topic: Can economists be converted?[9] By conversion she signifies not only a religious experience but, following Lonergan, also a cognitive process.

Jane Collier was disappointed that church leaders she observed discussing economics on television always argued morally instead of tackling the technical arguments of economists. They used *their* language in terms of morality, rather than that of the economists. Moral arguments are in this instance irrelevant because the mechanics of economy (say the economists) are given. Whether we like it or not, the Thames flows downwards into the sea—no argument, whether theological or moral, can change the law of nature which governs its flow. The free market, too, functions according to given laws.

---

[9] Collier, *Economism*.

Instead of arguing morally, Mrs. Collier takes on this technical argument, saying: economics is not a neutral science which informs us on the mechanism of economy—it uses hidden and open prejudices and value judgments. These value judgments Mrs. Collier calls "the culture of economism"; they correspond to the thrones and powers, the cosmic forces of our biblical example. Mrs. Collier proves that these value judgments function only within a secular faith option. Then she returns to her disappointment with the church leaders, and suggests that instead of arguing morally, they should call economists to scientific honesty. One cannot expect economists to be moral, but one can expect them to be good scholars.

Mrs. Collier follows her own prescription. While remaining strictly within the framework of economics, she shows how the decisions of the economists—and in fact all so-called scientific decisions—are always also determined by faith options. She shows convincingly that the culture of economism is a system of faith. To hold such a faith, she adds, is the right of economists; without it, they could not function. Only they should call their faith option a faith option, and not a given law.

In her chapter on conversion Mrs. Collier shows that there are also other faith options for economists, namely those options which do not "believe" in the powers and thrones, and which reckon with the fact that Christ has taken their power away.

Here we have a theologically responsible syncretism: the gods of capitalism and the world view of economy are not *a priori* denied. She does not say: your mechanisms and powers are not in the Bible, ergo they do not exist. But she says:

1. Economics is not—as you say—an objective science but a faith option. And that this is so is proved by the very instruments which economists use.

2. This world view is open for a theologically responsible syncretism if you see that these powers and mechanisms do not exist independently, but belong to the created world, and therefore can be questioned, changed, and re-arranged.

3. We want to show you the consequences of your system. Is it really the best system? We theologians are not qualified to judge, but we call on your scholarly integrity to admit that you cannot prove these so-called laws exist "in nature"; that they are simply your faith. If you put this faith aside for a moment, you might come to other insights.

A system which depends on producing enormous surpluses on the one hand and hunger on the other, which depends on the stimulus of a huge arms industry, this surely cannot be the best system you can develop. A system which pushes a little girl of twelve to write the following poem cannot be the best which you can invent:

My mother is called sorrow.
In summer she cares for water,
in winter she cares for coal
and the whole year through for rice.

During the day she cares for daily food,
during the night she cares for her children
and each day is filled with sorrow.
That's why my mother is called sorrow
and my father is called raving madness through drunkenness.
And I am called tears and sadness.[10]

---

[10] Quoted in Johanna Linz, "Meine Mutter heisst Sorge," in *Die Weltmission Das Wort in der Welt*, 1990/5, 4.

II

THE CATHOLIC ROOT

Any observer of Pentecostalism will see that it is particularly successful in Catholic cultures. This has its reasons. One of them is that Pentecostalism has not only oral black but also Catholic roots. To these roots are due its strict Arminianism (the doctrine of free will[1]); its belief in two worlds, a supernatural and a natural; its hierarchical church structure; and its doctrine of two (or sometimes) three stages in the *ordo salutis*, the decisive element being a second (or sometimes a third) religious crisis experience beyond salvation. Wesley mediated these Catholic elements to Pentecostalism and to the American Holiness Movement. That is why we now follow the emergence and changes of the doctrine of perfection in Wesley and its reception in the Holiness Movement.

---

[1] Synan, "Boundaries."

CHAPTER TWELVE

Wesley's Catholic Roots

Perfectionism in Swiss and German Methodism

In studying the Swiss and German Pentecostal Movement I was struck by the discovery that most of their doctrines were not invented by them. They had accepted them from the German and Swiss Holiness Movement, and this Holiness Movement had in turn been heavily influenced by Methodism. Main sources for this statement are the Methodist periodicals from the beginning of our century and Jacoby's *Handbuch des Methodismus*.[1] The theological gist of the Methodist publications is: There is a need for, and in fact a possibility of, perfection. That does not exclude error, ignorance and a thousand other weaknesses; it does not exclude "sin improperly so called, that is an involuntary transgression of a divine law, known or unknown." But to call this sin is a mistake. Jacoby, who had a profound influence on Switzerland and Germany as seminar teacher and editor of their periodicals,[2] defends Wesley's definitions of perfection and sin.[3] "The German Sankey," Ernst Gebhardt, a Methodist pastor in Zurich from 1874 to 1877, interpreted R. Pearsall Smith in Zurich's Tonhalle. He spoke of the necessity of a baptism in the Spirit, by which he meant a sanctification

---

[1] I do not need to go into details on European Methodism in an English/American book. See *The Pentecostals*, 218–43; more detailed in the German version. The following is not intended as an overall interpretation of life and work of the giant John Wesley. It serves only as a *pointer* to the Catholic roots in Wesley, the Holiness Movement, and Pentecostalism. Those interested may consider the sources in my *Handbuch*, 05.28.001, 05.28.002, 05.28.003 and 05.28.004. See also Bundy, "European."

[2] Peter, *Geschichte*, 233.

[3] Wesley, "Plain Account," *WW* XI, 396; Jacoby, *Handbuch*, 265.

experience different from justification.[4] Many are the testimonies of those who claim that perfection in Jacoby's and Gebhardt's sense is a second experience after conversion.[5]

Following reports from the Welsh revival, expectations of experiences of Spirit baptism became more intensive. Evan Roberts, prominent leader in the Welsh revival, was hailed as a local preacher of the "Free Methodists."[6] Even some of the more enthusiastic features of the revival did not trouble the Swiss and Germans. The first outbreaks of Pentecostalism were therefore greeted with joy.[7] Speaking in tongues in Barratt's revival in Norway was not criticized; in fact, Barratt was presented as "the leader of our city mission in Christiana [Oslo], a man well known to us through the European Conference of Methodism in Zurich four years ago. He is a sober man."[8] The reports became more cautious only after the ecstatic outbreaks at Kassel.[9] Of Barratt it is said that he resigned from the Norwegian (Methodist) Conference "because of other pressing commitments."[10]

According to their church order Methodist pastors had at their ordination to answer the question "Do you expect to become perfect in love during your lifetime?" with "Yes."[11] When the Pentecostals disrupted some of the Methodist churches in Switzerland the Methodists wrote: "It is not a wrongly understood doctrine of sanctification which creates the foundation for Pentecostalism but a wrong ideal of the church with its false subjectivism,"[12] and "there is a Christian perfection which is attainable in this life."[13]

An intensive study of the Methodist literature of the time of Pentecostalism's emergence in Germany and Switzerland challenged me to find out what Wesley had to say on this. Had the Methodists indeed been faithful to Wesley, or had they misunderstood him?

---

[4] Schulz, *Die Bedeutung,* 117, 120. *SE* 12.11.1898, 364. On Smith see below chapter 14, note 7, p. 183.
[5] *SE* 23.5.1896, 162. Hug, "Haben." *SE* 28.5.1898, 172f., 180. *SE* 23.7.1898, 236f., 30.7.1898, 241f., 6.8.1898, 325f. *SE* 17.9.1898, 302. 8.10.1898, 325f. *SE* 5.11.1898, 353. 12.11.1898, 361. 1.11.1898, 369. *SE* 20.5.1899, 156. *SE* 22.6.1900, 172f. 22.6.1900, 173. 22.2.1902, 61. 29.2.1902, 68. 8.3.1902, 76. 15.3.1902, 85. 22.3.1902, 92. 29.3.1902, 100. 5.4.1902, 108. 21.5.1904, 169. 211.5.1905, 164. 14.10.1905, 324. 14.10.1905, 327. 21.10.1905, 329f. 21.10.1905, 164. 14.10.1905, 324. 14.10.1905, 327. 21.10.1905, 329f. 21.10.1905, 334. 24.6.1906, 294. 30.9.1906, 310. 18.3.1905, 84f. 6.5.1905, 143. 10.6.1906, 180. 5.8.1905, 246. 29.7.1905, 328. 6.10.1906, 318. 19.8.1908, 263. 9.9.1905, 286. 13.4.1907, 116. 27.4.1907. 4.5.1907, 141. 11.5.1907, 148. 18.5.1907, 157.
[6] *SE* 18.3.1905, 84f.
[7] *SE* 19.8.1908, 263.
[8] *SE* 13.4.1907, 116.
[9] *The Pentecostals,* 223.
[10] *SE* 21.9.1907, 301.
[11] *Kirchenordnung,* § 103.3, 101.
[12] *Wächterstimmen,* Jan. 1910, 25.
[13] *SE* 29.10.1910, 697.

Wesley's Doctrine of Perfection

Wesley's doctrine of sanctification before his conversion was essentially influenced by Lorenzo Scopuli (1530–1610), a Catholic monk;[14] Henry Scougal (born 1650), a Scottish theologian;[15] Thomas à Kempis;[16] Bishop Jeremy Taylor (1613–67), Fellow of All Souls College and suspected of being a crypto-catholic because of his intimate fellowship with Franz a Santa Clara;[17] William Law (1686–1761), a teacher of perfection who was strongly influenced by Jakob Boehme;[18] Gregor Lopez (1542–96), a catholic Spaniard who lived

---

[14] Scupoli, born in Otrento, layman until he was forty, entered the religious order of the Theatines, was because of his zeal and influence persecuted and reduced to a layman (1585). He wrote *Il combattimento spirituale*. His authorship is however questioned. The *Enciclopedia universal ilustrada europeo-americano* (Vol. XII, 213 in an article on Juan de Castañiza; Barcelona, no date) says that it was wrongly attributed to Scopuli. Alamo, "Castañiza"; Andrei, "Scopuli"; Vezzosi, *Scrittori;* Steiner, B., "Untersuchungen"; Lang, "Scopuli"; Mercier, "Scopuli." The *combattimento spirituale* seems to have come to England via the Spanish adaptation by Juan de Castañiza (born in Iladiego, died 1598 in Salamanca); Philip II made him his chaplain and "censor de theologia entre los del Tribunal de la fe" (*Enc. univ.* XII, 213). Christian perfection is depicted as intellectualist and voluntarist mysticism. "To be ready for suffering is all, for God's intention points to the last." Many times the will in itself must be sufficient. Schmidt, Martin, *John Wesley* I, 48ff. Wesley learned about this from his mother.

[15] In his *Life* true religion is seen as "an Union of the Soul with God, a real participation of the Divine Nature, the very image of God drawn upon the Soul, or, in the Apostle's phrase, it is Christ formed within me," 30. " . . . that his Spirit shall be poured out on all flesh. This is most irreligiously restrained to the extraordinary effusion of the Holy Ghost on the Day of Pentecost or to the other miraculous gifts of the Spirit in those beginnings of Christianity: This is clearly contrary both to the promises of the Old Testament and the whole current of the New, and to nothing more than our Savior's most Divine Prayer wherein he expresses that he was not interceding for his Disciples only, but for all that should believe on his Name through their word" (edition 1733, 105; quoted in Schmidt, Martin, *John Wesley*, I, 55, 49ff. and note 8 [not in edition 1948]). Wesley was introduced to Scougal by his mother.

[16] Betty Kirkham, a clergyman's daughter, introduced Wesley to Thomas à Kempis (Schmidt, Martin, *John Wesley*, I, 95).

[17] In his *Discourse*, Taylor deals primarily with the Anabaptists; later bishop, translator of the Spanish Jesuit J. E. Nieremberg (Overbeck, "Taylor"). The *Dictionary of National Biography*, 1885ff., UK, 55.422–29. Brilioth, "Jeremy Taylor." He was called the Shakespeare of English prose. His *Rule and Experiences of Holy Living* and his *Rule . . . Dying* belong to the bedrock of English devotional literature. According to Taylor, love is the greatest gift which we can give God. The apostle calls it "the band of perfection" (Heber, *Jeremy Taylor*, 4.193, quoted in Schmidt, Martin, *John Wesley*, I, 78). Life according to the will of God appears in every detail as the "epitome of civil behavior" (Schmidt, Martin, *John Wesley*, I, 79): "Abstain from wanton and dissolute laughter, petulant and uncomely jests, loud talking, jeering, and all such actions which in civil account are called indecencies and incivilities" (Heber, *Jeremy Taylor*, 4.103, 138). Schmidt "misses the sense of the tragic" (Schmidt, Martin, *John Wesley*, I, 79). Wesley has read Taylor *(Journal* 14.5.1763; *WW* III, 212).

[18] He represented the doctrine of "inner light" (Fleisch, "Law," 1504). *Dictionary of National Biography*, 1885ff., UK, 32.236–40. Hobhouse, *Selected*. Perfection as a

for the greatest part of his life as an eremite in Mexico;[19] Jean-Baptiste de Renty (1611–1649), a French Catholic nobleman;[20] and others.[21]

However, for our purpose Wesley's doctrine of perfection *after* his conversion is more important. I introduce it by giving a chronological overview of Wesley's doctrine of perfection after his conversion.

In *August 1738* Wesley copied the definition of "full assurance of faith" by a Swedish Moravian, Arbid Gradin, in Latin and English into his Journal.[22] This definition, to which belongs the "deliverance from every fleshly desires and a cessation of all, even inward sins" he later accepts in his "Plain Account . . . "

Ca. 1738: The Character of a Methodist: The Methodist

> is therefore happy in God; yea, always happy . . . Perfect love having now cast out all fear, he rejoices evermore . . . He "loves his neighbor as himself"; he loves every man as his own soul . . . For he is "pure in heart." Love has purified his heart from envy, malice, wrath, and every unkind temper. It has cleansed him from pride, whereof "only cometh contention"; . . . There is not a motion in his heart but is according to his will. Every thought that arises points to him, and is "obedience to the law of Christ" . . . but has in all points "a conscience void of offence towards God, and towards man." Whatever God has forbidden, he avoids; whatever God has enjoined, he does. (*WW* XI, 371f.)

---

condition for eternal life means for him perfection in intention. "For surely it is a very different Case, to fall short of our Perfection after our best Endeavors, and to stop short of it, by not endeavoring to arrive at it. The one practice may carry men to a high reward in Heaven, and the other cast them with the unprofitable servant into outer darkness." Law, *Treatise*, 224 *(Treatise . . . ,* edition 1893, 6). Wesley knew Law's writings (Journal 14.5.1965, 186, *WW* III, 213).

[19] *Enciclopedia universal ilustrada europeo-americano,* XXXI, 113 ("Lopez"). What fascinated Wesley in this man was his longing for perfection in the love of God. Schmidt, Martin, *John Wesley,* I, 253.

[20] He founded "des sociétés d'artisans pour vivre ensemble comme les premiers chrétiens, en sorte que le gain de leur travail fût commun et que le surplus du nécessaire fût employé au soulagement des pauvres" ("de Renty"). Important for Wesley was de Renty's "holy indifference" at the death of his wife: "Madam sa femme fut très grièvement malade et pensa mourir . . . Monsieur de Renty . . . dit: Je ne peux pas nier que ma nature ne ressente une grande douleur de cette perte, mais mon esprit est remplis de tant de joie de me voir en état de donner et de sacrifier à Dieu une chose qui m'est si chère." *Le Chrétien réel ou la Vie du Marquis de Renty,* Cologne, 1701², 365, according to Schmidt, Martin, *John Wesley,* I, 213–15, quote 215.

[21] E.g., Tauler and Molinos (Schmidt, Martin, *John Wesley,* I, 753).

[22] "Repose in the blood of Christ; a firm confidence in God, a persuasion of his favour; the highest tranquillity, serenity, and peace of mind, with a deliverance from every fleshly desire, and a cessation of all, even inward sin." (Wesley, "Plain Account," *WW* XI, 369f.). "Requies in sanguine Christi; firma fiducia in Deum, et persuasio de gratia divina; tranquillitas mentis summa, atque serenitas et pax; cum absentia omnis desiderii carnalis, et cessatione peccatorum etiam interiorum. Verbo, cor quod antea instar maris turbulenti agiatabatur, in summa fuit requie, instar maris sereni et tranquilli" (*Tagebuch,* 37f.; "Plain Account," *WW* XI, 369); in *WW* the last sentence is missing.

Wesley explicitly says that he had presented this doctrine already in 1725 and more clearly in 1730 when he became "homo unius libri." Since that time he has, so he says, added nothing. (*WW* XI, 373.)

In 1730 he published a sermon on Christian Perfection (*WW* XI, 374–8) which showed that perfection did not mean being without error.

1741, Preface to the Second Hymn Collection (*WW* XI, 378–82). Here Wesley prints some extreme formulations but adds footnotes in which he corrects some of the most daring, especially the ones on "holy indifference" which he had taken over from de Renty.[23] Somebody who has only received remission of sins is nevertheless a child of God. Purification of the heart follows later. No person is known to him who had received in one and the same moment remission of sins, the abiding witness of the Spirit, a new, clean heart (*WW* XI, 380).

1742, Preface to the Third Hymn Collection (*WW* XI, 383–87). This is mainly a collection of Scripture passages.

1744, June 25th: First Preachers' Conference (*WW* XI, 387). Perfection means the overcoming of all inward sins.

1745, August 1st: Second Preachers' Conference (*WW* XI, 387): The majority of believers will only be sanctified shortly before death.

1747, June 16th: Fourth Preachers' Conference (*WW* XI, 388–91): Here Wesley shows from Scripture that only a very few of the addressees of Paul's epistles, and Paul himself, had been fully sanctified. But he continues to defend the doctrine of perfection because otherwise the prayers in John 17:20–23,[24] Eph 3:14 and 1 Thess 5:23 would be "mere mockery of God."

1759, Thoughts on Christian Perfection (*WW* XI, 394–407). This is a summary of all that Wesley has said so far on perfection.

1763, Further Thoughts on Christian Perfection (*WW* XI, 414–41). In this essay he examines whether the enthusiasts of a revival in London in 1762 were fully sanctified. He argues that very few have received perfection; most fall short in joy, kindliness, goodness, faithfulness, humility or temperance.

1777, A Plain Account of Christian Perfection as believed and taught by the Rev. Mr. John Wesley from the year 1725 to the year 1777 (*WW* XI, 366–446): This booklet contains all the above-mentioned writings and minutes and summarizes Wesley's doctrine in ten points (*WW* XI, 441f.):

- There is such a thing as perfection; for it is again and again mentioned in Scripture.
- It is not so early as justification; for justified persons are to "go on unto perfection" (Heb 6:1).
- It is not so late as death; for St. Paul speaks of living men that were perfect (Phil 3:15).
- It is not absolute. Absolute perfection belongs not to man, nor to angels, but to God alone.

---

[23] Above, note 20.
[24] See above Henry Scougal, note 15.

- It does not make a man infallible. None is infallible, while he remains in the body.
- Is it sinless? It is not worthwhile to contend for a term. It is "salvation from sin."
- It is "perfect love" (1 John 4:18). This is the essence of it; its properties, or inseparable fruits, are, rejoicing evermore, praying without ceasing, and in everything giving thanks (1 Thess 5:16 etc.).
- It is improvable. It is so far from lying in an indivisible point, from being incapable of increase, that one perfected in love may grow in grace far swifter than he did before.
- It is amissible, capable of being lost; of which we have numerous instances. But we were not thoroughly convinced of this, till five or six years ago.
- It is constantly both preceded and followed by a gradual work.

This doctrine of Wesley's has been heavily criticized by Zinzendorf,[25] by Böhler,[26] and above all, by the German Lutheran theologian and specialist on the German Holiness and Pentecostal Movements, Paul Fleisch. "In Wesley justification becomes merely a precondition for sanctification."[27]

Is Fleisch's critique correct? His judgment has two primary methodological flaws: (1) He works entirely on the basis of the "Plain Account" and disregards other writings by Wesley—perhaps these were not available to him. When I did my research in Zurich, the University library did not have Wesley's works—such was the ecumenical spirit of the University of Zurich at that time. I had to go to the Methodist Bishop's see where I found an amazing and extremely complete theological library, not only on Methodistica. (2) He worked on the basis of a faulty German translation.

The "Catholic" and the "Methodist" Wesley

The "Catholic" Wesley

Everybody conversant with Catholic literature of that time will discover a Catholic trend in these writings, which is not astonishing since Wesley was—as we have seen—heavily influenced by Catholic authors, and translated some of their books for his lay preachers. Walter Klaiber, the present bishop of the Methodists in Germany, tries to interpret Wesley in a Lutheran sense; and no doubt he is successful in many passages. But even he must accept that on the crucial difference between the Reformers and the Catholics, namely on the doctrine of predestination, Wesley was at least unsure. In his sermon on "Free Grace" he attacked the doctrine of predestination violently.[28] His

---

[25] Fleisch, *Heiligungsbewegung*, 43. Klaiber, "Aus Glauben" (quotes 329–31).
[26] Fleisch, *Heiligungsbewegung*, 45.
[27] Ibid., 42.
[28] Sermon no. 110, *WW* 3, 544–63. Significantly Wesley did not include this

adversary, George Whitefield (also a Methodist), says therefore: When Wesley speaks of "free grace" he means in fact "free will."[29] This is the decisive alternative: Free will or predestination? If asked in this way, no doubt not only the majority of Methodists but also Wesley himself would opt for "free will" against predestination—that is, for the Catholic option.[30]

However, taking into consideration Wesley's other writings, not just the "Plain Account," we find another side to the founder of Methodism.

The "Methodist" Wesley

In further writings by Wesley we also find passages which correspond to the "Plain Account."[31] But there are others. The most striking example is the famous entry in his Journal of January 24th, 1738—that is before his conversion. It shows without doubt an understanding of sin which is different from the one in the "Plain Account."

> I went to America, to convert the Indians; but O! who shall convert me? who, what is he that will deliver me from this evil heart of unbelief? . . . I think, verily, if the Gospel be true, I am safe: For I not only have given, and do give, all my goods to feed the poor; I not only give my body to be burned, drowned, or whatever God shall appoint for me; but I follow after charity, (though not as I thought as I ought, yet as I can,) if haply I may attain it (*WW* I, 74).

> I who went to America to convert others, was never converted to God. [Note at the bottom of the page: "I am not sure of this."] (*WW* I, 75) Are they read in philosophy? So was I. In ancient and modern tongues? So was I also. Are they versed in science and divinity? I too have studied it many years. Can they talk fluently upon spiritual things? The very same could I do. Are they plenteous in alms? Behold, I gave all my goods to feed the poor. Do they give of their labour as well as of their substance? I have laboured more abundantly than they all. Are they willing to suffer for their brethren? I have thrown up my friends, reputation, ease, country; I have put my life in my hand, wandering into strange lands; I have given my body to be devoured by the deep, parched up with heat, consumed by toil and weariness, or whatsoever God should please to bring upon me. (*WW* I, 76).[32]

> But does all this (be it more or less, it matters not) make me acceptable to God? Does all I ever did or can know, say, give, do, or suffer, justify me in his sight?

---

sermon in any of his sermon collections, Klaiber, "Aus Glauben," 332, note 78.

[29] A Letter to the Rev. Mr. John Wesley. Whitefield, *Works* IV, 53–73, quote 71.

[30] See the controversy between Luther and Erasmus and Zwingli and Erasmus on "Free Will," *ITh* 1, 320f. English: Hollenweger, "Zwingli," particularly 88f.

[31] *WW* IV, 156; Wesley, *Letters* VII, 102; VII, 322; Sermon no. 83, *WW* VI, 491; *WW* III, 308.

[32] The list in imitation of 2 Cor. 11 is no exaggeration. His American mission was connected to his ascetic ideal the more so as he was afraid of the sea. Witness his ascetic and disciplined soldiering in his diary (not to be confused with his *Journal*), in which he gave account of every one of his days in detail in shorthand and in secret writing from four o'clock in the morning until 9:30 at night. Notice also the strong social aspect of his thirst for sanctification.

Yea, or the constant use of all means of grace? (Which, nevertheless, is meet, right, and our bounden duty.)[33] Or that I know nothing of myself; that I am, as touching outward, moral righteousness blameless? Or (to come closer yet) the having a rational conviction of all the truths of Christianity? Does all this give me a claim to the holy, heavenly, divine character of a Christian? By no means. If the Oracles of God are true, if we are still to abide by "the law and the testimony;" all these things, though when ennobled by faith in Christ they are holy and just and good, yet without it are "dung and dross" meet only to be purged away by "the fire that never shall be quenched".

This, then, have I learned in the ends of the earth—That I "am fallen short of the glory of God;" That my whole heart is "altogether corrupt and abominable;" and, consequently, my whole life; (seeing it cannot be, that an "evil tree" should "bring forth good fruit:"). That "alienated as I am from the life of God", I am "a child of wrath", [Note at the bottom of the page: "I believe not."] an heir of hell: That my own works, my own sufferings, my own righteousness, are so far from reconciling me to an offended God, so far from making any atonement for the least of those sins, which "are more in number than the hairs of my head," that the most specious of them need an atonement themselves, or they cannot abide his righteous judgment; that "having the sentence of death" in my heart, and having nothing in or of myself to plead, I have no hope, but that of being justified freely, "through the redemption that is in Jesus" . . . (*WW* XI, 76–77).

Wesley knew, after as well as before his conversion, that sin is the human condition, irrespective of what one does or does not. But alongside of this understanding of sin he also held an understanding of sin as a concrete deed, a conscious and voluntary trespassing of a known law of God. His doctrine of perfection is in fact only possible with this second understanding of sin. Therefore Wesley was always oscillating between the two understandings of sin.

In his book *Checks to Antinomianism* (1771–75), Wesley's Swiss assistant John William Fletcher (also called the "Saint of Methodism") defended the doctrine of perfection.[34] He was the first to write in English using the term "baptism of the spirit" for the experience of perfection or sanctification.[35]

---

[33] Here Wesley quotes the Anglican Eucharist liturgy. "Means of Grace"—the eucharist.

[34] French: Guilleaume de la Fléchère, 1729–85, born in Nyon at the Lake of Geneva, read theology at Geneva, rejected the doctrine of predestination, and was a house teacher in England, where he got to know Methodism. After having received "full assurance of faith" (1757) he became pastor which he remained until his death at Madeley. Besides this he directed the seminary of the Countess Huntington in Trevacca (1768–71), but had to leave because of the disputes with Whitefield on Calvin's predestination. He never pretended to have reached "perfection in love" (Fleisch, "Fletcher"; Scott, "Fletcher"; "Fletcher," *Lexikon der Schweiz*, 3.171; Wesley, "Short Account"; Nuelsen, *Fletcher;* Brandt-Bessire, *Sources*, 63–72; Schulz, *Die Bedeutung*, 118; Dayton, "Roots," 7f.).

[35] Bundy, "European," 280.

Appraisal

It is difficult to bring Wesley's understanding of sin into line with Paul's. In spite of this Wesley in his time did more for the acceptance of Paul than many who quoted him correctly but not understandably. Why should we not interpret Wesley in his historical context as we do with any historical text? We might then consider the fact that Wesley had to do with a society and a church of ethical indifference (drunken clergy, people who were in prison because they could not pay their church taxes), of mysticism and pragmatism. In spite of his understanding of sin and perfection, which is probably different from Paul's, perhaps Wesley was nearer to Paul than his antagonists. These quoted Paul regularly, but seem not to have grasped the depth of Paul. Perhaps Wesley proclaimed the Gospel better—because more understandably—than they did. His offer of pardon and his demand for perfection *was socially and individually concrete.* His call to repentance had clear and experiential consequences. The price for this was to give up the Reformers' *simul iustus et peccator* (we are always sinners *and* justified), and their doctrine of predestination. These concepts are, in any case, an enigma for most people. To see this one has only to consult the article on Luther in the *Oxford Dictionary of the Christian Church*,[36] which says more about the English churches than about Luther. The understanding of unconditional grace taught in the Reformation is probably for many people a mere theory, or alternatively a heavy load, because it identifies people as sinners for the rest of their lives. Perhaps the dialectic understanding of grace and sin in Paul must be simplified and logically streamlined for most people.

That is what the tradition which flowed from the Catholic Wesley into the American Holiness Movement did, with all its practical positive and negative results. The advantage of this approach has been a socially and individually active Christianity. The disadvantage, perhaps, has been a tendency to forget that a good conscience is not necessarily proof of perfection. Blaise Pascal, the great French mathematician and theologian who had also experienced a "baptism of the Spirit," pointedly said: "No one ever does wrong so fully and so happily as when he does it with a clear conscience."[37]

---

[36] Luther's "central doctrines were a mirror of his temperament and of his experiences . . . Man is wholly under the power of evil and can do nothing but sin. Justification is something which is accomplished in man by a kind of legal fiction . . . though in reality he remains as sinful as before." Cross, "Luther." On this strange dictionary see *ITh* 2, 30f.

[37] "Jamais on ne fait le mal si pleinement et si gaiement que quand on ne le fait par conscience," Pascal, *Pensées*, Frag. 895. *The Pentecostals*, 328.

CHAPTER THIRTEEN

Pentecostals and Catholics

Before we continue the story "from the American Holiness Movement to Pentecostalism," I want to stop and glance at the Roman Catholic church; for, if Pentecostalism has one of its roots in Catholic spirituality, and if "there is greater relationship between Catholics and Pentecostals than between Catholicism and the historic Protestant churches,"[1] some repercussions of Pentecostalism in the Catholic camp are to be expected. This is the case at least in two directions; namely, in the growth of a Catholic Pentecostal or Catholic renewal movement, and in several important dialogues between Pentecostalism and the Vatican.

A Catholic Pentecostal Movement

Already by 1962 there were a few contacts between Catholics and Pentecostals in Holland[2] and in the USA. Some priests had taken part in meetings of the Full Gospel Business Men's Fellowship International (a lay organization within classical Pentecostalism)[3] and thereby experienced and accepted Pentecostal spirituality.[4] But the breakthrough came only in 1966–67, when

> several Catholic laymen, all members of the faculty of Dusquesne University in Pittsburgh were drawn together in a period of deep prayer and discussion about the vitality of their faith . . . Not satisfied with a life of ivory-tower scholarship, they concerned themselves with the problems of the renewal of the

---

[1] Vereb, Interview. Lundgren, "Dialog"; quoted by Sandidge, *Dialogue (1977–1982)*, I, 213.
[2] Zeegers, "R. K. Kerk."
[3] *The Pentecostals*, 6f., 8, 15, 43, 212, 356, 364f., 426, 268, 485.
[4] O'Docharty, "Tried." Schulgen, "Heaven."

Church . . . In recent years they had been involved with the liturgical and ecumenical movements, with civil rights, and with the concerns of world peace.[5]

Kevin and Dorothy Ranaghan, both university theologians, distinguished themselves in this group of Catholic intellectuals. At the end of 1966 they read the story of the Pentecostal evangelist David Wilkerson,[6] who had found prayer and the gifts of the Spirit to be the most efficacious means of combating juvenile drug addiction. Then, they read a report on neo-Pentecostalism within Protestant churches,[7] and became curious to get to know this charismatic movement themselves. Through the mediation of the Anglican Rector William Lewis they came into contact with a charismatic prayer group. Soon they received the gift of speaking in tongues. From Duquesne the movement spread to Notre Dame University and throughout the United States. Today the charismatic movement is one of the strongest sectors in the Roman Catholic church, having spread to Catholic churches around the world. There are also reports of a similar development in the Eastern Orthodox churches.[8]

In addition to the vast journalistic literature, there are some scholarly publications on the Catholic charismatic movement. For a critical understanding, the essays of Helder Câmara's former theological research assistant, Abdalaziz de Moura; of the Dominican professor of theology François-H. Lepargneur;[9] of the British Dominican Simon Tugwell; of the theologian J. Massyngberde Ford; and above all of the American Benedictine Kilian McDonnell, who has examined the revival and its roots thoroughly, are indispensable. McDonnell, de Moura and Lepargneur—unlike Ranaghan and O'Connor—do not belong in the narrower sense to the Catholic Pentecostals. Therefore their critical but sympathetic approach and their exact reports are particularly important.

Relation Between Catholics and Pentecostals

As the charismatic renewal movement grew, Catholic and classical Pentecostals in many cities began meeting regularly for prayer. The official publications of the classical Pentecostals were not sure how to interpret this new phenomenon. That is understandable, as among Pentecostals until recently the Catholic church has been seen as foreshadowing "the great whore," "lead[ing] to the

---

[5] Ranaghan, *Catholic Pentecostals*, 6. O'Connor, *Pentecostal Movement*, 105. Lundgren, *Ny pingst*. There was an explosion of literature on Catholic Pentecostalism in the late '60s and early '70s. Bibliographies: Melton, *Bibliography;* Lambert, *Bibliographique;* Hollenweger, *Pentecost Between Black and White*, 127–33; idem, *Christen*, 119–25; idem, *New Wine*, 60–75; and in the Spanish version of *The Pentecostals (El Pentecostalismo)*, 61–66.

[6] Wilkerson, *Switchblade*.

[7] Sherrill, *Tongues*.

[8] Kovaleski, "Charismen"; *Aion*, "Dialogue"; Stone, "Orthodox"; *Renewal*, "Orthodox."

[9] On these in detail in *The Pentecostals*, 101–7.

uniform, worldly and anti-Christian Super-Church, which is foretold in the Revelation of John."[10] On the other hand Catholics have in the past written, concerning the Pentecostals, mostly polemics based on ignorance.[11]

All of this is changing quickly, although not everywhere at the same speed. Classical Pentecostal churches and old-time Catholic specialists on sects cannot keep up with the changing situation. A reader from Maryland wrote, for instance, to the *Pentecostal Evangel*, wanting to know how the Catholics can receive the Spirit and "still go to confession and still have their idols? . . . Some of our people are going to Catholic prayer meetings and this disturbs me. As Christians we need wisdom to discern the spirits in these last days."[12]

Classical Pentecostals were "scandalized" that Catholic Pentecostals could smoke and drink and still claim to have had the baptism of the Holy Spirit. Vinson Synan of the Pentecostal Holiness Church says that classical Pentecostals will have to make "an agonizing reappraisal" of just what makes a Pentecostal, in light of the Catholic renewal.[13] Nevertheless one would have to agree with Mackay, who "foresees a more cordial rapprochement between the Catholics and Pentecostals than between adherents of mainline denominations." Rightly the Presbyterian theologian Rodman Williams indicates that the significance of official negotiations between Pentecostals and Catholics at the highest Vatican level "can hardly be over-emphasized."[14]

Signs of a change have been apparent for some time, for example in the publications of the French Pentecostals.[15] The current polemics of the German and Italian Catholic sect specialists against Pentecostalism, and the corresponding condemnations of the Catholic church by the Pentecostals, will soon be obsolete.

There are of course still remnants of past polemics, as for instance when the most important American Pentecostal periodical reported that the Second Vatican Council had "produced little worthy of note."[16] On the other hand, in more recent Catholic publications there has been an astonishing openness towards the classical Pentecostal movement;[17] sometimes even unashamed

---

[10] Duncan, M., *Revelation*. Further literature in *The Pentecostals*, 436–38. Overview in Bittlinger, *Papst*, 2–9. This type of polemics is not over yet, for instance when the pope called the Pentecostal sects "rapacious wolves" (see below, note 136), Robeck had to use all his delicacy, theological, and ecumenical skill to contain the damage (confidential correspondence in my possession).

[11] For instance some Italian Catholic in *The Pentecostals*, 257f.

[12] "Evangeletters."

[13] Torkelson, "Filled."

[14] Harper, "Dialogue." *Renewal*, "Dialogue." Williams, Rodman J., "Breakthrough." *One in Christ*, "Dialogue."

[15] The French Pentecostal periodical *Expériences* (Carhais 29N), especially the issues no. 2, 1971, and no. 8, 1972 with articles by O'Connor, Du Plessis, Ranaghan and French Pentecostals.

[16] Bolten, "Recent," 6f.

[17] Chéry, "Sectes"; idem, "Accusent"; Gaëta, "Chili" (1956!); Vergara, *Protestantismo;* idem, "Avance"; Zenetti, *Heisse,* 304–9. Particularly interesting is the change

admiration. Catholics and Pentecostals have a common problem: In an age when all authorities are declining, the authority of the clergy also declines. The modern world no longer asks for the Catholic or Pentecostal understanding of God but: Is God alive, and if so what does he do for me? Is there any sense in praying and trusting this God? Is the whole business of the church simply a vast and useless enterprise run at public cost, at best a "necessary illusion"? The answer the Pentecostal gives to all these questions is that of the man who was born blind: "Whether he is a sinner, I do not know; one thing I know, that though I was blind, now I see" (John 9:25).

On this the Dominican Tugwell comments: "People are dissatisfied with religion that does no more than preach and moralize; they want the real thing."[18] In his analysis of "The Ideology of Pentecostal Conversion," the Benedictine Kilian McDonnell aptly says that in the Pentecostal movement the problem of the "unbelieving believer" is not met by referring him to the "field" of abstract theological assertions in which he is hopelessly lost. He is capable neither of denying nor accepting the statements about this "theologians' " God. But—in McDonnell's view—in the Pentecostal liturgy he can experience being able to pray once again.[19]

There is no need to point out that the Pentecostal proof of God is insufficient, and in certain situations will even lead to the abolition of faith *qua* faith.[20] To some extent Pentecostals see this themselves (chapter 18, pp. 229–33). In spite of this the question remains: How does faith experience the real presence of Christ? It is worthwhile for Protestants and Catholics to meditate on this question.

Theological Characteristics

One can detect in Catholic Pentecostalism a tendency to accept from classical Pentecostals their experience but without its doctrinal articulation. For instance, fundamentalism is rejected as being opposed to charisms. "Too often in the past Christians experiencing baptism in the Holy Spirit have adopted not only the cultural environment of denominational Pentecostalism but also the thought categories of the fundamentalist milieu."[21] Yet it seems necessary for Ranaghan to interpret the charismatic dimension from different points of view, including that of critical exegesis, if the Pentecostal experience is for the whole church and not the particularity of one sect.[22]

---

which Damboriena underwent from a merciless critic to a tolerant partner: Damboriena, "Chile"; idem, "Algunos"; idem, "Fury"; idem, *Tongues*.

[18] Tugwell, *Receive*, 13.

[19] McDonnell, "Ideology." See also chapter 21, pp. 269–87 and chapter 26, pp. 356–60.

[20] Tugwell, *Receive*, 104.

[21] Ranaghan, *Catholic Pentecostals*, 261. McDonnell, "Catholic Pentecostalism," 41. See also idem, *Open*.

[22] Ranaghan, *Catholic Pentecostals*, 260.

From this it is concluded that charisms are not supernatural. Already the Protestant theologian Arnold Bittlinger has proved that there exists no criterion by which one could distinguish between genuine foreign languages and speaking in tongues. "Speaking in tongues," he says, "must be considered as a natural phenomenon, just as dreaming, laughing or weeping."[23] So the "supernatural" can be seen within an old Catholic tradition as "being precisely the fulfillment of our nature."[24] Using functional (and not ontological) categories, McDonnell poignantly affirms: "A gift is not a *what* but a *how*. A gift is less a new capacity and more the use of an old capacity as a function of Christ's kingdom. Quite secular activities can be gifts of the Spirit if they are used as functions of the kingdom."[25] Rightly Josephine Massyngberde Ford asks whether Handel's Messiah, Bach's passions, and the books of St. Thomas Aquinas are due to direct inspiration, or to human charismata. Her answer: "An excellent combination of both."[26]

One of the most articulate of these charismatic Catholic theologians is the Dominican Simon Tugwell from Oxford. He has presented several meditations on British Radio, one of them including a recorded segment of singing in tongues by three Catholic sisters, which provoked several hundred letters of thanks to the British Broadcasting Company. It was prayerfully and meditatively prepared in the studio (to the dismay of the technicians who did not appreciate this "waste" of valuable studio time and technical facilities "just for meditation"). The actual meditation was then broadcast live.

In several publications Tugwell has defended the use of speaking in tongues, which appears to him "to mean the production of genuinely linguistic phenomena, which may or may not be identified by someone present as some definite language, but which do not convey any ordinary semantic significance to the speaker himself."[27] It is not simply "praying in the Spirit," nor is it "God's kindergarten." "Prayer that we cannot ourselves fully understand is an essential part of Christian praying: Tongues is a particularly straightforward embodiment of this principle." But it is—from a phenomenological point of view—ambiguous. That applies—says Tugwell—to all pneumatic activities. He concludes that the New Testament does not put pressure on anyone to seek the gift of tongues, but it encourages those who receive it to use it to grow into fuller and richer experience of the Christian life as a whole. Thus Tugwell suggests that this gift does have a part in the wholeness of Christian life. "This does not in any way commit us to accepting the Pentecostals' understanding of it, nor to their kind of religion."[28]

---

[23] Bittlinger, "Glossolalie."
[24] Tugwell, *Receive,* 18.
[25] McDonnell (with Bittlinger), *Problem,* 53.
[26] Ford, J. M., *Baptism,* XII, 51.
[27] Tugwell, "Gift," 137.
[28] Ibid., 137, 139.

Tugwell goes on to state that "the Pentecostal doctrine is scripturally and theologically unwarrantable," and is for the theologian "cause for alarm." Yet he maintains that "Pentecostalism does represent a genuine eagerness for the original, undiluted message of the Gospel which is 'not in words of persuasive wisdom, but in demonstration of Spirit and power' (I Cor. 2:4), this too makes a legitimate demand on the theologian's interest and sympathy." He rejects the notion that the baptism of the Spirit adds anything more to Christian faith. "Anything more than fundamental Christianity is actually less than the Gospel."[29]

Tugwell uses categories of medieval mysticism in order to interpret his and his fellow Catholics' spiritual experiences. Mysticism, he says, "is not intrinsically Christian, but it can be made Christian." He differentiates between oracles and prophecy, between idols and icons. "An idol is a god, or a manifestation of god, or an experience of god, or a doctrine of god, that one has 'made a thing of.'" But "Christ is larger than his media of communication." Prophecy and icon "strip us down before God, peeling off our masks and pretenses, our false selves," while those using oracles and idols always try to get power over God, showing thereby how right they are.[30]

Tugwell knows of course that definitions and names (also a kind of idol) are sometimes necessary for our sanity, but they never capture God adequately. Only "when we have overcome" (Rev 2:17) shall we find our full identity, and only then will the reality of the experience of God fit its definition. That is why Tugwell sees no phenomenological difference between Christian and non-Christian mysticism, between oracle and prophecy, between idol and icon. The difference does not lie on the level of phenomenology, but on that of signification. From outside, both these mysticisms look exactly alike. Only by the function of mystical experiences, when they create room for freedom, do they become Christian. From this Tugwell draws the conclusion that in a charismatic community there must be freedom to speak in tongues and to offer extempore prayer, and also freedom to abstain from such kinds of spirituality without losing face. As among some German Protestant Neo-Pentecostals, Catholic Pentecostals similarly see in community work, journalism, and run-of-the-mill management,[31] even in music, poetry, and theology,[32] charisms of the Holy Spirit, approaching the black Pentecostal understanding of charisma.[33]

In fairness it must be added that Tugwell is regarded with suspicion by many Catholic Pentecostals, particularly in England. They see him more as

---

[29] Tugwell, "Reflections," 268, 269, 280. These and similar statements have provoked a protest from Michael Harper, see his review in *Renewal* 39, June/July 1972, 8.
[30] Tugwell, *Receive*, 95.
[31] Ranaghan, *Catholic Pentecostals*, 249. McDonnell (with Bittlinger), *Problem*.
[32] Ford, J. M., *Baptism*.
[33] See chapter 4, pp. 25–40 and chapter 17, pp. 218–27.

one of their outspoken critics than as a "Catholic Pentecostal." Tugwell himself does not want to be put into that category. On the other hand he is not the only one who has misgivings about the term and the concept of the "baptism of the Spirit." It is not surprising therefore that speaking in tongues is not recognized as the "initial sign," i.e., as the first and compulsory sign of Spirit baptism, by O'Connor.[34] But that does not hinder Catholic Pentecostals from seeing the spiritual and psycho-hygienic value of glossolalia. The usual dispensing of speaking in tongues as pathological is rejected.[35]

It is recognized that the term "baptism of the Spirit" was coined by the classical Pentecostals, who hardly have a theology of the sacrament;[36] also the Catholic roots of Pentecostal spirituality have nowhere—as far as I can ascertain—been recognized. A Catholic theology of charisms should speak rather of the renewal[37] of the Spirit received in baptism than of initiation into the life of the Spirit in Spirit baptism.[38] Although Kilian McDonnell knows that among the church fathers there were some who taught "two stages" of salvation similar to those taught in the classical Pentecostal churches, he maintains that for Paul "becoming a Christian and receiving the Spirit occur together."[39]

The theologians of the Catholic Pentecostal movement have stressed that Pentecostal spirituality does not hinder Catholic mariological spirituality, but on the contrary, promotes it.[40] In the preface to his book on the Spirit, Tugwell has included a prayer to and with Mary.[41] Catholics have rightly seen that the Pentecostals are—in contrast to their self-interpretation—not typically Protestant.

On the ethics of the Catholic Pentecostals one could at the beginning not discover any rigorist tendency. Also the political aspects of a Christian spirituality were at first kept alive. "It seems to be decisive," says a Jesuit observer, "that people who in the past could not see a Negro without becoming furious, can now embrace him."[42]

Ecumenical Significance of Catholic Pentecostals

The prayer-meetings of the Catholic Pentecostals shattered the "economic-deprivation"–theory that had customarily been set forth as an "explanation" of the older, classical Pentecostalism. It was not the uneducated but the

---

[34] O'Connor, *Pentecostal Movement*, 125.
[35] Jennings, "Glossolalia." Samarin, *Tongues*. O'Connor, *Pentecostal Movement*, 123.
[36] Ranaghan, *Catholic Pentecostals*, 249 and McDonnell (with Bittlinger), *Problem*.
[37] Caffarel, *Pentecôtisme*, suggests "effusion of the Spirit." Ford, J. M., "Catholicism," suggests "release of the Spirit."
[38] Clark, *Confirmation*. O'Connor, *Pentecostal Movement*, 132.
[39] McDonnell (with Bittlinger), *Problem*, 36.
[40] O'Connor, *Pentecostal Movement*, 59.
[41] Tugwell, *Receive*, 11.
[42] Altrichter, "Katholische."

intellectuals, not the uncritical but the critical exegetes, not frustrated Puritans but quite normal Christians who took part in these meetings. There was not only speaking in tongues but critical discussion of theological and social problems; not only the singing of hymns but the composition of hymns; not only praying, but eating, drinking and smoking. It was possible to laugh and weep, to clap hands—and also to leave the room when one did not like this style.[43] The Jesuit Sudbrack[44] therefore sees Pentecostal spirituality in relation to Harvey Cox's *Feast of Fools*. Social and political topics are not excluded from their meetings:

> Any genuine movement of the Holy Spirit will not stop at re-establishing unity in the family or small community or parish. It must move inexorably on towards creating freedom and justice in the larger community of the nation and among nations. Most of the participants [of the Conference at Columbia Feb. 19–23, 1973] had worked actively in concerns of social action.[45]

Harold F. Cohen goes even further in stating: "One finds an interesting parallel between the charismatic renewal and the statements of the documents of Medellín."[46] The review of the Full Gospel Business Men's Fellowship International reports the Mexican bishop Sergio Mendez Arceo as having said: "Only socialism can enable Latin America to achieve true development."[47] "The prayer-meeting is not an end in itself, but its point is to build a mature community of Christians."[48] Since autumn 1971 experiments in "communities"[49] have been under way which might perhaps not only bridge the ecumenical but also the political and social divides.

There has even been room for red-hot revolutionary talk, which has included a condemnation of "free trade," the revolutionary issues of the Third World, the necessity for the "spur of Marxism," and the inevitable interlinking of economics and spirituality.[50] These are of course important voices, but they do not represent the general feelings of rank-and-file Catholic Pentecostals.

The Catholic Pentecostal Movement has developed its own ecumenical momentum—an enigma for both classical Pentecostals and Evangelicals. It is true this was only possible after the Second Vatican Council, but the Catholic Pentecostals have translated its documents into experience at the local level, where *oikoumene* is not only discussed but lived. It is understandable that in

---

[43] Tugwell, *Receive*, 18 and passim.

[44] Sudbrack, "Im Spiegel der Zeit." On Harvey Cox and Pentecostalism see chapter 1, p. 2.

[45] *New Covenant*, 3/2, Aug. 1973, 26f.

[46] Cohen, "Renovación."

[47] Arceo, "Antorcha."

[48] *Introduction*, 10.

[49] Clark, *Building;* Connor, "Covenant"; Delespesse, *Church*. On the influence on existing convents see Cyprian, *New Covenant*, 2–5; Aymot, *New Covenant;* Reddy, *New Covenant*.

[50] McLeod, "Renew."

the joy of the ecumenical discovery, the theological differences between the different Catholic and Protestant churches have not been taken seriously enough, as Gelpi criticizes.[51]

The Catholics accept the fact that this revival has its roots outside the Catholic church. Though O'Connor does not allow any doubts on his Catholic orthodoxy, he answers the question of whether the Holy Spirit may conceivably be more at work in the classical Pentecostal churches than in that church which generally has accepted to be the most authentic church, as follows: "This may be God's way of demonstrating to members of the Church that He alone is sovereign Lord, and that all institutions and hierarchies on earth, even in the Church, are nothing but instruments and ministers . . . We need to have it demonstrated for us that God's action transcends the action of the Church."[52]

In contrast to the Protestant marginalization of the Pentecostal revival ninety years ago, and to the occasional social disqualifications of the renewal movement within Protestant churches today, the Bishops' Conference of the Catholic church in the USA has rather friendly relations with Catholic Pentecostalism. The bishops say: The movement has theologically legitimate reasons for its existence, and rests on a solid biblical basis. There are abuses here and there, but the movement as a whole should not be hindered. "Prudent priests" should accompany the groups and help them to maintain the impetus which they have received from the classical Pentecostal churches, without accepting their mistakes. Understandably an observer mockingly criticizes the bishops for preferring "tamed charismatics" to the revolutionary Berrigans.[53] Yet that might be a shortsighted judgment.

One thing is certain: the Catholic church (at least in Latin America but possibly also elsewhere) has only two choices: Either become a ghetto church by holding on to out-dated hierarchical and liturgical structures, or take on elements from the popular oral religion of Pentecostalism. The latter has of course happened in the setting up of "base communities" and in the giving of responsibility to lay leaders, the so-called "delegados de la palabra de Dios." That these "base communities" are a genuine Catholic form of Pentecostalism is obvious to any unbiased observer, even if this is not everywhere recognized. But they will also pose a number of problems. As in the case of the communists in the former Democratic Republic of Germany, so the Catholic church, too, will be confronted by a grass-roots base which will claim, "We are the church." A centrally-administered, monolithic Catholic church is no longer viable. The choice is clear: Either the Vatican will accept that it is a servant to the people of God, and that its hierarchy cannot in the long run continue to produce dogmas and moral decrees which people do not understand; or it will run out of funds and of people. The latter would not mean that the Vatican will disappear, but that it would sink into insignificance, for it cannot defend its

---

[51] Gelpi, *Piety*, 61–97.
[52] O'Connor, *Pentecost in the Catholic Church*, 28f.
[53] Weber, Karl, "Amerika."

monopoly with the Swiss guard. The alternative is a Vatican which is a real enabler, a *"pastor pastorum,"* a spokesman (or perhaps even a spokeswoman) for the convictions, aspirations and longings of the Catholic people of God.

Catholic Pentecostals—Ecumenical or Denominational?

I am sorry that I have to conclude the section on the Catholic renewal movement on a somewhat critical note. The renewal movement in the Catholic church, or "Catholic Pentecostals" as they called themselves at the beginning, started—like the Pentecostal movement itself—as an ecumenical renewal movement. The prayer meetings were ecumenical, for example, as I have demonstrated in chapter 2 (pp. 6–15). Important initiatives came from those prayer meetings. But perhaps by 1980 this ecumenical spirit had waned. Catholics and Protestants had organized their own denominational prayer groups, and some of them had become new Pentecostal churches, as we shall see later.

The Roman Catholic priest Peter Hocken detected this shift at an early stage in his painstaking research on the beginning of the charismatic renewal in England.[54] In contrast to most writers on the baptism of the Spirit, Hocken has seen in this crisis experience a *cognitive* element. The fact that people from evangelical to Catholic backgrounds, from conservative to liberal theological persuasion, have undergone an experience which they perceived to be identical, asks for a new look at our received theologies.

This was certainly the case for the ecumenical Pentecostal pioneer David Du Plessis. Du Plessis correctly saw that Pentecostals are not simply to be understood as the left wing of Protestantism. There are too many Catholic elements in their history and spirituality. Therefore it is foolish—in the opinion of Du Plessis—to exclude either the World Council of Churches or Rome from the sphere of the Spirit's visitation.[55]

It is, however, true that neither Pentecostals nor mainline churches are equipped to deal with the theological queries which arise from such an observation. Hocken writes:

> While there was a genuine communion in the Spirit between the Spirit-baptized, there was not a common understanding of the movement and of its purpose in God's sight. The possibility of a common understanding was dependent on the participants being willing to allow their received theologies, especially their ecclesiologies, to be challenged and expanded in common fidelity to the grace of baptism in the Spirit and in parallel fidelity to the work of God at the heart of each tradition.[56]

---

[54] Hocken, *Streams.*
[55] Hocken, *Streams,* quotes Du Plessis (p. 129 from a tape). Pentecostals "have denied being Protestants," they have much in common with Roman Catholics (*Elim Evangel* 10 March 1962, 146; *Elim Evangel* 29 June 1963, 402) Hocken, *Streams,* 146.
[56] Hocken, *Streams,* 178f.

Hocken's hermeneutical approach can be defended as Roman Catholic. But in the context in which he presents his findings this hermeneutic can also be called Pentecostal, Protestant or Anglican. In fact it reveals a critical edge in relation to *all* ecclesiologies, including the Roman Catholic.

Thus Peter Hocken sees the uniqueness of the charismatic renewal in the fact that for the first time since the Reformation, an ecumenical grass-roots movement has emerged which has crossed the frontiers between evangelicals and Catholics. This indeed is of great significance. The basis of this ecumenical approach is the fact that Christians have discovered a common experience, which is at the heart of their spirituality—and this in spite of their differing theologies and interpretations of this experience.

However, the charismatic movement has developed in other directions. Having failed to throw the baptism in the Spirit out of their churches altogether, denominational theologians are busy on all sides proving that it can be "contained" within the traditions of their denomination. And it is perhaps right that they try to do so, because it is always easier to accept something new by showing that it is in fact not that new. Proof of this process is Kilian McDonnell's massive three volume collection of one hundred church statements on the charismatic renewal.[57]

These signs of acceptance and integration are encouraging. But if this work is of the Spirit, as its adherents believe, then *it is also of the Spirit that it began as an ecumenical movement*. A recapturing of this original ecumenical spirit might lead us to discover new hermeneutical possibilities for the new crises of our day. In other words, the baptism of the Spirit introduces a critical and cognitive element into the liberal, evangelical, and Catholic camps. Evangelicals discover that it is possible to be a committed and Spirit-filled believer without accepting evangelical theological propositions. Critical liberals discover that the oral Pentecostal tradition is a potent vehicle for communicating important ecumenical and social insights in a milieu which the liberals can never reach. Catholics discover that it may be possible to be a fully-fledged Catholic without accepting the infallibility of the Petrine ministry. Protestants discover that Roman Catholic priests take Scripture and in fact the Reformation tradition just as seriously as they do.

In further publications Hocken[58] has developed his thinking by calling for the avoidance of two extremes: on the one hand, the non-denominational "home church" which breaks with the past and starts anew, and on the other a charismatic renewal which leaves everything as it is, does not ask any questions but just gives one's own denomination a few good songs, some warm prayer meetings and speaking in tongues. Hocken advocates a third way. The renewal is a new thing, and it calls for a dual loyalty from its members: loyalty to one's denomination *and* loyalty to the ecumenicity of the Spirit.

---

[57] McDonnell, *Presence.*
[58] Hocken, *One Lord;* idem, "Charismatic"; idem, "Renewal."

Cecil M. Robeck comes to very similar conclusions from the Pentecostal side.

> Our best confessional formulations of the Truth and the praxis of our churches which we often guard jealously, are in some ways ultimately marred or distorted. Herein lies the potential for pain . . . Sometimes in dialogue, certain people or groups, blinded by their own *apparent* success, will assume that they should argue from a position of "strength" or that they must have the upper hand. They may seat themselves at the head of the dialogue table, thereby exhibiting an air of superiority. They may attempt to manipulate the agenda to serve their own exclusivist ecclesiastical interests, oppose the Truth rather than submit to it, engage in arrogant or triumphalistic behavior which consummates in a form of theological imperialism or practical tyranny, or demand changes in the actions of their dialogue partners before dialogue has even begun. This behavior ignores the teachings of Jesus (Luke 14:7–11) who rightfully sits at the head of the table. Vulnerability of one dialogue partner without a similar openness and respect by the other actually nullifies the dialogue process, sabotages genuine communication, and dampens any authentic quest for Truth . . . An early revelation of the dialogue process is that most of us work with relatively *exclusive* definitions of the Church. We standardize our experiences of God and make them normative. We then judge the experiences of others according to those norms . . . Luke recorded that Jesus' disciples were proud, perhaps even arrogant in the exclusivity of their right to use the name of Jesus. On one occasion they triumphantly declared that they zealously stopped an "outsider" from doing so, thereby "safeguarding" the use of that name. Jesus admonished them (Luke 9:50).[59]

How far Robeck's advice has been followed in Pentecostal circles will occupy us later. For the time being we deal with the renewal movement in the Catholic church, and here it has to be said that the critical-ecumenical function of this movement has been largely lost. As an example I mention the important dissertation by Lucida Schmieder,[60] written under the supervision of Professor Heribert Mühlen in Paderborn.

Lucida Schmieder is a Benedictine missionary sister. After her studies she worked in Brazil and later in Germany. She traces the tradition of Spirit baptism to the revival movements in the sixteenth and seventeenth centuries, forwarded by such leaders as Huldreich Zwingli, the anabaptist Balthasar Hubmaier, and the spiritualist Kaspar Schwenckfeld. She does not claim historical interaction, but shows parallel structures of thought and experience. Then she goes on to discuss Wesley (without mentioning his Catholic roots) and the American and German Holiness movement in detail. For our purposes the fourth part of her book is most important. Here she tries to present the renewal movement as good Catholic spirituality, from which neither secular nor ecclesiastical authorities have anything to fear. One gets the impression from Lucida Schmieder's book that this new spirituality does not change any

---

[59] Robeck, "Du Plessis." See also idem, "Growing."
[60] Schmieder, *Geisttaufe*.

of our theological melodies, but it changes the rhythm and sometimes the key. It does not change the Catholic church, but it lights it up. It does not change its ministry, but it makes it more credible. It does not change its ecumenical commitment, but it makes it more alive. How far this is an expression of church politics I cannot judge. (This presentation now largely corresponds to the facts, at least in relation to the charismatic movement in the West.)

Thus Schmieder marginalizes the ecumenical and critical beginnings of charismatic Christianity; for instance the theologically explosive significance of women, blacks, the poor, and lay people in the inaugural years of classical Pentecostalism. Coming from Brazil, it is astonishing that Schmieder does not consider Paolo Freire, Leonardo Boff, or Helder Câmara, with their interpretation of Pentecostal popular religion, and their emphasis on an ecumenical understanding of the Catholic church. It is astonishing that in her work the Holy Spirit speaks eloquently on private and religious experiences, but is equally eloquently silent on the great problems of oppression, injustice, hunger, and discrimination. However, it must be said that her work represents the majority of the present-day Catholic renewal movement, in spite of some critical voices, such as those of Peter Hocken and others.

That there is also another way of dealing with Catholic Pentecostalism has been demonstrated by the Catholic Sister Mary Hall. In her *Quest for a Liberated Christian* she compares a man, a movement, and a mission. The man is Helder Câmara, the movement Catholic Pentecostalism, and the mission the Catholic schools in Pakistan where she had worked as a missionary sister. In dealing with Catholic Pentecostalism, she highlights its liberating but also its domesticating potential.

We move now from our overview of the Catholic renewal movement to the subversive work of the Spirit in another arena, namely that of the official Roman Catholic/Pentecostal dialogue.

The Vatican/Pentecostal Dialogue

Neither the secular nor the religious press, nor in fact the many Pentecostal periodicals, have reported one of the most important events in the religious scene of our century; that is, the Catholic/Pentecostal dialogue which took place from 1972 onward in four quinquennia. One of the reasons for this silence may be that the Pentecostal participants have been afraid to talk about it. Sometimes they have even asked that their identity be hidden. The American Assemblies of God put the spanner in wherever it could, and discouraged its own executive members from participation. "Why this refusal to participate?" asks Jerry Sandidge. It seems, he writes, to have been due to the involvement of David Du Plessis. Du Plessis was "still an embarrassment" to the Assemblies of God.[61] "So the Pentecostal team entered the 1977 Dialogue

---

[61] Sandidge, *Dialogue (1977–1982)* I, 366. Carmichael, William, Letter, 30.6.1982. Thomas Zimmerman, General Superintendent of the Assemblies of God,

session and the second quinquennial series with very little support from the leaders of the major classical Pentecostal denominations."[62] Du Plessis tried to put the dialogue on the agenda of the World Pentecostal Conference in whose beginning he had played a leading role. It was turned down.[63] The Advisory Committee of the World Pentecostal Conference advised its members not to participate in the dialogue.[64]

Nevertheless the dialogue took place. Its reports[65] and a number of highly scholarly analyses[66] are available in print. The time has come to tell this story. One of the most courageous ecumenists, the Assemblies of God professor of theology Cecil M. Robeck, says:

> Not to carry reports of the international Roman Catholic/Pentecostal Dialogue in Pentecostal periodicals may be good Pentecostal politics. But the question needs to be asked whether it helps or hinders the kingdom of God. Pentecostals and Roman Catholics owe it to themselves to learn as much as they can about one another since they both claim to be part of the same Body of Christ. Pentecostals have hardly begun to realize the enormity of change that has taken place among Roman Catholics since Vatican II. For Pentecostals to continue to respond to Roman Catholics with descriptions based upon time-worn stereotypes or ungracious over-generalizations is to insist upon the continued presence of specks in Roman Catholic eyes without due consideration to the logs in Pentecostal eyes. To withhold information which might help to remove both specks and logs is to participate in the perpetuation of misunderstanding.[67]

The First Quinquennium, 1972–76

The Catholic/Pentecostal dialogue was not concerned "with the problems of imminent structural union, although of course its object [was] with Christians coming closer together in prayer and common witness."[68] After a number of preliminary meetings in which David Du Plessis had an important hand, the dialogue sessions took place in Zurich (1972), Rome (1973), Craheim, Germany (1974), Venice (1975) and Rome (1976). The participants

---

was personally opposed to the dialogue (Sandidge, *Dialogue (1977–1982)* I, 331) but seemed to reconsider his position when Du Plessis gave up his leading role (Sandidge, *Dialogue (1977–1982)* I, 365).

[62] Sandidge, *Dialogue (1977–1982)* I, 176.

[63] Ibid., I, 333.

[64] Ibid., I, 175. Synan, Letter to Robert McAlister (Oklahoma City, Okla.), 5.1.1977 (copy was sent to Du Plessis). Sandidge, *Dialogue (1977–1982)* I, 324.

[65] The final reports from all three quinquennia are published in *Pneuma* 12/2, Fall 1990. A good overview in McDonnell, "Improbable Conversations," 20–31, and idem, "Five Defining Issues," 110–21. See also the two Catholic dissertations: Terrance Robert Crowe, *Pentecostal Unity*, and Lee, Paul D., *Ecclesiology;* also Hocken, "Ecumenical Dialogue"; Robeck, "Catholics."

[66] In particular Bittlinger, *Papst;* Sandidge, *Dialogue (1977–1982);* Robeck, "Pentecostals and Ecumenism"; Sandidge, "Dialogue."

[67] Robeck, "Specks," 82.

[68] Point 4 of the report of the first quinquennium, *Pneuma* 12/2, Fall 1990, 85.

included a broad spectrum of Catholic scholars and charismatic and Pentecostal leaders (although not including representatives from the Third World). The resulting talks represent the only dialogue undertaken by the Roman Catholic church with an unofficial movement[69]—and indeed, one represented not by its official leaders but by the personal friends of one catalytic leader (David Du Plessis). In a sense this early stage closely resembles the beginning of the World Council of Churches. I shall always remember how Visser t'Hooft told me that the World Council of Churches was originally a group of friends ("an old-boys' network") who decided to do something about the disunity of the churches. That is why the official documents do not tell the real story. What happened *between* the sessions, over the meals, at worship services, in personal conversation, was probably more important for the change of climate than the official proceedings. Bittlinger's work has been a very important window into this process, because he has the rare gift for documenting such "unofficial" but nevertheless highly important events.

The topics discussed were "Baptism in the Spirit," the relationship between "Receiving of the Spirit and Christian Regeneration," "Spiritual Gifts," "Public Worship," "Discernment," and "Prayer and Praise."

The reports clearly show the different theological starting points of the three parties. At the outset, these differences were diffused by a long historical introduction into mysticism. However, David J. Du Plessis told the committee that the study of mysticism of the past was not of particular value.

> One can find very little in ancient writings that was written by those who had the experience, and we have to rely on secondary information from those who wrote about the experience of others, yet not knowing what it was all about . . . The study of mediaeval charismatic phenomena through secondary sources is as futile and unrewarding as an attempt by a young man to make love to his sweetheart through the efforts of an interpreter.[70]

Perhaps Du Plessis was also reflecting here on the difficulties with interpreters.[71] Although Du Plessis does not do justice with his statement to solid historical research, he expressed a fundamental insight of a genuine Pentecostal. It is this: there are things which can only be communicated very incompletely through propositional language. Religious language—and theological language—is more an art than a science. It is not for nothing that our departments of theology are in Faculties of Art.

As those who had experienced the Spirit, it was the declared purpose of participating classical Pentecostals to testify to their experience, sometimes with remarkable success; on the other hand, their attempts at scholarly language

---

[69] Sandidge, *Dialogue (1977–1982)* I, 384. "In retrospect it is amazing that an official Church office would agree to meetings with an unofficial group of Christians described by one participant as 'David Du Plessis and his friends'" (Hocken, "Extraordinary," 204).

[70] Du Plessis, "Background," 178.

[71] Bittlinger, *Papst*, 356–57, note 5. Also Sandidge, *Dialogue (1977–1982)* I, 273.

met only with mild smiles from the Catholic dialogue partners.[72] (Note that this has changed in the meantime. Pentecostals have developed a rigorous scholarly tradition; whether that is to their profit is quite another question.)

These historical excursions, however, were only preliminaries. The real differences appeared when the exegetical methods of biblical studies were displayed. For classical Pentecostalism the Acts of the Apostles are the normative document of the normative church. The Secretariat and some of the charismatic scholars, on the other hand, used the critical tools of biblical scholarship.[73] Thus the latter accepted a pluralistic understanding of the church, of the Holy Spirit and of theology in general, while the classical Pentecostals regarded the pneumatology of Luke as the one and only true understanding of the Spirit, under which the other pneumatologies of the Bible had to be subsumed.

It is astonishing that the dialogue did not break up at this point, and that a second quinquennium was arranged, to which only the representatives of the Secretariat and classical Pentecostals would be invited.

More important than the reports of the dialogue is the fact that it took place. Classical Pentecostals had always said: Pentecost is an experience, not a doctrine. Now the Catholics had had the same experience. What did this say about the Roman Catholic church? Originally the Pentecostals had expected the Spirit-filled Catholics to leave the Catholic church and become members of a Pentecostal church. The Assemblies of God minister David Wilkerson had predicted in a vision great persecutions for the Catholic Pentecostals which would force them to abandon their church. The assumed options were: either they would leave the Catholic church and become a kind of classical Pentecostal, or the Holy Spirit would leave them.[74]

Such an "either or" became impossible for the Pentecostals who had taken part in the dialogue. Du Plessis rejected Wilkerson's vision,[75] and R. Douglas Wead, a former Assemblies of God minister, has since described in a disturbingly honest way the process of his own ecumenical education in his contact with Catholic Pentecostals.[76]

The Second Quinquennium (1977–1982)

We are given insight into the second quinquennium by a superb work in two volumes by Jerry L. Sandidge. Sandidge was an extraordinary man. Born in 1939 in Tulsa, Oklahoma, his "spiritual roots" went down in a small Pentecostal church in his home city. The only pastor he had as a child and teenager was a man who never finished the sixth grade. In spite of his lack of education and training for the ministry, the Rev. Johnny "Pappy" Stubblefield was "a true

---

[72] Hocken, "Extraordinary."

[73] Sandidge, *Dialogue (1977–1982)* I, 185. A thorough discussion of Pentecostal hermeneutics in chapter 23, pp. 307–25.

[74] Wilkerson, *Vision;* Sandidge, *Dialogue (1977–1982)* I, 400, 419.

[75] Du Plessis, "Persecution"; Martin, R., "Vision."

[76] Wead, *Charismatics.*

man of God."[77] Sandidge attended Central Bible College, Springfield, Missouri (the Bible School of the Assemblies of God) where he earned a BA in Bible (1961) and an M.A. in Religious Education (1964). In the spring of 1962 he served as the photographer for an archaeological expedition to Tell Dothan. He served as minister in several Assemblies of God churches, from 1966–1971 in their International Headquarters for the Sunday School and youth department. He earned an M.Ed. in guidance and counseling from the University of Missouri, Columbia, Missouri.

In 1971 he and his wife were approved for foreign missionary service with the Assemblies of God. They served the Assemblies of God in Belgium for ten years, two of which he acted as Dean of Students at the Continental Bible College, St. Pieters-Leeuw (1972–74), and for eight as founder and director of University Action, Leuven (1974–1982) (a kind of ecumenical university chaplaincy). In 1976 he completed the M.R.Sc. degree from the Catholic University of Leuven and in 1977 a special PhB from the Higher Institute of Philosophy in Leuven.[78]

He then embarked on a most ambitious program; namely, on a Ph.D. dissertation at Leuven in which he described and analyzed the Catholic/Pentecostal dialogue—especially the second quinquennium. That an Assemblies of God minister receives the greater part of his education from a Belgian Catholic university is in itself remarkable (although he was not the only one; there were a number of Pentecostals studying at Leuven). During his time there he was introduced by Du Plessis into the Catholic/Pentecostal dialogue and was subsequently given access to all confidential documents of the dialogue at the Secretariat in Rome. Du Plessis also allowed him free use of his extensive personal files (now in the David Du Plessis Center in Pasadena, California).

During the second quinquennium Sandidge read a paper on "A Pentecostal Perspective on Mary,"[79] a remarkable piece of research accomplished in the face of serious illness and hospitalization for a throat cancer. On the basis of unconfirmed and highly exaggerated press reports on the discussion on Mary during the dialogue, Sandidge lost his financial support from the Assemblies of God (although not his ministerial credentials). His wife stepped in and provided for the family;[80] he remained undeterred in bringing his work to a conclusion. During the years 1985 to 1987 he served as Assistant Professor of Church History at the School of Theology and Missions, Oral Roberts University, Tulsa, Oklahoma. Following several years on the faculty at CBN University, Sandidge accepted a pastoral call at Evangel Temple, Springfield, Missouri, until his untimely death in 1992. I follow closely Sandidge's work.

The discussion on the second quinquennium centered on such questions as "Speaking in Tongues," "Faith and Experience," "Hermeneutics," "Healing,"

---

[77] Sandidge, *Dialogue (1977–1982)* I, v.
[78] Ibid., I, 284f.
[79] Ibid., II, 289–351. See also the following notes.
[80] Ibid., I, iii.

"The Church as a Worshipping Community," "Traditions and Tradition," and "Mary." The venues for the sessions were Rome (1977 and 1979); Venice (1980); Vienna, Austria (1981); and Collegeville, Minnesota (1982). Since I shall deal with hermeneutics and other issues mentioned in later chapters, I will highlight here only three controversial areas: (1) Mary, the mother of Jesus, (2) the place of women in the ministry, and (3) the Eucharist.

(1) Mary

Sandidge was asked to give the paper on Mary from the Pentecostal side. His first discovery was "a great dearth of material written by Pentecostals about Mary."[81] "In fact it could almost be said that we do not even have a 'view' of Mary, unless it would be in negative terms. i.e., those things which we universally do *not* believe about her."[82] So Sandidge read the Catholic mariological literature and commented upon it from a Pentecostal point of view. He was overwhelmed by the wealth of material and by the fact that there seemed to be a pluralistic approach to Mary in the Catholic church. "There is room for various theologies of Mary."[83] He then goes on to give the biblical and historical bases of Catholic Mariology, including the dogma on Immaculate Conception of 1854, clearly pointing out the differences between Pentecostals and Catholics. The press release stated: "The topic which was anticipated to be extremely controversial ended with deeper consensus than anticipated."[84] This phrasing was perhaps unfortunate, in view of the liveliness of discussion on Mary.[85]

Certainly Sandidge's paper indicated the areas of agreement (for instance the virgin birth), as well as a broad area where more understanding was possible. Sandidge showed in his paper a great sensitivity for the religious practice on Mary, and gave examples from the Pentecostal side where popular religion was practiced because of pastoral needs. However the outcome for Sandidge was a near catastrophe. The press titled their report: "Pentecostals and Catholics Agree on Mary."[86] On the basis of unconfirmed and faulty press reports the executive of the Assemblies of God "asked Sandidge to change the topic of his doctoral dissertation for the Catholic University of Leuven" (in spite of the fact that they had previously agreed to it) and to discontinue any involvement in the dialogue with Roman Catholics.[87]

---

[81] Ibid., II, 290.

[82] Ibid.

[83] McDonnell, "Protestants," 29, quoted by Sandidge, *Dialogue (1977–1982)* II, 293. There is also room for an evangelical Mariology in the Protestant churches. See my play *Mary, the Mother of Jesus* (written for a Swiss actress) and Hollenweger, "Ave Maria"; idem, "Devotion."

[84] Sandidge, *Dialogue (1977–1982)* I, 363.

[85] Ibid., I, 236ff.

[86] Ibid., I, 244, 336, 397.

[87] Correspondence between Assemblies of God executives and Sandidge in Sandidge, *Dialogue (1977–1982)* I, 340, 397.

It is of course one thing to criticize the Catholic church for its censuring of Catholic theologians such as Hans Küng and Leonardo Boff, and quite another to accept pioneering thought and action from one's own missionaries and theologians. I suppose however that by now the Assemblies of God regret their harsh action in relation to Sandidge, and more so in relation to Du Plessis.[88]

(2) The Place of Women in the Ministry

The Pentecostals, who in certain countries have women among their ministers, put this "hard question" to the Catholics: "Why is the ministry of women in the Roman Catholic church seemingly relegated to such archaic practices? Pentecostals believe in a valid ministry for laypersons. How does the Roman Catholic church address the issue of ministry for the 'grassroots,' the layperson?"[89] Sandidge does not record the answer of the Catholics except for noting the well-known Catholic theological definitions of ministry. On the other hand he reports on an interesting development in the British Pentecostal movement: "an appeal for a religious order of women to be raised up to minister to those in need," under the title "Pentecostal Nuns." This term is not one of derision, but is rather used positively "to suggest an order of women dedicated to the work of the Lord in the same way that today the Anglicans, Roman Catholics and Salvation Army have vast numbers of women filled with the Holy Ghost, dedicated to the vast area of social care."[90] Catholic influence?

(3) On the Eucharist

On this subject the Pentecostals put another "hard question" to the Catholics: "If the eucharist is the heart of worship, in the light of Acts 15:5–11 and 1 Cor 12:12–13 how can Roman Catholics in good conscience exclude anyone from the table of the Lord? Where in Scripture do you find justification to use the Lord's Table (the heart of worship) as a disciplinary tool, i.e., a closed table (cf. I Cor 11:2, 11:28, Mt. 26:25)?"[91] The Pentecostals were disturbed that they were not allowed to take part in the Catholic Eucharist, but Catholics "whose lives do not conform to the Gospel are admitted to the eucharist simply on the basis of their supposed Catholic faith."[92] Furthermore they asked: Is the "mediation of Christ" exclusive to Roman Catholic ecclesiology? Who and what are the "separated brethren?"[93]

---

[88] On Du Plessis see chapter 26, pp. 350–55.

[89] Sandidge, *Dialogue (1977–1982)* I, 260.

[90] Quy, "Nuns"; Sandidge, *Dialogue (1977–1982)* I, 435. More on women's ministry in the Pentecostal Movement in the chapter on ecclesiology, chapter 20, pp. 267f.

[91] Sandidge, *Dialogue (1977–1982)* I, 220.

[92] Ibid., I, 227.

[93] Ibid., I, 220.

Robert McAlister asked the pertinent question: "Why do you call us brethren and refuse to share the Table with us, hypocrites!"[94] "The Apostle Paul makes it very clear that our burden is not whether our brother or sister or some other denomination is worthy or not worthy of the Table of the Lord. He points out that our sole responsibility is examining ourselves."[95] In further discussion the Pentecostals confessed to a Zwinglian understanding of the Eucharist, rather than a Lutheran one.[96] However it is doubtful to me whether they—or in fact most people who use the term "Zwinglian"—were aware of the transubstantiational aspect of Zwingli's Eucharist (transubstantiation of the *people* into the body of Christ) which has left deep traces in Anglican theology and liturgy.[97] It should be noted that the Pentecostal position on this was not as strong as it looks here, for later in the dialogue they had a heated debate among themselves on the Lord's Supper. "The Roman Catholic delegation sat quietly while the inner-dialogue was in progress."[98] William Carmichael came to this conclusion: "It is true (and a sad fact) that there is often sharp disagreement within the Pentecostal tradition. We are indeed a 'mixed bag.' "[99]

The Third (1985–89) and Fourth Quinquennium

The onset of the *third quinquennium* was postponed until 1985, in part because of the death of Popes Paul VI and John Paul I in rapid succession. The Pentecostal team was reorganized and included this time a number of official delegates.[100] Also included were two female delegates, a black and a Mexican

---

[94] McAlister letter to William Carmichael, Rio de Janeiro, 24 November 1980; Sandidge, *Dialogue (1977–1982)* I, 225.

[95] Sandidge, *Dialogue (1977–1982)* I, 225.

[96] Ibid., I, 226.

[97] See on this Hollenweger, "Einfluss." See also the Jesuit Albert Ziegler (*Zwingli*). According to Ziegler the reason for the reformation was the inflexibility of the Catholic hierarchy which treated symptoms instead of going to the root cause of the plight in the church. He draws explicit parallels with today's Catholicism and points out that the reformation did not start with a controversy on fundamental truths but in the realm of practical Christianity (celibacy of priests, the Bible in the language of the people, changes in the liturgy) and sees in Zwingli's reformation an "Ecclesial Basic Community" not unlike present-day communities in Latin America. He describes Zwingli's eucharist as ecumenical. There is room for Zwingli's eucharist in the Catholic Church. Ziegler deals with Zwingli's ecumenical and conciliar understanding of the universal church, which he calls "a very topical insight." The ministry of the Pope in its present historical form is not the only possible catholic form of a Petrine ministry. There are other, more ecumenical and more conciliar forms of expressing the unity of the church in the Catholic tradition. Therefore he invites his Catholic colleagues to read Zwingli ecumenically. The same invitation must be addressed to the reformed and Pentecostal theologians.

[98] Sandidge, *Dialogue (1977–1982)* I, 232.

[99] Carmichael, William, Letter, 22 Oct. 1980; McAlister, Letter, 30 December 1980. Sandidge, *Dialogue (1977–1982)* I, 232.

[100] Sandidge mentions three denominations that sent official delegates: the In-

Pentecostal (a Pentecostal and a Catholic), and in general a broad spectrum of younger Pentecostal leaders and scholars, including representatives from Eastern Europe. David Du Plessis stepped aside to allow for a transfer of leadership to his younger brother Justus Du Plessis. The topics and places of the dialogue were: Riano, Italy (1985): "Communion of the Saints"; Sierra Madre, California (1986): "The Holy Spirit and the New Testament Vision of Koinonia"; Venice, Italy (1987): "Koinonia, Church, and Sacraments"; Emmetten, Switzerland (1988): "Koinonia and Baptism"; and Rome (1989): the writing of the Final Report.

Since I have no direct information on the exchanges during these sessions, the discussion which appeared after the dialogue must serve as an overall conclusion.

There is to be a *fourth quinquennium* under the new chairmanship of Cecil M. Robeck, Jr., an Assemblies of God minister and professor of ecumenics and church history at Fuller Theological Seminary, Pasadena. The official topic is "Evangelism and Mission" but the *real* issue is the charge of proselytism,[101] made by Catholics especially against the Latin American Pentecostals (see p. 180, "The Style of the Dialogue"). Cecil M. Robeck's suggestion of Santiago, Chile as the venue for the dialogue session on proselytism—because the issue is particularly important for Latin American Catholics and Pentecostals and because of the deep ecumenical commitment of Chilean Pentecostals (chapter 27, pp. 367–71)—was turned down, not by the Pentecostals, but by the Catholics, who felt this was "not the right moment for such a dialogue." This is in my opinion an important missed opportunity to get to the heart of the issues between Pentecostals and Catholics.

Appraisal and Discussion

Together with the three final reports of the three quinquennia, *Pneuma* also published a number of reactions from leading Pentecostals and other theologians.[102] All of them expressed their appreciation of the report. It is a miracle that in spite of the fact that at times the dialogue "verged on the comic,"[103] the report appeared in the end. One should also not underrate the many technical problems which jeopardized the project. These problems included the following: The Pentecostals had to pay their own travel and hotel costs, which of course made for a selection of the participants. The Pentecostals

---

ternational Church of the Foursquare Gospel, the Church of God (Cleveland), and the Church of God of Prophecy (Cleveland). Sandidge, *Dialogue (1977–1982)* I, 382. Hocken mentions in addition the Broederschap van Pinkstergemeenten in Holland and the United Evangelical-Pentecostal Church of Poland. Hocken, "Extraordinary," 205, note 11.

[101] "Proselytism" is a term which never appears in Pentecostal literature.

[102] *Pneuma* 12/2, Fall 1990, contains responses from David K. Bernard, Fr. Frank Colborn, Fr. Donald L. Gelpi, S. J., J. L. Hall, Walter J. Hollenweger, David A. Hubbard, Harold D. Hunter, Leonard Lovett, Jesse Miranda, Fr. Thomas P. Rausch, S. J., Vinson Synan, George Vandervelde, Jakob Zopfi.

[103] Hocken, "Extraordinary," 202.

were also in constant fear—at least during the first two quinquennia—of being harassed by their denominational "popes" at home. Finally, because of illness and other problems the composition of the dialogue group changed all the time; sometimes nobody except Du Plessis knew who was a member of the group and who was not.[104]

In the introduction to the final report it is stated that the theme *koinonia* was chosen because the subject "communion of saints" emerged from the discussion on Mary; because of the importance of the concept in other bilateral dialogues; and because of the theme's fruitfulness in reflections about ecclesiastical self-understanding taking place in many Christian churches and communions.

On the *interpretation of Scripture* a significant divergence emerged:

> In Roman Catholicism the interpretation of Scripture goes on daily in the lives of the faithful at many levels, such as in the family, in the pulpit, and in the classroom. The whole body of the faithful, who have an anointing that comes from the Holy One cannot err in matters of belief (cf. I John 2:20, 27). Roman Catholics hold that the teaching office of the Church is not above the Word of God, but serves it, teaching only what has been handed on, listening to it devoutly, guarding it scrupulously and explaining it faithfully by divine commission and with the help of the Holy Spirit (*Dei Verum*, 10).[105]

If the Catholics had left it at that one would have to admit that they have a much more Pentecostal approach to the interpretation of Scripture than the Pentecostals, for Pentecostals "look with skepticism on any claim that the whole body of the faithful cannot err in matters of belief."[106]

This of course has to do with the thorny question of *papal infallibility*. David Du Plessis had already tried to defuse the issue by stating in a sermon that God was "using the doctrine of the infallibility of the people to realize Vatican Council II and also to allow for the charismatic renewal within Catholicism by virtue of Pope John XXIII's prayer for a new Pentecost."[107] This statement appeared in the press as "Protestant Evangelical Says Papal Infallibility is True."[108] It took all of Du Plessis's wit to set the record straight.[109] During the second quinquennium the Catholics put the following "hard question" to the Pentecostals: "When Pentecostal ministers exercise their authority and speak the truth, submission is expected. Who decides and how is it decided what truth is in the case? If the answer is 'the biblical message', who decides among the various interpretations of the biblical text?"[110]

---

[104] Ibid., 202–3.

[105] Final Report, point 25, *Pneuma* 12/2, Fall 1990, 122.

[106] Ibid., point 26, 122.

[107] Du Plessis newsletter, "A Season for Peace and Praise," 1976–77; Sandidge, *Dialogue (1977–1982)* I, 176 (Sandidge discusses here Du Plessis' misunderstanding of papal infallibility).

[108] Sandidge, *Dialogue (1977–1982)* I, 176.

[109] Ibid., I, 177.

[110] Ibid., I, 259.

Anybody knowledgeable about Pentecostalism will have to agree that this question is unanswerable for Pentecostals, which of course does not mean that the Roman Catholic position is the solution to the dilemma.

In the final report this complex issue was summarized as follows:

> Pentecostals believe that church order demanded by *koinonia* is not satisfactorily expressed in some important aspects of Roman Catholic ecclesiology. Even within the context of collegiality, examples which seem to bear this out include those passages where it is stated that "the episcopal order is the subject of the supreme and full power over the universal Church," and even more importantly, when it is stated that "the Roman Pontiff has full, supreme, and universal power over the Church", which "he can always exercise . . . freely" (*Lumen Gentium*, 22). On the whole, Pentecostals propose that presbyterial and/or congregational ecclesial models express better the mutuality or reciprocity demanded by "*koinonia.*"[111]

That in my opinion is a very tame Pentecostal protest. A Roman pontiff who has "full, supreme, and universal power over the Church" is in my opinion probably the greatest hindrance to growth and spirituality in the Catholic church and to ecumenical fellowship with other Christians. This is realized by many Catholics. They oppose the "full, supreme, and universal power of the pontiff over the Church," both in theory and in practice, and they do not cease to be Catholics (in this Hans Küng is not alone). Some Catholic researchers have told me that only Protestants still believe in the infallibility of the Pope. One would have wished a more thorough discussion on this great obstacle to ecumenism and on this controversy *within* the Catholic church. That does not mean that there is no room for a "Petrine ministry," but there is no room for a juridicial power for the pontiff. Perhaps Pentecostals did not dare to tackle this point because they know only too well that they themselves have become very clerical and that some Pentecostal pastors or executives have powers which would make the Pope envious. But would that not be a case for mutual repentance?

Another bone of contention was *baptism*. This issue was included in the final report "because of the difficulty which baptism and the practice of baptism have in our dialogue."[112] Jakob Zopfi, a Swiss Pentecostal and editor of *World Pentecost*, comments in his evaluation of the dialogue on the sentence "Pentecostals and Roman Catholics differ in that Roman Catholics understand baptism to be a sacrament."[113] He says: "This one issue makes all the difference in the world, the difference being that the infant baptism is a dead baptism, and dead baptism leads to a dead organization."[114] This is an extraordinary statement, for all of a sudden the vital difference between Catholics and Pentecostals is no longer a *Pentecostal proprium* but the Baptist understanding

---

[111] Point 87 of the final report, *Pneuma* 12/2, Fall 1990, 135.
[112] *Pneuma* 12/2, Fall 1990, 126; Sandidge, *Dialogue (1977–1982)* I, 129.
[113] Final Report, *Pneuma* 12/2, Fall 1990, point 41, 125.
[114] Zopfi, "Candid Thoughts," 182.

of baptism (it is doubtful whether Baptists would express it so harshly). I wonder what Zopfi has to say about the Methodist church or the Chilean Pentecostal movement (chapter 10, pp. 117–31), which are far larger than his own Swiss Pentecostal Mission and which practice infant baptism? Are they dead organizations?

The difference on baptism found its way also into the final report: "For all Pentecostals there is no coming to Christ apart from a person's turning away from sin in repentance. . . Baptism is withheld until after a person's conscious conversion."[115] Here the question is: What constitutes a conversion (see chapter 19, pp. 246–57)? A turning away from the sin of violence and racism, from the sin of greed and lust for power? If that is part of "turning away from sin," the Pentecostals would have to withhold baptism from a considerable number of their members. But if it is not part of conversion, what kind of conversion is this? Or to take the example of Frank Chikane (chapter 5, pp. 48–50): who has turned away from sin and experienced a conscious conversion—the Pentecostal torturer, or the tortured Frank Chikane, both, or neither of them?

Of course I do not oppose the practice of adult baptism, but, if "conscious conversion" is a pre-condition for baptism, the term "conversion" must either be so watered down as to make it virtually meaningless or else—and this would be the way forward—adult baptism must not be administered on the basis of a person's turning away from sin, but on the basis of his or her confession, in hope and faith that Christ *begins* a new work in him or her. This would render adult baptism much less substantially different from infant baptism.[116]

The Style of the Dialogue

A very interesting comment comes from Jesse Miranda, District Superintendent of the Pacific Latin American District of the Assemblies of God, who is pleading for an understanding of pluralism within the global village. There is a spiritual revolution going on in Latin America, says Miranda, but "it has been ignored and remains massively invisible. Increasingly, classical Pentecostals are becoming middle-class and leaving their counterparts searching for new ways and paradigms for a biblical expression of Christian unity of *koinonia.*"[117] Leonard Lovett, a black Pentecostal, brings the whole debate into focus. The final report suffers not by what it states but by "its glaring omissions." In particular, it suffers from a lack of Third World participation.

What an opportunity to have engaged the issues of sharing with regard to power, poverty and powerlessness. The document tends to dwell too much on issues

---

[115] Final Report, point 47, *Pneuma* 12/2, Fall 1990, 127.

[116] Particularly important on this is the Yugoslavian Pentecostal minister Miroslav Volf; see on him the chapter on ecclesiology, chapter 20, p. 261.

[117] Miranda, "A Response," quote 171.

which address inward piety with little or no concern for concreteness. Any discussion about the Incarnation that does not address concrete ways it can be realized within the blood, guts and tissues of society is meaningless (points 14–16). What about the sharing of power within the usual elitist ecclesiastical hierarchy of the church in which major decisions affecting the destiny of many are usually "handed down"? What about the sharing of wealth by the Vatican hierarchy in Third World countries in concrete ways other than "bricks and mortar"? Who is to caution Pentecostals about their new obsession with buildings, prestige, power and those who have bought the "prosperity" message with its cultural baggage [see chapter 18, pp. 228–43] and by the very presuppositions it embraces indicts Third World persons whose poverty is for the most part cultural? The breaking of bread in Acts 2:42 and the sharing of "all things in common" is restricted if it is viewed only in terms of sacramentalism. Both Catholics and Pentecostals alike have the opportunity during this final quarter of the twentieth century to begin the crucial task of sharing "all things in common" beyond its "sacred institutional walls." The conditions are ripe all over the world for such engagement.[118]

According to Lovett the final report on *Koinonia* completely omits such emphases.

All of this represents—as I have stated elsewhere—"The Koinonia of the Establishment."[119] This ethos emerged from the one-sided composition of both dialogue groups, although unsuccessful attempts were made to secure more Third World participation.[120] Miriam Castiglione, a critical observer of the Italian scene, states in another context that ecumenical neo-Pentecostalism is an attempt to defend Christian ghettoism and to avoid the more difficult debate with non-Christians and the issues of this world.[121]

Sandidge also realized this deficiency, and the fact that it goes beyond the composition of the dialogue group. What is needed, he notes, is the inclusion of other than Western styles of discussion.[122] "The pre-literary element of Pentecostalism needs to be a part of the dialogue."[123]

The dialogue seemed to be "tilted" in favour of the Roman Catholic approach to theology, i.e., discursive, scientific, and intellectual approaches. There were "Pentecostal" elements within the dialogue but little place was given to oral or narrative theology, testimony, spiritual experience validating truth, and the exercise of spiritual gifts as a context for theological exchange.[124]

---

[118] Lovett, "Response," 169.

[119] "The Catholics and the Pentecostals of the West have met (with a few exceptions) to talk about koinonia." Hollenweger, "Koinonia," 156.

[120] Sandidge, *Dialogue (1977–1982)* I, 268, 327. Bittlinger discusses this aspect passim and quotes Du Plessis: "The Catholics bring their top scholars, and we should invite Negroes and women?" Bittlinger, *Papst*, 447, note 1.

[121] Castiglione, *Italia.*

[122] Sandidge, *Dialogue (1977–1982)* I, 268, 327, 323, 326.

[123] Ibid., I, 351.

[124] Ibid., I, 123.

"Thus such patterns of dialogue could hardly do justice, for example, to the Kimbanguist Church in Africa (chapter 6, pp. 54–80) any more than they can to the Pentecostals."[125]

Indeed this is a fundamental problem in all ecumenical dialogues. I know of only two places in the world where a genuine dialogue between the oral and the literary cultures takes place: The first are the meetings of the Society for Pentecostal Studies, where a number of highly educated black Pentecostals use arguments, songs, testimonies, and prayer simultaneously and are respected by their white counterparts. This is also a meeting place between Trinitarian and Oneness, between black and white Pentecostals, between men and women, and between classical Pentecostals and charismatics (including Catholic charismatics).[126] Similar things can be said of the research group which gathers around Jean-Daniel Plüss and the brothers van der Laan in Europe. The second such "meeting place" is the school for black worker-pastors in Birmingham (chapter 9, pp. 106–16).

This meeting of theological styles must become a priority in future dialogues. It is interesting that the *Protestant charismatics* very early wanted to "see representatives of Pentecostal Churches not yet represented, for instance the independent African Churches." This was objected to, with rather weak arguments, by both classical and Catholic Pentecostals. The latter argued that many of these Christians would be ex–Catholics (as if that were an argument). At the close of the first quinquennium it was again suggested that persons from the independent African Pentecostal churches be invited to the second quinquennium. This was immediately rejected by the South African chairman David Du Plessis, on rather weak grounds: it was thought that the World Pentecostal Conference would then never become interested in the dialogue.[127]

Sandidge summarizes the problem as follows. In the world Pentecostal family there are at least six distinct groups:

(1) There are those classical Pentecostals identified with the Pentecostal World Conference and strongly associated with the Evangelical wing of Christianity (in fact a minority within Pentecostals, only 60 million of the whole charismatic/Pentecostal community of over 400 million).[128]

(2) The Pentecostal churches belonging to the World Council of Churches. They are few (chapter 27, pp. 384–87) but they would probably display a more ecumenical openness than the first group.

(3) The numerous indigenous churches in the Third World which are not re-lated to the Pentecostal World Conference or to North American or Euro-pean Pentecostal missionary societies.

---

[125] Hocken, "Extraordinary," 211.
[126] Robeck, "Society."
[127] Sandidge, *Dialogue (1977–1982)* I, 180, 334.
[128] The figure of 60 million in Vanelderen, "Conference."

(4) A large number of independent Pentecostal congregations having no denominational affiliation but maintaining high levels of activity in evangelism, missions, and church planting.

(5) The many good-sized, middle-class, independent, charismatic/Pentecostal congregations which have recently begun forming in North America and parts of Europe. (Some figures are as high as 60,000 local churches in the United States.) Many of these groups, known by Du Plessis, were just emerging into the charismatic renewal scene at the start of the dialogue.

(6) Those Pentecostal groups and denominations which are largely isolated from the rest of the Pentecostal world because of race, theology, or choice.[129]

At first Du Plessis approached the first group. As he was largely turned down he tried the smaller groups; but he never really touched the large Third World independent Pentecostal movement.[130]

Finally it must be said that because of the dialogue the climate has changed dramatically on both sides. Some of the early antagonists have been won over, for instance Alfred Missen from Great Britain,[131] and perhaps even Thomas Zimmerman.[132] Ludwig Eisenlöffel, a German Pentecostal, has published a most appreciative review of Bittlinger's *Papst und Pfingstler,*[133] as has the Catholic *Schweizerische Kirchenzeitung.*[134]

Peter Hocken, in his brilliant review of Sandidge, admonishes his Catholic co-religionists: "It would seem that many Catholics still readily attribute unworthy motives to Pentecostal missionaries seeing their advent primarily in terms of sectarian aggression and sinister subversion of the Catholic faith."[135]

I do not know whether the Holy Father in Rome listens to Peter Hocken, but he should. In the opening address to the Fourth General Conference of the Latin American Episcopate, John Paul II gave a somewhat triumphalistic speech on the Catholic mission in Latin America.[136] The speech is otherwise most enlightening because it admits the *de facto* pluralism and the questioning of the papal authority in the Catholic church (although all of this is of course

---

[129] Sandidge, *Dialogue (1977–1982)* I, 328f., 325.

[130] Ibid., I, 329.

[131] Ibid., I, 374. Hocken, "Extraordinary," 208, note 21.

[132] Sandidge, *Dialogue (1977–1982)* I, 331, 365.

[133] Eisenlöffel, "Papst."

[134] Moser, "Dialog."

[135] Hocken mentions in particular the Catholic statement from Mexico bracketing together the Assemblies of God and Jehovah's Witnesses as aggressive sectarian proselytizers. "It is a violation of ecumenical principles to place together classical Pentecostals and sub-Christian groups such as the Jehovah's Witnesses. Catholics should also distinguish between the indigenous Pentecostal movements in Latin American and those imported from North America. The evidence points to the former growing at a faster rate." Hocken, "Extraordinary," 212, note 29. See also the following.

[136] John Paul II, "Address."

rejected). He also mentions the invasion by the sects in Latin America, lumping by this term Jehovah's Witnesses and others together with Pentecostals. Not differentiating between those with whom his own Secretariat has been for years in an intensive dialogue and those who have no concern for the ecumenicity of the church is a regrettable oversight, one which has been criticized by a number of Catholics[137] and Pentecostals.[138]

One thing is sure: the new ecumenical climate among Pentecostals, especially in America, is due in part to this dialogue (more on this in chapter 27, pp. 371–74).

This is a prayer for Catholics, Protestants, and myself:

Prayer of the Mosquito

God,
Sometimes I feel like a mosquito.
In the morning, when the sun is shining,
I hum away happily.
But then an urge comes over me:
I must sink my sting into somebody;
I must draw blood in order to survive.
God, I have not made this sting.
Why must I be a mosquito?
I would prefer to be a fly,
who lives on sugar-water
or a butterfly who drinks honey.
Why must I be a mosquito,
who can only survive by stinging others.
I did not make myself.
You did not ask me whether I wanted to be a mosquito,
neither did my parents.
Dear God, will there also be mosquitoes in the kingdom of God?
What are you going to do with those that have to sting others?

---

[137] Cleary, "Misreading," 7f. Robeck, "Taking Stock." Cleary's article appeared also in Spanish: "El maltrato de la Jerarquía Católica a los Pentecostales."
[138] Robeck, "Pope." Overview in McDonnell, "Death," 14–19.

III

THE EVANGELICAL ROOT

We now pick up the thread again from chapter 12 (on Wesley) and follow the traces of Wesley's doctrine of sanctification through the American Holiness movement up to the beginning of Pentecostalism.

CHAPTER FOURTEEN

From the American Holiness Movement to Pentecostalism

"The Higher Christian Life"

"The Higher Christian Life" is the title of a historically influential book by the Holiness preacher W. E. Boardman (1810–1886).[1] The term also describes the spirituality and religious climate of the Holiness movement in America and Europe in the last century. Until now researchers into early Holiness and Pentecostal history have had to journey to North American and British libraries to find the source material for their research. Even then they have often failed to find what they were looking for, because established libraries have not acquired and catalogued this highly influential religious literature. Now Donald W. Dayton and his friends have edited facsimiles of some of the more important works.[2] Their selection is competent and extremely valuable. It will help to establish a relationship between perfectionism and the anti-slavery movement, and perfectionism and the feminist movement.[3] Perhaps it will also help to find out whether and when revivalism lost most of its social and political teeth.

In chapter 12 (pp. 144–52) I argued that Methodism represents a variety of Catholic spirituality. While it is not clear just how far Wesley accepted the ideas of his Catholic mentors, he certainly accepted their plea for a second religious crisis experience subsequent to and different from conversion. This experience, in turn, played a major role in the nineteenth century American Holiness movement.

---

[1] Boardman, *Higher.*
[2] Dayton, *Higher.*
[3] Dayton, *Defending.*

The movement's best-known representatives were the Oberlin theologians, so called after their spiritual and organizational center: Oberlin College, Oberlin, Ohio. These spokesmen included: the preacher, systematic theologian and president of Oberlin College, Charles Grandison Finney (1792–1876);[4] Asa Mahan (1857–1889),[5] a popular evangelist who attracted great crowds on both sides of the Atlantic;[6] and the couple Robert Pearsall and Hannah Whitall Smith (1827–1898; 1832–1911),[7] who were the "stars" at the Holiness conference in Oxford (1874) and Brighton (1875).[8] The reports of the European theologians and church leaders on Oxford and Brighton filled the pages of religious periodicals for many weeks. Most of these reports were highly enthusiastic; they are a first-class documentation of the religious climate at these conferences, and of the longing of many for the "Higher Christian Life." Thus the Oberlin theologians managed to win a number of church leaders to their specific understanding of the higher life—at least until some rumors of Robert Pearsall Smith's "unsavory" (but never specified) actions and doctrines put an end to his public appearances.

The Oberlin theologians stressed the necessity for holiness and sanctification, sometimes called "second blessing" or "baptism of the Spirit," but they were also men and women of action. They saw their social and political pioneering as part of this religious experience. Their causes included, for example, the inclusion of black and female students in their educational institutions, a more democratic and sharing organization of industry (Pearsall Smith was himself a glass manufacturer) and of society (this was modeled at Oberlin),[9] and a plan for world peace through an international institution similar to the present-day United Nations.

Another fruit of the Holiness Movement was the work of the Swiss Henri Dunant (1828–1910), founder of the Red Cross. He shared with the Holiness Movement, not only its eschatological fervor, but also its concrete understanding of the consequences of sanctification for political action. His Thursday Club in Geneva became one of the first sections of the Swiss YMCA. This section drafted the earliest confession of the Evangelical Alliance, which in

---

[4] Finney, *Lectures.* Documentation in *Handbuch,* 02a.02.002, and in Dayton, *Roots* (see index of names), Schmieder, *Geisttaufe,* 80–86 and Brandt-Bessire, *Sources,* 93–101.

[5] Mahan, *Out.* Documentation in *Handbuch,* 02a.02.003, in Dayton, *Roots* (see index of names), Schmieder, *Geisttaufe,* 173–80, and Brandt-Bessire, *Sources,* 93–101.

[6] Documentation in *Handbuch,* 02a.02.004, in Dayton, *Roots* (index of names), Schmieder, *Geisttaufe,* 224–27.

[7] Smith, Robert Pearsall and Hannah Whitall, *Devotional.* Smith, Hannah Whitall, *Unselfishness.* Documentation in *Handbuch,* 02a.02.004, Dayton, *Roots* (index of names), Schmieder, *Geisttaufe* (index of names) and Brandt-Bessire, *Sources,* 107–15.

[8] *Account. Record.*

[9] Fairchild, *Oberlin,* vol. 15. On Jean-Frédéric Oberlin (1740–1926) see below, ch. 28, p. 398.

turn became the model for the basis formula of the World Council of Churches. Here again, although this is mostly ignored, we can trace the fruits of this type of holiness in political and ecumenical activities to our time.[10]

While most leaders of the nineteenth century Holiness movement were men and women of action, one powerful thinker, Thomas Cogswell Upham (1799–1872) must be mentioned for his contribution to Christian thought.[11] His description of his "baptism in the Spirit" was widely known. For him, to be filled with the Spirit, to be sanctified, had cognitive repercussions. He applied sanctification not only to action but also to thinking, and tried—remarkable for his day—to disprove Kant. He also published a *Manual of Peace* that contained: (1) Evils and Remedies of War, (2) Suggestions on the Law of Nations, and (3) Considerations of a Congress of Nations.[12]

Very quickly, however, this side of the message of sanctification was forgotten. The translations of the pioneer Holiness theologians' works into French and German omitted all the passages that interpreted sanctification or the "second blessing" as having repercussions on the fight against slavery, for a female ministry in the church, and so forth.

In his introduction to volume 1 of the series "The Higher Christian Life," Dayton rightly stresses that

> many of the popular social movements of the nineteenth century cannot be understood without attention to this material. Recent scholarship has revealed the extent to which the antislavery movement was rooted in antebellum perfectionist revivalism, but there are still only hints in the literature to the extent to which the feminist movement of the nineteenth century was itself carried by the perfectionist currents.[13]

Dayton and his friends distinguish between the Holiness movement proper, "distinguished by its effort to maintain an American variation on the Methodist doctrine of 'entire sanctification' as a 'second blessing,' " and the Keswick movement, "named for summer conventions held in the Lake District town of Keswick in England, which represents a more moderate form of the teaching."[14]

Anybody with only slight knowledge of Reformation theology will understand why the evangelists and missionaries at least of Holiness proper, were rejected outright by most theologians of the Reformation tradition in Europe. Something that was "higher" than pure grace could only be a travesty of the pure gospel. Nevertheless, the holiness conferences in Oxford (1874) and Brighton (1875) and the public meetings of Dwight L. Moody, Robert Pear-

---

[10] See on the relation between the YMCA and the WCC, Hollenweger, "Content."

[11] Upham, *Life*. Documentation in *Handbuch*, 02a.02.007, Schmieder, *Geisttaufe*, 186–90, and Dayton, *Roots* (index of names).

[12] Upham, *Manual*, and idem, "Congress."

[13] Dayton, "Higher," viii. See also above note 3.

[14] Dayton, *Higher*, ix.

sall, and Hannah Whitall Smith produced a remarkable response in the religious (as well as the secular) press.[15] Paul Fleisch, a German Lutheran and prince abbot of the monastery of Loccum near Hanover, produced a number of historically very relevant publications on the subject, in spite of the fact that he thoroughly disagreed with the holiness preachers because of the underlying Catholic spirituality of the "higher Christian life."[16] His theological and historical judgment, however, which saw in the holiness preachers the semantic, theological, and spiritual forerunners of Pentecostalism, proved in the long run to be true in spite of the sharp counterclaims of many of the adherents of the holiness movement, particularly in Germany. The connection is now well established and competently demonstrated by a Catholic[17] and two Protestant researchers.[18] The shaping of early holiness doctrine into the Pentecostal doctrine proper can be followed in detail in the works of T. B. Barratt,[19] Frank Bartleman,[20] Agnes N. O. LaBerge,[21] Aimee Semple McPherson,[22] Charles F. Parham,[23] A. J. Tomlinson,[24] and others.[25]

Frank Bartleman

Some Pentecostals who stand at the transition between the holiness and the Pentecostal movement must specially be mentioned. In a brilliant essay[26] Cecil M. Robeck, Jr. (a Fuller Theological Seminary professor and pastor of the Assemblies of God), traces the editions and re-editions of Bartleman's seminal writings, and notes changes to them (most of them posthumous). He re-established the original Bartleman, and indeed I was greatly astonished to encounter a very different Bartleman from the one presented in the standard Pentecostal histories. Bartleman was reared by a Catholic father and a Quaker mother. This ecumenical family background shines through his whole life. Although one of the first to recognize the Pentecostal revival at Los Angeles, he was also critical of it because of its lack of humility and its unecumenical, almost sectarian, attitude. In particular he criticized Pentecostals (and other Christians) for their nationalism. A Bartleman tract on World War I reads like the opening chapters of Amos: Belgium was judged "for her Congo

---

[15] For the reaction in Switzerland see *Handbuch*, 05.28.002 and 05.28.003.
[16] Fleisch, *Gemeinschaftsbewegung*.
[17] Schmieder, *Geisttaufe*.
[18] Dayton, *Roots;* Brandt-Bessire, *Sources*.
[19] Barratt, *Works*.
[20] Robeck, *Witness*.
[21] LaBerge, *What*.
[22] McPherson, *This*.
[23] Parham, Sarah E., *Life;* Parham, Charles F., *Sermons*. This volume contains also his British (and American) Israel theories, which might explain his racist position vis-à-vis Seymour (above chapter 3, pp. 20–23).
[24] Tomlinson, *Conflict*.
[25] *Pentecostal Tracts*.
[26] Robeck, "Frank Bartleman." See also idem, "Bartleman."

atrocities,[27] France for her infidelity and devil worship, Germany for her materialism and militarism (and) England for her hypocrisy, bullying over weaker nations and her overwhelming pride."[28] Russia was judged for her religious intolerance and despotism. Italy was perceived as slick and diplomatic, wanting only to be on the winning side. The US would soon be judged as well for worshipping what he called "the money gods."[29]

Bartleman also judged that the United States were not—as they pretended—neutral. To believe English reports without giving equal weight to German reports was not to be neutral. And the US got their punishment when the Lusitania was torpedoed with ammunition that the Americans had provided. The First World War was not started for the reasons given by the politicians, but to defuse internal political issues. War was used largely by American interests to guarantee economic supremacy. The "free" press, he continued, had been captured by the government.

In the end, what else could one expect from greedy, unrepenting nations, but that their church behaved like a "War Church," a harlot. Preachers who preached military preparedness for wars were, in Bartleman's opinion, blasphemous. Their "business is to preach, not to murder."[30]

In matters of economics he rejected communism just as much as capitalism. He wrote brilliantly about the "wheat gamblers" (the commodity exchange and trade in futures), the "servant class" in England and the poor in the US. "Will God not curse us for this?" he asked. Added to this is his firm stand in favor of the "Oneness" or "Jesus only" tradition in Pentecostalism, which was represented mainly by poor blacks.

Thus Bartleman tried to carry the holistic understanding of holiness from the nineteenth century into the twentieth century Pentecostal movement. No wonder that *this side* of his evangelical conviction is shamefully silenced. One can be all the more thankful that this side of early holiness/Pentecostal spirituality is now available to those who want to know the roots of Pentecostalism. No doubt American researchers who are familiar with this style of language will be able to analyze these texts much better than I. In any case, the ferocious mutilation of early Pentecostal writings by Pentecostal publishers will perhaps open the eyes of Pentecostals to what happens to texts, for instance to New Testament texts, when they are passed down in a changing social context and when their message becomes uncomfortable. Pentecostals should be in a good position to understand this since their own texts have been changed—without acknowledgment.

Bartleman is not the only representative of this type of early Pentecostalism, just the best known. Mention should also be made of the controversial Dr. Finis

---

[27] Bartleman did not of course know Simon Kimbangu but his comments fit well into what we know from the former Belgium Congo (chapter 6, pp. 61–64).

[28] Bartleman, "Present" and "Danger." All in Robeck, "Frank Bartleman," xvi.

[29] Bartleman, "Money," in Robeck, "Frank Bartleman."

[30] Bartleman, "Preparedness," 115. Robeck, "Frank Bartleman," xvii.

Ewing Yoakum (1851–1921).[31] He at one point held the Chair of Mental Diseases at Gross Medical College in Denver, but gave up his lucrative medical career (he reportedly earned $18,000 a month) to enter a career in "faith healing." Following a near fatal accident in 1894, he had come to Los Angeles, where he was healed through prayer by a holiness pastor. He began to preach divine healing, and had a Pentecostal experience, although he remained somewhat distanced from the Assemblies of God. Following a vision, he set up what became known as the Pisgah Home Movement. It provided help for the homeless, and for the poor social outcasts such as alcoholics, drug addicts, and prostitutes. By 1911 he was supplying 9,000 clean beds and 18,000 meals each month.

Pacifism

Most Pentecostals were originally pacifists.[32] Mention must be made particularly of Arthur Booth-Clibborn, son-in-law of Salvation Army founder William Booth. Arthur Booth-Clibborn became an influential Pentecostal leader at the beginning of our century. His book *Blood Against Blood* was highly praised by Pentecostal periodicals.[33] Booth-Clibborn states: "The Scripture shows us that organized sin [today we would speak of "structural injustice"] is much worse in the sight of God than are sins of the individuals." The church, to its shame, has compromised itself at times by legitimizing "the organized slaying of millions in the wars" through an "unholy alliance" with emperors and governments.[34] Economically, wars result in the increased disparity between the rich and the poor: the rich get richer and the poor get poorer until finally "The rich man's dog gets more meat than the poor man's family."[35] The capitalists view the war as a commercial enterprise which

---

[31] Robeck, "Ethics," (on Yoakum 105), see also his article "Yoakum."

[32] Beaman, *Pacifism* (see also the excellent review of this book by Murray W. Dempster in *Pneuma* 11/1, 1989, 59–64). In addition to Beaman what follows is mainly based on Dempster, "Borders." The black Pentecostal pioneer C. H. Mason was tried and persecuted for his pacifist stance. Details in Lovett, "Black Holiness-Pentecostals," in particular 81 and Clemmons, "Mason."

[33] In 1915, for example, *Word and Witness*, under the editorship of E. N. Bell, ran repeated ads on behalf of the Gospel Publishing House for *Blood Against Blood;* in one instance calling it "a most striking, realistic and forceful book by Arthur Sydney Booth-Clibborn, an English Pentecostal Evangelist and Elder, who has put into words the principles burning in the hearts of all the Pentecostal saints on the subject of whether a Christian should go to war or not." The *Weekly Evangel* was more explicit in identifying what the principles were which burned "in the heart of all the Pentecostal saints" in its promotion of the book: "The Gospel Publishing House is now in possession of a powerful book *Blood Against Blood*, written by Arthur Booth-Clibborn, an English Pentecostal brother. . . . We recommend that you purchase it and become imbued with the spirit of its contents, in a complete opposition and protest against war and the shedding of blood" (19.6.1915, 1), quoted in Dempster, "Borders," 28, note 6.

[34] Booth-Clibborn, Arthur, *Blood*, 87f.; Dempster, "Borders," 10.

[35] Bartleman, "Last"; Dempster, "Borders," 13.

provides a way to make a profit. The profits come, however, from exploiting the misfortune of others. During a war economy, the prices for munitions, wheat, and the other staples of life are driven up for profit. And who are the beneficiaries of the price hypes? Bartleman lists them: "Wall Street interest, Pork Barrel administration, Brewer's Corporation, Syndicate and Monopoly, Steel Trust and Armor Plate, Powder Trust, etc. without end."[36] The irony is that politicians who have enough power to "commandeer a nation" into war do nothing about this "handful of exploiters."[37]

From the outset of the First World War, the pacifists emphasized that it was the American wealthy class that profited financially from the bloody transaction of human killing. Samuel Booth-Clibborn, for example, recalled how the rich profited without regard to human suffering when the Allies looked to US firms for millions of tons of munitions. "Did these millionaires 'stand by the president' by keeping him strictly neutral??? No!!! Not while there was a chance of piling up dollars, even though every one of them was dripping with the blood and tears of tortured Europe."[38]

This was official policy of the Assemblies of God. In 1917 the Assemblies of God sent a statement to President Woodrow Wilson officially declaring itself a pacifist church: "Every branch of the movement, whether in the United States, Canada, Great Britain or Germany . . . " is pacifist. This is astonishing for today's readers but it is clearly the case. It is possible, however, as Dempster supposes, that the official position adopted by the church may not have reflected the majority position of the movement.[39] Dempster offers this as an explanation of the denomination's later abandonment of pacifism.[40]

Compare to this the analysis by Stephen Lloyd Holmes on the Pentecostal movement in the US army. He quotes Brigadier General Curry:

> One of the greatest blessings of baptism with the Holy Spirit for our family has been a new clarity in understanding the Bible. Among them is what I wonder to be God's attitude toward war. At times, the question of whether Christians should be members of the Armed Forces seemed fuzzy to us. Now it is clear. God intends that Christians do not only make the military a career, but when they go to war they are to fight better than unbelievers. The Christian's action in combat should be an inspiration to others . . . [Christians] should be in the front ranks, in support units, in fighter planes and warships. They should be in positions of responsibility and leadership, as well as in the fighting ranks. . . . When a nation goes to war, Christians should go to war, Christians should obey the laws of the government as God requires . . . Satan has not only confused some Christians, leading them out of war, he has used rebellion to sap the strength and vitality of

---

[36] Bartleman, "War," 83; Dempster, "Borders," 13.
[37] Bartleman, "War," 4; Dempster, "Borders," 13.
[38] Booth-Clibborn, Samuel, *Should,* 42; Dempster, "Borders," 14.
[39] "Conscription"; Dempster, "Borders," 23.
[40] See also Robin, "Chronology." He shows how the Assemblies of God oscillated between pacifism and patriotism.

our nation and shed blood if required. We cannot "fight the good fight of faith", as we are instructed by God, unless we believe in fighting.[41]

So far the Pentecostals have moved away from their own roots. How is it possible that modern American revivalism, with its deep roots in the nineteenth-century holiness movement, can be either so ignorant of or so antagonistic to many of its own tenets, as for example its stand for equal rights for women and slaves, and its fight for peace and justice? How is it possible that a powerful religious movement which directed its religious energies to the solution of the structural ills of its time could become so individualistic and almost blind to its own past? Of course, there are important exceptions to this historical blindness within the root holiness movement itself, such as Timothy Smith,[42] Donald W. Dayton,[43] Melvin Easterday Dieter,[44] and others.[45] Also it has to be said that today this past is being re-discovered in other quarters as well, and revived in a critical context (see on this part IV on the "Critical Root," pp. 201–331).

William Faupel gives a provisional answer to our questions.[46] He points out that around 1900, eschatology was profoundly changed. Originally the holiness preachers had believed that the rapture would take place after the millennium (postmillennialism). They had also believed that their endeavor for holiness would contribute something to the establishment of the kingdom of God on earth, focused in the millennium. When this proved to be unsuccessful, and instead of the millennium the Great War and the economic crisis arrived, postmillennialism was replaced by premillennialism, i.e., by the expectation of the rapture *before* the millennium. It was now necessary to prepare the believers for the rapture which would save them *out* of the world before everything broke down, and before the Great Tribulation. They would then feast with Jesus in the clouds and celebrate the wedding of the lamb until Christ established the millennium and they would be invited to rule with him. This is the eschatological doctrine of many Pentecostals and evangelicals today. It is also the most potent obstacle to an involvement in the struggle against structural evils.

---

[41] Curry, "Fight," quoted in Holmes, *Pfingst-*, 10–11.
[42] Smith, Timothy, *Revivalism*.
[43] Dayton, *Discovering*.
[44] Dieter, *Holiness*.
[45] For example the collection edited by Runyon, *Sanctification and Liberation*, or Shuman, "Patriotism."
[46] In his dissertation "Kingdom."

CHAPTER FIFTEEN

Pentecostalism and Evangelicalism

Pentecostalism and Fundamentalism[1]

"How are Pentecostalism and Fundamentalism related? In what way are Pentecostals Fundamentalists?" This is the topic of a paper which Russ Spittler, a New Testament professor at Fuller Theological Seminary, Pasadena, California, and an Assemblies of God pastor, presented at an international conference at the University of Calgary, Canada.

His first observation was that, regarded as movements within religious history, *Pentecostalism preceded Fundamentalism.* Pentecostalism arose at the turn of the century. Fundamentalism appeared just before the First World War.

Furthermore, Pentecostalism, fundamentalism, and neo-orthodoxy—in that sequence—can be viewed as unrelated reactions to the state of religion at the close of the nineteenth century. Fundamentalism is an intellectual reaction. Barth argued, as did fundamentalism, for a recovery of classic Christian beliefs, even if the menu varied. Both fundamentalism and neo-orthodoxy proposed an essentially cognitive rescue of the church from its lassitude.

Pentecostalism on the other hand profoundly distrusted the intellectual enterprise. The Pentecostal critique focused not so much on diluted theology as upon withered piety. The problem, to Pentecostals, lay not in wrong thinking so much as in collapsed feeling. Not the decline of orthodoxy but the decay of devotion lay at the root of the problem. It was not that the church was *liberal,* but that it was *lifeless. What was needed was*

---

[1] The following is largely based on Spittler, "Fundamentalists," 103–16.

not a new argument for heads but a new experience for hearts. Fundamentalists and the neo-orthodox mounted arguments. Pentecostals gave testimony.

Far from being a part of the fundamentalist movement, Pentecostalism became one of its targets. By 1928 the fundamentalist organization had formed a sufficiently strong opinion about the Pentecostal movement to adopt the following resolution:

> Be it Resolved, That this convention go on record as unreservedly opposed to Modern Pentecostalism, including the speaking in unknown tongues, and the fanatical healing known as general healing in the atonement, and the perpetuation of the miraculous sign-healing of Jesus and His apostles, wherein they claim the only reason the church cannot perform these miracles is because of unbelief.[2]

The Pentecostals had been no major players in the famed Scopes trial which popularized the fundamentalist/modernist controversy in the mid 1920s and led to Harry Emerson Forsdick's exclaiming in his famous sermon: "The God of the fundamentalists is one God and the God of liberals another." Early Pentecostals, therefore, while they shared most beliefs of the fundamentalists, were neither offered nor sought affiliation with fundamentalism. By the middle 1920s, Pentecostalism and fundamentalism were separate and often hostile movements. G. Campbell Morgan, one of the contributors to *The Fundamentals,*[3] even spoke of the Pentecostal movement as "the last vomit of Satan."

Spittler's view is confirmed by other Pentecostal scholars. William Faupel, a former Assemblies of God pastor and now a professor at Asbury Theological College, said in his presidential address to the Society for Pentecostal Studies (1992): "I concede that I originally also thought that Pentecostalism arose in competition with liberalism. However, as I studied the original Pentecostal sources, it slowly began to dawn on me that theological liberalism was not even in the consciousness of the adherents of the initial Pentecostal revival. Certainly, it was not the subject of their critique" [note that they did criticize it, they knew very little of the liberal critical school].[4] "Rather, I have to believe that Pentecostalism arose, in large part, as a critique directed at an emerging fundamentalism which was attaching itself to the Old Princeton Theology."[5]

---

[2] "Tenth Annual Convention," 3–10, quote 9. However, the resolution was "adopted by the ruling of the chair [W. B. Riley] by a majority of four votes." See Spittler, "Fundamentalists," 115, note 11.

[3] *The Fundamentals,* 12 vol. 1910–15. The quote by G. Cambell Morgan without primary documentation appears in Synan, *Holiness-Pentecostal,* 144; Spittler, "Fundamentalists," 110.

[4] See chapter 21 of *The Pentecostals,* 292ff., and passim.

[5] Faupel, "Whither?" 21. For this interpretation of fundamentalism Faupel refers to Sandeen, *Roots,* where Sandeen develops the thesis that fundamentalism arose when "future premillenialists" adopted Princeton theology to support their interpretation of Scripture.

Faupel quotes George Fry:

I am convinced that liberalism and Pentecostalism are in fact fraternal twins [having] arisen out of precisely [the same] conditions [and] are derived from the same sources. For a century Liberalism had preached experience—then Pentecostalism suddenly produced it! No wonder the Liberal and Neo-Orthodox theologians were at a loss when the Pentecostals started talking. How could they condemn the rampant empiricism and subjectivism of Pentecostalism when that is precisely the approach they had previously recommended. Pentecostalism is the logical end of Liberalism.[6]

Faupel's conclusion is therefore: The historiography of Pentecostal doctrine will follow one of two competing visions.

One vision sees the movement as a subgroup of Evangelicalism, sharing its assumptions, its agenda and its mission. This view can only be sustained through a selective reading of Pentecostal history and through an abandonment of many of the initial Pentecostal assumptions . . . The second vision is still emerging, its shape is not yet clear. Certain characteristics, however, are apparent. Those holding this view feel that the initial impulse which gave rise to the movement, must be recovered—not in a naive sense, but in the sense that Paul Ricoeur means by "second naiveté."[7]

Pentecostals have of course themselves contributed to the understanding of their movement as being a "fundamentalism plus." For example, J. R. Flower:

We can say like Paul, "I am a fundamentalist, of the strictest sect of the fundamentalists am I one." But that is not enough. Paul was more than a Pharisee. The Pharisees believed in the resurrection; they believed in angels; they believed in the supernatural—but it was all in the past. Paul believed in it—the past and in the present also. We are fundamentalists, but we are more than that.[8]

Probably Vinson Synan is nearer to the truth when he states: "In the opinion of this writer the breaks with fundamentalism in 1928 and 1943 turned out to be a blessing that freed the rising Pentecostals from the dead cultural and theological baggage of a discredited movement and opened up the way for unparalleled influence and growth in the last half of the twentieth century."[9] This was achieved by an alliance with evangelicalism, a "milder form of fundamentalism."

Pentecostalism and Evangelicalism[10]

In spite of early Pentecostal interest in the National Association of Evangelicals (NAE), full participation did not come easily. Pentecostals were chary

---

[6] Fry, "Perspective," 182, 192; Faupel, "Whither?" 22.
[7] Faupel, "Whither?" 29–30.
[8] Flower, *PE,* 23f; *The Pentecostals,* 41.
[9] Synan, "Fundamentalism," 327. See also his article "Evangelicalism."
[10] The following is largely based on Robeck, "National."

of the response they were given by these "Calvinists," and as J. R. Flower noted, some Pentecostals kept their "fingers crossed" lest they lose this "good fortune." Harold Ockenga did much to alleviate Pentecostal fears, arguing repeatedly that Pentecostals and holiness groups such as the Free Methodists and the Nazarenes should have an equal voice with others who called themselves evangelical. For many the issue of Pentecostal participation peaked in April 1944 when Carl McIntire published several articles in his paper, the *Christian Beacon*, repudiating Pentecostals. "Tongues," the paper claimed, "is one of the great signs of the apostasy." The real gift of tongues had long since ceased to exist. McIntire announced his willingness to merge his American Council of Christian Churches into the NAE, *if* the National Association of Evangelicals would, among other things, ". . . get rid of the . . . tongues groups."

Flower wondered aloud whether the NAE had hurt its chances of representing evangelical Christians in the US by including Pentecostals in their numbers. But Ockenga reassured him that Pentecostals would participate. As late as 1947 Ockenga was still defending that decision. Flower, with E. S. Williams' encouragement, had led the Assemblies of God into organization. G. H. Montgomery had urged participation in the NAE, and the Church of God (Cleveland) took its cue from J. H. Walker, Earl P. Paulk, E. L. Simmons, M. P. Cross, and E. C. Clark. Since the NAE's founding meeting, these groups have been joined by the Christian Church of North America, Church of God of the Mountain Assembly, Elim Fellowship, Full Pentecostal Association, International Church of the Foursquare Gospel, International Church of Christ, Pentecostal Church of God, and the Pentecostal Evangelical Church, as Pentecostal member churches.

By 1987 the Pentecostals constituted a majority in the NAE. Out of the five million members in the NAE denominations, 3.1 million were Pentecostal. Three times Pentecostals have served as presidents, most notably Thomas F. Zimmerman,[11] general superintendent of the Assemblies of God. However, no black Pentecostal church and no Oneness Pentecostal group is a member. They have formed their own national organizations.

This move has gained respectability for the Pentecostals, as they have become "a typical middle-class evangelical movement."[12] But they have also lost something. "The 'evangelicalization' of Pentecostals has brought them into dialogue with evangelical Christians, but this interaction has been at the risk of certain distinctives." They have lost, for example, their pacifist conviction, and have instead appointed military chaplains. "More often than not,

---

[11] So strong was Zimmerman's loyalty to evangelicalism that he asked for his papers not to be put in the archives of his own denomination, the Assemblies of God, which he served for a quarter century, but in the archive at Wheaton College, which has sometimes been labeled the "Evangelical Vatican." Spittler, "Fundamentalists," 112. Nothing of this can be found in *World Pentecost*, "Zimmerman," 6f.

[12] Horn, "Experience," 135.

they identify with the political right and have been hard on those with whom they have disagreed." The role of women in Pentecostal churches has also suffered from the intensive dialogue with evangelicals. They have accepted such evangelical tenets of faith as "the inerrancy of scripture." And finally they have accepted from the evangelicals their suspicion of the National Council of Churches and the World Council of Churches. "Thus Pentecostals have effectively been cut off from meaningful interaction with the conciliar sector of the church."[13]

In Germany the dialogue did not go so smoothly because of the ill-fated and long-drawn-out animosity between the *Gnadauer Verband* and the Pentecostals therefore described the *Gnadauer Verband* as "God's state attorney."[14]

Similar variety can be seen in Pentecostal attitudes towards biblical studies. Pentecostals took part in the translation of the *New International Version* of the Bible. In France a Pentecostal collaborated on the project of a new French Bible translation.[15] This is not, however, the end of the story. Russ Spittler mentions those members of the Pentecostal tradition who have adopted an informed exegetical style characteristic of the left wing of evangelicalism—as found at such schools as Wheaton, Regent, Fuller, and to some extent Dallas, Trinity, and Gordon-Conwell, as well as within many of the biblical faculties of colleges of the classical Pentecostal churches themselves.

So wide is classical Pentecostalism today that among its card-carrying teachers are those whose method of biblical interpretation would almost precisely align with ideological fundamentalism, along with others who, with no sacrifice of biblical authority—as they would understand the term—have made friends with redaction criticism and other modern approaches to the study of Scripture. That raises the question of the relationships between Pentecostalism and academic theology.

Pentecostalism and Academic Theology

The Past

There was a time when Pentecostals called modern academic theology a tragedy, whose fruit is empty churches. The decline in the churches is the result of our "theologizing to death," they said. The theological intellectuals had their chance in past centuries and have lost it; they have shown what man accomplishes. "Now there is a theology emerging that is proving what God can do."[16] In this and many similar phrases, Pentecostals distanced themselves

---

[13] Robeck, "National," 636.

[14] See *The Pentecostals,* 218ff., more detailed in the German version. The *Gnadauer Verband* is a fellowship of evangelical congregations (within and without the established churches) in whose midst German Pentecostalism was born. The last quote in Müller-Bohn, "Zungenreden-Weissagung."

[15] Sandidge, *Dialogue (1977–1982)* I, 20.

[16] The following is based on a lecture given on the occasion of the presentation of the Festschrift in honor of Walter J. Hollenweger at the University of Utrecht on

from academic theology. Karl Barth,[17] and Adolf Schlatter[18] were not exempt from this criticism. Accordingly Pentecostal Bible Schools produced a crude rationalism in the form of fundamentalism. Since Aristotelian logic was accepted unconsciously root and branch, contradictions had to be harmonized or explained away—a fact which obscured the individual profile of biblical writers. They all had to say the same thing in order not to fall into the trap of contradiction.

Now it is unquestionable that Aristotle made a great discovery. He said that if of two propositions one is the exact contradiction of the other, one must be wrong. The trouble with that logic is that it is foreign to the biblical testimony. There God can repent, he can change his opinion, for example in the book of Jonah. He can say: "Only forty days and Nineveh is destroyed," and then decide not to destroy it, much to the chagrin of Jonah. God is—like a partner in marriage—not without contradiction, but totally reliable. He is not reliable like a computer, he is reliable like—well—like only himself.

Furthermore, we know now that truth—even mathematical truth and truth in natural science—is not necessarily without contradiction. It is even possible that some phenomena can be accurately described only by using different and contradicting paradigms.

If it is true of mathematics that one must accept contradictions in order to describe the whole truth, how much more true is it of theology? Furthermore, we know that the observer is part of the things he observes: his or her point of view, his or her questions, his or her approach is part of the process of observation. What things really are, we shall never know. We only know how they appear to us or to our instruments of observation.[19] Some of this was already evident in Pentecostalism in the '60s.[20]

Del Tarr in a recent analysis of homiletics and communication is well aware how much Western thought and also Pentecostal theology is affected by these "canons of Western logic" from which America is not exempt. It shows itself in the homiletical style so typically symbolized by "Three points and a poem." "Sounding like a debate, preaching in the West has for centuries sounded as if the preacher were making a case in court. As if logos were apologia. Preaching, per se, has meant marshaling an argument in logical sequence, coordinating and subordinating points by the canons of logic, all in a careful appeal to the reasonable hearer."

Quite apart from the fact that the biblical authors would fail miserably if judged against this yardstick, these "canons of Western logic" "are

---

September 9th, 1992. Hollenweger, "Pentecostalism." See also Jongeneel, 1992. The quotes are from van Gijs, *Het*, 36. Chinn, "Speak?" See *The Pentecostals*, 291–310, esp. 293.

[17] Atter, *Cults*, 18f.; *The Pentecostals*, 292.

[18] Lohmann, "Wie?"; *The Pentecostals*, 296.

[19] Discussed in detail in *ITh* 3.

[20] E.g., an article by Russel Evans, a university lecturer from the Elim Churches in England: Evans, "Science"; *Handbuch* 07.425.008; *The Pentecostals*, 297f.

ill-equipped to penetrate the cognitive expectations of non-Western countries, where the majority of missions activity takes place."[21] Probably they are also not very suitable in the West.

The Swiss Pentecostal Jean-Daniel Plüss presents a similar argument in his article on the "liturgical practice" of Pentecostalism. He comes to the conclusion that "ambiguity and truth are not necessarily diametrically opposed."[22] Others have begun to realize that not all that academic theologians produce is drawn from their tobacco pipes, and that we would, for example, have no reliable biblical translations and manuscripts without their patient work.

Correspondingly, academic theologians to this very day have been largely ignorant of the ever-growing Pentecostal revival. The greatest revival movement of our time is largely ignored by professional theologians, probably because its strongest side is its *oral* theology. Oral theology operates, as we have seen

> not through the book, but through the parable,
> not through the thesis, but through the testimony,
> not through dissertations, but through dances,
> not through concepts, but through banquets,
> not through a system of thinking, but through stories and songs,
> not through definitions, but through descriptions,
> not through arguments, but through transformed lives.

These are exactly the categories which have priority not only in the biblical records—as Bultmann has shown in his exegetical works—but also in Third World cultures. Through form-criticism, Bultmann and others have developed a tool to understand the oral processes of biblical tradition. A remarkable achievement! But Bultmann did not realize that he was describing not only a biblical process but also the communication-process of the most important missionary movement of our century. What a fatal intellectual oversight! And Pentecostals did not realize that Bultmann's exegetical work was much nearer to their lived religion than all that the fundamentalists have produced.

Until very recently, academic theology did not seem interested in what the Spirit is doing today, because the work of the Spirit has been relayed mainly in oral forms. In order to get to the roots of this movement one has to do field research, and that not only in Europe and America. No wonder that anthropologists, ethnologists, and sometimes sociologists have been the first to discover Pentecostalism (however, mostly without seeing its theological and

---

[21] Tarr, "Preaching," 121f. The inner quote is from Wardlaw, *Preaching,* 12. In this fascinating article Tarr is well aware of the complexity and specificity of Aristotelian logic. He also quotes Korzybski, *Science,* which was published by the International Non-Aristotelian Library Publishing Company.

[22] Plüss, "Public," 7.

academic relevance). For these scholars, Pentecostals have been interesting objects of research—not teachers in a global art of communication.

That today we have institutes and specialists in every possible and impossible theological topic, but not one single library, not one single institute, not one specialized doctoral supervisor in Europe for the hundreds and perhaps thousands of young Pentecostal scholars worldwide who are knocking at the doors of our academic establishments, this is a theological scandal without precedent! It can certainly not be right that we theologians have only to do with the past of Christianity. It cannot be right that our dialogue partners are only philosophy and sociology, psychology and politology. Our partners are also, and in a growing way, the new academics who are beginning to emerge from Pentecostalism.

The Present

The climate among Pentecostal intellectuals is changing. They are awakening to the question of race; discovering the enormous political and social potential of their own past; and beginning to enter the scholarly dialogue and the political debate on many issues. This should make us listen. Achtemeier[23] and Walter Wink[24] have shown that our historical-critical exegesis and our critical theology are bankrupt. Students learn them only to pass examinations, then later find them irrelevant in their practical work. Critical exegesis is not bankrupt because it is wrong, but because it cannot make its insights fruitful for the normal believer; and this in turn is because it is not tested in liturgical and homiletical praxis. Perhaps Pentecostals can help in this dilemma. They learn critical exegesis not to pass examinations but because they want to know; they do not accept everything in critical theology but they test it with a view to its usefulness.[25] Such students and fellow-researchers, such teachers and professors are needed.

The church lost the working class after the Second World War. Later it lost the intellectuals (because of positions which were not tenable) and the aristocracy. It became more and more a bourgeois or petit-bourgeois club. Now it is about to lose this section of society too, because they are demanding tangible religion—a commodity which Pentecostals and Charismatics can deliver.

Would it not be healthy for both theological academics and Pentecostals to accept the challenge of a lived religion which does not leave its head together with its hat at the church entrance? Would it not be a good thing to interpret not only the miracles and visions in the Bible but also such things in our daily life—by learning from biblical miracles and visions? All this is in any case

---

[23] Achtemeier, *Inspiration.*
[24] Wink, *Bible in Human Transformation,* discussed in detail in Hollenweger, "Exegesis," and idem, "Theology."
[25] An example: Fee, *First Corinthians,* reviewed by J. L. Karsten in *EPTA Bulletin* 8/4, 1989, 183f. See also Zeegwart, "Apocalyptic." Martin, R. Francis, "Apocalypse."

needed for successful dialogue with our own Third World partner churches; missiology without these aspects becomes a purely Western intellectual game. The question however is, how will the academic establishment react to such suggestions? Will it say: We are ecumenical, but within limits; we are fighting for the poor, but we do not want to fight together with the Pentecostals; and above all, we have our own problems. We must help our own Western churches to come to grips with the modern world. We cannot be side-tracked by exotic studies such as Pentecostalism.

Such a response might be a mistake. Neither the Pentecostals nor the World Council of Churches can solve the crying problems of international cooperation and communication. About half of the non-Roman and non-Orthodox churches in the Third World are not members of the World Council of Churches,[26] and the great majority of these are Pentecostal or Pentecostal-like. What does that mean for the ecumenicity of the ecumenical movement? These churches do not know how to work within an international organization, and that means that their contribution is lost. Only those churches which have been shaped to think, talk and argue as we do, have a chance to be heard.

The international Pentecostal organizations are no better—with a few exceptions such as the European Pentecostal Theological Association,[27] and the Society for Pentecostal Studies,[28] both small academic minority organizations. The Pentecostal World Conference has certainly not solved the problem—it has simply placed another international bureaucracy alongside those already existing. The result is that only about sixty million of the over four hundred million Pentecostals/charismatics/independents are represented in some way in these Pentecostal World Conferences. The majority are entirely uninterested.[29]

Yet, "no one can be truly ecumenical without being evangelical, just as no one can be truly evangelical without being ecumenical."[30] If that dictum be true, then we—that is the ecumenical movement, the theological academics, the Pentecostal scholars—have to put our resources together; we have to learn how to act and speak internationally in oral categories, in liturgies and songs, in prayers and bible studies (and this does not mean speaking unpolitically); thus might we have a chance. Hans Ruedi Weber from the World Council of Churches and others have shown the way.[31]

It could also be that some of our own problems can be solved in working with the Pentecostals; for example, we might discover an oral homiletic; a

---

[26] Vanelderen, "WCC," 1100.

[27] *EPTA Bulletin* (EPTA=European Pentecostal Theological Association).

[28] *Pneuma.* Journal of the Society for Pentecostal Studies.

[29] Vanelderen, "Conference."

[30] Curlee–Curlee, *Springtime,* iv, quoting John A. Mackay from an unpublished manuscript (Presbyterian Historical Society, Philadelphia, "Mackay papers"; interview William Rodman).

[31] Weber, H.-R., *Experiments.* See also Vogt, *Bibelarbeit.*

church music which is nearer to the people;[32] participatory services; inclusion of charismata which are almost absent in our Western culture; and finally a ministry to the heavy-laden and weary which is not directed by so-called charismatic healers from overseas, but by the community of the local congregation, which cooperates with doctors and psychiatrists, avoiding the ugly features of big healing campaigns.[33] In the process we might discover that it is possible to speak in tongues and be a critical scholar, or to be a reputable researcher who undertakes scholarly work equally well in both literary and oral categories.

There is one who has shown us the way: it is our Lord. His parables are models of content and communication. He could be deep and scholarly, yet oral. Oral people are not stupid people. They are just oral, as we have shown in the Centre for Black and White Christian Partnership (chapter 9, pp. 106–16). This school has discovered in part how theology can break out of its bourgeois and literary ghetto. Who knows, the study of and with Pentecostals could inspire us in this.

From the Pentecostal side one must ask, now that there is a slow distancing of Pentecostalism from certain aspects of evangelicalism: Why should Pentecostals restrict their contacts to evangelicals?[34] Do not catholics and the conciliar movements need the testimony of Pentecostalism even more, especially as evangelicals have proved to be some of the most resistant to the Pentecostal witness?

Here is a prayer for my fellow evangelicals and for myself:

Prayer of the Turtle

God,
sometimes I feel like a turtle.
I carry this big shell on my back.
It protects me.
But it also makes it difficult for me to meet other people.
I cannot get through to them and they cannot get through to me.
But dear God,
I have not chosen to be a turtle.
Neither my parents nor you did ask me whether I wanted to be a turtle,
nor indeed, whether I wanted to be born or not.
So I am here, just here.
Sometimes I would prefer to be a flamingo,
or a deer, or a swallow, or an eagle, or a mighty roaring lion.
But I am none of these.
I am simply a turtle.
And so I ask you, O God,
be a little patient with me
when I do not understand you
when I do not understand your children,

---

[32] See chapter 21, pp. 269–87.
[33] See chapter 18, pp. 233–37.
[34] Bridges-Johns, "Adolescence," 3–17.

just be a little patient when I am slow to understand your love
and your generosity,
your truth and your wisdom.
Please, help me to live the life of a turtle
who feels loved, accepted and useful,
who feels the rays of your love through my shell.

IV

THE CRITICAL ROOT

"Pentecostalism is anti-intellectual, evangelical-fundamentalist and anti-ecumenical." These are three characterizations which can no longer be accepted without qualification. It is true one finds a lot of anti-intellectualism in Pentecostalism—this has reasons, as C. van der Laan explains in the case of Gerrit Polman, the founder of Dutch Pentecostalism. "Polman was not equipped with the tools to develop a theology in which inconsistencies are acceptable and ended up as a sectarian against his will. Surely this was not his fault alone. He received no help from the Evangelical colleagues nor from the academic theologians."[1]

But now this has changed, as I will try to demonstrate. A number of Pentecostals are engaged in a critical reassessment of their own roots. The trouble is that their publications are not read by Pentecostal leaders (not to speak of the rank and file), who in general have no idea what a mine of insight and dedicated scholarship they are missing (however, here, Pentecostals are not very much different from other churches). In most cases the Pentecostal periodicals do not report the critical yet deeply spiritual and helpful essays and dissertations of their own scholars. This is all the more reason for the mainline theological journals and publishers to take them up: they would be astonished what a wide market this research could command. However, it is my own experience that most mainline publishers want easy, sensational or simply "up-lifting" manuscripts from Pentecostals, not specialized analyses on Pentecostalism and ecumenism, Pentecostalism and social ethics, Pentecostalism and pacifism, Pentecostalism and feminism, Pentecostalism and critical exegesis, and so forth. On all these issues Pentecostals have original contributions to make which are based on grass-roots experiences.

---

[1] C. van der Laan, *Sectarian Against His Will*, 306; see chapter 25, pp. 345–47.

As to the characterization of Pentecostals as Evangelical Fundamental-ists,[2] it must be said that for a long time Pentecostals tried to present themselves as a kind of "Evangelicals plus"; that is, Evangelicals plus fire, dedication, missionary success, speaking in tongues, and gifts of healing. But that will no longer do, especially because of the heavy dispensationalism one finds in evangelicalism, that conflicts with a Pentecostal hermeneutics which refuses to relegate the gifts of the Spirit to the formative period of Christianity.[3] Pentecostalism is thus a denomination *sui generis:* its roots in the black, oral tradition of the American slaves, in the Catholic tradition of Wesley, in the evangelical tradition of the American holiness movement (with its far-reaching political, social, and ecumenical programs), in the critical tradition of both the holiness movement and critical Western theology, in the ecumenical tradition—all this qualifies it as a movement which is not just a sub-division of evangelicalism on fire. This, despite the fact that most Pentecostal denominations' official statements use out-dated confessional concepts of the turn of the century and pseudo-rationalist thought patterns of the last century which in no way express their dynamic and inspiring spirituality, and which are only magnified by a sometimes frightening Pentecostal triumphalism.

Yet, the men and women whom I discuss in this volume deserve to be taken seriously by both Pentecostals and non-Pentecostals. Most of them do theology in the context of memories of suffering and defamation, of being ridiculed and persecuted (sometimes by their own brothers and sisters in the faith who either do not understand them and are therefore frightened, or have "gone over" to the right-wing money aristocracy of this world). They use the standard methods of historical and exegetical research. Because of their specific religious socialization they refuse to drive a wedge between "the spiritual" and "the material," and thus take seriously the praxis of early Pentecostalism (but not its ideology). They try to articulate a theology which expresses, in a true biblical way, God's interest and love in *this* world without giving up the convictions that God is always beyond our experiences of God, and that the Spirit of God is not identical with how we experience Him (or Her). The Spirit still has something new in store for us, of which we have not thought. Unity and diversity in the Christian church needs an expression which goes beyond the bureaucratic organizational models and the conceptual patterns of the Western world: perhaps the God who came to terms with the KGB and the Stasi in the former communist countries may also come to terms with this Pentecostal movement. Remember the book of Jonah! God could deal aptly with the monstrous state of Nineveh, its concentration camps and its secret police; he could work with the wild sea and with the pagan seamen; but the question remained open: could he also come to terms with his prophet

---

[2] See above, chapter 15, pp. 190–92.
[3] Sheppard, "Dispensationalism."

Jonah? So today the question may be put: can he also come to terms with the power structures of Pentecostalism; with its ideological hard-liners and its amazing capacity to forget its history—the "history of the slaves who came out from Egypt," from the religious rat-race, the money-based power structures and the conformism with this world?

CHAPTER SIXTEEN

Battle Against Unjust Structures

Social Ethics: Making the Truth Visible

United States Pentecostals generally have a difficult time imagining that there are Pentecostals in Latin America who value major elements of Liberation Theology, who supported the Sandinista government in Nicaragua, who aided the Socialist President Salvador Allende to rise to power in Chile,[1] or who hold and value membership in the World Council of Churches.[2] Americans do not have to go to Latin America to find such conundrums. There are difficult discoveries much nearer to home, among Hispanic Pentecostals in the United States. On March 13, 1981, at the Riverside Church Conference on the Church and the City, the Coalition of Hispanic Leadership disrupted a panel on "Liberation Theology" to protest the exclusion of Hispanics from the conference program. The chant of protest (Basta ya! No nos pueden ignorar!) echoed the sentiments of millions of Hispanics[3] living in American urban centers whose cry is not being heard by the religious establishment. Three of the original five members listed in the "Riverside Manifesto"[4]

---

[1] Gaxiola-Gaxiola, "Latin American," in particular, 123.

[2] Robeck, "Southern," 103.

[3] A "Hispanic" is a US citizen with Latin American roots. See Villafañe's comprehensive overview of Hispanic culture and religion in the US (not just Pentecostal) in his *The Liberating Spirit*.

[4] The Manifesto stated: "The Coalition of Hispanic Christian Leadership as a prophetic act of conscience charge the American religious establishment with the following complaints:

were Pentecostals, including the chairperson Rev. Benjamin Alicea.[5]

This manifesto is an extraordinary document, reflecting a new type of political ethics among Hispanic Pentecostals. It criticizes the churches and the state for its oppressive policy, including Reagan's economic and foreign policy in Latin America. It deplores the fact that Hispanic music, theology, liturgy and language is denied its rightful place in the American religious community, thus depriving the religious establishment of important Hispanic contributions. The universities and theological seminaries are not excluded from this criticism because they refuse to hire indigenous Hispanic faculty. Bilingual education, very important for a multi–cultural society, is rejected. "There has always been plenty of rhetoric, but very little action or financial and academic support." This is a truly Pentecostal document reflecting not only the economic plight but more so the cultural and religious marginalization of Hispanics. It highlights forcefully the interplay between the cultural, the spiritual, and the political.

---

1. The social issues relevant to the Hispanic community are not seriously addressed in the conferences, radio and television programs funded and staffed by the Mainline Protestants, Conservative Fundamentalists and Establishment Evangelicals. Social issues of particular interest to Hispanics are: undocumented workers, U.S. foreign policy in Latin America, the impact of multinational corporations in Latin America, bi-lingual education in America and the adverse impact of Reagan's economic policy on Hispanics.

2. The contributions of Hispanic people in the life and ministry of the Church in the city are systematically and categorically ignored. National and regional conferences (such as the Riverside Church Conference on the City, Washington '80 and the American Festival on Evangelism) exclude significant participation of indigenous Hispanics in the planning and implementation stages. The absence of Hispanic speakers in regional and national events deprive the Christian community of an Hispanic perspective.

3. The American religious establishment must assume its share of the responsibility for (1) the decay of urban areas and the deplorable conditions under which Hispanics must live in American cities, and (2) the Church's policy to neglect, desert or undermine the resources of the Hispanic people. The only churches that have remained to service the spiritual needs of the Hispanic people residing in the inner cities of our country are the indigenous and independent Hispanic churches.

4. Hispanic liturgy and theology have been denied their rightful place in the American religious community. Our music, theology, literature and language have been rejected. The Church has served as an instrument of assimilation instead of human liberation and fulfillment. The Church has perpetuated paternalism, division and oppression which have aggravated and deprived the American religious establishment of the contributions of the Hispanic religious experience.

5. Theological seminaries and graduate schools of religion have discriminated against Hispanics by refusing to hire indigenous Hispanic faculty, provide supportive services and allocate financial resources. The educational establishment has rejected the legitimacy of bi-lingual theological education as a viable and indispensable ingredient for men and women in the ministry. There has always been plenty of rhetoric, but very little action or financial and academic support. Quoted in Villafañe, *The Liberating Spirit*, 70f., and in Costas, *Outside*, 115f.

[5] Villafañe, *The Liberating Spirit*, 69.

White American Pentecostals might also be astonished to hear North American history told by one of their fellow Pentecostals "from the other side," namely from the side of those victimized, when half of Mexico was "given" to the United States (1848), "leaving several thousand Spanish and Mexicans 'captive strangers in their own land.' "[6] They might be surprised to hear Reis Lopez-Tijerina stating that for him "The struggle for land[7] is not only a political question; it is also a spiritual mission of justice against the oppression of Chicanos in the South West by the United States government."[8] In his protest, Lopez-Tijerina even went so far as to raid the courthouse of Tierra Amarilla. Tijerina is admittedly a controversial person, and many Pentecostals do not claim him. Nevertheless, says the Hispanic Pentecostal scholar Eldin Villafañe, he "represents that 'spirit' of the oppressed among Hispanic Pentecostals that see the Gospel's concern for social justice and wholistic liberation."[9]

Villafañe is one of the foremost Hispanic Pentecostal theologians.[10] He is professor of Christian Social Ethics at Gordon-Conwell Theological Seminary. He was founder-director (1976–1990) of the Center for Urban Ministerial Education (CUME) in Boston. He is an ordained minister of the Hispanic Eastern District of the Assemblies of God, and served as the first president of La Comunidad of Hispanic Scholars of Theology and Religion. He earned his Ph.D. in Social Ethics from Boston University. In *The Liberating Spirit* he discusses the pitfalls and promises, the pains and joys of oral theology in relation to social ethics. He manages to engage in dialogue not only with his own roots but also with the world of learning—theological, sociological, and political.

Another impressive document of a change in Pentecostal social ethics is a volume of essays on "Global Mission in Pentecostal Perspective."[11] The editors state: "Pentecostal missiological literature has not kept pace with the explosive growth of the Pentecostal churches worldwide."[12] This task is taken up in the book by a number of authors, in a dynamic expansion which produces

---

[6] The Catholic Church then "ousted the native Mexican clergy and bishops and replaced them with French and Spaniards. These were replaced in turn, in the twentieth century, by Irish and German Americans. This trend has continued to exist to this date with attempts at redress beginning to appear in the 1960s and early 1970s." "That there are only 400 native-born Hispanic priests—so few in proportion to the Hispanic population—seriously affects the relation of the Hispanics with the (Catholic) Church in America." Father Ritilio del Riego in Lucas, *Browning*, 40; quoted in Villafañe, *The Liberating Spirit*, 47.

[7] In this instance the Kit Carson National Forest in New Mexico which in 1848 was "skillfully and manipulatively extorted by the 'gringos'." Villafañe, *The Liberating Spirit*, 97.

[8] Guerrero, *Chicano*, 36f., quoted in Villafañe, *The Liberating Spirit*, 97.

[9] Villafañe, *The Liberating Spirit*, 97.

[10] See his *The Liberating Spirit* and "Call."

[11] Dempster–Klaus–Petersen, *Called.*

[12] Ibid., xv.

"a theology on the move," whose "character has been more experiential than cognitive, more activist than reflective." Astonishingly the authors start their missiological reflection with the thesis "that the roots of our conviction about the global mission of the church are to be found in Jesus' proclamation of the kingdom of God."[13] This New Testament foundation of mission (laid by one of Pentecostalism's most gifted New Testament scholars) is decisive for the rest of the book.

In the following chapter, "Evangelism, Social Concern, and the Kingdom of God,"[14] the missiological task is expressed not as one of *preaching* social concern, but as one of acting as a Christian social witness, thus "making the truth visible."[15] The gospel requires "the validation of a living community that translates proclaimed truth into social practice."[16] Furthermore, Christian social action itself must aim at "changing the system."[17]

> One of the purposes of the church's social action programs is to desacralize the political power of human governments. By maintaining the option of what Stephen Mott has labeled as the way of "strategic non-cooperation," the church can reserve its right to say its "no" to Caesar through organized action-plans; . . . the gospel of the kingdom, more than anything else, can undemonize the state with its totalitarian pretensions and demythologize its claim to autonomy.[18]

Only in the third place does the article's author, Murray W. Dempster, mention the social programs of the church. Their function is to construct "alternative systems of justice."[19]

Elsewhere, the Swiss Jean-Daniel Plüss asks: "When will the disciples of Jesus hold their conference of disarmament?"[20] Even in Chile, where the CIA has tried to influence Pentecostalism, the Pentecostals sent an open letter to Pinochet expressing their dismay relating to the gap existing between the "sad reality in this country and the official reports on television."[21]

Finally Kathleen Harder has demonstrated the "expanding politicization of the World Pentecostal Movement,"[22] showing that "Pentecostals are becoming more political, but about different things."[23] Based on the American

---

[13] Fee, "Global," 7. With the same starting point but with another goal: Suurmond, "Christ King."

[14] Dempster, "Evangelism." See also idem, "Mandate."

[15] Dempster, "Evangelism," 29.

[16] Ibid., 30.

[17] Ibid., 35.

[18] Ibid. As a positive example of such action, Frank Macchia points to Christoph Blumhardt: "the inseparability of spiritual from bodily existence . . . made Christoph a socialist" (Macchia, "Waiting and Hurrying," n.p.).

[19] Dempster, "Evangelism," 12.

[20] Plüss, "European," 44. Plüss quotes here a leader of the German Pentecostal movement, C. O. Voget.

[21] *EPTA Bulletin* 5/3, 1986, 119f.

[22] Harder, "Expanding."

[23] Ibid., 12.

experience, she expected to find Pentecostals worldwide to be mainly politically conservative. "Surprisingly the majority of the respondents, 32 of the 56,[24] asserted that there was no such pattern, and most explained that Pentecostals were spread out among the parties."[25] As we have already seen in our analysis of black Pentecostals in the USA, Pentecostals of that group have marched and demonstrated for or against certain public policies. In the lower house of Brazil's Congress, thirty-five Pentecostals were serving by 1990; nineteen were members of the same Assemblies of God congregation.[26]

Pentecostalism and Theology of Liberation

The usual picture which is given of Latin American Pentecostalism is this: Latin American Pentecostals do marvelous evangelistic and charitable work, which constitutes a viable alternative to political and economic structural change. But that is not the whole truth. It is quite true that Pentecostals use an individualistic language, and that they concentrate on the personal (not societal) evils. They fight violence against women, they build schools, they combat drunkenness, they offer the poor and silenced people a language. It is clear that if this was all they did, they would be highly praised by the national and multinational companies, which respect the good workers Pentecostalism produces.[27] However, there is also another side to the story.

For a number of Pentecostals dialogue with theology of liberation has become imperative. This is the task to which Douglas Petersen[28] sets himself.

> To be relevant, theology simply must respond to the questions that the poor are asking. The marginalized are not interested in the traditionally scientific/theological ideas, rather, they want to know how God could abandon them so totally in the physical realm. Unless the church is a participant in this question, the liberationists argue, it has no reason for being.

Petersen discusses this hermeneutical approach in detail and agrees with it to a great extent, although he has, like Segundo and others, some reservations on a wholesale acceptance of the Marxist basis.

Some Pentecostal critique has also been directed at the mainly Catholic theology of liberation. This theology is confusing, says Harold D. Hunter, "because social activists often speak of liberating the poor but seem to have little appreciation for those (like Pentecostals) who minister to the working class."[29] In echoing what Catholics themselves have perceived, Cecilia Loreto

---

[24] Ibid., 17. She interviewed a selected number of Pentecostal participants at the Conference of Brighton, England, 1991.

[25] Ibid., 10.

[26] Ibid., 19; Marcom, "Fire."

[27] Ströbele-Gregor, "Indios."

[28] Petersen, "Kingdom," 47.

[29] Harold D. Hunter in a review of Harrell, *Oral Roberts,* in *EPTA Bulletin* 5/2, 1986, 59–61, quote 60.

Maríz[30] says: "The Catholic Church opts for the poor because it is not a church of the poor. Pentecostal churches do not opt for the poor because they are already a poor people's church and that is why the poor people are opting for them." Nevertheless, a number of Latin American Pentecostals are seeing the necessity for dealing with structural injustice,[31] acknowledging that personal ethics is necessary, but not sufficient. Carmelo E. Alvarez, for example, notes that the search for a just life and a just community involves dealing with economic and political structures.[32]

The most explicit author on this topic is probably the Chilean Pentecostal Juan Sepúlveda. Along with Dempster Sepúlveda sees the Pentecostal church as a "healing community." "Healing is not just understood as a medical term but also as a social term. The church is an alternative to society."[33] He compares Pentecostalism and liberation theology at the ecclesial rather than the propositional level.[34] The two types of church entities he analyzes are the Catholic Base Ecclesial Communities and what he calls Criollo Pentecostalism (i.e., autochthonous and indigenous Latin American Pentecostal communities as over against the Pentecostalism which has been imported from the US). In these new ecclesial experiences he sees affinities and differences. The differences lie in the fact that the members of Criollo Pentecostalism have typically gone through a traumatic conversion experience, which has given them new meaning and a new community—but has also separated them from society. In the Catholic Base Ecclesial Communities, on the other hand, such conversion experiences are less dramatic. Criollo Pentecostals see in this world the reign of the "prince of this world." Base Ecclesial Communities, on the other hand, developed in a setting of effervescent hope for change, in particular after Vatican II. For both, however, salvation is not an immaterial thought but a concrete reality in the here and now.[35] Carmelo E. Alvarez rightly detects in the majority of works analyzing Latin American Pentecostalism (especially the ones which deal with church growth) a kind of "Manichean reading," which does not see these material, positive elements in the movement.[36] On the other

---

[30] Maríz, *Coping*, 138.

[31] Special issue of *Pastoralia* 7/15, December 1985 on "Pentecostalismo y teología de la liberación." Ramón Flores, "Hermit" (an interesting combination of Pentecostal spirituality with social and political ethics).

[32] Alvarez, *Santidad*, reviewed by David Bundy, *Pneuma* 8/2, Fall 1986, 187. See also Alvarez, *Pentecostalismo*, reviewed by Anders Ruuth in *Evangelio y Sociedad* 18, July-Sept. 1993, 26–27. See also Bundy's review in *International Review of Missions* 83/331, Oct. 1994, 637–39.

[33] This is based on a paper by Sepúlveda, "Reflections."

[34] Sepúlveda, "Liberation."

[35] Volf, "Materiality."

[36] See the important booklet *Algo mas que opio* [Something more than opium] (eds. Boudewijnse/Droogers/Kamsteeg). Quote in the introduction by Carmelo E. Alvarez, 11. Julio de Santa Ana also makes a difference between the "rural" and the "urban" Pentecostals (similar to Sepúlveda); the rurals engage in a fight for land ("la lucha per la tierra"), the urbans conform more or less to the laws of capitalism if left

hand, the Catholics have learned from the Pentecostals that the absence of a priest does not mean the end of the church.[37]

Another difference is found in the two groups' approach to the Bible. For many Pentecostals, the Bible was their first contact with the written word. Some have learned to read by using it; thus, all reality is seen through the Bible "lens." In the Base Ecclesial Communities the readers come to the Bible with their daily problems (as, for example, in the method developed by Ernesto Cardenal[38] and Carlos Masters).[39] This would seem to be a fundamental difference. Methodologically the Pentecostals use an *exe*getical process, even if it is rustic, and are generally literal and not critical in their interpretation. The Catholics use an *eis*egetic process. In practice, this means that in Criollo Pentecostalism the Bible is read, interpreted and proclaimed by abstracting the problems, tensions, and questions of real life, resulting in a "spiritualization" of the biblical message. The Base Ecclesial Communities, for their part, seek in the Bible a mirror in which they may see themselves and discover a theological justification for their social struggle, thus "politicizing" the message.

Although this impression is partially correct, at least as a tendency (and on the conscious level), a more rigorous analysis shows that Criollo Pentecostalism also reads the Bible from a real life viewpoint. As with the Catholics, the Bible helps them to understand themselves in their context. Therefore Sepúlveda comes to the conclusion that a dialogue between the two approaches is necessary and helpful. In his opinion Criollo Pentecostalism and Catholic Base Ecclesial Communities have more in common than is generally acknowledged. They are not contradictions but come to the same truth from opposite ecclesial, biographical, and social contexts.

In his treatment of Base Ecclesial Communities, Adoniram Gaxiola correctly observes that these communities were "intended as a means of stopping Protestantism." But the "result was instead 'a parallel church, and, in the last instance, a schismatic church,' "[40] He is seconded in this by Harvey Cox, who writes:

> The intention of the ecclesial machinery in giving life to the Ecclesial Base Communities was to re-organize the periphery and to direct it towards a centralized power [, but] this time the mechanism "went hay-wire," and the periphery distanced itself still more from the centralized power. The base communities rebounded against . . . the vertical structure and dismantled it.[41]

---

in peace. Interview by Schippers with Julio de Santa Ana ("Julio"), quote in Boudewijnse/Droogers/Kamsteeg, *Algo*, 56.

[37] *Eclesiogenesis*, 13.
[38] Cardenal, *Love in Practice*.
[39] Masters, *Colección*.
[40] Gaxiola, "Poverty," 169.
[41] Cox, *Religión*, 111, quoted in Gaxiola, "Poverty," 169.

In returning to this chapter's main topic, namely an emerging social ethics in Latin America, I want to draw attention to the works of a specialist who has done extensive field research in Central America, and who was won for Christianity by Pentecostals. His conclusions:[42] Pentecostals are expecting the return of their Lord. "This understanding of the world corresponds to their experience, i.e., their earthly fate cannot be changed by them." Theirs, then, is the strategy of survival of the despondent, for example in Guatemala. Very different voices, however, emerge from the charismatic renewal. Schäfer calls it the Neo-Pentecostal money aristocracy in Central America. They hold their prayer meetings in exclusive hotels and actively support police terror and torture. That means in certain cases they are torturing their own brothers in the faith, the poor Pentecostals. In contrast to these brothers, the charismatics have as their own aim freedom for big business and suppression of social protest through an authoritarian state. All this is biblically camouflaged as the fight of the good against the evil. That "the evil" can also be their own brothers and sisters in the faith who happen to be on the other side of the social divide, is a particularly cruel irony of this story. However, the independent and indigenous Pentecostal churches (those which Sepúlveda called Criollo Pentecostals) have discovered that they are not helpless victims of a cruel world-law. They know that God gives them power and hope to change the world. They organize themselves and even accept political mandates. "God demands from us a prophetic stance."[43]

Dennis Smith, a Presbyterian working in Guatemala, confirms Schäfer's picture of the charismatic money aristocracy: Some of them "were well-connected in local and international politics." They "embraced New Right politics as a logical extension of their new found gospel." He pointedly asks:

What about the businessman who participates in a Full Gospel Businessmen's prayer every Tuesday, and attends worship at a Neo-Pentecostal church three or four times a week? Does his faith affect his business ethics? Will he permit his employees to organize a union? Will he continue to fire and rehire his production workers every six months so that he can avoid paying Social Security benefits? Will his home continue to be plagued with domestic violence? In a highly polarized society like Guatemala's, those who have wealth and power and who

---

[42] Schäfer, " . . . und erlöse uns von dem Bösen" See also his "Dualistische." Schäfer wrote his doctoral dissertation on a related theme under the supervision of Konrad Raiser, now General Secretary of the World Council of Churches (Schäfer, *Zentralamerika*). Will this open the door to a more serious commitment of the WCC for the poor Pentecostals? A very different presentation of the situation in Guatemala in Wilson, E. A., "Passion and Power," on Guatemala, 77ff.

[43] Schäfer, " . . . und erlöse uns von dem Bösen" quotes from a Spanish document in detail (Declaración de la consulta de lideres educationales de la Iglesia de Dios: Desarrolle de un modelo pastoral pentecostal frente a la teología de la liberación, in *Pastoralia*, San José, Costa Rica, No. 15, 10/1989, 102f.).

claim to have had their lives transformed by the Spirit of God are faced with a special responsibility to practice justice, humility and mercy.

And how about those who now hold high public office? Will they be less corrupt and less abusive of human rights than their predecessors? So far President Serrano and his closest advisers have shown that they are fond of the trappings of office. Pomp and protocol are practiced religiously. In classic Neo-Pentecostal style, Serrano and his advisers are very conspicuous consumers of luxury automobiles, exclusive clothing and the finest culinary fare. Serrano preaches fiscal responsibility, but has chosen not to eliminate the huge Presidential discretionary fund that has been a major source of corruption in the past. Human rights violations have increased sharply since Serrano assumed office in January 1991. Drug traffickers and human rights violators in the army continue to operate with impunity.[44]

Less critical is Karl Braunhart, who wrote his theological dissertation at the University of Heidelberg on the neo-Pentecostals in Honduras. Although numerically not very strong, this group is politically influential.[45] According to Braunhart one of the neo-Pentecostal churches ("Vida Abundante") attracts mainly "professionals, well educated specialists of middle and higher ranks. A great percentage of church members has one or two university degrees. 40–50 engineers, besides lawyers, doctors and architects are members."[46] Braunhart gives a detailed picture of these churches; but he is mainly interested in their social and political positions. He shows that "seen from the point of social and political science they diagnose and describe the problem of the country correctly."[47] As to the solutions, they prefer neo-liberal measures. Their structural priorities are "democratization of capital," participation of workers in enterprise capital, and so on. On the political task of the church Braunhart reports: "A part of the membership denies that the church has to take sides in political matters. She should concentrate on spiritual issues. . . . The Neo-Pentecostal Benjamin Villanueva who is also finance minister of Honduras represents this position clearly."[48]

> Another part of the membership affirms a strong political involvement and sees in the lack of such an involvement the weakness of the Protestant churches in Honduras. According to Pastor Peñalba the Catholic Church has loosened its relationship with the powerful and rich. But the Protestants have yet to find a political role in their fight against injustice. Pastor Peñalba includes explicitly his own church in this judgment.[49]

---

[44] Smith, Dennis, "Coming," 139.

[45] According to Braunhart (*Heiliger Geist,* 39, 41), 37% of Protestants in Honduras are in classical Pentecostal churches. In addition to this, there are 4%–5% Neo-Pentecostals (they are the object of his research).

[46] Ibid., 58.

[47] Ibid., 127

[48] Ibid., 143, xxix–xxxii.

[49] Ibid., 143.

To sum up, Braunhart says:

> The problems of society are clearly seen. However, the status quo is not questioned. They try to improve it by involving converted Christians in the political process. . . . De facto Honduras has a policy which is geared to the needs of the middle and upper-middle classes and consequently neglects the poor. For this policy Neo-Pentecostals take some responsibility. That is why their demands for more justice lack teeth. This is underscored by their lack of social ethics.[50]

> The Neo-Pentecostals churches address the problem of insecurity in a society of crises. They offer stabilizing norm-systems and concrete advice for individuals. Some, however, are involved in the political arena. . . . Neo-Pentecostal theology and spirituality is therefore a religion of success and corresponds to the interests of those who have worked hard and try to defend their newly acquired status.[51]

The neo-Pentecostal churches, in other words, meet the needs of an emerging middle and upper class—needs which the Catholic church could not meet. Consequently they represent a neo-liberal economic and social system. Whether this is sufficient for Honduras is another question. However, the situation in Honduras is not very different, it seems to me, from that of the rest of Protestant churches in the world, including the church of Wurttemburg, of which Karl Braunhart is a pastor.

In relation to the dilemma between the poor Pentecostals and the Pentecostals with money and power, Harvey Cox (who considers himself "a sympathetic fellow traveler" of Pentecostalism and has "developed a genuine fondness for the movement" knowing "how much the world needs its message and its spirit") nevertheless sees cause for genuine concern. He writes:

> In America, most white Pentecostals have become terribly comfortable with "this world." They started out as a faith that brought hope to the rejects and the losers. Today some of their most visible representatives have become ostentatiously rich. They started out as a rebellion against creeds. Today many of their preachers cling doggedly to such recently invented dogmas as the verbal inerrancy of the Bible. They started out teaching that signs and wonders that took place in their congregations were not some kind of spectral fireworks but harbingers of God's new day. Today some Pentecostals have become so obsessed with the techniques of rapture that they have forgotten the original message. They started out as radical antagonists of the status-quo, refusing to fight the bloody wars of this fallen age. Many have now turned into flag-waving super-patriots, easy marks for the demagogues of the new religious right. They started out as a radically inclusive spiritual fellowship in which race and gender virtually disappeared. That is hardly the case, at least in most white Pentecostal churches today.

> But I have not given up hope. In fact what impressed me most about the people I met at the Society for Pentecostal Studies was not just their openness to dialogue but also their commitment to rescue their own movement from the

---

[50] Ibid., 150.
[51] Ibid., 157.

distortions it has suffered, especially in recent years. What I found there was an expanding company of young Pentecostal leaders who are determined not to barter the power of their remarkable movement for a questionable batch of currently religious and political slogans.[52]

That Dennis Smith's and Harvey Cox's concern is shared by not a few Pentecostal leaders can be seen from the fact that they published these scholars' reflections in a Pentecostal periodical. The ability for critical self-examination has always been a mark of the Spirit.

Pentecostalism and Marxism

Peter Kuzmič[53] from former Yugoslavia, wrote his dissertation on the Serbo-Croatic Bible translation at the Catholic Faculty of the University of Zagreb. He has discovered that the topic of Marxism can "generate more heat than light," and agrees with Paul Tillich: Marx's name "has become so potent a political and semi–religious symbol, divine or demonic, that whatever you say about him will be used against you by fanatics on both sides."[54] He is aware that dogmatic Marxism is dead. "Even if the process were reversible by sheer use of military power, the people would not take it any longer. Where all of this will lead is impossible to predict."[55]

In Kuzmič's opinion Marxism is neither monolithic nor is it—as is sometimes said—neutral science. Christians must know that Marxism and Christianity are "actually relatives, relatives historically and philosophically at odds with each other." "Nicolai Berdyaev argued that communism and Christianity are rival religions, and William Temple explained the similarity of Christian and Marxist social ideas by pronouncing the latter a Christian heresy."[56]

In Eastern Europe Pentecostals have learned to distinguish between "dogmatic" (rigid, inflexible, bureaucratic, consistently anti-Christian) and "non-dogmatic" (humanist, tolerant, philosophically open for dialogue) Marxists. We also must differentiate between Marxism where it is in power, where it is a marginal or emerging force, and where it is outlawed and thus underground. Kuzmič quotes the "excellent Lutheran document 'Theological Reflection Upon the Encounter of the Church with Marxism in Various Cultural Contexts' "[57] and outlines these similarities and differences in detail. He agrees with Hugo Assman's comparison of "non-dogmatic Marxism and authentic Biblical Christianity" on the functional, although not on the ideological, level.

---

[52] Cox, "Reflections," 34.

[53] Sandidge, "Kuzmič."

[54] Tillich, "Marx," 906.

[55] Kuzmič, "Respond," 144. This article contains a detailed bibliography of Kuzmič's work on Marxism.

[56] Cf. Lyon, *Karl Marx*, 11–12; Kuzmič, "Respond," 147.

[57] "Theological Reflections on the Encounter of the Church with Marxism in Various Cultural Contexts," in Mojzes (ed.), *Varieties of Christian-Marxist Dialogue,* 67.

Both have a specific relationship to truth. Both understand truth as something which happens. Truth is not something which simply exists but which emerges. Both are therefore in opposition to objectivism and idealism.

> The perception that Christianity and Marxism are irreconcilable enemies which can meet only on a battle-ground has enormous destructive potential for the international community and the future of humanity. This crusader mentality is a betrayal of the gospel for it reduces the Christian faith to a politico-ideological force. It may also be a distortion of Marxism . . . While in the East, Christian truth and values are officially opposed, in the West they are often verbally honored while practically they are ignored or even totally rejected.[58]

"Christianity is not the official ideology of the West and capitalism is not the economic theory of Biblical faith. Old extreme positions must go: Christianity should no longer be identified with anti-communism nor should Marxism be reduced to militant atheism."[59] That does not mean for Kuzmič that the Christian church must make compromises with the communists. He agrees with Jan Milič Lochman, a Czech theologian, that "any attempts to relate the gospel too closely to an ideology is dangerous for its integrity and identity."[60]

He is well informed on Pentecostals in China and in the former Soviet Union and points to their strength and growth. As the Marxist specialist Aleksei Trofimovich Moskalenko has also discovered, prayer and glossolalia are a strength of these movements: "Such is the influence of the prayer meetings of the Pentecostals on the consciousness and feelings of believers. It is one of the most powerful means of religion's influence. Very often only two or three visits to these meetings are quite sufficient for the leaders of the congregation to turn a novice into a religious fanatic, a zealous adherent of the Pentecostal sect."[61] The largest Pentecostal church in Romania (in Timisoara) has an attendance of about 5,000, with over 3,000 active members, but it has never had one salaried minister.[62] In China, the Marxist revolution, which wanted to destroy the church by separating pastors from their congregations and by confiscating the church buildings, "has strengthened the Chinese church. It was forced to discover New Testament principles of congregational life."[63]

Kuzmič also sees the weakness of Pentecostals in these countries: the generation gap, a lack of concern for larger human and social issues, and a retreat from the world.

For Pentecostals, however, it is imperative to discover that Marxist criticism of religion—with all its stereotypes, abuse of science and false

---

[58] Kuzmič, "Respond," 152.
[59] Ibid., 153.
[60] Lochman, *Encountering Marx*, 15. Kuzmič, "Respond," 155.
[61] Moskalenko, *Piatidesiatniki;* Kuzmič, "Respond," 156. On the Pentecostals in Russia see *The Pentecostals*, 267–87 and Fletcher, *Soviet.*
[62] Kuzmič, "Respond," 157.
[63] Ibid.

propaganda—"is not all wrong, and we have come to acknowledge that the rise
and spread of Western and Marxist atheism is proportionately related to the
shrinking credibility of the institutional Christian church." He refers explicitly to Hromádka.

> We must humbly acknowledge that religion was frequently used as a manipulat-
> ive tool of the powerful and mighty, often serving as an ideological screen to
> justify the actions of powerful oppressors to pacify the poor and exploited.
> White-washing unjust wars, justifying economic injustices and blatant exploita-
> tion, and smoke-screening racial discrimination are only some of the obvious
> evils that the church has practiced for ages . . . The Pentecostals as "the church
> of the working class"—as they have been occasionally labeled—and as a move-
> ment of the "whole/full gospel," are in a unique position to overcome this
> criticism and other Marxist prejudices and stereotypes.[64]

In my chapter on Italy I have described this working class, which many
times voted for the communists. For whom else could they vote? Perhaps for
the Democrazia Cristiana with its violence against Pentecostalism?[65]

I finish this chapter on the "Battle Against Unjust Structures" with a
prayer with and for all those who are manipulated in the present world.

Prayer of the Cow

O my God,
Sometimes I feel like a cow,
a big, beautiful milk cow.
I must eat to make milk and manure.
In the past I had a name
and the farmer came in the morning
and scratched me between my horns.
Now I am only a unit of production
and I produce milk and manure.
In the past the bull came once a year
now only the veterinary doctor comes.
Why must I be a cow?
Why can I not be a beautiful hart or an eagle or a butterfly?
Why am I just a unit of production
who is judged according to her profitability?
And when I cease to produce I am superfluous.
Could I not be a more human cow?
How can I do that?
Yes, I could do something.
I could produce an almighty heap of manure
and submerge the whole country in it.
But is that a solution?
I would drown myself.

---

[64] Ibid., 161.
[65] *The Pentecostals*, 251–66. This situation has in fact probably now changed, but
I have no exact information.

Perhaps I could cry, I could moo like mad
until all cows know that we are not just units of production,
machines which produce milk
until our bosses know that we have a name and ask themselves:
What does it help to gain the whole world and lose our souls?
My God, show me a solution.
You do not want us to be mere units of production.[66]

---

[66] When I prayed this prayer in a Swiss village I got into trouble with a Member of Parliament (who happened to be the secretary of the Farmers' Union). He thought I was being polemical against Swiss agriculture. However, the workers in the congregation understood that I was not praying about Swiss cows but about all the workers, all the units of production. On this see Hollenweger, "Efficiency," in more detail in *ITh* 2, 214–25. See also Tonks, *Decision-Making*. I was research assistant to Professor Rich, the leading social ethics scholar in Switzerland.

CHAPTER SEVENTEEN

Rethinking the Spirit

A Western or an Eastern Pneumatology

Remarkably Pentecostalism has not developed a pneumatology which fits its experience. One would expect Pentecostals and charismatics to be strong on pneumatology; this is not the case. They are strong on experience of the Spirit, on pneuma*praxis*, but they are weak on the interpretation of these experiences.

Generally Pentecostals adhere to a Calvinistic pneumatology. It is strictly christological, despite demurrers. The Spirit is allowed no dignity on his (or her) own, but is constrained by the doctrine of the *filioque* (although the *filioque* is seldom discussed). Schematically Western understandings of the procession of the Spirit look like this:

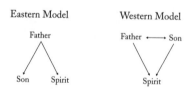

Unfortunately in praxis Western pneumatology looks rather like this:

Thus in the West, what is spiritual is determined exclusively by christology. In turn, proper christology is determined in the Catholic church by the *curia*,[1] and in the Protestant and

---

[1] See Vischer, *Spirit*. Discussion and exact sources in *ITh* 3, 305–7.

Pentecostal churches by the confessional declarations and the local pastors. The Eastern Orthodox churches complain bitterly, saying that this is not a doctrine of the Spirit but a device by church authorities to control and domesticate the Spirit in Pentecostal, Catholic, and Protestant churches. Hence the charge that the West does not have a proper pneumatology. Some Orthodox go even so far as to say that the *filioque* is in the first instance a doctrine about the pope and his infallibility.

There are a number of Western theologians who have had second thoughts on the *filioque*, including some in the Anglican Church, the Catholic author Yves Congar,[2] and a number of Dutch theologians.[3] But even if one operates within Reformation theology, one must admit that Huldreich Zwingli[4] and John Calvin[5] were not prepared to reduce pneumatology to christology, and recognized the Spirit outside the churches and outside the influence of the Christian gospel. For the Pentecostals the problem can be formulated as follows:

- if an important element of Pentecostal spirituality comes from the black slave religion and therefore ultimately from their pre-Christian African past;
- if many elements of pre-Christian African religions have been selectively integrated and transformed in African Pentecostal churches (chapters 6, pp. 54–80 and 5, pp. 41–53);
- if elements of Korean Shamanism re-emerge in Korean Pentecostalism (chapter 8, pp. 99–105);
- if elements of American Indian culture re-emerge in Latin American Pentecostalism (chapter 7, pp. 81–98);
- if elements of Western middle-class culture become dominant in Western Pentecostalism (chapter 18, pp. 228–45); and
- if all these elements are clearly decisive for the growth and strength of Pentecostalism, then we must ask whether these elements might belong to the order of God's creation, to the realm of the *Creator Spiritus*, to the good but confused order of creation and not exclusively to the order of the prince of this world.

A pneumatological way of understanding this would be to see the Holy Spirit as "ruach Yahwe"—the life-giving, life-sustaining Spirit of God—following the Old and New Testament (for example, Acts 2:17: the Holy Spirit is poured out on *all* flesh, not just on Christian or religious flesh). Moltmann calls this option *panentheism* (not pantheism), a technical term which means that God's Spirit is both person *and* life-giving power. He (or she, "ruach" is female) is present in all life, not just in Christian life.[6]

However, if such a pneumatology (the details of which I have elaborated elsewhere)[7] were to emerge, this would make a relevant doctrine of the Trinity

---

[2] Congar, *Crois.*
[3] O. Noordmans, G. J. Hoenderdaal, A. A. van Ruler, discussed in *ITh* 3, 323ff.
[4] Literature and discussion on Zwingli in *ITh* 1, 327ff and *ITh* 3, 157ff.
[5] "Ille (Spiritus Sanctus) enim est qui ubique diffusus omnia sustinet, vegetat et vivificat in coelo et in terra," Calvin, *Institutio* I 13, 14; cf. Krusche, *Wirken*, in particular chapter II ("Der Heilige Geist und der Kosmos"). Also Moltmann, *Creation*. A positive review of Moltmann by William K. Kay in *EPTA Bulletin* 6/3, 1987, 107–9.
[6] On this the work by Daniel Lys is vitally important: Lys, *"Rûach."*
[7] Hollenweger, "Creator"; idem, "Creatures"; idem, "L'expérience." Eldin Villafañe

vital. Otherwise spirituality might disintegrate into a form of all-embracing New Age religion (chapter 11, pp. 132–41). It seems to me that such a doctrine of the Trinity is called for because most Pentecostals do not have a trinitarian spirituality, but rather a kind of Jesus-religion or God-Father religion.

I also do not postulate such a trinitarian theology because it is a Christian tradition, but because it is necessary if we are to safeguard a *Creator Spiritus* pneumatology. In any case, such a theology would have to focus on the following question: What is the relation between the mode of God's being which transcends our experience, spirituality, and theology (the Father, God's transcendence); and the modes of God's being which operates as life giving ruach Yahwe in all religions, cultures, and perhaps even in parts of nature (the Spirit); and the mode of God's being which manifested himself in an historical person, namely Jesus of Nazareth (the Son).

The term "mode of being" of God (*Seinsweise*) is taken from Karl Barth's doctrine of the Trinity, and signals an attempt to overcome the restrictions of the language of the "persons of God," which in our age and culture can only be misunderstood.[8]

Such proposals are not taken entirely out of thin air. Some Pentecostals have begun to think in this direction. Stanley M. Burgess states that

> even Pentecostals, who are interested in the Spirit experientially, hardly give the divine Third Person lip service theologically. This should not be surprising given the strong Christological emphasis of Western christology. Our concentration on Christ as savior results from the negative anthropology which has characterized Western theology since Tertullian (ca. 160/170–ca. 214/220), and Augustine (354–430). Eastern Christianity does not portray humankind as so badly fallen, and hence does not have a strong Christology. They attempt to stress each member of the Trinity equally. This results in a stronger Eastern pneumatology, and also in certain doctrines which are distinct from the West.

Burgess goes on to discuss the *filioque*, which modern Pentecostals in the West have adopted without question. He includes not only the Byzantine church in his essay (Greek, Russian, Romanian, Bulgarian, Albanian etc.) "but

---

heads his chapter on "The Holy Spirit and Social Spirituality: A Pneumatological Paradigm" with a quote from Karl Barth: "At the end of the 'postscript' Barth also told his dream—which he had also occasionally mentioned in conversations—that someone, and perhaps a whole age, might be allowed to develop a 'theology of the Spirit', a 'theology which now I can only envisage from afar, as Moses looked on the promised land.' He was thinking of a theology which, unlike his own, was not written from the dominant perspective of Christology, but from that of pneumatology." Busch, *Barth*, 494, quoted in Villafañe, *The Liberating Spirit*, 163. The inner quote is from Barth's "Nachwort."

[8] Discussed in *ITh* 3, 325ff. David Gill, in his discussion of Oneness Pentecostalism, even goes so far as to say that "their understanding of Trinity approaches that of Karl Barth. Their use of the term *modo* (Seinsweise, modes of being) . . . reflects this tendency." Gill, "Oneness," 109.

also the East Syrian (Assyrian or 'Nestorian') church which rejected the decrees of the Council of Chalcedon in 451."[9]

Burgess is well aware of Eastern spirituality. "Because of their belief that all Christians are prophets who are guided by the Holy Spirit, local congregations in Eastern Christianity are lay-led."[10] They practice healing through prayer or Unction of the Sick[11] and have a wider range of "gifts of the Spirit" than the Pentecostals. He also sees their weakness. "There seems to be a natural tendency to pass from seeking the truth to defending it against those who seek it in new ways." He concludes: "Perhaps a more healthy response for all people would be to learn from each other."

Gerald T. Sheppard observes that Pentecostals can agree with the Eastern Orthodox criticism of the *filioque* clause as entailing the danger of making the Spirit an inferior member of the Trinity, and that Pentecostals would benefit from a greater familiarity with the Orthodox tradition and the argumentation of the Greek fathers.

This, in turn, would lead automatically to a positive appreciation of Moltmann's approach to *God in Creation*,[12] and to the insight that "the Spirit—on a cosmic scope—is preparing the way for the new creation."[13] Take for example, Richard J. Mouw who, after a discussion of Pittinger, can ask the question whether D. H. Lawrence was directly inspired. Mouw then continues:

> For me the most interesting questions arise in very different contexts. When after thousands of years of hostility between Egyptian and Jew, the leader of the Egyptian people proclaims, to the utter surprise of friend and foe alike "I will go to Jerusalem," and when the leader steps off the plane to embrace the political leader of Israel, is that the identifiable work of the Holy Spirit? Is it legitimate to identify the cries of revolutionary movements in Southern Africa with promptings of the Spirit? Can we hear the recognizable voice of the Spirit in feminist calls for an end to patriarchal oppression and in the protests of those who cry out on behalf of the unborn? Note that I am not asking whether it is reasonable to assume that the Spirit is somehow at work in such events and movements. I think so. My question is whether the Spirit is identifiably at work there and whether the Spirit's movements in the realm beyond that community in which the name of Jesus is confessed are recognizable and chartable by Christians.[14]

---

[9] Burgess, "Implications," 24. See also Dayton, "Issues"; reviewed by J. D. Plüss in *EPTA Bulletin* 6/2, 1987, 46–48.

[10] Burgess, "Implications," 27.

[11] Ibid., 30f.

[12] Sheppard, "Nicene," reviewed by H. Zeegwaart, *EPTA Bulletin* 7/3, 1988, 95–98. There is also a note on the *filioque* in Villafañe, *The Liberating Spirit*, 183, note 63.

[13] Mouw, "Life," 120. Mouw is a member of the Christian Reformed Church and president of Fuller Theological Seminary, Pasadena, Calif., but his article was published in the leading American Pentecostal scholarly periodical.

[14] Ibid., 120f.

Another commentator adds: "A genuine gospel will always be concerned with human justice rather than with the cultivation of a warm inner-glow."[15] In short, the ministries of all the gifts of the Spirit are given "to engage the world."[16]

Baptism of the Spirit: "Subsequent to and Different from Conversion"

Another issue which is widely discussed among Pentecostal scholars is the question of the baptism of the Spirit's subsequence to and difference from salvation and conversion. Classical Pentecostals taught for a long time that a person can be saved but not baptized in the Spirit. In many Pentecostal denominations the "initial sign" of the baptism in the Spirit is speaking in tongues. This doctrine has, however, already been questioned by the Chilean Pentecostals (who have a strictly Methodist doctrine [chapter 10, pp. 117–31]), by the Mulheim Association in Germany,[17] and by Leonhard Steiner from Switzerland.[18] These German-speaking Pentecostals have collapsed Spirit baptism into regeneration or baptism in water, as has Brick Bradford, longtime general secretary of the Presbyterian Charismatic Communion.[19] For Spittler, subsequence is a "non-issue": "The early Pentecostals did not intend to frame a new *ordo salutis*, an algorithm for piety."[20]

The Pentecostal New Testament scholar Gordon D. Fee suggests "that there is in fact very little biblical support for the traditional Pentecostal position," but he argues further that this is of little real consequence to the doctrine of baptism in the Holy Spirit. He gives a number of "Historical Reasons for the Rise of Separate and Subsequent Experience." We now have churches where

> people can be in the church, but evidence little or nothing of the work of the Spirit in their lives . . . It is precisely out of such a background that one is to understand the Pentecostal movement with its deep dissatisfaction with life in Christ without life in the Spirit and their subsequent experience of a mighty baptism in the Spirit. If their timing was off as far as the biblical norm was concerned, their experience itself was not . . . The fact that this experience was for them usually a separate experience in the Holy Spirit and subsequent to their conversion is in itself probably irrelevant. Given their place in history of the church, how else might it have happened? Thus the Pentecostals should probably not make a virtue out of a necessity. On the other hand, neither should others deny the validity of such experience on biblical grounds, unless, as some do, they wish to deny the reality of such an empowering dimension of life in the Spirit

---

[15] Jeffrey T. Snell adapts here Padilla, *Mission*, 41.
[16] Snell, "Beyond the Individual," 56f.
[17] See *The Pentecostals*, 236ff.
[18] Ibid., 325, 335.
[19] Williams, Rodman J., "Baptism," 43.
[20] Spittler, "Suggested," 43.

altogether. But such a denial, I would argue, is in fact an exegeting *not* of the biblical texts but of one's own experience in this later point in church history and making that normative.[21]

In other words, Fee and others want to stress the fact that Pentecostals, Charismatics, and others have had a valid experience which is important for their lives and which they call baptism in the Spirit. But they suggest that Pentecostals should not make a dogmatic statement of their subsequent experience.

This leads Roland H. Wessel to the question: "Is it not now time that the Biblical scholars in the Assemblies of God turn from the patterns of interpretation of Pentecostal experiences developed in the 19th century Holiness Movement in order to wrestle with the pneumatologies of Paul, Luke and John, and so to interpret them from within the writings of each?"[22] To this Lederle adds that "only 35% of all members (of Pentecostal churches) have practiced the gift [of tongues] either initially or as an ongoing experience."[23] In other words: There are different pneumatologies in Pentecostal practice and in the New Testament which should not prematurely be harmonized.[24]

Perhaps here again Pentecostal scholars are not so far away from modern Catholic scholars like Kilian McDonnell and George T. Montague who, in a monumental work, show that it is possible to integrate "Baptism in the Holy Spirit" into a long Catholic tradition of "Christian initiation." Baptism in the Spirit can happen either in a sacramental context or through personal prayer. The main thing is that it happens, and that charisms become a normal part in the life of the church.[25] I am sure many Pentecostals would sympathize with

---

[21] Fee, "Baptism," 88, 96–98.
[22] Wessels, "Distinguished," 23, note 69. See also Bush, "Development," 24–41.
[23] Lederle, " 'Initial Evidence.' "
[24] This is taken seriously in the article by Hurtado ("Spirit"), where he quotes among others E. Schweizer's article "πνεῦμα" in the *Theological Dictionary of the New Testament* 6.332–455. For Hurtado "Spirit of God does not simply mean 'non-physical,' and does not carry overtones of asceticism in later Christian usage" (804). See also Lederle (*Treasures*) in which he shows the *many* understandings and interpretations of Spirit Baptism in the Pentecostal/Charismatic movements. An interesting and so far unsolved question is the place of Edward Irving in Pentecostal theology. As of late David W. Dorries from Oral Roberts University, Tulsa, Okla., has established on the basis of a careful study of the sources that with his doctrine of Spirit baptism (including the initial sign of speaking in tongues) Edward Irving precedes the outbreak of Pentecostalism. Dorries concedes that no historical link between the Irvingites and the Pentecostals has been established. He also touches on Irving's christology and states to my astonishment "that it has achieved distinction in Neo-Orthodox circles in our century as a valuable contribution to Reformed theological discussion" (C 17). That is not exactly the impression I got from reading the valuable and striking book by Strachan, *Pentecostal Theology*. It is true, however, that Strachan considers Irving to be a "Reformed Pentecostal Theologian," and that he presents a workable theology for the Pentecostal revival within the Reformed church. Dorries, "Doctrine."
[25] McDonnell with Montague, *Initiation*.

me when sometimes in a moment of vision I wish that Kilian McDonnell and his friends were *periti* in Rome.

Natural and Supernatural

Another controverted issue in Pentecostal pneumatology is whether speaking in tongues is the "initial sign" of baptism of the Spirit. Within and outside of Pentecostalism there is criticism of this doctrine. Many Pentecostal churches have a great proportion of members (and sometimes even some pastors) who have never spoken in tongues. If a third of all members do not speak in tongues,[26] this leads to enormous pastoral problems. It divides the church into first and second class Christians; and many times the "second class Christians" are the pastor's most faithful co-workers. If he sticks to his doctrinal tenets he is in trouble. If he does not stick to this doctrinal tenets he is also in trouble. What should he do?

This is perhaps why the Pentecostal scholar Russ Spittler says: "Glossolalia is a human phenomenon, not limited to Christianity nor even to religious behavior . . . The belief that *distinguishes* the movement can only wrongly be thought of as describing the *essence* of Pentecostalism."[27]

I think that Spittler is right. The notion that glossolalia (or in fact any other gift of the Spirit including healing and precognition) is essentially "supernatural" is in my view biblically and scientifically untenable. *Biblically* it is untenable because the list of charismata in the New Testament includes so-called extraordinary gifts (healing, prophecy, glossolalia) *and* so-called ordinary gifts (management, teaching, giving money to the poor, even being married or unmarried). Paul's criterion for a charism is not ontological or phenomenological but functional. *Pneumatikos, sarkikos,* and so forth are not ontological but functional terms. A charism is a natural gift which serves *pros to symphéron* (for the common good), which operates in an ecclesiological and christological context (nobody can say *anathema Iesous* in the Spirit) and which is open to judgment by the ecumenical community.[28]

Scientifically, speaking in tongues has been demonstrated to be a human ability which may or may not be used in Christian spirituality. It is not abnormal, only uncommon in certain cultures. Just as music, normal speech and the bread in the Eucharist are common gifts of creation and may be transformed in the liturgical context, so speaking in tongues is a natural gift which many human beings may possess. As they live in societies in which speaking in tongues is considered eccentric or even insane, they do not have a chance to discover this natural ability, just as in a society in which singing or dancing were stigmatized, few people would dare to discover their gifts in these fields.[29] The same is true for the gift of healing.

---

[26] See above note 23.

[27] Spittler, "Glossolalia," 340. See also chapter 3, p. 22.

[28] See *The Pentecostals,* 320ff. for details.

[29] Samarin, *Tongues;* Williams, Cyril, *Tongues* (reviewed positively by George C. Batson in *EPTA Bulletin* 2/4, 1983, 88–91); Christie-Murray, *Voices.* See also the

The function of speaking in tongues is similar to that of dreaming, singing or dancing, or even being silent. It is, as Spittler says "a form of right-hemisphere speech." Speaking in tongues is non-cognitive, but meaningful nevertheless.[30] It is a means of communicating without grammatical sentences, a kind of atmospheric communication. When a whole congregation sings in tongues in many harmonies (without following a set piece of music), Pentecostals are building a "cathedral of sounds," a "socio-acoustic sanctuary," which is particularly important for people who have no cathedral or have left it. Just as a cathedral is built of ordinary stones, so glossolalia is made of ordinary sounds. And just as, when put together in a masterpiece, the stones in a cathedral do not change ontologically but functionally, so speaking in tongues can become a piece of art which, like the cathedral, proclaims: God is here.

In this connection one might consider a comparison between Dadaism and Pentecostalism. I have observed the following points of contact: Dadaism emerged during World War I in Zurich in a multi-lingual and international milieu of immigrants—similar to Pentecostalism in Los Angeles. Not far from the Cabaret Voltaire, the meeting point of the Dadaists, one finds also the first Swiss Pentecostal church.[31] That church grew also in a milieu of uprooted people. The poems of the Dadaists (rendered simultaneously in several languages) appeal directly to the senses. They lack a semantic meaning. The vocals and sounds are in themselves the message. Every listener makes his or her own interpretation, similar to speaking in tongues. Thus Dadaism (and speaking in tongues) creates a community across languages and definitions. It is furthermore no coincidence that after Dadaism and Pentecostalism a new expression of art, Cubism, emerged. It created multi-perspective images, images which present an object simultaneously from different view points—just as the Dadaistic poem combines several languages, or as singing in tongues creates a piece of art simultaneously in several languages. Whether there are social parallels between the mentioned expressions of art and Pentecostalism I do not know. However, the similarity of the phenomena, and the appearance at the same time and at the same place, cannot be an accident. A researcher who understands more about these forms of art might take up this issue. Perhaps the fact that Hugo Ball presented a Christmas play without words (only sounds) in the Cabaret Voltaire would be of significance for this research.

Such an understanding of glossolalia would also open the way for a "more catholic" understanding of sacraments. This is the suggestion of Frank Macchia,

---

special issue of *Discours.* Bibliography: Mills, *Glossolalia.*

[30] Spittler, "Suggested," 52.

[31] Swiss Pentecostalism is not properly researched. I have gathered a considerable amount of material and attempted an interpretation in my *Handbuch,* 05.28.025ff. The first meetings were at Mühlebachstr. 126 and at Waisenhausgasse 10 (*Handbuch,* 05.28.033a).

who wrote his Th.D. thesis on Johann Christoph and Christoph Blumhardt at Basel University. For him, glossolalia is a kind of "sacrament." It "accents the free, dramatic, and unpredictable move of the Spirit of God." It is "a kind of primary sacrament or kairos event. . . . Tongues are the 'new signs of the Christian Church' according to Thomas Barratt,[32] the 'root and stem' out of which all other spiritual gifts grow, according to Edward Irving, and the 'spiritual rest of the new covenant', according to the Oneness Pentecostal J. L. Hall."[33] Thus "Pentecostals have parted significantly from the conservative Evangelical preoccupation with subjective conversion" and have been led into the vicinity of the Lima document (BEM).[34]

This new, broader understanding of tongues would also do away with the dichotomy between the natural and the supernatural. The modern Catholic understanding of the sacraments does not argue ontologically, but rather asks: What are they, for the gathered community? Furthermore, the New Testament does not know the word "hyperphysikos" (supernatural), and it is quite impossible to translate "supernatural" into Hebrew—the concept does not exist. Both realms of reality—the one which we think we understand (the so-called "natural") and the one which we do not (or not yet) understand (the so-called "supernatural")—are God's creation and the realm of his reign. He reigns even in *sheol*, which some Bible translators render somewhat inexactly as "hell" (Ps 139:8).

This has been clearly seen by the Pentecostal Miroslav Volf, from former Yugoslavia, who did his doctoral dissertation with Jürgen Moltmann on "Human Work, Divine Work, and New Creation."[35] By "work," Volf does not mean "work in the church," but work in general. "Charisms should not be defined so narrowly as to include only ecclesial activities." The Spirit of God is active not only in the fellowship (of the church) but also through the fellowship in the world. The Spirit who is poured out upon all flesh (Acts 2:17ff.) also imparts charisms to all flesh: they are gifts given to the community irrespective of the existing distinctions or conditions within the community."[36]

> Very frequently charismatic is taken to mean extraordinary. Ecclesiologically this restricted understanding of charisms can be found in some Pentecostal (or "charismatic") churches which identify charismatic with spectacular. A secularized form of this "supernaturalistic reduction" is found in the commonly

---

[32] Cited in McGee, "Early Pentecostal Hermeneutics," 126; Macchia, "Tongues," 69.

[33] Cited in Dorries, " 'Standard Sign,' " 49; Macchia, "Tongues," 69.

[34] The whole passage from Macchia, "Tongues," 63, 69, 70. See also idem, "Sighs too Deep for Words." As to Macchia's criticism of the so-called Zwinglian understanding of the sacraments, see chapter 13, p. 172, note 97. Macchia wrote his dissertation at the University of Basel ("Spirituality and Social Liberation. The Message of the Blumhardts in the Light of Wuerttemberg Pietism").

[35] Volf, "Human Work." His published dissertation has the title *Zukunft der Arbeit—Arbeit der Zukunft. Das Marxsche Verständnis der Arbeit und seine theologische Wertung* [Work in the Spirit. Toward a Theology of Work].

[36] Volf, "Human Work," 184.

accepted Weberian understanding of charisma as an extraordinary quality of a personality. One of the main points of the Pauline theology of charisms is to overcome this restrictive concentration on the miraculous or extraordinary.[37]

Volf is seconded in this by the charismatic theologian J. Veenhof, who also does not want to use the terms "natural/supernatural" in connection with the charismata.[38]

The Spirit of God is—as the charismatic theologian Jean-Claude Schwab says—always mediated through human media: through understanding, experience, or emotions.[39] The consequences for further research and for Pentecostal educational institutes have been well formulated by Russ Spittler. Such studies, he says, "ought to be done in a university-related environment," The "vanity publishers should be avoided." We need an "Institute for Pentecostal Studies." Such an Institute "would focus on published research, for which there is no substitute." Some Pentecostal graduate schools have forsaken the genius of Pentecostal piety and replicate, not very well, evangelical theological education better accomplished elsewhere. In other words, Spittler pleads for genuine Pentecostal research, education, and theology which seeks its own way, and does not imitate evangelical theology.[40]

[37] Ibid., 185.
[38] J. Veenhof in a review of Suurmond, *Ethical,* in *EPTA Bulletin* 4/1, 1985, 16–19. See also Veenhof, "Charisma."
[39] Schwab, "Charismes."
[40] Spittler, "Suggested," 54–55.

CHAPTER**EIGHTEEN**

Signs and Wonders

This chapter has a threefold purpose. In the first place I want to document the necessity and the possibility of a therapeutic function of the Christian community. (Things are moving in this area in all churches, even the most rationalist ones.) In the second place I want to document the critique by Pentecostalism of a hitherto facile and superficial treatment of this topic. This critique will astonish many readers, since Pentecostals are not known for their critical analysis of our topic. However, they have considerable experience in prayer for the sick, and this shows in some of the more enlightened treatments of the subject. In the third place I shall try to establish some theological guidelines for treating the whole field of medicine, alternative medicine, and prayer for the sick—their interrelatedness and their differences.

"Preach, as you go, saying, 'The kingdom of heaven is at hand'. Heal the sick, raise the dead, cleanse lepers, cast out demons. You received without paying, give without paying." (Matt 10:7f.) That is how Matthew formulates the Great Commission, the missionary command of the church. "The message of the nearness of the Kingdom of God is conceived in such realistic terms that the disciples actually bring it in their words. They do not just talk about it."[1] Such an understanding is uncomfortable for many. Usually we replace it with the "easier" Great Commission at the end of the Gospel of Matthew, where it seems that we are "only" expected to speak, to teach and to baptize.

That, however, is too simple a way out, as Eduard Schweizer and Gerd Theissen (both non-Pentecostal New Testament

---

[1] Schweizer, *Matthäus,* 156; my translation (English: *Matthew,* 241).

scholars) point out. Texts, and in particular biblical texts, "are specific forms of human actions."[2] They are "not 'enacted parables,' which mean something quite different, the overcoming of sin or the like; they are concerned with real poverty, real distress."[3]

In our time it is mainly the health professions, including alternative medicine, which deal with the real needs in the realm of medicine. Medical doctors and alternative healers feel let down by the theologians in this work. Doctors anyhow have long understood that they are only "treating" the sick person—that healing comes from somewhere else. "From nature," say some. Christians say "from God," or to be more precise, "from the life-giving 'Ruach Yahweh,' " who is the basis of all life.[4]

Since Ruach Yahweh does not operate only in Christians but is the basis of all life, a responsible theologian cannot avoid the critical dialogue with representatives of medicine, alternative medicine, and the praxis of healing in pre- or non-Christian cultures.

It should be clear to the theologian that the place where wholeness and healing may be expected (and not merely discussed) is the Christian community. Health and sickness are not private; they belong to the realm of public liturgy with and for those who need help. That is why this chapter aims at a community liturgy involving the "weary and heavy-laden."

The Critique by Pentecostals on the Healing Evangelists

Pentecostals have always had a praxis of prayer with the sick; their books and periodicals are full of healing testimonies. After World War II, the key figure for the emergence of a special kind of Pentecostal healing evangelist is William Marrion Branham (1909–65).[5] He possessed an extraordinary diagnostic gift and could identify the illnesses (sometimes even the names) of persons he had never seen. Unfortunately his healing prognosis was accurate only in rare cases. The excuse of the healing evangelists in such cases has always been: The patient did not really believe; for they were convinced that faith leads automatically to health.

There was immediate criticism from some Pentecostals; for instance, from Leonhard Steiner. He repeated his critique at a Pentecostal World Conference[6] but was—at that time—ignored and removed from the international scene. Only when the healing evangelists started to organize their own financial basis was there strong criticism from the Pentecostal churches. The lifestyle of many of the healing evangelists (often including luxurious villas, air-conditioned

---

[2] Theissen, *Urchristliche,* 37 (English: *Miracle,* 32).

[3] Ibid., 43 (English: *Miracles,* 32). Richardson, *Miracle,* 57.

[4] Very important on this is the book by Lys, *"Rûach."*

[5] Weaver, *Branham;* Wilson, D. J., "Branham"; *The Pentecostals,* 354ff. Chappel, "Healing." This is an excellent historical survey but it is theologically and medically uncritical.

[6] Steiner, L., "Healing"; *The Pentecostals,* 357.

dog kennels, highly-priced cars and designer clothes, and sometimes sexual extravagances) made their glory pale. That is the reason why they now look for other markets, preferably in European hard-currency countries.

It seems to me that the charismatic leaders of the European mainline churches have learned nothing from the debacles of the past. They continue to invite these evangelists—now selling the same product under the new trading label of "The Third Wave"—and this in spite of the severe criticism by American Pentecostals and the Fuller Theological Seminary in Pasadena.[7]

The Pentecostal W. MacDonald describes these healing evangelists as follows: Single women, especially widows, are the preferred diet of this species of religious wolf. The evangelist weeps and melts the heart of the woman. He declares that the kingdom of God is about to go under and his own soul is in danger unless substantial financial resources are sent to him immediately. We may compare this behavior to that of Paul, who never collected money to build up his organization. "The greatest threat to the Pentecostal/Charismatic movement in the last two decades of this century will be the rise and fall of *personal* kingdoms, because when they fall, as inevitably they must, the faith of those who do not have their eyes on Jesus, will fall with them."[8]

Some pretend they will live to the age of 110 and then die of old age (not of sickness). Others believe that they will not die at all. They exploit their fans without mercy. If one of them goes bankrupt, they say: "Sorry, you did not really believe; this is your own fault." Others drive out demons by the hundreds—they provide plastic buckets into which the patients can vomit the demons. To this Robeck says: The suffering of Paul spoke louder than his miracles.[9]

Many of these evangelists do not call themselves Pentecostals but—as mentioned—"Third Wavers." They see the world as a cosmic and moral duality. There is no room for the natural: everything is either divine or demonic. They reject historical-critical research in favor of their own experience. "We are successful," they say, "so why ask questions?"[10]

Against this many critical Pentecostals argue: we find that Jesus did not make a fuss about demons. Robert A. Guelich quotes Theissen in noting that exorcism was not a sign of faith in New Testament times.[11] There is no spiritual war in Scripture between the faithful and the demons; the exorcism

---

[7] Pratt, "Dialogue." Peter Hocken in *EPTA Bulletin* 7/3, 1988, 104–8. Smedes, *Ministry* (mainly on John Wimber).

[8] MacDonald, "Cross."

[9] Farah, "Analysis"; Robeck, "Signs." See also Lovett, "Positive."

[10] Thomas Pratt and Peter Hocken, as in note 7. See also the editorial to *Pneuma* 12/1, 1990, 1. Bradley, "Miracles," or the very critical review of Kenneth McAll, *Healing the Family Tree* by Brian Russell-Jones in *EPTA Bulletin* 3/4, 1984, 140–42. In Germany most criticism has come from medical and theological scholars outside Pentecostalism: Albrecht, "Opium"; Engemann, "Paradigma."

[11] That is perhaps not quite true, see Mk. 16:17. The complex topic of exorcism will be treated in a forthcoming volume, see *ITh* 3, 61–120, and Wink, *Engaging*.

of these evangelists resembles more the doings of pagan exorcists than it does
New Testament exorcism. The battle is won already (Barth)—*that* is what we
confess.[12]

Allan Anderson, from South Africa, also criticizes the "power concept" of these evangelists. "There are not always instant solutions to life's
vicissitudes."[13] Boasting about their financial and building successes does not
show the spirit of Jesus. "Recently I read about a charismatic church which
boasts it has more square footage than any other church building. So
what?"[14] Pentecostals have discovered—contrary to Bruce Barron[15]—that
"the faith message [namely the conviction that those who believe will be
healed automatically] does not have its origins in the Charismatic renewal."
It was taken from E. W. Kenyon.[16] Some read James 5:13–18 and say: "It may
be that James deliberately chose words that are ambiguous to allow breadth
of meaning. Thus, instead of specifically clarifying their meaning to reveal
a promise to the sufferer of physical healing (whether forgiveness or encouragement or spiritual sustenance or eschatological salvation or any combination), James offers in his words a message that by its very nature and
presentation brings hope for the future in both areas." This passage is also
interesting for the order in which things happen: first healing, then forgiveness, then confession of sins. For most theologians this is in every respect the
wrong order.

This theme is further elaborated by Keith Warrington, Lecturer in New
Testament, Elim Bible College, Cheshire, England. In a rigorous examination
of the meaning of the words in James 5:13–18, comparing the passage with
texts from religious and secular writers of the first century, he comes to the
conclusion: "Most commentators interpret this passage to refer to physical
healing either by medical therapy or supernatural power and there appears to
be no good reason for doubting this possibility. However, it may be that James
anticipates a wider form of healing, depending on the suffering concerned."
Warrington adds, "It is proposed that James avoids a dogmatic route and
instead chooses to be deliberately ambiguous to provide the possibility of a
wider benefit to the sufferer. . . ."[17]

On another level Eldin Villafañe takes up John Wimber's *Power Evangelism* and comments: "The tendency of many, including Wimber, is to see this
struggle [against demonic powers] too individualistically and not see that
spiritual warfare must correspond with the geography of evil—the sinful and

---

[12] Guelich, "Warfare." Guelich is not a Pentecostal but his essay was published
in *Pneuma*.

[13] Anderson, "African," 74.

[14] Mathai, "Whatever."

[15] Barron, *Health*, 71f.

[16] McConnell, *Different*. This dissertation, which was submitted to Oral Roberts
University, is reviewed by D. D. Smeeting in *EPTA Bulletin* 8/1, 1989, 34–36. See
also Brandon, *Health*, reviewed by David Petts, *EPTA Bulletin* 8/2, 1989, 93–94.

[17] Warrington, "Observations." See also already Gee, *Trophimus*.

evil structures of society. . . . They must see that the texture of social living makes no easy distinctions between the personal and the social."[18]

When I was at Wimber's Vineyard Church in Anaheim (California) in July 1993 I understood what Villafañe meant. There was not much "power" in the service, possibly because Wimber was "out of commission," suffering from serious nose and throat cancer. The text was Romans 7, and I expected the preacher to say something on the rampant racism also among Christians in that very region. In the same week a Fascist youth group had planned to blow up the African Methodist Episcopal Church in Los Angeles. Indeed a topic for Romans 7. But no, the only examples the preacher could think of in his forty-five minute sermon were: bigamy, divorce (an increasing problem in American Pentecostalism), and pornography. Not with a word did he mention the obscenity of those young people who dressed in SS uniforms, said publicly that the "down breeding" must stop and that they were starting a race war against all Hispanics, Blacks, Asians, and Jews and their fellow travelers. God seems, in the view of these Christians, more interested in what happens in the bedrooms than in what happens in the boardrooms. Thank God, the following Sunday I enjoyed a real Pentecostal service at West Angeles Church of God in Christ.

As to the difficult question of demon possession and sickness, John Christopher Thomas, Associate Professor of New Testament, Church of God School of Theology, Cleveland, Tennessee, comes to the following conclusion:

> In ways somewhat similar to James, Paul is not hesitant to assign the origin of certain illnesses to God. Although not always the case, Paul sometimes sees a clear connection between sinful behavior and sickness or death. In only one text does Paul identify the Devil as having a hand in illness, but even there, Paul suggests that Satan does not work without the co-operation of God himself. The precise nature of that co-operation is not altogether clear. Paul and the "Paul of the Pastorals" (if such a distinction needs to be made) can also treat illness as a "normal" part of Christian existence . . . If the evidence from the Pastorals can be trusted, it seems that Paul is not opposed to advocating the use of certain "medical" remedies in the case of sickness.[19]

It is only logical that Mark E. Roberts gives the following advice: "Challenge and reject popular cultural notions of successful leadership that devalue the criteria of apostolic servanthood exemplified in Jesus and Paul." "Turn from seeking social legitimation as a goal for ministries to attain."[20]

In his opening address for the 24th Research Conference of the Society for Pentecostal Studies (Wheaton College, Ill., 1984) Roger Stronstad criti-

---

[18] Villafañe, *The Liberating Spirit*, 201. Wimber, *Power;* Wagner, "Vineyard"; idem, "Wimber."

[19] Thomas, "Deliverance"; idem, "An Angel From Satan." The best book on exorcism I have found so far is Solomon, *Living.* See for an extensive discussion *ITh* 3, 61–120 ("Geist und Geister").

[20] Roberts, Mark E., "Weakness," 23–24.

cized the "individualistic, self-centered, and, even, narcissistic" tendencies. Thus prophecy is "trivialized and/or commercialized." The prophecies often "borders on the credulous, the absurd, the blasphemous and the exploitative." They deal with new revelations and novel and authoritative interpretations of the Bible, with who to marry and when to have babies, with material prosperity and careers. "All over the world there are prophets who, like Balaam, prostitute the gift of prophecy for money and power." This emphasis totally misses the first century function of prophets.[21]

What is astonishing in this short overview is not so much the eccentricities of the money evangelists (who make much of their money by leasing and selling their data banks), but the decisive, exegetically and theologically clear critique by Pentecostal theologians. All the sadder that, of all people, some charismatics with a decent theological education still give a platform to the apostles of "signs and wonders."

It is clear that this critique does not solve the problem of the need for a liturgically and theologically sober healing ministry in our local churches, Pentecostal and non-Pentecostal. Here as elsewhere it is true: the best critique of the false is the praxis of the true. That is why I now turn to what I consider "the praxis of the true."

A Community Liturgy for Sick and Healthy People

During my studies at the University of Zurich we examined in detail the healing stories of Jesus. We analyzed the vocabulary, the structure, and the variations in these stories.[22] I was already then astonished that hardly anybody dared to apply the practices described in these stories to our time. In a seminar paper on blind Bartimaeus (Mark 10:46–52) I therefore raised the question of the contemporary relevance of these passages. The professor—an eminent New Testament scholar—wrote in the margin in red: "Author should concentrate on exegesis!"

"Diseases and their cures have natural causes, and do not depend on the actions of evil spirits. This puts an end to the New Testament miracles as miracles."[23] We are taught that miracle-workers were commonplace in Jesus' time. Miracle stories were simply intended to illustrate the love and majesty of God; they were a sign of the Kingdom of God.[24] The same is true in the churches today: Listen to the preachers up and down the country. They tell us that our sick world is promised God's protection; that our political, economic, and personal relationships must and can be healed. At best, then, the

---

[21] Stronstad, "Diversity," 18–19.

[22] Bultmann, *Geschichte.*

[23] Bultmann, "Neues Testament"; quoted in Theissen, *Miracle,* 34.

[24] Theissen rejects this oversimplification. He writes: "We must firmly reject assertions that primitive Christians' belief in the miraculous represented nothing unusual in the context of this period." Theissen, *Urchristliche,* 272 (English: *Miracle,* 276). Similarly Twelftree, *Christ Triumphant.*

sensational propaganda of contemporary healing evangelists is rejected. If healing in the literal sense is mentioned, our preachers refer to doctors and nurses.

Now this is all true. Only why should these texts not also really mean what they say? That is, that the proclamation of the gospel, that the community of Jesus Christ, has something to do with ministry to the sick; that in the Christian church we believe that God is interested not only in our souls but likewise in our bodies? "The variety of possibilities in the pastoral and liturgical realm is not exhausted by far (prayer for healing, services for the sick, anointing the sick, blessing of the sick with laying on of hands, traditional and therapeutic counselling)."[25]

The Christian Church will exercise this ministry—just as the Christian doctor—knowing that all healing comes from God, whether somebody is healed by an operation, by a reasonable diet, by prayer or by a combination of these different therapies. In all cases healing is not automatic. Neither a reasonable lifestyle nor prayer nor operations guarantee healing. It is therefore important that the topic of illness and health becomes part of our liturgies. "If a theological system cannot accommodate the reality of Christian healing, then there is something wrong with the theology."[26] There are practical beginnings to such a balanced healing liturgy in some of the European and American mainline churches (Africa and Asia have never completely forgotten this dimension of the gospel). But these beginnings have so far not been taken seriously by academic theology, because their implicit ideas of what is "true" are based "on obsolete scientific theories."[27]

For the Christians from the Third World, however, healing in the liturgy is a matter of course; and these believers now compose the majority of Christianity. For them, illness is always also an expression of a disturbed relationship, either to oneself, to other people, to the dead, the ancestors, to the clan or tribe, or to nature.

Unfortunately, this ethos of healing has been ignored in the exporting of our medical industry to the Third World, with catastrophic consequences (as noted by the World Health Organization in Geneva).[28] If we trample the convictions of our patients because we cannot share them, we can at best treat these patients, but we cannot heal them. Can we imagine what it means for an African, who understands his illness to be a result of a broken relationship, when, in the hour of crisis in sickness, he is separated from friends and family, is touched by foreign people and is obligated to

---

[25] Fritsche, "Heilung/Heilungen," 773.

[26] Parsons, *Healing*, 151. In the avalanche of literature on Christian and alternative healing (detailed bibliography in *ITh* 3), Parsons's book is an exceptionally sober and open-minded approach.

[27] Ibid., 142.

[28] Djukanovic–Mach, *Alternative;* Newell, *Health;* Pfleiderer–Bichmann, *Krankheit.*

swallow foreign food and medicine? Such disrespectful treatment depersonalizes the patient—making him or her feel like a car put into the garage for repair. This approach has led not only in Africa but also in the West to wrong diagnosis and to illnesses which have been *caused* by the medical profession (a fact long known and noted in medical literature).[29] We Europeans also are not ill or healthy in private; it is the whole community, the *soma Christou* which participates in the illness and health of the individual. It is therefore not astonishing that in Europe we find approaches to illness and health similar to those used in Africa. I take the example of an Anglican hospital chaplain. He uses the old Anglican liturgy of "anointing the sick": before an operation he invites the surgeon, the nurses, the family of the patient, and some parish councilors for a short eucharistic service with laying on of hands and anointing with oil (James 5:14).

One such chaplain told me that he has observed three different results: First, the operation goes well. Everybody—including the surgeon—is pleased, and the patient is calm. This is also one reason why the doctors participate in the liturgy, whether they are committed Christians or not.[30] They have discovered that the short postponement of the operation is justified because it prepares the patient better for surgery. Prayer and operation work together.

Secondly, it may also happen that the patient dies during or shortly after the operation. But this is not to be considered as a failure, since healing does not depend on the faith of the patient, nor on the faith of the minister, nor on the holiness of the other persons participating in the service. It depends solely and wholly on the incalculable mercy of God. Therefore neither doctor nor pastor are to be blamed for the death of the patient. But it makes sense to accompany the patient on his last difficult journey. If somebody emigrates to Australia we would also say farewell in a proper way, organize a little "liturgy," a farewell party, and wish him or her a good journey. Why should a Christian not be properly sent on his way when he goes on his or her last difficult journey? The Catholic Church has realized this too: the sacrament which in the past was called "last anointing" is now called "anointing of the sick," indicating that the anointing can be either a rite for recovery or a farewell ceremony.

The third possibility is for us the most interesting because it makes the operation unnecessary; that is, the patient is healed without surgery. It is the most interesting case but also the most difficult to explain. And we have no means of knowing whether the first, the second, or the third possibility will result from our intervention.

The Anglican experience has paved the way for many similar experiences in Protestant churches on both sides of the Atlantic. This praxis of the true—it

---

[29] Wilson, Michael, *Hospital*. Sampson, *The Neglected Ethics*.

[30] If they are Muslims (which is often the case) they will not take part in the Eucharist, but they will be present.

seems to me—is the best and most credible criticism of the sensational and sometimes damaging practice of certain healing evangelists. The challenge has also been taken up by the World Council of Churches (and that not just by its Medical Commission). In the Ecumenical Centre in Geneva, liturgies for ill members of staff have been conducted. They were introduced by the World Council's African secretary, the late Hank Crayne. After a long battle he realized that he had to give up his resistance to the application for membership by the Kimbanguist Church from Zaïre (chapter 6, pp. 54–80) and in fact he learned from them a more biblical approach to illness—his own illness. Reconciliation with the Kimbanguists was in itself a healing story; and the introduction of healing services in the World Council's headquarters in Geneva is probably the last thing one would expect from an international church bureaucracy. This story has not been picked up by the religious or secular press, but it could become an example for dealing with problems of tension and illness in many areas of our working life, including the headquarters of churches.

The World Council of Churches and the Deutsches Institut für ärztliche Mission at the University of Tübingen have for many years emphasized the need for a wholistic approach to health, a "primary health care." They have dealt in detail with the contribution of "non-white indigenous churches" to this topic, and researched the consequences both in Third World and European churches.[31] In the course of discussions on this chapter with Cecil M. Robeck, Jr., a Pentecostal scholar teaching at Fuller Theological Seminary, Pasadena, he recommended that I underline the sacramental and corporate character of these services as over against the show business performances of television evangelists. Indeed, the former usually take place in a eucharistic context (as in the Zwinglian churches in Switzerland). Thus people are realizing that sacraments are not about hocus-pocus but about the real presence of Christ among his people. Many Christians (and non-Christians) have said to me, if only Christ were walking down the aisles of the church, I would throw myself at his feet and ask him to put his hands on me. It is my duty and my privilege as a *Verbi Divini Minister* of the Swiss Reformed Church to say to them: Christ is *realiter* present in His word and sacrament, in prayer and anointing; this is the common testimony of all Christian churches including the Pentecostal and Zwinglian churches (see chapter 13, p. 172, note 97). Let people call me a sacramentalist, if by this is meant the generally acknowledged belief that in anointing the sick and heavy-laden, Christ is present in His word and in the prayer of His people, in the partaking of wine and bread.

The healing stories of the New Testament "demonstrate in symbolic actions a radical protest against the negations of human existence which is not rooted in our experience." Theissen, who wrote this, probably would not agree

---

[31] See the periodical *Contact* of the World Council of Churches; McGilvray, *Gesundheit;* idem, "Verwaltung"; and Grundmann, "Heilung."

with my extrapolations of his exegesis. He is of the opinion that these healing stories are "the expression of a human race in its childhood," therefore not applicable to an adult (or perhaps even senile) humanity. "Miracles are alien visitors in our world."[32]

I suggest that Theissen is wrong on this issue. My experience shows me that under the surface of Western culture and science there is not only the desire but also the faculty for a bodily understanding of these healing stories. In Switzerland and Germany the liturgies for such services (sometimes even involving Catholics and Protestants together) are usually prepared by a team of church members including people from the very margin of the parish, usually people from the medical profession or alternative practitioners. Thus the liturgy becomes for them the place par excellence where the protest against the negation of life in our society is celebrated and demonstrated, where the purely mechanical understanding of health and sickness is overcome not just in theory but also in practice.

"All Nations Were Deceived by Your *Pharmakeia*"[33]

The title for this section is a quotation from Rev 18:23. This is the seer John's verdict on commerce and conduct in the city of Babylon. "*Pharmakeia*" means "medicine," but also "witchcraft," "sorcery," and the like. The translation "sorcery" in our Bibles does not show the ambiguity of the original text. I do not want to give the impression that today's medicine is a form of sorcery; but two observations show us that our health industry is in serious crisis. The first observation results from conversations with doctors with whom one has to sympathize—in spite of their high income and their high social status. A doctor in Germany explained to me that a consultant needs a high income to compensate for his professional and human frustration. Doctors have become technicians. They have become the servants of their rich patients, the insurance companies, the state bureaucracy, the pharmaceutical industry, victims of medical propaganda, and medical lawyers. Patients expect them to heal all

---

[32] Theissen, *Urchristliche*, 297 (English: *Miracle*, 302); see also pp. 285, 295 (English: 289, 300).

[33] This section deals critically with Western medicine. I do not want to be aligned with Ivan Illich's verdict on the medical profession (Illich, *Limits*). I know Illich and I am sure that he exaggerates in order to make himself heard (see R. Huber in a review of Illich's book in Kaltenbrunner, *Pillenpest*, 164–67, and the discussion between Hans Schaefer and Ivan Illich in *Medizin statt Gesundheit*). A personal note is therefore necessary. Doctors have always treated me well. Contrary to those accusations in the literature, the doctors who treated me have always talked to me and explained the cause of my illness. In most cases they considered their therapy as "supporting actions," once they had explained to me how I had to change my life-style. I am convinced that at least once a doctor saved me from a serious stomach ulcer by explaining the origin of an ulcer and my wrong reaction to the pain. It took him some time which he could not charge to my sickness insurance. The only question is whether he can do this with all his patients and not go bankrupt.

their illnesses; however, they cannot. They must, however, maintain the fiction that they can, which leads to dangerous passivity in the patient. The pressures from the pharmaceutical industry are indicated in the enormous publicity budget, which in the USA in 1958–59 already amounted to three times more than the running costs of all their eighty-five medical schools taken together.[34]

Worse, however, is the fact that the doctor does not know *for what* he should heal a patient. Only to send him back into the production process? Neither the doctor nor the patient knows for what they should be healed. A leading German medical professor, Hans Schaefer, criticizes our present medical situation. He calls it an "inhumane medicine" *(Medizin ohne Menschlichkeit)*—the price which we pay for progress. As examples he mentions the medical dissertations heaping up as scrap-paper, the competition between medical academics; the many instances of planting catheters in veins and electrodes in the brain, of puncturing arteries and even the heart purely for research purposes.[35]

Psychosomatic medicine is, in spite of a few important successes, no way out. Either this branch of medicine works according to scientific rules—but how can we measure and quantify relationships between "body and soul"?—or else it presupposes a valid model of what makes a human being human, on which there is no agreement at the present time. Such a model cannot be elaborated on the basis of empirical research. "Since humans have not made themselves and have also not observed their making they know nothing about the relationships between psyche and soma."[36] What they believe they know are convictions, "faith statements," dogmas, and metaphysics. And such statements are not—as in exact sciences—falsifiable or verifiable. They rest on the self-understanding of man—his faith.[37]

The second observation relates to the catastrophic failure of Western medicine in the Third World. It has overstepped its limits when it has stated that "that which cannot be does not exist." For example, the verified and recognized cases of healing in Lourdes should make medical science more cautious.[38] Statements outside their competence have been issued by medical professionals in many countries, for instance in Brazil (where Zè Arigo was twice condemned in spite of his recognized healings),[39] and also in the Philippines,[40] Switzerland, and Germany;[41] although not in England.[42] It is

---

[34] Rappleye, "Medicine," quoted in Schaefer, *Medizin,* 277.

[35] Schaefer, *Medizin,* 111, 140. See also Muschg, "Arzt."

[36] Schaefer, *Medizin,* 156.

[37] Ibid., 161.

[38] Eagle, *Alternative,* 25. Stelter, *Psi–Heilung,* 224.

[39] Puharich, *Arigo.* Stelter, *Psi–Heilung,* 119ff.

[40] Stelter, *Psi–Heilung,* 172.

[41] Aktenzeichen 1 Str. 389/77, quoted in *Der Stern* Nr. 47, 10.11.1977 and in Gerlach, "Magische," 74.

[42] At least 5,000 healers work in England in 1,500 hospitals. See also *Daily Telegraph,* London, 26.9.1985. Eagle, *Alternative,* 7.

in my opinion unscientific to pretend that nothing can happen outside of our structures of plausibility. Such dogmatics must take heed of the research of the World Health Organization and other experts who tell us that our medical services are only suited to a minority of the world's population, that they may be inefficient or even damaging in other cultures,[43] and that even in our own cultures they are slowly but surely becoming too expensive. If dogmatic medical professionals deny the alternatives they become—according to their own understanding of science—unscientific.

Neither medicine nor chemistry can explain how it was possible for Harry Edwards to heal a patient in a London hospital telepathically, without even telling the patient. We do not know how the Brazilian healer Zè Arigo used an ordinary knife to cut a small tumor from the arm of the doctor Henry Pharish without pain and without causing an infection.[44] We do not know how the Philippino ghost-healers effect their operations.[45]

I do not want to enter into the polemics of the authenticity of such phenomena. As in all such areas, some may be charlatans, but some are genuine. Stelter has shown with all due accuracy how resistant our so-called scientific establishment is when it comes to acknowledging facts which are outside our plausibility structures. He mentions the American, Dr. Nolen, who has acknowledged that he totally altered facts, claiming that the ends justified the means.[46] A long chapter could be written on the reasons for such falsifications "in the interest of science." John Hasted, Professor of Experimental Physics at the University of London, has tried to explain the mechanisms responsible for the rejection by scientists of the results of experiments which contradict their ruling dogma.[47] Truth is very difficult to establish, especially when it threatens the privileges of ruling opinion makers.

However, the Philippino healers are not unique. On May 31st, 1947, Mirin Dajo put a sword through his breast in the presence of a number of medical experts at the University Hospital of Zurich. The spectators expected a trick. But when they saw what had happened they asked for Mirin Dajo to be x–rayed. The sword was clearly visible. After twenty minutes the sword was taken out. Only a small scar was left.[48]

---

[43] Ranger, "Medical"; Wilson, Michael, "Materialism"; Goba, "Role"; Nxumalo, "Pastoral"; Hoerschelmann, *Christliche Gurus;* Becken, *Theologie;* Lartey, *Pastoral Counseling;* Mostert, "Men"; Edwards, "Attitudes"; Farrand, "Choice"; Bührmann, "Aspects"; Booyens, "Ethnological."

[44] Stelter, *Psi–Heilung,* 119ff. (lit).

[45] Ibid., 147ff. and Sherman, *Wonderhealers.* Naegeli–Osjord, *Logurgie;* Chapmann, *Operationen.*

[46] Stelter, *Psi–Heilung,* 305.

[47] Hasted, *Metal-Benders.*

[48] Stelter, *Psi–Heilung,* 145. Walker, B., "Physical," 193.

Finally, let me quote an example from South Africa. Dr. G. L. Johnson from Durban, South Africa, knew the leader of the Church of the Nazarites,[49] Shembe. When she visited him in Ekupakameni with a group of Englishmen,

> a Negro came with the message that a girl had been bitten by a poisonous snake and that she was dying. The group went to the injured girl. She was still alive but the arm was swollen. In the shadow of a holy tree Shembe prayed to his God, went to the girl, put his foot on the injured arm. To the great astonishment of all those present the girl shook and got up. One could see how the swelling was disappearing. At the same time the snake, which had been caught, coiled up and died.[50]

Here,

> common sense strikes (or what we hold for it) and reason protests because that which cannot be should not be. Before we accept that our world-view is challenged we suspect bluff and fraud. "Fraud"—that is what the secretary general of the French Academy of Science thought, when the first record-player was demonstrated to a circle of scientists. He thought it was a trick by a ventriloquist. He threw himself at the man, held his throat in order to demask him—but to the astonishment of all the machine continued to talk.[51]

> When in 1893 the young Berlin surgeon, Carl Ludwig Schleich, wanted to present at a medical congress the method of local anesthesia which he had developed, he was thrown out by the medical pundits of his time. In 1910 at a congress of German neurologists and psychiatrists a discussion on psychoanalysis was announced. Professor Wilhelm Weygandt hammered his fist on the table and exclaimed: "This is not a topic for a scholarly meeting. This is a topic for the police."[52]

Why do scholars react with mockery or fury when something new is presented to them? This would be itself a topic for psycho-analysis. One suggested answer: "The younger scholars usually have to accept the opinions of their teachers and colleagues if they want to get on in their careers."[53] This is, of course, in flagrant contradiction to the declared ethos of science. Another suggestion: "It is likely that psychological forces are at work here against which man is helpless as long as he does not see through them."[54] This is the case not only in natural science but also in theology, both evangelical and liberal. Altogether, these factors may account for the fact that many discoveries in our century have been made not by the established experts but by scholarly outsiders.[55]

---

[49] On this church see Schlosser, *Eingeborenenkirchen*, 219–91. Oosthuizen, *Theology*.

[50] Stelter, *Psi–Heilung*, 24. Bozzano, *Uebersinnliche*. Cf. Mk 16:18.

[51] Pauwels/Bergier, *Aufbruch*. Stelter, 1.

[52] Stelter, *Psi–Heilung*, 9–10.

[53] Naegeli–Osjord, *Besessenheit*, 56.

[54] Stelter, *Psi–Heilung*, 12.

[55] Rhine, "Introduction," 12. Naegeli–Osjord, *Besessenheit*, 56. Cf. also Lyttleton, "Knowledge."

In his pioneering book on the miracle stories of early Christianity, Gerd Theissen does not seem to be far off the mark when he writes: "Superstition (Aberglaube) is the faith which is rejected in a society . . . Faith (Glaube) is the superstition accepted in a society. Where the line has to be drawn is decided by the ruling opinion makers." Thus Christianity was rejected as "superstition" or even "atheism" in the first centuries of its existence.[56]

We know, however, that many present-day illnesses are caused by our medical institutions. In Berlin 22% of patients in one survey suffered the side-effects of medical treatment.[57] For the USA, figures as high as 30% have been quoted, and similar statistics may be found for England.[58] We must therefore examine the alternatives to the methodologies and technologies of the medical establishment.

Non-Christian and Non-Medical Healing

It is urgent that we develop a better understanding and a more discriminating approach to non-Christian and non-medical healing practices. What are these practices? Kofi Appiah-Kubi reports:

> In 1962, the regional sports organizer in the Eastern Region of Ghana had a very grave motor accident. He was admitted to the Military Hospital in Accra, the then most up-to-date and best-equipped hospital in Ghana. After some weeks of observation and treatment, the specialists decided to amputate one arm and one leg. The man's family was consulted, but after several meetings and discussions they decided to remove him against medical advice and try the services of the traditional bone-setters. After some months of treatment, he regained the use of his limbs. He returned to his job as the regional sports organizer without difficulty; he was still at his post at the time of the survey.[59]

The author of this report is a lecturer and research fellow at the University of Science and Technology in Kumasi, Ghana. At the time of writing he was working on his doctorate in Public Health at Columbia University. His appraisal cannot be lightly set aside. He has a high opinion of the know-how of African healers, Christian and non-Christian:

> The priest-healers are expert doctors, and they administer medicine. They have a wide knowledge of the properties of many roots, barks, herbs and leaves. At the same time they seek to interpret the mysteries of life, convey the messages of the gods, give guidance in the daily lives of the people, settle disputes, uncover the past, explain the present, and foretell the future.[60]

---

[56] Theissen, *Urchristliche,* 230 (my translation; English: *Miracle,* 232). The quote goes on " . . . those parts of society in the Roman Empire which were convinced that Christianity was an eccentric superstition."

[57] *Frankfurter Allgemeine Zeitung,* Nr. 249, 26.10.1977, 30, quoted in Gerlach, "Magische," 64.

[58] Eagle, *Alternative,* 10.

[59] Appiah-Kubi, *Man Cures,* 58f.

[60] Ibid., 39.

This is why a missiological congress held in Harare, Zimbabwe, in 1985 stated, concerning traditional African medicine: "The Church recognizes increasingly the contribution of traditional African medicine for the Christian understanding of healing."[61]

Kofi Appiah-Kubi considers Western medicine too expensive. One hospital alone (Korle Bu Hospital, the teaching hospital of the Ghana Medical School) accounts for fifty per cent of the national drug bill. "Is this the most efficient way to distribute the money available?"[62] he asks. However, he also sees the disadvantages of the healers—mainly their lack of hygiene. But, he continues, it is time to incorporate "faith healing" into our national health services, since it is accepted by a great percentage of the population. One should allow the traditional healers to dispense certain basic drugs and medicines. Young nurses and doctors should be apprenticed to the traditional healers.

> We can no longer exist with the lazy belief that more police will stop crime, more school buildings and teachers will make children more brilliant, and more hospitals and doctors will make society healthier. Constructive methods of bridging the gap between rich and poor, urban and rural, and educated and uneducated groups are an essential step toward achieving reasonable comprehensive health care services.[63]

The relative success of alternative medical approaches can no longer be denied. For the Christian the question here is: how do we understand, interpret, and evaluate these alternative practices? Many times when I posed this question, I found that Pentecostals were afraid of the roots of alternative medicine in non-Christian religions. This fear is strange, since it does not also apply to our own medical praxis, which also has roots outside of Christianity, which sometimes uses very dangerous drugs and practices, and which often creates long-lasting medically-induced dependencies and deficiencies. No such questions are asked in relation to our Aristotelian theological methods (chapter 15, pp. 194–96 and chapter 11, pp. 132–41); our rites and organizational patterns; and our values borrowed from society at large, which are sometimes anything but Christian. Unlike today's Christians, the authors of the Bible were not afraid to adapt and change religious and cultural material from their non-Jewish and non-Christian context—from the temple in Jeru-

---

[61] Becken, "Begegnung," 294. Also idem, "Kirche." See also his *Theologie;* idem, "Heilungen"; Klöcker, *Gesundheit;* Becken, *Glaube;* idem, "Heilen"; the ecumenical collection *Auf der Suche* (with reports from many parts of the world and a commission report of the Christian Medical Commission of the WCC). Shorter, *Jesus;* Stiglmeyer, "Medizinmann"; Hilton, "Future"; Adegoke/Hollenweger, "Praxis."

[62] Sai, "Planning," quoted in Appiah-Kubi, *Man Cures,* 143.

[63] Appiah-Kubi, 148. He continues: "Too often in the rush to resolve urgent problems, important values are lost sight of. In an age where *paper* is more important than *person,* when *money* is more important than *man,* when *number* is more important than *name,* perhaps the greatest contribution of Akan culture is its emphasis on the value of the name, the man, the person. It is hoped that this may change our concept of development and give it a human face."

salem (built by pagan craftsmen and according to pagan plans) to the astrologers at the cradle of Jesus (at least according to Matthew) to the generous use of hellenistic christological titles in Paul.

Pentecostals might also be interested to learn that the famous Pentecostal missionary to Zaïre, William Frederick Padwick Burton (1886–1971) was saved several times from death by using the method of dowsing in order to find water wells. Dowsing is usually associated, by Pentecostals, with demonism or at least with non-Christian religions—a fact which explains the silence of Pentecostal literature on this important aspect of Burton's missionary work.[64]

But not all Pentecostals today share these fears. Out of his understanding of the Spirit's working in the world, along with his positive interpretation of Hispanic culture, the Pentecostal scholar Eldin Villafañe can appreciate the work of the *curandera* or *curandero* (traditional healers in Latin America).[65]

In the chapter on syncretism the question was asked: What do we learn from these biblical examples for our own dealing with non-Christian and non-medical healing practices? Which of them can and should be included in our liturgy? What happens to non-Christian healers who become Christians? Should they forswear the gifts which they have been given by the *Creator Spiritus* and adapt to our cultural brand of medical practice? Such questions cannot be answered in detail here. A thorough examination of the whole complex of Spirit and spirits would have to be conducted before some guidelines could be established.[66] However, a few theological guidelines seem to be clear.

Conclusion

A Christian theology of healing must start with creation. God has made humans (not only Christian humans) so wonderfully that they have in themselves gifts of healing. The Bible tells us that we live because God breathed his Spirit into us. If he takes his Spirit away we die. It is therefore not astonishing that this Spirit of God liberates forces of healing in Christians and non-Christians alike.

This is not an attempt to make everybody Christian. I am merely taking seriously the biblical testimony that all of us live through God's Spirit. This is also the reason why non-Christians are able to become Christians: they recognize something in the gospel which has found an echo in their tradition and life. It is the reason why rites and customs, thoughts and insights from pre-Christian times have found a place in our Christian tradition—not only in the Third World, but also in Europe and America.

---

[64] On Burton see Cartwright, "Burton." My information is based on oral communication from Desmond Cartwright.

[65] Villafañe, *The Liberating Spirit*, 113.

[66] This is done in detail in *ITh* 3.

However, not all of these rites have a place in Christian faith. Manipulating our neighbors, for example, or the attempt to explain all suffering logically—for these there is no room in the Christian gospel. What is foreign to the gospel is the attempt to make somebody Christian in *our* way, according to *our* understanding. If this is true, then a few things which we call "orthodox" in theology and medicine have to be questioned. My observation so far has been that the doctors are readier to accept this questioning than the theologians. Why this is so I cannot explain.

Finally one would like to ask: are there not specifically Christian elements in healing? Yes, there are: Christian healing is rooted in the belief of God's sovereignty. It is in fact very rare that God allows us to look into his notebook. From this I draw five practical insights:

1. A causal connection between the sin of a patient (or the sin of his ancestors) and his or her illness is *expressis verbis* rejected by the gospel. Of course the Bible knows that there might be a connection. After all, if we persist in poisoning our food, our air and our water, then it is not surprising that we become sick. But—and this is the difference—it is not necessarily those who sin who become sick. It is often the innocent who are affected.

2. The Christian knows that there are healthy sinners and sick saints. Faith does not automatically lead to health, nor is unbelief automatically the cause of illness. Many healers are themselves ill. Christians believe in God in sickness and in health.

3. It is not true that faith is always a condition for healing. There are many healing stories in the New Testament where faith plays no role. This has also been my own experience.

4. In their healing ministry Christians must avoid all propaganda, and must not trumpet their successes. They must not confuse success with blessing and failure with curse.

5. The place where Christian healing can and should be expected is in the worshipping local community, not in a *virtuoso* healer. Christian healers should be integrated into our liturgy, even if they are not ordained. Healing seems to be a charisma which appears more often in lay-people, especially in women. It is necessary to show them the "craft" of anointing, so that they can deal adequately with the "energies" and emotions which emerge.[67]

In conclusion: what is Christian in our liturgies for the sick is the insight that prayer is not the infallible last resort which certainly works when all else fails. Of course there are such cases in our experiences—people who have been given up by the doctors are healed. But it is not true to say that Jesus is the

---

[67] Practical indications in Hollenweger, "Heilt die Kranken."

answer to all our questions. Some of our questions are stupid, and some of our questions are unanswerable, even by Christ. He does not answer all our questions—but he helps us to live with unanswered questions. He himself died with an unanswered question on his lips: "My God, my God, why hast thou forsaken me?"[68]

---

[68] My own development in relation to services of anointing is documented in *The Pentecostals*, 353–76; idem, "Heilt die Kranken" (also in French: *Hokhma, Revue de réflexion théologique* 42, 1989 65–89; and in *Perspectives missionaires* 20, 1990, 49–61. See also, idem, "Healing through Prayer" (in Danish, *Praeste Foreningens Blad* 1990, 3, 657–63). In the meantime, many churches in Switzerland and Germany have published liturgies and little manuals on the topic. Cf. also Heinzer, *Mit Kranken beten*. This chapter is a summary of Hollenweger, *ITh* 3, 21–59.

CHAPTER NINETEEN

Soteriology: Who Is Saved?

In speaking of Pentecostal soteriology one must distinguish between *expressed* soteriology and *lived* soteriology—the two are not the same. When a black worker pastor in Birmingham says: "Hallelujah, I am saved," he means that he has literally been saved (like "sozein" in the New Testament). He owes his physical, psychological, cultural, and spiritual existence to the saving power of this Jesus Christ and his saving community. Without Jesus, he would be lost—literally dead. Nobody would care for him, and he might well be crushed in the machinery of the modern city. But when an insurance agent in Holland who has been converted in a charismatic prayer group says: "Hallelujah, I am saved," he means something very different. He would not be dead without Christ—he could still live on. But he has found a direction and a religious meaning for his life; sometimes also a spiritual family and a shift in priorities; which is certainly not to be despised. But it is very different from the salvation experience of the black worker pastor in Birmingham.

This is why "salvation" means different things to different Pentecostals. However, this intercultural understanding of salvation is very new in theology, and has not yet reached the official declarations of Pentecostalism. Perhaps the fact that the new *Dictionary of Pentecostal and Charismatic Movements* (which is otherwise a fairly representative Pentecostal lexicon) has no entries on "salvation" or on "sanctification" is an indication of this present uncertainty.

In the following I will first present the *theoretical statements* on salvation in Pentecostal literature; secondly, I will deal with the *experience* of salvation; and finally, I will try to bring the two together.

Soteriology: The Theory of Salvation

For the Pentecostal believer, the fundamental experience necessary to salvation is conversion, or regeneration. In numerous hymns and choruses the Pentecostal sings of "the miraculous transformation which takes place in the soul and life of the sinner in the moment in which he repents and declares his sincere faith in Christ Jesus as his Savior."[1]

At the end of the gospel meeting, when the Pentecostal preacher makes the call to sinners to turn to Jesus, the angels look down from heaven with rapt attention. Their harps are silent and they fold their wings in awe, for "they have never felt what moves a poor sinner whom Jesus leads home."[2]

The Finnish Pentecostal preacher Hokkanen finds it difficult to describe the process of regeneration, and yet he knows that something real happens. The godless life comes to an end. Someone no longer dances, no longer drinks, now loves God's word and God's people. "If you are not reborn, open your heart to Jesus the King of sorrows, and the miracle of grace will take place in you too—you will be reborn to a living hope."[3]

The conditions for regeneration have been fulfilled on God's side in Jesus. "It is received quite freely through grace alone; yet for a man to accept it requires a conscious and free decision of his will . . . Regeneration does not take place gradually, but in a moment."[4]

It is clear from these statements that the Reformation doctrine of election is replaced here by the Catholic doctrine of "free will of man"—a point to which I shall return later.

The International Church of the Foursquare Gospel declares: "We believe that the change which takes place in the heart and life at conversion is a very real one; that the sinner is born again in such a glorious and transforming manner that old things are passed away and all things are become new."[5]

The older Pentecostal churches know, however, that the experience of conversion was more dramatic in early days. Today their children become

Christians in a milder manner, without being able to point to a definite emotional crisis taking place at a definite time. Some of the very best saints of the church

---

[1] Asambleas de Dios (Dominican Republic), *Reglamento.* This chapter started as a contribution to a symposium on "Salvation Today" at the Interuniversity Institute for Missiological and Ecumenical Research, Utrecht, Holland, Fall 1992; published: Hollenweger, "Salvation."

[2] *Pfingstjubel,* no. 205, verse 2; *The Pentecostals,* 315.

[3] Hokkanen, *Oletko;* quoted by Schmidt, Wolfgang, *Finnland,* 211; *The Pentecostals,* 316.

[4] Pejsti, *Zasady,* chapter 11; *The Pentecostals,* 316.

[5] *Declaration of Faith* compiled by A. S. McPherson. The crucial text for Pentecostals is 2 Cor. 5:17, but the Authorized Version follows the false reading of Marcion, which introduced the word "all" into the Pauline text: "The old has passed away, behold *all things* have become new." Paul wrote: "The old passed away, *it* has become new." *The Pentecostals,* 316.

bear testimony to this quiet type of conversion experience, which results from a lengthy period of Christian training . . . On the other hand there are thousands in modern society who are unreachable except by means of a crisis experience.[6]

J. E. Campbell, from the Pentecostal Holiness Church, accuses the Reformation churches of neglecting the preaching of conversion and of not believing in the supernatural new birth.[7] "We believe that the church lost something vital when she began to neglect that old landmark, the altar, where people may come together and 'pray through' until empowered and unified."[8] Added to these complaints there are numerous lamentations at the "largely unbelieving clergy."[9]

> Is it not a well known fact that the vast majority of the theologians who preach in the pulpits of the established church have experienced neither conversion nor regeneration, still less biblical sanctification and endowment by the Holy Spirit. . . . However, in the Pentecostal meetings the word of God is . . . a power such that every person who receives it is made new and set free from all the constraints that weighed upon him, all vices and sins, all fetters and lusts. . . . [10]

In practice things are not so simple. Even in the Pentecostal movement there is no exact knowing who is really saved. Of course bitter attacks have been made on Bishop James A. Pike because he will not limit salvation to people "who happen to have heard the news and heard it well."[11] On the other hand, it is asserted that "innocent children," who have been neither converted nor born again, will take part in the rapture.[12] There are also Pentecostal groups who declare the conversion which normally takes place in the Pentecostal movement to be invalid, because in their view confessions of sins are necessary for a valid conversion. Some say that this must take place before the pastor, others before the person who has been offended, and others again before both.[13]

"All endeavors in prayer and singing, in weeping and fasting, and all other devotional practices are worthless in the eyes of God if sins are not confessed with godly repentance and contrition, and the past restored to purity."[14]

Others even demand confession not only of *remembered sins*, but also of *forgotten sins*, a practice made possible by the aid of prophetic messages.[15]

---

[6] Campbell, *Pentecostal*, 122, 132; *The Pentecostals*, 317.

[7] Campbell, *Pentecostal*, 60; *The Pentecostals*, 317.

[8] Wyatt, *Birth*, 10ff.; *The Pentecostals*, 317.

[9] Hutten, *Seher*, 529; *The Pentecostals*, 317. On the "unbelieving pastors," see chapter 11, p. 135.

[10] Hermann Lauster, in: *Die Wahrheit* 15/4, April 1962; *MD* 23, 1962, 108; *The Pentecostals*, 318.

[11] James A. Pike, *Christian Century*, 77/51, 21.12.1961, 1496ff.; *PE* 2444, 12.3.1961, 3. *The Pentecostals*, 318. On Lauster see *Handbuch*, 07.823, 001.

[12] Williams, Ernest S., "Your Questions."

[13] Church of God in Christ, *Year Book*, 88f.; quoted in Moore, Everett LeRoy, *Handbook*, 178ff.

[14] Widmer, *Kampf*. Cf. also Drollinger, *Offener*, 17; *The Pentecostals*, 318.

[15] *The Pentecostals*, 142ff., 319.

With regard to the condition of man before conversion, Pentecostal doctrine strictly follows the Western orthodox doctrine of "the utter depravity of human nature" (as opposed to the Eastern orthodox doctrine, which does not see man as utterly depraved). Also, most Pentecostals believe that it is possible to fall back from the state of grace after conversion,[16] although some believe in the "eternal security" of the converted. All agree that "however great a sin may be committed by a person before he receives the Lord Christ, if he believes in him and accepts him, the sin is forgiven."[17]

Sins committed after conversion fall into the wide field of Pentecostal pastoral care. There is disagreement about what to think of children of God who sin. In the view of the Congregação Cristã do Brasil,

> sins committed after the Lord has been received should be judged by the church always in accordance with the word of God, with the exception of mortal sin, which in accordance with the word of God is unforgivable. One of the mortal sins is committed when there is resistance to the work of the Holy Spirit (Matt. 12:32).[18]

The existential problem of sins committed by the converted led the Holiness and Pentecostal movements to add a second stage to regeneration or conversion. This is the experience of sanctification, through which sins are finally rooted out. Ultimately salvation depends on this final overcoming of sin: only those who overcome sin will inherit the kingdom of God. The result is that in spite of the formal affirmation of the doctrine of justification by faith, the doctrine of justification is emptied of meaning and reduced to a preliminary stage for beginners. Röckle expresses this view in a critique of Hutten's famous book on Sects and Free Churches by writing: "Hutten's basic error is that he speaks of grace without conditions, and the Bible knows of no such thing. The doctrine of grace without conditions is Satan's master-stroke, with which he has already deceived millions of people and led them to damnation."[19]

This view has led to a long, unresolved discussion on the context and status of sanctification. What is sanctification, and is it a condition for salvation?

No outsider can imagine the anguish undergone by earnest Pentecostals who struggle to live a holy life. In their worship they sing the hymns of total victory.

Troubles almost 'whelm the soul;
Griefs like bellows o'er me roll;

---

[16] Apostolic Church, *Fundamentals*, 3; Conn, *Evangel*, 13.

[17] Congregação Cristã do Brasil, *Estatutos*, Art. 27; *The Pentecostals*, 319.

[18] Congregação Cristã do Brasil, *Estatutos*, Art. 27. Mark the catholic influence in this formulation!

[19] Röckle, "Biblische," 3; *The Pentecostals*, 319. On Röckle see *Handbuch*, 08.200.001.

Tempters seek to lure astray,
Storms obscure the light of day;
But in Christ I can be bold,
I've an anchor that shall hold.[20]

On the basis of the Bible, their pastors promise them the "total and complete sanctification of the sons and daughters of God."[21] But their everyday lives bring numerous sins. What can be done? The answers given by Pentecostals vary, and the same group or the same pastor can hardly ever be tied down to any one of the possible answers. Sometimes they follow John:

The biblical norm is: Do not sin! (1 John 2:1) For this we were redeemed and born again. But supposing that you are a young child and make a slip and sin, what then? Come to Jesus and tell Him that you have sinned, confess your sin to Him, and then He will forgive you them, for He intercedes for you.[22]

But at the same time they affirm:

When many people say that we are not delivered from our sins, the devil has the last word, for then the trick the devil tried to play in paradise has succeeded. This makes the devil more powerful than God. But these are thoughts that border on blasphemy. Redemption consists of the total removal of the consequences of the fall.[23]

Occasional objections are made to this doctrine of sanctification. For example, it is pointed out that it is incorrect to apply the expression "sanctified" to Christians who have received a "second experience" after conversion. Paul uses the term "sanctified" for all Christians. One could also add: even such Christians, as for example the Corinthians, whom we would hardly consider sanctified, he calls "saints."[24]

That is why all the newer Pentecostal movements go back to the original teaching. "If the Lord has purified us and set us free from sin, then the source from which all the hateful sins appeared in the past is now empty . . . and now the heart cannot sin, because there is no longer any sin in it, so that sin can no longer come forth from it" (1 John 3:6, 9 and 5:18).[25]

The inevitable problems which arise from this doctrine are solved by taking a leaf from Wesley: only "the voluntary transgression of a known law"[26] is sin. Unintentional or forced acts, or those which spring from good intentions or ignorance, are not sin.

---

[20] Martin, W. C., *Hymns; The Pentecostals*, 325.

[21] Confession of Faith of the "Bruderschaft: Der König kommt!"; *The Pentecostals*, 325.

[22] Krüger, "Ein"; *The Pentecostals*, 325.

[23] Regehly, "Sehend"; *The Pentecostals*, 325f.

[24] Full Salvation Union, *Manual*, n.p. 1964; quoted in Moore, Everett LeRoy, *Handbook*, 298f.; *The Pentecostals*, 327.

[25] Krige, *Paar*, 19; *The Pentecostals*, 327.

[26] *WW* XI, 396. For a full discussion see *Handbuch*, 05.28.004a, and chapter 12, pp. 146–52.

The reduction of sin to what can be experienced emotionally and subjectively has two consequences: (1) sin that is *experienced as such* (that is, as willful and conscious) is taken more seriously than in the Reformation churches; but (2) unconscious sins (the neglect of social and ethical responsibility; the condemnation of other Christians through ignorance or mental inertia) may be committed with a good conscience. "No one ever does wrong so fully and so happily as when he does it with a clear conscience" (Pascal).

This understanding of salvation was not invented by Pentecostals. It goes back through the Holiness Movement and Wesley to Catholic spirituality, as the following story will show: A young man was condemned to death for embezzlement. Those present took pity on the young man, who had fallen into evil ways. The King gave $900 from the treasury to make good the debt, the Queen gave $90, the young Crown Prince gave $5, and the people in the public gallery passed the hat round and collected another $4.90. But since the condemned owed $1000 in all, the judge said: "It is no use, the man must be hanged." In despair the man went through his pockets and, to the acclaim of those in the court, produced the last vital dime from his trouser pocket.

This example illustrates the understanding of salvation in the Pentecostal movement (but also in some Reformation churches). Admittedly, the last dime is a very small contribution compared to the large donation from the King and the Crown Prince, but this last dime is the one that saves. Without this last dime, without this minimum of sanctification for which God looks, there is no redemption.

Anyone knowledgeable of the history of spirituality will recognize this pattern of salvation. Ultimately it does away with God's grace given unconditionally.

Let me contrast this story with the experience of salvation by Martin Luther, who is for me not the final word in this matter, but needs to be quoted here because he is often misunderstood by Pentecostals. Luther had learned from Gabriel Biel (1410–95): If man does his uttermost *(facere quod in se est)*, God will forgive him. This was meant to be a pastoral counsel to those Christians who were tormented in their conscience by their shortcomings. But this minimal request was turned into a whip in the hands of a conscientious thinker like Martin Luther. In studying Gabriel Biel's writing he had to ask himself continually: When am I really doing my uttermost? Who can give me the assurance that the fear of hell *(attritio)*, which drives me into the confessional, is this uttermost *quod in me est?* Is not the repentance of the heart *(contritio)*, which flees out of love to the arms of God, this uttermost which God justly requires of us—rather than the fear of damnation? But precisely this minimum, this *contritio* of heart, was impossible for Luther to achieve. Even though as a young monk he had sat with wide open mouth and nose, smacking his lips out of devotion[27] when he heard that every renewal of the

---

[27] Scheel, no. 281 ("Kleine Antwort," Fall, 1533; *WA* XXXVIII: 148f.): "Wir jungen Münche sassen und sperreten maul und nasan auff, schmatzten auch für

monk's vow had the same virtue as the first decision for a life as a monk, he now became convinced on the basis of Biel's soteriology that he could not flee from hell through his life as a monk.[28] Reading the Bible did not ease his conscience. He recognized that "there was no corner in his soul that was not full of the most bitter bitterness."[29] "O my sin, sin, sin, sin!" he complained in a letter to Staupitz. He was made desperate by the incomprehensible phrase in Psalm 31: "In thy justice deliver me *(in iustitia tua libera me),*" which for a Latin understanding of justice (Luther read daily in the Latin psalter) appeared to him to be gross nonsense. Justice—this could mean for him only the Latin distributive; that is, the punishing justice of God, which distributes to everyone according to his merits. For a realistic, self-examining man such as Luther, this meant deserved punishment, not liberation.

His troubles were not eased by reading the New Testament. Even in Paul's epistle to the Romans (1:17) he found this punishing justice of God, so that he was greatly tempted to curse God.

> So I was raging with a wounded and perturbed conscience; in great thirst I knocked again at Paul's door in order to find out what he really meant by this passage, until after days and nights of thinking I observed more exactly the context [*connexio verborum*]. "The justice of God is revealed in the Gospel" and "The just shall live by faith."[30]

In the same manner he examined Psalm 31:1:

> Praise God, when I understood the context (*res*) and saw that "justice of God" meant "justice that justifies us through the given justice in Christ Jesus," then I understood the grammar and I began to enjoy the Psalter.[31]

That is, Luther discovered that the genitive "justice of God" meant the justice which God *gives* us, and not a justice which he demands of us.

---

andacht gegen solcher tràstlicher rede von unser heiligen Müncherey. Und ist also diese meinung bey den München gemein gewest."

[28] Scheel, *Dokumente,* no 397 (Sermon on John 3:16, June 29, 1538; *WA* XLVII, 90: "Ich will der hellan entlauffen mit meiner Muncherej und Orden").

[29] *WA* I, 558 ("Resolutiones disputationum de indulgentiarum virtute," 1518: "Nec est ullus angulus in ea non repletus amaritudine amarissima."

[30] *WA* LIV, 186 (Introduction to vol. I of the Opera Latina, 1545): "Furebam ita saeve et perturbata conscientia, pulsabam tamen importunus eo loco Paulum, ardentissime sitiens scrie, quid S. Paulus vellet. Donec miserente Deo meditabundus dies et noctes connexionem verborum attenderem, nempe: Iustitia Dei revelatur in illo, sicut scriptu est: Iustus ex fide vivit, ibi iustitiam Dei coepi intelligere eam, qua iustus dono Dei vivit." For the Reformed tradition see *ITh* 1, 299–328 (on the very different and social consequences of salvation), also *ITh* 3, 157–59 (on the salvation of "pagans," in particular Muslims). Hollenweger, "Zwinglis" (on the very considerable influence of Zwingli on Anglican theologies, liturgies, and Bible translations).

[31] Scheel, no. 449 ("Tischreden," V, no. 5247, between September 2 and 17, 1520): "Gott lob, da ich die *res* verstunde und wiste, das *iustitia Dei* hiess *iustitia, qua nos iustificat per donatam iustitiam Christi Jhesu,* da verstunde ich die *grammatica,* und schmeckt mir erst der Psalter."

Immediately he tested his discovery on similar genitives in the Bible, and found that the Hebrew word "justice" *(zedaqa)* did not mean the mechanical, Latin concept, but God's personal, sovereign justice—his free, unconditional justice. This is the reason why the same word can sometimes be translated in the Bible as "mercy."[32]

The Praxis of Salvation: Experience

In this section I want to remind us of the salvation *experience* of Pentecostals. Let us take the Chilean peasant. He is torn from his traditional extended family and locked into the processes of industrial work and still, after years, ill at ease in the life of the modern city. But he finds help from the Pentecostals. Without this help he often falls victim to drunkenness, hopes to win large sums of money by gambling, or tries to forget his misery in the arms of prostitutes. Often the only people to have any concern for him are the street singers of the Iglesia Pentecostal. They visit the shanty towns and sing to the accompaniment of guitar and mandolin:

Rolled away, rolled away, rolled away
All the burdens of my sins rolled away,
I remember when my burdens rolled away,
That I feared would never leave night or day;
Jesus showed to me the loss,
So I left them at the cross.[33]

At first he may laugh with the rest of the bystanders, but then he is convinced by the faces of these Pentecostals: in the midst of the filth of the city they are already in heaven. Through curiosity and boredom he walks along with them. He hears a preacher who like himself has to struggle for daily bread for his family. He says to himself, "This is one of us," and after attending a number of services he joins the Pentecostals. He is now no longer at the mercy of uncertainty, hunger, unemployment, drunkenness, boredom, and homelessness, because he has once again become part of a "family," because he has "brothers" and "sisters" who help him and give his life moral direction. They may not teach him to write, but they teach him to read and underline the important passages in the Bible. He learns to read not only the Bible but also the newspapers, and sends his children to school. And because he no longer throws his money away, he may be able to send one of his sons to study at the university. Because industrialists have found out that Pentecostals are loyal and careful workers, they ask Pentecostal pastors for advice when they want to hire more people. So, the pastor recommends him and he has a stable job. All this he owes to the Savior who has rolled away the burden of his sin—who has led him out of the prison of sin, indifference, and hopelessness; and to the

---

[32] *WA* V, 155. On Luther see also Volf, "Materiality," in particular, 449–54.

[33] A "chorus" which has been carried by oral tradition throughout the world. Steele, "Burdens" (has a slightly different version).

Holy Spirit who has not just to be believed in, but whom one can experience in all sorts of marvelous healings, visions, and utterances in unlearned tongues (chapter 10, pp. 117–31).

Or take the Indian woman who is to be baptized in Pachuco. There she stands at the microphone for the first time in her life, in front of two thousand people. She has been asked to give her testimony in Spanish, which is a foreign language for her. There she stands—her face wrinkled, her back bent, overwhelmed by the many people, unable to speak. But then she begins to sing of her liberation. Every note is wrong, but the congregation helps her, prays for her, sings with her, and explodes in a great chorus of praise when she finally arrives at the end of her song. This again is an experience of becoming human, of becoming a person—it is an experience of liberation.

John Davis,[34] one of my former post-graduate students, told his fellow researchers about a mission by thirty Californian business men to Thailand. They arrived by jumbo jet and distributed tracts on which John 3:16 was printed in Thai. Now, every Thai will gladly accept what a foreigner gives him. He is far too polite to refuse. And if the foreigner asks him, "Do you want to give your life to the Lord Jesus Christ?" he will of course say, "Yes." One does not say "no" to a foreign guest. After their two week evangelistic campaign, the Americans held a great farewell meeting at which they said that they had converted more people in two weeks than the missionaries had in ten years.

That hurt my doctoral student greatly, for he was the director of an Evangelical Theological College in Thailand. So he told his fellow researchers what a Buddhist Thai understands when he reads John 3:16 in Thai. First there is the question of God. Whether there is a god or no god, who can know that? But anyhow foreigners believe in a god, so let it be conceded. But a God who loves, furthermore a God who loves the world, and a God who has a son, that is either great nonsense or even a blasphemy. And a God who promises life eternal—no thank you! That would be like a Protestant offering a Catholic eternal purgatory if he converted to Protestantism. Life eternal is the last thing a Buddhist wants. He wants to get out of this continuous circle of reincarnations; he wants to be freed from the power of karma. So in this context salvation means not "life eternal" but the end, the breaking out of this eternal circle.

Other cultures experience and interpret salvation in positive ways appropriate to their own traditions. For example, in Africa salvation now often entails acceptance of traditional healing practices as gifts of the Holy Spirit, rather than their proscription as the work of demons (as under many missionaries in the past). For many African Independent Pentecostal churches the Holy Spirit is already present in their pre-Christian healing praxis, as in other aspects of their culture. The old healing practices are taken up, purified, liturgized, and criticized in the light of biblical healing records. A church in Africa which has neither a small medical station with a midwife or a nurse

---

[34] See Davis, John R., *Contextualized*.

(certainly no big computerized hospital) *nor* a healing ministry in its liturgy can survive only with subsidies from America and Europe. *Sozein,* salvation, means for Africans salvation for soul *and* body: Africans do not separate the two.[35] Therefore—as in the healing ministry of Jesus—these churches deal also with the bodies of their "clients." In a survey of the reasons for conversion we found that in the Third World—but perhaps not only there—people usually become converted either because of a healing (of themselves or of a friend or family member), because of a dream or vision, or because they have a friend who is a Christian. We have found not one single instance where somebody was saved on the basis of arguments, nor on the basis of a sermon, nor certainly on the basis of a hell-fire sermon. The sermon seems to have other functions: to those who have already experienced salvation, it gives a language and provides a narrative community in which they can articulate their newly-found freedom.

What does this all mean for Europe? Salvation essentially means a shift in priorities, a new community and a new direction; this, at least, has certainly been my own experience.[36]

Towards a New Soteriology

While the fear of eternal damnation might be present in certain sectors of Pentecostalism, in general it plays a role only in theoretical discussion, where the question is sometimes asked: Will those who have not accepted Christ personally be condemned to eternal damnation? As long as this is a purely theoretical question, it is easily answered. But as soon as one has a Muslim in the family (as is the case in many African churches), then it becomes much more difficult. The same applies to Europe. As soon as a pastor gets a Muslim son-in-law, the question is dealt with much more cautiously.

Moreover, although eternal damnation for the unsaved is sometimes a (theoretical) motivation for mission, it cannot sustain mission work.

What one seldom finds in Pentecostal soteriological literature is a discussion of the reasons for eternal damnation. For here some discoveries are to be made. Who goes to hell in the New Testament? Not the unbelievers (this is the case in only one or two passages, one of which is the inauthentic ending of the Gospel of Mark), but the rich (the parable of the rich man and Lazarus), the merciless (the parable of the goats and sheep, where those saved are "unbelievers" in the cognitive sense and those who are condemned to utter darkness where there is howling and gnashing of teeth are firm believers), the cowards, and so forth (Rev. 21:8).

Furthermore in Pentecostal theology—at least according to the Chilean Pentecostal Juan Sepúlveda—

---

[35] Anderson, "African"; idem, *Moya; The Pentecostals,* 149–75. Chapters 5 (pp. 41–53) and 6 (pp. 54–80).

[36] See on this van der Laan, P., "Hollenweger."

the idea of "perdition" takes on more significance: the world is "perdition" in the sense that life before conversion is a life that is lost, it is an unsustainable way of living; it is to lack a "livable life." In short "world of perdition" refers to a place where life and the individual "are lost," where identity is impossible and the fall is visible; a world of loneliness, of hate, of sadness, of fear, of shame, of envy, of neglect, of moral degradation.[37]

This is why Miroslav Volf sees theologies of liberation and Pentecostal theologies not as "prime examples of radically opposing theologies," but as containing certain commonalities. In his article on the "Materiality of Salvation," Volf argues "that in one crucial respect they agree and that precisely in this respect they differ most radically from classical Protestantism: both liberation and Pentecostal theology emphasize the *materiality* of salvation." It is therefore "of ecumenical importance for liberation and Pentecostal theology to recognize each other as feuding *family* members."[38] This seems, in fact, to be happening, at least from the Pentecostal side. For example, Lidia Susana Vaccaro de Petrella has noted the increasing attention some Latin American Pentecostals have paid "to denouncing corruption and sin, not only the sin of individuals . . . but also the sin embodied in power structures."[39]

Volf summarizes his findings by stating:

A responsible contemporary theology of salvation needs to integrate the distinctive soteriological characteristics of all three traditions discussed—the *personal-spiritual* aspect of salvation emphasized in classical Protestantism, the *individual-physical* aspect emphasized by Pentecostalists,[40] the socioeconomic aspect emphasized by liberation theologians—while also developing the ecological aspect of salvation.[41]

The integration of these three aspects does not happen through simple addition, but by showing how each of these areas of salvation is a different aspect of one and the same "full Gospel."

This is why I believe that the time has come for Pentecostalism to deal with its soteriology against the background of its own experience—both the experience of being freed from fear (fear of life and fear of death) and the experience of liberation and of becoming a human person—and to harness the potential of critical traditions which are also present in Pentecostalism, and which are today coming more and more to the forefront. Such a critically developed,

---

[37] Sepúlveda, "Pentecostalism," 83.
[38] Volf, "Materiality," 447, 449.
[39] De Petrella, "Tension," 35, quoted in Volf, "Materiality," 463.
[40] The first tradition is exemplified by Volf in a careful interpretation of Luther; for the *material* aspect in the second tradition Volf refers to healing.
[41] Volf, "Materiality," 667; using material of his doctoral supervisor Jürgen Moltmann, he adds a fourth aspect, that of ecology: Moltmann, *Creation*, 250.

experientially-aware soteriology would have consequences for christology: it would relativize the theoretically believed but practically not really experienced doctrine of *satisfaction:* For "Jesus did not live in order to die, as some theories of reconciliation fixated on the cross seem to say. He died as he lived."[42] That too is charismatic theology!

---

[42] Suurmond, *Word and Spirit at Play*, 51.

CHAPTER TWENTY

Ecclesiology:
Who Belongs to the Church?

Charisma and Institution

In the writing—years ago—of the first volume of *The Pentecostals*, I noted that Pentecostalism must deal with the tension between charisma and institution.[1] Since that time, Pentecostals themselves have begun to discuss this topic. One of those involved in the discussion is Margaret M. Poloma.[2] In an article in *The Christian Century* she discusses the well-known sex scandals of Assemblies of God television evangelists: "The public thus became aware of the Assemblies of God not because of its rapid growth, but because of the misdeeds of its televangelists." Of course, this is an unfortunate critique, for mainline churches take the easy way out if they discuss an important movement on the basis only of the extravagances of some individuals (even if they are prominent). Poloma continues: "As sociologist Peter Berger noted some years ago, religious experiences, whatever else they are, are institutionally dangerous. The Assemblies of God learned this lesson early in its history." Recently, they have been confronted with this same lesson again in the conflict with the "Signs and Wonders" movement (chapter 18, pp. 228–45).

On what basis does Poloma make these assertions? In a survey, she found that of 1,275 Assemblies of God adherents from 16 different congregations, only 30 percent were raised in the Assemblies; an additional 10 percent were converts from other Pentecostal "sects."

---

[1] *The Pentecostals*, 33ff., 424ff.
[2] Poloma, *Crossroads*. In the following I quote widely from her article "Charisma."

These converts have brought not only an enthusiasm to many staid and established Assemblies of God churches but also their middle- and upper-middle-class status, which has legitimated greater openness to the range of the "gifts of the spirit." Due largely to this influx from mainline churches, confirmed membership in Assemblies of God congregations jumped from 646,000 in 1970 to over one million in 1980. Perhaps the greatest factor in Assemblies of God growth has been the fact that the charismatic movement has never been fully accepted in mainline denominations and has been rejected by most fundamentalists. The movement reached its height during the 1970s as charismatic renewal groups formed in every major Protestant denomination, in Roman Catholic and Orthodox churches and among Jewish converts.[3] This movement seemed to lose momentum during the 1980s, reducing the pool of readily available recruits. After years of steady growth, the Assemblies of God reached a plateau, with membership figures for 1988 and 1989 actually declining slightly. This plateau can be attributed to several interrelated factors. Besides the waning of the charismatic movement in general, the Assemblies of God felt the impact of new charismatic ministries and the effect of the televangelism scandals. Independent charismatic groups such as the newer Maranatha Fellowships,[4] Word-Faith Churches,[5] and Vineyard Ministries[6] promise fewer institutional restrictions. Unfettered by older Pentecostal history and traditions, these new sects attract experience-hungry charismatics who long for fresh spiritual encounters and who often mistrust institutional church ties. As for the Swaggart,[7] and Bakker[8] scandals, although the denomination was commended for its handling of these situations, the publicity accentuated how far the Assemblies of God had moved from its earliest restorationist vision. Unbridled wealth, sex scandals and competitive bids for power make great television drama but don't attract moralistic Christians."

A greater problem confronting the Assemblies of God—one that may underlie the aforementioned issues—is sociological: the tension between the charisma that initiated and renewed the Assemblies of God, and the rise of a bureaucratic organization that necessarily undergirds the successful denomination. Charisma—elusive, fragile, affective rather than rational—is particularly difficult to maintain in a modern and secular society";

that is, at least, if charisma is understood to have the spontaneous and selective meaning given it by the early Pentecostals, and also by Max Weber (chapter 17, pp. 224–27).

Just as other once-charismatic religious movements have followed the path of over-institutionalization and over-regulation, which in turn has discouraged much of the original charisma, the Assemblies of God suffer of the chilling effects of routinization. . . . The institutional mechanisms that demand credentials

---

[3] Rausch, *Messianic;* Juster, "Messianic"; idem, "Union."
[4] McGee, "Maranatha."
[5] Lovett, "Positive."
[6] Wagner, "Vineyard."
[7] Stout, "Swaggart."
[8] Burgess, "Bakker."

over calling and encourage large bureaucratic congregations rather than small charismatic ones are easing the prophetic daughters out of the ordained ministry [we will return to this point later]. Paradoxically, the institution that developed out of charisma and has been strengthened by fresh outbursts seeks to tame and domesticate the spirit. It remains to be seen whether—and how much—charisma will rule over bureaucratic forms and regulations, or whether organizational concerns will stifle the Spirit.[9]

As I have already mentioned, this argumentation holds water only if we understand charisma in a "Weberian," and not a Pauline, sense, for it can be argued according to Paul's usage of charisma that the *proïsthameno* (Rom. 12:8)—the managerial organizer—may also be gifted by the Spirit, and should be measured not only against his so-called efficiency but much more against his ministry and service to the whole church of God.

A similar development is discussed among Swedish Pentecostals. As long as Lewi Pethrus was the unchallenged leader of Swedish Pentecostalism, the official ideology was that of a strict congregationalism. No organization higher than the congregation was tolerated. "The ideology of non-organization had the function as a denominational standard."[10] It gave Pethrus an unchallenge-able power over the whole movement through his Filadelfia church in Stock-holm. But when Pethrus resigned from his pastorship in Stockholm "he pushed the idea of both the autonomy and hegemony of the [local] church into the background" and organized a whole string of national institutions—above all, publishing companies, periodicals and joint companies, including "The Lewi Pethrus Foundation for Philanthropic Activity."[11] Bertil Carlsson, a well-known Swedish Pentecostal, has untiringly unveiled this process.[12]

---

[9] Poloma, "Charisma."

[10] D. Bundy in his review of Struble, *Samfundsfria, EPTA Bulletin* 3/1, 1984, 12–16, quote 4. Lindberg, "Swedish."

[11] Lindberg, "Swedish."

[12] Carlsson, "Pingstväckelsen aller Pingströrelsen?" *Veckotidning* Nr. 51.52 1973. Idem, "Objektiva fakta är into så farliga," *Dagen* 11.1.1973. Idem, "Yrkesfördelnin-gen bland beslutsfattarna inom pingströrelsn," *Dagen* 28.3.1972. Sjögreen, "Ping-strörelsens organisationsfromer." Carlsson, "Svenska Pingströrelsen en folkrörelse I blickpunkten," *Dagen* 30.9.1977. Idem, "Svensk Pingstmission" 60 år, *Dagen,* 30.11.1973. Idem, " 'Trafikregler' for de kristna församlingarna," *Dagen* 5/2/1988. Idem, "Vad lör Pingströrelsen I centrale kristna frågor?" *Dagen* 5.2.1988. Idem, "Möt 90–talets utmangingar ma medömdjikeet," *Dagen* 17.7.1990. Idem, *Människan, um-hället och Gud, Grunddrag I Lewi Pethrus kristendomsuppfatning* (see the review on this last book by David Bundy in *Pneuma* 12/1, 1990, 69–70).
This is part of an ongoing debate in Swedish Pentecostalism. Carlsson has summarized his arguments and facts in English in *Organization*. This is a basic document. The books on Pethrus are not yet closed. His life was clouded by controversies and jealousies with other important leaders (for the controversy with Lidman, see chapter 28, pp. 395–97). He actively stopped his colleague Törnberg from being elected to the national parliament. "He could tolerate no competition to his leadership and forced talented individuals such as Sven Lidman (journalist) and A. P. Franklin (missiologist) to work outside the movement." Bundy, "Pethrus," *Dictionary,* 711f.

In conclusion one can say: Pentecostals have to wrestle in all countries with institutional problems similar to those faced by other churches. What is new is that they are becoming aware of the problem. Is it unrealistic to think that they could perhaps come forward with a form of organization that gives way to charisma in the Pauline sense, and does not, for example, exclude women from leading positions? As to the place of women, one must accept that even many Presbyterian churches are "more charismatic" than most Pentecostal churches.

Baptism

For many Pentecostal churches today adult baptism has become a more important issue than the gifts and life in the Spirit. This, in spite of the fact that adult baptism was not even mentioned in the first "declaration of faith" of Pentecostalism, and in spite of the fact that for instance in Germany the Protestant church has baptized (not re-baptized!) more adults than the whole German Pentecostal movement.[13]

Cecil M. Robeck and Jerry L. Sandidge, both of them Assemblies of God ministers, have examined this question in detail: "Fr. Donald Gelpi has noted that 'the most serious doctrinal differences dividing Catholic charismatics and Protestant Pentecostals lie in the area of sacramental theology.'[14] Undoubtedly, this observation could be applied equally to Roman Catholics and Pentecostals in general. What may not be so obvious is that one aspect of 'sacramental' theology, baptism, has led to more intense debate and divided more Pentecostal churches than any other issue the movement has faced."[15] The authors then go on to discuss the different modes and interpretations of baptism within Pentecostalism. They mention immersion and sprinkling, infant baptism and adult baptism. Some demand rebaptism if the mode was in their view not correct or if it took place *before* conversion. Some dip the candidate only once, others thrice. The condemnation of infant baptism is not equally strong in all Pentecostal churches. As in the case of "Spirit-baptism" Pentecostalism displays a rich, pluralistic approach to the praxis, mode, and interpretation of baptism, and to the baptismal formula as well.[16] It is also not clear among Pentecostals whether baptism is an ordinance or a sacrament, and it is furthermore not clear whether baptism is necessary for salvation or not. Readers who deny this

---

[13] "Confession of the Apostolic Faith," *Apostolic Faith*, Los Angeles, Sept. 1906, see *The Pentecostals*, 513. On adult baptism in the German Protestant churches (Evangelische Kirche in Deutschland) see Berg, "So viele waren," 15: "67,645 people joined the Protestant Church in 1991, 22,914 through adult baptism. 16,169 who had left the church once returned alone in the churches in West Germany."

[14] Gelpi, "Ecumenical," 180, quoted by Robeck, "Ecclesiology," 505.

[15] Robeck, "Ecclesiology," 505.

[16] *The Pentecostals*, 31–32, 390–95.

pluralism may argue with their own fellow-Pentecostals, and with Sandidge and Robeck, whose closely-argued and richly-documented essay I need not repeat.

Most important is the authors' theological conclusion:

> What most Pentecostals fail to take as seriously as the witness to an individual's identification with Christ in this act is the testimony it contains to the identification with Christian *koinonia*, to corporate identification, the relationship between the person being baptized and all others who have been baptized and who share in their identification with Christ.[17]

In other words, baptism is an ecumenical sacrament. It expresses identification with the whole church of God.

If baptism "is to bear witness to that koinonia with God in Christ through the Spirit, then it cannot be done in isolation. It is meant to be undertaken within the context of the community of faith. Private baptism undermines baptism's community nature."[18]

It is furthermore seen in terms of *anamnesis:* "the Risen Lord is present through the Holy Spirit who comes to indwell the new believer. Baptism then becomes sacramental by bringing reality to the presence of the one who died and was resurrected. . . . " The *koinonia* of baptismal identification means the "church as a whole"—including those previously baptized. "The implications of this are both social and ethical. At each baptism the question must be asked again: Do we accept them as our brothers and sisters? Are we willing to be responsible for them? Are we also willing to recognize that they now have a responsibility to/for us?"[19]

This may place the issue of the legitimacy of believers' and infant baptism in a new light. The biblical data seem generally to favor believers' baptism, regardless of age.

> However, the question must be raised regarding at what point in what way such baptism becomes efficacious. Within much Pentecostal theology, the faith of the one seeking healing is often understood to be essential to a person's healing, but the person who is sick may not be able to exercise the "necessary" faith. It may be exercised, however, by the community of faith on behalf of the sick or injured person, and the community of faith anticipates that its faith will be effectual . . . ; for those who view baptism non-sacramentally and who practice believers' baptism, there is no clear and efficacious role for the faith of the koinonia, of other believers, to be exercised on behalf of the baptismal candidate.[20]

---

[17] Robeck, "Ecclesiology," 525f.

[18] Ibid., 527.

[19] Ibid., 528. That is why the Dominican, Prof. LeGrand, from the Insitut Catholique in Paris asked (at the Vatican/Pentecostal Dialogue Session in Brixen, Italy, July 1995): "You say that the Catholic infant baptism is no baptism. Yet you want to celebrate the Lord's Supper with us. How come that you celebrate the eucharist with non-baptized people?"

[20] Robeck, "Ecclesiology," 528.

For instance, Nelson notes[21] that since the sinner must first repent and believe, "this excludes children (infants) who are too young to repent and believe, and invalidates 'baptism' of those who were not regenerated when they submitted to the ordinance." However, that is not what I read in the Scripture. I mention only two passages. Peter says to the inquirers in Acts 2:38: "Repent, and be baptized everyone of you in the name of Jesus Christ for the forgiveness of sins *(eis aphesin ton hamartion hymon)*." There is no question that they need forgiveness of sin *before* their baptism, and that baptism is only a public sign of what has already happened. Baptism is "for the forgiveness of sins," whether we like it or not. Even stronger is Mark 2. Here a paralytic is brought before Jesus. The evangelist Mark says: "And when Jesus saw their faith [that is, the faith of the four who brought him], he said to the paralytic: 'My son, your sins are forgiven.'" Fortunately Mark did not have to send his gospel for approval to any church, Pentecostal or not; for this passage means that sins are forgiven in this instance on the basis of the faith of others; in other words, of the *koinonia*.

Sandidge and Robeck argue in a similar way. "One theological document suggests that the baptism of infants may be considered a baptism of 'corporate faith,' and believers' baptism of 'personal confession.'"[22] No wonder that these Pentecostal authors then recommend the ecumenical *Baptism, Eucharist and Ministry.*

They then discuss very intelligently the pastoral problems, for instance when somebody who has been baptized as an infant demands to be baptized as a believer. They quote the Catholic priest Francis MacNutt: "Rather than deny their sacramental baptism as infants, he told them they could 'enact' the conversion that many of them had truly experienced...." MacNutt immersed each person three times

> calling the person's name and saying, "I renew your baptism in the name of the Father, and of the Son, and of the Holy Spirit." ... If Roman Catholics can accept the baptism of persons immersed in the name of the Trinity by a Pentecostal minister, is it too much to anticipate that Pentecostals might also accept the reaffirmation of sacramental baptism received as an infant through a rite of renewal by immersion, whether by a Roman Catholic priest or a Pentecostal pastor?[23]

(I wonder what my Swiss Pentecostal friends would say to this.) Sandidge then goes on to recommend an ecumenical discussion of the issue within Pentecostalism, since Pentecostals already have a wide variety of praxis and interpretation of baptism.[24]

---

[21] Nelson, P. C., *Doctrines,* 65, quoted by Robeck, "Ecclesiology," 528f. (Nelson was originally a Baptist, *Handbuch,* 08.021.001).

[22] Ford, John, "Findings," note 13, manuscript 21, quoted by Robeck, "Ecclesiology," 529.

[23] McNutt, "Solution," 61, quoted by Robeck, "Ecclesiology," 531.

[24] On a similar topic see van der Laan in chapter 25, pp. 345–47.

Who Belongs to the Church?

As one might expect, Pentecostals from former Yugoslavia take the lead in addressing the question of what exactly constitutes a "church." Miroslav Volf takes a position much more sober than that expressed by the groups around John Wimber,[25] and by Kopfermann and the neo-Pentecostals and charismatics in general. Volf says:

> A church is a community of people who congregate in order to call on, to testify and to confess Christ the liberator. . . . They do not need to be characterized by a certain grade of personal or social holiness in order to be called the church. The church . . . lives solely on the sanctifying presence of Christ, who promised, to be wherever people congregate in His name. . . . The Church is therefore not a club of the perfected but a community of people who confess to be sinners and pray: *debita dimitte* (forgive us our sins). Any group which gathers around the one Christ, around God in his salvific devotion to men *(Zuwendung zum Menschen)*, who celebrate in him their liberator and Lord, who is open to all people and where all people have the same dignity, such a group is a church because Christ has promised to be present among them.[26]

> Although I am not prepared to deny ecclesiological quality to those Christian communities which reject sacraments and ordinances, I am of the opinion that the sacraments above all display the essentially ecclesial character of Christian life, because nobody can give himself or herself the sacraments (although they must be accepted in person).[27]

What is interesting in this ecclesiology (which was published in one of the leading German theological periodicals and which was expressly classed under "free-church perspectives") is the influence of the orthodox context from which Volf comes. Even more striking is the blatant difference between Volf's formulation and earlier Pentecostal ecclesiologies, in which clear lines of demarcation were drawn based on criteria of personal and social holiness.[28] This earlier ecclesiological ideology has in fact, for a long time, been out of use both in the West and in the Third World. This is however, to my knowledge, the first time that an ecclesiology has been published by a leading Pentecostal scholar who has given up earlier ecclesiologies. Perhaps the turmoil and suffering in Yugoslavia sharpen the theological mind. At any rate, he "sensed an unexpressed expectation to explain why he, as a Croat still had friends in Serbia and did not talk with disgust about the backwardness of Byzantine-Orthodox culture." In his "Theological Reflections in the Wake of 'Ethnic Cleansing,' "[29] Volf gives a moving example of reconciliation *and* sharp politi-

---

[25] Wagner, "Wimber," see also note 6.

[26] Volf, "Kirche," 64, 66.

[27] Ibid., 68, note 65.

[28] *The Pentecostals*, the chapter on Ethics ("Religion is what you must not do") 399–412, and 413ff.

[29] Volf, "Exclusion and Embrace," 232f., 241. Cf. also idem, "Vision," 195–205.

cal analysis—a reconciliatory ecclesiology which is badly needed in all ecumenical relationships, but in particular between the Orthodox and other Christians. Important also is his definition of sin: *"The real sinner is not the outcast but the one who casts the other out . . .* Sin is not so much a defilement but a certain form of *purity:* the exclusion of the other from one's heart and one's world."

Volf is not alone in this approach. The Hispanic Pentecostal scholar Eldin Villafañe also sets the ecclesial demarcation lines very differently from earlier Pentecostals. Because the church is a liberated community, he says, "It is committed to reconciliation. Because it has an ethic of liberation, it plays a major role in bringing about a new, reconciled national church and society."[30]

As to the abandonment of the earlier lines of demarcation in practice, I invite any reader to go to a long-established Pentecostal church and see for himself or herself what has changed in the last twenty years in the areas of dress, cosmetics, life-style and even sexual ethics, including an increasing rate of divorce in Pentecostalism. This latter issue, however, creates problems. If the divorcée is powerful and/or rich, nothing happens,[31] or sometimes his or her earlier marriage is annulled (as in the Catholic church). If he or she is an ordinary member, church discipline is rarely applied. But if he or she is an ordinary pastor with not much power or money, that person gets into real trouble.[32] Another indication of the changing situation is an article of the British Assemblies of God on "Cohabitation and the Church," in which cohabitation is not condemned as "unbiblical."[33] One more is the fact that in the Dutch charismatic movement homosexual pastors are actively engaged, and that the American homosexual and lesbian Pentecostals publish a periodical.[34] That British Assemblies of God pastors celebrate more marriages and funerals than weddings[35] further points to the process of denominationalization.

For the Third World one may consult Allan Anderson, who points out an interesting interaction between Pentecostalism and the African background in South African Pentecostalism. Only about half of those interviewed had ever spoken in tongues but many had offered sacrifices to ancestors, and a few actively reverenced ancestors. Almost all consulted diviners, a few practiced polygamy, and a few drank beer and smoked. A majority had a clear preference for Nelson Mandela as political leader for South Africa.[36]

---

[30] Villafañe, *The Liberating Spirit,* 105, quoting Costas, "Social," 224.

[31] See the story of Aimee Semple McPherson, *The Pentecostals,* 488.

[32] Eisenlöffel, *Wenn* (being the tragedy of Eisenlöffel's divorce and the treatment he got from the German Pentecostals).

[33] Hudson–Warrington, "Cohabitation," 63–73.

[34] *Pentecostal Coalition: Newsletter of the Pentecostal Coalition for Human Rights, Supporting Black, Hispanic, Women's and Gay Liberation,* Howard University, Washington, DC.

[35] Kay, "Characteristics."

[36] Among the questions which Anderson asked his Pentecostal sample, one finds:

This just shows how much the African context has influenced the lines of demarcation in the church, just as in Europe and America society at large has also influenced Pentecostals. Perhaps in Africa the *reverence of ancestors* needs some explanation. For Catholics this is perhaps not so strange as for Protestants, since Catholics reverence their saints and have a much more complete ritual for dealing with ancestors. For Western Protestants this is only a problem as long as they do not realize that we too have a relationship to our ancestors; only, we give it a different name. Since the Protestant churches have cut off every formal relation with the ancestors, they return in our dreams (as with the Africans), where they enter the domain of psychiatric analysis. Perhaps we then call it father-complex or mother-complex or super-ego. One can justly ask the question whether or not the Protestant churches should leave all this to psychiatry. On the other hand, we have to develop a critical relationship to our ancestors (to tradition, to father- and mother-complexes), otherwise we become the slaves of the past. The same would apply to Africans, but in their case, it seems to me that this process is already in full swing.

I have been unable to come to a clear understanding of what is going on in Africa in relation to ancestor spirits. Perhaps a European theologian is unable to find categories for this kind of spirituality, as was already my impression when discussing the "presence" of Simon Kimbangu in the Kimbanguist Church.[37] Allan Anderson also gives several perspectives on this problem. In a recent article he tries to interpret ancestors in a pneumatological context:

	yes	no	unsure
Baptism by immersion	98%	1%	
Does your church have speaking in tongues	81.3%	14.9%	3.7%
Have you spoken in tongues?	51.5%	48.5%	
To whom do church members offer sacrifices?			
to God	0%		
to ancestors	80%		
to both the ancestors and to God	20%		
Do church members reverence ancestors?	3.6%	96.4%	
Do church members consult diviners?	3.6%	95%	1.4%
Do church members practice polygamy?	0.7%	99.3%	
Do church members drink (African) beer?	2.2%	97.8%	
Who would you like to be president of a new South Africa?			
Nelson Mandela	44.9%		
F. W. de Klerk	31.2%		
the PAC leader	2.2%		
another person	2.9%		
undecided/refused to answer	18.5%		

Source: Anderson, *Bazalwane*, 129ff. Anderson also gives figures broken down between Pentecostal mission churches and independent Pentecostal churches. There are some variations in this but the tendency is the same everywhere.

[37] See chapter 6, pp. 64–66, 77–80.

The fact that most of our interviewees had a clear understanding of the Holy Spirit and were opposed to the practice of the ancestor cult by Christians, tends to negate the view of earlier researchers that the ancestor cult has found new expression in the emphasis on pneumatological beliefs and manifestations in African Pentecostalism. These views were mostly based on European theological presuppositions that could not really be substantiated by empirical research. The fact that the Holy Spirit has taken over some (or all) of the *functions* of the ancestor does not mean that he has thereby *become* an ancestor. It means rather that the doctrine of the Holy Spirit has become relevant in this very important African context, in that the Spirit has become the Counselor and Guide as portrayed in Scriptures. Far from being a resurgence of traditional ancestor spirit possession, once we have separated the forms of the Spirit phenomena from their meaning, the revelations of Holy Spirit in African Pentecostalism point to a realistic encounter and confrontation between the new Christian faith and the old traditional beliefs. Christianity thereby attains an authentically African character, realistically penetrating the old and creating the new.[38]

On *polygamy*, perhaps the following will help clarify the issue: "Only the males are denied the ordinances, the women are allowed all ordinances and offices even if they are a third or a fourth wife."[39]

From the important Assemblées de Dieu in Borkina Faso[40] and Togo (West Africa) we learn that American Assemblies of God missionaries in these areas originally demanded from their polygamistic converts that they divorce all of their wives but one. Consequently, converts kept the youngest wife, and the remaining women had no other choice but prostitution. Now that the Assemblées de Dieu have become independent, the converts are no longer forced to divorce their women. They are baptized together with all their wives and take part in the eucharist. However, after baptism no further polygamistic marriage is allowed.[41]

Women

In volume I of the *Pentecostals* I have already documented the important role of women in the Pentecostal church.[42] In most countries women were essential at the beginning of Pentecostalism; examples may be found in France,[43] Switzerland, the USA[44] (including American Hispanics),[45] Scandinavia,[46]

---

[38] Anderson, "Ancestor," 38f.

[39] Mann, "Polygamy," quoted in Aigbe, "People," 175, 179, note 20.

[40] Barrett, *WChE*, 732: "Assemblées de Dieu en Haute-Volta: 80,000." For Togo, see ibid., 670.

[41] Communication by Dr. Del Tarr, former missionary of the Assemblies of God in West Africa and now president of the Assemblies of God Theological Seminary, Springfield, Missouri.

[42] *The Pentecostals*, 486ff.

[43] Pfister, *Soixante*.

[44] Lawless, *Peculiar*.

[45] Villafañe, *The Liberating Spirit*, 131, in particular on Mama Leo, 96.

[46] Hoaas–Tegnander, *Kvinnen*. Review, D. Bundy in *EPTA Bulletin* 5/4, 1986, 139–42.

Great Britain,[47] the Black Churches in Britain,[48] Chile,[49] Holland,[50] and other places. R. M. Riss gives a detailed and competent overview of women ministers in the USA at the beginning of Pentecostalism.[51] Today the issue is controversial in spite of the important role of women in the past. Generally they are barred from leadership roles, and often they are not allowed (officially) to celebrate the eucharist, or to baptize or receive converts into church membership.[52] Edith L. Blumhofer gives some embarrassing details on this. She observes how important women have been in the Assemblies of God, but also how stubbornly the male leaders (especially E. N. Bell[53] and Ernest S. Williams[54]) have objected to accepting them as equals. They filled in the gaps left by men, and were considered "second best" in God's eyes.[55]

Several reasons have been suggested for this. The most plausible to me is offered by Cecil M. Robeck: "As evangelical values have been adopted by Pentecostals, the role of women in ministry has suffered."[56] Whether this will change with Pentecostals' rediscovery of the important role of women at the beginning of their movement is difficult to say. On the basis of many interviews, David G. Roebuck is rather pessimistic.[57] Nevertheless, many things have changed in recent years in Pentecostalism, and recent biblical research on the roles of women among the early Christians has produced some revelations.[58] In the end, Pentecostals who want to be biblical in all respects might have to revise their attitudes here too.

---

[47] Cartwright, "Daughters."

[48] Foster, *Black Women.*

[49] Slootweg, "Mujeres"; Tamez, "Mujer" (a very critical and well-documented essay on women in the Pauline corpus by a Pentecostal); see also Tamez, *Contratoda* (quoting Conzelman's commentary on *1 Corinthians*). Esparza, "Question." Bridges-Johns, "Women."

[50] Graf, "Vrouw."

[51] Riss, "Women" (very competent article with rich bibliography).

[52] Roebuck, "Brothers," in particular F, 12. Cf. also Best, "Loosing the Women"; Lozano, "Crossroads." *Pneuma,* 17/1, 1995 is dedicated to the topic of "women in Pentecostalism" with some enlightening documentation.

[53] Warner, "Bell."

[54] Robeck, "Williams."

[55] Blumhofer, *Assemblies,* in particular, 26.

[56] Robeck, "National," 635.

[57] Roebuck, "Brothers," F 16–19.

[58] Especially important because of her precise and competent exegetical analysis is the Austrian professor of theology Susanne Heine. See her *Women,* in particular p. 40, where she shows that the name Iounias (Rom 16:7 "fellow prisoners and of note among the apostles") is pure fantasy by the editors of the Greek text. The oldest manuscripts have Iounia, "noted among the apostles." Only in the 13th century was this female apostle "transformed" into a man by giving her a name which appears nowhere in Greek literature (Iounias). Susanne Heine gives many more such examples and backs them up with solid scholarship.

CHAPTER TWENTY ONE

Music and Liturgy:
How to Worship in Public?

In the following chapter I draw on my personal experience in Pentecostal churches (and to a limited extent in charismatic groups). I believe that there are some important lessons to be learned from certain musical and liturgical traditions in Pentecostalism; but I also believe that it is generally neither desirable nor possible to transplant these experiences directly into another social and cultural context. What is important to recognize, however, is that the original impetus of all church liturgy and music was *for and with the people of God* (and not just the liturgical and musical experts). This applies as much to mainline churches with their liturgical traditions as to Pentecostal churches which have outgrown their original cultural context.

A Genuine Oral Liturgy[1]

Pentecostal liturgy—is this not a contradiction in terms? How can a spontaneous and sometimes enthusiastic understanding of worship produce a liturgy? This question only shows how far *our* understanding of liturgy has departed from the New Testament understanding of what is a proper order of worship. For, if spontaneity and enthusiasm are essentially a-liturgical, how then do we explain that the first Christians—who could obviously be a rather enthusiastic crowd—very early on produced a kind of liturgical tradition? It is true that the early liturgies were not printed—how could the illiterate slave in

---

[1] Some of the material in this section has been published in my article "Significance." J. W. Shepperd approaches the topic more conventionally in his article "Worship."

Corinth follow a printed liturgy? (Slaves made up the majority in the Corinthian church, but there were other classes involved in the church at Corinth—it was truly heterogeneous.)[2] Nor were those earliest liturgies even always written out in the first place—but that did not prevent the first Christians from having some order in their worship. Printed prayer books and agendas are not the only form of ordering a service—nor perhaps even the best one. The first Christians had what I would call an "oral liturgy"; that is, a liturgy which could be memorized by the congregation. Their liturgy was continually "in the making." It was a liturgy which was shaped and reshaped by the people of God according to principles laid down by tradition (1 Cor 12 and 14).

One might expect an oral liturgy among oral people. Oral people are not necessarily people who do not read and write[3]—although the illiterates surely belong to them; they are people whose main medium of expression is the oral form—story, proverb, parable, joke, dance, song (chapter 2, pp. 6–15, section I, pp. 19–141)—in short, all the forms in which (as form-criticism has shown us) were framed the elementary, original source material of the Bible. Today the fact that not only illiterates, but also people from middle-class backgrounds and highly trained intellectuals find the "oral order" more satisfying than the written one is demonstrated by the great attracting power of the charismatic movement within the mainline churches.

Pentecostal worship has been described many times, but no description replaces personal acquaintance with the Pentecostal service. The following example from personal experience in Chile[4] is not of course representative of all Pentecostal churches, but may serve as an introduction to Pentecostal worship.

I was asked to sit in front of the congregation in the red plush seat reserved for honored guests. An ocean of faces floated before my eyes, 2,000 to 3,000 faithful, some shod with sandals made from car-tires rather than shoes. As soon as the trumpet blew the first melody, those faces, creased with the lines of age-long oppression, came to life. In a circle the people danced slowly the dances of their Indian ancestors. Those who did not dance stood reverently and clapped their hands in slow rhythm. A woman prophesied in a deep, soulful voice. All of a sudden there was silence! The whole congregation fell down on their

---

[2] See on this Hollenweger, *Conflict* and *ITh* 1.
[3] For a discussion on this cf. Hoggart, *Uses.*
[4] Examples in Pope, *Millhands;* Meyer, "Brasilien"; Calley, *God's People;* Maurer, "Pentecôtisme"; Lalive d'Epinay, *Haven of the Masses.* For a Catholic description, see Zenetti, *Heisse,* also my *Pfingstkirchen,* 301–6, and the highly interesting liturgiological reflections of de Moura, *Importância das Igrejas Pentecostais,* and "Pentecostalismo" (English summary in *The Pentecostals,* 105ff.). Ample literature in my *Pfingstkirchen,* 396–466. Passim in *The Pentecostals,* in chapter 2 (pp. 6–15), and in the conclusion of this book (chapter 28, pp. 398–400). Also Hollenweger, "Liturgies." On Pentecostal dance in Chile see Robeck, "Taking Stock," in particular 50. On dance and liturgy with professional dancers see Leinberger/Hollenweger/Bubmann, *Getanztes Leben.*

knees in order to thank God for the dance he had given them. Above in the left-hand gallery sat 50 to 100 gray-bloused *ciclistas.* These are the bicycle-evangelists, who cycle every Sunday into the surrounding villages to preach, sing, and heal the sick. This evening they will return and the congregation will greet them with a loud "Gloria a Dios!" They will draw behind them a queue of curious people, many of whom will be converted right in the service.

"Do you also dance?" they asked me. This was the test-question. They wanted to know whether I despised them or not. Some American missionaries had told them that dancing was not of the Spirit. "I would like to," I answered sincerely, "but I do not know your dances." They were satisfied with this answer. Their own preachers do not dance either; their duty is not to dance, but to interpret the dances.

From this description it is clear that the most important element of an oral worship is the active participation of every member in the congregation, even if this amounts to several thousand people: dancing, singing, pilgrimages, praying individually and collectively, playing all kinds of instruments (from the hand-harmonica to triangle and drum; from the saxophone to the violin), and appreciating or judging the sermon with inspiring shouts or critical remarks and questions.

In the structure of the Pentecostal liturgy one might find most of the elements of historical liturgies: Invocation, Kyrie, Confession of Faith, Gloria, Eucharistic Canon, and Benediction. Yet these parts are hardly ever named, and for most observers are not recognizable as such, since the elements according to which the different parts of the service are structured are not the rubrics and the nigrics,[5] but the so-called choruses, that is, short spontaneous songs, known by heart by the whole congregation. Some of the key choruses[6] indicate the transition from one part to another.

Key choruses vary from one congregation to another, yet everyone in the congregation understands these signals. During the time of participation by the whole congregation if someone sings a song of praise in the Kyrie part, or gives a prophecy in the Invocation part, he or she will be corrected by the pastor, or by an elder, or, if the person persists, by immediate and spontaneous singing by the whole congregation. Most Pentecostals are not aware of the liturgical function of these choruses, yet they are clearly observable. The Pentecostals thus demonstrate that the alternative to a written liturgy is not chaos, but a flexible oral tradition, which allows for variations within the framework of the whole liturgical structure, similar to the possibilities in a jam session of jazz musicians—another black heritage.

---

[5] "Rubric" is that which is printed in red in the liturgical books (what the priest reads). "Nigrics" would then be that which is printed in black (for the congregation).

[6] This seems to be an old tradition as the Calvinistic liturgy also contains the so-called "chants spontanés." But they are today only called spontaneous, as they are sung from the book. Place, tune, and words are prefixed in the liturgy. Nonetheless, they are beautiful and could easily be sung spontaneously.

Speaking in tongues can play a similar "democratizing" role, because it allows prayer in non-rational meditative language. This is an important prayer experience for the rationally unskilled as well as for the intellectually over-burdened academic. As the apostle Paul said, "He who speaks in a tongue edifies himself" (1 Cor. 14:4).

Jean-Jacques Suurmond has written a fascinating book on this topic. Suurmond is a Dutch Reformed pastor who was for a long time a Pentecostal pastor, and is in contact with the Dutch charismatic renewal. Suurmond uses the well-known Dutch tradition of the *homo ludens*, seeing in the "uselessness" (for instance of glossolalia) its usefulness and political significance. As such, it is "justification brought to life." This is important in a neurotic civilization such as ours, says Suurmond, which is obsessed with utility and a desire to perform and to dominate (no one is more obsessed with order than the neurotic). Salvation, he says, lies in the church at play. "A real game consists in the creative integration of order (word, rules) on the one hand and the spontaneous contribution of dynamic enthusiasm of all participants on the other."[7] Thus the minister is not "the star" of the play but a religious producer.

The Future of Pentecostal Liturgy

If one considers the future of Pentecostal worship, there are two possibilities open. On the one hand, *classical Pentecostalism* can adapt itself to the mainline churches, adopting a fundamentalistic theology and a written liturgy. This process was until recently in full swing for most of the European and North American Pentecostal churches. Oral liturgy can become as fixed and dull as written liturgy, when it becomes dominated by a few individuals and is no longer the open-ended expectant experience of the whole congregation. Donald Gee (1891–1966), a British Pentecostal leader, says that the result of this "is to produce meetings so stereotyped that, for all their boasted freedom, they become more barren than the very liturgical services they deprecate—and with less aesthetic appeal."[8] One can therefore observe an increasing production of liturgical forms and agendas within the white Pentecostal community.

So the Assemblies of God (USA) have published a three-volume Minister's Manual[9] with agendas for burials in general, for burials of devout Christians, children, church or civic leaders, for non-Christians, for the installation of pastors and associate pastors, for baptism and children's dedication. In the foreword they state:

> It hardly needs to be said that set forms of devotion are uncongenial to those who practice a simple mode of worship and who stress spiritual liberty in prayer and

---

[7] Suurmond, *Word and Spirit at Play*, 59
[8] Gee, "Lead"; *The Pentecostals*, 385–89.
[9] Pickthorn, *Manual*. But see the violent protest of the Italian Pentecostal against written liturgies (Bracco, *Potenza;* quoted and discussed in the excellent doctoral dissertation by the late Miriam Castiglione, *Aspetti*).

preaching. Yet, while recognizing this fact it still remains true that there are special occasions where an appointed order is necessary for a well-conducted service. And if this is so, why be content with forms that are crude or badly prepared? Jesus in the Scripture portion known as the Lord's Prayer instructed the disciples: "When you pray, say. . ." The prophet Hosea once said to his countrymen: "Take with you words, and turn to the Lord, and say to Him. . ." (Hos. 14:2). There need be no morbid fear of lifeless ritual. As long as the spiritual vitality of the church is maintained the use of necessary forms will never become merely formal.

The other possibility would be the development, using all the know-how of Pentecostal oral culture, of a really post-literary liturgy, where the main medium of communication would be not the written word but the proverb, not the doctrinal proposition but the parable, not the statement but the story, not the Gregorian hymn but the chorus. This liturgy could be adapted to non-proletarian cultures, but its main mission would be in the Third World and among the subcultures of the younger generation in the West.

The *charismatic movement* in the mainline churches also has two options. In emphasizing the personal aspect of Christianity it can develop into a spiritual revival movement for higher social classes, which would lead to worship services refreshing and equipping the individual but relatively unaware of corporate sins and potentials. The other possibility is that the charismatic renewal might develop its charismatic worship—following the Pauline rather than the Lucan pneumatology[10]—to include among the charismata not just those common to classical Pentecostalism, but also charismata in the social, political, and artistic fields—the charismata of those people who are not generally considered to be fitting members of liturgical commissions, and are not commonly found within the worshipping congregation. This would be a healthy ecumenical complement to the classical Pentecostal understanding of worship.

The Social Implications of an Oral Liturgy

By confining liturgy to written liturgy—albeit read orally in church, but read from a book in written language—we have excluded in our historical churches the majority of the people of this world; namely, the oral people. (No wonder that the Pentecostals said at the Full Assembly of the World Council of Churches at Uppsala [1968]: "These people are religiously underdeveloped. They *read* prayers! [laughter]"[11]) Thus we have not only sanctioned the separation of the world into haves and have-nots, whites and non-whites, but also excluded from worship oral people! One looks in vain for the theological justification of such an atrocity.

Look, however, at Pentecostals in the Third World: If the inarticulate *peon* in Latin America realizes that he or she has something to say, if the despised

---

[10] Schweizer, "Spirit," see *The Pentecostals*, 335–41 (detailed discussion).
[11] Ramírez-Ramírez, "I Could Have Danced"; de Melo, "Participation."

Indian of Mexico begins to sing and make music with the instruments of his persecuted ancestors, if the Chilean begins to dance the dances of his forefathers, if the member of the Guru churches in India[12] begins to use the drama and dance of her pagan forefathers, which for centuries have been categorized as heathen and primitive, if these people realize that what they have is good enough for the worship of God, that God accepts "the thank offerings of their lips"—this seems to me to possess a more revolutionary quality than does the imitation of Western revolutionary theories, which makes those imitating into puppets of a foreign (albeit a so-called revolutionary) ideology.

I want to elaborate on this by commenting on the Faith and Order Consultation on "Worship in a Secular Age,"[13] beginning with the essay by Raymundo Panikkar. He has put his deliberations under a motto from Satapatha Brahmana: "Worship, above all, is truthfulness."[14] He says: "Only worship can prevent secularization from becoming inhuman, and only secularization can save worship from being meaningless."[15] "Probably one of the reasons (effect or cause, I leave it open) of the deep crisis of the United Nations Organization is that it could not or knew not how to develop a really common and thus universal and meaningful liturgy, cult, worship."[16] Panikkar sees in worship the place where those things which are logically contradictory—the earthly and the heavenly, transcendence and immanence, human and divine, rubrics and nigrics,[17] the principle of Martha and that of Mary—are not *dialectically balanced* but are experienced together in a *form of art* (Panikkar is an Indian). (Note that even in the West, theology and liturgiology are taught in Faculties of *Art*, which means that liturgy [and theology, for that matter] is not only a scholarly but also an artistic faculty.)

The place where this art is forged is not in the philosophical academy, nor in the theological faculty, but in the dialogical togetherness of Christians: theologians and artists, beggars and businessmen, doctors and hippies, mathematicians and singers. The task of liturgy is to make this dialogue possible, and to enable the voice of the Spirit to be heard in these contradictions, relating them to the tradition of the church. It is true that such a dialogue would demand a different theological education for priests and pastors, an education

> in which artistic intuition has the same right as critical exegesis. Practical theology would be matched with training for preaching in the open air. The sociological analysis would be paralleled by the spontaneous improvisation in

---

[12] Hoerschelmann, *Christliche Gerus.*

[13] Report in *Studia Liturgica* 7/2–3, 1970. I quote from the off-print edition: Vos, *Worship.*

[14] "Satyam eva upacâta," Satapatha Brahmana II.2,2,20. Panikkar, "Secularization," in Vos, *Worship,* 28.

[15] Panikkar, "Secularization," in Vos, *Worship,* 28.

[16] Ibid., in Vos, *Worship,* 53.

[17] According to Panikkar both must be changed fundamentally. Panikkar, "Secularization," in Vos, *Worship,* 56–70.

words, images and music. The professor of homiletics would stand side by side with the author of a scenario, the liturgiologist beside the producer, the systematic theologian next to the choreographer and the ballerina (all of them being concerned with synthesis, "bringing together," only through different media). This is commonly rejected as being utopian. But how can we know before we have tried it?[18]

I have tried it with astonishing results, and will report on this in the next section.

The German theologian Will Adam tackles the same problem from an exegetical basis. Adam remarks[19] that the alliterative epigram of the section on worship in Uppsala ("Worship for a Christian is not a problem, but a privilege") avoids the *real* problem. He says: "Certainly worship today is not an unquestioned matter. But it never has been."[20] From his profound knowledge of modern exegetical research Adam reveals the attitude of Jesus to worship as relevant for us today. By dealing with publicans, prostitutes, and sinners Jesus not only broke political and social taboos of his time, but violated that which was considered at that time to be the will of God—*in order to do the will of God*. In inviting culturally impure people to his communion-meals he determined what *he* considered to be worship.

Similarly, in the Corinthian Eucharist Paul was criticizing not the cultic unworthiness of the Corinthians, but the fact that the rich did not wait for the poor (1 Cor 11:33); that is, he criticized a liturgically camouflaged social misbehavior. That in the communion of the first Christians the barriers between rich and poor, men and women were overcome—not logically, nor on the basis of a social theory, but in the actual event of worship—made this worship one of their most powerful instruments of mission. Here, in their celebration, in their salvific communion, they anticipated something which the world did and does not know. No one can imagine what a dynamic power would flow from such a worship today into our fragmented world.

It could also happen that such a missionary worship would destroy some aspects of our current ecclesiology—the very thing which happened to the first Christians. The success of their missionary outreach among the Greeks forced the first Christians to change their self-understanding (Acts 11). Today, too, worship services which take seriously the liturgical conscientization of the people of God lead to a serious shaking of our ecclesiological concepts. In many ad hoc ecumenical worship services—sometimes with strong Pentecostal overtones—the artificial barriers of denominations are pushed aside in order to anticipate the overcoming of the *real* barriers of race, social status, and education.

---

[18] Hollenweger, "Spiel."
[19] Adam, "Outdated," in Vos, *Worship*, 96–119. The German original version duplicated "Veraltete." Quotations English, 97, German, 1.
[20] Adam, "Veraltete," 24 in the German text (not in the English).

I experienced this dramatically when I organized an anointing service in the cathedral of Berne with students from the University. The students knew what everybody in Berne knows—that the drug addicts and prostitutes congregate around the cathedral. Therefore they invited them to the anointing service. When people were invited to come forward to be anointed, these prostitutes and drug addicts came in great crowds. For once they were not being told off, but some young students wanted to be tender with them, to anoint them and to give them a word of blessing. (That such a service has to follow strict liturgical rules and must be well-prepared is another matter, which I discussed in chapter 18). Many of these non-church-goers wept, others sat in amazement, ringed by three students who were anointing people for the first time in their lives. Also for the first time, these "sinners" realized what a Christian liturgy can be: an anticipation of liberation.

In order to understand this properly one has to realize what usually happens in this cathedral. Famous preachers preach here. The aristocracy of Berne comes down from their suburbs by taxi and jump—without looking right or left—into the church, where they hear a tremendous sermon on the solidarity of Jesus with sinners and prostitutes. After an elaborate organ postlude they jump into a taxi again and go home to their Sunday lunch.

No wonder that the sacristan of the cathedral—he wears a beautiful uniform in the colors of the republic of Berne, black and red—told me after our service: "Professor, you have violated the dignity of this cathedral!" Unfortunately that's how it often is: when that about which we talk in our sermons is put into (liturgical) action, we violate the dignity of the church—not only in Reformed but also in middle-class Pentecostal churches.

At the end of his article Adam asks the question: "What kind of worship do the Christians owe to the world, for which worship is as important as daily bread?" His answer: a worship in which that which we talk about is done, and in which the postulate of the general priesthood of all believers is not merely declared but lived (as with my students, none of whom were ordained). This is—if I have understood Adam rightly—part of his appeal for an extension of the hermeneutical reflection to include not just the sermon but the whole of worship. Protestant and Catholic theologians[21] are asking today for a liturgy where things are done in common by the whole congregation. This kind of liturgy would more closely approximate the patristic Eucharist and the liturgy of the Reformers. Only how do we achieve a liturgy—a worship—in common? It is hardly possible for us to take refuge in the spontaneous worship of the Chilean Pentecostals.

Yet are the alternatives to the liturgical dance of the Chileans, to the glossolalic prayer and the improvised singing of the whole congregation, our *pre*-printed, *pre*-worded and *pre*-thought liturgical agendas? I do not believe

---

[21] Klauser, *Western Liturgy.* See on this *The Pentecostals,* 387f.

so. I do not believe it because I am convinced by many experiences in several countries that our historical churches too can discover the charismatic dimension of worship, including some of the aspects of Pentecostal churches but not confined to those.[22] In the following section I shall discuss some of the experiences which have convinced me of this.

Pentecostal Music: Problem and Promise[23]

The following section approaches the neglected issue of Pentecostal/ charismatic singing and music, and discusses the contribution of this music to the non-Pentecostal churches, along with its problems and promises. Since my cultural and musical background is thoroughly European, I am above all discussing the issues which arise in this context. The Americas have a different and more flexible approach to church music.[24]

> It has long been a concern of mine that we in the Hymn Society would come to grips with what is happening in the Pentecostal movements. We tend to look at their songs and to judge them purely in the way we would judge a traditional hymn, and whereas surely some of the criteria apply there must be reasons why a huge number of our fellow Christians take up a kind of song that we normally would not touch.

These are the words of Alan Luff, the secretary of the Hymn Society, a renowned church musician in the British scene. Among other things he was responsible for all the music for the wedding of the Duke and Duchess of York. I can put his statement more bluntly: indeed mainline churches have a problem on their hands, the problem being that what they consider as rather cheap and inferior musical noises is very popular among many Christians.[25]

I do not believe that the way forward in matters of church music is to accept the Pentecostal songs as they are. On the other hand, Pentecostal spirituality represents a tradition which is becoming increasingly important; namely, the tradition of black music. Pentecostalism was born—as we have seen—in the context of black slave religion in the United States. That is where its musical roots lie—although much of these roots have been obscured in the process of upward social mobility in white Pentecostalism, not least under the influence of our criticism of early Pentecostalism. Black music is the music of an oppressed people who—by the very medium of their music and stories—were

---

[22] Examples below and in Hollenweger, *Kirche*, in Simpfendörfer, *Offene Kirche*, and passim in the three volumes of *ITh*.

[23] This section started as a lecture for the British Hymn Society, published under the title "Music."

[24] See Alford, "Music," with detailed historical discussion and an extensive bibliography which was not fully available to me.

[25] There is a special issue of *The Hymn*, Hymn Society of America (Minneapolis), on Pentecostal and charismatic music and singing (38/1, Jan. 1987). See also *The Pentecostals*, 464–67.

saved from cultural and physical extinction.[26] It is the music of an oral people: spirituals and choruses are spread orally.

The tradition of the ballad or the song with a chorus is therefore very important in Pentecostalism. It is also common to many strands of European folk music. The chorus allows the audience to join in a song and to take the chorus home. One is reminded of the tradition of the great German oratorios, with their chorales which could be sung by the congregation; or the tradition of some English promenade concerts, where the audience is invited to sing certain parts with the orchestra and choir.

There have been attempts to learn from this musical tradition. I think of the music published by the monks from Taizé.[27] This music moves in the "folk" direction, but avoids both the cheap and superficial scoring and the trivial and sometimes pompous wording of both the Pentecostal choruses and the proms. The music of the Taizé monks blends the Reformation musicality with ad hoc scoring and singability. That is why their liturgical pieces can be accompanied by all kinds of instruments, from the guitar to the trombone, the saxophone and the drum—and in any combination. This of course is another important feature of modern Pentecostal music: it does not have a fixed score in the classical sense, just a pattern of melodies, rhythms, and harmonies, which can be varied by various configurations of instruments and singers, ad lib.

In the following I first want to describe my own personal introduction into this field, so that it becomes clear against which experiential background I am arguing. Secondly, I want to sketch briefly the musical and social context in which Britain operates. Thirdly, and most importantly, I want to offer a few suggestions for a way forward for that church music; one which takes seriously its theological mission of reconciliation.

I am not a trained musician. The little I know I have picked up by playing the recorder and later the French horn in an orchestra. My most formative musical experience, however, was the study of the scores of the great masters. As a boy, I discovered some parts of Beethoven's First Symphony in a loft. Having been brought up as a Pentecostal, I had never been allowed to go to concerts, first because it was too expensive, and secondly because it was considered to be too worldly. Time wasted studying the music of a worldly musician was also, of course, considered a sin. So I waited for my parents to go to bed, then lit a candle and studied that great work (the second movement in particular). All alone in the night, I tried to reconstruct the score with the help of the parts I had found, trying to imagine how it would sound. How could anybody write something so beautiful, so simple and so deep? Only very much later—when I had the freedom to do so—did I buy a full score and get the opportunity to hear the symphony played by an orchestra.

---

[26] See Cone, *Spirituals and the Blues*, and my article "Spirituals."
[27] Berthier, *Taizé*.

I tell this story to highlight the enormous difficulty many people have with classical music, both church and secular. Even if they are not forbidden by religious taboos to enter into this world of music, there are cultural and social taboos which bar them from it. Musical taste is formed by education and custom; thus when children are fed with the trivialities of modern light music they may simply not recognize as music the sequences of harmonies and melodies of classical music. Such sequences can sound like a foreign language to them—the language of those who have the leisure and the money to indulge in such luxurious and unnecessary pastimes.

I was fortunate, because my musical context was the folk hymns which I learned at home and in school, and the Pentecostal hymns, with their echo of the black slave music. This background provided a bridge to classical and also modern music, for example Tippett's *A Child of Our Time,* Arthur Honegger's *King David,* and the like. Most people raised in separation from classical musical forms, however, remain prisoners of the simple and sometimes trivial harmonies and rhythms of everyday music. This is a dangerous situation for the church, because it strengthens another parallel development which separates the producers and the consumers of theology.

In theological language, as in classical music, a level of abstraction has been developed which is not accessible to ordinary people—very often not even to the clergy. In the liturgy a mastery of English is expected which is also not accessible to many people. In other words: certain cultural preconditions have to be fulfilled before people are allowed to praise God together with the "cognoscenti." No wonder that many emigrate from our churches, to produce their own self-made music, theology, and worship—if they do not decide to leave the church altogether.

The British Context

Britain is the most musical country I know. The reason for this is probably the musical tradition of the Church of England, the Methodist Church, and lately the black Pentecostal churches (chapter 9, pp. 106–16). Britain has also an astounding tradition of secular music. Radio Three, the many music competitions, the huge number of very competent amateur musical societies, and the contributions of schools and universities (although the latter is now under threat), all add to this musical culture.

But that is only one side of the story. The other side is the fact that what is good music, also good church music, is decided by those who have privilege and power in church and society. Their taste and their judgment can be challenged only by their peers, and not by musical outsiders, even if these outsiders are the overwhelming majority of the population. The number of people following these opinion-makers in church music is very small indeed—a tiny minority in society at large. But since the majority is considered incompetent, the only thing left to the majority, which has no power and no say in these matters, is to demonstrate their dissent by absenting themselves *from* our music and our liturgies. The quality programs of Radio Three are listened to by a minority. Our church music touches a very small minority. The majority of our people listen to other music.

At the larger level of liturgy as a whole, my judgment is based on an analysis of the religion of fifty workers in the Birmingham area, carried out by one of my doctoral students.[28] He interviewed each of these men from a working class area for between one and three hours. The researcher was an American, Roger Edrington. He had the gift of listening. That is why many of the interviewees told him what they had so far told nobody else—not even their own wives. They were astonished that somebody was actually interested in their ideas and their lives.

Now this research was on belief and unbelief, but it is relevant as I want to approach our topic from a theological point of view. Anyone familiar with the religious scene in Europe would expect the usual results from this research: mistrust of church and clergy, arguments from science and science fiction against Christian beliefs. All this is contained in the research, but not as prominently as one would expect. What comes through as more important and with unambiguous clarity is the genuine modesty, honesty, and lostness of these men. These are three great words which need some explanation.

Modesty is shown in the way the men confess their ignorance on vital issues of their lives. They neither know what they believe nor what they disbelieve. They are almost equally critical of atheistic slogans as of the tenets of the Christian faith. And if they have some convictions or some knowledge they phrase them in very cautious language. Very little propaganda, much pain in grappling with the issue, and many times a resigned confession: "I would say that I was a Christian and an agnostic." They term themselves a "not–sure religious Christian," a "don't–know believer." Sometimes a mild criticism of the official voices of religion comes through: "It's all right for these blokes to write books, but they don't tell you, they don't put it plain enough for you to understand. I don't think they know theirselves [*sic*]."

To many of them God is—as one told the researcher—like that "captain in the Gurkha rifles" who "carried me across the paddy fields and the Japs were shelling over him and he was ill himself. He was rotten with dysentery. I've never seen him since and I don't know his name, but I think of him." Many of them have had religious experiences which have made a deep impression on them. But they cannot articulate their experiences. They do not know the name of the one who saved them "but they think of him."

Honesty comes through in the way both believers and unbelievers among those interviewed volunteered their experiences of prayer—and this in spite of the fact that with the exception of four, none of them had gone to church since the age of ten (except for the obligatory christenings, weddings, and funerals). But their prayer is a very private prayer. "Don't tell the Missus that

---

[28] Edrington, *Everyday.*

I am praying." "The best place to pray is the [water] closet." They never talk to anybody about religion. It is taboo. Yet they let the researcher tape their accounts of visions, answers to prayer in war and peace, and anger at the years lost in the war. They expressed their criticism at the misuse of God's name by the military:

> You take the Falkland Islands. Our lot blessing our boys going out there and their priests blessing their men, instead of as the Bible says . . . It's stupid! You're going out to kill each other and you don't even own an ounce of the land and you don't own nothing here. Most of the people at home, they've got nothing. They haven't even got control over their rent. They've got nothing and they're going out to massacre each other. And their priest on the dock blessing them, you know. Fellows carrying the picture of the Virgin Mary on his gun. Poor old Argentinian, he's dead now, you know. Okay, he might have had a belief, but is that belief going to keep your family? It's not. So as far as beliefs are concerned, I'm afraid it's a no-no with me. Never convince me.

Lostness: "Our opinion don't count for much. We don't have any opinion any more, we just live from day to day." "Anyhow, if the government cannot save us, God can [*sic*] neither." It appears that not only do they not talk about religion among themselves, but "they don't have any opinion any more." People whose language and whose songs do not count lose the will and the ability to communicate and to sing—except in those places where it still matters: perhaps in the family and the pub.

What are we to conclude from testimonies like these? I believe that the church is the community which creates, tests, and inspires language (including musical language) about the meaning of life and death. But this church is absent in much of British working-class culture, and is replaced by nothing. Because the workers interviewed had never been asked to contribute anything to the church—the church had only talked at them and wanted to "educate" them—it would have been a strange thought to them that they are actually vital for the survival of the church, for its ministry of reconciliation in its liturgy, in its message, in its music. Their experiences count for nothing. And so the cultural divide in Britain is mirrored in the church: the ever-speaking and ever-proclaiming and ever-performing church, and the almost-silenced workers. The cultural elements which could build a bridge over the abyss of the two cultures are almost absent in the church. These elements are: prayer in which they can join (whether sung or spoken); faith which is expressed with their hands; dialogue in small groups where they can join in.

There are of course flourishing working-class congregations in England—one hundred and twenty of them in the Birmingham area alone, about eight hundred in the UK. But they are black. In spite of slavery and repression, the blacks are not silenced. They have created their own vigorous language of faith, filling some of the abandoned Anglican churches with their resounding songs, their inspiring dances, their electrifying rhythms. I believe that if there is ever to be a revival in our churches—both musical and spiritual—we have to learn from these black churches.

It is part of our ministry as the church to help people who have been carried through the paddy fields of life's danger to get to know the name of the one who carried them through. In order to do this we must dig deep into our memories. We must do this together with others who were also carried through the shell-fire, questioning them, comparing our memories, visions, and songs. This search for the names is called theology. The celebration of this search is called church music. It therefore has a vital place in our ministry of reconciliation.

The Way Forward

What follows is based on experiences in many seminars with clergy and musicians in Switzerland, Germany, England, and France; and with musical development in the churches in Poland, Czechoslovakia, and East Germany, and above all the German *Kirchentag,* which has virtually become a singing *Kirchentag* (without losing its political and theological teeth). In all these contexts, theological insights are put into music—either spontaneously, as in the black churches, or with the help of musicians who put themselves at the service of the people of God. Of course much of this music is evanescent, but once in a while something lasting emerges. That, however, is not this music's most important feature. The most important thing is that it helps people learn to express themselves in the middle of hot theological and political arguments (for politics is not excluded, for example, from the *Kirchentag;* in fact, it has become compulsory for all leading politicians to come and *listen* at the *Kirchentag,* even if they are not invited to speak!).

The insights which I have gained from these experiences apply equally to theology as to liturgy and church music, and they are these:

1. Let us start with the gifts *of the people!* If we discover prayer experiences of the kind described by the workers from Birmingham, this is the starting point for our theology. If we have only a saxophone or a drum or a guitar among the people we want to celebrate with, let us consider this a challenge for making really good music with them, but on the drum and the saxophone, in the language and with the musical vocabulary they know and understand and at the level of their musical skill. Arthur Honegger once complained to Stravinsky that for the première of his *King David* he had only a small brass band in a Swiss village. Stravinsky told him: every fool can write music for a full symphony orchestra. But to write within the restrictions of a mediocre brass band and to write a masterpiece, that is real art. And out of this came Honegger's *Le roi David.* Let us therefore start with the musical culture of those we want to win, with their folk songs, with the elements of light music they know.

2. This does not mean that we just imitate or repeat "popular religion" and "popular music." For that would be a betrayal of the gospel. It does not

mean we must sing only the cheap and superficial tunes to which the people are accustomed; for this is in many cases the easy way out which the charismatic movement has chosen. It would mean giving up our work as musical educators. But most of all it means—theologically and musically—using popular vocabulary, popular culture, as a starting point, as the main medium of communication, in ways which are recognizable to the great majority of people. It means further trying to express that which we have to say in the grammar and the vocabulary of the people.

Let me give just one example. I am not the only one experimenting with this kind of liturgy, but the experiments in which I have been involved are the ones I know best. I wrote a little oratorio or musical called *Jonah—A Child of Our Time*, for which a young German musician, Fritz Baltruweit, wrote the music. It tells the story of Jonah—but with a difference. First, the historical-critical exegesis is not ignored. It shows in a dramatic and narrative form that the historical Jonah is a man about whom we only know his name. The book of Jonah is not about the historical Jonah but it is a Jewish satire which tries to open the eyes of the author's contemporaries to their own chauvinistic, narrow views. It wants to show them that their God cares for all the nations, even for their enemy, the mighty city of Nineveh. Jonah of course does not like this: he does not like to make a fool of himself. So—in his narrowness—he becomes a child of our time.

The main play is set "within a play," a staging of the premiere of 'Jonah' in the first century, at the church of Sinope on the Black Sea, which is the church of the evangelist Luke.[29] This is appropriate, since Luke reacts to the problems of his church in the way he selects and shapes his material: to stresses between rich and poor as many civil servants and high financiers had joined his third-generation church (hence the story of Zacchaeus); relations with the military, as Roman officers wanted to be baptized (hence the story of Cornelius); racial tensions as blacks became members (hence the story of the eunuch); and the changing role of women, as many had become prominent in

---

[29] For text and music of the musical see Hollenweger, *Jona*. On the exegetical hypothesis about Luke, see Schmithals, *Lukas;* another application in Hollenweger, *Wagnis*. The Metanoia Verlag has published many of my plays, oratorios, cantatas, etc. which I wrote for such evangelisms and for the unchurched, particularly in Switzerland and Germany. Among them are: *Jüngermesse* (The Disciples' Mass); *Mirjam, Mutter Jesu* (Miryam, the Mother of Jesus); *Michal: Die Frauen meines Mannes* (Michal: The Wives of My Husband); *Gomer* (the wife of Hosea); *Fontana, die Brunnenfrau und der siebte Mann* (Fontana, the fountain-woman and the seventh man, John 4); *Ostertanz der Frauen* (Easter: Dance of women); *Veni Creator Spiritus* (Pentecost liturgy); *Requiem für Bonhoeffer; Hiob im Kreuzfeuer der Religionen* (Job in the cross-fire of religions); *Oratorio Jürg Rathgeb* (a famous painter and peasants' leader of the sixteenth century); *Ruth, die Ausländerin* (Ruth, the foreigner); *Der Kommissar auf biblischer Spurensuche* (a detective superintendent examines a number of biblical persons); *Christmas Oratorio*, etc. Some of them exist also in English translation (typescript) since I tried them out with students and others in Birmingham (also available from Metanoia Verlag, Kindhausen, Switzerland).

his church—especially when the men were in prison (hence the prevalence of women in his Gospel accounts). Redaction criticism has shown us these relationships between social, political, and theological controversies in Luke's church, as reflected in his writings.

By placing the première of Jonah in Luke's church, I can show the problems the early church had with the Old Testament. I can also describe their world outlook: They lived at a time when the gods had lost their power to anonymous entities (which still bore divine names)—to laws of the universe which nobody could control, not even the state. The sky was no longer the expression of eternal harmony, but it was full of demons, uncontrollable rays, poison and animosity towards the people. They felt caught, imprisoned, lost.

To such a people Jonah says: "Only forty days and Nineveh is destroyed." And modern singers and speakers realize—without any abstract exegetical explanation—that they sing and talk not only about the end of the first century but about themselves, about their own lives today. They know that this earth will be destroyed if things go on as they are. And to give articulation to this fear, the children—the children of Sinope and the children of Birmingham—assemble on the stage and sing the "Children's Doomsday Song," in which they protest about the inheritance we are going to leave with them.

So audience and choir ask Jonah and themselves: "What have you done now, Jonah?" The message of the musical comes as a surprise. Because the people repent, God repents. He is sorry and changes his decision. This is not in line with what our church audiences think, nor what the workers from Birmingham think. That God could say that he feels sorry for the great and sinful city of Nineveh "with over one hundred and twenty thousand people who do not know the difference between right and left and many cattle too," such a God with a human heart is foreign to them, yet it is he who is the father of our Lord Jesus Christ.

If I present such a message in a lecture or a sermon, it may be difficult to understand. But if people sing and act it, if they are allowed to change the words to make it more understandable, then they wrestle with the issue. Here the fact that English is not my mother tongue becomes an advantage. I can always say: Please change it, English is a foreign language to me. Put your own words into the script—even if you change my theological and musical intentions. What you decide has priority.

I presented these ideas to clergy and lay people in a public lecture at the University of Birmingham. Afterwards one of the vicars asked me: Couldn't we do what you have been talking about? We want to perform a kind of a festival for the nine hundredth anniversary of our church in Northfield. What would you suggest? I said tell me what musicians, singers, speakers you have in your congregation, in your schools and in your wider community. It does not matter whether they are committed Christians or not, or not Christians at all. It does not matter either whether they are trained musicians and singers or not. All that matters is that they want to do something together, using the gifts they have.

The response was overwhelming. Fifty children, seventy singers in the choir, a dozen speakers and soloists, two violinists, two viola players, two cello players, one pianist, two flautists, one oboist, two trumpeters, two trombonists, an excellent classical recorder quartet, and a jazz drummer offered their help. This is not exactly a classical ensemble—so I had to rewrite all the choruses (which were to be sung with the audience), the solos, and the canons for this score, taking into consideration the level of skill of the musicians and singers (which was very uneven). Some were just beginners, others were accomplished musicians. For example, the string players were very weak. They could not count the bars when they had to be silent. Also they could not enter at the right pitch when it was their turn. They came in a third too high or too low, which was usually all right for the first chord but produced disaster later on. The jazz drummer could not read music. Some of the singers could not keep time.

But, amazingly, after just one rehearsal with the choir and one other rehearsal with choir and instrumentalists, they were able to play and sing the piece. I asked the string section to sit near me so I could give them their entry exactly and sing to them the pitch of their first note. Being musical children they immediately picked up the right pitch and corrected their mistakes by intuition. Thus the cellist, who was smaller than his big instrument, even played a solo. Think how proud his mother was! The jazz drummer I led with eyes and baton—always a bar before he actually had to enter.

Of course this performance had many flaws from a musical point of view, but it brought together over one hundred and fifty people in a musical/theological event. It made them think together. It gave them a voice. It made them sing not just their own songs and words, but music and words which they could recognize as their own because they had participated in the making. It made the silenced speak and the songless sing. Of course with such an arrangement there is no need to put an announcement in the newspapers. We had one hundred and fifty public relations agents. So the church was filled as never before. More than this, the congregation and the singers quickly learned the songs by heart. They took them home. They became part of their theological and musical memory, of their daily talk.

Behind this experience lies the conviction that that which makes people *think* and *learn* has priority over a flawless performance. Is it not strange that a Swiss theologian writes a score for this performance in an Anglican church—in spite of all the many church musicians around who are much better qualified than he? But alas, many of these "professionals" do not want to do this kind of thing. They fear for their musical reputations. They stick to their ideas, their standards, instead of taking what is there and using it to create an opportunity for musical and theological exploration.

Space forbids me to go into the details of many similar experiences, or to discuss the methodology and the craftsmanship which is required from an enabler and co-ordinator of such an experience. Probably the most important is that of giving a strong input at the beginning, in both emotion and content, but then letting the people take over and change whatever they like in the course of the experience, according to their understanding. Most clergy opt for the opposite approach. At the beginning they are all for a non-directive method, with the result that people get off to a very slow start. But then, when things begin to move, they want to control the theological, ethical and liturgical development, with the result that people lose heart.

That it pays to trust our lay people was demonstrated at a Liverpool diocesan conference for lay people. The *Liverpool Echo* (21.6.88) reported:

> There was a Swiss professor, telling some 200–plus Church of England people from all over the Liverpool diocese, that they were suddenly going to turn into singers, actors, and dancers. And perform in front of an audience. Can you imagine it? Funny thing is, though, that's just what happened. People discovered talents they didn't know they had . . . Oh yeah? You could see the doubt on people's faces. Let's face it you don't associate C of E worthies with those sorts of "goings-on." They're just not the type. . . Don't you believe it. . . The result was a weekend of total magic, leaving a kaleidoscope of memories. There were three St. Peters, on stage at different times, all with different accents, including broad Scouse. There was even a female St. James, who shook her stick angrily at everyone.

If people find out that we are really interested in their elementary theology, in their rudimentary gifts and music, if they realize that we love them as they are, miracles happen. Then they are also prepared to work with us and even to learn from us. This does not require less theological and musical skill. On the contrary it will stretch us to the limits. But it is also very rewarding because it places church musicians where they belong: in the middle of the praying, doubting, cursing, celebrating, dancing, repenting, weeping, and laughing people of God.

Music is just as necessary for the ministry in the church as theology. It is not an adornment, a decoration which we may take or leave. As Pentecostals always knew, "Music unites people; music transmits social values; music denounces injustice; music influences human behavior; music can tranquilize and put to sleep or can awaken and be a challenge for the struggle."[30] But if this is true, then we must find a way to develop it with and in the people of God—in Europe as in America and the Third World—and even with those who do not know the names of the one who carries them through the shell-fire of life.

Is this perhaps a legitimate translation of my own Pentecostal experiences into a different ecclesial and cultural context?

Prayer of the Singing Bird

Holy Spirit,
Sometimes I feel like a singing bird.

---

[30] Rosas, "Música," quoted in Villafañe, *The Liberating Spirit*, 11.

I fly on the highest tree and I sing and sing and sing.
And people say: If only that bird would stop his noise.
And young people put on their walkman and listen to the sound of the drum.
And sometimes it seems to me that I sing for nothing.
Why am I a singing bird?
Why am I not a flamingo, or an eagle or a mighty roaring lion, only a singing
 bird?
I did not make myself.
And you, Holy Spirit, you did not ask me whether I wanted to be a singing bird.
My parents did not ask me either
whether I wanted to be a singing bird or whether I wanted to be at all.
That's why I am what I am, an ugly bird, who can only sing.
And now you tell me:
What would the world be without your song?
You tell me: You are more important than all the walkmen of the world.
Sing, singing bird, you make the world a better place.
Yes, Holy Spirit, I want to sing
for those who listen and for those who don't listen.
Holy Spirit, could you not tell those people to put their walkmen aside
and listen to my song. That would be nice.

CHAPTER TWENTY TWO

Mission:
What Kind of Missionaries?[1]

The following chapter is written from the perspective of a European who has for many years been involved in the education of theologians from all over the world, among them many Third World and many Pentecostal scholars. This experience is the source of my examples. The chapter is also written by an educator who at the end of his academic career is dissatisfied with the general trend of mission education in Europe and in the United States, including his own endeavors.

Introducing the Topic

In terms of numbers, the modern missionary movement is a success story. Missionaries *from* the Third World[2] are increasing at a decadal growth rate of 248%, that is, from 2,951 missionaries *from* the Third World in 1972 to 35,924 in 1988. 162,360 missionaries *from* the Third World are projected for the year 2000. "What is established is that the Two-Thirds World missions movement is growing at a rate which is five times the growth rate of Western missions."[3] In the year

---

[1] Some of the material in this chapter was part of my farewell lecture at the University of Birmingham, published as "Mission."
[2] Missionaries *from* the Third World are defined as follows:
    1. Their agency is led and administered by indigenous, non-Western leaders.
    2. They go across significant cultural and/or geographical boundaries, *or* they are supported across significant cultural or geographic boundaries.
    3. Their primary funding is from non-Western indigenous sources.
    Pate, "Pentecostal Missions from the Two-Thirds World," 244.
[3] Pate, "Pentecostal Missions from the Two-Thirds World," 243.

2000 there will be more missionaries from the Third World than Western missionaries.[4]

There are now more Christians in the Third World than in the West. Extraordinarily, this raises some questions. Why are the descendants of black slaves in the Caribbean and in the United States, Christians? Why are the blacks of South Africa Christians, and not Marxist or Muslim? Certainly not because of the example of their overwhelmingly Christian white slave masters. Or, to take another example, why were there more Christians in the Soviet Union than members of the Communist Party, even after seventy years of official state propaganda, and that before the *revivrement* by Mikhael Gorbachev?[5]

The success of Christianity, and of Pentecostalism in particular (by the year 2000 85–90 percent of the Christians in the Third World will be Pentecostal/Charismatic),[6] also raises many questions. What does it mean that our Western form of Christianity and of Pentecostalism is by now a minority form, and that these other Christians, these other Pentecostals, are different—very different—from us? What does that mean for our own European/American understanding of Christianity, theology, education, politics, medicine, and so forth?

I often think of the story John Mbiti told[7] about one of the first Africans to gain a doctorate of theology in Germany. It had taken him nine and a half years from the time he left home, and had involved his learning from scratch three ancient and two modern European languages. When he returned home, Mbiti continues, great festivities were organized by his people to celebrate the achievements of their native son. There were dancing and eating—great jubilation all around. Suddenly there was a shriek. A woman had fallen to the ground. The great theologian said she had to be taken to hospital, but the people pointed out that she was possessed by a spirit, and the chief insisted that a religious leader must be able to perform an exorcism. But when he looked up his precious volumes of Bultmann they gave him no help—the spirits about which the New Testament speaks have all been demythologized. The people are astonished: "What is the use of studying in Europe? Before you went you could heal people; now you can't!"

Mbiti insists that his story is entirely fictional. But it is not fantasy, "for these are the realities of our time." The question behind his story remains:

---

[4] Ibid., 246.

[5] Religious statistics in the Soviet Union are notoriously difficult to determine, but see Barrett, *WChE*, 689ff. And Beeson, *Discretion*.

[6] Pate, "Pentecostal Missions from the Two-Thirds World," 250. On statistics, see chapter 4, note 52, p. 34 and the following:

54,000 new members every day, 19 million new members a year, 332 million affiliated church members worldwide, 66 percent membership in the Third World, majority of the world's megachurches, 34 billions (1988; 37 billions 1990) annually donated to Christian causes, 2/3 of all global evangelization plans.

Barrett, "20th"; *Dictionary*, 810–29; and Barrett, "Signs."

[7] In his 1974 article "Impotence."

"How can an African be introduced into a western, critical understanding of the reality of our time without being made useless in his home context?"

This was the question with which I went to Birmingham University. I was promised that I could experiment with a new type of theology, an intercultural type, that does not transform vital and spontaneous Christians into detached intellectuals. And, I am glad to say, the promise was kept. The only limits of my work were not the limits of institutions and organizations, but my own limits—the limits of my ignorance, of my inertia, of my lack of perception. And what discoveries we made! Ninety-nine postgraduates of all ages came (the eldest of them over seventy, the youngest in their early twenties);[8] many pastors, teachers, church leaders, even a trade union leader; college and university teachers from such countries as Korea, Kenya, the former East Germany, Ghana, the Caribbean,[9] West Africa, Mexico,[10] Malaysia, Argentina, Australia, India, Indonesia,[11] Thailand,[12] Switzerland, Romania, Ireland, Holland, Britain,[13] and the United States; men and women; Catholic nuns, priests,[14] and lay people; Baptists, Methodists,[15] Presbyterians, Lutherans, and Anglicans,[16] even Eastern Orthodox, Seventh Day Adventists,[17] Pentecostals,[18] and members of African independent churches and of black British churches.[19]

Their topics ranged from a study of the culture of economism (the "state religion of Britain")[20] to voodooism (the folk religion of Haiti);[21] from research into the gospel of prosperity in Argentinian Pentecostalism,[22] to the ecumenical promise of Dutch Pentecostalism;[23] from intercultural pastoral care in Ghana,[24] to shamanism in Korea;[25] from a theological reading of Dürrenmatt,[26] to a rigorous and highly technical debate on gene manipulation in the Soviet Union and the United Kingdom (with the help of Birmingham's

---

[8] Rose, *Sent.* The following is a selection of published research; see review in Hollenweger, "Intercultural." A more detailed list in Jongeneel, 1992, 359–66.

[9] Lewis, *Moravian.*

[10] Gaxiola-Gaxiola, *Mexican.*

[11] Haire, *Character;* Prior, *Indonesian;* Haire, "Animism."

[12] Davis, John R., *Contextualized.*

[13] Thurman, *New;* Hall, Mary, *Quest.*

[14] Kinne, *People's.*

[15] Kamu, *Samoan.*

[16] Binyon, *Concepts.*

[17] Graham, Roy E., *White.*

[18] Faupel, "Kingdom"; idem, "Durham."

[19] Mazibuko, *Education;* MacRobert, *Racism;* idem, *Black Pentecostalism;* idem, "Black Roots"; Gerloff, *Plea;* idem, "Education."

[20] Collier, *Economism.*

[21] Mulrain, *Theology.*

[22] Saracco, *Argentine.*

[23] van der Laan, C., *Sectarian Against His Will.* van der Laan, P., *Question.*

[24] Lartey, *Pastoral Counseling.*

[25] Yoo, *Korean Pentecostalism* (see also bibl.).

[26] Weber, Emil, *Friedrich Dürrenmatt.*

medical faculty);[27] from worship and theology in a communist country, to business ethics (or the lack of it) in the USA; from non-Christian religions, to the churches in China;[28] from a critical reading of Fynn's *Mister God, this is Anna,*[29] to Forster's *A Passage to India;* from biographies of missionaries, ecumenical leaders,[30] and Pentecostal pioneers, to an analysis of the fears and faiths of Birmingham workers;[31] from an interpretation of the songs of Zambia,[32] to the stories of independent churches in India,[33] Africa, and Latin America; and from a study of the liturgies of the Orthodox churches, to an analysis of worship, preaching style, and the role of women in British black churches. Much of this research has been published. As the established theological publishers did not want to take the risk of publishing this innovative theology, the late Professor Margull (Hamburg), Professor Friedli (a Dominican from Fribourg University, Switzerland) and I founded the trilingual series, "Studies in the Intercultural History of Christianity," which has been very successfully marketed for the last twenty years through an international publishing company in Germany, France, and the United States.

As one can imagine, the research undertaken by my students opened my eyes to the problems and promises of the worldwide *oikoumene,* the universal church. Coming from a small country like Switzerland, I received an education in global theology, liturgy, economics, and educational theories, from my student researchers.

It became necessary to institutionalize some of this work, for example in the Centre for Black and White Christian Partnership in Birmingham; in the Centre for New Religious Movements, also in Birmingham; and in Springdale College, an American school that gives American pastors the opportunity to break out of their own American monoculture. But all this is now history, and I prefer to address the question: "*Quo Vadis?* What about the future of mission and the mission of the future?"

Before I do this I would like to add a personal note. When I came to Birmingham it was thought necessary to give me a secretary whose mother tongue was English. The one appointed was not very attracted to mission studies. Coming from South Africa, she had seen some of the more ugly sides of mission history. She filled that post for eighteen years with friendliness, dedication, and competence. In the course of her work she made several discoveries:

1. She soon realized the human quality, the determination, the integrity, and the intellectual potential of the postgraduate mission researchers, many of whom became her friends.

---

[27] O'Mahony, *Question;* idem, *Swords.*
[28] Hood, *Mission.*
[29] Tonks, *Decision-Making.*
[30] Jackson, Eleanor M., *Tape;* Morse, *Koyama.*
[31] Edrington, *Everyday.*
[32] Castle, *Hymns;* idem, "Blue-Prints."
[33] Raj, *Christian Folk Religion.*

2. She realized too that mission studies are not about increasing the power base of the church or of the missionary society, but about a self-critical process that goes to the heart of the matter, asking: "What is the gospel in a given context?"

3. She also discovered that the history of the English language and the history of Jesus of Nazareth have many parallels. English was—so to speak—invented in England. Today more people speak English who are not English. But they also change it. The Americans, Irish, Indians, Germans, all speak English their own way. And what is English, proper English, can no longer be determined in a normative way by the English. Some of the non-English speakers (like the Irish or the Indians, or the Americans) have become experts in their own way of using the English language. Some of the greatest English writers are not English, but Irish, Indian, or American. And so it is with Jesus of Nazareth. Jesus of Nazareth no longer belongs to the Christians alone. Many marxist, agnostic, Hindu, and Muslim followers of Jesus write and think about him. Jesus has been liberated from domination by Christians. He is a truly universal figure. Some of the best interpreters of Jesus call themselves non-Christians.[34] And much of what the non-English do to the English language, much of what the non-Christians do to the image of Jesus, does not meet with the approval of either the English or the Christians. But that is inevitable, and who knows whether this is not a way of showing us that there is more to English than the English know, that there is more to Jesus of Nazareth than the Christians realize.

This brings me straight to the heart of this chapter. If mission and mission studies are to have a future, they must be rigorously *ecumenical*. Ecumenical means that we have not just to cooperate with all Christians, but also to listen to non-Christians' interpretations and criticisms. This is important if we are to deal constructively with the issues facing us; namely, the search for a just world order, the threat of nuclear war, the ecological crisis, the global drug mafia, and widespread starvation with its devastating migration problems. All this needs understanding on a global scale. And since war and greed start in the hearts and heads of people, there is no world peace without peace between the religions, and between religious and agnostic people.[35]

The Academic Task of Pentecostal Studies

Given the enormous political, social, cultural, and religious weight of the oral Pentecostal culture, the level of academic research on this topic is laughable. In Europe, for instance, we have not one specialized university chair, not one specialized institute, not one library holding more than random collec-

---

[34] See for example Machoveč, *Marxist,* or Birmingham's extra-mural professor in New Testament Studies, Michael Goulder (chapter 9, pp. 109–10, 113).

[35] See on this the preamble of the UNESCO convention and in detail Friedli, *Frieden.*

tions on Pentecostalism. Where can the many hundred Pentecostal/Charismatic/Independent scholars earn their doctorates so that they do not repeat the experience which Mbiti mentioned? In America the situation is somewhat better; but still, it is irresponsible to have institutes dedicated to studying all thinkable and unthinkable topics but not one for researching the most vigorous (and perhaps also the most dangerous) Christian revival movement of our time. Perhaps in the future the Pentecostals themselves will remedy this situation, but clearly such research is best done in proper academic surroundings, on an ecumenical and intercultural basis.

The study of oral cultures is particularly important for theology, because *oral culture* is the majority culture in the world (not just in the Third World). Our universities are children of our European tradition: they have served us well and have made important contributions to world cultures. But if the university does not want to be just a place where local (Western) cultures and insights are reflected and discussed, then we have to consider our relationship to oral theology, oral medicine, oral education, and so forth.

Let me give you an example. If somebody should hand in the Gospel of Mark as a piece of theological research, it would be turned down by any Western examiner, including myself. We would say:

1. This is not scholarly but anecdotal.

2. Mark has borrowed the title *"euangelion"* from his surrounding culture without indicating that he is using this word in a different way.

3. Although Mark uses a hidden hermeneutical key, he never spells it out clearly.

4. Mark uses sources and never acknowledges them.

5. Finally—most unfortunately—Mark offers no conclusion, which led a later copyist to add a conclusion, which in turn produced only confusion.

Now, my question is this: Is it not extraordinary that one of the most important theological and literary works ever written, a piece of seminal research, can at the present time not be recognized as such due to the limitations of our university culture? Has a university first to be loyal to the cultural tradition of the native tribe in which it operates, or is it—as I always thought it should be—interested in original, seminal, pioneering research?

I can give another example from our century. Karl Barth's *Commentary on Romans* is one of the most important pieces of theological writing in our century. Although he was given about twenty honorary doctorates, Barth never earned a doctoral degree from any university! When he wrote *Romans* he was a country pastor in Safenwil, wrestling with unemployment and organizing a trade union. He never submitted his research to a university because he knew that it would be turned down. I have asked many New Testament scholars and they have confirmed to me that Barth's *Commentary on Romans* never had a chance of being recognized by a university. Now, is it not interesting that we are not able to recognize research which is this vital and decisive?

This, of course, is not a purely theological phenomenon. It is only—as is many times the case—specially highlighted in theology. It is true also in medicine, and in physics. Einstein was never recognized in Switzerland; he was considered to be an eccentric. Many of the pioneering medical discoveries were—and still are—ridiculed by the academic establishment (see chapter 18, pp. 237–43).

Since I myself belong to this establishment, it concerns me. Why can we not recognize that work which is dealing with the problems of the future? Why do we find it so much easier to accept the repetition of the truths of the past? What a topic for a missiologist!

I have mentioned the Gospel of Mark. This is an example of oral theology. Oral theology is based not on an Aristotelian framework of logic, but on the cohesion of the tradition in a community. It operates like a computer: The people are the microchips. Different people have different stories or sayings in their memory data bank. The whole memory can be called upon only when the community comes together, when the microchips are connected. This dynamic can be observed for example among South American Indians, or in African churches. Mark has recorded the community memory of his church and put it into a theological framework, without destroying the traditional oral elements.

All of this points up the need for Pentecostal studies. There are hundreds, perhaps thousands, of young Pentecostal intellectuals who are looking for a place to study for their doctoral degree. Just to make them good Protestant scholars is not good enough; they have to be allowed to liberate their Pentecostal oral competence from the enslaving Pentecostal ideology, and see its truly worldwide significance. Pentecostal research is not an easy research into the enthusiasm of unenlightened people. A supervisor of Pentecostal studies is ill-equipped if he knows only Ronald Knox's book on enthusiasm. He has to know how to discover, translate, and handle the individual oral elements and he must—like Mark—help his researchers to put these elements into a theological framework that does not destroy the beauty and precision of the oral raw material.

At a time when secular historians have begun to take seriously oral tradition and oral history, it could be argued that a methodological study of oral theology might be indicated, especially in relation to Africa, certain regions in Latin America, and also our own post-literary culture. Oral theology is not a primitive theology; it is a very sophisticated form of thinking, evaluating, analyzing—as can be seen, for example, in the documents of the old Mexican oral culture. And it has produced, for example, technological miracles at which we can only marvel. Neither does oral theology mean theology which cannot be written down; but if it is written down, it follows other rules than the written essay. The technique resembles much more a good television play than a book.

Christian theology has always been both oral *and* literary. The gospels belong to the oral genre; the epistles to the literary genre. Academic theology so far has not developed sophisticated oral theologies. I have been experimenting with this form at the German *Kirchentag*—with an astonishing result. Some English students and pastors attending the *Kirchentag* in Germany confessed to me that although they knew only a little German they understood the Bonhoeffer *Requiem*[36] or the Bible study because it was given in an oral form—with music, choreography, and audience participation. Language is about more than cognitive information; it is also about creating a framework of trust, of acknowledging one's own and others' view of reality.

We theologians have failed our churches badly in this. How would one otherwise explain the fact that a conservative man like the Bishop of Durham can upset the whole of the United Kingdom by saying things that every student of theology knows after the first year? The answer is that we have not communicated our insights in the proper oral form. We have kept them secret by hiding them in literary language. So people still do not know that a critical reading of the Bible does not harm religion but makes it more mature, more adult, and also more truthful.

So here too we need missionaries. A missionary in this context is a theologian who is "bilingual." He knows the literary conceptual language of the minority *and* the oral language of the majority. Mission studies are bridge studies between orality and literacy.

Practical Implications

The tasks of the future are enormous. In the field of *university education* (in theology and in other disciplines, such as psychology, history, music, medicine, and economics) we must break out of the monocultural methodology and topics of the past. Political, economic, and religious development can no longer be measured solely against the yardstick of Western tradition. It may well be that democracy can find other forms than the parliamentary forms of the West. It may well be that effective economic development in the Third World will require a return to so-called intermediate technology, in a man-power-intensive but low-capital economy. It may even mean that the West will have to reintroduce or help to reintroduce the machinery of the thirties, the old mechanical sewing machines, the horse- or cattle-drawn agricultural machinery. High-tech development is one reason for the disastrous dependence of Third World economies on Western capital and know-how. As for the techniques of education itself—many of the sophisticated oral techniques of the Third World could and should be developed. This would also mean for the World Council of Churches that even more than before, it must develop international forms of cooperation that are not biased towards Western bureaucratic and parliamentary ways of communication. Beginnings are being

---

[36] Hollenweger, *Requiem*.

made, but they demand great sacrifice and patience from all concerned, for this level of change will not happen in one day.

In the field of *mission organization* there are some encouraging signs. Some old mission societies have reorganized their executive committees to give their partner churches equal—and sometimes even greater—say in the decision-making process. Mention should be made of CEEVA (the former Paris Mission), the Council for World Mission[37] (the former mission arm of the United Reformed Church in Britain) and the Basel Mission in Switzerland. These are small but important beginnings. The task, however, of communicating this power-shift to the donors has not yet been solved. Giving money does not automatically make one competent to decide "how this money should be spent": this insight has not yet filtered through. Mission executives—and even more so the public relations specialists of development agencies—fear, rightly, that giving up their old marketing strategy would mean a drastic reduction in income. They can no longer say, "Every penny you give goes directly to the Third World," because this is either patently untrue or foolish.

Let me give an example. Some high-powered mission executives (in a country which, out of Christian concern, I shall not name) once invited me for a frank talk on these issues. Each one of them introduced himself by saying, "My name is XY; I represent the mission of such-and-such a church. My budget is twenty million (or five million)." When I had ended my talk they said, "We know only too well that our so-called projects in the Third World help neither the churches nor the societies there. The educational, medical and media infrastructures introduced by our societies do not fit the context. In many cases they favour an already privileged elite. We should have programs that cost much less, are nearer to the people and can be administered by them. But then, what are we going to do with the millions that we have to spend each year?"

My answer was: 1) You use part of your millions for telling your constituency the truth. 2) You use part of your millions to find the projects that really help the people. That costs money. Do not say to your donors: "Every single penny that you give goes directly to the needy." That is blatant nonsense. Tell them that to bring the money to where it is needed is a very costly process. 3) If you begin to tell your sponsors the truth, you might get less money. So be it. Other agencies might even spring up who will go back to the old PR pattern and take some of the millions that you got. So be it. It is better to have a little less money for long-term profitable investment than too much money for prestige projects.

Another encouraging example is discussed in the basic volume on *Global Mission in Pentecostal Perspective*. Reporting on the third mandate of the Theological Education Fund (TEF) of the World Council of Churches (1970–77), Byron D. Klaus and Loren O. Triplett say:

---

[37] Hollander, *Council.*

The clergy-laity dichotomy present in WCC-affiliated churches becomes a focal point of discussion and debate. The consequences of hierarchical ministerial structures was an elite clergy separated from their parishioners. In July 1976 the TEF Committee met in San Jose, Costa Rica, in a Consultation on Ministry with the Poor in Latin America. They saw new believers in Pentecostal churches incorporated into the community of "ministers." Every member seemed to feel a responsibility as a debtor to God and the world and thus felt called to be a "missionary." The new believer was encouraged to preach, not based on preparation, but zeal, and no one was excluded . . . The local church was the "school" in which the Pentecostal pastor was formed. These basic forms of leadership emergence and ministry participation were observed by the Consultation to reflect theologically and structurally the key components of "excellence in ministry" that TEF was so valiantly trying to foster.[38]

Finally, it is very important that some *Third World theologians help us in the West to develop our congregational life and our theology.* These Third World theologians should not only be recruited for service to their own so-called ethnic minorities, i.e., Chinese for the Chinese in California, Caribbeans for the Caribbeans in England, Africans for the Africans in France. Western congregations and the Western faculties of theology should include representatives of another type of Christianity. When an Indian baptizes a little Swiss girl, when a Caribbean celebrates a white English marriage, when a German congregation receives communion from the black hands of an African, this does more to help us see and overcome our monoculturism than many learned articles. After all, we still send Europeans and Americans into all the world to teach the gospel—even if these missionaries have sometimes only a flimsy knowledge of local culture and languages. So why should we not have the experience from the other side, and accept pastors and teachers who have to wrestle with the culture and language of Switzerland, France, or Germany?

When a Swiss publican somewhere in the mountains discovers that the Indian smoking a pipe in his pub is a pastor he will ask, "Aha, a Muslim pastor or a Hindu pastor?" "No," replies the Indian, "a Swiss Reformed pastor from a little village nearby." For a moment the publican is speechless. This man is an Indian all right; his hands are brown, so is his face. Yet he speaks a Swiss mountain dialect, as flawlessly as a Christian from Switzerland. On top of this he pretends to be a Swiss Reformed pastor. How strange! The Indian continues, "I have just presided over the marriage of the couple who are celebrating their wedding in your pub." The publican asks, "But why are you not a Muslim? Why are you a Christian?" And he adds, "Are Indian Christians different from Swiss Christians?" This evinces a more evangelistic and intercultural dialogue than my lectures at the university. It helps the publican to understand what mission can mean today, namely the celebration of that wonderful worldwide sharing of insights, resources, cultures and spiritualities. But if he reads the above sentence in a mission magazine—if indeed he reads

---

[38] Klaus–Triplett, "National," 233; Leinemann-Perrin, *Relevant,* 190–93.

mission magazines—he has no idea of what it means. That is the difference between oral and literary theology. The credibility and indeed the meaning of oral theology depend on the presence of the witness. My printed message in this book, on the other hand, travels independently from my own person, and is therefore (I fear) less credible.

The mission of the future costs not only patience but also money. It costs money to bring a Ghanaian to England, an Indian to Switzerland, a Caribbean to Germany. It costs money to train him and her, to look after their children, to overcome the many difficulties of a cultural clash. But remember the mission executives who asked me, "What shall we do with the many millions?" Here is a fruitful field.

It could even be that the non-theological disciplines (if indeed there can be such)—schools and hospitals, police and state administration—begin to understand that we too need expertise from outside, not just from the USA or from Germany. We need people who have another approach to medicine, to education, to administration, to the police, and who are ready to share these insights with us and to help us develop our own institutions for the future.

For we Europeans and Americans have a future only if we radically change our "culture of economism" (which we have exported into the Third World, with catastrophic results). Maybe there is still time for repentance in our churches and schools, in our administrations and universities, in our businesses and hospitals. "Maybe that God then sees our works, that we turn from our evil way; and God may repent of the evil, that he has said that he would do unto us" (Jonah 3:9). Maybe.

Pentecostal Missiology: Promise and Problem

How does Pentecostal missiology fare in this ecumenical discussion? First let me mention *the promise:* Pentecostal mission has, after a somewhat shaky start,[39] resolutely taken the line of Roland Allen's *Missionary Methods: St. Paul's or Ours?*[40] It is astonishing that this high Anglican missionary to China "unwittingly exerted a profound influence on Pentecostal mission through his writings."[41] So deep was his influence that he shaped not only the thinking of Pentecostal missiology but also the activities of Pentecostal mission. This can best be demonstrated in the life and work of Melvin Hodges,[42] a leading Pentecostal missiologist. In 1950 he asked a simple question: Why the weakness of many of the mission churches in the Third World? His answer: Because missionaries have treated people like irresponsible children. They mistook the scaffolding for the building. Missionaries, says Hodges, are not intended to be

---

[39] Early Pentecostals believed that "speaking in tongues" was xenolalia which would enable the recipients for mission work. In detail McGee, "Missions"; McClung, "Missiology."

[40] On Allen's influence see also Klaus–Triplett, "National," 266.

[41] McGee, "Missions," 620.

[42] McGee, "Hodges." Also Smeeton, "Missiology."

a permanent factor. They must work themselves out of a job. Mission work has been centered too long on the mission station rather than on the local church. Too many missionaries have been sent. And in Hodge's opinion all this amounts to a lack of faith.[43]

> The book proved to be the most significant work on missions strategy and theology that the Pentecostal movement had produced. [Hodges] asserted that "the faith which Pentecostal people have in the ability of the Holy Spirit to give spiritual gifts and supernatural abilities to the common people . . . has raised up a host of lay preachers and leaders of unusual spiritual ability—not unlike the rugged fishermen who first followed the Lord."[44]

The application of Hodges's teachings, and in particular his insertion of Allen into Pentecostal practice and conviction, "played a major role in the spectacular spread of Pentecostalism overseas, particularly in Latin America."[45]

His statements were meant in the first instance as a criticism of the mainline mission societies at a time when Pentecostals were poor and could not rival them. In the meantime Pentecostal churches in the West have become rich. Now whilst the original missiology and mission praxis is still upheld, there are grave departures here and there from this strategy. That is why for instance Rubén Zavala Hidalgo describes how the Assemblies of God missionaries formed a national leadership dependent on *their* (the missionaries') funds and detached from the values and needs of the local culture. His book is a "devastating critique of the missionaries [in Peru] who retained orthodoxy by isolating the mission churches from their larger cultural context."[46]

This leads me to *the problem* of Pentecostal mission. A most interesting discussion of the problem of Pentecostal mission comes from a number of younger Pentecostal scholars. They say:

> Our almost reflex affirmation of the indigenous church must not keep us from concerted reflection upon whether or not we are allowing authentic indigenous processes to emerge from each culture by the Spirit's direction. The church of Jesus Christ, which we can expect to emerge in a culturally appropriate form in any culture, can easily be localized if it becomes overly dependent on another potentially localizing institution, i.e., education, particularly as a formal structure.[47]

Pentecostals who value the development of national leadership must also nurture and encourage representative theologians from the two-thirds world. Russell P. Spittler suggests that a way be found to identify in non-Western emerging nations, those who will become the Pentecostal theologians of the twenty-first

---

[43] Hodges, *Indigenous*, 6–24. Other publications on the subject are: Pomerville, *Third;* McClung, *Azusa;* McGee, *Gospel.* Some of these books are discussed in Hollenweger, "Intercultural."

[44] McGee, "Missions," 621.

[45] Ibid.

[46] Hidalgo, *Perú,* reviewed by David Bundy in *Pneuma* 13/1, Spring 1991, 94–96.

[47] Klaus–Triplett, "National," 235.

century, potentially expressing the first truly indigenous Pentecostal theology. He reflects that the first native theology of Pentecostals may come from south of the equator, be in Spanish, and have no footnotes.[48]

The emergence of a truly non-Western theology is at the same time a threat and a promise, and will be discussed later.

The topic is approached from another angle by Larry D. Pate. He looks at the missionaries *from* the Third World.[49] Although 85 to 90% of the Christians in the Third World will be Pentecostal/Charismatic/Independent in the year 2000, only 41% of the missionaries and agencies from the Third World will be Pentecostal/Charismatic. This gives cause for serious self-examination. Pate identifies a number of factors which have led to this imbalance.

The first is *a faulty missionary ecclesiology.* So determined about evangelism have the Pentecostal missionaries been

> that there was an unspoken but clear message to indigenous church leaders: "You evangelize your people and we will be the missionaries." This is perhaps the single greatest reason cross-cultural ministry was so slow in catching on among Western related Pentecostal/Charismatic denominations in the two-thirds world.[50]

The second reason is what Pate calls "*Missionary 'People Blindness.' "* Most Pentecostal/Charismatic missionaries

> received inadequate training concerning the realities and implications of culture before going to the field. They often did not recognize that the greatest barriers to the gospel (other than sin) were cultural, not geographic . . . Though there were some obvious differences, they did not seem so terribly important. The assumption therefore prevailed that the gospel could spread rapidly throughout the country if the indigenous Christians could simply be trained to evangelize "their people." That has not happened often enough. The gospel might often spread among *one* people group, but many surrounding groups would remain virtually untouched.[51]

The third related reason Pate gives is a "*Monocultural Training System.*" In sum, there is insufficient attention given to the role of culture as a barrier to the gospel.

Pate discusses the issue at length and comes to the conclusion:

> The fact that the rise of the missionary movement in the two-thirds world does threaten traditional forms of missions structures must be faced squarely in the Western church. Twenty-five years ago few Westerners would buy a Japanese car. Today, too few are available for the demand. As it came to be accepted that Japanese automobiles offer greater value for money, people switched to Japanese cars by the millions. In a parallel manner, it is now becoming recognized that many missionary roles can be performed *as well or better by non-Western missionaries,*

---

[48] Ibid. 237, quoting Spittler, "Implicit."
[49] For definition of a missionary *from* the Third World, see note 2.
[50] Pate, "Pentecostal Missions from the Two-Thirds World," 251.
[51] Ibid.

and for much less money than their Western counterparts . . . No amount of denial on the part of Western missionaries and missionary leaders will change that fact.[52]

"The greatest need in mission today is not to find more laborers for the harvest, as important as that is. The greatest need is for effective management of the global missionary task." This means more global cooperation, and above all an intercultural education.

In the future, it may be possible for missionaries from any part of the world to gain higher level training in or near the country and culture of their calling. The training faculty may be representative of many parts of the world, and the training may be offered in more than one international language. It may become as common to see representatives of many cultures undergoing training in one place in much the same way as it is common in many universities today.[53]

In other words, Pate sees mission education in future as radically intercultural, and perhaps also ecumenical.

However, this is not just—as a European reader might perhaps think—a technical and managerial argument. A new generation of Pentecostal mission scholars will discover that the Holy Spirit was already present before the Pentecostal missionary or any other missionary arrived on the mission field, that the Holy Spirit also works through the Celestial Church in Anglophone West Africa, the Kimbanguist Church in Francophone Africa, and the independent churches in Indonesia, Korea, Latin America, and the Caribbean. Most of these churches have had initial contacts with Pentecostal missionaries, but then they became independent, financially and theologically. They have produced their own theologies, liturgies, and ethics.

But here tensions arise between the Pentecostal churches in the Third World and Pentecostal mission headquarters in Europe and America. I mention just an example.

In the statistical section of the *Dictionary of Pentecostal and Charismatic Movements,* the truly amazing growth of the worldwide movement is discussed. Within less than a century, Pentecostals are in the process of out-growing all other Protestant churches taken together.[54] But in the historical and theological sections of the same dictionary (as in the body of Pentecostal theological work as a whole) one finds very little material from the numerical and spiritual center of Pentecostalism, that is, from outside the Western world. Had the traditions of this majority Pentecostalism been included, a picture of a genuine and growing Third World movement would have emerged, with all its theological contradictions, social pains, and political compromises. "Pentecostals are multi–cultural, but we have not yet learned how to act like it without hurting one another."[55]

---

[52] Ibid., 254f., emphasis mine.
[53] Ibid., 255, 257.
[54] Above, note 6.
[55] Robeck, "Taking Stock," 45.

In other words, Pentecostal missiology must now address this question: How do we cope theologically with the bewildering pluralism within Pentecostalism worldwide? So far the theological contributions of Third World Pentecostalism have largely been ignored. Apart from human pride and weakness, from which Pentecostalism is not exempt, there are several practical reasons for this failure. To begin with, many documents are not in English. Secondly, they are difficult to get hold of. Thirdly, more often than not the theology of Third World churches is not contained in their confessions of faith (if in fact they have written such a document, and not just "received" one from missionaries) but in their songs, prayers, liturgies, and testimonies; that is, in their oral theologies. A type of research is required which can deal with these forms of theological documentation (which, as I have suggested, are nearer to biblical forms of theology than to Western theologizing). Often the *overt* meaning of such documents hides the *hidden* but true meaning. An uninformed Western theologian might take the overt meaning for the true meaning. Pentecostals, however, know that they have to dig for the hidden but real meaning—a kind of research which calls for considerable competence in interpreting language and culture.

One way of solving the dilemma for Pentecostal research would be to acknowledge the diversity and the unity of spiritualities, theologies, and liturgies which we find already in the biblical witness, following such evangelical researchers as James Dunn on the biblical material and Charles Kraft from Fuller Theological Seminary on the missiological material.[56]

We have seen that there are beginnings of such thinking; for example, H. V. Synan, in the *Dictionary of Pentecostal and Charismatic Movements*, states that "the breaks of Pentecostalism with Fundamentalism turned out to be a blessing."[57] This dictionary also contains a farewell to the old theory of verbal inspiration and inerrancy.[58] Instead one speaks now of the reliability and authority of Scripture. Whether one is prepared to accept the conclusion that not all "inerrant statements" are also reliable and not all "reliable statements" are necessarily inerrant, I do not know. Every marriage partner, however, should know this by experience (chapter 15, p. 195). Further evidence of re-thinking may be found elsewhere in the same source; for example, in the discussion on the Virgin Birth by a Catholic charismatic author Josephine M. Ford (the New Testament makes no explicit connection between the divinity of Jesus and his virginal conception);[59] in the growing acknowledgment of pluralism within Pentecostalism in an article by D. A. Reed defending Oneness Pentecostalism;[60] in an article on black theology;[61] and in

---

[56] Dunn, *Unity*, see note 43 and Kraft, *Culture*. From the Pentecostal side: Agosto, "Diversity."

[57] Synan, "Fundamentalism," see also Spittler, above in chapter 15, pp. 190–92.

[58] Arrington, F. L., "Hermeneutics."

[59] Ford, J. M., "Mary."

[60] Reed, "Oneness."

[61] Lovett, "Black Holiness-Pentecostals," and idem, "Black Theology."

a remarkable critique of the "gospel of prosperity" by the black Pentecostal theologian L. Lovett.[62]

In his refreshingly polemical missiology (*The Third Force in Mission*), Paul A. Pomerville also takes up some of these issues. As far as I know this book is, for instance, the first appreciative American Pentecostal treatment of the African Independent Churches (but see chapter 6, pp. 56–57). Pomerville, however, does not deal with the fact that the general approach to these churches among Pentecostal missionaries was, and sometimes still is, one of hostility or indifference. The pioneers who first drew attention to these contextualizing Holy Ghost theologians in the Third World were not the Pentecostal missiologists and historians but the conciliar theologians who recognized God's Spirit at work in places where no missionaries were in control. The discussion will become the more interesting once Pomerville begins to debate his findings with his Pentecostal missionary colleagues in South Africa, West Africa, India, Korea, and Latin America.[63]

Pomerville sees one of the great deficiencies of Western theology as its tendency (both in Fundamentalistic and in other forms) towards what he calls "Protestant Scholasticism." It is a joy to watch a Pentecostal scholar taking his insights on the dynamics of the Spirit into cognitive academic dimensions—with far-reaching consequences. Pomerville says farewell to so-called academic objectivity. Instead he makes clear that a scholar has to state his point of departure, the biographical and cultural *Sitz im Leben* of his arguments. This is more scholarly, he says, than claiming absolute, universal truth for a theology worked out in Western categories, then wreaking havoc in Third World contexts by applying that theology as if it represented "the" truth. Since I have already discussed the issue of "natural/supernatural," I do not have to treat his claim for "supernatural mission." The God of the Bible (and the God of oral Africa) is the God of nature *and* of "super-nature" (chapter 17, pp. 224–27).

What I did not find in Pentecostal missiology were statements on the eternal lostness of non-Christians.[64] Pentecostal scholars seem to shy away from this highly explosive issue, except in some popular essays.[65] Just how difficult this topic becomes as soon as one has "non-saved" friends was demonstrated to me at the Evangelism Congress in Berlin 1967. In one of the large discussion groups the eternal lostness of non-Christians was the topic. A converted Jew rose to his feet and said: "All my relatives, all my friends were exterminated in concentration camps. They were Jews. Are you going to tell

---

[62] Lovett, "Positive."

[63] In his criticism of Sundkler, Oosthuizen, myself and others, one often gets the impression that Pomerville judges them from today's hindsight. Sundkler's *Bantu Prophets* was at the time a breakthrough in spite of its weaknesses. Whoever moves into new ground is bound to tread on a few mines.

[64] I have dealt with this question in detail in Hollenweger, *Evangelism*, 55–75.

[65] E.g., Zopfi, "Sind."

me that they are lost for ever?" The reaction of the meeting was the only one possible—silence. What else could one do in such a situation? However, the incident was not reported in the congress report.[66] It is also my experience that as soon as a Pentecostal pastor has a Muslim (or perhaps a Mormon) son-in-law, the whole discussion takes on another shape.

Another example comes from the Evangelism Conference in Lausanne in the summer of 1974, where over 2,000 participants from almost 150 countries met to celebrate, discuss, and commit themselves to the evangelization of the world. In his opening address Billy Graham stated that "evangelism and the salvation of souls is the vital mission of the church . . . Thus, while we may discuss social and political problems, our priority for discussion here is the salvation of souls."[67]

In the foyer was a clock which counted the souls lost every second, every minute. Speakers referred to this clock by saying, for instance: "Since the beginning of this conference so many souls have died without salvation. They are eternally lost." This was not, however, the approach of some of the main speakers. "I refuse to drive a major wedge between a primary task, namely the proclamation of the Gospel, and a secondary (at best) or even an optional (at worst) task of the church," said René Padilla[68] from Buenos Aires. Michael Green from England, added: "What God has joined together we are not at liberty to put asunder."[69]

Samuel Escobar, then General Secretary of the Inter-Varsity Christian Fellowship of Canada, began his paper on "Evangelism" with a story by Clifford Christians:

> Imagine that all the population of the world were condensed to the size of one village of 100 people. In this village 67 of the 100 people would be poor; the other 33 would be in varying degrees well off. Of the total population, only seven would be North Americans. The other 93 people would watch the seven North Americans spend one half of all the money, eat one seventh of all the food, and use one half of all the bathtubs. These seven people would have ten times more doctors than the other 93. Meanwhile the seven would continue to get more and more and the 93 less and less.[70]

But that is not the whole story. The wealthy seven of which—he continued—we are part, continually try to evangelize the other 93.

> We tell them about Jesus and they watch us throw away more food than they can ever hope to eat. We are busy building beautiful church buildings, and they scrounge to find shelter for their families. We have money in the bank and they do not have enough to buy food for their children. All the while we tell them that our Master was the Servant of men, the Savior who gave his all for us and bids

---

[66] Henry–Mooneyham, *One Task.*
[67] Graham, Billy, "Lausanne," 31f.
[68] Padilla, "Evangelism," 144.
[69] Green, "Evangelism," 175.
[70] Éscobar, "Evangelism," 303; from Christians/Schipper/Smedes, *Who,* 125.

us give all for him . . . We are the rich minority in the world. We may be able to forget about that or consider it unimportant. The question is, can the 93 forget?

It is against this background of reality that René Padilla, then Associate General Secretary for Latin America of the International Fellowship of Evangelical Students, Buenos Aires, criticized the American "church growth" school. He said: "There is no place for statistics on 'how many souls die without Christ every minute' if they do not take into account how many of those who die, die victims of hunger." But today, this question is not asked. On the contrary, "the Gospel is truncated in order to make it easy for all men to become Christians." So from the very outset we lay the basis for an unfaithful church. As a black teacher at Fuller Theological Seminary, Pasadena (where the church growth school is located) once told me: "Church Growth is a way out for the churches to go on sinning under a respectable name. Not all that grows is the church. Cancer grows too." (See chapter 26, p. 364.)

But that is not all. Padilla looked for the root cause of what he considered to be unbiblical theology, and found it in the cultural imprisonment of much American and European theology to Descartes.

René Descartes's formula "I think, therefore I am" failed to take into account that man is not a mind, but a mind-body (a psychosomatic being), living and acting in the world, and that the "subjective" and "objective" aspects of reality are therefore inseparable in knowledge. The failure resulted in the split of reality into two levels: the upper level of the "subjective" (feelings and religion) and the lower level of the "objective" (facts and science). This split is behind much of modern thinking in the fields of science, philosophy and theology.[71]

While the speeches of Padilla's opponents, the Americans McGavran and Lindsell, "were greeted with stony silence,"[72] Padilla received the warmest applause of any speaker at the Congress. This is all the more astonishing as Padilla and Escobar flatly contradicted Billy Graham's opening address.

What was Billy Graham's reaction to this outspoken criticism? The story goes that he took Padilla's paper, went immediately to his hotel room, read and studied it together with his wife, prayed about it and came to the conclusion that it was a genuinely biblical paper. So Bruce Kaye was inspired to write: "The fact that Billy Graham said publicly that he was in substantial agreement with René Padilla's paper, and thought it to be one of the outstanding papers of the congress, is a sign and an assurance of a new humility."[73]

Padilla concluded:

If the church is really one, then there is no place for the assumption that one section of the church has the monopoly on the interpretation of the Gospel and the definition of the Christian mission. The problem is that one version of culture-Christianity, with an inadequate theological foundation and conditioned

---

[71] Padilla, "Evangelism," 132f., note 9.
[72] Kaye, "Tomorrow"; idem, "Challenge."
[73] Ibid.

by "fierce pragmatism"—the kind of pragmatism that in the political sphere has produced Watergate—should be regarded as the official position and the measure of orthodoxy around the world.[74]

Now that things seem to be moving in the evangelical camp, Pentecostals are also beginning to reconsider their position. Many Pentecostals were at Lausanne. It is possible that in the end, at the meeting point between problem and promise, something new—a genuine Pentecostal theology—will emerge, different from our Western-based (Catholic, Protestant, evangelical and Pentecostal) theologies and missiologies. This seems especially likely to happen if the question of the hermeneutic principle, the basis from which Scripture is interpreted, becomes a focus of reflection. This will be the topic of our next chapter.

---

[74] Padilla, "Evangelism," 140. The conference volume by J. D. Douglas is a mine of important reflections and new thinking in the evangelical camp, unfortunately all too often ignored by evangelicals and their opponents. See also, Stott, "Twenty Years," 50–55.

CHAPTER TWENTY THREE

Hermeneutics:
Who Interprets Scripture Correctly?

Who interprets Scripture correctly? Most Pentecostal believers would answer: every believer does, because Scripture is clear in itself. That was—as we know—also the position of the Reformers, until they discovered that believers were coming to answers different from their own. Thus confessions of faith were introduced; in the Reformation churches, and in Pentecostal churches. But such confessions have not solved the problem for Pentecostal Bible readers—they still come to very different conclusions among themselves (as is clear to any reader who has followed the argument of this book so far). There are many different "Pentecostal" positions on the church, on the Spirit, on ethics, on politics, on glossolalia, and even on the Baptism of the Spirit—the heart of Pentecostal spirituality.

Why is it that *bona fide* believers come to different conclusions on the meaning of Scripture? Furthermore, what do we do if the Scriptures say different things in different places; for example, on the Spirit, on the church, on christology, and so on? And what about those important issues where the Scripture is silent; for instance, on all the activities of "civil religion" (burials, weddings, and so forth), not to speak of many important ethical questions of our modern time?

These questions have led a number of Pentecostal scholars to open the debate on hermeneutics, an overview of which I want to give in the following chapter.

Why Hermeneutics?

All people can understand the Bible; how is it that they come to different conclusions? Is it because I (or my group) understand better and more deeply what the text says, and others are dull, disobedient, or simply inaccurate? That is too easy a way out; we can no longer say "The Bible says," and then quote a verse of Scripture. We have to account for the principle of our selectivity. For example:

Why do some Pentecostals take literally the command by Jesus in the Gospel of John to wash each others feet, and others do not?

Why are black (and some white) Pentecostals uneasy about Paul's obvious hesitation to attack the institution of slavery, while some of these same people take literally his condemnation of homosexuality—and still others have founded a Pentecostal association for homosexuals?

Why do most (not all) Pentecostals reject infant baptism because it is not in the New Testament, yet appoint army chaplains, organize Bible schools, celebrate December 25th as the birthday of their Lord, and do extended youth work—none of which is mentioned in the New Testament?

Why do Pentecostals and charismatics teach so many different doctrines on the baptism in the Spirit?

My own conclusion from all of this is that we must plead for a theologically responsible syncretism. That Christianity (both today and in the New Testament) is a syncretism *par excellence* seems to be irrefutable (chapter 11, pp. 132–44). One has only to think of the temple which was planned according to Canaanite models and built by Canaanite craftsmen; or of the magi who found their way (at least according to Matthew) to the cradle of Jesus on the basis of their pagan astrology, while the Bible-reading scribes in Jerusalem tried to kill little Jesus. Any responsible (including evangelical and Pentecostal) exegesis has to reckon with the fact that without this syncretism the Bible could never have been written. So the question arises: What is a theologically responsible syncretism, as over against a theologically irresponsible syncretism? The signposts for answering this question are the biblical authors who—with skill, responsibility and competence—decided to use or not to use certain religious or cultural rites, thought-patterns, and even moral precepts (think of Paul's *Haustafeln*, household codes) from their surrounding world. So if today some bury their lords in their churches, if we act as religious celebrants at patriotic celebrations (such as Remembrance Day or the swearing-in of a new president), or if we accept the thought-patterns of Aristotelian logic in our theology (after all, Aristotle was a pagan philosopher), we have to have reasons for these choices. I do not want to be misunderstood: there might be perfectly legitimate reasons for these forms of syncretism. But those reasons must be demonstrated, not just taken for granted. The issue becomes urgent when churches from other cultures in which Aristotle is not predominant begin to articulate their Pentecostal theology, or when they integrate into their theologies and liturgies *their* patriotism, *their* ancestors and *their* nationalism (or their revolutionary and anti-patriotic ideas), as well as their "non-Aristotelian" logic. Examples are plentiful in the churches in China, in Korea (chapter 8, pp. 99–105 and 20, pp. 264–67) and in semitic or pre-literary cultures in Africa whose patterns of thinking are probably closer to that of the biblical authors than are ours.[1]

More importantly, we ask: why is it that only Christian fringe groups take seriously the historical precedent of "having all things in common" set by the early Christians, which was after all an important fruit of the first Pentecost?[2] And why is it that even fewer Christians (whether Catholic, Pentecostal, Protestant, or evangelical) live according to the Sermon on the Mount—including those who take this sermon to be the actual words of Jesus?

It is not only the Pentecostal who "tends to exegete his experience";[3] historical-critical exegetes also do this, as I have argued elsewhere.[4] What remains to be done in this situation is to recognize this, and to be aware of one's own bias and limitation.

The necessity for this sort of hermeneutical reflection became even clearer to me when I tutored Pamela Binyon, an English High School teacher. She had studied theology in Oxford and taught religion in an English Girls' High School. Religion is a compulsory subject in English schools; thus lessons are taught in a "scholarly" and "objective" way—neither as worship nor as evangelism. And since religion is a topic like any other, in which information, facts in their interrelatedness, and models of interpretation are discussed and examined at the final examination, both Catholic and Protestant interpretations of the Gospel must be considered.

Ms. Binyon belongs to the Church of England, and she had to present the different streams in her church as well, from liberal to evangelical. The important minorities in Britain such as the Methodists, the Baptists, the Presbyterians, and the Catholics were also considered. And finally there were significant Muslim, Buddhist, and Hindu minorities to be accounted for, not to forget the many who do not know where they belong religiously and have rather flimsy religious convictions.

Binyon also belongs to the evangelical wing of the Church of England. To her, theological studies at Oxford looked like an intellectual game which by-passed the most important issue, the personal decision in her life. Nonetheless, she continued her studies in order to become a teacher. She tried to shape her lessons in such a way that her students at least considered seriously

---

[1] On semitic thought patterns and language see e.g., Moore, Rich D., "Canon," including a discussion of *dabar* and *yada*. Also Johns/Bridges-Johns, "Yielding," 109–34, in particular: "We have found the rationalism of twentieth-century evangelical Christianity to be an inadequate vehicle for passing on a faith which honors the active presence of the Holy Spirit in the contemporary world" (110) or a quote from Down ("Contours"): "When the only 'language game' in town is rationalism it is not hard to understand why an experiential, relational, emotional and moral faith would choose not to play by the rules" (Johns/Bridges-Johns, "Yielding," 110), or also a discussion of *yada* on p. 128.

[2] Gee, "End"; *The Pentecostals*, 212.

[3] Fee, "Precedent," 120. Also Anderson, Gordon L., "Hermeneutics," 15.

[4] Hollenweger, "Exegesis."

the gospel as an important signpost for their lives. Some of her students understood and accepted this, to the extent that they became Anglican nuns.

The process of choosing a topic for her research was a difficult one. She always said that she was looking for a language which her students could understand; I pointed her to the books of Emil Brunner. But Brunner was not convincing for her. One day she said to me: "I give up. I am either too stupid or unable to write a decent theological dissertation."

I asked her once again: "What do you want to find out? As a teacher you know that the most important thing in teaching is to have a precise goal." Then she began to speak. She had an extraordinarily expressive face on which many years of hard intellectual and physical work had left its traces. Her sentences were always of astonishing clarity and lucidity. She gave the following answer: "First: I have not studied properly. That is a disadvantage today. The critical tools of modern theology are necessary for my work. Second: I was converted in the Students' Mission in Oxford; however, I cannot teach my conversion—I must teach the whole field of experience and thinking in Christianity. Third: Two years ago I was at a charismatic conference. What I heard and saw there has convinced me that I must risk a move into a less doctrinaire position. How does one do this? I do not want to become a victim of the opposite position; that of the many Christians who do not really know what they believe, nor what they disbelieve."

This was, of course, more than a scholarly program. But Pamela Binyon found her way. She had been trained in the English philosophy of language—a capital which she could now draw from. She examined the language in which the prophets of the Old Testament, the evangelist Luke, the apostle Paul, the Catholic Pentecostals, a famous neurosurgeon (William Sargent), and an equally famous Swiss psychoanalyst (Carl Gustav Jung) described phenomena which are typically considered, within the faith, to be manifestations of the Spirit or of spirits.

For our topic, the most important comparison was the one between the neurosurgeon, the psychologist, and the biblical authors. Binyon started with the assumption that they described the same phenomena; just as a geologist, a photographer, or a mountaineer describes the Himalayas differently, so they described religious experiences in different languages. Furthermore, it mattered whether they described the Himalayas from the foot of the mountain, from another mountain, or from an airplane. Always the Himalayas appear in a different way; and yet it is the same mountain range. Conversions and religious experiences such as healing or Spirit-Baptism appeared to the neurosurgeon as bio- or electro-chemical functions of the nervous system; to the biblical authors as signs of God's love; to the psychologist as processes through which somebody can understand repressed feelings and memories in his subconscious and integrate them into his whole person.

Which one is the correct language? The question has no answer. There is no language which describes the Himalayas "objectively," that is to say simultaneously, from all points of view and in the language of all observers. All human language, including biblical language, is provisional. That is why the Bible speaks of God in languages which differ according to author, time, and context.

There are, however, yardsticks which measure the relative truth of language. The specialized language of a pastry-cook is not completely, but relatively, unsuitable for describing the Himalayas. In fact, some "technical" languages are only accessible to specialists, but are otherwise unusable. Some languages even tend to change their point of reference in the middle of a sentence; these are confused languages, which do not give a clear image.

Pamela Binyon's work was published in 1977 in the "Studies in the Intercultural History of Christianity."[5] After she had finished her work, I asked her to talk to my other candidates who were wrestling with their dissertations just as she had wrestled. She said: "Whether my little book is of any scholarly value I do not know. For me, however, it was important. It showed me the relative significance of my own evangelical language and also the significance (and the limitations) of other languages. Furthermore I learned the art of translation from one language into another. It is no longer necessary for me to consider somebody as an inferior Christian because he does not understand (or perhaps because in my opinion he wrongly understands) the biblical or the evangelical language. The wrong language is that language which thinks it has the monopoly in explaining God's mysteries. There *are* wrong languages. But these are not the languages which say something wrong but languages which think they have a monopoly on truth."

This is certainly not all that Pamela Binyon has to say on the subject. I cannot enter into a detailed and extensive epistemological discussion of the co-determination of language by culture, biography, religion, politics and social context (in the Bible and in present-day language). Most helpful for me personally were the discussions with mathematicians and physicists who deal exactly with this kind of problem, and who have long overcome the old ideology of "objectivism" without falling into a new subjectivism. They discuss in detail for which parameter, under which condition, a statement is true or false, verifiable or falsifiable.[6]

The Problem Recognized

I want to return now to hermeneutics among Pentecostals, for Pentecostals themselves have recognized the problem.[7] Gordon Anderson for instance states that Pentecostals do not conduct penetrating discussions on how biblical principles translate into behavior.

That might be a partial answer to the puzzling question of why the Pentecostal world had been virtually comatose prior to the public disclosures of the sexual

---

[5] Binyon, *Concepts.*
[6] Discussed at length in my *ITh* 3.
[7] See also Stronstad, "Trends"; *EPTA Bulletin,* 7/3, 1988, 116f.; Johnston, "Hermeneutics."

misconduct of a major Pentecostal minister who was guilty, not only of sexual immorality, but by any. Christian measure, other serious breaches of biblical principles as well . . . Why is it that the Pentecostal church, along with its many positive features, is also such a fertile field for a bumper crop of poor or heretical theology, embarrassing personalities, outrageous visions and revelations, preposterous fundraising schemes, financial impropriety, and, in some cases, scandalous moral failure? A good deal of the answer lies in the fact that many Pentecostals have an inadequate means by which they establish biblical principle and apply it to the moral issues of everyday life.[8]

Richard D. Israel goes a step further: "A Pentecostal ideology is no hermeneutic at all; it is the obliteration of the horizon of the text by the interpreter." Using Habermas and other specialists on communication he says:

If one cannot establish comprehensibility, there can be no mutual language and no conversation. If you cannot redeem the truth claim, there will be no shared knowledge and understanding. If the sincerity is left unredeemed, trust and understanding is not established. Finally, unless all the first three claims are satisfied, there cannot be legitimation. There will be no shared values and no interpersonal relationship.[9]

Whatever else this means, it reveals an uneasiness with the present state of Pentecostal hermeneutics.

Mark D. McLean adds:

A strict adherence to traditional evangelical/fundamentalist hermeneutical principles leads to a position which, in its most positive forms, suggests the distinctives of the twentieth century Pentecostal movement are perhaps nice, but not necessary; important but not vital to the life of the Church in the twentieth century. In its more negative forms, it leads to a total rejection of Pentecostal phenomena.[10]

On the issue of creation he says:

From a Pentecostal perspective, what can be more natural than the God who created all things, manipulating the stuff of creation in ways that do not violate that creation, but are in harmony with the realities of creation which our sophisticated scientific study, as great and as valuable as it is, has not yet discerned, let alone understood.[11]

One of the first who put hermeneutics on the Pentecostal agenda was Gordon D. Fee (born 1934). He is a remarkable Pentecostal: ordained in 1959 as minister of the Assemblies of God, a graduate from Seattle Pacific College and of the University of Southern California (Ph.D. 1966), professor of New Testament at Regent College, Vancouver, B.C., he now also serves on the

---

[8] Anderson, Gordon L., "Changing," 3.
[9] Israel, "Pentecostalism," A 9, A 32.
[10] McLean, "Hermeneutic," 37. See also idem, "Gap."
[11] McLean, "Hermeneutic," 45.

American executive committee of the International Greek New Testament Project, co-chairing its patristic section.

> As a teacher, Fee is known for his contagious enthusiasm and passionate love for Scripture. He also has a reputation for insisting on conscientious and careful scholarship. . . . Within Pentecostal circles Fee is both admired and denounced. To some, Fee epitomizes the heretofore oxymoron "a Pentecostal scholar." His careful regard for "the text" and his skills as a New Testament exegete render him a voice to be reckoned with; moreover, his zeal behind the pulpit and his passion for the Pentecostal message of the Spirit's presence in this age authenticate him as one deeply committed to the Pentecostal experience. Yet, to others, Fee's hermeneutic challenges the traditional Pentecostal hermeneutic (which Fee labels "pragmatic" . . .) and is regarded as an implicit threat to the Pentecostal doctrine that tongues are the "initial physical evidence" of the Spirit baptism.[12]

Furthermore, Fee teaches regularly overseas, which points not only to a deep commitment to mission but also to an intercultural understanding of theology.

At the second annual meeting of the Society for Pentecostal Studies in Oklahoma City (1972), Fee shook his audience by mercilessly exposing the deficiencies of Pentecostal hermeneutics:

> Two observations should be made about hermeneutics within the traditional Pentecostal movement. First, their attitude toward Scripture regularly has included a general disregard for scientific exegesis and carefully thought-out hermeneutics. In fact, hermeneutics has simply not been a Pentecostal thing. Scripture is the Word of God and is to be obeyed. In place of scientific hermeneutics there developed a kind of pragmatic hermeneutics—obey what should be taken literally; spiritualize, allegorize, or devotionalize the rest. Pentecostals of course, are not alone in this. Furthermore, gifted men tend to apply the hermeneutics with inspired commonsense.[13] Therefore, although exegetical aberrations abound in Pentecostal pulpits and sometimes in their pamphlets, the mainstream of traditional American Pentecostalism has treated Scripture in very much the same way as have other forms of American fundamentalism[14] or evangelicalism. The differences have been over *what* is to be literally obeyed. Secondly, it is probably fair—and important—to note that in general the Pentecostals' experience has preceded their hermeneutics. In a sense, the Pentecostal tends to exegete his experience.[15]

Fee continues, "In defense of the Pentecostal, it should be observed that although he has tended to arrive at the biblical norm by way of his experience, he is not alone in establishing norm on the basis of historical precedent rather

---

[12] Alexander, "Fee." See also Fee, "Baptism."

[13] Perhaps "inspired commonsense" is a new and interesting gift of the Spirit.

[14] And I might add as many highly trained pastors in Europe, see below, pp. 322–23.

[15] Fee, "Precedent," 121f.

than on the explicit teaching of the Scripture."[16] After discussing hermeneutics in Catholic, Baptist, and other churches he comes to the crucial question:

> *How* is the Book of Acts the Word of God? . . . If the primitive church is normative, *which* expression of it is normative?[17] . . . Jerusalem? Antioch? Philippi? Corinth? That is, why do not all the churches sell their possessions and have all things in common? Or further, is it at all legitimate to take descriptive elements as normative? If so, how does one distinguish those which are from those which are not? For example, must we follow the pattern of Acts 1:26 and select leaders by lot?

"It is of interest that the Assemblies of God sees baptism by immersion as 'commanded by Scriptures' but makes no statement on the frequency of the Lord's Supper."[18] Or, he adds, "to use Jesus' cleansing of the temple to justify one's so-called righteous indignation—usually a euphemism for selfish anger—is to abuse the principle of the norm of a biblical precedent."[19]

Before we now turn to the guidelines for a Pentecostal hermeneutics, let us take a brief look at Pentecostals' criticism of the hermeneutics of others.

Criticism of Non-Pentecostal Hermeneutics

It is to be expected that Pentecostals would criticize a rigid dispensationalism (which states that the gifts of the Spirit ceased with the completion of the biblical canon); this is too well-known to need documentation. Only, it is strange that in all other matters Pentecostals still use a dispensational approach which fits neither their experience nor their understanding of the Bible.[20] Less known are their arguments with the Catholics, documented by Sandidge: They confronted their Catholic dialogue partners in the Vatican/Pentecostal dialogue with a "pneumatic exegesis" or "spiritual criticism," in opposition to critical exegesis (in spite of the fact that the former methodology seems to be highly criticized by their own Pentecostal scholars).[21] Yet they could have

---

[16] Ibid., 122.

[17] On this very issue see the important works by Schweizer *(Order)* and Dulles *(Models)*.

[18] Fee, "Precedent," 123 and 123, note 13.

[19] Ibid., 129.

[20] Sheppard, "Dispensationalism." Sheppard finds it unfortunate to "wed a Pentecostal ecclesiology to a dispensational eschatology. I am concerned to describe the attempt by Pentecostals to find acceptance and legitimation from the dispensationalist-fundamentalist. I hope to show both that Pentecostals were not originally dispensationalist-fundamentalist and that efforts secondarily to embrace such views have raised new problems . . . " (5). There is no "pre-tribulation rapture among the doctrinal statements of the Church of God in Christ, Memphis" (10). Sheppard shows how the doctrine of the pre-tribulation rapture emerged slowly in the Assemblies of God and how they suddenly accepted what they earlier had rejected (11). His conclusion: "They would be wiser to look for eschatology and ecclesiology of the black and hispanic churches" (33).

[21] Sandidge, *Dialogue (1977–1982)* I, 185, 209, 386f. For criticism on the "spiri-

learned from the Catholics that the originally Protestant critical method can also be used in another framework, in this case in the Catholic framework. So why not in the Pentecostal framework? This is in fact what most Pentecostal exegetes state: that they use the same tools for exegesis as any other scholar.[22] Did the Pentecostal dialogue-partners in the Vatican/Pentecostal dialogue not know what is taught in their own Bible colleges? How else could one explain that they paralleled the German critical methodology with the Old Antiochian exegesis, "that was emphatically rejected by the Council of Ephesus (AD 431)"? The Catholics answered: Critical methodology is not specifically German, nor Catholic, but they added a very pastoral note: "Roman Catholics went through the same stage Pentecostals are now passing and they asked the same questions. Catholics, therefore, understand the Pentecostal concerns on this hermeneutical point."[23] Gerald T. Sheppard expressed the Pentecostal situation like this: " . . . the best Pentecostal practice of interpreting Scripture is not fundamentalistic but dependent on a spiritually informed discernment and intuition. It is a form of interpretation open to ordinary people with an extraordinary book."[24]

On the other hand they clearly detect the faults in some devotional books, for example, on John's Revelation: "In order to arrive at a correct understanding of Revelation 20:4–6 one must realize that John was influenced by both the biblical and extra-biblical books mentioned." Far from intending to give a blueprint for the future, John was a proper prophet in that he prophesied against the evil of his time—for instance, against a Caesar who claimed to be *Dominus et Deus*. In today's Pentecostalism Revelation "became increasingly an object of dogmatic speculation" which is not its intention.[25] Thomas Ruchelka also states that the prophetic passages in the Old Testament have "to be first understood in the historical sense before prophetic/christological conclusions are drawn."[26] And R. F. Martin says clearly that Revelation is

---

tual exegesis" see below, pp. 321–22. On "soul marriages" (an "identification of one's sexual desires with the promptings of the Holy Spirit") see McLean, "Hermeneutic," 51, note 6. On Wilkerson's *Vision* (against mainly the Catholic Church) see Robeck, "Authority." Anderson, Gordon L., "Hermeneutics," 6f. Anderson takes issue with Arrington, F. L. ("Hermeneutics," 382) and Ervin ("Option," 16, 23). He finds their work "confusing" and "elitist" because they say that there are certain things in the Bible which Pentecostals understand better than others.

[22] Fee, "Precedent," 124. See also his *First Corinthians*, for instance, on the possibility that 1 Cor 14:34–35 is an inauthentic gloss is carefully considered and affirmed, although other opinions are clearly stated (183). "Fee incorporates the best of Barrett and Conzelmann, with whom he more often agrees than not." Reviewed by John L. Karsten in *EPTA Bulletin* 8/4, 1989, 183–84. Anderson, Gordon L., "Hermeneutics," 1, 8, 11. Arrington, R. L., "Hermeneutics," in particular, 387.

[23] Sandidge, *Dialogue (1977–1982)* I, 204f, see also 207.

[24] Sheppard, "Tradition," 19, quoted in Sandidge, *Dialogue (1977–1982)* I, 209.

[25] Zeegwaart, "Apocalyptic," 23.

[26] Liebi, *Erfüllte Prophetie*, critical review by Thomas R. Ruchelka in *EPTA Bulletin* 9/2, 3, 1989, 74–76.

neither a cryptically coded prediction of all future history nor an imaginative flight from the harsh realities being faced by those to whom it was addressed. It is rather a symbolic interpretation of history deriving from the experience of the author's time and laying down the ultimate principles of Christian existence for all time as these came to the author of the "revelation of Jesus Christ."

John uses terminology which was intelligible to his readers (but not necessarily to us).

This is prophetic teaching on the ultimate meaning of what John's audience was suffering . . . Those who have insisted that the text must refer to realities in this world are correct: this is a word of prophecy for the disinherited. Those who see the application of this and other teachings of Revelation to their own time are also correct, and there have been people who have so understood the text in nearly every century.[27]

A similar situation is described in the dissertation of Peter Kuzmič on the Serbo-Croatian Bible translation.[28] This is an astonishing piece of research and impressive in its scholarly breadth, with notes from English, French, Russian, German, Serbian, Croatian, and Latin sources. Kuzmič offers a critique of the activities of the British and Foreign Bible Society in his country. The Society's involvement in the Serbo-Croatian translation

illustrates the problems and weaknesses of a centralized bureaucratic system which ignores the advice of its agents and fails to recognize the complicated social, cultural and historical context of the Balkans; and it demonstrates the strengths of such a system as it became willing to subsidize scholarly activity and publishing by leading Serbian and Croatian literary figures.

One thing becomes clear in Kuzmič's critique: a Bible translation is not just a translation; it is also a social, political, and theological statement. In fact, everybody who has tried to translate passages from the Bible will testify to this. Therefore, hermeneutics is inevitable for every Pentecostal, even (or even more) if he or she uses a translation.

Elements of a Pentecostal Hermeneutics

As far as I can see, Gordon D. Fee was the first to tackle the problem of Pentecostal hermeneutics in any substantive way. Among his "General Principles of Interpretation" he mentions first:

It should be an axiom of biblical hermeneutics that the interpreter must take into account the literary genre of the passage he is interpreting, along with the questions of text, grammar, philology, and history. Such a principle would appear to be self-evident, yet it is seldom applied to the New Testament . . . The point is that not every biblical statement is the Word of God in the same way.

---

[27] Martin, R. Francis, "Apocalypse."

[28] Kuzmič, *Vuk-Danicicevo,* reviewed by David Bundy in *EPTA Bulletin* 4/1, 1985, 7–10.

The fact that the Psalms are poetry, that the prophets are primarily a collection of spoken oracles, that Ecclesiastes and Job are Jewish wisdom literature, that Daniel and Revelation are apocalyptic, that the epistles are letters, and that Acts is historical narrative must be a primary consideration in interpretation in order to avoid the non-contextual, "promise-box" approach to Scripture. For instance, the epistles must be taken seriously as letters, not treated primarily as theological treatises . . . They are not systematic treatises on theology.[29]

Coming to Acts he first criticizes "the monumental works of Dibelius and Haenchen."[30] "They tend to treat Acts first as theology and only secondarily as history. I demur. Theology there is aplenty, and theology is most likely a part of Luke's intent; but it is cast as history, and the first principle of hermeneutic is to take that literary genre seriously, . . . even if one disregards its historical value."[31]

But as Fee continues, he concedes that Acts is a *Tendenzschrift*, a narrative with a "broader intent." For instance, the story of the conversion of Cornelius "serves his broader interest not simply to 'represent a principle . . . of higher historical truth' (so Dibelius), nor simply to illustrate Christian conversion in general or the baptism in the Holy Spirit in particular (so the Pentecostals). Rather, Cornelius serves for Luke as the first-fruits of the Gentile mission."[32]

He now comes to his main thesis: *In order to have normative value, historical precedent must be related to intent,*

> that is, if it can be shown that the purpose of a given narrative is to *establish* precedent, then such precedent should be regarded as normative. For example, if it could be demonstrated on exegetical grounds that Luke's intent in Acts 1:15–26 was to give the church a precedent for selecting its leaders, then such a selection process should be followed by later Christians. But if the establishing of precedent was *not* the intent of the narrative, then its value as a precedent for later Christians should be treated according to the specific principles of the next section of this paper.[33]

He then goes on the distinguish between primary and secondary levels of doctrinal statement. The first describes the principle, the second its applications. The second is not unimportant, but is not on the same level as the first, and might sometimes yield other applications today than are described in the text.

---

[29] Fee, "Precedent," 124.
[30] Dibelius, *Studies;* Haenchen, *Acts.*
[31] Fee, "Precedent," 125.
[32] Ibid.
[33] Ibid., 126. These "Specific Principles for the Use of Historical Precedent" state among others: "The use of historical precedent as an analogy by which to establish a norm is never valid in itself. . . . Whether we can reproduce the manner of exegesis which the New Testament authors applied to the Old Testament is a moot point. . . . For a biblical precedent to justify a present action, the principle of the action must be taught elsewhere, where it is the primary intent so to teach" (Fee, "Precedent," 128f.).

On the basis of his hermeneutical reflections, Fee comes to the conclusion that the Pentecostal doctrine of tongues as "the initial evidence" is an over-statement of Luke's intent. "To insist that it is the only valid sign seems to place too much weight on the historical precedent of three (perhaps four) instances in Acts."[34] That does of course not undo the value and importance of speaking in tongues, but it places it in a different theological framework.

One can imagine the storm of protest which this observation has produced among Pentecostals—not so much because of Fee's hermeneutical method, as because of its application to a *pièce de résistance* of Pentecostal self-identification (in spite of all which has been said earlier in chapter 17, pp. 222–24). However, in order to remain faithful to their commitment to a scholarly exegetical method, Pentecostals have had to deal with Fee's hermeneutical argument.

One of Fee's outspoken critics is Gordon L. Anderson.[35] Anderson's presupposition seems to be:

> The correct view is to recognize that the work of theology is that of systematizing the objective meanings of individual verses into a coherent whole. In this method the original meanings are gotten through the historical-grammatical method, grounded in the assumption that they have fixed and objective meanings. The system is constructed by the theologian, but without claiming that any particular verse means what is revealed as a composite from a synthesis of the whole of Scripture. One must first do biblical theology and then systematic . . . A good Pentecostal argues for the uniformity of language and logic.[36] . . . Pentecostals reject the pluralism that ensues when the language and logic of the Bible are taken to be culture specific.

The Bible does not have a variety of meanings, only a variety of applications.[37] To this Anderson adds that for him the narrative has no less value than the propositional (a position which in my opinion he seems wrongly to attribute to Fee). The Bible is also "a true record" in its narratives. "The document is valuable for the facts it records."[38]

In one way Mark McLean agrees with Anderson: "We will assert that the mode of God's presence in and among his people is the same today as it was in biblical times," hence the value of biblical narratives. In another sense, it seems to me, he disagrees with Anderson by stating that we must turn away "from the nostalgic longing (evidenced in much of orthodoxy) for an ontologically distinct era in which God spoke audibly and acted concretely in history."[39]

---

[34] Ibid., 131.

[35] Anderson, Gordon. L., "Hermeneutics," 8.

[36] One is reminded of the old mediaeval dispute on the *universalia* in a new form: *nomen est omen.*

[37] Anderson, Gordon. L., "Hermeneutics," 11.

[38] Ibid., 15.

[39] McLean, "Hermeneutic," 49f.

F. L. Arrington, whom Anderson finds "confusing," tries to get away from the "coherence syndrome" by quoting James D. G. Dunn:

> The common error . . . is to treat the New Testament (and even the Bible) as a homogeneous whole, from any part of which texts can be drawn on a chosen subject and fitted into a framework and system which is often basically extrabiblical . . . To avoid this error, which Dunn rightly notes,[40] the interpreter must make an effort to search out the particular theological concerns of the individual writer.[41]

Arrington nevertheless comes, of course, to different conclusions from Dunn and Fee. He sees in Luke (with Stronstad[42]) "a theological framework from the whole of the Lukan corpus and offers that framework to the interpreter as a template with which to interpret the historical narrative of Luke–Acts," basically a similar approach to Fee but opting for a "Pentecostal framework" of Luke and thus vindicating the usual Pentecostal interpretation.

Kilian McDonnell criticizes: "F. L. Arrington claims both a special Pentecostal tradition and a unique Pentecostal hermeneutic." McDonnell "supports the first but sincerely doubts the second, because it sequesters the charisma and the Spirit. Some years ago this same question was discussed in Europe outside of Pentecostal circles."[43]

Finally some very different approaches are found in the Dutch Pentecostal movement. There *myth* as an adequate category of theological synthesis and expression of "coherence" is re-discovered.[44]

As far as I can see the hermeneutical approach of Louis Dallière, a French charismatic of the 1930s (chapter 25, pp. 338–42) has not been discussed among the Pentecostals. Yet, it could be important for them. In dialogue with T. Fallot, Dallière accepts the "law of intermediaries," which allows him to avoid a fundamentalist reading of Scripture and to avoid a rupture between science (including psychology and sociology) and religious life. "All aspects of knowledge, when applied critically to the biblical text, make the text human, social, real, and able to be responded to in life and worship."[45]

Others look for help among their fellow Pentecostals in the Third World:

> We need the doctrinal leadership of the Third World leaders, scholars, and pastors who not only grapple with American and European exported doctrinal

---

[40] Dunn, *Baptism*, 39.

[41] Arrington, F. L., "Hermeneutics," 387.

[42] Stronstad, *Luke*, 75–76. See also idem, "Experiential," and idem, "Trends"; *EPTA Bulletin* 7/3, 1988, 116f.

[43] Kilian McDonnell in a review of the *Dictionary* and Arrington's entry on "Hermeneutics" (376–89) in *Pneuma* 13/1, 1991, 83–85, quote 83. For a Pentecostal critique of this so-called Pentecostal hermeneutics see above Gordon L. Anderson, note 21.

[44] J. L. Karsten in a review of Willis (ed.), *Kingdom* in *EPTA Bulletin* 9/2, 3, 1990, 79–83, Zeegwaart, " 'Myth' " (discussion with Hollenweger, *ITh* 2).

[45] Bundy, "Making," 47; Dallière, "Fonction," 254f.; Fallot, *Comment.*

heresies (areas such as extreme faith and prosperity, kingdom now, new age etc.) but also address life and death issues from their own regions . . . I wonder if it is seriously believed by North American and European Pentecostals.[46]

"I dream of a time when our politicians, scientists, psychologists, economists, teachers, and others will search for common ground with Pentecostal-charismatic theologians and church leaders in pooling and mobilizing our resources for the struggle," for liberation needs all the resources available.[47]

How such a hermeneutic would look from the underside is documented by Eldin Villafañe:

The witness of Scripture is clear that while the Gospel is for all, the rich and powerful (including the religious "powers-that-be") because of their grasping or dependence ("idolatry") on their financial or religious advantage, hear it as "bad news." This is part of the meaning of the "hermeneutical advantage of the poor."[48]

I do not want to enter into this hot intra-Pentecostal debate. The main thing for me is that it is taking place. I want only to add a few questions, to highlight what I consider the strength of Pentecostal hermeneutics, and then to offer my own lifelong experience in interpreting the Bible with small groups and before crowds of many thousands at the German *Kirchentag*.

First the questions: Some Pentecostals ask for coherence[49] in theological statements. If by "coherence" is meant a logical coherence in the sense of Aristotelian logic, those who ask for this do not have the Bible on their side, for the God of the Bible can change his mind (Jonah!); he can repent. He is the same all the time, he is true and utterly reliable, but he does not fit our logical categories. So what does coherence mean? Furthermore, why should Pentecostals reject a pluralistic approach to the Bible[50] when the Pentecostal movement itself is a shining example of "unity and diversity"? What is meant by "objective meaning"? This concept has been given up by most scientists in the so-called hard core of science, in physics and mathematics. The observer, it is admitted, is part of the observed. We do not know what is; we only know how we perceive it.[51] So while God is an objective reality (if such an almost blasphemous sentence is allowed) we know him (or her), only in part, as he or she is revealed to us. This means for hermeneutics that no system is ever final, only a contribution to the continuing process of knowledge in the whole

---

[46] McClung, "Interdependence."

[47] Lovett, "Liberation," 169. Lovett is a black Pentecostal, Ph.D. in Social Ethics at Emory University, founding-president of the Charles Mason Theological Seminary, the first fully accredited Pentecostal seminary in the U.S., now pastor of the Church at the Crossroads, Los Angeles.

[48] Villafañe, *The Liberating Spirit*, 106.

[49] "Coherence" is also a key-word for Johnston, "Hermeneutics," 62, also for Ervin, "Option," 12.

[50] Dunn, *Unity*.

[51] This is discussed in detail in my *ITh* 3, especially in part IV.

oikoumene. It does *not* mean that the biblical authors did not have something clear in mind when they wrote. But can we always grasp it?

The strength of Pentecostal hermeneutics is in fact that it takes into consideration the *hermeneutes* and his experience. That is how one could interpret the insistence on "pneumatic exegesis." "Pneumatic exegesis" is not a kind of intuition. It can simply mean that the Pentecostal interpreter has a greater *Einverständnis*[52] with the text than others because of his cultural and spiritual background. That is certainly true for certain passages, and untrue for others, where for instance Catholic and Orthodox Christians have a greater empathy; which is why we need each other. This was dramatically shown to me in the teaching process at the Centre for Black and White Christian Partnership in Birmingham (chapter 9, pp. 106–16). The New Testament teacher analyzed miracle stories and healing texts according to the well-known critical method. The Pentecostal students busily took notes. There was no objection from them. Why should they not learn how these texts had been shaped in a long oral process? That is their daily experience. But all of a sudden one of them asked the teacher: "Have you ever experienced a healing?" The lecturer was dumb-founded. He repeated the results of his research on redaction criticism and form criticism. But the student was not to be put off: "Have you ever experienced a healing?" "No," the teacher said. "But *we* have . . . ," said the students and began to tell their stories. The teacher was introduced into a world quite unknown to him. The continuation of the story is too personal to be printed in this book but it shows that the experiential horizon of the interpreter can help or hinder biblical exegesis.

Or to take another example which Pentecostals will perhaps not like. For many centuries it was written in the Greek manuscripts that there was a female apostle among the early apostles. This is also confirmed by the church fathers.[53] Yet the commentaries which I consulted said, in effect: "Yes, that is what is written in the text, but it must be a mistake. There could not have been a female apostle." The text was therefore read as Iounia*s* (a man's name) rather than Iounia (a woman's name—the original reading). The text was "objectively" there for anybody to read for many centuries. But it could not be "taken in" by male commentators because it was contrary to experience and conviction. When the feminists, on the other hand, read the Bible, they discovered the female contribution; they asked different questions, and got different answers. This is not a plea for subjectivism: the text is there for everybody to read. Any male exegete, once he has been enlightened by the feminist exegetes, can check it for himself. But it needed the specific question which came from a specific female experiential, social, and cultural background to bring this

---

[52] Anderson, Gordon. L., "Hermeneutics," 15, quoting Fuchs, *Horizons*, 343f. Similarly Moore, Rich D., "Approach": "There is a vital place for emotion as well as reason, for imagination as well as logic" (quoted in Arrington, F. L., "Hermeneutics," 388).

[53] See above chapter 20 (p. 268), especially note 37 and Heine, *Women*.

insight to light. I am sure that it is on *this* level, by asking hitherto suppressed questions, that Pentecostals can make a contribution to hermeneutics. How this happened in my own life is the topic of the next section.

Hermeneutics as I Lived It

This is the testimony of my own hermeneutical pilgrimage: I was raised in the experiential and oral spirituality of Pentecostalism. But I was trained in the most rigid methods of historical-critical exegesis. Among my teachers were Hans Conzelmann, Eduard Schweizer, Gerhard Ebeling and Karl Barth. I knew Rudolf Bultmann and Ernst Käsemann personally. I have great respect for the spirituality and integrity of these men. What they said was extremely helpful as long as it was *critical* and *historical*. What can a Pentecostal say when he is shown that some of his presuppositions were based on wrong translations or on very late biblical manuscripts, and not on the best available ones? What can he say when he is shown that the process of handing down an oral culture follows certain rules, which he recognizes only too well from his own experience in the oral culture of Pentecostalism?

But when it came to what the Americans call "the New Hermeneutics,"[54] I could only react with a mild smile. It looked to me like the worst of Pentecostal exegesis (not of the text but of the exegete), with the remarkable difference that a Pentecostal lay preacher who uses a biblical text in order to give significance to his daily sorrows and joys in the factory or in the family at least speaks of *real* experiences in a given social field, while the New Hermeneutics seemed to be speaking of an inner world of the individual, while denying that this was a kind of Christian psychology.

When I began to teach pastors in further education classes (Catholic, Lutheran, and Presbyterian) I was amazed at how little they had absorbed from their university education.

> Having been exposed to a critical reading of Scripture in their seminary education, it is difficult for pastors to return to a pre-critical reading of the text. But once the pastor enters his or her first parish the tools of historical criticism remain a closely guarded secret. Very little that the pastor learned about how to read and interpret Scripture is passed on to the laity . . . For various reasons pastors apparently either cannot or will not lay their exegesis on the table for the congregation.[55]

This is why Walter Wink considers historical-critical exegesis to be "bankrupt":[56] not because it is not true, but because it cannot convey its insights to where they are badly needed, and because future pastors are not taught how

---

[54] What was called at that time *existentiale Interpretation*, mainly based on Heidegger and other existentialist philosophers.

[55] Stroup, *Promise*, 28.

[56] See chapter 15 (pp. 197–99) and Wink, *Bible in Human Transformation*.

to communicate in this way (which is probably, in turn, because their teachers do not know either).[57]

I can put it much more bluntly. We theologians learn Greek, Latin, and Hebrew. We are drilled in all the methods of critical exegesis and critical thinking. In form-criticism we learn to distinguish between myth and history, between parable and allegory, between the literary structure of the gospels and a biography of Jesus. We learn in redaction-criticism that biblical texts are the theological product of authors who are responsible to and sometimes in conflict with a narrative community. Yet in our churches almost nothing of this is made fruitful for the people of God. While we are trained in the details of critical theology, our church members still discuss whether or not Adam and Eve, Noah and Methuselah, were historical persons. They still discuss whether or not God could have created the universe in seven days. They still read the gospels as straightforward biographies.

If I as a theologian would pretend that the *Kleine Nachtmusik* (by Mozart) is written by the Beatles and *Winnie the Pooh* by Shakespeare, I would be considered ignorant, although I am not a literary or music historian. But if similar things and worse are said about the Bible—if genres, times, and authors are mixed up with each other—then this is called "faith." This has nothing to do with faith. It is just ignorance.

This situation is the focus of Eugen Drewermann's work. He uses a parable and says: "If a nomadic tribe leaves an oasis it has two possibilities to secure its water supply. The first is: It takes water provisions on its journey. Only these provisions will soon be used up. One cannot live on this water a whole life long. The second: They dig wells. They bring fresh water from the depths to the surface." Drewermann compares the historical-critical research with the water provisions which we carry. "Here they go, the caravans, through the desert of scholarship and do not even realize that their water bags are empty and that they are condemned to death. To distract themselves on the way they discuss who has the nicer water bags or the older camels (or more modern, or more evangelical, or more catholic)."

Then Drewermann presents his psychological interpretation. We do not need bags full of water, he says, but we must dig deep into the depths of our souls. There we might find wells of fresh water.[58]

Drewermann's critique is justified. He is also not the only one who sees the crisis.[59] The question is only whether his program can fulfill its promises. Digging into the depths of our souls might produce water. Many a Pentecostal

---

[57] Conservatives do not fare better; see Achtemeier, *Inspiration:* "Since no autograph [of the Bible] is known to have survived, it would appear that the conservatives have not only an impregnable position—one cannot prove an error in something one does not possess—but also a highly dubious one. Of what use is an inerrant Scripture which is unavailable?" (52).

[58] Drewermann, *Tiefenpsychologie,* I, 14f.

[59] Ebeling, *Studium,* 23; Stuhlmacher, *Neuen Testaments.*

has found this for instance in prayer. But we might also hit a cesspool, or an oil-well. That is, something useful but not fit for drinking. The depths of our souls also contain some ugly things: it is good that this stuff comes out, but it is not necessarily the pure water of God's revelation. To distinguish between the two is only possible if we can in fact still recognize the difference between clean well-water and chlorinated water; and the taste for good water is given to us in the Bible.

I am not against diving into our own depths. But we should not do it uncritically. There are sources *extra nos*, outside of us. That is why we need map readers—navigators who help us to find our way through the desert. It seems to me that Drewermann does not know much about nomads. No nomad would go all alone into the desert and dig a hole: he would die. He operates within the tribe and within a tradition where there are memories of waterholes and oases. Likewise, no Christian can be a Christian all alone with his Bible. We need "the tribe," the whole universal church in this case, to help us to find our way through the desert.

That the business of navigation and map reading has been made boring or incomprehensible is no reason to give it up. What is the alternative? The alternative is what I call "narrative exegesis." This is not bibliodrama. The bibliodrama asks the question: What do *I* hear, feel and understand in this text? This might be a legitimate exercise in some cases, but it is not what a theologian is called upon to do. Narrative exegesis asks the question: who has written this text, for whom and why? For the biblical texts have not been written for us but for the addressees indicated in these biblical texts. In studying these testimonies of past wanderings through the desert we will discover their extraordinary quality.

That is why I never start Bible studies with an indication that this is the Word of God. I am convinced that it is, both in its linguistic beauty and in its ideas—in this I am more fundamentalistic than the fundamentalists. But why not let listeners discover that for themselves?

This experience is even more powerful when non-church people are asked to take an active part in the production of a narrative exegesis such as those I have been involved in producing. The script is based strictly on historical-critical research, but the exegesis is not presented in the dry form of a lecture. The different layers of Scripture, the social, cultural, and religious context, the conflicts among the narrative community are made visible through music, dance, and drama. With non-Christian dancers and musicians, with folk music groups and male choirs, with brass bands and gymnastic societies, with professional and lay actors (most of them not church-goers), we have produced liturgies, Eucharists, evangelistic campaigns, and biblical and religious musicals. It is amazing how these people, especially the dancers and actors, react to biblical texts. Some Marxist dancers and musicians in the former German Democratic Republic, with whom I produced a play on "the prodigal son," asked me: "Why is it that your texts are so different from the ones we are usually given? Do you have more of them?" "Yes, I have," I answered, "but they are not my texts. This story was first told by a certain Jesus of Nazareth who had to lose his life because he told stories which upset the religious and political leaders of his time." They said: "Nonetheless they are good stories." Certainly they are. That explains why I concentrate on biblical texts. What else could we take? Mark Twain, Shakespeare, the Koran? It is my professional duty to read some of these other texts, but none of them shows the quality of biblical texts. And that is invariably recognized by those who act them, and by those who put them to music and choreography. Some of their reactions have put me to shame. These people realize first and foremost that this is something special, when the biblical texts are not used as proof-texts for *my* ideology but as texts which are our *common* vis-à-vis. Whether these people become Christians or not is not my responsibility, but the responsibility of the Spirit of God. Perhaps it is not even desirable that they become members of a church. The churches might destroy their emerging faith. On the other hand, the churches might repent their ghetto existence and welcome those who try to become Christians in a different way. Thus they will discover aspects of the gospel which they have ignored so far. Here too, even in hermeneutics, I come back to my main topic, and that is: how do we become evangelists, and not just propagandists, of biblical ideas and concepts?

So the answer to the question of this chapter is: no one person interprets Scripture correctly on his own. It is only in conflict, debate, and agreement with the whole people of God, and also with non-Christian readers that we can get a glimpse of what Scripture means.[60]

---

[60] An example of this approach is given in chapter 21, pp. 202–86, where the scripts are mentioned in detail (note 29). See also Hollenweger, "Narrative Exegese"; Korthaus, "Sprechende Bibel" (on an experience at Fuller Theological Seminary).

CHAPTER TWENTY FOUR

Historiography: Who Tells the Pentecostal Story Correctly?

Controversies

Two controversies dominate Pentecostal historiography. The first is: who is at the root of the modern Pentecostal movement? Is it William Joseph Seymour, the black ecumenist and pioneer from Los Angeles, or is it Charles Fox Parham, the "inventor" of the doctrine of tongues as the initial, outward sign of the Baptism of the Spirit? This controversy has been described in detail in chapter 3 (pp. 20–23). It is not just a historical but also a theological controversy, for it decides what one considers to be the heart of Pentecostalism. The fact that most printed Pentecostal declarations of faith contain the "initial evidence" doctrine speaks for the second answer. On the other hand, the fact that in many Third World Pentecostal churches (and as of late also in many Western Pentecostal churches) speaking in tongues does not seem that prominent,[1] and that many Pentecostals have never spoken in tongues, speaks for the first answer. And in fact the weight among Pentecostals does seem to be shifting slowly to the first answer. This is not without difficulty, for the first answer begs the question: "what then is the characteristic of Pentecostalism"? One must remember that "arguments about one's true history are usually struggles between forms of legitimacy."[2]

---

[1] See chapter 10 (pp. 117–31 on Chile); chapter 17 (pp. 218–27); chapter 5 (pp. 41–53 on South Africa).

[2] Wacker, "Bibliography," 75.

This leads us to the second historical controversy: "What is a tenable definition of Pentecostalism?" I consider this question unanswerable for the time being; the definition I gave earlier seems to be inadequate now: "All the groups who profess at least two religious crisis experiences (1. baptism or rebirth; 2. The baptism of the Spirit), the second being subsequent to and different from the first one and the second usually, but not always, being associated with speaking in tongues."[3] Kilian McDonnell suggests an alternative definition: "Those Christians who stress the power and presence of the Holy Spirit and the Gifts of the Spirit directed toward the proclamation that Jesus Christ is Lord to the glory of God the Father."[4] Finally, from inside the Pentecostal movement comes a third definition: "All Pentecostals agree on the presence and demonstration of the charismata in the modern church, but beyond this common agreement there is much diversity as in all the other branches of Christianity."[5]

It seems to me that before we can define Pentecostalism we have to know more about it as a worldwide movement: its convictions, history, liturgies, and social practices. Unfortunately the historiographical situation is not as good as one would wish it to be. We have very few scholarly histories and descriptions of Pentecostal churches. There are some good denominational histories in the USA,[6] one (historically out-dated) from Germany, some histories from Scandinavia,[7] a beginning of a history in France and Portugal,[8] and works on Pentecostalism in Belgium,[9] Holland,[10] and Great Britain.[11] But we are not

---

[3] In *The Pentecostals*, xxi.

[4] McDonnell (with Bittlinger), *Problem*, quoted by Villafañe, *The Liberating Spirit*, 85, and Synan, "Pentecostalism," 32. Synan's paper is an excellent overview of the different variations in Pentecostalism.

[5] Villafañe, *The Liberating Spirit*, 121, quoting from the draft of Synan's "Pentecostalism" (presented at the consultation on Confessing the Apostolic Faith from the Perspective of Pentecostal Churches, Fuller Theological Seminary, Pasadena, Calif., October 22–24, 1986), 2 (unpubl.). I did not find this quote in the printed version of Synan's paper (note 4); Villafañe summarizes Synan.

[6] Good overview in Wacker, "Bibliography." Histories include: Kendrick, *Promise Fulfilled* (see Burgess, "Kendrick," 516); Menzies, *Anointed to Serve* (see Spittler, "Menzies," 602); Brumback, *Suddenly* (see Wilson, D. J., "Brumback," 100); Blumhofer, *Assemblies*; Poloma, *Crossroads*. An important history on Hispanic Pentecostals in the U.S. comes from de Leon, *Silent*. One of the best sources for the U.S. is Everett Le Roy Moore's *Handbook of Pentecostal Denominations in the U.S.* (unfortunately unpubl.).

[7] Fleisch, *Pfingstbewegung;* Strand/Strøm/Ski, *Urkristendommen;* Bloch-Hoell, *Pinsebevegelsen;* Schmidt, Wolfgang, *Finnland;* Sundstedt, *Pingstväckelsen.*

[8] Stotts, *Pentecôtisme;* Pfister, *Soixante;* idem, "Culture"; Dudley, "Portugal," 49–63.

[9] Bundy, "Belgium"; idem, "Rietdijk"; idem, "Renewal"; Brandt-Bessire, "L'implantation," 5–23.

[10] van der Laan, C. and P., *Pinksteren* (for more literature by the brothers van der Laan see Short Titles List). Wumkes, *Pinksterbeweging,* 1917.

[11] Kay, *Inside;* Massey, *Sound*. This is an extraordinarily careful historical research based on hitherto unknown sources, unfortunately unpublished. Extracts:

well-served with histories from Eastern Europe,[12] and there are no histories of the important Brazilian[13] and Chilean movements,[14] not to speak of the rest of Latin America.[15]

There are only glimpses from Africa,[16] Asia,[17] and Australia,[18] and even such an important country as Italy[19] has still to wait for its history of Pentecostalism. I expect a newer generation of Pentecostal scholars to produce monographs not just on their own Pentecostal denomination but on the whole of Pentecostalism in their respective countries.[20] Once this work is done, we

---

"Flirtation with Elim" and in the popular (poorly footnoted) *Another Springtime.* More on Gee in Ross, *Gee,* and idem, "Sectarian" and Bundy, "Gee" and in *The Pentecostals,* 208–13. Further: Kay, "1930s"; idem, "War Years"; Hocken, "Layman"; idem, "Polhill"; idem, *Streams;* Cartwright, *Evangelists* (on Jeffreys); idem, "Jeffreys"; Gerloff, *Plea;* Worsfold, *Great Britain.*

[12] Sandru, "Rumänien"; idem, *Doctrinele* (reviewed by Bundy: "What one finds here is one of the first attempts by a Pentecostal theologian to wrestle seriously with the classical Christian heritage of East and West, early and modern, patristic and Romanian Orthodox, Charismatic and Reformed Evangelical. It is quite a remarkable achievement." Bundy, *EPTA Bulletin* 9/3+4, 1989, 76–79, quote 79; also in *Pneuma* 12/1, 1990, 56–57). Bundy, "Roumanian" (Bundy speaks of a "deep and sincere appreciation for and loyalty to the government," 21). On the former USSR see *The Pentecostals,* 267–87; Ceuta, "Romania."

[13] Novaes, *Os;* Rolim, *Pentecostais.* See also *The Pentecostals* (75ff.) for older literature.

[14] Lalive d'Epinay, *Haven of the Masses.* Martin, David, *Tongues.* These and most other literature on Pentecostals in Latin America is not historical but sociological. But see in this book chapters 7 (pp. 81–98) and 10 (pp. 117–31).

[15] Westmeier, *Reconciling* (on Bogota); Gaxiola-Gaxiola, *Mexican;* Saracco, *Argentine;* Gill, *Contextualised;* Flora, *Colombia;* Huamán, *Primera;* Hidalgo, *Perú;* Domínguez, *Pioneros;* Peréz-Torres, *Puerto Rico.*

[16] See the respective chapters in my *Handbuch. The Pentecostals,* 111–75 (lit.); Turner, *Independent Church;* Mitchell–Turner, *Bibliography* (basic) and follow-up by the same authors in *Journal of Religion in Africa* 1, 1968, 173–210. Turner, "Nigeria"; Oshun, "Perspective." Chapters 5 (pp. 41–53) and 6 (pp. 54–80) in this volume. Important is the *Centre for New Religious Movements,* founded by H. W. Turner at the Selly Oak Colleges, Birmingham. It has files on every country and on most independent churches throughout the world.

[17] The respective chapters in my *Handbuch.* Hoerschelmann, *Christliche Gurus;* Yoo, *Korean Pentecostalism* (chapter 8, pp. 99–105 in this book lit.); Raj, *Christian Folk-Religion;* Bergunder, "Die südindische Pfingstbewegung."

[18] Chant, "Australien"; idem, *Heart;* Worsfold, *New Zealand;* Smith, Denis and Gwen, *River.*

[19] Traettino, *Pentecostale;* Tortorelli, *I Pentecostali;* Castiglione, *Movimento;* Schiavone, *I Pentecostali;* Moscato, "Alcuni"; Lucente, *Movimento;* Cito, *Movimento;* Bonanno, *Aspetti.* Most of these are unpublished dissertations at the University of Bari; they are discussed in the Spanish edition of *The Pentecostals* (*El Pentecostalismo,* 233ff.) For earlier research see *The Pentecostals,* 251–66. A new publication by Rochat, *Regime* (reviewed by David Bundy in *Pneuma* 14/1, Spring 1992, 94–95).

[20] One of the most careful overviews of international Pentecostalism was the typescript by Du Plessis, *Brief History.* It contains very extensive lists and

can take stock, look at the whole picture, and try to define what it is we are looking at. The purpose of the footnotes in this chapter (as incomplete as they are) is to help future researchers find the more scholarly and more accurate dissertations and books (the popular books are well-known enough) in these areas.

I believe that there is something unifying in the Pentecostal movement, but it is probably not on the level of doctrine. It is a way of doing theology: experience-related, open to oral forms, ecumenical (by virtue of its many worldwide forms), and expressing itself in categories of pneumatology.

Pentecostalism is in a position similar to that of the early church, around the year 100 AD. At that time there was barely a unifying confession of faith. Different confessions for baptism were in use. However, the Lord's Prayer, a body of hymns, and above all an emerging corpus of canonical writings (the Gospels, the Pauline epistles) served as a bond between the different expressions of Christianity. Perhaps something similar could happen in Pentecostalism.

Research Reviews, Bibliographies, etc.

The source situation is rather good. That is why a *consortium* has been founded towards the task of photocopying all available Pentecostal periodicals worldwide, and offering this collection to university libraries and Pentecostal colleges.[21] It is an important step forward, but it is not clear whether this ambitious program will come to fruition.

There are a number of good bibliographies (but mostly on American and Western literature)[22] and a few limited research reviews.[23] There are the research conferences which Jean-Daniel Plüss has organized in Europe[24] and the research conferences of the Society for Pentecostal Studies (SPS)[25] which

---

descriptions of Pentecostal churches for certain countries (e.g., Nigeria). This typescript has—as far as I can see—only been used by me. See also his *Brief History of American Pentecostal Movements* (unpub.).

[21] *Pentecostal Research and Preservation Consortium.* Founding meeting March 2–3, 1992 at Krattigen, Switzerland. Present were Vinson Synan, Bill Jernigan, Paul Chappell, Jim Zeigler, William Faupel, Ken Gill, David Bundy (all USA), Walter Hollenweger, Jean-Daniel Plüss (both Switzerland), Cornelius van der Laan (Holland), Desmond Cartwright (Britain), and Bertil Carlsson (Sweden).

[22] Jones, C. E., *Perfectionist;* idem, *Holiness;* idem, *Pentecostal.* (Bundy: "As it is, the volume perpetuates the myth that U.S. Pentecostalism is *the* major focus of the Pentecostal movements, giving the false impression that nothing has been happening in Pentecostal circles in Europe, Africa, Mexico, South or Central America . . . or other Third World countries," Bundy in a review of Jones, *Pentecostal,* in *EPTA Bulletin* 4/1, 1985, 5–6.) Mills, *Charismatic;* Wacker, "Bibliography," note 2.

[23] Hollenweger, "Ein Forschungsbericht." This is the first and as far as I know still the only international polyglot research review. It is of course out-dated and inadequate. Idem, "Priorities"; idem, "Europe"; idem, "After"; *The Pentecostals,* 497ff.; Spittler, "Suggested"; Bundy, "Scholarly"; Hocken with Cartwright, "European," 267–78.

[24] Bundy, "Perspectives." See also the important volume *Conference.*

[25] The conference papers of the SPS are available from SPS, *Pneuma,* Gaithersburg, Md.

regularly produce important papers on limited subjects. Finally, there are three scholarly periodicals[26] which no university library and no Pentecostal college can afford to be without.

A word might be said on my own research. My own *Handbuch der Pfingstbewegung* was an almost foolhardy attempt at describing the worldwide Pentecostal movement.[27] That it has not been superseded, as David Bundy says,[28] is astonishing. It is now out-dated and badly needs an institute or a group of scholars to produce something better. So far, however, this has not happened. In a limited sense, the *Dictionary of Pentecostal and Charismatic Movements*[29] took up this task. Since its publication this *Dictionary* has been my constant companion. It is critical and ecumenical, both in its scope and the wide range of its contributors from many different churches. It also represents (probably for the first time) a kind of inner-Pentecostal ecumenicity, by including for instance the Oneness and black Pentecostals. The articles on the US are precise and well written, those on Europe are short but extremely valuable, battling valiantly with sources in many different languages (and succeeding, primarily due to the input of David Bundy and Peter Hocken). The articles on biblical books are conservative but acceptable; those on ecumenical topics are of an astonishingly wide horizon. Not surprisingly, the articles by Catholics and on Catholic issues breathe a completely new spirit of understanding.

Compared to the *Handbuch* the first volume of *The Pentecostals*[30] is even more patchy. This was rightly pointed out by reviewers, although I was fully aware, in the writing, of the ommission of certain stories which are included in my *Handbuch* but had to be excluded from *The Pentecostals* to avoid giving a complete history of Pentecostalism in each country; instead, I concentrated on some of Pentecostalism's characteristics, using examples to highlight each

---

[26] *Pneuma. The Journal of the Society for Pentecostal Studies,* 1979ff. (Gaithersburg, Md.). *EPTA Bulletin,* 1981ff. (Elim Bible College, Nantwich, England). *Journal of Pentecostal Theology* (Sheffield Academic Press, 1992ff.).

[27] For a description of the *Handbuch* see *The Pentecostals,* xvi, 497–98.

[28] Bundy, "Scholarly."

[29] A most interesting review of the *Dictionary* by Kilian McDonnell may be found in *Pneuma* 13/1, 1991, 83–85.

[30] Some reactions to the German version of *The Pentecostals* are included in *The Pentecostals,* 499–502. The English version was received well on the whole, but Pentecostals did not know what to think of it. British Pentecostals did not like it, perhaps because I had given too much prominence to Donald Gee, or perhaps because I had relied too heavily on Bryan Wilson's *Sects.* Wacker, "Bibliography," 65, mentions "numerous factual mistakes," but on request he was not able to mention one. I am, of course, sure that there are "many factual mistakes," both in that volume and in this one. In such a complex work, this is inevitable. Zopfi had started a critical series on *The Pentecostals* (*The Pentecostals,* 500), but he was stopped from continuing the series probably by his colleagues for reasons unknown to me. Later he used the book as propaganda with Catholic priests. Now it is used in most Pentecostal colleges (see back cover of the third edition of *The Pentecostals*).

aspect. A complete history of each country would have amounted to a very boring and less useful book.

Equally, this volume is not a complete overview of the problems and promises of Pentecostalism, but rather an articulation of the state of the debate at the present, as I see it. Others will have to take up the torch.

In the future we need good archives, a network of international scholars, scholarly conferences, and historical (not just sociological[31]) monographs on specific countries. It looks as if this is going to happen. However, why should it not be a task for the *World Pentecostal Conference*?

---

[31] I was also guilty of giving too much prominence to sociological works because they were less polemical than the theological ones.

V

THE ECUMENICAL ROOT

CHAPTER TWENTY FIVE

Ecumenical Beginnings

In this chapter I want to establish the fact that Pentecostalism started in most places as an ecumenical renewal movement in the mainline churches, not unlike the charismatic movement in the '60s and the so-called "third wave" in the '80s. That this renewal movement developed later in most places into Pentecostal free churches is an important indication of what is likely to happen to the charismatic movement, unless we learn from the mistakes of the past on both sides. This matter is obviously of concern only if one considers the fragmentation of Pentecostalism into so many churches and organizations to be undesirable and inconsistent with the proper functioning of the kingdom of God.

Since the early 1910s a charismatic movement has existed in Europe within the traditional churches. In many cases it was the starting point of "classical Pentecostal churches," but in some cases it existed and exists alongside Pentecostal churches.

Obviously I have to be highly selective, presenting only a few of the more outstanding of these ecumenical charismatic theologians.

Jonathan A. A. B. Paul (1853–1931)[1]

Jonathan Paul was a Lutheran pastor in Germany. His father was *Diaconus* at the church of St. Stephen in Garth an der Oder. His mother came from a doctor's family. At his

---

[1] Some of the material in this chapter has been published in Hollenweger, " 'Touching.' " There is a scholarly and reliable biography by Giese *(Pastor)*. See also Bundy, "Paul"; *The Pentecostals*, 231–41 and passim (index of names); *Handbuch* 08.097; Hocken, "Mülheim"; More in the German version of *The Pentecostals* (*Enthusiastisches Christentum*, 201–43). Jonathan Paul was not the only Lutheran pastor in the German Pentecostal Movement who remained a Lutheran infant baptizing pastor to the end of his life (see e.g., K. Ecke, in *Handbuch*, 07.390).

baptism, his father "pledged little Jonathan to become at some time a preacher of the Gospel." Jonathan Paul wrote later about his (infant) baptism:

> My father had five sons. It is only me whom he had pledged by God's providence to become a pastor. And I am the only one that in fact became a pastor of all the five sons. I can therefore not deny that the words uttered at my baptism were of prophetic significance.[2]

The significance of this experience might be one reason why all his life Paul defended infant baptism[3]—while not denying the possibility of believer's baptism—and why his Mülheim Association of Christian Fellowship[4] (a federation of Pentecostal communities partly of a free-church character, partly within the existing established Lutheran and Reformed churches) practices both infant *and* believer's baptism up to the present day.

These churches, although the oldest Pentecostal organization in Germany, have been consistently ignored by most Pentecostal authors writing in English,[5] with Michael Harper even calling them "a very small group and barely Pentecostal."[6] This is all the more reason to bring to light the leader and pioneer of this group. Paul became a conscious Christian through the sermons of his father.[7] Then, in Stettin's gymnasium, he discovered the richness of German literature. In 1872 he passed his matriculation examination and went to the university. He would have preferred to study medicine, but in obedience to his father's pledge, he took up the study of theology at Greifswald and Leipzig. There, he passed his second theological examination with a thesis on "The Doctrine of the Holy Spirit" (written in Latin!). Although a successful pastor and youth worker, Paul was constantly searching for a deeper spiritual life. One day, when performing a child funeral, Paul read from the Lutheran liturgy, "Like as a father pitieth his children, so the Lord pitieth them that fear him." When he came to the passage, " . . . unto such as keep his covenant and his testimonies," his conscience awoke and asked him: "You, pastor, when will you begin to keep his covenants?"[8]

On June 17, 1890 Paul underwent an experience of sanctification, associated with a vision, which led him among other things to abstain from smoking. He did not regard smoking as a sin in itself, but he wanted to devote the money saved to the church's mission. His biographer, the Lutheran pastor Ernst Giese, says that Paul's experience of sanctification

> . . . is by no means of a mystical or ecstatic nature. If the account is read closely, it can clearly be seen that it is dictated not by an extraordinary mental impulse,

---

[2] Paul, "Krone."
[3] Paul, *Taufe;* idem, *Die Taufe.*
[4] On this see *The Pentecostals*, 218–43.
[5] Carmichael, "Pentecost"; Nikoloff, "Awakening"; but not Gee, *Pentecostal* and astonishingly *not* Robeck, "Ecclesiology," in particular, 510.
[6] M. Harper, *Renewal* 41 (Oct.–Nov. 1972) 10.
[7] Krust, *Fünfzig.*
[8] Paul, "Krone."

or any exalted emotion, but by a perfectly sober self-criticism, which was the basis of this decisive crisis experience. Therefore Paul never regarded himself as a mystic or ecstatic.[9]

Paul thought that, according to Scripture, this experience of sanctification—also known as the baptism of the Spirit—ought to occur suddenly. But he was unwilling to assert that those who had not experienced this sudden baptism of the Spirit did not possess the gift of the Holy Spirit.[10] On various occasions Paul testified about his own experience, and he laid particular stress on one point: "I would like to express the wish that . . . what I have said should not be understood as a doctrine but as what it is, a *testimony* of what the death and resurrection of Jesus have brought *me.*"[11] But for him one thing was certain: "One who is reborn not only desires to do the will of God, but is also able to do it."[12]

In accordance with that part of the early Pentecostal movement which had strong ties with the holiness movement, Paul's understanding of regeneration and Spirit-baptism (sometimes the two terms are identical) had a strong connotation of sanctification. Yet Paul's teaching of sanctification has not been properly understood, either by his opponents[13] or by his friends. Admittedly the responsibility for this lies to some extent with the obscure and contradictory nature of his accounts, which is the result of the different pastoral situations in which they were offered.

Paul's doctrine of sanctification is expressed in a laborious and inflated style in his voluminous writings. If one attempts to reduce it to a clear formula, however, it turns out to be a Wesleyan doctrine of perfection.[14] This can be seen clearly from his concept of sin:

> Only culpable failings are sin, not blameless ones . . . Where there is disobedience, there is sin; and where there is obedience, there is no sin, but human short-sightedness and limitation . . . Consequently, a pure heart is a heart purified of disobedience (Heb. 8:10). We see from this that what matters is not the extent of the knowledge one possesses, but obedience . . . Thus what matters is that *according to one's* knowledge one is obedient to the Spirit of God and allows oneself to be led by him.[15]

---

[9] Giese, *Pastor,* 27.

[10] Paul, *Kraft.*

[11] Quoted in Fleisch, *Gemeinschaftsbewegung,* 127.

[12] Paul, *Kraft,* 41, quoted by Giese, *Pastor,* 51. (I could not find this passage in the third edition of Paul's book).

[13] Pastor Thimme, *Auf der Warte* (1920–21), quoted in Fleisch, *Pfingstbewegung* 273; cf. Paul, "Antwort."

[14] "In the view I hold I am in the fullest sense a follower of John Wesley; I have been conscious of being in full agreement with the substance of Stockmayer's doctrine in his tract *Gnade und Sünde,* even though I have used other expressions, in accordance with my own understanding of Scripture" (quote in Giese, *Pastor,* 223). On Otto Stockmayer see *Handbuch,* 10.879 and 05.28.047.

[15] Paul, "Herz," 19f.

This is confirmed by comments in his translation of the New Testament, the so-called Mülheim Testament.[16]

From the very beginning Jonathan Paul and his colleagues[17] rejected the doctrine of the "initial evidence." Already in the first issue of his magazine *Pfingstgrüsse* he wrote: "It is not our view that only those who have spoken in tongues have received the Holy Spirit."[18] Speaking in tongues was to be desired as a gift of the Spirit (and in fact Paul himself practiced speaking in tongues frequently), but—in contrast with the teaching of many other Pentecostals—it was not considered to be the sign that the baptism of the Spirit had been received.[19] Paul also considered speaking in tongues a natural human gift, which the Holy Spirit could use if He wished.[20] This has been the doctrine of the Mülheim Association until this day.[21]

Since 1968, ecumenical contacts have been established between the Mülheim Association, the World Council of Churches, and other (Catholic and Protestant) churches in Germany.[22] In spite of this recent ecumenical spirit the Mülheim Association has been from its beginning the target of more harsh attacks than any other Pentecostal church in the world. In the *Berlin Declaration* (1909) it was stated that the spirit in Pentecostalism is "not from above but from below."[23] None of the newly emerging congregations from the charismatic movement in Germany has even considered joining the Mülheim Association. Ecumenicity and sober theological work does not pay! What is valued in our world is aggressive, market-oriented religion!

In summary, the pioneering ministry of Paul and his colleagues is important for the following reasons: They practiced spiritual gifts, including speaking in tongues, within a loose federation which contained "Pentecostal free churches" *and* associations within the established churches;[24] they did not teach a baptism of the Spirit with speaking in tongues as the initial sign, but believed in growing into deeper experiences of the Spirit; and they did not discard theological scholarship. In fact, they were the first (1914) and so far the only Pentecostals to produce

---

[16] *Das Neue Testament in der Sprache der Gegenwart*, 1914, 1968[7].

[17] E.g., the Reformed pastor C. A. Voget (*Handbuch* 08.543), the Lutheran pastor R. Lettau (*Handbuch*, 07.843) and Karl Ecke (see note 24).

[18] Paul, "Sollen." See also Krust, "Geistesbewegung."

[19] Paul, "Beantwortung"; cf. *Kampf*, 2f and 6f.

[20] Quoted in Fleisch, *Pfingstbewegung*, 79f.; cf. Lettau, "Briefmappe"; Paul, "Verhältnis."

[21] Krust, *Glauben*.

[22] Krust, "Churches"; idem, "Mülheimer"; idem, "Pfingstbewegung"; idem, "Mülheim-Ruhr"; idem, "Ökumenische"; idem, "Uppsala"; idem, "Heilige Geist"; Rottmann, "Mülheim-Ruhr"; Steiner, L., "Oekumenische"; Lemke, "Begegnung"; *The Pentecostals*, 442–44.

[23] Hocken, "Berlin," discussed in detail in the German version of *The Pentecostals*.

[24] Already in 1911 (!) Karl Ecke, a Lutheran charismatic pastor, began publishing the results of his research on Kaspar Schwenckfeld. For sources see Short Titles List under Karl Ecke.

a translation of the New Testament.[25] Furthermore, they rejected the doctrine of the verbal inspiration of the Bible as unchristian.[26] On the other hand, they saw clearly that theological learning is of only relative importance.

Louis Dallière (1887–1976)

A very old and highly indigenous charismatic movement exists in France (after all, the tradition of the Camisards has never been completely forgotten[27]) and in French-speaking Switzerland.[28] Pentecostalism has always had some friends and supporters within the French Reformed Church. Already in the thirties the Swiss Reformed minister Fritz de Rougemont had opened his church to Pentecostal preachers such as Douglas Scott and Donald Gee.

One of the leading charismatic pastors within the Reformed Church of France was Louis Dallière.[29] He

> has been a historiographical enigma. Although he was actively involved in the beginnings of the Pentecostal movement in two countries [France and Belgium], because he did not "come out" of the Reformed Church he was removed from Pentecostal historiography (both written and oral) and his participation minimized.[30]

His biography is most interesting.

> It was in Chicago on 4 July 1887 that he was born, the son of an English Anglican mother and a French Catholic father. The father was employed there by a French bank. After the family's return to France, Dallière was baptized as an Anglican in 1901 in Nice. There was apparently little family religious involvement until 1907 when the death of a younger sibling brought the family into contact with the Reformed Church and Dallière into Sunday School.[31] Shortly thereafter, in 1910, he had an initial conversion experience.[32]

In 1915, he experienced a second conversion. Part of that experience was a sense of call to the pastoral ministry; thus, he studied at the Faculty of

---

[25] Note 16.

[26] Krust, *Glauben*, 117, 120; C. O. Voget, *Pfingstbotschaft*, 1921, 201ff., quoted in Krust, *Fünfzig*, 237ff.; Gericke, *Christliche*, 16.

[27] Gagg, *Kirche;* Poujol, *Cévenne.*

[28] On this see the German version of *The Pentecostals* (*Enthusiastisches Christentum,* 279–80), and *Handbuch*, 08.212.

[29] The following is based on the sources, given in the footnotes and on excellent articles by Bundy, "Making"; idem, "Louis Dallière"; appeared in an extended form under the title "Apologist"; idem, "Belgium"; idem, "Renewal"; idem, "L'émergence." Bundy's writings contain detailed and commented bibliographies. See also Dallière, *D'aplomb.* Lovsky, *Louis Dallière;* and Robert, "Dallière" (based on unpublished official and private notes). Hocken, "Dallière."

[30] See as an example Stotts, *Pentecôtisme.* The quote from Bundy, "Apologist," 85 and similarly Bundy, "Louis Dallière," 60.

[31] Dallière discussed the influence of his mother on his spiritual development in "Toi."

[32] The quote from Bundy, "Apologist," 88. Similarly in Bundy, "Making," 42.

Theology in Paris (1915–1921), receiving his theological formation from figures such as Eugène de Faye, Maurice Goguel and especially Wilfrid Monod.[33] He spent one year of this period in the military.

During 1921, he received his *baccalauréat en théologie,* began serious studies in philosophy, and married Marie-Caroline Boegner, daughter of Pastor Alfred Boegner (later the president of the French Reformed Church). Boegner's other daughter had married Gabriel Marcel, an important French philosopher. The relationship with his brother-in-law appears to have been rather influential in the development of Dallière's thought—Marcel introduced Dallière to the philosophy of the American William E. Hocking.[34] In 1922 Dallière spent the academic year studying at Harvard with Hocking. He returned to Paris for the year 1923–1924 where he finished a licentiate in theology[35] and began to prepare for doctoral studies (which he never finished). As pastor in Charmes-sur-Rhône he read widely, and seems at one point to have experienced a crisis of spirituality.[36] For one year (1932–1933) he taught at Montpellier, where he also invited Donald Gee to meet the faculty. However, his appointment was not renewed, primarily because of his growing sympathy with Pentecostalism.[37]

> The British Pentecostal evangelist Douglas Scott, who had been greatly aided and defended by Dallière, soon found it impossible to work with him. Here the socio-economic factors became important. Scott, the uneducated musician turned evangelist,[38] had most influence among the lower middle class and lower classes. Most of his converts were from among the alienated and disaffected Roman Catholic population. The Protestant Church remained middle class. Neither side was able to work with the other for long. However, a "charismatic" tradition was maintained within the protestant churches of France . . . The tragedy is that the two expressions of the movement, the one with a sophisticated intellectual analysis and the other based on the function of therapeutic narratives and on eschatological expectations, could not find grounds for mutual appreciation as well as cooperation.[39]

With the French Reformed Church, too, relations were uneasy, although Dallière remained pastor to the end of his life in Charmes-sur-Rhône. The bone of contention was baptism: Dallière argued for both forms of baptism, which now is accepted by the French Reformed Church and to some extent also by the Reformed Church in francophone Switzerland. At the time,

---

[33] Bundy, "Making," 42; idem, "Apologist," 89.

[34] Marcel, "W. E. Hocking."

[35] Dallière's thesis for the licentiate was: *Peut-on démontrer que l'apôtre Pierre est mort a Rome? Sujet d'un livre récent de H. Lietzmann.* On the basis of this work, Dallière published "Mort."

[36] Bundy publishes a telling text by Dallière in French: Bundy, "Making," 43; idem, "Apologist," 89.

[37] Bundy, "Apologist," 94. Thoorens, *L'Union,* 36–37.

[38] On Scott see Hocken, "Scott" and Stotts, *Pentecôtisme.*

[39] Bundy, "Making," 59.

however, this did not seem possible. Dallière gave up publication and served quietly as a country pastor[40] until his death.

> Dallière's vision for the Pentecostal movement is that it be a revival within the Church, that it be theologically orthodox, mission-oriented and ecumenical. He was fighting against two tendencies, that of the French Protestant Churches to draw theological and ecclesiological boundaries which would exclude the revival, and that of the English band leader turned evangelist, Douglas Scott, who wanted to establish a new denomination on the English and American models.

Dallière was, as Bundy confirms, one of the first really charismatic theologians.[41] The *Union de Prière*, which he founded and which exists to this day, is a cross between the new charismatic organizations and the Catholic or ecumenical "charismatic communities."[42] The participants sign a "commitment card" which contains twelve points. These include:

> In the morning of every day I will give my first thought to God by speaking a short prayer, reciting a Bible verse or a stanza from a hymn.
>
> Every day I will have my quiet time . . .
>
> In remembrance of Jesus I will take part in the Lord's Supper whenever there is an opportunity.
>
> I will give ten percent of my income for the work of the Lord.
>
> Every day I will pray for the revival of my church and for the coming of the Kingdom of God . . . [43]

It was not expected that all participants would fulfill all the requirements. On the back of the card is written: "In order to use this card properly, one chooses at the beginning only one or two resolutions which one wants to carry out. One writes the number of the resolution and the date on the back of the card, signs and carries out this pledge faithfully."

This movement has not led, as one might think, to the formation of new sects. On the contrary, ecumenical relations very soon were taken up with other Protestant churches, with Orthodox churches[44] (rare in Pentecostal circles!), and recently also with the Catholic churches.

In the thirties this Prayer Union invited Pentecostals such as Douglas R. Scott, George Jeffreys, and Donald Gee to their conferences. In the region of

---

[40] Bundy, "Apologist," 110; idem, "Louis Dallière," 78.

[41] Bundy, "Louis Dallière," 69. Bundy, "Apologist," 102.

[42] Hocken, "Communities."

[43] Schaerer–Richemond, *Retour*. Speeches given August 24, 1969, in the Reformed Church of Charmes (mimeographed), 4. See also Roux, *Désunion*.

[44] In his report to the Reformed Regional Synod of Tournon of November 10, 1958, L. Dallière said: "I was in complete concordance with the Greek fathers, and above all with Gregory from Nyssa, for whom the whole mystical life is inspired and indissolubly tied to the sacramental life . . . " (Dallière, "L'Eglise," quoted by Lienhard, *Aspect*, 77).

Ardèche (where the Prayer Union is strongest) Pentecostalism has not created any divisions, writes Henri Schaerer.[45] This is probably exaggerated, for one can find in the yearbook of the French Assemblées de Dieu some assemblies in this very region. Nevertheless, these came much later, and were not splits from the Prayer Union. The relation between the Prayer Union and the classical Pentecostals is described by Jean Paul Lienhard as follows: In spite of the obvious similarity of the Prayer Union to the classical Pentecostal churches (which came into being ten years later!) the Prayer Union has little contact with those churches and in fact with other evangelical circles.[46] Louis Dallière confirms this, writing:

> My ministry and my thinking have been certainly enriched by the Pentecostal movement. The Prayer Union is open to certain teachings of the Pentecostals. In this respect there is rapprochement. But there is no real dialogue. For these brethren I am more of a "black sheep." In their opinion I should have left the Reformed Church and joined them. Because I have not done this, I am a compromiser, an unfaithful, I am wrong.[47]

Yet the Prayer Union has built up a charismatic movement within the Reformed churches of France which is resolutely determined to serve the whole church, and which rejects all attempts at sectarian isolation. The possibility is not excluded that the Prayer Union, having fulfilled its purpose, might be dissolved.[48]

The "Charter" of the Prayer Union is one of the most interesting theological documents one can find in the Pentecostal and charismatic movement. It tries to combine the dynamics of a kind of non-monastic "Pentecostal religious order" with the breadth and generosity of the Reformation-based concept of faith. Here is an example:

> It is well possible that the number of the saved ones at the last judgment is greater than the number of the people who have been converted and have consecrated their lives to Christ. And the reverse is possible also: that among those who consider themselves to be converted there might be hypocrites who will be rejected at the last judgment. Despite these provisos we believe that the church is normally composed of "living stones," i.e., of those people who have met Jesus, who have been gripped by him (that being the reality of baptism) and who serve him with all their heart within the church (that being the meaning of the eucharist) (1 Peter 2:5).[49]

In a most instructive chapter on the Jewish people, the Charter describes "the conversion of the Jewish people, prophetically foretold in the Scriptures" as "a general subject for the intercession of the Prayer Union,"[50] an insight

---

[45] Schaerer–Richemond, *Retour*, 8.
[46] Lienhard, *Aspect*, 78.
[47] Letter of L. Dallière to J. P. Lienhard (quoted in Lienhard, *Aspect*, 78).
[48] Schaerer–Richemond, *Retour*, 17.
[49] *Charte*, pars. 5–7.
[50] Ibid., par. 25.

which the authors of this document gained when studying again Romans 9–11 during the persecution of the Jews under the German occupation.[51] This has had far-reaching consequences—obviously under the influence of Karl Barth, who seems also to have influenced their understanding of baptism.[52] But a mission to the Jews is radically rejected, "because the goal assigned here to prayer is not that some Jews might be converted (which has always happened), but that all that which is from God in Judaism might be integrated at once into the body of Christ."[53] "One can expect that God will raise among the Jews themselves apostles who will speak of Christ to their brothers."[54]

On the "visible unity of the body of Christ" the Charter has this to say:

> The Prayer Union prays that within the Catholic church more and more people might become faithful disciples of Christ, a fact which will overcome the tremendous difficulties between Rome and the other two branches of Christianity.[55]

The Prayer Union is not against culture and education.[56] Yet on the subject of money it is rather critical: "This idol has to be struck down in order that Christ might reign,"[57] a program which, it is suggested, may be carried out by means of generous financial giving (about which every member decides individually). The spiritual gifts which are known in the Pentecostal movement are practiced but "these experiences are in no case a condition for becoming a member of the Prayer Union. The members who do not feel called to exercise these gifts are fully free in this respect."[58]

It is clear that these French charismatic Protestants have made an original theological, ecumenical, and political[59] contribution, which combines ecumenical breadth and biblical discipline within the framework of a Pentecostal spirituality. Without exaggerating, one can say that the charismatic movement in France not only came thirty years before American neo–Pentecostalism, but pioneered a "theology on living and thinking charismata" which seems to have overcome some of the weakness of classical and neo–Pentecostalism.

---

[51] Schaerer–Richemond, *Retour,* 12; *Charte,* par. 45.

[52] Schaerer–Richemond, *Retour,* 12.

[53] *Charte,* pars. 25–29. That is not quite what Bundy writes about the "conversion of Jews" on the basis of Dallière's article "L'anti–judaisme." Bundy, "Making," 46f. On this topic see also *Expérience* (22/85, 1992), a French Pentecostal periodical.

[54] *Charte,* par. 30.

[55] Ibid., par. 37.

[56] Ibid., par. 111, and Dallière's report to the Synod of Tournon (see note 44), quote in Lienhard, *Aspect,* 77.

[57] *Charte,* par. 110.

[58] Ibid., par. 104. See also Dallière, "Mouvement"; Bundy, "Apologist," 99; idem, "Louis Dallière," 65.

[59] The fact that they reject a mission to the Jews means that they accept them as equal partners, and this acceptance is in itself a highly political testimony. It means of course that they were part and parcel of that company of Christians in France who risked their lives in hiding the Jews from the Germans.

Alexander A. Boddy (1854–1930)[60]

Another of these ecumenical pioneers of Pentecostalism is the Anglican rector Alexander Boddy, who remained in the service of his church until the end of his life, baptized infants, and was at the same time the unchallenged pioneer of early British Pentecostalism.

Boddy was originally a lawyer. He traveled widely in the world (including Russia), wrote many travel books, and was made a fellow of the Royal Geographical Society (England) and of the Imperial Geographical Society (Russia). The Keswick movement[61] and the Welsh revival[62] influenced him greatly. He studied theology at Durham University and was ordained by Bishop J. B. Lightfoot, the famous New Testament scholar. After his ordination, he was sent to a run-down parish, the miners' village of Sunderland (near Durham), where the previous priest had been a drunkard. Boddy built up that parish by hard work, street preaching, and taking active part in helping the striking miners.

In 1907 he traveled to Oslo and invited T. B. Barratt[63] to his parish. Before long, Boddy had experienced the baptism of the Spirit, and his parish became the focal point of emerging Pentecostalism in Britain, if not in Europe. His wife was healed of asthma and herself exercised the gift of healing. Among those who received the baptism of the Spirit when she laid hands on them were Gerrit R. Polman from Holland (see below, pp. 345–47), the Bradford plumber Smith Wigglesworth (who prophesied later to David Du Plessis that he would become an instrument of Pentecostal ecumenicity[64]). Stanley Frodsham[65] was also baptized in the Spirit in Sunderland, and Jonathan Paul (see above, pp. 334–38) received an important impetus from his visit to Sunderland.

Boddy provided a link between the different Pentecostal groups through his paper *Confidence,* his Whitsuntide Conventions in Sunderland, and the *Pentecostal Missionary Union,*[66] which he founded together with Cecil

---

[60] The sources for this section are: van der Laan, C., "Portret"; Bundy, "Boddy"; Cartwright, "Boddy"; Blumhofer, "Boddy"; Kay, "Boddy"; Robinson, *Clergymen; The Pentecostals,* 184f.

[61] Bundy, "Keswick."

[62] *The Pentecostals,* 176–84; Jones, C. E., "Welsh."

[63] Bundy, "Barratt."

[64] Warner, "Wigglesworth" (without mentioning his prophecy to Du Plessis!), but Hywel-Davies, *Baptized,* discusses the prophecy extensively, 152ff. Hywel-Davies is a British Pentecostal, staff member of Kensington Temple, London, and a distinguished radio broadcaster with the BBC. His Wigglesworth biography is popular but well-researched.

[65] Warner, "Frodsham" (Frodsham was one of the first Pentecostal "historians," editor of the *PE;* he left the Assemblies of God in 1949).

[66] Hocken, "Union." A rich archive (many handwritten letters) and complete accounts of the Pentecostal Missionary Union are lodged at the Assemblies of God Bible College in Mattersey, near Duncaster, England.

Polhill.[67] Polhill, a former missionary to Tibet, had been one of the "Cambridge Seven," and was squire of Howbury Hall near Cambridge—a man of means, culture, and lineage.

Boddy did not introduce Pentecostal practices into his regularly scheduled Anglican services. Rather, he added separate prayer and teaching sessions on the subject of the Pentecostal experience. From these meetings the message was carried across Britain, often in the homes of his or Polhill's acquaintances.

After the First World War the emerging Assemblies of God and other Pentecostal groupings grew apart from Boddy and Polhill.[68] The reasons for the failure of Boddy's original ecumenical vision are (in my opinion) the following:

1. Boddy was an aristocrat, Polhill belonged to the landed gentry. Many of the early Pentecostals were either self-taught lower middle class (such as Donald Gee, whose son became an Anglican vicar, and the brothers Jeffreys), or rough but highly gifted men such as Smith Wigglesworth. What openings were there for these men, who felt a vocation into the ministry (and for whom university studies were unavailable)? At first they were sent to the mission fields (Salter,[69] Burton[70]), but there was no financial basis in the Pentecostal Missionary Union to support their development. The Church of England was (and still is) totally unable to accommodate such highly gifted, but uneducated people among their ministers, although the church badly needs their ministry. Most churches with a university-trained ministry suffer the same problem, and Pentecostal churches in future times will likely not be excluded. The problem is similar to that of the buoyant black churches and their leaders in Britain, which none of the established churches so far can accommodate (not even the established Pentecostal churches!); and yet it is exactly this kind of minister which they need (chapter 9, pp. 106–16). Similarly, the only avenue open to these men in Boddy's time was to found their own churches—an option the exercise of which spelled the end of Boddy's ecumenical vision.

2. Boddy was a patriot. He supported the British war ideology in *Confidence*. "While Polhill was ending the prayer meetings at Sion College with the national anthem other Pentecostal pioneers were suffering indignities as conscientious objectors."[71] Polhill even objected to praying for the people on both sides during the war. The abyss between the early British Pentecostals and Boddy is clearly documented by David Allen, Lecturer at the Assemblies of God College, Mattersey.[72]

---

[67] Hocken, "Polhill."

[68] Hocken, "Layman": Although he had in earlier days generously financed Pentecostal causes, "he left £ 96,000 in his will, with bequests to a number of Christian bodies, *none of them Pentecostal*" (137, *The Times*, April 26, 1938, 10d).

[69] Cartwright, "Salter."

[70] Cartwright, "Burton."

[71] Hocken, "Layman," 134; Gee, *Wind and Flame*, 101f.

[72] Hocken, "Layman," 135, and above all, Allen, D., "Ostrich," 50–62; this is a

In conclusion, one can say that Boddy's and Polhill's ecumenical vision *did not fail because of theological differences,* but because of cultural and class differences, which were then rationalized with half-baked theological arguments. It is in general much more difficult to overcome psychological and cultural barriers than theological ones.

Gerrit Roelof Polman (1868–1932)[73]

"The purpose of the Pentecostal revival is not to build up a church, but to build up all churches."[74] This remained Gerrit R. Polman's conviction all his life, although he failed as an ecumenist.

We are well served by an excellent dissertation on Polman by Cornelis van der Laan. Van der Laan is a first-generation Dutch Pentecostal, an ordained pastor, leader, and teacher in his native Pentecostal church. He presents a meticulously researched and closely argued biography of the founder of Dutch Pentecostalism, placing Pentecostalism in the context of social, political, and ecclesial history. In this book, he does not gloss over the deficiencies of the movement and its founder, but treats them with tact and frankness.

In his researches Van der Laan searched for and found an amazing array of sources on Pentecostalism in public records, private collections, the testimonies of eye-witnesses, church periodicals, and in early Pentecostal publications, not only in his native Holland but also in Germany, Switzerland, England, the United States, and Sweden. This clearly demonstrates that Pentecostalism was in its formative years a close international community.

On the basis of hitherto unknown documents, van der Laan discovered that Polman was declared at his birth to be "onecht," a "not-genuine" or illegitimate child, because his mother was his father's stepdaughter. Van der Laan documents the struggle for survival by the Polman family in the small rural community of Westenholte, and the early influences on Polman of the Salvation Army and John Alexander Dowie.[75] In so doing, he brings to light many details on these revival movements which are not generally known. He describes how Polman saw Pentecostalism as an ecumenical revival movement which was not called to build up its own church organization but to build up all the churches, including the ones that attacked him and his work. Van der Laan was helped in this by one of the most lucid historians of early Pentecostalism, the Frisian pastor Dr. Wumkes,[76] whose works are practically

---

spicy article against political naiveté in the British Assemblies of God. The article analyzes today's situation in Great Britain and shows how the Pentecostals lost their early political teeth (e.g., pacificism). Among others, he quotes Dietrich Bonhoeffer and Edward Irving.

[73] Sources include: van der Laan, C., *Sectarian Against His Will;* idem, "Theology."

[74] van der Laan, C., "Theology," 23, quoting from *Spade Regen* 12/3, June 1919, 37.

[75] *The Pentecostals,* 116–20; *Handbuch,* 02a.02.047; Blumhofer, "Dowie."

[76] Wumkes, *Pinksterbeweging,* 1917. A first-class historical and theological analysis by one of its fairest critics.

unknown outside Holland. Van der Laan used Wumkes's large collection of letters (having to learn Frisian in order to understand them).

Van der Laan calls Polman a failed ecumenist, "a sectarian against his will." Certainly Polman was an ecumenist born before his time. He was a "go-between" for the Germans and the British during the First World War. Unlike many of the German and British Pentecostal leaders he was also a pacifist. For him the strident nationalism depicted in the pages of *Confidence* (the leading British Pentecostal periodical at that time) and *Pfingstgrüsse* (the corresponding German periodical) was a denial of Christ's work of reconciliation. Consequently he visited German prisoners of war in England and British prisoners of war in Germany. He refrained from writing a declaration of faith because he felt such a document would raise unnecessary walls between the churches. Water baptism—that bone of contention for Pentecostals in many ecumenical discussions (see chapter 20, pp. 261–63)—was considered by Polman to be of minor importance, but was administered by immersion upon request.[77] Polman gladly confessed that Pentecostalism was born in the crucible of the black slaves' suffering in the United States, and rejected the fashionable claims that Pentecostalism was simply a development of the American white Holiness movement—I know of no other early Pentecostal leader who puts himself so squarely and fairly on the side of the "onecht" ("not-genuine") black citizens of America. But then he knew that in God's eyes the despised children of Israel were the people of God, the despised early Christian slaves were his church, the down-trodden descendants of America's slaves were the founders of the most vital 20th century denomination, and he himself, the illegitimate son, had been made legitimate.

So why did Polman fail as an ecumenist? Van der Laan summarizes his dilemma succinctly:

> Polman's ecumenical heart collided with his fundamentalistic Evangelical head. His Spirit baptism had generated a loving attitude towards all fellow Christians, but he was unable to fully assimilate this ecumenical experience into his thinking. . . . Surely this was not his fault alone. He received no help from his Evangelical colleagues nor from the academic theologians.[78]

They were either too busy condemning the fledgling ecumenical movement, or they simply ignored it.[79]

---

[77] van der Laan, C., "Theology," 24. Wumkes, "De Pinksterbeweging," 1916, 267.

[78] van der Laan, C., *Sectarian Against His Will*, 305.

[79] This has also been observed by Bill Menzies. Early Pentecostals were largely ignored by the liberals. "Fundamentalists, on the other hand, bitterly opposed the Movement and charged adherents with theological heresy. . . . Even as they were losing their war with the Modernists, Fundamentalists regarded Pentecostals an equal threat to Orthodox Christianity." Menzies, *Anointed to Serve*, 179–81, summarized by Faupel, "Whither?" 22.

Can the early ecumenical spirit of Dutch Pentecostalism be recaptured? This is no easy task. Van der Laan discusses the conditions which would make such a thing possible. In the first instance conflict must be recognized as a necessary context for innovative theology.

> This requires an ecclesiology in which pluriformity becomes a hallmark of the church, a dynamic pluriformity that allows room for conflict and change. It calls for a theology that refuses to make its own position normative; a theology that partakes in an intercultural learning process. A true Pentecostal/Charismatic theology should welcome conflicts as being essential for the continuous work of the Spirit. Conflicts provide the context in which the charismata operate.[80]

This is not an appeal for an "anything-goes" attitude. It is a theology which takes Paul seriously: our knowledge, including theological and biblical knowledge, is provisional (1 Cor 13:8). It is a theology where the heart pleads with the head and the head informs the heart—in fact, a "body-of-Christ" theology which promises to rekindle in Dutch Pentecostalism that early ecumenical spirit.[81] Indeed, we need to develop categories of thinking and acting ecumenically which allow us to bring the different theological and spiritual approaches in the worldwide Church into contact *and* conflict.[82]

The promising ecumenical start of Dutch Pentecostalism failed "because on the one side the Pentecostals did have the right heart for the matter, but lacked the means to develop an adequate corresponding theology,[83] while on the other side the churches possessed the means, but lacked the necessary ecumenical heart."[84]

Other Ecumenical Pentecostals

The four Pentecostal pioneers mentioned have not been alone. I hope that some day Cecil M. Robeck, Jr., will publish his research on early and present Pentecostal ecumenicity. For the time being I can give only a short overview based on his seminal research, in which he points out that early Pentecostals "were hopeful that this revival would bring about worldwide Christian unity."[85]

---

[80] van der Laan, C., *Sectarian Against His Will*, 306f.

[81] It is not by accident that one of the best and the earliest ecumenical documents on Pentecostalism was produced in Holland (Nederlands Hervormde Kerk, *De Kerk*, see *The Pentecostals*, 433ff.).

[82] Dayton, "Expansion."

[83] By this van der Laan does not mean a rationalist/evangelical (or rationalist/critical) theology but "a theology in which inconsistencies are acceptable," van der Laan, C., *Sectarian Against His Will*, 306. This topic needs expansion. The question is: How can we build a new type of coherence which is not based on logical consistencies?

[84] van der Laan, C., *Sectarian Against His Will*, 327.

[85] For this section I have been drawing heavily on an unpublished paper by

One of the least expected among these early Pentecostal ecumenists is Charles Parham (chapter 3, pp. 20–23), the founder of the Apostolic Faith Movement in the midwest. Parham thought of himself as "an apostle of unity," and wrote:

> Unity is not to be accomplished by organization or non-organization. Unity by organization has been tried for 1900 years and failed. Unity by non-organization has been tried for several years and resulted in anarchy, or gathered in small "cliques" with an unwritten creed and regulations which are often fraught with error and fanaticism. . . . We expect to see the time, when baptized by the Holy Ghost into one Body, the gloriously redeemed Church without spot or wrinkle, having the same mind, judgment, and speaking the same things.[86]

Likewise W. F. Carothers[87] wrote: "The restoration of Pentecost means ultimately the restoration of Christian unity."[88]

The black ecumenist William J. Seymour has already been mentioned (chapter 3, pp. 18–20). However, "he differed from Parham and Carothers for he believed that doctrinal unity was as essential as spiritual unity."[89]

Robeck also mentions Thomas Ball Barratt from Norway. Barratt noted the transdenominational character of the NorwegianPentecostal revival, which included Roman and Greek Catholics, and which, he said, " . . . must be the very Revival Christ had in His mind when He prayed that *all His disciples might be* one."[90] Yet Barratt acknowledged there would continue to be disputes over doctrines, the significance of the sacraments, and questions regarding church organizational structure. He vowed that those within Pentecostalism would not seek to undermine other evangelical denominations, but would actively promote their welfare, attempting to live out Jesus' prayer of John 17. "We are therefore to be found in all denominations, as well as among Christians who do not belong to any denomination,"[91] Barratt wrote.

The subject of ecumenism was addressed too by William H. Durham[92] and Frank Bartleman.[93] Bartleman argued that what had occurred at Azusa Street was the beginning of the "final outpouring . . . A heterogeneous body was thrown together, 'baptized in one Spirit.' "[94]

Robeck, "Perspectives," 4. See also McDonnell (with Bittlinger), "Problem," 29; Krust, "Churches" 343; Cronje, "Influence," 115.

[86] Parham, Charles F., *Voice*, 65, 64f.

[87] Robeck, "Carothers."

[88] Carothers, *Baptism*, 25.

[89] Robeck, "Perspectives," 8. As further witnesses Robeck mentions J. M. Pike, the medical doctors Amelia and Lilian Yeomans, and William Hamner Piper. Idem, "Pike"; idem, "Yeomans"; Blumhofer, "Piper."

[90] Barratt, *In the Days*, 145; emphasis his.

[91] Ibid., 223.

[92] Riss, "Durham."

[93] Robeck, "Bartleman."

[94] Bartleman, "Earthquake," 38. "Earthquake" was a tract which he had written in April, 1906.

Robeck concludes:

It is clear that most of these early Pentecostals believed in the invisible and visible churches, and that the true unity of Christians was accomplished by the work of the Cross. Some were more generous than others in their identification of Christians with whom they had doctrinal differences. As time went on, though, more and more Pentecostal denominations were founded and questions of Pentecostal organizations as well as visible alignment with the larger Church became increasingly significant.[95]

The ecumenical work of Donald Gee has already been mentioned in the first volume of *The Pentecostals*. Robeck traces Gee's commitment to unity within the Pentecostal movement and unity within the larger church in great detail. "The dream of creating one worldwide denomination out of the Pentecostal Movement can be dismissed as hopeless. If it were ever achieved we may be almost certain it would no longer be Pentecostal."[96] His clear support of ecumenism in the editorials of *Pentecost*[97] "outraged" British and especially American Pentecostals, "and in the strongest terms possible Gee was advised to cancel any commitments" [to the World Council of Churches].[98] The most ardent spokesman of this anti-ecumenism[99] was Thomas F. Zimmerman,[100] then newly elected president of the National Association of Evangelicals and general superintendent of the American Assemblies of God. Gee did not give up, and reminded the Pentecostals that "the complete answer to modernism is not fundamentalism, but Pentecost in all its fullness."[101] He also observed, as has been stated many times, that the bitterest opponents of the Pentecostal movement have been the fundamentalists.

---

[95] Robeck, "Perspectives," 14.

[96] Gee, "Possible."

[97] A much less complete analysis of Gee's ecumenical commitment in *The Pentecostals*, 208–13. Robeck ("Perspectives") has 24 (15–39) carefully footnoted pages on Gee.

[98] Ross, "Sectarian," 99. Twelve of the famous editorials by Gee in *Pentecost* have been published separately in book form as Gee, *All with One Accord.*

[99] "In a sense Zimmerman was also ecumenical, but very choosy and political about with whom to be ecumenical," Robeck, in a conversation, July 1993.

[100] Burgess, "Zimmerman." After his death a rift between Zimmerman and the Assemblies of God became apparent. No Assemblies of God representative was allowed to speak at Zimmerman's funeral. His papers were lodged not in the Assemblies of God archives but at Wheaton College.

[101] Gee, "New Delhi."

CHAPTER TWENTY SIX

An Ecumenical Follow-Up

David J. Du Plessis

Probably the most important prophecy in the history of the Pentecostal movement is connected with David J. Du Plessis (1905–1987).[1] It was given in December 1936 by Smith Wigglesworth (1859–1947),[2] an extraordinary English Pentecostal evangelist who could hardly read or write. While in South Africa Wigglesworth laid his hands on Du Plessis' shoulders, pushed him against the wall and began to prophesy:

> You have been in "Jerusalem" long enough . . . I will send you to the uttermost parts of the earth . . . You will bring the message of Pentecost to all churches . . . You will travel more than most evangelists do . . . God is going to revive the churches in the last days and through them turn the world upside down. . . .[3]

Then Wigglesworth began to tell him details of visions he had been seeing that morning and which God had told him to share with Du Plessis. It was all too fantastic: according to Wigglesworth's visions even the Pentecostal movement would pale into insignificance compared with the revival God was

---

[1] The basis of this section are personal reminiscences (I interpreted for Du Plessis many times; he was a great inspiration for my own ecumenical biography); Robinson, *To the Ends of the Earth;* Spittler, "Du Plessis"; and Robeck, "Du Plessis." The personal papers of David Du Plessis are housed in the David Du Plessis Center at Fuller Theological Seminary, Pasadena, California.

[2] The article by Warner on "Wigglesworth." Chapter 25, note 64, p. 343.

[3] See *The Pentecostals,* 346. The prophecy grew over the years and it was re-interpreted (Robinson, *To the Ends of the Earth,* 85–91). It is an interesting case where we can follow a prophecy and the process of *Nachinterpretation* (later re-interpretation) which we know from the Old Testament prophets.

bringing to the churches. Wigglesworth went on to specify that all this would not happen until after his own death. Wigglesworth died in 1947; by 1957 Du Plessis was becoming the best known Pentecostal ecumenist worldwide.

Who was David Du Plessis? He grew up in one of the most conservative Pentecostal churches, the South African Apostolic Faith Church.[4] In England I met a black Christian from one of the South African Independent Pentecostal churches[5] whose father played an important role in Du Plessis's youth and had been influential in Du Plessis becoming a Christian. Du Plessis rose very quickly in the denomination and ended up as general secretary from 1936 until 1947. In 1947 he resigned to concentrate on his global ministry, which started with the first World Pentecostal Conference (1947, Zurich), and continued as Du Plessis acted as unpaid general secretary of the World Pentecostal Conferences (1949, Paris; 1952, London; 1955, Stockholm; 1958, Toronto).

In between conferences Du Plessis tried to bring Pentecostal churches worldwide together, but with little success.[6] In 1955 he joined the American Assemblies of God (having in the meantime become an American citizen), and from 1956 to 1959 he worked with Gordon Lindsay's *Voice of Healing Fellowship.*[7]

It is not entirely clear what had activated Wigglesworth's long dormant prophecy in Du Plessis, especially as Du Plessis shared the general Pentecostal belief of that time, namely that the mainline churches—and in particular the Roman Catholic Church and the World Council of Churches—were hopelessly lost. Perhaps his long convalescence after a serious car accident matured in him the decision to share with these churches his convictions, and to start the process of forgiveness with groups for whom he (as "God's state attorney," as he once put it) had previously had nothing but contempt. What is certainly known is that Du Plessis at one point visited the World Council of Churches offices in New York, uninvited and unannounced.[8]

Hearing some hard words for Latin American Pentecostals from John Mackay, president of Princeton Seminary, Du Plessis wrote to Mackay, and the two became friends. Mackay was Du Plessis's gate into organized ecumenism. As president of the International Missionary Council, Mackay brought Du Plessis to the 1952 meeting at Willingen, Germany, and had him address the 210 delegates. Probably because of Du Plessis's interviews with more than half of the global ecclesiastical representatives, most of whom had never seen a rational Pentecostal, he there earned the title "Mr. Pentecost." At Willingen, W. A. Visser t'Hooft invited Du Plessis to the 1954 World Council Assembly at

---

[4] *The Pentecostals*, 120–22.

[5] Sydney Sibusiso Nkosi, who prepares a theological defense of some of the South African Independent Pentecostal churches.

[6] His two manuscripts (*History* and *Brief History*) were probably the first attempt at taking stock of global Pentecostalism. See also Robinson, "David Du Plessis," in particular, 144.

[7] Bundy, "Lindsay"; Spittler, *loc. cit.*, 252.

[8] Spittler, "Du Plessis," 252; Robinson, "David Du Plessis," 146.

Evanston, Illinois. By 1959 Du Plessis was giving lectures at major theological centers—Princeton, Yale, Union, Colgate, Bossey, and others. He was received by three Roman Catholic pontifs—John XXIII, Paul VI, and John Paul II.[9]

Du Plessis was also instrumental in strengthening the charismatic renewal in the historic churches (chapter 26, pp. 362–66) and was the driving force behind the Vatican/Pentecostal dialogue (chapter 13, pp. 165–180).

Two incidents may serve as examples of his "Pentecostal style" in dealing with ecclesiastical dignitaries and scholars. One happened at the Uppsala Full Assembly of the World Council of Churches (1968). He traveled to Uppsala with the Benedictine Kilian McDonnell (the other main inspirer of the Vatican/Pentecostal dialogue). McDonnell asked Du Plessis: "How do we get into this meeting?" Du Plessis answered: "The Lord will provide." When they came to the conference site I met these two friends. Du Plessis smiled and said to McDonnell: "You see, the Lord provides." Du Plessis had asked for press status at the conference but—since he was not expected—was denied a press-card. What else could I do then but go to my colleague in charge and protest? "Du Plessis," he said and raised his eyebrows, "isn't that the man who was disfellowshipped from the Assemblies of God?" "Yes, he is," said I, "and do you know why?" "Of course not, it does not interest me," answered the colleague. "But it should interest you," I continued. "He was disfellowshipped because of his endeavors to create contacts between Pentecostals and the World Council of Churches. Are you going to punish him for trying to make our work understood in Pentecostal circles?" That obviously did the trick, and Du Plessis got his press-card.

Many times Du Plessis was asked his opinion on Barth, Bultmann, and other theologians whose works he had never read. But he was a teacher with a difference. In Germany he was asked by a disciple of Bultmann, "What is your program?" Du Plessis replied, "To demythologise the Scriptures." Curious at such a reply, his questioner asked, "How will you do this?," to which Du Plessis responded, "It's very simple, we Pentecostals take the things in the Bible that you say are myths and we make them happen today so that they are demythologised!"[10]

Obviously this answer does not solve the problem of myths in the Bible, and Pentecostal scholars nowadays have much more sophisticated analytical tools to deal with myths in Scripture.[11] Nevertheless Du Plessis hit the nail on the head when he pointed out that "the things in the Bible" are not supernatural and extraordinary. They are part and parcel of a Christian's life, *cum grano salis*, of course. Thus many times he quoted Acts 2:17, where it is said that the Holy Spirit is poured out on *all* flesh. From this Du Plessis concluded that the

---

[9] Spittler, "Du Plessis," 252. More details in Curlee–Curlee, *Springtime*, 1ff. This is an excellent study on Mackay and Du Plessis based on original archive research. See also Curlee–Curlee, "Bridging the Gap."

[10] Robinson, "David Du Plessis," 152.

[11] See chapter 23, note 44, p. 319.

Holy Spirit is also in the unbelievers, and that they too have charismata, although they might perhaps not understand or use them correctly—an extraordinary statement for a Pentecostal.[12]

In time Du Plessis knew most of the ecclesiastical leaders in the Pentecostal, Roman Catholic, and Protestant churches. Although he had never received an academic theological education, his narrative style, his honesty, his large heart, his burning love for all Christians (and non-Christians), and his wit won him many friends—but he also gained enemies among his Pentecostal constituency. Thus he was unsuccessful in presenting the Vatican/Pentecostal dialogue to the World Pentecostal Conference (chapter 13, pp. 165–80), and once complained that he was not even allowed to say "Hallelujah" in this Pentecostal gathering.

> The leaders of the Assemblies of God were embarrassed by Du Plessis' work among ecumenical leaders, and, in 1962, presented an ultimatum to Du Plessis. He must either cease his ecumenical ministry or lose his ministry credentials with the Assemblies of God. Naturally, given his new understanding of the nature of the Pentecostal Movement, it was impossible for him to agree to the demand of the Assemblies leadership and he was expelled as a minister. For Du Plessis this expulsion meant more than just the loss of his ministry-credentials. From now on it would be almost impossible for him to work with the official Pentecostal structures. Ironically, it was as if the Pentecostal leaders were wishing to place themselves outside of the new Pentecost that Du Plessis was discovering. Du Plessis did not miss the irony that it was the evangelical churches which had previously proved the most resistant to the "baptism of the Holy Spirit" who were now successfully urging the Pentecostal churches to reject the development of this same experience in the more ecumenical of the historic churches.[13]

As an insider of the Assemblies of God, Russ Spittler describes this incident more precisely. He concentrates on the fact that

> the North American Pentecostal establishment luxuriated in its postwar acceptance among Evangelicals. In 1961 Thomas F. Zimmerman, who in 1959 had become general superintendent of the Assemblies of God, was returned for a second year to the post of elected president of the National Association of Evangelicals. It was an era that completed the evangelicalization of Pentecostalism.[14]

It was impossible for Zimmerman to remain president of the National Association of Evangelicals and to tolerate one of the most outspoken ecumenists among the Assemblies of God. From 1962 until 1980, when Du Plessis was reinstated as an ordained minister, Du Plessis served as an uncredentialed and unofficial Pentecostal ambassador-at-large. When Du Plessis was showered

---

[12] *The Pentecostals*, 343. Du Plessis in Wogen, *Jesus*, 223–50. However, the mediation of charismatic spirituality to the churches by the South African Du Plessis also has its drawbacks; see Suurmond, *Word and Spirit at Play*, 16.

[13] Robinson, "David Du Plessis," 149.

[14] Spittler, "Du Plessis," 252.

with honors from the ecclesiastical and secular establishment towards the end of his life,[15] it became necessary for the Pentecostal establishment to claim him again as a minister of the Assemblies of God—of course without any discussion or apology.

God's ways are astonishing. Two of the most influential Pentecostal ecumenists have come from the conservative Apostolic Faith Church of South Africa: Frank Chikane (chapter 5, pp. 49–50) and David J. Du Plessis. These two were not the only ones, however, who had to pay dearly for their ecumenical commitment; Daniel Brandt-Bessire[16] was another. However, things are changing rapidly—as we shall see in chapter 27.

One agent of this change is Cecil M. Robeck, Jr., an Assemblies of God professor at Fuller Theological Seminary, Pasadena, California. Robeck combines a burning ecumenical heart with a thorough knowledge of internal church policy; he follows the ecclesiastical code of conduct by informing his superiors in detail about, and securing their agreement on, every important step of his ecumenical journey.

Robeck is the son of an Assemblies of God minister. He was ordained in 1973 in the Assemblies of God. He was trained at San Jose City College (1967), at Bethany Bible College (1970), and at Fuller Theological Seminary (M.Div. 1973, Ph.D. 1985). He has acted in various administrative and academic positions mainly at Fuller and is now Professor of Church History and Ecumenics at Fuller. He is presently co-chairing the Vatican/Pentecostal dialogue. He is also a member of numerous ecumenical bodies, among others of the Working Group (formerly Commission) on Faith and Order of the National Council of Churches (1985ff.) and of the World Council of Churches. He acted for many years as editor of *Pneuma*, the journal of the Society for Pentecostal Studies.

His wife is a trained nurse with major administrative responsibility. In a telling article she describes what she must do when somebody steps into the hospital, uninvited, to pray for a patient. "As the patient's advocate, I must protest their right to privacy and redirect this unrequested visitor."

---

[15] Complete list in Spittler, "Du Plessis," 253.

[16] Daniel Brandt-Bessire, a Swiss Pentecostal, was ordained in the Assemblées de Dieu de Belgique in 1976 but had to withdraw because of the antagonism of the Assemblies of God USA missionaries to his ecumenical commitment. The beneficiaries of this were the Swiss Reformed churches who appointed him as pastor in a holiday resort. Bundy in his review on Daniel Brandt-Bessire, *Aux sources de la spiritualité pentecôtiste* in *Pneuma* 9/2, Fall 1987, 204. Many European Pentecostals so far hardly know how to deal with some of their most gifted and highly educated young theologians. Another case is Dr. Jean-Daniel Plüss, a graduate from Louvain for whom there does not seem any place in the Swiss Pentecostal movement. The Reformed Church made him president of one of their richest congregation in Zurich. See also the adventurous journey of Jerry L. Sandidge (chapter 13, pp. 168–71). There are, however, important exceptions: Holland (see chapter 25, pp. 345–47) and England, where the Swiss Pentecostal theologian Dr. S. Schatzmann was made president of the Elim Bible College.

Robeck is a theologically-trained historian who specializes in Patristics and Pentecostalism—a most interesting and necessary combination. His ecumenical heart is best documented by the following quote:

> The Corinthians quarreled, drank to excess, visited temple prostitutes, held secret knowledge over others, monopolized the Lord's table for personal gain, advocated immoral behavior, abused God's gracious endowments, and even denied the reality of the resurrection from the dead. Even so, Paul did not call them "Not-Christians." Rather, he addressed them as "the church of God in Corinth . . . sanctified in Christ Jesus and called to be saints" together with all others who called on the name of the Lord Jesus Christ (1 Cor 1:2). He did not require change before he recognized them as Christians. So how could I do less?[17]

Four Phases of Ecumenical Development

One can detect four phases in the ecumenical development of Pentecostalism:

First Phase: Pentecostalism begins as an ecumenical renewal movement, breaking through racial and denominational barriers (chapter 25, pp. 334–49. It sees in the experience of the Holy Spirit the one important force which sweeps away all denominational, racial, educational, and social divides.

Second Phase: This ecumenical movement then develops into locally organized congregations heavily influenced by evangelicalism; by defending themselves against severe attacks from the evangelicals, Pentecostals perhaps accept much of the thought categories of their antagonists.

Third Phase: National and international Pentecostal denominations are organized. Catechisms, Bible colleges, extensive building programs, successful media policies, pension funds for the pastors, centralized church bureaucracies, aggressive fund-raising programs and so forth, were all established. Pentecostalism is no longer an ecumenical renewal movement but becomes visible as a group of highly clericalized new denominations.

Fourth Phase: Pentecostals begin to return to their ecumenical root by starting a dialogue with the Roman Catholic Church and organized ecumenism (as discussed in chapter 27, pp. 367–88). This, however, leads in certain cases to splits from the denominations. The separated groups start the process again at phase 1.

In general a phase takes a generation (25 years). What is important for our topic is the fact that the older classical Pentecostal denominations are now somewhere between phases 3 and 4, while the charismatic renewal in the mainline churches has to be placed between phases 1 and 2. Whether the charismatic renewal can skip phases 2 and 3 is in my opinion uncertain. All indicators point in the direction of new Pentecostal churches, although this is

---

[17] The section on Robeck is based on private notes. The quotes are from Robeck, Patsy, "Ecumenical Ministry in the Hospital," 9, and Robeck, "Growing," 7.

officially denied and although the new organizations take on new names ("third wave," "charismatic center," "Christian center," and so on).[18]

Kilian McDonnell

Due to Kilian McDonnell's fundamental work,[19] we are well informed on the reaction of the churches to the charismatic renewal.[20] McDonnell has collected, translated, and interpreted one hundred documents—mainly from the churches in Europe, North and South America. The documents represent all denominations, from the classical Pentecostal to the Protestant and Roman Catholic Churches. Some of the most interesting documents come from unexpected sources, for example the statement by the Protestant Churches in former East Germany,[21] or the document from the Mekane Yesu Church in Ethiopia (the only document which reviews the position of the main denominations in other continents systematically and ecumenically before it comes to its own judgment).[22] Some churches have resources within their own tradition for dealing with the renewal, like the Roman Catholic Church, the Methodist Church, the Czech Brethren and—amazingly—the Presbyterian Church (USA) (the latter drawing heavily on modern scholarship). Other churches, like some American Baptists and the Missouri Lutherans, find it difficult or impossible to accommodate the renewal within their tradition. So it is criticized and rejected as *theologia gloriae,* as un-Lutheran, or un-Baptist. This is probably a fair judgment, since there are important trends in Pentecostalism and in charismatism which deviate from the tradition of the Reformation. But perhaps—*horribile dictu* for an ordained minister of the Swiss Reformed Churches—the reformation of the 16th century is not the last word on Christianity. The Roman Catholic Churches in Costa Rica, Puerto Rico, and Brazil also criticize the renewal because it introduces "Protestant ideas" into the Roman Catholic Church, as if this were an argument in our present ecumenical era.

It is obvious that the creation of ecumenical links at the grass roots level (especially between evangelicals and Catholics, see chapter 2, pp. 10–11) is both an embarrassment and a source of rejoicing for church leaders and ecumenists. Ecumenists and church leaders become afraid of their own (verbal) courage when at last the people of God put their

---

[18] On the history and the extensive literature of the Charismatic Renewal see the excellent article by Hocken, "Movement" (with a precise write-up of the history and denominational service organizations). Reimer, H.-D., *Wenn der Geist in der Kirche wirken.*

[19] On McDonnell, see Robeck, "McDonnell."

[20] Some information on the early Charismatic Renewal ("Pentecost Outside Pentecost") in *The Pentecostals,* 3–20.

[21] McDonnell, *Presence* II, 453–83. This document was reviewed (in its original German version) by David Bundy in *EPTA Bulletin* 3/3, 1984, 92–96; Kirchner/Planer-Friedrich/Sens/Ziemer, *Charismatische.*

[22] McDonnell, *Presence* II, 150–82.

ecumenical appeals into practice. Furthermore, the charismatic renewal creates ecumenical facts which might force us theologians to rethink some of our denominational theologies.

Kilian McDonnell published his collection in 1980, at the end of phase 1 of the charismatic renewal. During this phase Arnold Bittlinger,[23] Simon Tugwell,[24] and Kilian McDonnell were considered the forward-pointing signposts of ecumenism. My impression today is, however, that these early pioneering approaches have largely been forgotten in favour of either a conservative catholic or a narrow evangelical approach. This is certainly true of the majority of European charismatics, although perhaps the situation in the Church of England is somewhat different.[25]

Because of its importance for our subject one of the first of Kilian McDonnell's publications must be mentioned. In *Charismatic Renewal and the Churches*, McDonnell dealt with the many theories of the causes and motivations behind the charismatic movement. Probably the majority of researchers in this field have described glossolalia and the charismatic communities in terms of pathology and subnormality. McDonnell quotes with approval William Samarin,[26] who suggests a scholarly investigation of the psychological profile of those researchers who show a bias against the glossolalics. Why is it, McDonnell asks rightly, that much of the research on this topic gets away with rather flimsy empirical evidence, provided that the researcher confirms the popular belief that charismatics are highly emotional, disturbed, suggestible people? In fact E. and J. Hilgard[27] have shown that normal subjects are more easily hypnotized than those who border on the neurotic, so—if the allegations of hypnosis and of suggestion in charismatics is true, this could certainly not be used as evidence against the normality of the people attending these meetings. McDonnell further states that much of this research is done without ever checking the findings against a control group. The fact that this research is widely quoted does not alter the grave methodological weakness of its "one shot" design.[28]

Some of these researchers, however, score better than others. Kilian McDonnell considers the German book on glossolalia by Eddison Mosimann, written in 1911 (which most modern researchers ignore),[29] and the

---

[23] On Bittlinger see *The Pentecostals*, 245ff. Also Failing, "Neue." As far as I can see these ecumenical pioneers have been marginalized, left the movement and lost interest, or were simply silenced.

[24] On Tugwell, see chapter 13 (pp. 157–59).

[25] Elbert, "England"; Hunt, "Wimberites."

[26] William Samarin in a review of Kildahl's *The Psychology of Speaking in Tongues*, in *Sisters Today*, 44 (August-September 1972), 44; quoted by McDonnell in *Charismatic Renewal*, 147.

[27] Hilgard–Hilgard, *Hypnotic*, 295, 331, 349, 374. Quoted in McDonnell, *Charismatic Renewal*, 80.

[28] McDonnell, *Charismatic Renewal*, 150.

[29] Ibid., 87f.; Mosimann, *Das Zungenreden; The Pentecostals*, 227f.

unpublished dissertation by the Pentecostal psychiatrist Vivier from South Africa,[30] among the most reliable research works on glossolalia. On the other hand he severely criticizes Cutten's widely-quoted work[31] and even more John P. Kildahl's *Psychology of Speaking in Tongues*, and rightly so. McDonnell says the overall judgment on Kildahl's research must be negative: "There is an appended bibliography [to Kildahl's book] but there is no indication in the text that the author is acquainted with the content of the research there reported."[32] This observation every careful reader of Kildahl's book will find confirmed.

McDonnell also deals with the different deprivation theories. These claim that people become charismatic because they lack money, status, prestige, or a combination of these. With the emergence of the renewal movement in the upper middle-class this theory was shattered, so a new theory had to be created. This time it was to be "affective deprivation"[33] on which McDonnell comments: One wonders, whether this is not a universal condition,

> something which is constant in all human beings. Who among us thinks that he or she receives the love deserved? Where are the persons who have attained a kind of parity between the expected love and love received? Since affective deprivation . . . is considered a factor in the rise and growth of the (charismatic) community, is one not explaining a variable (the charismatic community) by a constant (affective deprivation)? In social science a constant cannot be used to explain a variable.[34]

Another researcher who uses a constant in order to explain a variable is Robert M. Anderson.[35] Anderson has provided a competent and important *Social History of the Early Twentieth Century Pentecostal Movement.*[36] The mistake which he makes, however is to conclude, from the emergence of Pentecostalism in a deprived social milieu that social deprivation provides the reasons for its emergence. He realizes the trap and asks: Why did all similarly deprived people not become Pentecostals? Why did some (and probably the majority) seek relief in crime, delinquency, violence, heavy drinking, drug addiction, gambling, prostitution, and sexual promiscuity? (To which list one could also add: political utopianism, fascism, and escapist music.) Anderson is not able to give a sociological answer to this question. Instead he introduces two psychological factors. He says that socio-economic deprivation leads to the making of a Pentecostal only if two further individual factors come into play; namely, personal stress and a religious disposition.

---

[30] Vivier, *Glossolalia*, and idem, "Glossolalic"; McDonnell, *Charismatic Renewal*, 90–93 and passim. *The Pentecostals*, 342f.

[31] Cutten, *Speaking;* McDonnell, *Charismatic Renewal*, 88f.

[32] McDonnell, *Charismatic Renewal*, 134.

[33] Ibid., 25.

[34] Ibid., 26.

[35] Anderson, Robert Mapes, *Vision of the Disinherited.*

[36] This is the title of Anderson's Ph.D. dissertation.

Anderson is probably correct in his reading of these factors as associated with Pentecostalism. His material shows that personal stress and religious influences in childhood have been constituent factors in most of the lives of early Pentecostal leaders. But does this prove anything? The majority of people suffer stress, and many are religiously influenced at some time in their lives. The question is: are these factors causal or coincidental?

What of our observation that the charismatic renewal does not fit the picture of the socially deprived? Anderson responds: The charismatic renewal is the answer to real or *imagined* deprivation of respect and prestige.[37] Of course, this sort of influence can be used as an explanation for the founding of any social institution, from a university to a political party. No doubt someone will explain that the Gothic cathedrals of the Middle Ages were the product of frustration, imagined or real, and that Brahms's Requiem is the outcome of a continuous stream of frustration (which is perhaps true). But does this really explain anything? Many people suffer frustration, but not all write a masterpiece or build a cathedral. Where is the person who thinks that he or she receives all the recognition she/he deserves?

Two questions are not discussed in McDonnell's book on theorists of the renewal. The first is: On the basis of what criteria do we judge a person to be psychologically and medically normal? As far as I know there are no objective standards—only statistics—upon which to base such a judgment. This is increasingly recognized by medical researchers: the lack of criteria for establishing "normality" is felt not only in the psychiatric but also in the purely medical field.

The second question is: What is the ecclesiological and charismatic function of people who are considered neurotic? Could it not be that they have important charismata to contribute to a world and a church which believes itself to be fairly healthy, but is more endangered by the "disease" of normality than it knows? Is God not also a God of the neurotics? Does he not use them in their neurotic states? One should not forget that some of the greatest thinkers and musicians (such as Kierkegaard, Nietzsche, and Robert Schumann), and some of the great prophets (such as Hosea and Ezekiel) were—in the modern clinical sense—psychologically disturbed.

Kilian McDonnell does not stop at taking facile sociological explanations to pieces. What is even more important in his analysis is his disagreement even at this early stage with much that is written by those within the charismatic renewal. For him, "a charism is a fully human activity and is not under the control of some force outside the person." "All charismatic activity is, in the first instance, ambiguous. The ambiguity is removed by a discerning process (1 Cor 12:30, 14:5, 29) which is essentially a community function though certain individuals may play a more pronounced role in such a process."[38]

---

[37] Anderson, Robert Mapes, *Vision of the Disinherited*, 229.

[38] McDonnell, *Charismatic Renewal*, 6f. Karl Braunhart, for instance, did not observe trance among the tongue-speaking Neo-Pentecostals in Honduras (Braunhart, *Heiliger Geist*), 66, 72.

"There is theologically no reason why a certain ability cannot be both a 'natural' ability and a gift of the Spirit."[39] He even goes so far as to describe glossolalia using the psychological term "learned behavior." But "this does not militate against it being a gift of the Spirit."[40]

> It is not true that what can be described in psychological terms is therefore not a true exercise of a charism, not of the Holy Spirit. This supposition would relegate the Spirit to some Platonic ideal world as it would presuppose that the Spirit operates in a psychological void. On the contrary, only what can be described in psychological terms is a true charism, even though the religious meaning and content is not adequately accounted for in psychological terms.[41]

In short a charism "is less a what and more a how."[42] Charisms are not defined phenomenologically but in relation to their function in church and society.

That understanding of a fully human charism, of a gift of the Spirit within the context of the presence of the Spirit in all creation, demands a pneumatology which comes near to what is described in chapter 17 ("Rethinking the Spirit"). "Such a theology is essentially cosmic and developmental in its preoccupation."[43]

The United Presbyterian Church, USA and the Charismatic Renewal

One of the best reports on the charismatic renewal (called in the report "neo-Pentecostalism") was prepared in 1970 by the United Presbyterian Church USA. In the following I quote from this report.[44]

> The committee is grateful to observe the rapid breaking down of barriers that have separated Protestant denominations from our brethren in the Roman Catholic and Greek Orthodox Churches. Similarly, we are glad to note the beginning of a breakdown of the barriers that have deprived us of fellowship with Pentecostal denominations . . . In the United Presbyterian Church the number of clergy and laity involved in charismatic experiences is comparatively small, although your committee finds that in some areas these numbers are growing significantly. This involvement in such experiences has sometimes led to dissension within our Church. Occasionally where pastors have been involved, the pastoral relationship has been terminated. As a result, many have found it

---

[39] McDonnell, *Charismatic Renewal*, 84.
[40] Ibid., 154.
[41] Ibid., 155.
[42] See chapter 13 (pp. 218–27).
[43] McDonnell, *Charismatic Renewal*, 156, more lit. by McDonnell in the Short Titles List.
[44] McDonnell, *Presence* I, 221–82; *Minutes of the 182nd General Assembly*, 145–98. "It was the most thorough [report] ever done by a major denomination" (Synan, *Explosion*, 168). On the dramatic story of the genesis of this report see Curlee–Curlee, *Springtime*.

necessary to seek an "independent ministry-evangelism," and some to demit the ministry of the United Presbyterian Church.[45]

In case of conflict, stated the report, the Church should remember its Westminster Confession of Faith, Chapter XX, on "Christian Liberty and Liberty of Conscience."

> We plead for that tolerance, good will, and Christ-centered love which is at the heart of the thirteenth chapter of First Corinthians. . . . It is evident to your committee that the silence of the Book of Confessions on any matters of faith or practice does not prohibit the introduction of such beliefs and practices into the life of a congregation so long as such beliefs and practices are not destructive to the external peace and order which Christ has established in the Church.[46]

In an extensive exegetical section the report deals with the different interpretations of the Spirit in Scripture. The writers state, however (together with some classical Pentecostals[47]), that the term "baptism of the Spirit" seems to be a sectarian over-interpretation. "We do not find warrant in the New Testament for a doctrine of *two* Spirit-baptisms as normal for the Christian life."[48] It seems to me that the Assemblies of God New Testament scholar Gordon Fee is more helpful on this topic by stating that the *two* Spirit-baptisms (one for salvation, the other for endowment with the Holy Spirit) has no exegetical foundation (in spite of all that his fellow Pentecostals say) but that this does not prevent people in specific cultural and social contexts from *experiencing* two or more Spirit-baptisms and that these experiences might even be fundamental for their lives.[49] Certainly this was my own experience. Without the experience of Spirit-baptism I would never have become a pastor nor a theologian, but a banker (of course some think this might have been better). But my own experience does not make me assume that all Christians have to follow this *ordo salutis*—that this second Spirit-baptism is necessary for all Christians.

On the other hand, the writers of the report under discussion see no evidence for the belief that the gifts of the Spirit ceased with the death of the apostles.[50] "The practice of glossolalia should be neither despised nor forbidden; on the other hand it should not be emphasized nor made normative for the Christian experience."[51] The report quotes modern Protestant scholars (Karl Barth, Emil Brunner, Paul Tillich) in order to make clear that the Spirit is not just a christological cognitive category, but also a creative force in the world and in the church. In an exhaustive section on

---

[45] McDonnell, *Presence* I, 223.
[46] Ibid., I, 224.
[47] See above chapters 17 (pp. 222–24) and 23 (pp. 313–14).
[48] McDonnell, *Presence* I, 229, 270.
[49] See above G. Fee in chapter 23 (pp. 313–14).
[50] McDonnell, *Presence* I, 230.
[51] Ibid.

psychological interpretations of the charismatic renewal, the report comes to the conclusion that this type of spirituality (including speaking in tongues) is not a sign of a disturbed personality. It is not the result (or the cause) for neurotic breakdowns, high emotional tensions and the like. Although these notions are very popular, there is hardly any evidence to support them in empirical research.[52]

The report states that "if a psychologically sick individual experiences a charismatic gift, it neither validates nor invalidates the gift." God is also a God of the neurotic.[53] "A person may be emotionally disturbed: this however does not prove his religious experience to be imaginary."[54] In other words, the report follows more or less the lines drafted by Kilian McDonnell (chapter 26, pp. 356–60). In a brief section it tackles the problem of exorcism and evil spirits, and even has a good word to say for psychic research (parapsychology), which is "often a creditable, dignified pursuit, conducted by persons of integrity and responsibility."[55]

In its practical guidelines the report asks for tolerance and the dissemination of more precise information on the charismatic renewal, from both practitioners and non-practitioners. This wish remains unfulfilled to this day, in my opinion. I have seldom read such a well-informed, balanced, theologically and psychologically sober report, written with a pastoral heart for those who disagree, and seeking to preserve the United Presbyterian Church as a home for practitioners of different spiritualities. However, I doubt that the report stopped the "draining" of the charismatics to independent and Pentecostal churches.

The Protestant Charismatic Renewal, Ecumenical or What?

In 1978 Kilian McDonnell wrote: "The Charismatic Renewal is the single most potent force on the ecumenical scene today. And it is here to stay. Both it and its ecumenical significance are permanent elements in the life of the Roman Catholic Church."[56] I wonder whether he would write that today?

---

[52] Alland, "Possession"; Boisen, "Economic"; Gerlach–Hine, "Non-pathological"; idem, "Factors"; Gerrard/Gerrard, *Scrabble Creek*. (These Jewish researchers compared a snake-handling Pentecostal church with a conventional denomination as a control group. There is very little difference between the two groups with regard to mental health "but whatever differences there are seem to indicate the serpent-handlers are a little more 'normal' than members of the conventional denominations," quoted in McDonnell, *Presence* I, 240.) Lapsley–Simpson, "Token"; idem, "Song of the Self"; McDonnell, "Holy Spirit and Pentecostalism"; idem, "Catholic Pentecostalism"; Pattison, "Speaking"; idem, "Effects"; idem, "Behavioral"; Vivier, *Glossolalia;* Wood, *Culture.* See also chapters 13 (pp. 157–58) and 17 (pp. 218–27).
[53] McDonnell, *Presence* I, 239.
[54] Ibid.
[55] Ibid., I, 245.
[56] McDonnell, *Ecumenism,* 113.

Certainly in the seventies it was true. At that time he and many others (including myself) hoped that the charismatic renewal would become an ecumenical grassroots movement. Perhaps that potential still exists. However, Peter Hocken, writing ten years later, was more cautious: "It is falsifying the nature of this grace when Catholic charismatic renewal, Lutheran charismatic renewal, or any other denominational renewal is regarded as a distinct movement, rather than as a part of one worldwide transdenominational outpouring of the Spirit of God."[57] Others have observed that the charismatic renewal had run out of steam by the late 1970s. Richard Quebedeaux attempted "to document how a young maiden was embraced by the religious *status quo* and given the kiss of death."[58]

Perhaps Quebedeaux exaggerates. But it is obvious that after a promising start, which included both the ecumenical and the critical root of Pentecostalism, the charismatic renewal is now in a dilemma—or at least at a turning point. It can take one of the following directions:

1. It can develop a dual loyalty: loyalty to one's denomination and loyalty to the ecumenical community. This is a difficult and unstable situation and I doubt whether the majority will follow this line. An important example of a group which has taken this option is the charismatic renewal in the Presbyterian Church of Ghana, which has existed since the thirties, not as an import from Europe but as an indigenous movement.[59]

2. It can become a conservative force within a given denomination. This is certainly the case in most European churches, and may even remain the case if—as seems to be more likely—the renewal there does not develop more along the lines of numbers 3 and 4.

3. Charismatics can leave their denominations and join some of the existing Pentecostal churches. This has certainly been the case throughout the USA.[60]

4. Charismatics may found their own Pentecostal churches, and continue the process which was sketched above (p. 355) with phase 2. This seems to be the trend in Europe and in the USA.[61]

---

[57] Hocken, "Movement," 159.

[58] Quebedeaux, *The New Charismatics* II, 239, reviewed by Donald D. Smeeton in *EPTA Bulletin* 2/3, 1983, 62–66.

[59] Hocken, *One Lord*, reviewed by Vinson Synan in *Pneuma* 10/2, Fall 1988, 162f.; Omenyo, "Ghana."

[60] Sometimes in connection with the New Order of the Latter Rain. Holdcroft, "Order"; Riss, "1948," 32–45 (especially 45); Poloma, "Empirical" (she reports that the Assemblies are "reaping" the benefits of the charismatic movement, Poloma, "Empirical," 75, note 1). See also chapter 20 (pp. 258–61). Similarly Hocken, "Charismatic Movement in the U. S.," 191–214, esp. 212.

[61] Hocken speaks of an "explosion of nondenominational charismatic assemblies." Hocken, "Movement," 141; idem, "Independent." For Europe see below, notes 63ff.

The last development is the least desirable, but obviously the most in vogue; it is a shame that this fragmentation of the Christian witness is traded under the label of "church growth." In the German language the travesty of this label is even more glaring: "church growth" is translated as "building up the community" *(Gemeindeaufbau)* while in actual fact it entails the destruction of flourishing communities.[62] Ingrid Reimer reports for instance from Germany that she is aware of over 200 new congregations; these separatist and individualistic congregations, usually centered around one or two leaders, are growing like mushrooms not only in Germany, but in Switzerland,[63] England,[64] and (in a different form) in the USA.[65] Moreover, it is not known in Europe that the "church growth" ideology is controversial even at Fuller Theological Seminary, where the "church growth" institute is located, and this at the level of students and staff. (More on this in chapter 22, p. 305.)

In relation to the growth of the "third wave," Roswith Gerloff says:

> When Reinhard Bonnke makes ten thousand people speak in tongues in half a minute or when he stages miracle after miracle in his services, then religion is marketed like a new shampoo or a disco song. That is neither renewal of the church nor of society. I have been asked many times how such meetings compare on the one hand with the services of my black friends and on the other hand with the mass psychosis of a *Reichsparteitag,* a Nazi meeting of the Third Reich.

The representatives of the "third wave" have reacted with loud protest against this comparison;[66] however, rather than criticizing here it would be better to examine and answer this question of a theologian who has devoted the greater part of her life to researching the inter-racial dynamics of charismatic spirituality. Rather than protesting against Roswith Gerloff, it would be better to reflect on the *difference* between the modern psycho-boom and the work of the Holy Spirit.

---

[62] The most spectacular (but by no means the only) case was Wolfram Kopfermann, Hamburg, who envisages the foundation of 5,000 new congregations by his Anskar Church. It does not seem that he will achieve even 10% of this. Hummel, "Kopfermann." Birnstein, *Geist,* reviewed by J. D. Plüss in *EPTA Bulletin* 6/4, 1987, 131–33.

[63] Reimer, I., "Neue Gemeindebildungen," 245–52. See also the excellent article by Hempelmann, "Glaubens-Gemeinde." Sturm, "Stadtmission." The ideology was provided in a dozen books by Christian A. Schwarz, e.g., under the pretentious title *Die Dritte Reformation* ("The Third Reformation"). An excellent overview by Hempelmann, "German Protestantism." Schmid, "Die Dritte Welle," and idem, "Christliches." See also "Die Propheten kommen," 51–52.

[64] Here the new congregations are often connected with the "House Churches." Kay, "Interactions"; Birkey, *The House Church;* Walker, Andrew, *Restoring,* reviewed by William Kay in *EPTA Bulletin* 7/3, 1988, 108–110; Davies, William R., *Rocking,* reviewed by Jean-Daniel Plüss in *EPTA Bulletin* 5/3, 1986, 114; Munden, "Encountering;" *EPTA Bulletin* 4/1, 1985, 27f.; Thurman, *New;* O'Sullivan, "Ichthus Fellowship."

[65] Macchia, "Confused Situation," see also note 61.

[66] Gerloff, "Afrikanische Diaspora," 198.

I suggest that this difference can be seen most clearly in the life and work of William Joseph Seymour (chapter 3, pp. 18–24), the founder of the Pentecostal/charismatic movements. For Seymour the Holy Spirit showed himself in speaking in tongues and perhaps also in other manifestations such as "falling down in the service" (that which is often today called the "Toronto Blessing").[67] However, his decisive criterion for identifying the presence and working of the Holy Spirit at Azusa street was that *racism and the idea of the master-race had been overcome.*

The use of the spirituality of the black and Third World Christians as a religious "product," for the promotion of church growth, is unbiblical. It is bad enough that we exploit these Christians politically and economically; religious exploitation is even worse. For these Third World Christians and the black charismatics, these manifestations—their songs and dances—were their only means for saving their culture from destruction through colonialists, missionaries, and political powers. They are an expression of their inner revolt and hope. When Mahalia Jackson would sing at a black meeting in Chicago before ten thousand people "Go down, Moses, way down in Egyptland. Tell old Pharaoh, let my people go," she was expressing both a political *and* a religious hope. She was testifying that the Pharaohs of this world—the businessmen, the generals, and the politicians—do not have the last word. All too often, however, such expressions in a white service are reduced to novel samplings of black folklore. When a congregation in Chile spontaneously breaks out singing in tongues, it is an attempt of these whom we have silenced to find a new language. They are testifying that God has not forgotten them. What function, however, has this expression in a white congregation, where speaking in tongues is manipulated from the platform? That is the question on which we need more clarification.

Thus the "church growth" of splintering new congregations is "almost always the expression of a failed process of communication between the historic churches and the charismatic groups."[68] Neither side has yet learned to come to terms with different styles of spirituality. Another problem is the difference between the USA and Europe. In most European countries there are two main denominations: a Catholic and a Protestant. The country is divided up into parishes. There is no space for new organizations except within the framework of the historically established churches which have—among their ecclesiastical duties—important functions as guarantors of "civil religion" (a very important function *for society,* also in the USA), and as sources of diakonia and social work. (In Germany, for instance, many great hospitals and

---

[67] On the newest discovery of the charismatic spirituality, the so-called Toronto Blessing (including, e.g., falling down, laughing, crying during the worship service), see Baumert, "Phenomena." See also Oropeza, *Laugh*; Hempelmann, "Toronto," 33–43 (bib.); Merz, "Toronto"; *The Guardian* 30.1, 1995. Overview in Föller, *Charisma und Unterscheidung.*

[68] Schäfer, "Wo der Geist des Herrn ist," 4.

social institutions are run by the two main churches.) Furthermore, in most countries the churches provide religious instruction in the schools (pupils who do not want to take advantage of this can in most cases opt out). Where the relations between free churches and the established churches are good, there is always a possibility for the free churches to work together with the established churches. Such relationships exist for instance with Methodist and Salvation Army groups. But where new charismatic movements deny that the established churches are *charismatic* (albeit in a different way from them), where they understand charismata more as a "what" and not as a "how," where they judge their presence or absence according to phenomenological-religious criteria (and not, as Kilian McDonnell and many Pentecostal authors quoted in this volume suggest, according to their function in church and society), there the conflict is programmed.

Thus as the established churches fall back into the old clichés against the charismatics, criticizing their religious manipulations and separatist maneuvers, the charismatics call the established churches dead and unfaithful to the Bible. The Catholic Church is in general better placed to contain these renewals, since it has more practice in dealing with revivals within the church. However, if the charismatic renewal develops in the direction of new Pentecostal denominations—as if we had not already enough Pentecostal denominations—it will lose its momentum and its influence in society and on individuals. It will become just another group of Christians. If the charismatics are intent on leaving the historical churches, why do they not at least join one of the existing Pentecostal churches?

To deny the historical churches charismatic qualities reveals a very narrow and unbiblical understanding of charismata. Are not the ecumenical, inter-racial meeting described in chapter 2 (pp. 6–15), the anointing services described in chapter 18 (pp. 233–37), and the musical evangelism with believers and non-believers described in chapter 21 (pp. 282–86) genuinely charismatic? All these activities describe charismatic and Pentecostal activities in a different cultural and organizational context. Are they disqualified because the "incarnation" of the charismata is different from that experienced in the charismatic renewal?

So what happens to the ecumenical vision which inspired the early charismatic movement and which is still supported by such ecumenists as Peter Hocken and Kilian McDonnell? Is it fading away, or is the ecumenical torch being handed back to the classical Pentecostal churches? That question will be examined in our next chapter.

CHAPTER TWENTY SEVEN

Dialogue with Organized Ecumenism

Latin America

"Without a doubt, Pentecostals in Latin America have played the single most significant prophetic role among the worldwide Pentecostal Movement with respect to the formal ecumenical movement," said Cecil M. Robeck at the Conference on Pentecostal and Charismatic Research in Europe (Kappel, Switzerland, 1991). "They have led and continue to lead the way in membership and cooperation with the World Council of Churches, and with regional ecumenical organizations such as the Consejo Latinoamericano de Iglesias (CLAI), the Latin American Council of Churches. Nowhere else in the world is this ecumenical commitment by Pentecostals quite so free as it is in Latin America." And the Chilean Pentecostals back this up by stating: "Therefore it is not surprising that both Latin American and world ecumenism are increasingly focusing their attention on this issue and thinking about the possibility of *a massive incorporation of Pentecostalism in the ecumenical task.*"[1]

The Latin American Council of Churches consists of some hundred-plus denominations, including many Pentecostal churches, such as the Iglesia Cristiana de Cuba, the Iglesia

---

[1] Cecil M. Robeck in his extraordinary paper "Pentecostals and Ecumenism." Robeck and Manuel Gaxiola-Gaxiola also edited a whole issue of *Pneuma* (13/2, 1991) on Latin American Pentecostalism. See also on CLAI: Sepúlveda, "3a Asamblea" (interview with Felipe Adolf). The quote by Sepúlveda in Sepúlveda, "Pentecostalism," 80, emphasis mine. See also *MD* 58/4, 1.4, 1995, 120–21: "Oekumenismus im Wandel. Wachsende Pfingstbewegung verändert die ökumenische Bewegung in Lateinamerika." WCC, *Consultation.*

Pentecostal de Chile, the Misión Iglesia Pentecostal de Chile, the Unión Evangélica Pentecostal Venezolana, and the Asociación de la Iglesia de Dios of Argentina. The Council was most successful in enlisting those Pentecostal churches "which have the fewest external controls."[2]

Eugene Stockwell, a well-known World Council of Churches figure, was present at an all-Latin American Pentecostal encounter (Encuentro Pentecostal Latinoamericana; EPLA I, 1988, Salvador, Bahia). He reported that there was a "good deal of negative feeling about North American dominance and about North American missionary and European immigrant dominance." In particular the Assemblies of God came under heavy criticism. Perhaps it is felt that the Assemblies of God are too "evangelicalized" or "tied too closely with conservative political thinking." Stockwell came away convinced that further exclusion of Pentecostalism from World Council of Churches circles, whether by neglect or by design, was to the detriment of the ecumenical movement at large. He notes:

> Latin American Pentecostals have a feeling that the historic churches and the ecumenical movement in general, look down on them, exclude them, give them little importance. They know that some Pentecostal churches are members of the World Council of Churches and of the Latin American Council of Churches but that does not suffice to dispel their feeling. I believe they are right in this feeling of exclusion. There is much evidence that the historic churches and the ecumenical movement, including I believe in the World Council of Churches, care little about them.[3]

At a second meeting of Latin American Pentecostals in Buenos Aires (EPLA II, 1989) an action and study program was set up, among other things "to investigate and explore the historical origins of our Pentecostal faith, . . . to review the theological heritage which Pentecostals received from Western Protestantism in general, which has been characterized by confronting social problems in the light of individual ethics, . . . to take into consideration the growing demand for a Christian formation, . . . to go deeply into the experience of 'ecumenism of the Spirit,' . . . [and] to examine the mass effects of televangelism and radio broadcasting, which in many ways mutilates a great part of the richness of community experience and personal testimony."[4] The topics and breadth of the papers presented is impressive.

At a third meeting in Santiago, Chile (EPLA III, 1990) the topic was to be "Pentecostalism y Liberación" (chapter 16, pp. 208–16). It called for a renewed search for "the good and perfect will of God, the promise of justice,

---

[2] Sinclair, "Solidarity," 83, in Robeck, "Pentecostals and Ecumenism," 28. For earlier Pentecostal/ecumenical relationships in Latin America see *The Pentecostals*, 99–107.

[3] Stockwell in an unpublished internal paper: "Pentecostal Consultation," quoted in Robeck, "Pentecostals and Ecumenism," 31f. Robeck gives a complete list of the participants, uses the Spanish minutes, and is aware of all the papers presented.

[4] From the minutes of the 1988 and 1989 consultation (*Si ahora vivimos*, 2) quoted in Robeck, "Pentecostals and Ecumenism," 33f.

peace, and joy in the Holy Spirit," and the ability to follow, from the perspective of the poor, the way of the Spirit's fellowship toward "the ecumenical movement and the mission of the Church."[5]

In a paper given at the North American Academy of Ecumenists (1991)[6] Donald Dayton, an expert of Pentecostal/ecumenical relationship in Latin America, vividly describes the fears and difficulties which block further dialogue, and is rather harsh with organized ecumenism. He describes the subtle disdaining of "Pentecostal Christianity" and related movements in the supposedly more mature and tolerant ecumenical circles. He is surprised at the extent to which both Protestants and Catholics attempt to interpret Pentecostalism in Latin America in the categories of the "problem of the sects"—and testifies to having a whole shelf of books by Protestants, Catholics, and secular journalists on topics like the "irruption of the sects" and "the problem of the sects," lumping together "marginal Christian movements" like the Unification Church (Moonies) with Pentecostalism.

During a sabbatical in Geneva Dayton describes having been astonished to hear, at a meeting of the Commission of World Mission and Evangelism, the cavalier and flat rejection of a proposal which had recommended that one plenary session at the Canberra Full Assembly of the World Council of Churches (1991) be devoted to exploring the missiological significance of Pentecostalism. It is obviously one thing to title such a meeting "Signs of the Spirit"[7] and another thing to read these signs, especially if they appear "not in the official context."

"Ecumenical" has become in many circles an "invective," and in others a party label which describes the work of those already committed to each other, and which carries the connotation of "enlightenment" (subtly denigrating those who do not see the world through the "party's" glasses). Indeed, the movement *is* becoming institutionalized. Probably the greatest challenge to this institutionalization is posed by Pentecostalism and the questions it raises—in particular its complex, informal, and "polycephalous" oral style of organization. (In Argentina there are for instance over a thousand separate Pentecostal bodies ["juridical persons"] registered with the government). Dayton also describes having observed many times, in a variety of ecumenical contexts, fierce infighting over the application of grid and quota systems which carry with them the pretention of having the whole world wrapped up, but which leave no room for new or missing partners in ecumenical dialogue.

One further indication of the current state of affairs is the important file in the archives of the World Council of Churches in Geneva on "failed negotiations" with Pentecostals. It would be a real contribution if a young scholar could take this topic as the theme for a doctoral dissertation.

---

[5] Robeck, "Pentecostals and Ecumenism," 35.
[6] Dayton, "Turning." Since I base my information on the draft of this lecture, I am not allowed to quote verbatim.
[7] Kinnamon, *Signs*.

On the other hand, there are the untiring work of Marta Palma, a Chilean Pentecostal who occupies the Latin American and Caribbean desk concerned with human rights in the World Council of Churches;[8] the nudgings of the already-mentioned Eugene Stockwell, an old hand in ecumenism;[9] the sympathy of Emilio Castro, a Methodist from Uruguay and a former General Secretary of the World Council;[10] the writings of Juan Sepúlveda, an ecumenical Pentecostal from Chile;[11] and the analyses of Carmelo E. Alvarez.[12]

Psychological and institutional obstacles are responsible for the fact that the Latin American experience (not just the Pentecostal) is profoundly marginalized in the life of the World Council of Churches, despite the two past General Secretaries who have come from this region (Philip Potter from the Caribbean and the already-mentioned Emilio Castro). Out of 900 or so delegates at the Full Assembly of the World Council at Canberra, only twenty represented Latin America, mainly because the largest blocks of Christians in Latin America (Roman Catholics, Pentecostals, and other Pentecostal-like evangelicals) are not formally linked to the World Council of Churches. Dayton recalls the protest of a Lutheran woman from Latin America that there was only one Latin American Lutheran on the Central Committee and that this was unacceptable because Lutherans make up two-thirds of Latin American Christians. She quickly corrected herself to say two-thirds of those belonging to member churches of the World Council of Churches (in fact a tiny minority of Latin American Christianity).

This situation will not change unless there are strong and clear decisions taken and priorities set. Dayton believes—as I have proposed for a long time[13]—that things will not change unless a desk is established with the explicit assignment to create workable relationships with Latin American Pentecostals.

In Dayton's opinion the discussion is still too Eurocentric. Even if, for example, Lutherans and Roman Catholics are able to agree on "justification," this has no impact on the Latin American context, where a majority of Protestants do not stand in the line of Luther and do not, for the most part, take their identity from this Protestant tradition (see chapter 12, pp. 146–52).

Other indications show that Latin Americans take the lead in ecumenical/Pentecostal relationships, for instance at a consultation "Toward the Common Expression of the Apostolic Faith Today," organized by the Com-

---

[8] Palma, Marta, "Conciliar Movement."

[9] Eugene Stockwell, see above note 3.

[10] Castro, "Pentecostalism."

[11] Sepúlveda, "Pentecostalism," where he argues that a fuller understanding of Pentecostalism is essential for ecumenism.

[12] Alvarez, "Latin." See also his *Santidad* (reviewed by David Bundy in *Pneuma* 8/2, Fall 1986, 186–88, above chapter 16, p. 209); idem, *People.* A helpful report and bibliography by Wilson, E. A., "Potential."

[13] See my article "Verheissung," in particular 286f., but see also—as of late—WCC, *Consultation.*

mission on Faith and Order of the National Council of Churches of Christ, USA. The highest ranking ecclesiastical leader at this consultation was Jesse Miranda, an Hispanic superintendent of the American Assemblies of God. He "drew on his identity as a classical Pentecostal and a Hispanic"—there are now between 25 and 30 million Hispanics in the US—

> to talk about the intersection and interaction of cultures: "I am a Christian who sees the church, *now and in eternity*, as a multi–racial, multi–cultural, *multi–doctrinal* community—a beautiful tapestry, a colourful mosaic." . . . With Synan, he emphasized the diversity within the Pentecostal movement in both theology and culture. He was more hopeful about the "new bread" of Pentecostal scholars who are providing "more viable and adequate" theological statements.[14]

North America

For twenty years official historiography presented the American Assemblies of God as a strictly anti-ecumenical church. This history—whether by ignorance or by opportunism—does not correspond to the facts. Far into the '60s the Assemblies of God worked intensively in several committees of the National Council of Churches in Christ. They even had an office in "Babylon," the headquarters of the NCCC in New York. Only in the '70s did they sever their relationships with the ecumenical agencies, mainly under pressure from the fundamentalists. We owe this rather sensational discovery to the research of Cecil M. Robeck. He writes:

> One can only wonder, because in the end, Assemblies of God leaders, for whatever reason, found it more expedient to break with old friendships, embrace the agenda of an old enemy, capitulate to questions of a new set of "friends," and compromise what appears to be a basic Pentecostal distinctive with the enactment of a Bylaw which limits with whom Pentecostals can talk or work, than they did to act without guile. The earliest Pentecostals including the Assemblies of God believed that their way was the answer to Jesus' prayer in John 17:21.[15]

In this connection we have also to mention the Pentecostal Fellowship of North America (1948)[16] This fellowship grew out of the relationships developed among the Pentecostal members of the National Association of Evangelicals. It was a limited fellowship, since it included no Hispanic, Afro-American, or Oneness Pentecostals.

The Oneness Pentecostals have also organized the "Apostolic World Christian Fellowship," a loose fellowship of Oneness Pentecostal denominations

---

[14] Jeffrey Gros, FSC (Director of the Commission on Faith and Order of the National Council of Churches of Christ in the USA), "Confessing," 12–13, emphasis mine.

[15] Robeck, "Ecumenical Cooperation" (from the ms, p. 46). See also idem, "Mission"; idem, "Unity" (forthcoming); and Cole, "Ecumenical Tensions."

[16] Warner, "Pentecostal Fellowship." "Dwindling interest and attendance in recent years prompted the Pentecostal Fellowship of North America participants to change the meetings from rally to leadership type and was open by invitation" (704).

(1970). The role Pentecostals have played in the National Association of Evangelicals has already been documented.[17] In 1962 a smaller counterpart of the National Association of Evangelicals was founded in Los Angeles, California; it is an association for Afro-American evangelicals and Pentecostals.[18]

There have also been several dialogues pursued over the year, including an evangelical/Roman Catholic dialogue and an Assemblies of God/Roman Catholic dialogue. More decisive has probably been the inclusion of a number of Pentecostals in the Commission on Faith and Order of the National Council of Churches of Christ, USA. Participants included Cecil M. Robeck, Jerry L. Sandidge, Harold D. Hunter, Edith Blumhofer, and David Daniels.[19] It seems that the impetus for this ecumenical beginning came not only from the Pentecostals, but also from a Catholic, namely Jeff Gros.[20] The papers of the consultation were published in *Pneuma*[21] and in *One in Christ* (23:1–2, 1987).

> The consultation brought together about seventy-five conciliar Protestants, Orthodox and Roman Catholics, as well as a number of Pentecostals for a period of candid and fruitful discussion. It resulted in a desire by those involved in the consultation to continue discussion between Pentecostals and members of the National Council of Churches of Christ, USA.[22]

Besides the important paper by Jeffrey Gros, in which he quotes the amazing statement by the Assemblies of God superintendent Jesse Miranda, one should mention Claire Randall (General Secretary of the National Council of Churches of Christ, USA, 1974–84). Randall asserted that the Oneness Pentecostals can sharpen the questions raised in the Faith and Order Commission in relation to its understanding of the trinitarian doctrine.[23] She also touched on their contribution to the understanding of folk religion and the black Pentecostal experience. Robeck addressed "fear as a key issue" in ecumenism. He gently but critically pointed to weaknesses in American Pentecostalism, especially in their endeavor to please the evangelicals. "The price of

---

[17] See above, chapter 15, pp. 192–94.

[18] National Black Evangelical Association; Robeck, "Pentecostals and Ecumenism," 9 (not in *Dictionary*).

[19] Robeck mentions: Dr. Edith Blumhofer (Assemblies of God), David Daniels (Church of God in Christ), Dr. Harold Hunter (Church of God of Prophecy), Dr. Donald W. Dayton (Wesleyan Church), Stephen Land (Church of God), Dr. Jerry L. Sandidge (Assemblies of God), Dr. Vinson Synan (Pentecostal Holiness Church) Robeck, "Pentecostals and Ecumenism," 19, note 54.

[20] Gros, "Confessing."

[21] Besides J. Gros's paper (note 20), the following papers were published: Rusch, "Theology" (Rusch is the Ecumenical officer for the Lutheran Church in America and presented a fairly traditional protestant interpretation of the *filioque*); Synan, "Pentecostalism"; Claire Randall (see below, note 23); Cecil M. Robeck (see below note 25); Everett Wilson (see above, note 12); Jerry L. Sandidge (see below note 28); Carmelo E. Alvarez (see above note 12); Horgan, "Consultation."

[22] Robeck, "Pentecostalism and Ecumenism" (note 1), 17f.

[23] Randall, "Importance," 56.

acceptance has included changes which are viewed by some Pentecostals precisely, as 'compromises,' " for example, on pacifism[24] and on the "traditionally. . . wide ranging opportunity to women in ministry." This latter characteristic, well established in early Pentecostalism, has been eroded in recent years.[25] As a true disciple of Du Plessis, Robeck mentions at the end of his paper the need for "forgiveness of past hurts." He also knows that

> early Pentecostals tended to be more open to doctrinal diversity than they are today. Lilian B. Yeomans, MD, noted that "the Church in all her divisions recognizes the Holy Spirit as indispensable to her life and genuine growth . . . *Differing theologies have nothing to do with it,* nor differing Church nomenclature. The need confessed by all churches is greater spirituality."[26]

It is amazing that such a statement was expressed in the Faith and Order Commission of all places. However, if coherence is not to be achieved through theology, we must ask: through what, then, is it to be achieved?[27]

Jerry Sandidge hit the nail on the head when he concluded:

> Pentecostals need "bridge people" who will step into the ecumenical arena with their gloves on, confronting all the issues of the conciliar movement. Those same people, then, must enter the "sweat box" of their own tradition to explain that it is good to be in the ring. Somehow, leadership in the classical Pentecostal denominations must be shown, enticed, encouraged—in some way convinced—into seeing the value and necessity of participation in the ecumenical family . . . The conciliar movement needs to nudge the Pentecostals into expressing a greater concern for threatening world issues, aching social problems, women, poor, and economically and culturally marginalized peoples; discussion of areas of common witness, possibilities for the mutual recognition of ministry, and the sharing

---

[24] See chapter 14, pp. 187–89.

[25] Robeck, "Implications," in particular 69, 70, 71, 75. There is a most interesting follow-up paper by Robeck ("Apostolicity"), in which he probes the different "apostolic traditions" (Oneness and others) within Pentecostalism as to their ecumenical relevance. The issue of the erosion of female ministry in Pentecostalism was also addressed by Barbara Brown Zikmund (United Church of Christ), quoted in Gros, "Confessing," (note 20), 13.

[26] Note 2.

[27] This was picked up already in 1985 by Jakob Zopfi: "We are very happy that liberal theologials (*sic*) are baptized in the Holy Spirit. But what does it help to talk if they go on in their liberal understanding of the Bible? And praise God again, when pastors of the state church are baptized in the Holy Spirit! But if they stay in their state church ecclesiology—what should we speak about? Of course, we could speak with many, many people of this whole world. We are not against that. But when the Holy Spirit, who wants to lead in all truth, does not have more success, does anybody in this world believe that our talks will be more fruitful? I am not talking about nonessential Bible understanding. Ecclesiology is of vital importance to me." Zopfi, "Now What?" and "Answer." Leaving aside Zopfi's Helvetian English one might compare this with the chapter on Pentecostal ecclesiology in this volume (chapter 20, pp. 264–67). Nevertheless, the question of coherence and identity of an ecumenical movement which is not mainly theologically defined has to be addressed in the final chapter.

of theological insights . . . The Pentecostal misunderstanding of the ecumenical movement as a super world-church needs to be corrected.[28]

Europe and Africa

In Europe the ecumenical impetus will come either from the Pentecostals in Eastern Europe (who already under the Communist regime studied at universities and established relationships with non-Pentecostal churches) or from the black Pentecostal churches in Britain, or both. I do not have up-to-date information on Eastern Europe, but on the black British scene we are well informed by Roswith Gerloff. From among this group, the Shilo United Church of Christ Apostolic (Worldwide) was the first Pentecostal church to be received into membership of the European Council of Churches (1984). This episcopal church with both trinitarian and oneness elements is an interesting new blend of Christianity. It is a member of the British Council of Churches and has worldwide relationships (among others, with the Old Holy Catholic Church).[29]

The second church to enter the European Council of Churches was the Council of African and Afro-Caribbean Churches from Britain (1990).[30]

---

[28] Sandidge, "Consultation Summary."

[29] Oral communication by Jean Fischer, Conference of European Churches, May 25, 1993. Gerloff II, no. 151.

[30] Information from Jean Fischer, Conference of European Churches, letter May 24, 1993. Below a list of the member churches of the Council of African and Afro-Caribbean churches (068) (numbers relate to Gerloff's list). The document which the Council submitted to the Conference of European Churches has a different list from Gerloff's. As the names are sometimes interchangeable I cannot sort out the problem. The document lists 18 churches, 40 congregations, 12,000 members, 120 ministers, 300 local and lay preachers and 2,500 children and young people as affiliated to their council.

    004 (African) Pentecostal Revival Church of Jesus Christ
    006 Aladura International Church (UK and Overseas)
    029 Celestial Church of Christ
    030 (Cherubim and Seraphim) Holy Church of Christ
    031 Cherubim and Seraphim Society
    033 Christ Apostolic Church (UK)
    062 Church of the Lord (Brotherhood)
    065 Church of the Universal Prayer Fellowship
    069 Divine Prayer Society 1944
    080 Eternal Sacred Order of the Morning Star and St. Michael Star
         Foundation of Life Mount Zion
    093 (1) Christ Healing Church = All Saints Born Again Christ Healing Church
         (2) Christ the King Pentecostal Church
         (8) Holy Mount Zion Revival Church
    095 Hackney Pentecostal Apostolic Church
    122 Musama Disco Christo Church
    146 Seventh Church of Melchizedec
    175 (8) All Saints (Aladura) Church of Christ

Other churches and church clusters (such as the International Ministerial Council of Britain[31]) are members of the British Council of Churches.

Some of these mainly black church clusters are small, but together they represent an impressive pioneering move in European Pentecostalism. Some of them express themselves in fundamentalistic language. However, they are in a process of

> distancing themselves slowly from this unsavory white heritage. People who fight in their own existence against racism or (like the black woman) against sexism, who refuse to be separated in social classes, who act and propagate self-help programmes, who take a stand for their youth and who (as in Britain) become ecumenical partners in the struggle for social justice, have little in common with a fundamentalism, who wants to preserve the status quo. If at all, it is a "liturgical fundamentalism" (James Barr) which preserves the beauty of the biblical word and a theology which returns to biblical "fundamentals" and refuses to be determined by foreign thought categories.

The ecumenical significance of these "black churches" in Britain (and elsewhere) consists in recognizing the fact that the Holy Spirit helps people "to survive on a technically manipulated and exploited earth."

---

(23) Cherubim and Seraphim (IMOLE)
(24) Christ the Resurrection Church
(38) Eternal Sacred Order New Temple (CS) Church
(39) Evangelic Church of Christ
(75) New Church of God

The Council has links with France, USA, Netherlands, Germany, Ghana, and Nigeria. It is also a member of the British Council of Churches and of the Free Church Federation Council. Gerloff, no. 068.

[31] The member churches of the International Ministerial Council of Great Britain (107) are:

002 African Methodist Episcopal Church
004 (African) Pentecostal Revival Church of Jesus Christ (Streatham)
020 Bethel Apostolic Church
035 Church of God and True Holiness
039 (038?) Church of God Fellowship in Great Britain
057 Church of Jesus Christ of the Apostolic Faith
069 Divine Prayer Society 1944 (The Church of the Family of God and of Jesus Christ)
075 Emmanuel International Revival Church (Calvary Healing Temple)
086 Faith Apostolic Church = Universal Evangelical Church
093 (5) Divine Healing Pentecostal Church of Christ (UK and Ghana)
101 Holy Tabernacle of Christ Jesus
129 (2) Pentecostal Church of God
151 Shilo United Church of Christ Apostolic (World-Wide)
175 (36) Elim Pentecostal Church (B1)
Walworth Methodist Church.

The International Ministerial Council of Great Britain (107) is a member of the British Council of Churches (Gerloff, 107).

The "Black-out" of ways of biblical interpretations different from the Western approach has robbed the language of the church of a communicative power. Only churches which offer experience instead of dogma, living testimonies instead of consistent arguments, sisterhood and brotherhood instead of rational proofs, songs instead of books, are able to rediscover the biblical message.[32]

It is no accident that the black churches in Europe have been the first to take up the ecumenical challenge, although they have done it in their own way, and so will create much headache for the conciliar church bureaucrats. But who knows, perhaps they will force the mainline churches to develop ecumenical incarnations which are nearer to the people. Every expert knows that the average Christian in Europe couldn't care less about the ecumenical movement, although their leaders make big pronouncements at the international level. It is different, however, in the black churches. Their members care about ecumenical cooperation. It seems that they—like the Kimbanguists (chapter 6, pp. 54–80)—consider ecumenical fellowship not as a luxury in which one indulges when one has nothing more important to do, but as the very essence of ecclesiology. That this concern has social and cultural roots is clear.

Why is it that these black churches have developed such ecumenical activity? One of the reasons is their understanding of the church: they operate in fellowship with other churches, including those which Pentecostals consider to be liberal. After all, it was neither the evangelicals nor the Pentecostals in Britain who opened the door to a university education to these black Pentecostals (chapter 9, pp. 106–16), but the so-called "liberals." Working together with them has corrected, for these black churches, many a cliché about Protestant and Catholic mainline churches. Black Pentecostals have gotten to know theologians like Roswith Gerloff as well as the teachers at the University and the Selly Oak Colleges, and even a Roman Catholic bishop— Dr. Patrick Kalilombe, the former director of the Centre for Black and White Christian Partnership. Recently (1994) Gerloff introduced at the University of Leeds BA and MA degree programs on "black Religion and black Christianity in Great Britain." This personal cooperation has made ecumenicity visible and concrete to the black churches.

One encouraging sign among other European Pentecostals was an important meeting at Gunten, Switzerland, featuring representatives from the World Council of Churches, the Pentecostal European Conference,[33] and several national Pentecostal organizations. There have also been some contacts between Pentecostals and evangelicals (mainly in Britain and Scandinavia). The Fédération protestante de France has two Pentecostal member organizations, namely the Pentecostal Gipsy mission (*Mission évangélique tzigane de France*, 30,000) and the Church of God (*Eglise de Dieu*, 1000).[34] But by and large white European

---

[32] Gerloff, "Schwarze Kirchen."

[33] *The Pentecostals*, 442–51; Hocken with Cartwright, "European," 268–78, esp. 278.

[34] As of late see Gerloff and van Beek, *Report*. On France, see Baubérot/Willaim, "Fédération."

Pentecostals keep to themselves, and find it difficult enough to keep peace *among* themselves. This will change only once they follow the example of their black, Latin, and North American brothers and sisters.

As for Africa, at the Full Assembly of the World Council of Churches in Nairobi a number of African Pentecostal churches became members of the World Council.[35] The intensive ecumenical debate in South Africa has already been discussed (chapter 5, pp. 41–53).

Consultation in Bossey (1980)

On August 31st, 1979 Philip Potter, then General Secretary of the World Council of Churches, wrote a letter to all member churches asking them for help in identifying the issues in relation to the charismatic renewal.[36] The reaction was overwhelming. Philip Potter did not

> remember in the history of the World Council of Churches any letter coming from the General Secretary which was so generously and copiously responded to—and that is saying something. There were nearly 70 official replies and with those replies were many documents taken out of synods and General Assemblies of churches and personal experiences expressed.[37]

This response encouraged the World Council to hold a consultation on Pentecostalism/Independentism/Charismatism in Bossey, Switzerland (*"Consultation on the Significance of the Charismatic Renewal for the Churches"*).

Suffice it to quote a few significant examples from the vast material: "The Kimbanguist church, in whose midst there are permanent charismatic manifestations, although not yet having made an official declaration on this subject, wishes to participate and provide a living witness of its experience in this matter."[38]

"The history of the Salvation Army, and particularly its very rapid expansion from a small London mission to a world movement in twenty years, is only intelligible as a work of the Holy Spirit. For this reason, the Salvation Army could itself be called a charismatic movement and its early meetings resembled . . . charismatic meetings of today."[39]

"More important than liturgical movements and innovation in worship is the transition from a structure of worship dominated by the single voice of the pastor to one which is charismatic and congregational."[40]

---

[35] For a full list of Pentecostal member churches of the World Council of Churches see below, pp. 386–87. I have no up-to-date information on Asia.

[36] In *Bossey*, 39. *Bossey* is a highly important collection of material on Pentecostalism/Charismatism/Indepentism and the World Council.

[37] Potter, "Charismatic Renewal," 74.

[38] *Bossey*, 42.

[39] Ibid.

[40] Evangelical Churches of Westphalia, Germany; *Bossey*, 43. Similarly the United Church of North India; *Bossey*, 49, and the Church of the Czech Brethren Czechoslovakia; *Bossey*, 49.

The renewal in the highlands of New Guinea, "while it may be expressed in charismatic language, in fact is deeply dependent on traditional responses in animistic religion and is a superb illustration of the cultural relativism of spirit type responses."[41] In this connection, "Is it not important to build a bridge to forms of group ecstasy already there in local cultures rather than culturally alienating people by the use of stereotyped imported material?"[42] This last point was taken up by Chung Hyun Kyung at the Full Assembly of Canberra (1991).[43]

The United Society for the Propagation of the Gospel reflected on the charismatic experiences in Britain, concluding that these charismatic groups are "divisive in the sense that the unity they proclaim 'across denominational barriers' is a unity of the like-minded."[44]

In Ghana, "Many of the newer churches which have burst out of this situation are headed by men of little education who have gifts of leadership which they could not exercise within the older churches."[45] The Pentecostal experience in Ghana is not only a reaction "against the Western forms of liturgy but also against the older churches' bureaucratic organization and conservativism."[46] "The older churches are growing at between 30 and 45%, the Pentecostal churches seem to be growing nearly 70% over the same period."[47]

From Canada, this assessment of the charismatic movement: "This is the largest grassroots ecumenical movement in 800 years . . . The World Council of Churches has brought together Catholic and Protestant traditions, but it has not been a grassroots movement, nor does it have the potential of becoming one as long as it is based mainly on discussion."[48] "Therefore the question must be raised: What can the ecumenical movement learn from the charismatic movement? Characteristics of the latter must be examined: spontaneous; lay-oriented; dynamic; worship- and mission-oriented; trans-denominational."[49]

From Ghana again: "It seems to me that while the charismatics pay more attention to the physical needs of the people, the non-charismatics are more concerned with the spiritual needs of the people, such as salvation and Christian growth."[50]

---

[41] United Theological College; *Bossey*, 49.

[42] Pacific Conference of Churches; *Bossey*, 45.

[43] See below, pp. 383–84 and the chapter on "Syncretism," chapter 11, pp. 132–41.

[44] United Society for the Propagation of the Gospel, UK; *Bossey*, 51.

[45] Bible Reading Association, Ghana; *Bossey*, 52.

[46] Bible Reading Association, Ghana; *Bossey*, 53.

[47] Bible Reading Association, Ghana; *Bossey*, 53. Cf. also above, ch. 26, "The Protestant Charismatic Renewal: Ecumenical or What?"; on Ghana, see note 59, p. 363.

[48] Hope Reformed Church, Canada; *Bossey*, 56f.

[49] Hope Reformed Church, Canada; *Bossey*, 56f.

[50] Ghana Baptist Convention; *Bossey*, 62.

From Germany: "What brings young people into these groups is not convincing arguments but the fact that they feel themselves emotionally attracted to it,"[51] and the observation that in Protestant theology "there is no systematic reflection on piety and the religious life."[52]

This random choice from documents from all over the world shows how different Pentecostal/charismatic phenomena are viewed by the member churches of the World Council. Some state categorically that they are already "charismatic,"[53] others want to learn from the charismatic movement, others see its divisive influence, and others again see in their own pre-Christian culture the Spirit of God at work already, which has to be discovered, cleansed, and integrated into a Christian framework of priorities.

Philip Potter's first remark on this material was his astonishment. "I didn't realize how vast the phenomenon of the Charismatic Renewal was and the vastness of the literature."[54] Up to this day this kind of lack of awareness is widespread, both within and outside the World Council. In the end, Potter, a Methodist, took the line that charismatic concerns have been central to all Christian churches, from the Orthodox and the Catholic to Wesley and beyond. The charismatic renewal thus "confirms the goal of the ecumenical movement."[55] It "provides a link between the churches of the Reformation, the Roman Catholic Church, the conservative Evangelicals," and the Orthodox.[56] This can also be seen in the fact that both [Charismatics and Ecumenists] are criticized on the same ground—that of authority. The churches regard both the World Council and the charismatic/Pentecostal movement as not sufficiently under their authority.[57] "The whole ecumenical movement has been in fact a Charismatic Renewal."[58] Theologically this is of course true: one would like to see a bit more of this kind of response.

In response to Potter's opening speech, the consultation developed a new style of working and thinking together, a style which had already begun at Bangkok[59]

---

[51] EKiD (Federation of Protestant Churches in Germany); *Bossey*, 63.
[52] EKiD; *Bossey*, 64.
[53] Above, notes 38 and 39.
[54] Potter, "Charismatic Renewal," 75.
[55] Ibid., 79.
[56] Ibid.
[57] Ibid., 81.
[58] Ibid.
[59] The conference volume of Bangkok appeared only in German (Potter, *Das Heil*). Bangkok was a "wild" but creative conference. It did not, however, solve the problem of combining creativity with analysis. This was better solved in *Bossey* and in later WCC conferences. Bangkok produced a wide range of international reactions in many languages (see Hollenweger, "Reviews Bangkok"). I tried to give an aperçu of Bangkok in "Goes to Bangkok," and in a novel (only printed in German as *Glaube*). English publishers were not interested in this theological novel. Parts of it appeared in several periodicals (see bibliography in Jongeneel (ed.), 1992, 311–70, in particular nos. 73.31, 74.03, 75.14, 76.18, 76.20). Chapter 2 of this volume is the concluding chapter of the novel on Mr. Chips. In German Mr. Chips is called "Professor Unrat."

and had been continued at the Full Assemblies of Nairobi, Vancouver, and Canberra. This "style" had much to do with the composition of the consultation: Participants came from many different backgrounds. There were well-known theologians[60] and members of the World Council's working group on Renewal and Congregational Life (people usually described as ecumenical church bureaucrats). Present were in addition a nuclear physicist/chairman of the cabinet of the chef spiritual of the Kimbanguist church,[61] the General Secretary of the African Israel Nineveh Church from Kenya,[62] and a black choir from the Church of God in Christ[63] (England) with their pastor (a driving instructor by profession and a student at the Centre for Black and White Christian Partnership in Birmingham[64]). One of the worship services was led by the Senior Apostle of the Cherubim and Seraphim Society from Birmingham[65] according to the liturgy of his church, which is identical, word for word, with the old Anglo-Catholic liturgy—except that he celebrated it without reference to a printed liturgy and with all the dramatic panache and deeply-felt reverence of an African who actually knew and experienced that he was praying in the presence of "angels and archangels, the cherubim and seraphim and all the company of heaven." Prophecies and speaking in tongues fitted easily into this age-old liturgy.

How does one lead such a diverse group of people in a study and consultation process? Philip Potter solved this problem by describing his own thoughts, joys, comments, and criticism when reading through the thick file of responses to his initial letter. By personalizing his theological analysis, he made it possible for everybody—the academics and the "worker pastors"—to follow his critical analysis. The consultation became itself not only an observation and study of the charismatic renewal, but a cognitive charismatic/Pentecostal process. That this transformation did not militate against critical thinking is seen from the "Report of the Consultation."[66] Among a number of interesting theological prognostications, the consultation's most important "Hope for the Future" was this:

> In order to bring the main Charismatic Renewal of the Third World into proper focus, we also hope that in future consultations Latin American Pentecostal churches, North American Black Pentecostal churches, African Independent

---

A German professor (Prof. Beyerhaus of Tübingen) thought he recognized himself in this description, wrongly, because Chips/Unrat is a composite fictional personality.

[60] Bittlinger, "Opportunity"; Dunn, "Models"; Hocken, "Survey"; McDonnell, "Reactions," plus reports from Africa, New Guinea, Europe, Latin America, North America, etc.

[61] Bena Silu.

[62] See below, p. 386.

[63] Jones, C. E., "Church of God in Christ," and Gerloff, *Plea* II, no. 042.

[64] Pastor Alvin Blake, Luton, UK.

[65] John Adegoke. The Cherubim and Seraphim Church belongs to the same family as the "Church of the Lord" (below, p. 386). Gerloff, *Plea* II, no. 032.

[66] *Bossey*, 201–12.

churches, and Asian Pentecostal churches (member and non-member churches of the World Council of Churches) can be more adequately represented.[67]

In response to the report of the consultation, the Sub-Unit on Renewal and Congregational Life submitted a statement to the Central Committee, in which the "unusually large number of responses to the letter of the General Secretary" was noted. It recommended that the Central Committee "pay attention to the report from the Consultation, comment on it, and pass it on through the General Secretary, to the member churches, together with its own comments . . . It is the intention of the sub-unit to continue the study and the consultative process."[68] This statement was unanimously accepted by the Central Committee of the World Council in August 1980. What has resulted?

My impression is that hardly anybody in Geneva has noticed the report and its accompanying papers, some of which were of very high quality. It seems the World Council went into a kind of hibernation on this issue. Impulses to deal with the issues surrounding the renewal certainly had not come from the General Secretariat, nor from the Sub-Unit on Renewal and Congregational Life. The bureaucracy was occupied with other things. However, new impulses had come from different quarters, as we have seen above.[69] In the end, this had some marginal repercussions on the World Council.

In a sense the Brighton Conference on World Evangelization (1991), organized by the International Charismatic Consultation on World Evangelization, took up the Bossey concerns. That is, at the margin of the Brighton Conference a number of Pentecostal/charismatic and ecumenical theologians treated some of the issues raised at Bossey. This attention started with a pneumatological paper by Jürgen Moltmann,[70] to which Miroslav Volf[71] and others reacted. Then the issue of an "African Independent Church Pneumatology"[72] was treated in detail. Others addressed the topic of women in ministry,[73] "Charismatic Churches and Apartheid in South Africa,"[74] "Pentecostalism and Liberation Theology: Two Manifestations of the Work of the Holy Spirit for the Renewal of the Church,"[75] and the historical controversy on whether Pentecostalism/charismatism started with the black ecumenist Seymour or with the white racist Parham.[76] Finally, a new challenge was the

---

[67] Ibid., 211.

[68] Ibid., 230.

[69] See chapter 27, pp. 369–74, and chapter 13, pp. 165–80.

[70] Moltmann, "Life"; see chapter 17, pp. 218–22.

[71] Volf, "Rhythm."

[72] Daneel, "African." See chapter 5, pp. 51–53.

[73] Bridges-Johns, "Women." See chapter 20, pp. 267–68.

[74] Poewe-Hexham/Hexham, "Apartheid." Responses by Nico Horn and Wynand J. de Kock in the same volume. See chapter 5, pp. 41–52.

[75] Sepúlveda, "Liberation." On this important paper by Sepúlveda see also chapter 16, p. 209. Also Cook, Guillermo, "Church."

[76] Robeck, "Origins." Contra Robeck: Goff, "History." On the whole controversy see chapters 3 (pp. 20–24) and 24 (pp. 326–29).

consideration of non-Christian religions as falling within the sphere of the Spirit's activity. This challenge was taken up by Jean-Jacques Suurmond. Suurmond does recognize gifts of the Spirit as being at work in non-Christian religions, and states: "Had Pentecostalism not quickly been infiltrated by fundamentalist views, there might have been a charismatic *renewal of the religions.*"[77]

Pentecostals at the Full Assembly of Canberra (1991)

The late Jerry L. Sandidge, a pioneer in Pentecostal ecumenism, states bluntly: "There should be some contact between the Pentecostal side of the [Vatican/Pentecostal] Dialogue and the World Council of Churches."[78] Certainly, there should, but how is it going to happen? One harbinger of such contact was the attendance by a number of Pentecostals of the Full Assembly of the World Council at Canberra. Included among them was the indefatigable Cecil M. Robeck. He was an "accredited visitor," and states that he met with interest and was very well treated. Besides Robeck there were eight official delegates from Pentecostal member churches, plus an assortment of advisors, stewards, and staff; in all, sixteen people out of 4,500.[79]

Robeck noted, among other things, the "horse-trading" which goes on at election time, probably not very different from what is going on in the Christian churches, including the Pentecostal ones. He was also aware of the fact that for instance the Orthodox do not recognize women in the ordained ministry. Therefore other groups were required to send more women to meet the Assembly's quota. He was impressed as well by the statement of an Iraqi Christian about the allied bombing of his country (but it did not change his overall judgment of the Gulf war).

More centrally, Robeck was uneasy about the limits of pluralism. The presence of Jews, Muslim, Buddhists, Hindus, and Sikhs raised problems for some people—although it did not bother Robeck himself. Increasingly, he finds such people in his own neighborhood. "I must come to terms with that . . . I want to affirm what I see in other religions that contributes to the dignity of humanity and to world peace." He was aware that much of what we call "theological" is in fact "cultural" and that many Christians "had not dealt with national guilt for the destruction of peoples . . . in the name of mission." They saw the "reaffirmation of culture and in some cases the reaffirmation of non-Christian religions as a way of solving their guilt."

---

[77] Pinnock, "Evangelism." See also chapter 28, p. 399. Quote from Suurmond, *Word and Spirit at Play*, 208.

[78] Sandidge, *Dialogue (1977–1982)* I, 446. An earlier attempt by the WCC staff member Davies, Rex, *Locusts* (reviewed by Donald D. Smeeton, *EPTA Bulletin* 2/1, 1993, 5–6 ["the major Pentecostal churches are almost completely ignored," 5]).

[79] Robeck, "Canberra", 1993, 111, 112, 116. See also Dayton, "Layer"; idem, "Limits."

He also commented on the contribution by a Korean Presbyterian professor, Chung Hyun Kyung.

> At points, I found her to be genuinely prophetic. At other times, I was very uncomfortable. I worried that she had passed outside the bounds of orthodoxy as, for example, when she "summoned" various spirits of *Han*, spirits of those who had been touched by anger, resentment, bitterness and grief.

It seems to me that this subject of ancestor spirits will need further discussion by Pentecostals, Independents, and non-Pentecostals. Certainly the question is a major one, and not only for Third World Christians. Anyone knowing the Protestant, Catholic, and Pentecostal churches in the Third World knows that there is widespread belief in the presence of ancestor spirits among Third World Christians, and that this belief has almost never been properly addressed by missionary theology, including Pentecostal and charismatic theology. In the West we would describe these spirits in psychological categories (some of the most important problems in the West are not dealt with by priests and pastors but by psychiatrists). What is the ontological difference if the grandmothers and grandfathers who appear in Western or Third World dreams are called spirits, or father- or mother-complexes? Those very churches whose old cathedrals are full of tombs, who are not ashamed to have the "Stars and Stripes," the "Union Jack" or even the "Swastika" (as far as I know these are not Christian but pre-Christian symbols) prominently displayed, shout out when a Korean woman confirms the presence of her ancestors in an ecumenical meeting. The fact that this issue has produced so much dissension and discussion shows that it aggravates a weak spot in Western theology. Just to label such beliefs "psychological" or "superstitious" does not solve the problem.

Robeck states that he could identify at certain points with the Korean *minjung* concerns. "But the summons of departed spirits to come to the Assembly, if that is what was really intended, seemed to me to be more akin to the liturgies of Spiritism or was more rooted in ancestor worship than it was in the classical expression of Christianity."[80]

> In spite of this by no means minor question, I thought that her point was well taken by many . . . Indeed, it is possible that her intent was not so much to summon spirits as it was to enable her audience to identify with a theology from the perspective of suffering and oppression. I believe that were there greater evangelical and/or Pentecostal participation in such a gathering, more significant headway, that is, headway with more genuine Gospel integrity might have been forthcoming in that discussion. As it was, it was left almost totally to the Orthodox to raise up the centrality of Jesus Christ.

All in all Robeck came away with the conviction that the Assembly of the World Council is "an honest and legitimate attempt to demonstrate a form or

---

[80] Robeck, "Canberra", 1993, 112. On the ancestors see above chapter 20, pp. 266–67 and the chapter on syncretism (chapter 11, pp. 132–41). See also, idem, "World Council."

expression of visible Christian unity, as well as an incredibly valuable instructional forum for the churches which participate." For Robeck the time to stand back and criticize is over. The World Council needs the Pentecostals. The Pentecostals need the World Council.

Perhaps some issues would be dealt with more realistically if African and other Third World Pentecostals were to be included in the coming dialogue. It might become visible that some of our Western theological positions are not as biblical as we believe them to be.

It would also, in my opinion, be important to develop a style of discussion in which worship and prayer is as important as cognitive analysis. I believe that the World Council has tried this out on several occasions, not least in Canberra. But the link between "praying and worshipping together" and "thinking and discussing together" has not been achieved. As in most churches, thinking and praying in the World Council appear divorced.

Furthermore, I do not see why the World Council should appear only as a kind of global parliament. This has no attraction and little communicative value. Why not learn from the pope, who in spite of his authoritarian ideology, attracts many people by the fact that he celebrates masses, blesses marriages, and baptizes children. The World Council could organize anointing services of the kind described in chapter 18 (pp. 233–37), common baptismal services, and other liturgies in which some of the "bodily" elements[81] of Pentecostalism (and other churches) are made visible. The people and the money are there; so why not do it?

Pentecostal Member Churches of the World Council of Churches[82]

Nobody seems to know exactly how many Pentecostal churches are members of the World Council of Churches. There are several reasons for this. First, there is no universally accepted definition of a Pentecostal church. If one applies the criteria which I set out in chapter 3 (p. 18), on "The Oral Black Root" (including the Confession of Faith of the first Pentecostal church, the "Apostolic Faith" in Los Angeles[83]), then a great number of the Third World churches belong to Pentecostalism. If, however, one takes as a guideline the full evangelical confessional framework of the American Assemblies of God,[84]

---

[81] See above the remark of the Ghana Baptist Convention, footnote 49.

[82] On the early history see Sandidge, *Dialogue (1977–1982)* I, 13ff. and *The Pentecostals,* 438ff.

[83] Text in *The Pentecostals,* 513 (no "initial sign," no water baptism, no doctrine on scriptural inspiration, etc.). But see the attempts at defining Pentecostalism by Kilian McDonnell and Vinson Synan in chapter 24, p. 327. Also Robeck: "Seymour moved away from a theology of tongues as the initial physical evidence of baptism in the Spirit. In point of fact, Seymour ultimately repudiated the 'initial evidence' teaching as providing 'an open door for witches and spiritualists and free loveism' " (Robeck, "Azusa," 36).

[84] *The Pentecostals,* 29ff. However, this evangelical/Pentecostal framework is now becoming shaky, as is clear from the discussions in this book.

then not even all the churches represented in the Pentecostal World Conference belong to Pentecostalism.[85] If—as a way out—a church is *asked* whether it is Pentecostal or not, then the answer will depend very much on the context of the question: there are situations where it is to the disadvantage of a church to call herself Pentecostal (because "Pentecostal" can mean a specific Western brand of Pentecostalism with which that church does not want to identify, or for social or prestige reasons).

Secondly, the "world confessional families" (Reformed, Lutheran, Anglican, Roman Catholic, Orthodox, Baptist, Methodist, etc.) have been developed in Europe and America, based solely on theological categories derived from written confessions. The theologies of the Third World churches, on the other hand, are very often to be found not in their confessions but in their liturgies (as in New Testament times)—in their hymns, histories, and testimonies. This is clearly seen by Villafañe: "The 'culto' is the clearest reflection of the theology of the community of faith . . . Our theology . . . is not a lineal, horizontal, written reflection."[86]

More adequate categories must be developed if we are to group the world churches in a truly representational way: the Western confessional divisions are inadequate. There is a world of difference between a Roman Catholic in Germany and one in Flores (Indonesia); or between a member of the British Pentecostal Elim Church[87] and a Mexican[88] or Arab Pentecostal; or between a Dutch Lutheran and a Lutheran from Indonesia.[89] On the other hand there is more common ground between German Catholics and German Protestants, and between American Pentecostals and American mainline churches, than between these bodies and many of their co-religionists in other parts of the world.

Furthermore, it is doubtful whether the theological categories as formulated in the official documents of the churches play a significant role in the life and spirituality of ordinary church members, or even of pastors and priests. This also applies to the Roman Catholic church, which is—from a global point of view—much more pluralistic than its leaders would like it to be.

---

[85] For instance some German Pentecostals (*The Pentecostals*, 231ff.). A German was the first Pentecostal to address a Full Assembly of the WCC (Krust, "Churches"). The Chilean Pentecostals (chapter 10, pp. 117–31) and others would also not qualify.

[86] Villafañe (*The Liberating Spirit*, 124) quoting Costas, *Protestantismo*, vii. Villafañe rightly refers to my colleague, the Swiss liturgiologist J.-J. von Allmen *(El Culto)* and Cullman *(La Fé)*.

[87] Prior, *Indonesian*. For "Elim," *The Pentecostals*, 197ff.

[88] Gill, *Contextualised*. Gaxiola-Gaxiola, *Mexican*.

[89] Some Indonesian churches have joined the Lutheran World Federation for reasons of convenience.

In the following list, I have included a dozen churches which clearly show Pentecostal characteristics, according to my definition of "Pentecostal" in *The Pentecostals* (pp. xxi–xxii):

Pentecostal Member Churches of the World Council of Churches[90]
*African Church of the Holy Spirit (Kenya)
- 20,000 members (*Handbook*, 44); 5,400 members (Barrett, *WChE*, 435). "The pioneer of the community in the Kakamega district of Kenya was Mr. Chilson who taught fellow human beings to pray and to confess their sins. They were baptized by him in the Holy Spirit by the laying on of hands. Converts spoke in tongues" (*Handbook*, 44; *Handbuch*, 01.17.017 lit.).

African Israel Church, Nineveh (Kenya)
- 350,000 members (*Handbook*, 45); 100,000 members (*CC* 1988, 7); 76,000 adherents (Barrett, *WChE*, 435). Ex Pentecostal Assemblies of Canada[91] (*Handbook*, 45; Barrett, *WChE*, 435). They practice "infant baptism and the baptism of adults by the Spirit. Baptism with water is not practiced" (*Handbook*, 45; *Handbuch*, 01.17.019).

Church of the Lord Aladura (Nigeria)[92]
- 1,103,340 members (*Handbook*, 51); 750,000 members (*CC* 1988, 7) (Barrett, *WChE*, 531). "The Church is one of the first three Pentecostal churches in Nigeria which have brought considerable revival among African Christians" (*Handbook*, 51; *Handbuch*, 01.28.018).

Eglise de Jésus-Christ sur la Terre par le Prophète Simon Kimbangu (Zaïre)
- See chapter 6 (pp. 54–80). "It remains the deep desire and longing of the Church that the charismatic element break through again and again" (*Handbook*, 69). According to the statistics of the WCC (*CC* 1988, 8; *Handbook*, 69) this church has 5,000,000 members, while all the other member churches of the WCC in Zaïre together have only 1,360,000. Even if one doubts the accuracy of these statistics, this is by far the biggest member church of the WCC in Zaïre.

Eglise Evangélique du Congo
- 110,461 members (*Handbook*, 37); 101,000 members (*CC* 1988, 7). "Because of its charismatic approach and revivalist enthusiasm, the use of African musical instruments and dynamic evangelistic campaigns, this church has a distinct impact on society." It was founded

---

[90] Sources are mainly *Handbook* and *CC*, 1988 An asterisk (*) means "associated member." I was greatly helped in establishing this list by two staff members of the WCC: Hubert van Beek of the General Secretariat and Mr. Beffa from the library. I want to thank them although the result perhaps does not please them in all respects.
[91] Kydd, "Canada."
[92] Turner, *Independent Church* (on the "Church of the Lord").

by the so-called Örebro Baptists (Sweden), a Baptist Church with a specifically Pentecostal spirituality.[93] It is the only member church of the WCC in the People's Republic of the Congo.

Iglesia de Dios (Argentina)
- 40,000 adherents (*Handbook*, 257). Independent, founded by Pentecostal missionaries from Sweden and the USA.

Iglesia de Missiones Pentecostales Libres en Chile
- No statistics in the WCC, nor in Barrett, *WChE*. Whatever the statistics, the three Pentecostal member churches of the WCC in Chile have about 50 times more members than the other member church (Lutheran).

Iglesia Pentecostal de Chile
- 90,000 members (*Handbook*, 265; *CC* 1988, 11; Barrett, *WChE*, 229). This was one of the first Pentecostal churches to join the WCC (*The Pentecostals*, 438–41, *Handbuch*, 02b.08.052).

Igreja Evangélica Pentecostal de Angola
- 3,000 adherents (Barrett, *WChE*, 144); 13,600 members (*Handbook*, 31). Ex Assembleias de Deus.

International Evangelical Church (USA)
- 168,000 members; covers USA, Brazil, Italy, Nigeria (*CC*, 1988, 12; *Handbook*, 223f., *The Pentecostals*, 254, 438). "John McTernan, founder of the International Evangelical Church was the first secretary of the Pentecostal core committee of the Roman Catholic/Pentecostal Dialogue. The Roman Catholic chairman of the Dialogue, Kilian McDonnell, took McTernan to Geneva to discuss with WCC leaders the possibility of the International Evangelical Church becoming a member. This is a direct and positive development from the early years of the Dialogue." Jerry L. Sandidge, *Roman Catholic/Pentecostal Dialogue* I, 43.

Misión Iglesia Pentecostal (Chile)
- 12,000 members (*CC* 1988, 11; *Handbook*, 267f., Barrett, *WChE*, 229; *Handbuch*, 02b.08.061).

Union of Evangelical Christians/Baptists of USSR[94]
- 547,000 members (*Handbook*, 183), 1,014,000 members (*CC* 1988, 10). "In 1945, the Pentecostals joined" (*Handbook*, 183).

---

[93] See the literature in *Handbuch*, 01.19.001, 05.27.005, and statistics by Hocken with Cartwright, "European," 273.

[94] *The Pentecostals*, 267ff.

Appropriately this ecumenical section ends with the

Prayer of the Frog

Sometimes, I feel like a frog,
happy in the waterpond—until I run out of air and creep on land.
Happy in the fresh air, until my skin hurts in the glaring sun
and I plunge back into the water.
O God,
Why did you make me an in-between creature, neither fish nor fowl?
Why am I not a flamingo, or an eagle or a mighty roaring lion?
Just a frog?
You did not ask me whether I wanted to be a frog,
nor whether I wanted to be at all,
nor did my parents ask me.
So, I am, what I am, an in-between being.
When I am with the feminists they call me "macho"
  because I want to pray "Our Father."
When I am with the men they call me a feminist
  because I believe that we should not suppress what is female in us.
When I am with the pacifists they call me a war-monger
  because I do not believe that the abolishment of the Swiss Army serves world
    peace.
When I am with the military they call me a pacifist
  because I find it a scandal how we treat the conscientious objectors.
When I am with the Christians, they say I am not a Christian
  because I find many of their convictions superfluous.
When I am with the non-Christians they say I am a Christian
  because I believe in Jesus Christ
When I am with the progressives they say I am conservative
  because I do not know how to re-organize world trade justly.
When I am with the rich people they say I am a leftist
  because I expect them to share their riches.
When I am with the Catholics they say that I am a Protestant
  because I do not believe in the infallibility of the pope.
When I am with the Protestants they say I am a Catholic
  because I like the Catholic liturgy.
When I am with the Ecumenists they say that I am a Pentecostal
  because I would like to see more of the Spirit in the ecumenical movement.
When I am with the Pentecostals they say I am an ecumenist
  because I am convinced that they need the ecumenical movement.
When I am with the critical exegetes they call me "pious"
  because God sometimes speaks to me in Scripture.
When I am with the uncritical Bible readers they say that I do not believe in the Bible
  because I do not accept their facile interpretations.
O God, you alone know what I am.
Help me to believe that this is enough.
You made me an in-between being so that I can be an evangelist.
But God, it is a tough job.
Sometimes I am confused and terrified.
Strengthen my faith so that I am
a cheerful in-between creature, a happy frog.

CHAPTER TWENTY EIGHT

Conclusion: Problem and Promise

Problem: The Victims

Ex-Pentecostals Anonymous

In order to focus on the *problem* of Pentecostalism I want to remind Pentecostal and non-Pentecostal readers of the many ex–Pentecostals. Pentecostalism—like other religions and ideologies—also has its victims. These victims usually do not write books and articles, so they are difficult to document.[1] One finds them as students of theology at universities and colleges (where they prepare for the ministry in mainline churches). One finds them also at pastors' conferences. Because of my publications they make themselves known to me. It is a fact that the mainline churches have profited greatly from these former Pentecostals. In general they abandon Pentecostal theology but try to safeguard their Pentecostal experience. However, since most Protestant theologies have little room for Pentecostal experience, they are sometimes torn between their experience and their theology. Perhaps this book will help them to resolve this dilemma.

Others have digested their Pentecostal experience and matured in the struggle to sort out their lives and their ideology, and they acquire a healthy suspicion of one hundred per cent and total claims by any brand of religion or ideology, Christian or otherwise. It is astonishing how many ministers and leading lay people who have "fled" Pentecostalism for the historic churches play an important role in their new religious environment. Of course for some Pentecostals these ex–Pentecostals

---

[1] Exceptions: Robinson, *Spoke;* Babcox, *Search.*

are now non-persons. They are nearly always blotted out from the Pentecostal memory and historiography. This is understandable because, as the Pentecostals see the situation, these are people who have tasted the best and the highest, but are now content to feed on crumbs.

Certain neo-Pentecostal churches also practice such "blotting out" of ex-members; for instance, the "Biblische Glaubensgemeinde" (Stuttgart), probably the biggest Pentecostal church in Germany. "Persons who criticize the church and leave are disciplined according to 1 Cor 5:11ff. They are excommunicated from the body of Christ (!), even if they inform the Pentecostal leaders that they do not want to leave the body of Christ but only this particular congregation. The 'Biblische Glaubensgemeinde' risks such to give the impression that it speaks for the whole body of Christ in Stuttgart."[2]

Many carry all their lives the scars of the wounds received from their former friends. Pentecostalism is a high-tension religion and is not for everybody. These victims say: "I was once a hundred per cent Christian. It proved to be a failure. So I prefer to give it up altogether." There are more such people around than one might think. For these ex-Pentecostals, there is no question of accepting the "lukewarm Christianity" of those churches they have known only from the descriptions of disappointed critics. If they cannot be Christians on fire, Christians with a clear witness, Christians with no compromises (all of this meaning "Pentecostal Christians") it is better to leave the faith altogether. I feel profoundly sorry for these ex–Pentecostals. Since for them Christianity means *per definitionem* a "high voltage religion," the ordinary Protestant churches hold no attraction for them. In general they do not even consider catholicism. Forms of Christianity other than the ones they know are believed to be bad or distorted copies of the real.

Thus at an academic conference an otherwise normal anthropologist or sociologist (seldom a theologian) can suddenly burst forth in an emotional explosion which is—seen from a purely academic standpoint—inexplicable.[3] I have learned to recognize in such cases old wounds which are beginning to bleed again. The injured parties cannot come to terms with what they have been told is "lukewarm ordinary Christianity," because they have been programmed for an all-or-nothing religion. Since "all" is no longer available to them, they opt for "nothing."

Few have become outright antagonists of Pentecostalism. Once, one of the most outspoken critics of German Pentecostalism and a staunch defender of the ill-fated "Berlin declaration"[4] (in which Pentecostalism was essentially declared to be inspired from below) asked me to forswear in public all Pentecostal connections. "How can I?" I asked him. "In spite of all its shortcomings, I became a Christian through Pentecostalism. One does not forswear one's

---

[2] Hempelmann, "Glaubens-Gemeinde," 140. As to the other examples, I do not think it is fair to give names and places of such incidents, although I easily could.

[3] Poewe, "Introduction," 1–29, esp. 15.

[4] Hocken, "Berlin."

mother." Since he was unsuccessful, he wrote to my doctoral supervisor warning him of this ex–Pentecostal who was still unrepentant and not fully healed of his heresy. My supervisor showed me the letter and smiled: "What does he think? Does he really believe that I am unable to supervise your dissertation critically?" Much later I met this man again. He was now already approaching his eighties. Again he tried to convince me of the error of my ways and, as the one and vital proof of his utter condemnation, he told me that as a young man he had been in love with the daughter of one of the Pentecostal leaders, a respected man in society since he was an important high school teacher. "Do you know what this man said to his daughter?" He said: "My dear daughter, you are not going to marry one of these despised lay preachers when you can marry any one of the respected men in our community." Having played his last trump-card he expected me to accept his arguments. Of course I was not convinced, but I said nothing. I understood. The Pentecostal antagonist had had his self-esteem shattered, and therefore he regarded Pentecostalism as anathema.

A different story is the novel *Portofino* by Frank Schaefer. Schaefer's father (Francis Schaefer) was a missionary of a fundamentalist American Presbyterian Church (probably the Presbyterian Church of Christ and Covenant United States of America) to the idolatrous catholics and the nominal Presbyterians of Switzerland. In this novel, his son now describes the miseries and joys of this missionary family and seems to transfer his ill-feelings against his father onto the country of the missionary's calling. He calls Switzerland a "clockwork state run by chronographic fascists." I doubt whether any member of this missionary family had any deep knowledge of Swiss culture, language, or religion. It is clear that they were singularly unfit to help Swiss churches to overcome their shortcomings and to bring to life their Swiss Reformation tradition, or their Catholic tradition for that matter.

More to the point is Schaefer's portrait of the missionary son's parents. The father had frequent and ugly rows with the mother which were thinly papered over by an embarrassingly "Christian" and "evangelical" witness. They were absolutely sure that "the others" were not converted and therefore ripe for eternal perdition. And yet the father was deeply miserable. The mother sought comfort in the arms of a fellow missionary and the boy (clearly, the author as well) could not square the Christian missionary rhetoric with the harsh reality of his family. So he took refuge in lies. I do not think that this is a typical evangelical, nor a typical Pentecostal family. Nevertheless the novel shows—through clearly autobiographical detail—what damage can be done by people who confuse their religious ideology with the gospel. And this is true even if the author claims that "this is a work of fiction."

Some ex–Pentecostals have become famous singers, movie stars, or writers, for same gifts which make a good Pentecostal pastor also make a good entertainer or communicator (just as the reverse is also quite common: jazz musicians, singers, and actors who become Pentecostal pastors). Usually these artists hide their Pentecostal past, but to those properly sensitized, it shines through in their works of art. I want to present two writers of this ilk here, namely James Baldwin, a Black American, and Sven Lidman, a famous Swedish author.

James Baldwin

Consider the following description of a Pentecostal service. Admiration and contempt are both very apparent. A writer does not invent such stories. They are deeply engraved on his memory.

The Sunday morning service began when Brother Elisha sat down at the piano and raised a song. This moment and this music had been with John, so it seemed, since he had first drawn breath. It seemed that there had never been a time when he had not known this moment of waiting while the packed church paused—the sisters in white, heads raised, the brothers in blue, heads back; the white caps of the women seeming to glow in the charged air like crowns, the kinky, gleaming heads of the men seeming to be lifted up—and the rustling and the whispering ceased and the children were quiet; perhaps someone coughed, or the sound of a car horn, or a curse from the streets came in; then Elisha hit the keys, beginning at once to sing, and everybody joined him, clapping their hands, and rising, and beating the tambourines.

The song might be: "Down at the cross where my Savior died!" Or: "Jesus, I'll never forget how you set me free!" Or: "Lord, hold my hand while I run this race!" They sang with all the strength that was in them, and clapped their hands for joy. There had never been a time when John had not sat watching the saints rejoice with terror in his heart, and wonder. Their singing caused him to believe in the presence of the Lord; indeed, it was no longer a question of belief, because they made that presence real. He did not feel it himself, the joy they felt, yet he could not doubt that it was, for them, the very bread of life—could not doubt it, that is, until it was too late to doubt. Something happened to their faces and their voices, the rhythm of their bodies, and to the air they breathed; it was as though wherever they might be became the upper room, and the Holy Ghost were riding on the air. His father's face, always awful, became more awful now; his father's daily anger was transformed into prophetic wrath. His mother, her eyes raised to heaven, hands arched before her, moving, made real for John that patience, that endurance, that long suffering, which he had read of in the Bible and found so hard to imagine.

On Sunday mornings the women all seemed patient, all the men seemed mighty. While John watched, the Power struck someone, a man or woman; they cried out, a long, wordless crying, and, arms outstretched like wings, they began the Shout. Someone moved a chair a little to give them room, the rhythm paused, the singing stopped, only the pounding feet and the clapping hands were heard; then another cry, another dancer; then the tambourines began again, and the voices rose again, and the music swept on again, like fire, or flood, or judgment. Then the church seemed to swell with the Power it held, and, like a planet rocking in space, the temple rocked with the Power of God. John watched, watched the faces, and the weightless bodies, and listened to the timeless cries. One day, so everyone said, this Power would possess him; he would sing and cry as they did now, and dance before his King. He watched young Ella Mae Washington, the seventeen-year-old granddaughter of Praying Mother Washington, as she began to dance. And then Elisha danced.

At one moment, head thrown back, eyes closed, sweat standing on his brow, he sat at the piano, singing and playing; and then, like a great, black cat in trouble in the jungle, he stiffened and trembled, and cried out. "Jesus, Jesus, oh Lord Jesus!" He struck on the piano one last, wild note, and threw up his hands, palms upward, stretched wide apart. The tambourines raced to fill the vacuum left by his silent piano, and his cry drew answering cries. Then he was on his feet, turning, blind, his face congested, contorted with this rage, and the muscles leaping and swelling in his long, dark neck. It seemed that he could not breathe, that his body could not contain this passion, that he would be, before their eyes, dispersed into the waiting air. His hands, rigid to the very finger-tips, moved outward and back against his hips, his sightless eyes looked upward, and he began to dance. Then his hands closed into fists, and his head snapped downward, his sweat loosening the grease that slicked down his hair; and the rhythm of all the others quickened to match Elisha's rhythm; his thighs moved terribly against the cloth of his suit, his heels beat on the floor, and his fists moved beside his body as though he were beating his own drum. And so, for a while, in the center of the dancers, head down, fists beating, on, on, unbearably, until it seemed the walls of the church would fall for very sound; and then, in a moment, with a cry, head up, arms high in the air, sweat pouring from his forehead, and all his body dancing as though it would never stop. Sometimes he did not stop until he fell—until he dropped like some animal felled by a hammer—moaning, on his face. And then a great moaning filled the church.

We owe this description of a Pentecostal worship in the "Temple of the Fire Baptized" to James Baldwin's novel *Go Tell It On the Mountain.*[5] In this story Baldwin describes a part of his own biography. As a son of a black minister and himself a junior pastor he knew by experience the beauty and the weakness of the black Pentecostal church. However, he left the church very soon, because he could not answer the question: Why does my mother "come here, night after night, calling out to a God who cared nothing for them—if, above this flaking ceiling, there was any God at all?" He was in revolt against his father, who made sin responsible for all the evils of the black people, for unemployment and sickness, for hatred in the harassed black families. "It was sin," his father preached,

> that drove the son of the morning out of Heaven, sin that drove Adam out of Eden, sin that caused Cain to slay his brother, sin that built the tower of Babel, sin that caused the fire to fall on Sodom—sin, from the very foundations of the

---

[5]Baldwin, *Go*, 14–16. There are several Pentecostal churches in the USA with this name; cf. Fire Baptized Holiness Church (Wesleyan) (*Handbuch*, 02a.02.025; 02a.02.110a; Synan, "Fire-Baptized," 309); Fire-Baptized Holiness Church of God of the Americas (*Handbuch*, 02a.02.088; Synan, "Fire-Baptized"); Fire-Baptized Holiness Church; Pentecostal Fire-Baptized Holiness Church (*Handbuch*, 02a.02.107; Stout, "Fire-Baptized," 309).

world, living and breathing in the heart of man, that causes women to bring forth their children in agony and darkness, bows down the backs of men with terrible labor, keeps the empty belly empty, keeps the table bare, sends our children, dressed in rags, out into the whore-houses and dance halls of the world![6]

That is why Baldwin puts the following words into the mouth of one of the leading figures in the novel: "I'm going to have my baby and I'm going to bring him up to be a man. And I ain't going to read to him out of no Bibles and I ain't going to take him to hear no preaching. If he don't drink nothing but moonshine all his natural days he be a better man than his Daddy,"[7] who was a preacher.

Baldwin describes himself as "one of those people who have always been outside it [the church], even though one tried to work on it."[8] This did not hinder the World Council of Churches from inviting him to speak at the Fourth Full Assembly in Uppsala (1968), where he gave—hors programme—his testimony as a former Pentecostal preacher who still sees in the gospel a power to change the world and to redeem the races, but has got the impression that this gospel has been forsaken by all the churches:

> I watched what the Christian church did to my father, who was in the pulpit all the years of his life. I watched the kind of poverty, the kind of hopeless poverty, which was not an act of God, but an act of the State, against which he and his children struggled, I watched above all, and this is crucial, the ways in which white power can destroy black minds, and what black people are now fighting against, precisely that.[9]

After reminding his audience of the passion history of his own ancestors, he mentioned the Black Power leader Stokely Carmichael, considered by the press as a very dangerous, radical black fanatic racist.

> But everyone overlooks the fact that Stokely Carmichael began his life as a Christian and for many, many years, unnoticed by the world's press, was marching up and down the highways in my country, in the deep south, spent many years being beaten over the head and thrown in jail, singing "We Shall Overcome," and meaning it and believing it, doing day by day and hour by hour precisely what the Christian Church is supposed to do, to walk from door to door, to feed the hungry, to speak to those who are oppressed, to try to open the gates of prisons for all those who are imprisoned. And a day came, inevitably, when this young man grew weary of petitioning a heedless population and said in effect, what all revolutionaries have always said, I petitioned you and petitioned you, and you can petition for a long, long time, but the moment comes when the petitioner is no longer a petitioner but has become a beggar. And at that moment one concludes, you will not do it, you cannot do it, it is not in you to do it, and therefore *I* must do it.[10]

---

[6] Ibid., 121, 165.
[7] Ibid., 135.
[8] Baldwin, "Racism," 371.
[9] Ibid., 374.
[10] Ibid., 373.

According to Baldwin, what has to be done could be the destruction of a church which has lost its vocation. This church has too long taken sides with the mighty ones, too long has she told black history in white, too long has she destroyed the spontaneity and musicality of the black people.

Is Baldwin right? Or can his prophecy awaken us to a new ecumenicity, in which black and white learn from each other?

Sven Lidman

We find quite a different story in Sven Lidman. He explores another feature of Pentecostalism, the radical retreat into one's own soul, the will of uncompromising openness, the confession of all vice in public, sometimes grotesquely exaggerated. Lidman, later a famous Swedish writer, was born in 1882. After studying law, he published a number of erotic novels between 1904 and 1913.[11] In 1917 he became a Christian.

> The Swedish State Church had no attraction for him. He almost became a catholic, although he belonged to a family of Lutheran pastors. If a Catholic priest had visited him he would have been prepared to convert to the Catholic church in Sweden. But no priest came. And so he became a member of the Pentecostal church in Sweden. He wrote: "I understood that there is another way than the Catholic church, namely the way of radical pietism. In the first case the human soul becomes a spouse of God. In the second case he or she enters a marriage of conscience—a much steeper and more dangerous way."[12]

As a Pentecostal pastor he edited the Swedish Pentecostal periodical *Evangelii Härold* (1922–1948) and published Augustine's "Confessions."[13] E. Briem and L. Stampe find his published sermons fascinating.[14]

It is clear that such a strong personality would create conflicts with the popular Pentecostal leader Lewi Pethrus.[15] In 1948 Lidman was excommunicated from the Filadelfia Church in Stockholm. Pethrus and Lidman accused each other of unspiritual behaviour, authoritarianism, and commercialization of the revival. Lidman became a member of the "Free Pentecostal Church Ostermalm."

---

[11] *Paisphaë* (1904). *Primavera* (1905). *Källorna* (1906). *Elden och alteret* (1907). *Imperia* (drama, no date). *Härskare* (1908). *Stensborg* (1910). *Thure Gabriel Silverståål* (no date). *Köpman och krigare* (1911). *Carl Silverstååhls upplefversen* (1912). *Tre dräktens barn* (1913). (Lidman's works are not included in the bibliography).

[12] According to Braun, *Schweden*, 105.

[13] Works of this time: *Bruggan håller* (1913). *Personlig frälsning* (1924). *Bethlehemsstjärnen och båglampen* (1926). *Förgangelsens träler ochffrihetens söner* (1928). *Människan och tidsandan* (1932). *Ovoligt var mitt hjärta tills de fick find I dig. En själs biografi I dikter* (1933). *På resan genom livet* (1934). *Guds eviga nu* (1935). *Blodsarv* (1937). *Var inte förskräckt!* (1939). *Utvald av Gud* (1940). *Glädjebudbärare* (1941). *Från Coventry till Bethlehem* (1942). *Ingen lurar Gud* (1945). *Fjäril och vilddjur* (1947).

[14] Briem, "Pingströrelsen." See also other articles by this excellent scholar on Swedish Pentecostalism in the same lexicon: "Barratt"; "Glossolali"; "Lewi Pethrus." Stampe, "Pinsebevegelsen."

[15] See above chapter 20, p. 260.

R. Braun, obviously a Catholic author, deals with Lidman in detail in his critical book on Swedish literature. According to Braun "radical pietism" offered too narrow a space for the writer and poet Lidman—he could not live there for long. "Perhaps I am only a small singing bird," Lidman wrote in his farewell letter to the Filadelfia Church, "who feels that the atmosphere is slowly but surely poisoned and who flees in order to save his life and his soul."[16]

After his polemics against Pethrus,

> Lidman's literary production changed. He wrote his memoirs. These are not the idyllic memories of an old man but rather a return to the position which he had left a quarter of a century before. The memoirs did not deal with sermons and devotion. What mattered now, he said, was to bring into focus his own innermost being. He took as his example Thomas Mann. The one who does not deal with himself is lost. But he did not want to present this position as a flight into his own self (not unlike a number of secular authors of his time). Much more he tried to reconcile his literary work with his former existence as a preacher.[17]

The three volumes of memoirs[18] were a tremendous sensation in Sweden. They reached editions of 60,000 and more, which is considerable in a population of seven million. The enormous excitement which these memoirs produced can be seen in the reviews and discussions which filled the Swedish newspapers for many months.

The new and sensational thing in Lidman's memoirs is "his sexual autobiography in which he goes much further than the already extreme rebels of the North. This man of seventy-two goes further than any of them." The author is gripped by a burning desire for honesty, and runs amok in his determination to go to the very depths of his own soul.[19] This "honest, simple, naked description" of himself, this "journey of a Christian into the cesspool" is a detailed description of his sexual experiences, reaching back to his earliest childhood and leaving out no taboo, even the description of something approaching the action of Noah's sons, when his father was lying dead. "In Lidman's memoirs a man who sees himself as an important author and a leading Christian puts his understanding of sovereign freedom and Christian confession into practice, for the first time at least in Sweden," a position which Braun utterly condemns.[20]

On the other hand Meyer's Handbook on literature points out the "particular value" of these utterly honest but subjective autobiographical works,[21] and Elovson sees a certain coherence in Lidman's development. The common element in Lidman's life is his "lyrical aestheticism," "the Roman, moral

---

[16] Braun, *Schweden*, 105.
[17] Ibid., 106.
[18] *Gossan I grottan* (1950). *Logan och lindansaren* (1952). *Mandoms möda* (1954).
[19] Braun, *Schweden*, 106.
[20] Ibid., 108.
[21] *Meyers Handbuch über Literatur*, 552.

heroism" which one finds also in the Pentecostal pastor's "passionate rejection of all lukewarmness and ambition in his thoughtful humanism."[22]

Lidman's development certainly shows one of the paths open to Pentecostalism. The "radical pietist" withdraws from the injustice of the world and the lameness of the churches into the innermost chamber of his own memories, even if this means a Christian's journey into the cesspit. It focuses on his own soul, on his own purification and sanctification. If Pentecostalism chooses this way, it would not mean that it has to follow the genius of Lidman with all his radical passion. It could tame this process liturgically and rationally, as is the case in many traditional churches. One has only to think of the confessions of sin in our liturgies.

The other possibility is the way which is shown by some authors in this book. Which way will Pentecostalism go? Will it become a religion of the soul; will it celebrate one's own innermost being; or will it develop a passion for the kingdom of God in which the personal and the social are seen in their complementarity?

If This Movement Be of the Spirit . . .

The problem and promise of Pentecostalism are two sides of the same coin. Both are rooted in its identity and in its history. It would be bad advice to recommend to Pentecostals that they become Presbyterians, Baptists, Methodists, or Catholics of a sort. They must discover instead what it means to be genuinely Pentecostal. Genuine Pentecostalism is distinguished by faithfulness to its roots. For if this movement be of the Spirit—which I believe with all my soul—then it is also of the Spirit that:

- it began with a black ecumenist, in the black, oral Afro-American culture, with all that implies;
- it integrated important elements of Catholic spirituality;
- it was inspired by the social and political interpretation of holiness developed in the American Holiness Movement;
- it developed—from its very beginning—critical elements in relation to dispensationalism, inspiration of Scripture, hermeneutics, social and political issues, and modern theological scholarship.
- It began as an ecumenical renewal movement. With Dale T. Irvin we observe: "I believe we have yet to realize the ecumenical implications of Seymour's theology."[23]

All these things are part and parcel of the Pentecostal heritage. Take them away, and what is left of the work of the Spirit in Pentecostalism?

It is no accident that Pentecostalism has been marked not only by Wesley and Seymour but also—indirectly, via the holiness evangelists of Oberlin

---

[22] Werin–Elovson, "Lidman."
[23] Irvin, "One Bond," 53.

College (chapter 14, pp. 182–85)—by the Alsatian pastor Jean-Frédéric Ober-lin (1740–1826) from Waldersbach,[24] whose parishioners emigrated to Ohio, where they founded the city of Oberlin with its college. The connection between Oberlin, the Holiness Movement, and early Pentecostalism is obvi-ous. Oberlin was a pietist, a Lutheran pastor, a medical doctor, friend of the French Revolution (he was president of the local Jacobine Club), builder of streets and bridges, initiator of home-industry, and reformer of schools in the spirit of Jan Amos Komenius. His spirituality included both ecumenical openness and political and social action as a matter of course. He would show his pupils a picture which—seen from the left—showed a bird. But if one looked at it from the right, one saw a rose. He called it "reconciliation." He wanted to instill to his pupils the principle that what we see and conceive depends on the point of view from which we approach the world, politics, theology, and the Bible—and that it is part and parcel of holiness to look at the world also from the point of view of "the other" in order to understand his (or her) views. All this has been transmitted to the American Holiness Movement and from there to Pentecostalism. When, therefore, the Assemblies of God at their General Council of 1995 supported their anti-ecumenical decision by citing their "historic position," they betrayed not only their own pioneers but also those of the Holiness Movement on whose foundation they stand.

Promise

Since Pentecostalism is now at a turning point, it can release its potential in several areas. For example, it can help the sleepy *theological faculties and theological colleges* (particularly in Europe) once again to become places where religion is not only discussed but lived *and* analyzed; where thinking *and* praying are complementary; where oral theological scholarship and homiletics is discovered and tested; where the prison of propositional theology (and liturgy!) and of Western theological jargon is broken up; where ecumenicity is not the hobby horse of a few experts but part and parcel of theological thinking and ecclesiastical practice, where biblical pluralism is not doctrinally domes-ticated but recognized as one of the most important gifts of biblical tradition, and where therefore several different spiritualities are not only accepted but tried and tested; where Pentecostalism/charismatism/independentism is seen not as an embarrassment but as an invitation to study them seriously; and where the "problem of the sects" is seen not just in others but also in one's own exclusivity, at the same time recognizing the psychological need for sectarian structures in specific psychological and cultural situations.

A new and dangerous thought was recently expressed by Bodo Leinber-ger, a German protestant pastor, in his report to his superiors on the charis-matic renewal in Germany. In his report, he expresses the wish that the

---

[24] Sources and biographies (also on his visionary experiences) in Zwink, "Ober-lin," 720–23.

charismatic renewal could draw inspiration from its inter-cultural and ecumenical roots for the benefit of inter-religious dialogue. And this indeed seems to be a way out of the narrow, defensive, fundamentalistic position of many Christians. Pentecostal roots lie in the soil of oral, narrative, bodily, and therefore biographical theology. This kind of inductive theology is not adequate to defend orthodoxy, but it is adequate for mission, testimony, and dialogue. Because a movement which understands itself from the third article ("I believe in the Holy Spirit") is essentially tolerant and open to new, so far unknown moves of the Spirit, such a return to the ecumenical roots of this movement could be a decisive contribution to a world conference on Religion and Peace, and to a global ethos of love.[25]

No doubt such a move would make Pentecostalism/charismatism even more suspect to some evangelicals; however it would make clear that this segment of the church is not just "evangelicalism on fire" or a defender of orthodoxy, but a pioneer in new areas of the workings of the Spirit, as is clearly seen in the work of David Du Plessis and other Pentecostal ecumenists.

What Bodo Leinberger says here is probably true. However, it would have to be supplemented with a rigorous trinitarian reflection of the kind discussed in chapter 17 (pp. 219–20)—not in the interest of orthodoxy, but in the interest of faithfulness. Thus it could become visible that to be faithful and true is not always the same as being theologically orthodox; and in fact that in certain cases orthodoxy is a hindrance to faithfulness, as the history of Pentecostals and their antagonists shows clearly. The contribution of the Oneness Pentecostals could easily fit into such a trinitarian reflection, and thus perhaps solve the controversy between Oneness and Trinitarian Pentecostalism.

The place where these insights and experiences can be tested, applied and worked through is the *World Council of Churches*. Neither the World Council nor the Pentecostals can work out a global system of communication and cooperation alone. Together they might have a chance. The Pentecostal example, finance, skill, institutional and personal network, and man- and woman-power constitute a formidable force, which could really make a difference. So, why not invest time, money, and persons in the World Council of Churches and bring it to life again?

Perhaps mainline churches will reach the conclusion that they could learn something from the Pentecostals. But, just as it would be a pity for Pentecostals to imitate the mainline churches, so it would be a pity for the mainline churches to imitate Pentecostalism. Presbyterians and Catholics, Methodists and Anglicans may wish to discern the Holy Spirit in their *own* context and in their *own* tradition, for instance in the common Christian conviction that the church is not synonymous with priests and bishops but that the church consists of the interplay between different charismata.

---

[25] Certainly, such thinking may also be found in the Pentecostal/charismatic literature (e.g., chapter 27, note 77, p. 382).

Charismata of oral culture are present in all churches, but in most of them they are suppressed. What is the reason for this, if not fear and unbelief? In all churches there are testimonies, in all there is healing and there are other gifts. Why not recognize these and integrate them into the life of the church? How do these gifts find their rightful place; how do we articulate and live the conviction of the Reformation churches, for instance, that we are saved by grace alone and not by correct thinking? This does not devalue hard critical thinking, but it puts it in its relative place. Catholic and Anglican Churches could articulate and live their conviction that the church (or at least their denominations) appears in culturally and socially diverse liturgical forms and theological expressions and that the unity of the church can and should also be expressed in forms other than the ones which we have developed in the Mediterranean propositional tradition. All this is also part of the mainline churches' tradition.

If Pentecostals and Catholics, independents and Anglicans, Methodists and charismatics, Presbyterians and "non-white indigenous churches" dig deep enough into their own traditions, they might discover some considerable common ground (both of content and of form) for a global system of cooperation and communication. This, it seems to me, is as necessary for the world and the church as is our daily bread.

The Prayer of the Ostrich

O God,
Sometimes I feel like an ostrich,
a bird with wings—yet he can only run
a bird with wings—yet he has only the memory of flying.
And so I run over the hot sand and spread my wings,
yet only a poor hop is the result.
I am a Christian with the memory of the early Christians,
when in one day the gospel emerged in a foreign culture,
when in one day that which was considered essential, faded away,
when in one day for the sake of a foreign officer's salvation,
your servant crossed the frontiers of what he considered to be the
limits of the Gospel,
when in one day more of the Gospel was discovered than we could hope
in a hundred years.
Why must I be an ostrich, the laughing stock of the world?
I did not make myself. You did not ask me whether I wanted to
be an ostrich, nor whether I wanted to be at all, nor
did my parents ask me.
So, I am a bird and I cannot fly.
And yet I see other birds taking to the sky.
So I bury my head in the sand, in the Bible, in the tradition, in scholarship.
Today I pray just for one thing, one little thing,
O God,
Help me at least not to hinder the other birds from flying.
Help me not to think that because we cannot fly, other birds shouldn't either.
Help me to rejoice in the sight of those who fly higher than I can ever dream.

Short Titles List

The following literature list is by no means a complete bibliography of Pentecostalism. It is merely an indication of the books and articles cited (not of all those used) in the present work. For research reviews and bibliographies see Part Three of my *Handbuch* (05–11), my *Die Pfingstkirchen*, 317–466 and chapter 24 (pp. 326–31) of this volume.

Abrams, *Fire*
    Abrams, Minnie. *The Baptism of the Holy Ghost and Fire,* Kegdaon, Poona, India, ca. 1907.
Abrams, "Mukti"
    ———. "The Baptism of the Holy Spirit at Mukti." *Indian Witness* 26.4.1906; *The Missionary Review of the World* 19/8, August 1906, 619–20.
Achtemeier, *Inspiration*
    Achtemeier, Paul J. *The Inspiration of Scripture. Problems and Proposals.* Philadelphia: Westminster Press, 1980.
Account
    Account of the Convention for the Promotion of Scriptural Holiness Held at Oxford, August 29 to September 7, 1874; reprint in: *The Higher Christian Life,* vol. 2.
Adam, "Outdated"; German: "Veraltete"
    Adam, Will. "Outdated and Modern Forms of Worship." In Wiebe Vos (ed.), *Worship and Secularization,* Bussum, Holland: Paul Brand, 1970, 96–119.
    German: "Veraltete und moderne Gottesdienstformen." Faith and Order Paper 69:31, Geneva: WCC, September 1969 dupl. original version of the above.
Adegoke/Hollenweger, "Praxis"
    Adegoke, John, and Walter J. Hollenweger. "Markus 9:17–27: Heilung—Theorie und Praxis." *Predigtstudien* III/2, Stuttgart: Kreuz Verlag 1981, 225–31.

Agosto, "Diversity"
 Agosto, Efrain. "Diversity in Leadership: Paul's Commendations in Their
 Greco-Roman Context." SPS 1994.
Ahlstrom, *History*
 Ahlstrom, S. C. *Religious History of the American People.* New Haven and London:
 Yale University Press, 1972.
Ahn, *Kirche*
 Ahn, Byung-Mu. *Draussen vor dem Tor. Kirche und Minjung in Korea.* Göttingen:
 Vandenhoeck & Ruprecht, 1986.
Aigbe, "People"
 Aigbe, Sunday. "Pentecostal Mission and Tribal Groups People." In *Called,* 165–79.
Aion, "Dialogue"
 Aion, Biannual Journal of St. Symeon's Fellowship, July 1972, 4: "Our Dialogue."
Alamo, "Castañiza"
 Alamo, Mateo. "Juan de Castañiza." *Dictionnaire de Spiritualité,* Paris 1953, II, 277.
Albrecht, "Opium"
 Albrecht, Horst. "Opium auf dem Bildschirm. Telekirchen in den USA—Botschaft, Erfolg,
 gesellschaftliche Wirkungen." *Wege zum Menschen* 41/2, Febr./March 1989, 103–14.
Alexander, "Fee"
 Alexander, Patrick H. "Fee, Gordon Donald." *Dictionary,* 305.
Alford, "Music"
 Alford, D. L. "Pentecostal and Charismatic Music," *Dictionary,* 688–95.
Alland, "Possession"
 Alland, Alexander. "Possession in a Revivalistic Negro Church." *Journal for the
 Scientific Study of Religion* 1, 1961, 204–13.
Allen, D., "Ostrich"
 Allen, David. "The Glossolalic Ostrich. Isolationism and Other-Worldliness in the
 British Assemblies of God." *EPTA Bulletin* 13, 1994, 50–62.
Allen, *Methods*
 Allen, Roland. *Missionary Methods: St. Paul's or Ours?* 1912.
Altrichter, "Katholische"
 Altrichter, M. "Katholische Pfingstbewegung." *Orientierung* 36/3, 31.3.1972, 70–72.
Alvarez, *Historia*
 Alvarez, Carmelo A. (et al.). *Historia de la iglesia pentecostal en Chile* (Serie
 Communidades). Santiago: Ediciones Rehue, n.d.
Alvarez, "Latin"
 _____. "Latin American Pentecostals: Ecumenical and Evangelical." *Pneuma* 9/1,
 Spring 1987, 91–95.
Alvarez, *People*
 _____. *People of Hope. The Protestant Movement in Central America with Selected
 Statements from the Churches.* New York: Friendship Press, 1990.
Alvarez, *Pentecostalismo*
 _____. (ed.). *Pentecostalismo y liberación. Una experiencia latinoamericano.* Costa Rica:
 Departamento Ecuménico de Investigaciones, 1992.
Alvarez, *Santidad*
 _____. *Santidad y compromiso: El riesgo de vivir el evangelio.* Mexico, D.F.: Casa Unida
 de Publicaciones, 1985.
Amerlinck y Assereto, *Ixmiquilpan*
 Amerlinck y Assereto, Maria Josefina. *Ixmiquilpan: un estudio comparativo de evangélistas y
 católicos* (Anthropological thesis, Universidad Iberoamericana, Mexico, 1970, dupl.).
Anderson/Stransky (eds.), *Mission Trends* no. 3
 Anderson, Gerald H., and Tom Stransky, (eds.) *Mission Trends* no. 3.
Anderson, "African"
 Anderson, Allan. "Pentecostal Pneumatology and African Power Concepts: Continuity
 and Change." *Missionalia* 19/1, April 1990, 65–74.

Anderson, "Ancestor"
———. "African Pentecostalism and the Ancestor Cult: Confrontation and Compromise." *Missionalia* 21/1, April 1993, 26–39.

Anderson, *Bazalwane*
———. *Bazalwane, African Pentecostals in South Africa.* Pretoria: University of South Africa, 1992.

Anderson, *Moya*
———. *Moya: the Holy Spirit in an African Context.* Pretoria: University of South Africa, 1991.

Anderson, Gordon L., "Changing"
Anderson, Gordon L. "The Changing Nature of the Moral Crisis of American Christianity." SPS 1990, V.

Anderson, Gordon L., "Hermeneutics"
———. "Pentecostal Hermeneutics." SPS 1992, BB.

Anderson, Robert Mapes, *Social*
Anderson, Robert Mapes. *A Social History of the Early Twentieth Century Pentecostal Movement.* Ph.D. Columbia University, 1969, Xerox copy.

Anderson, Robert Mapes, *Vision of the Disinherited*
———. *Vision of the Disinherited. The Making of American Pentecostalism.* Oxford University Press, 1979.

Andrei, "Scopuli"
Andrei, Francisco. "Scopuli." *Enciclopedia cattolica.* Vatican 1953, XI/1, 203f.

Andresen, "Literaturmisjon"
Andresen, Kiss. "Literaturmisjon." In Kåre Juul (ed.), *Til jordens ender,* 189–92.

Apostolic Church, *Fundamentals*
Apostolic Church. *Fundamentals being "things most surely believed." A brief statement of fundamental truths contained in the Scriptures and believed and taught by the Apostolic Church.* Bradford, England: Puritan Press, n.d.

Appiah-Kubi, *Man Cures*
Appiah-Kubi, Kofi. *Man Cures, God Heals. Religion and Medical Practice Among the Akans of Ghana.* Totowa, N.J.: Allanheld, Osmond Publ., 1981.

Arceo, "Antorcha"
Arceo, Sergio Mendez. "La Antorcha de la verdad." *La Voz* 1/1 (1966?), 18–20, 31.

Arrington, F. L., "Hermeneutics"
Arrington, French L. "Hermeneutics, Historical Perspectives on Pentecostal and Charismatic." *Dictionary,* 376–89.

Asambleas de Dios (Dominican Republic), *Reglamento*
Asambleas de Dios (Dominican Republic). *Reglamento local de la Iglesia Evangélica de las Asambleas de Dios en la República Dominicana* (written 1932 by Rafael D. Williams and Francisco Arizú, El Salvador; printed 1944 in Trujillo: Prensa Bíblica).

Asch, *Kimbangu*
Asch, Susan. *L'Eglise du Prophète Kimbangu. De ses origines à son rôle actuel au Zaïre (1921–1981).* Paris: Karthala, 1983.

Assemblies of God, *Our Mission in Today's World*
Assemblies of God (ed.). *Our Mission in Today's World. Council on Evangelism. Official Papers and Reports.* Springfield, Mo.: Gospel Publishing House, 1968.

Assemblies of God (Australia), *United Constitution*
Assemblies of God (Australia). *United Constitution of the Assemblies of God in Australia.* n. p., n. d.

Atter, *Cults*
Atter, Gordon F. *Cults and Heresies. The Student's Handbook.* Peterborough, Ontario: The Book Nook, 1963.

Auf der Suche
Auf der Suche nach einer christlichen Antwort auf die heutigen Gesundheitsprobleme. Evangelisches Missionswerk, Informationen Nr. 80. Hamburg, 1988.

Ayandele, "Appendix"

    Ayandele, E. A. "Appendix." In Fashole-Luke, *Christianity in Independent Africa.*

Aymot, *New Covenant*

    Aymot, Sr. Floretta. *New Covenant* 1/9, March 1972, 6–8.

Babcox, *Search*

    Babcox, Neil. *A Search for Charismatic Reality. One Man's Pilgrimage.* Portland, Oregon: Multnomah Press, 1985.

Baer, "Socio-Religious"

    Baer, Hans A. "The Socio-Religious Development of the Church of God in Christ." In Hans A. Baer and Yvonne Jones (eds.), *African Americans in the South. Issues of Race, Class, and Gender.* (Southern Anthropological Society Proceedings, no. 25), Athens and London: The University of Georgia Press, 1992, 111–22.

Baer–Singer, *African-American Religion*

    _____. and Merrill Singer. *African-American Religion in the Twentieth Century. Varieties of Protest and Accommodation.* Knoxville: The University of Tennessee Press, 1992.

Balandier, *Sociologie actuelle*

    Balandier, Georges. *Sociologie actuelle de l'Afrique noire. Dynamique des changements sociaux en Afrique centrale.* Paris: Presses Universitaires de France (1955), 1963.

Baldwin, *Go*

    Baldwin, James. *Go Tell It On the Mountain.* New York: Dell Publishing Company, 1969.

Baldwin, "Racism"

    _____. "White Racism or World Community." *Ecumenical Review* 20/4, Oct. 1968, 371–76.

Banda-Mwaka, "Kimbanguisme"

    Banda-Mwaka, J. "Le Kimbanguisme en tant que mouvement prépolitique che les Kongo." *Problèmes sociaux congolais* no. 92–93, March-June 1971, 3–53.

Barclay, *History of Methodist Missions*

    Barclay, Wade Crawford. *History of Methodist Missions.* New York: Board of Missions and Church Extensions of the Methodist Church, 1949.

Bårdli, "Skolarbeidet"

    Bårdli, Johannes. "Skolarbeidet, en grunnleggende faktor. Bibelskolen." In Juul (ed.), *Til jordens ender,* 176–88.

Barratt, *Works*

    Barratt, Thomas Ball. *The Works of T. B. Barratt.* Ed. Donald W. Dayton. Reprint 1907, 1927. The Higher Christian Life 4. New York: Garland, 1984.

Barratt, *In the Days*

    _____. *In the Days of the Latter Rain.* London: Simpkin, Marshall, Hamilton, Kent & Co. Ltd., 1909.

Barrett, "20th"

    Barrett, David B. "20th Century Pentecostal/Charismatic Renewal in the Holy Spirit with Its Goals of World Evangelization in A.D. 2000." *Int. Bulletin of Missionary Research,* Fall 1988.

Barrett, "AD 2000"

    _____. "AD 2000: 350 Million Christians in Africa." *Int. Review of Mission* 59/233, Jan. 1970, 39–54.

Barrett, *Schism and Renewal*

    Barrett, David B. *Schism and Renewal in Africa. An Analysis of Six Thousand Contemporary Movements.* Oxford: Oxford University Press, 1968.

Barrett, "Signs"

    _____. "Signs, Wonders, and Statistics in the World of Today." In Jongeneel, 1992, 189–96.

Barrett, "Statistics"

    _____. "Statistics, Global." *Dictionary,* 810–829.

Barrett, *WChE*
_____. (ed.). *World Christian Encyclopedia: A Comparative Study of Churches and Religions in the Modern World, AD 1900–2000.* Nairobi; New York: Oxford University Press, 1982.

Barrington-Ward, "Centre Cannot Hold"
Barrington-Ward, Simon. " 'The Centre Cannot Hold . . .' Spirit Possession as Redefinition." In Fasholé-Luke, *Christianity in Independent Africa*, 455–70.

Barron, *Health*
Barron, Bruce. *The Health and Wealth Gospel: What's Going on Today in a Movement That Has Shaped the Faith of Millions?* Downers Grove, Ill.: Inter Varsity Press, 1987.

Barth, "Nachwort"
Barth, Karl. "Nachwort." *Schleiermacher-Auswahl* (Siebenstern Taschenbuch 113/14, Munich and Hamburg 1968, 290–312).

Bartleman, "Danger"
Bartleman, Frank. "The War—Our Danger." *Word and Work*, Nov. 1915, 301.

Bartleman, "Earthquake"
_____. "The Earthquake" in *My Story: "The Latter Rain."* Columbia, S.C.: J. M. Pike, 1908, 36–54.

Bartleman, "Last"
_____. "In the Last Days." *Word and Work*, Sept. 1916, 393.

Bartleman, "Money"
_____. "The Money God." *Word and Work* (ca. 1916/1917), 375.

Bartleman, "Preparedness"
_____. "Christian Preparedness." *Word and Work* (ca. 1916), 115.

Bartleman, "Present"
_____. "The Present Day Conditions." *Weekly Evangel* no. 93, 5.6.1915, 3.

Bartleman, "War"
_____. "War and the Christian," *Word and Work* (ca. 1915). (All of the above documents by Bartleman in Robeck, *Witness*.)

Bartleman, *What Really Happened at Azusa Street?*
_____. *What Really Happened at Azusa Street?* Ed. John Walker. Northridge, Calif.: Voice Christian Publications Inc., 1962.

Bartsch (ed.), *Kerygma*
Bartsch, H. W. (ed.). *Kerygma und Mythos* I (5th ed.; Hamburg: Herbert Reich, Ev. Verlag, 1967). English: *Kerygma and Myth* (London: n.p., 1953)

Bastide, *Les religions africaines au Brésil*
Bastide, Roger. *Les religions africaines au Brésil.* Paris: Bibliothèque de sociologie contemporaine: Presses Universitaires de France, 1960.

Baubérot/Willaim, "Fédération"
Baubérot, Jean, and Jean-Paul Willaim. "Fédération protestante de France," in Pierre Gisel (ed.), *Encyclopédie du protestantisme* (Paris: Cerf; Geneva: Labor et Fides, 1995) 568f.

Baumert, "Phenomena"
Baumert, Norbert, S.J. "Concerning Extraordinary Bodily Phenomena in the Context of Spiritual Occurrences," *Pneuma* 18/1, Spring 1996, 5–32 (translated from the German by Veronika Ruf, et al., and edited by The Theological Commission of the Charismatic Renewal in the Catholic Church of Germany).

Bazola, "Kimbanguisme"
Bazola, E. "Le Kimbanguisme" *Cahiers des religions africaines* 2/3, Jan. 1968, 144–52.

Beaman, *Pacifism*
Beaman, Jay. *Pentecostal Pacifism. The Origin, Development, and Rejection of Pacific Belief Among the Pentecostals.* Hillsboro, Kansas: Center for Mennonite Brethren Studies, 1989.

Becken, "Afrikanisches"
Becken, Hans Jürgen. "Afrikanisches Arztpriestertum und westliche Medizin," *MD* 57/6, 1.6.1994, 153–66.

Becken, "Begegnung"

_____. "Begegnung mit Medizinmännern in Afrika." *MD* 48, 1985, 284–94.

Becken, *Glaube*

_____. *Wo der Glaube noch jung ist. Afrikanische Unabhängige Kirchen im südlichen Afrika.* Erlanger Taschenbücher 73. Erlangen: Verlag der Evangelisch-Lutherischen Mission, 1985.

Becken, "Heilen"

_____. "Heilen ist Versöhnen zur Gemeinschaft. Heilung in Afrika." *Jahrbuch Mission* 1990, 77–86 (Hamburg: Missionshilfe Verlag, 1990).

Becken, "Heilungen"

_____. "Heilungen in anderen Kulturen-Oekumenische Erfahrungen." *Zeitschrift für Mission* 17/1, 1991, 18–25.

Becken, "Kirche"

_____. "Die Kirche als heilende Gemeinschaft." *Zeitschrift für Mission* 12, 1986, *MD* 49, 1986, 321–24.

Becken, *Theologie*

_____. *Theologie der Heilung. Das Heilen in den Afrikanischen Unabhängigen Kirchen in Südafrika* (Verkündigung und Verantwortung 1). Hermannsburg, Verlag Missionsbuchhandlung, 1972.

Beeson, *Discretion*

Beeson, Trever (ed.). *Discretion and Valour. Religious Conditions in Russia and Eastern Europe.* London: Fontana Pub., 1974.

Béguin–Martin, "Kimbanguisme"

Béguin, Willy and Marie-Louise Martin. "Découverte du Kimbanguisme." In: *Le monde non-chrétien* 22/89–90, Jan.–July 1969, 5–37.

Benz, *Amerika*

Benz, Ernst. *Der Heilige Geist in Amerika.* Düsseldorf: Diederichs, 1970.

Berg, "So viele waren"

Berg, Stefan. "So viele waren wir noch nie." *Deutsches Allgemeines Sonntagsblatt* 41/43, 28 October 1994, 15.

Bergunder, "Die südinisches Pfingstbewegung"

Bergunder, n.i. "Die südinisches Pfingstbewegung im 20. Jahrhundert." SPS and EPTA Conference, Mattersey, England, July 1995.

Berinyuu, *Pastoral Care*

Berinyuu, Abraham A. *Pastoral Care to the Sick in Africa. An Approach to Transcultural Theology.* IC 51, 1987.

Bernal, *Cien obras*

Bernal, Ignacio. *Cien obras maestras del museo nacional de antropologia.* Mexico: José Bolea, 1969.

Berthier, *Taizé*

Berthier, Jacques. *Music From Taizé: Responses, Litanies, Acclamations.* London: Collins, 1978.

Bertsche, "Kimbanguism"

Bertsche, James E. "Kimbanguism: A Challenge to Missionary Statesmanship." *Practical Anthropology* 13/1, Jan.-Febr. 1966, 13–33.

Best, "Loosing the Women"

Best, Falcon O. "Loosing the Women: African-American Women and Leadership in the Pentecostal Church, 1890–Present." SPS 1994.

Biermann, *Las Casas*

Biermann, Benno M. *Las Casas und seine Sendung. Das Evangelium und die Rechte des Menschen.* Mainz: Matthias-Grünewald-Verlag, 1968.

Binyon, *Concepts*

Binyon, Pamela. *The Concepts of "Spirit" and "Demon." A Study in the Use of Different Languages Describing the Same Phenomena.* IC 8, 1977.

Birnstein, *Geist*
Birnstein, Uwe. *Neuer Geist in alter Kirche? Die charismatische Bewegung in der Offensive.* Stuttgart: Kreuz-Verlag, 1987.

Birkey, *The House Church*
Birkey, D. *The House Church. A Model for Renewing the Church.* Scottsdale, Pa: Herald Press, 1988.

Bittlinger, "Glossolalie"
Bittlinger, Arnold. "Die Glossolalie innerhalb der charismatischen Bewegung." *MD* 35/18, 15.9.1972, 275–79.

Bittlinger, "Opportunity"
———. "Charismatic Renewal—an Opportunity for the Church." *Bossey,* 7–13.

Bittlinger, *Papst*
———. *Papst und Pfingstler. Der römisch-katholische/pfingstliche Dialog und seine ökumenische Relevanz.* IC 16, 1978.

Bixler, "Ramabai"
Bixler, F. "Ramabai, Sarasvati (Pandita) (ca. 1858–1922)." *Dictionary,* 755–56.

Bloch-Hoell, *Pinsebevegelsen*
Bloch-Hoell, Nils. *Pinsebevegelsen. En underøkelse av Pinsebevelsens tilblivelse, utvikling og saerpreg med saerlig henblikk på utforming i Norge.* Oslo: Universitetsforlaget, 1956.

Bloch-Hoell, *The Pentecostal Movement*
———. *The Pentecostal Movement. Its Origin, Development and Distinctive Character.* London: Allen & Unwin; Oslo: Universitet, n.d.

Blomquist, *Svenska Pingstväckelsen*
Blomquist, Axel (ed.). *Svenska Pingstväckelsen femtio år. En krönika i ord och bild.* Stockholm: Förlaget Filadelfia, 1957.

Blumhofer, *Assemblies*
Blumhofer, Edith. *The Assemblies of God: A Chapter in the Story of American Pentecostalism.* Springfield, Mo.: Gospel Publishing House, 1989.

Blumhofer, "Assemblies"
———. "Assemblies of God." *Dictionary,* 23–28.

Blumhofer, "Boddy"
———. "Alexander Boddy and the Rise of Pentecostalism in Britain." *Pneuma* 8/1, Spring 1986, 31–40.

Blumhofer, "Dowie"
———. "Dowie, John Alexander (1847–1907)." *Dictionary,* 248.

Blumhofer, "Piper"
———. "Piper, William Hamner (1868–1911)." *Dictionary,* 716f.

Boardman, *Higher*
Boardman, William Edward. *The Higher Christian Life.* London 1896, reprint "The Higher Christian Life." vol. 6.

Boddy, "Ueber Land und Meer"
Boddy, Alexander A. "Ueber Land und Meer." *Pfingstgrüsse* 1912/13, originally published in *Confidence.*

Boff, "Syncretism"
Boff, Leonardo. "Christianity as One Huge Syncretism." In *Igreja, carisma e poder* (Petropolis). English: *Church, Charism and Power. Liberation Theology and the Institutional Church.* London: SCM, 1985.

Boisen, "Economic"
Boisen, Anton T. "Economic Distress and Religious Experience. A Study of the Holy Rollers." *Psychiatry* 2, 1939, 185–94.

Boka–Raymaekers, *Chants*
Boka, Simon and Paul Raymaekers. *250 Chants de l'EJCSK. Première série: 85 chants de Nsambu André.* Université Lovanium-Léopoldville, IREW, Notes et Documents vol. 1, no. 3, Léopoldville 1960 (dupl.)

Bolamba, *Diaconie*
    Bolamba, Baruti Ewololiya. *La diaconie au sein de l'Eglise kimbanguiste.* Mémoire de fin
    d'études, Kinshasa: Ecole de théologie kimbanguiste, 1977.
Boletin de Cencos
    Boletin de Cencos A. C. Nr. 4164, Mexico, 13.5.1970.
Bolten, "Recent"
    Bolten, C. A. "The Recent Vatican Council," *Pentecostal Evangel* 2703, 27.2.1966, 6f.
Bonhoeffer, "Bericht"
    Bonhoeffer, Dietrich. "Bericht über den Studienaufenthalt im Union Theological
    Seminary zu New York." In *Gesammelte Schriften.* Munich: Kaiser-Verlag, 1958, I,
    84–103.
Bonnano, *Aspetti*
    Bonnano, Maria Pia. *Aspetti della diffusione del protestantesimo nella provincia di Cosenza.*
    Ph.D. University of Bari, no date, unpubl.
Booth-Clibborn, Arthur, *Blood*
    Booth-Clibborn, Arthur. *Blood Against Blood.* New York: Charles C. Cook, n.d.
Booth-Clibborn, Samuel, *Should*
    Booth-Clibborn, Samuel. *Should a Christian Fight? An Appeal to Christian Young Men
    of All Nations.* Swengel, Pa: Bible Truth Depot, n.d.
Booyens, "Ethnological"
    Booyens, J. H. "The Ethnological Framework and the Diagnosis of Illness by Prophets
    and Sangomas: a Comparison." In C. G. Oosthuizen (ed.), *Religion Alive,* 116–25.
Børresen, "1955–1960"
    Børresen, Inger Marie. "1955–1960." In Juul (ed.), *Til jordens ender,* 165–69.
Bossey
    Arnold Bittlinger (ed.). *The Church is Charismatic. The World Council of Churches and
    the Charismatic Renewal* [at Bossey]. Geneva: WCC, 1981.
Boudewijnse/Droogers/Kamsteeg, *Algo*
    Boudewijnse, Barbara, André Droogers, Frans Kamsteeg (eds.). *Algo más que opio. Una
    lectura antropológica del pentecostalismo latinoamericano y caribeño.* San José, Costa Rica:
    Departamento Ecuméneco de Investigaciones (DEI), 1991.
Bozzano, *Uebersinnliche*
    Bozzano, Ernesto. *Uebersinnliche Erscheinungen bei Naturvölkern.* Bern, 1948.
Bracco, *Potenza*
    Bracco, Roberto. *La potenza della Pentecoste nel ministerio.* Marchirolo, 1965.
Bradley, "Miracles"
    Bradley, James E. "Miracles and Martyrdom in the Early Church: Some Theological
    and Ethical Implications." *Pneuma* 13/1, Spring 1991, 65–81.
Brandon, *Health*
    Brandon, Andrew. *Health and Wealth.* Eastbourne, England: Kingsway Publications,
    1987.
Brandt-Bessire, "L'implantation"
    Brandt-Bessire, D. "L'implantation des Assemblées Pentecôtistes en Belgique
    Francophone." *EPTA Bulletin* 10/1+2, 1992, 5–23
Brandt-Bessire, *Sources*
    ———. *Aux sources de la spiritualité pentecôtiste.* Geneva: Labor et Fides, 1986.
Braun, *Schweden*
    Braun, Robert. *Was geht in Schweden eigentlich vor? Analyse und Kritik einer
    Entchristlichung.* Nürnberg: Glock und Lutz, 1967.
Braunhart, *Heiliger Geist*
    Braunhart, Karl. *Heiliger Geist und politische Herrschaft bei den Neopfingstlern in
    Honduras.* Frankfurt: Vervuert, 1995.
Brazier, *Black Self-Determination*
    Brazier, Arthur M. *Black Self-Determination. The Story of the Woodlawn Organization.*
    Grand Rapids, Mich.: Eerdmans, 1969.

Brazier, "Origin"
_____. "The Origin of the New Testament." *Christian Outlook* (Pentecostal Assemblies of the World), East Orange, N.J. 39/4, April 1962, 3.
Brazier, "Upgrading"
_____. "Upgrading Education in the Inner City." In Sol Tax (ed.), *The People vs. the System. A Dialogue in Urban Conflict. Proceedings of the Community Service Workshop Funded Under Title I of the Higher Education Act 1965 and Held at the University of Chicago.* Chicago: Acme Press, 1968, 198–201.
Bridges-Johns, "Adolescence"
Bridges-Johns, Cheryl. "The Adolescence of Pentecostalism: In Search of a Legitimate Sectarian Ideology." *Pneuma* 17/1, 3–17.
Bridges-Johns, "Women"
_____. "Pentecostal Spirituality and the Conscientization of Women." *Brighton,* 153–65.
Briem, "Barratt"
Briem, Efraim. "T. B. Barratt." *Svensk Uppslagsbok* III (1947), 175.
Briem, "Glossolali"
_____. "Glossolali." *Svensk Uppslagsbok* XI, 839.
Briem, "Lewi Pethrus"
_____. "Lewi Pethrus." *Svensk Uppslagsbok* XXII (1951), 913f.
Briem, "Pingströrelsen"
_____. "Pingströrelsen." *Svensk Uppslagsbok* XXII (1951), 1066f.
Brighton
Hunter, Harold D., and Peter D. Hocken (eds.). *All Together in One Place. Theological Papers from the Brighton Conference on World Evangelization.* Sheffield Academic Press, 1993.
Brilioth, "Jeremy Taylor"
Brilioth. "Jeremy Taylor." *Die Religion in Geschichte und Gegenwart,* 2d ed., (1931), 5.1030.
Brooks, *Azusa Street Revival*
Brooks, André David. *Azusa Street Revival: A Docudrama Based on the Origins of Modern Pentecostalism and William J. Seymour, the Man That Led This Movement.* Photocopied M.A. thesis, California State University, Los Angeles, 1991.
Brown–York, *Covenant*
Brown, John Pairman, and Richard L. York (eds.). *The Covenant of Peace. A Liberation Prayer Book by the Free Church of Berkeley.* New York: Morehouse-Barlow Co., 1971.
Bruderschaft "Der König kommt!" "Confession"
Bruderschaft, n.i. "Der König kommt!" "Confession of Faith" *Bruderschaft "Der König kommt!"* Ferndorf, Kreis Siegen: H. Kocks, 1946.
Brumback, *Suddenly*
Brumback, Carl. *Suddenly From Heaven. A History of the Assemblies of God.* Springfield, Mo.: Gospel Publishing House, 1961.
Buana-Kibongi, "Kimbanguisme"
Buana-Kibongi, D. "L'évolution du Kimbanguisme." *Flambeau* no. 10, May 1966, 75–81.
Buck, "Logos"
Buck, J. "Logos Report One. Melody and Miracles Mark Third Holy Spirit Conference." *Logos Journal* 1/7, Jan.-Feb. 1977, 40f.
Bührmann, "Aspects"
Bührmann, Vera. "Some Aspects of Healing Methods Among Black South Africans." In C. G. Oosthuizen (ed.), *Religion Alive,* 105–15.
Bultmann, "Neues Testament"
Bultmann, Rudolf. "Neues Testament und Mythologie. Das Problem der Entmythologisierung der neutestamentlichen Verkündigung" (1941). In H. W. Bartsch (ed.), *Kerygma und Mythos* I (Hamburg, 1948, 1967^5), 15–48. English: "New Testament and Mythology." In H. W. Bartsch (ed.), *Kerygma and Myth* I (London, 1953), 1–44.

Bultmann, *Geschichte*

———. *Die Geschichte der synoptischen Tradition.* Göttingen, 1958[4]; English: *The History of the Synoptic Gospels.* (Oxford: Blackwell, 1963).

Bundy, "Apologist"

Bundy, David D. "Louis Dallière: Apologist for Pentecostalism in France and Belgium." *Pneuma* 10/2, Fall 1988, 85–115.

Bundy, "Barratt"

———. "Barratt, Thomas Ball (1862–1940)." *Dictionary*, 50.

Bundy, "Belgium"

———. "Pentecostalism in Belgium." *Pneuma* 8/1, Spring 1986, 41–56.

Bundy, "Boddy"

———. "Boddy, Alexander Alfred (1854–1930)." *Dictionary*, 90f.

Bundy, "European"

———. "European Pietist Roots of Pentecostalism." *Dictionary*, 279–81.

Bundy, "Gee"

———. "Gee, Donald (1891–1966)." *Dictionary*, 330–32.

Bundy, "Keswick"

———. "Keswick Higher Life Movement." *Dictionary*, 518f.

Bundy, "L'émergence"

———. "L'émergence d'un théologian pentecôtisant: Les écrits de Louis Dallière de 1922 à 1932." *Hokhma, Revue de réflexion théologique* (Switzerland) 38, 1988, 24–36.

Bundy, "Lindsay"

———. "Lindsay, Gordon (1907–73) and Freda Theresa (1916–)." *Dictionary*, 539–41.

Bundy, "Louis Dallière"

———. "Louis Dallière (1932–1939): The Development of a Pentecostal Apologetic." *EPTA Bulletin* 8/2, 1989, 60–93.

Bundy, "Making"

———. "The Making of a Pentecostal Theologian: The Writings of Louis Dallière, 1922–32." *EPTA Bulletin* 7/2, 1988, 40–68.

Bundy, "Paul"

———. "Paul, Jonathan Alexander Anton (1853–1931)." *Dictionary*, 664.

Bundy, "Perspectives"

———. "Historical Perspectives on the Development of the European Pentecostal Theological Association." *Pneuma* 2/2, Fall 1980, 15–25.

Bundy, "Pethrus"

———. "Pethrus, Petrus Lewi (1884–1974)." *Dictionary*, 711f.

Bundy, "Renewal"

———. "Charismatic Renewal in Belgium: A Bibliographical Essay." *EPTA Bulletin* 5/3, 1986, 76–95.

Bundy, "Rietdijk"

———. "Johannes Rietdijk: Belgian Pentecostal Theologian." unpubl. paper given at the European Pentecostal Research Conference at the University of Birmingham, 1984.

Bundy, "Roumanian"

———. "The Roumanian Pentecostal Church in Recent Literature." *Pneuma* 7/1, Spring 1985, 19–20.

Bundy, "Scholarly"

———. "Early European Scholarly Perspectives on Pentecostalism." *EPTA Bulletin* 5/1, 1986, 4–23.

Bundy, "Taylor[a]"

———. "Bishop William Taylor and Methodist Mission: A Study in Nineteenth Century Social History." *Methodist History* 27/4, July 1988, 197–210.

Bundy, "Taylor[b]"

———. "Bishop William Taylor and Methodist Mission: A Study in Nineteenth Century Social History." *Methodist History* 28/1, Oct. 1989, 3–21.

Burgess, "Bakker"
    Burgess, Stanley M. "Bakker, James Orsen ('Jim') and Tammy Fay (La Valley) (1940–)." *Dictionary*, 38–40.
Burgess, "Implications"
    _____. "Implications of Eastern Christian Pneumatology for Western Pentecostal Doctrine and Practice." In Jongeneel, 1991, 23–34.
Burgess, "Kendrick"
    _____. "Kendrick, Klaude (1917–)." *Dictionary*, 516.
Burgess, "Zimmerman"
    _____. "Zimmerman, Thomas Fletcher (1913–)." *Dictionary*, 910f.
Burton, "Kongo"
    Burton, William. "Auf biblischen Wege an den Kongo gesandt." Latter Rain Evangel. *Verheissung des Vaters* 15/6–7, June/July 1922, 19ff.
Burton, *Mafundijyo*
    _____. *Mafundijyo a ku mukanda wa Lesa*. Mwanza, Elisabethville, n.d. (ca. 1950).
Burton, *Man*
    _____. *When God Changes a Man. A True Story of this Great Change in the Life of a Slave Trader*, London: Victory Press, 1929.
Burton, *Missionary*
    _____. *When God Makes a Missionary, Being the Life Story of Edgar Mahon*. London: Victory Press, 1936.
Burton, *Pastor*
    _____. *When God Makes a Pastor*. London: Victory Press, 1934.
Burton, *Signs*
    _____. *Signs Following*. London: Elim Publishing Co. 1949, 1956[3].
Burton, *Village*
    _____. *When God Changes a Village*. London: Victory Press, 1933.
Burton, *Working*
    _____. *God Working With Them. Being 18 Years Congo Evangelistic Mission History*. London: Victory Press, 1933.
Busch, *Barth*
    Busch, Eberhard. *Karl Barth: His Life from Letters and Autobiographical Texts*. Philadelphia: Fortress Press, 1976.
Bush, "Development"
    Bush, Timothy A. C. "The Development of the Perception of the Baptism in the Holy Spirit Within the Pentecostal Movement in Great Britain." *EPTA Bulletin* 10/1+2, 1992, 24–41.
Butler, "Walls"
    Butler, Anthea. "Walls of Division: Racism's Role in Pentecostal History." SPS 1994.
Caffarel, *Pentecôtisme*
    Caffarel, Henri. *Faut-il parler d'un Pentecôtisme catholique?* Paris, 1973.
Calley, *God's People*
    Calley, Malcolm J. *God's People. West Indian Pentecostal Sects in England*. Oxford University Press, 1965.
Calvin, *Institutio*
    Calvin, John. *Institutio* I.13,14.
Campbell, *Pentecostal*
    Campbell, Joseph E. *The Pentecostal Holiness Church 1898–1948. Its Background and History*. Presenting complete background material which adequately explains the existence of this organization, also the existence of other kindred Pentecostal and Holiness groups, as an essential and integral part of the total church set-up. Franklin Springs, Ga.: Pentecostal Holiness Church, 1951.
Cardenal, *Love in Practice*
    Cardenal, Ernesto. *Love in Practice. The Gospel in Solentiname*. New York: Orbis Books, 1976–77.

Carlsson, *Organizations*
    Carlsson, Bertil. *Organizations and Decision Procedures Within the Swedish Pentecostal Movement* (privately published by Bertil Carlsson, Spjugatan 41, 87100 Härnösand, Sweden, 1974); for his articles in Swedish periodicals see chapter 20, note 12, p. 260.
Carmichael, "Congo"
    Carmichael, Chr. "Congo." *PE* 2994, September 9, 1971, 19f.
Carmichael, "Pentecost"
    ———. "Pentecost in Germany." *PE*, August 20, 1961, 25f.
Carmichael, William, Letter, 30.6.1982.
    Carmichael, William. Letter to Jerry L. Sandidge, Sisters, OR, 30.6.1982.
Carothers, *Baptism*
    Carothers, Warren Fay. *The Baptism with the Holy Ghost and Speaking in Tongues.* Houston: W. F. Carothers, 1906–07.
Cartwright, "Boddy"
    Cartwright, Desmond W. "Boddy, Mary (d. 1928)." *Dictionary*, 91.
Cartwright, "Burton"
    ———. "Burton, William Frederick Padwick, 1886–1971." *Dictionary*, 103f.
Cartwright, "Daughters"
    ———. "Your Daughters Shall Prophesy: The Contribution of Women in Early Pentecostalism." unpubl. paper given at the SPS, Gaithersburg, Maryland, November 15, 1985.
Cartwright, *Evangelists*
    ———. *The Great Evangelists. The Remarkable Lives of George and Stephen Jeffrey.* Basingstoke, Hants.: Marshall Pickering, 1986.
Cartwright, "Jeffreys"
    ———. "Jeffreys, George (1889–1962)." *Dictionary*, 478f.
Cartwright, "Salter"
    ———. "Salter, James (1890–1972)." *Dictionary*, 766.
Casebow, Circular Letter No. 2
    Casebow, H. J. Circular Letter No. 2, 23rd April 1958 from Ngombe Lutete to Baptist Missionary Headquarters, in Baptist Missionary Society Archive, Casebow Papers.
Casebow, *Kimbanguisme*
    ———. *Mvutu mu Kimbanguisme.* Ngombe-Lutete, 1958.
"Castañiza, Juan." *Enciclopedia universal ilustrada europeo-americano* (vol. XII, 13) Barcelona, n.d.
Castiglione, *Aspetti*
    Castiglione, Miriam. *Aspetti e problemi del Pentecostalismo contemporaneo.* Unpublished diss. University of Bari, 1970.
Castiglione, *Italia*
    ———. *I neo-pentecostali in Italia (del "Jesus Movement" ai "Bambini di Dio").* Turin: Claudiana, 1974.
Castiglione, *Movimento*
    ———. *Il movimento pentecostale in Italia nelle polemiche del secondo dopoquerra.* Bari: Adriatica Editrice, 1972.
Castle, "Blue-Prints"
    Castle, Brian. "Hymns: Blue-Prints for Mission." *Missionalia* 21/1, April 1993, 19–25.
Castle, *Hymns*
    ———. *Hymns: The Making and Shaping of a Theology for the Whole People of God. A Comparison of the Four Last Things in Some English and Zambian Hymns in Intercultural Perspective.* IC 67, 1990.
Castro, "Pentecostalism"
    Castro, Emilio. "Pentecostalism and Ecumenism in Latin America." *Christian Century* (September 2, 1972), 955–57.
Catéchisme 1957
    Catéchisme 11.7.1957 quoted in full in Raymaekers, "L'EJCSK" *Zaïre* 13/7, 1959, 737–40.

Catéchisme 1958
    Kikonga catechism (1958) quoted in full in Raymaekers, "L'EJCSK", *Zaïre* 13/7, 1959, 737–40.
Catéchisme 1970
    Le Catéchisme concernant le prophète Simon Kimbangu. N'Kamba, 1970.
Cavendish, *Encyclopedia*
    Cavendish, R. (ed.). *Encyclopedia of the Unexplained: Magic, Occultism, and Parapsychology.* London: Routledge & K. Paul, 1974.
CC, 1969
    Minutes of the Central Committee of the WCC (Canterbury 1969). Geneva: WCC, 1969.
CC, 1988
    Minutes of the Central Committee of the WCC (Hanover 1988). Geneva: WCC, 1988.
Centre de Recherche et d'Information Socio-Politique (C.R.I.S.P.), "Kimbanguisme"
    Centre de Recherche et d'Information Socio-Politique (C.R.I.S.P.). "Le Kimbanguisme" (*Courrier hebdomadaire*, 8.1.1960, Brussels: C.R.I.S.P.).
Ceuta, "Romania"
    Ceuta, Ioan. "The Pentecostal Apostolic Church in Romania 1944–1990." *EPTA Bulletin* 13, 1994, 74–87.
Chalux, *Congo Belge*
    Chalux (pseudonym). *Un an au Congo Belge.* Brussels, 1925.
Chan, "Asian"
    Chan, Simon K. H. "An Asian Review." *Journal of Pentecostal Theology* 4, April 1994, 35–40.
Chant, "Australien"
    Chant, Barry. "Australien." In Hollenweger (ed.), *Die Pfingstkirchen*, 125–30.
Chant, *Heart*
    _____. *Heart of Fire. The Story of Australian Pentecostalism.* Fullarton, South Australia, Luke Publications, 1973.
Chapmann, *Operationen*
    Chapmann, George. *Operationen im Aetherfeld.* Remagen: Otto Reichl Verlag, 1979.
Chappell, "Healing"
    Chappell, Paul G. "Healing Movements." *Dictionary*, 353–74.
Chappell, "Roberts"
    _____. "Roberts, Granville Oral (1918–)." *Dictionary*, 759–60.
Charte
    Charte de l'Union de Prière. Charmes-sur-Rhône 1966[2] (mimeographed).
Chassard, "Essai de bibliographie"
    Chassard, Paul-Eric. "Essai de bibliographie sur le Kimbanguisme." *Archives de Sociologie des Religions* 16/31, 1971, 43–49.
Chéry, "Accusent"
    Chéry, H.-Ch. "Les sectes nous accusent." *Signes du Temps*, Jan. 1960, 9–11.
Chéry, *Offensive*
    _____. *Offensive des Sectes.* Paris 1954[2].
Chéry, "Sectes"
    _____. "Les sectes." *Lumière et Vie. Revue de formation doctrinale* no. 6. Oct. 1952, 67–108.
Chikane, *No Life of My Own*
    Chikane, Frank. *No Life of My Own. An Autobiography.* Maryknoll, N.Y.: Orbis Books, 1989.
Chinn, "Speak?"
    Chinn, J. J. "May We Pentecostals Speak?" *Christianity Today* 5, 1961, 880f.
Cho, *Fourth Dimension*
    Cho, Yonggi. *The Fourth Dimension* Plainfield, N.J.: Logos International, 1979.
Choffat, "Kimbanguiste"
    Choffat, F. "L'église kimbanguiste africaine et non-violente." *Cahiers de la réconciliation*, May–June 1966, 4.

Choi, "Comparative"
    Choi, Syn-Duk. "A Comparative Study of Two New Religious Movements in the
    Republic of Korea: the Unification Church and the Full Gospel Central Church." In
    James Beckford (ed.), *New Religious Movements and Rapid Social Change.* Beverly Hills,
    California: Sage Publications, 1986.
Chomé, *Kimbangu*
    Chomé, Jules. *La passion de Simon Kimbangu.* Brussels: Présence Africaine, 1959.
Christians/Schipper/Smedes, *Who*
    Christians, Clifford, Earl J. Schipper, Wesley Smedes. *Who in the World?* Grand Rapids,
    Mich.: Eerdmans, 1972.
Christie-Murray, *Voices*
    Christie-Murray, David. *Voices from the Gods. Speaking with Tongues.* London:
    Routledge & K. Paul, 1978.
Chung, *Struggle*
    Chung, Hyun Kyung. *Struggle to the Sun Again. Introducing Asian Women's Theology.*
    Maryknoll, New York: Orbis Books, 1990.
Church of God in Christ, *Year Book.*
    Church of God in Christ. *Year Book.* Memphis, Tenn.: Church of God in Christ, 1951.
Cito, *Movimento*
    Cito, Carmelo. *Il movimento pentecostale nel settore occidentale della provincia di Taranta.*
    Ph.D. University of Bari, 1970/71, unpubl.
CLAI
    Consejo Latinamericano de Iglesias
Clayton, *Melodies*
    Clayton, N. J. (ed.). *Melodies of Life.* Malverne, N.Y.: Gospel Songs Inc. 1946.
Clark, *Building*
    Clark, Stephen. *Building Christian Communities. Strategy for Renewing the Church.*
    Notre Dame, Ind.: Ave Maria Press, 1972.
Clark, *Confirmation*
    ———. *Confirmation and the "Baptism of the Spirit."* Pecos, New Mexico: Dove
    Publications, 1969, and Watchung, N.J.: Charisma Books, 1971.
Cleary, "Misreading"
    Cleary, Edward. "John Paul Cries 'Wolf'; Misreading the Pentecostals." *Commonweal*
    119, 20 November 1992, 7f.; Spanish: "El Maltrato de la jerarquía católica a los
    Pentecostales." *Pastoral Popular* no. 226, March 1993, 15–17.
Clemmons, "Mason"
    Clemmons, Ithiel C. "Mason, Charles Harrison (1866–1961)." *Dictionary*, 585–88.
Clemmons, "True Koinonia"
    ———. "True Koinonia: Pentecostal Hopes and Historical Realities." *Pneuma*, 3/1,
    1981, 46–56.
Coalition of Hispanic Christian Leadership, "Manifesto"
    Coalition of Hispanic Christian Leadership. "Riverside Manifesto" Riverside Church
    Conference on the Church and the City, March 13, 1981.
Códice Matritense
    *Códice Matritense de la Real Academia (textos en náhuatls de los indígenos informantes de
    Sagahún),* ed. facs. de Paso y Troncoso, Madrid, fototipia de Hauser y Mente, VIII,
    1906.
Cohen, "Renovación"
    Cohen, Harold F. "La renovación carismatico de la Iglesia Catolica." *Boletin Mensuel del
    movimiento de renovación cristiana en el Espíritu Santo* 1/6, March 1973, 1–3.
Cohn, "Das Modell der themenzentrierten Interaktion"
    Cohn, Ruth. "Das Modell der themenzentrierten Interaktion." In A. Faran/R. C.
    Cohn, *Gelebte Geschichte der Psychotherapie.* Gleh-Cotta, 1984, 352–75.
Cole, "Ecumenical Tensions"
    Cole, David. "Current Pentecostal/Ecumenical Tensions." *Ecumenical Trends* 24/5,
    May 1995, 1–16.

Collier, *Economism*
    Collier, Jane. *The Culture of Economism. An Exploration of Barriers to Faith-as-Praxis.* IC 65, 1990.
Cone, "Black Spirituals"
    Cone, James H. "Black Spirituals: A Theological Interpretation." *Theology Today* 29/1, April 1972, 54–69.
Cone, *Spirituals and the Blues*
    _____. *The Spirituals and the Blues. An Interpretation.* New York: Seabury Press, 1972.
Conference
    Conference on Pentecostal and Charismatic Research in Europe. Kappel (Switzerland), no place, 1991.
Congar, *Crois*
    Congar, Yves. *Je crois en L'Esprit Saint.* Paris, 3 vols. 1979/80. English: *I Believe in the Holy Spirit.* New York: Seabury, 1983.
Congregação Cristã do Brasil, *Estatutos*
    Congregação Cristã do Brasil. *Estatutos aprovados em 4 de Março de 1931 e reformados em 23 Abril de 1943, 29 de Novembre de 1944 et de 1946, em Assembleia Geral.* S. Paulo, n.d.
Conn, *Like a Mighty Army*
    Conn, Charles. *Like a Mighty Army Moves the Church of God.* Cleveland, Tenn.: Church of God Publishing House, 1955.
Conn, *Evangel*
    Conn, Charles W. *Church of God Evangel* 50/50, 15.2.1960.
Connor, "Covenant"
    Connor, John. "Covenant Communities: A New Sign of Hope." *New Covenant* 1/10, April 1972, 2–9.
"Conscription"
    "The Pentecostal Movement and the Conscription Law." *PE,* 4th August 1917, 6.
Conzelmann, *First Corinthians.*
    Conzelmann, *First Corinthians.* Philadelphia: Fortress Press, 1975.
Cook, Guillermo, "Church"
    Cook, Guillermo. "The Church, the World and Progress in Latin America, in Light of the Eschatological Kingdom." *Brighton,* 199–206.
Cook, William, "Interview"
    Cook, William. "Interview With Chilean Pentecostals." *Int. Review of Mission* 72, 1983, 591–95.
Corum, *Like as of Fire*
    Corum, Fred T. (ed.). *Like as of Fire. A Reprint of the Old Azusa Street Papers.* Fred T. Corum, 160 Salem Street, Wilmington, Mass. 01887; 1981.
Corum, *God's Glorious Outpouring*
    _____. *God's Glorious Outpouring. The Azusa Street Revival.* (1992) (documentary video available from CTL Productions, P.O. Box 1428, Whittier, CA 90609).
Corum, *Tragedy to Triumph*
    _____. *Tragedy to Triumph. The William Seymour Story* (1992) (documentary video available from CTL Productions, P.O. Box 1428, Whittier, CA 90609)
Costas, *Outside*
    Costas, Orlando. *Christ Outside the Gate: Mission Beyond Christendom.* Maryknoll: Orbis Books, 1982.
Costas, *Protestantismo*
    _____. *El Protestantismo en América Latina Hoy: Ensayos del Camino (1972–74).* San José, Costa Rica: Publicaciones INDEF, 1975.
Costas, "Social"
    _____. "Social Justice in the Other Protestant Tradition: A Hispanic Perspective." In Frederick Greenspahn (ed.), *Contemporary Ethical Issues in the Jewish and Christian Tradition.* Hoboken, N.J.: Ktau Publishing House, Inc. 1986, 205–29.

Cox, *Feast*
>   Cox, Harvey. *The Feast of Fools. A Theological Essay on Festivity and Fantasy.* Cambridge, Mass.: Harvard University Press, 1969.

Cox, "Reflections"
>   _____. "Some Personal Reflections on Pentecostalism." *Pneuma* 15/1, 1993, 29–34.

Cox, *Religión*
>   _____. *La Religión en la Ciudad Secular.* Madrid: Sal Terrae, 1985.

Cox, *Secular*
>   _____. *The Secular City. Secularization and Urbanization in Theological Perspective.* New York: Simon & Schuster Inc., 1984.

Cox, *Turning East*
>   _____. *Turning East—the Promise and Peril of the New Orientalism.* New York, 1977.

Cox, "Why"
>   _____. "Why God Didn't Die: A Religious Renaissance Flourishing Around the World. Pentecostal Christians Leading the Way." *Nieman Reports. The Nieman Foundation at Harvard University* 47/2, Summer 1993, 3–8.

CRISP
>   Centre de Recherche et d'Information Socio-Politique, Brussels.

Crompton, "Tide Has Turned"
>   Crompton, D. "The Tide Has Turned." *New Vision* 5/2, March/April 1980, 1–13.

Cronje, "Influence"
>   Cronje, F. H. J. "The Influence of Pentecostalism on Church Unity and Diversity." In W. S. Vorster (ed.), *Church Unity and Diversity in the Southern African Context,* Pretoria: University of South Africa, 1980.

Cross, "Luther"
>   Cross, F. L. "Martin Luther." In F. L. Cross (ed.), *The Oxford Dictionary of the Christian Church.* Oxford University Press, 1974, 846–48.

Crouch, *World Outlook*
>   Crouch, Archie R. "A Shoot Out of the Dry Ground: The Most Rapidly Growing Church in Mexico." *World Outlook,* April 1970, 33–35.

Cullmann, *La Fé*
>   Cullmann, Oscar. *La Fé y el Culto en la Iglesia Primitiva.* Madrid, Spain: Stadium, 1971.

Cunningham, "Social Concern"
>   Cunningham, R. C. "Social Concern Articulated." *PE* 2840, 13.10.1968, 5.

Curlee–Curlee, "Bridging the Gap"
>   Curlee, Mary Ruth, and Robert R. Curlee. "Bridging the Gap: John A. Mackay, Presbyterians, and the Charismatic Movement." *American Presbyterians* 72/3, Autumn 1994.

Curlee–Curlee, *Springtime*
>   _____. *God's Springtime: John A. Mackay, David J. du Plessis and Presbyterian Charismatic Origins.* Ms 1993, to be published in the USA.

Curry, "Fight"
>   Curry, Brigadier General Jerry. "Fight the Good Fight of Faith." *Military Chaplains Review,* Spring 1977, 59–60.

Cutten, *Speaking*
>   Cutten, George B., *Speaking With Tongues.* New Haven: Yale University Press, 1927.

Cyprian, *New Covenant*
>   Cyprian, Sr. *New Covenant* 1/9, March 1972.

Dallière, *D'aplomb*
>   Dallière, Louis. *D'aplomb sur la parole de Dieu. Courte étude sur le réveil de Pentecôte.* Valence: Imprimerie Chaprin et Reyne, 1932.

Dallière, "Fonction"
>   _____. "La fonction spirituelle du culte: III. La loi des intermédiaires." *Foi et Vie* 29/71, April 1926, 351–60.

Dallière, "L'anti–judaisme"

———. "L'anti–judaisme dans la pensée paulinienne." *Revue de l'histoire des religions* 93, 1926, 264.

Dallière, "L'Eglise"

———. "L'Eglise devant les reveils, en particilier les mouvements de Pentecôte, rapport du pasteur Dalliere presenté au Synode régional de Tournon le 10 novembre 1958." In Lienhard, *Aspect.*

Dallière, Letter

———. Letter to J. P. Lienhard (quoted in Lienhard, *Aspect*, 78).

Dallière, "Mort"

———. "La mort de l'apôtre Pierre et les récentes fouilles de Rome. A propos de l'ouvrage de Hans Lietzmann." *Revue d'histoire et de philosophie religieuse* 3, 1923, 145–55.

Dallière, "Mouvement"

———. "Le mouvement de Pentecôte." *Le Semeur* 35/1, 1.11.1932, 1–19.

Dallière, *Peut-on*

———. *Peut-on démontrer que l'apôtre Pierre est mort à Rome? Sujet d'un livre récent de Hans Lietzmann,* lic. thesis, Faculté libre de théologie protestante, Paris, 1922, unpubl.

Dallière, "Toi"

———. "Toi aussi, tu es de ces gens-là?" *Esprit et Vie* 2/23, April 1934, 167–69.

Damboriena, "Algunos"

Damboriena, Prudencio. "Algunos aspectos de la penetración protestante en Iberoamerica." *Arbor* (Madrid) 50/192, Dec. 1961, 60–75 (624–39).

Damboriena, "Chile"

———. "El protestantismo en Chile." *Mensaje* 6/59, June 1957, 145–54.

Damboriena, "Fury"

———. "Pentecostal Fury." *Catholic World* 202/201, Jan. 1966.

Damboriena, *Tongues*

———. *Tongues as of Fire. Pentecostalism in Contemporary Christianity.* Washington and Cleveland: Corpus Books, 1969.

Daneel, "African"

Daneel, M. L. "African Independent Church Pneumatology and the Salvation of All Creation." *Brighton,* 96–126; also *Int. Review of Mission* 82/326, April 1993, 143–66.

Davies, *Worship and Dance*

Davies, J. G. (ed.). *Worship and Dance.* Birmingham: Birmingham Institute for the Study of Worship and Religious Architecture, 1975.

Davies, Rex, *Locusts*

Davies, Rex. *Locusts and Wild Honey: The Charismatic Renewal and the Ecumenical Movement* Geneva: WCC, 1978.

Davies, William R., *Rocking*

Davies, William R. *Rocking the Boat: The Challenge of the House Church.* Basingstoke, Hants.: Marshall Pickering, 1986.

Davis, John R. *Contextualized*

Davis, John R. *Towards a Contextualized Theology of the Church in Thailand.* Unpubl. Ph.D. University of Birmingham, 1990.

Dayton, *Defending*

Dayton, Donald W. (ed.). *Holiness Tracts Defending the Ministry of Women.* Reprint 1853, 1891, 18??, 1905. Higher Christian Life. 11. New York: Garland, 1984–.

Dayton, *Discovering*

Dayton, Donald W. *Discovering an Evangelical Heritage.* 1976, Reprint. Peabody, Mass.: Hendrickson, 1988.

Dayton, "Expansion"

———. "The Holy Spirit and Christian Expansion in the Twentieth Century." *Missiology* 16/4, Oct. 1988, 397–407.

Dayton, *Higher*

> Dayton, Donald W. et al. (eds.). *The Higher Christian Life*, 50 vols. New York and London: Garland, 1984–.

Dayton, "Higher"

> ———. "The Higher Christian Life. A Bibliographical Overview." In *The Higher Christian Life*. vol. 1.

Dayton, "Issues"

> ———. "Pneumatological Issues in the Holiness Movement." *Greek Orthodox Theological Review* 31, 3+4, 1986, 361–67.

Dayton, "Layer"

> ———. "Yet Another Layer of the Onion! Or Opening the Ecumenical Door to Let the Riffraff In." *The Ecumenical Review* 40, 1988, 87–110.

Dayton, "Limits"

> ———. "The Limits to Evangelicalism: The Pentecostal Tradition." and "Some Doubts About the Usefulness of the Category 'Evangelicals.' " In Donald W. Dayton and Robert K. Johnston (eds.), *The Variety of American Evangelicalism*. Knoxville, Tenn.: The University of Tennessee Press, 1991, 36–56 and 245–51.

Dayton, "Roots"

> ———. "Theological Roots of Pentecostalism." *Pneuma* 2/1, 1980, 3–21.

Dayton, *Roots*

> ———. *Theological Roots of Pentecostalism*. 1987. Reprint. Peabody, Mass.: Hendrickson, 1991.

Dayton, *Three*

> Dayton, Donald W. (ed.). *Three Early Pentecostal Tracts*. Reprint 1910, ca. 1907, 1916. *The Higher Christian Life*, vol. 14. New York: Garland, 1984–.

Dayton, "Turning"

> ———. "Is Latin America Turning Pentecostal? The Ecumenical Significance of a Religious Revolution." unpubl. paper given at the National Academy of Ecumenists, 28 September 1991, St. Louis, Days Inn.

Decapmaeker, "Kimbanguisme"

> Decapmaeker, R. P. "Le Kimbanguisme." In *Devant les sectes non-chrétiennes. Rapports et compte rendu de la XXXième semaine de missiologie*. Louvain, 1961, 52–90.

"Declaration of Solidarity"

> "Declaration of Solidarity with the Relevant Pentecostal Witness from South Africa," at the "Conference on Charismatic and Pentecostal Research." In Kappel a. A., Switzerland, July 1991. With an introduction by Murray W. Dempster, in *Transformation* 9/1, January/March 1992, 32f., and in *EPTA Bulletin* 10/1, 1991, 34f.

de Kock, "Response"

> de Kock, Wynand J. "A Response to Karla Poewe-Hexham and Irving Hexham." *Brighton*, 91–95.

de Leon, *Silent*

> de Leon, Victor. *The Silent Pentecostals. A Biographical History of the Pentecostal Movement Among the Hispanics in the Twentieth Century*. Taylors, South Carolina: Faith Printing Company, 1979.

Delespesse, *Church*

> Delespesse, Max. *The Church Community Leaven and Life Style*. Ottawa: The Catholic Center of Saint Paul University, 1969, and Notre Dame, Ind.: Communication Center, 1972.

de Melo, "Participation"

> de Melo, Manuel. "Participation is Everything." *Int. Review of Mission* 60/238, April 1971, 245–48.

de Moura, *Importância das Igrejas Pentecostais*

> de Moura, Abdalizis. *Importância das Igrejas Pentecostais para a Igreja Católica*. Recife (duplicated typescript, de Moura, Rua Jiriquiti 48, Boa Vista), 1969.

de Moura, "Pentecostalismo"
_____. "O Pentecostalismo como fenômeno popular no Brasil." *Revista Eclesiástica Brasileira* 31/121, March 1971, 78–94.

Dempster, "Borders"
Dempster, Murray W. "Crossing Borders: Arguments Used By Early American Pentecostals in Support of the Global Character of Pacifism." In *Conference on Pentecostal and Charismatic Research in Europe, 1991, Kappel, Switzerland* (unpubl.).

Dempster, "Evangelism"
_____. "Evangelism, Social Concern and the Kingdom of God." *Called*, 22–43.

Dempster, "Mandate"
_____. "Pentecostal Social Concern and the Biblical Mandate of Social Justice." *Pneuma* 9/2, Fall 1987, 129–53.

Dempster–Klaus–Petersen, *Called*
Dempster, Murray A., Byron D. Klaus, Douglas Petersen (eds.). *Called and Empowered. Global Mission in Pentecostal Perspective.* Peabody, Mass.: Hendrickson, 1991.

de Petrella, "Tension"
de Petrella, Lidia Susana Vaccaro. "The Tension Between Evangelism and Social Action in the Pentecostal Movement." *Int. Review of Mission* 75, Jan. 1986, 34–38.

"de Renty"
"de Renty, Jean-Baptiste." In *Nouvelle Biographie Générale.* Paris, 1863, XXXXII, 3.

de Renty, *Le Chrétien*
_____. *Le Chrétien réel ou la Vie du Marquis de Renty.* Cologne 1701^2.

Desanti, "Golden Anniversary"
Desanti, Dominique. "The Golden Anniversary of Kimbanguism. An African Religion." *Continent 2000. Africa's Bilingual Monthly*, no. 19, April 1971, 7–19.

Dialungana, *Kisikulusa*
Dialungana, K. S. *Kisikulusa za Dibundu*, N'Kamba, EJCSK, 1960.

Dialungana, *Tanganinia*
_____. *Tanganinia Fu Ya Klisto.* N'Kamba, EJCSK, 1966.

Dialungana, *Zolanga*
_____. *Zolanga Yelusalemi dia Mpa.* N'Kamba, EJCSK, 1961, dupl.

Diangienda, "Coup"
Diangienda, K. (alias J.). "Coup d'Oeuil sur le Kimbanguisme." *Kimbanguisme* (Kinshasa), May 1960.

Diangienda, "Eglise et politique"
_____. "Eglise et politique." *Cahiers de la réconciliation*, nos 5–6, May-June 1966, 41.

Diangienda, "Kimbanguisme"
_____. "Le Kimbanguisme." *Courrier hebdomonaire du C.R.I.S.P.* 29.1.1960, 16f.

Diangienda, *L'histoire*
_____. *L'histoire du Kimbanguisme.* Kinshasa, 1984.

Dibelius, *Studies*
Dibelius, Martin. *Studies in the Acts of the Apostles.* London: SCM, 1956.

Dickson, *Theology*
Dickson, Kwesi A. *Theology in Africa.* New York: Orbis Books. London: Darton, Longman & Todd, 1984.

Dictionary
Dictionary of Pentecostal and Charismatic Movements. Ed. S. Burgess and Gary McGee. Grand Rapids: Zondervan, 1988.

"Die Propheten kommen"
"Die Propheten kommen." *Informationsdienst* (Switzerland) 28/3, Aug. 1991, 5f.

Dieter, *Holiness*
Dieter, Melvin Easterday. *The Holiness Revival of the Nineteenth Century* (Studies in Evangelicalism 1). Metuchen, N.J.: The Scarecrow Press, 1980.

Discours
  Le Discours Psychoanalytique 51/1, March 1983 (Services Masson, 64 bd
  Saint-German, Paris): "Les amants de la langue Autre. Travaux sur le bilinguisme, les
  glossolalies, la langue étrangère") (Special Issue).
Djukanovic–Mach, *Alternative*
  Djukanovic, J., and E. P. Mach (eds.). *Alternative Approaches to Meeting Basic Health
  Needs in Developing Countries.* A Joint UNICEF/WHO Study. Geneva: World Health
  Organization, 1975.
Domínguez, *Pioneros*
  Domínguez, Roberto. *Pioneros de Pentecostés en el mundo de Habla Hispana,* vol. III:
  Venezuela y Colombia. Terrassa, Barcelona: Libros CLIE, 1990.
Dorries, "Doctrine"
  Dorries, David W. "Edward Irving's Doctrine of Spirit Baptism." SPS 1992, C.
Dorries, " 'Standard Sign' "
  _____. "Edward Irving and the 'Standard Sign' of Spirit Baptism." In Gary B.
  McGee, *Initial Evidence.* Peabody, Mass.: Hendrickson, 1991.
Douglas, *Earth*
  Douglas, J. D. (ed.). *Let the Earth Hear His Voice. International Congress on World
  Evangelization. Lausanne, Switzerland [1974]. Official Reference Volume: Papers and
  Responses.* Minneapolis, Minn.: World Wide Publications, 1975.
Doutreloux, "Prophétisme"
  Doutreloux, A. "Prophétisme et 'leadership' dans la société Kongo." In *Devant les sectes
  non-chrétiennes, XXXIème semaine de missiologie.* Museum Lessianum, no. 42, Louvain,
  1961.
Down, "Contours"
  Down, M. B. "Contours of a Narrative Pentecostal Theology and Practice." SPS 1985.
Drewermann, *Tiefenpsychologie*
  Drewermann, Eugen. *Tiefenpsychologie und Exegese,* 2 vols. 1984/85.
Drollinger, *Offener*
  Drollinger, Christian. *Offener Brief auf die Erklärung des Herrn Methodistenpredigers
  Währer aus Signau, vom 28. Oktober 1937, in betreff der neuen Versammlung in Signau und
  anderwärts.* (Signau, Switzerland, 1937).
DuBois, *Negro Church*
  DuBois, William Edward Burghardt. *The Negro Church. A Social Study Made Under the
  Direction of Atlanta University* (1903).
DuBois, *Souls*
  _____. *The Souls of the Black Folk.* Chicago, 1903; 22d ed., 1940.
Dudley, "Portugal"
  Dudley, Roland Q. "History of the Assemblies of God in Portugal." *EPTA Bulletin* 12,
  1993, 49–63.
Dugan, "Mass Evangelism"
  Dugan, George. "Mass Evangelism *Called* of No Relevancy to Blacks." *New York Times*
  5.4. 1970.
Dulles, *Models*
  Dulles, Avery. *Models of the Church. A Critical Assessment of the Church in all its Aspects.*
  Dublin: Macmillan, 1974.
Duncan, M., *Revelation*
  Duncan, Mildred A. *A Revelation of End-Time Babylon. A Verse by Verse Exposition of
  the Book of Revelation.* Edgemont, South Dakota: M. A. Duncan, 1950.
Duncan, R./Western-Smith, *Ignorance*
  Duncan, Ronald, and Miranda Western-Smith. *The Encyclopedia of Ignorance,
  Everything you ever wanted to know about the unknown.* Oxford: Pergamos Press, 1977,
  1978, 9–17.
Dunn, *Baptism*
  Dunn, James D. G. *Baptism in the Holy Spirit.* Philadelphia: Westminster, 1970.

Dunn, "Models"
_____. "Models of Christian Community in the New Testament." *Bossey,* 99–116.

Dunn, *Re-examination*
_____. *A Re-examination of the New Testament Teaching of the Gift of the Spirit in Relation to Pentecostalism Today* (Studies in Biblical Theology, second series 15). London: SCM, 1970.

Dunn, *Unity*
_____. *Unity and Diversity in the New Testament. An Inquiry into the Character of Earliest Christianity.* London: SCM, 1977.

Du Plessis, "Background"
Du Plessis, David J. "The Historical Background of Pentecostalism." *One in Christ* 10/2, 1974, 174–79.

Du Plessis, *Brief History*
_____. *A Brief History of the Pentecostal Movements* (unpublished, unpaginated, no date).

Du Plessis, "Holy Spirit"
_____. "Holy Spirit in Ecumenical Movement," in Wogen (ed.), *Jesus,* 223–50.

Du Plessis, "Persecution"
_____. "Persecution for Charismatic Catholics." *New Covenant* 3/6, Jan. 1973, 13.

DuPree, *Biographical*
DuPree, Sherry Sherrod. *Biographical Dictionary of African-American, Holiness-Pentecostals, 1880–1990.* Washington, D.C.: Middle Atlantic Regional Press, 1989.

Eagle, *Alternative*
Eagle, Robert. *Alternative Medicine. A Guide to the Medical Underground.* London: Future Publications, 1978.

Earhardt, "Korea"
Earhardt, Byron H. "The New Religions of Korea: A Preliminary Interpretation." *Transactions of the Korea Branch of the Royal Asiatic Society* 49, 1974.

Ebeling, *Studium*
Ebeling, Gerhard. *Studium der Theologie. Eine encyklopädische Orientierung.* UTB 446, Tübingen: J. C. B. Mohr, 1976.

Ecke, *Durchbruch*
Ecke, Karl. *Der Durchbruch des Urchristentums seit Luthers Reformation. Lesestücke aus einem vergessenen Kapitel der Kirchengeschichte.* Altdorf/Nbg.: Süddeutscher Missionsverlag Fritz Pranz, 1950; second edition, n.d.

Ecke, *Luther*
_____. *Luther und der Gedanke einer apostolischen Reformation* (Berlin: Martin Warnweck 1911); abridged second edition: *Kaspar Schwenckfeld. Ungelöste Geistesfragen der Reformation. Kaspar Schwenckfeld's Schau einer apostolischen Reformation,* ed. H. D. Gruschka in connection with the Schwenkfeld Library, Pennsylvania (Memmingen: Missionsverlag für urchristliche Botschaft, 1965).

Ecke, *Pfingstbewegung*
_____. *Die Pfingstbewegung, Ein Gutachten von kirchlicher Seite.* Mülheim/Ruhr: Christlicher Gemeinschaftsverband GmbH, 1950.

Ecke, *Reformierende*
_____. *Der reformierende Protestantismus. Streiflichter auf die Entwicklung lebendiger Gemeinden von Luther bis heute.* Gütersloh: Bertelsmann, 1952.

Ecke, *Sektierer*
_____. *Sektierer oder wertvolle Brüder? Randglossen zu einem Sektenbuch.* Mülheim/Ruhr: E. Humburg, Verlagsbuchhandlung, 1951.

Ecke–Bibra, *Reformation*
Ecke, Karl, and O. S. von Bibra. *Die Reformation in neuer Sicht.* Altdorf/Nbg.: Süddeutscher Missionsverlag Fritz Pranz, 1952.

Eclesiogenesis
  Eclesiogenesis. Las Comunidades de Base Reinventen la Iglesia. Santander: Sal Terrae, 1980.
Edrington, *Everyday*
  Edrington, Roger. *Everyday Men: Living in a Climate of Unbelief.* IC 46, 1987.
Edwards, "Attitudes"
  Edwards, S. D. "Attitudes to Disease and Healing in a South African Context." In C. G. Oosthuizen (ed.), *Religion Alive,* 90–96.
Eisenlöffel, "Papst"
  Eisenlöffel, Ludwig. "Der Papst und die Pfingstler." *Wort und Geist* 8/2, Febr. 1979, 6–7.
Eisenlöffel, *Wenn*
  ———. *Wenn Christen in der Ehe scheitern. Ein Plädoyer für Barmherzigkeit.* Wiesbaden: Coprint, 1986.
Elbert, "England"
  Elbert, Paul. "The Charismatic Movement in the Church of England: An Overview." *Pneuma* 6/1, Spring 1984, 27–50.
EJCSK
  Eglise de Jésus-Christ sur la terre d'après le prophète Simon Kimbangu.
Enciclopedia universal
  Enciclopedia universal ilustrada europeo-americana: Etimologias sanscrito, hebreo, griego, latin, arabe, lenguas indigenas americanas, etc.; versiones de la mayoria de las voces en frances, italiano, ingles, aleman, portugues, catalan, esperanto. 70 vols. Barcelona: J. Espasa, 1912–1930.
Engemann, "Paradigma"
  Engemann, Wilfried. "Die intime Interne. Charismatik als pastoral-psychologisches Paradigma." *Wege zum Menschen* 41/2, Febr./March 1989, 87–103.
EPLA
  Encuentro Pentecostal Latinamericano.
EPTA
  European Pentecostal Theological Association.
EPTA Bulletin
  The Journal of the European Pentecostal Theological Association, Elim Bible College, London Road, Nantwich, CW5 6LW, England.
Ervin, "Option"
  Ervin, Howard. "Hermeneutics: A Pentecostal Option." *Pneuma* 3/2, Fall 1981, 11–25.
Éscobar, "Evangelism"
  Éscobar, Samuel. "Evangelism and Man's Search for Freedom, Justice and Fulfillment." In J. D. Douglas, *Let the Earth Hear His Voice,* 303–18.
Esparza, "Question"
  Esparza, Gabriella. "Let's Question the Ministry of Women." *Pneuma* 13/2, 1991, 157–60.
Espinosa, "Cinco"
  Espinosa, Arnulfo. "Cinco años de unificación." *Mensajero Pentecostés* 2/60, Febr. 1961, 3–8.
Espinosa, "Datos"
  ———. "Datos para la historia de la Unión de Iglesias Evangélicas Independientes." *Mensajero Pentecostés* 2/6, Jan. 1961, 9–11.
"Evangeletters"
  "Evangeletters" in *Pentecostal Evangel* 3018, 12/3, 1972.
Evangelical Witness
  Evangelical Witness in South Africa: A Critique of Evangelical Theology and Practice by South African Evangelicals Themselves. The Evangelical Alliance, Regnum Books (UK), 1986.
Evans, "Science"
  Evans, Russel. "Science and Christianity Today." *Youth Challenge* 2, 1963, 6f.

Failing, "Neue"
    Failing, Wolf-Eckhart. "Neue charismatische Bewegung in den Landeskirchen." In
    Hollenweger, *Pfingstkirchen*, 131–45.
Fairchild, *Oberlin*
    Fairchild, James H. *Oberlin: The Colony and the College.* 1883; *The Higher Christian
    Life,* vol. 15.
Fallot, *Comment*
    Fallot, Tommy. *Comment lire la Bible jour après jour.* Paris: Librairie Fischbacher, 1909.
Farah, "Analysis"
    Farah, Charles. "A Critical Analysis: The 'Roots and Fruits' of Faith-Formula
    Theology." *Pneuma* 3/1, Spring 1981, 3–21.
Farau–Cohn, *Gelebte Geschichte der Psychotherapie*
    Farau, A., and R. C. Cohn. *Gelebte Geschichte der Psychotherapie.* Stuttgart:
    Klett-Cotta, 1984.
Farrand, "Choice"
    Farrand, Dorothy. "Choice and Perception of Healing among Black Psychiatric
    Patients." In C. G. Oosthuizen (ed.), *Religion Alive,* 97–104.
Fasholé-Luke, *Christianity in Independent Africa*
    Fasholé-Luke, Edward, Richard Gray, Adrian Hastings, Godwin Tasie (eds.).
    Christianity in Independent Africa. London: Rex Collings, 1978.
Faupel, "Durham"
    Faupel, William. "William H. Durham and the Finished Work of Calvary." In
    Jongeneel, 1992, 85–96.
Faupel, "Kingdom"
    _____. "This Gospel of the Kingdom: The Significance of Eschatology in the
    Development of Pentecostal Thought." Sheffield Academic Press, 1996.
Faupel, "Whither?"
    _____. "Whither Pentecostalism? 22nd Presidential Address Society for Pentecostal
    Studies." *Pneuma* 15/1, 1993, 9–27.
Feci, "Kimbangu"
    Feci, Damso. "Vie cachée et vie publique de Simon Kimbangu selon la littérature
    coloniale et missionaire belge." *Les Cahiers du C.E.D.A.F.* no. 7, 1973.
Fee, "Baptism"
    Fee, Gordon D. "Baptism in the Holy Spirit: The Issue of Separability and
    Subsequence." *Pneuma* 7/2, 1985, 87–99.
Fee, *First Corinthians*
    _____. *The First Epistle to the Corinthians.* International Commentary on the New
    Testament. Grand Rapids, Mich.: Eerdmans, 1987.
Fee, "Global"
    _____. "The Kingdom of God and the Church's Global Mission." *Called,* 7–21.
Fee, "Precedent"
    _____. "Hermeneutics and Historical Precedent—A Major Problem in Pentecostal
    Hermeneutics." In Russel P. Spittler (ed.), *Perspectives on the New Pentecostalism.*
    Grand Rapids, Mich.: Baker Book House, 1976, 118–32.
Fehderau, "Prophetic Christianity"
    Fehderau, H. W. "Kimbanguism: Prophetic Christianity in the Congo." *Practical
    Anthropology* 9/4, July-Aug. 1962, 157–78.
Fidler, "History"
    Fidler, R. L. "Pentecostal History Lends Important Role to Blacks." *The International
    Outlook,* 4, 1971.
Finney, *Lectures*
    Finney, Charles G. *Lectures to Professing Christians,* 1837, reprint in *The Higher
    Christian Life,* vol. 17.
Fisher, *Negro Slave Songs*
    Fisher, Miles Mark. *Negro Slave Songs in the United States.* New York: Citadel Press,
    1953.

Fleisch, "Fletcher"
Fleisch, Paul. "J. W. Fletcher." *Die Religion in Geschichte und Gegenwart,* second edition (1928) II, 618.

Fleisch, *Gemeinschaftsbewegung*
_____. *Geschichte der deutschen Gemeinschaftsbewegung bis zum Auftreten des Zungenredens (1875–1907)* Vol 1 of *Die moderne Gemeinschaftsbewegung in Deutschland.* Leipzig: H. G. Wallmann 1912–14[3].

Fleisch, *Heiligungsbewegung*
_____. *Zur Geschichte der Heiligungsbewegung.* 1. Heft: *Die Heiligungsbewegung von Wesley bis Boardman.* Leipzig, 1910.

Fleisch, "Law"
_____. "William Law." *Die Religion in Geschichte und Gegenwart,* second edition (1927–32) III, 1504.

Fleisch, *Pfingstbewegung*
_____. *Die Pfingstbewegung in Deutschland.* Vol. II, part 2 of *Die moderne Gemeinschaftsbewegung in Deutschland.* Hanover: Heinr. Feesche Verlag, 1957. Reprint in Dayton, *The Higher Christian Life,* 18.

"Fletcher," *Lexicon der Schweiz*
"Fletcher, John W." *Historisch-biographisches Lexikon der Schweiz.* Neuchâtel, 1921–34.

Fletcher, *Soviet*
Fletcher, William C. *Soviet Charismatics: The Pentecostals in the U.S.S.R.* New York: Peter Lang Publishing, 1985.

Flora, *Colombia*
Flora, Cornelia Butler. *Pentecostalism in Colombia. Baptism by Fire and Spirit.* Cranburry, N.J./London: Associated University Presses Inc., 1976.

Flores, "Hermit"
Flores, Ramon. "The Hermit: A Prophetic-Pastoral Model for Latin America Today." *Pneuma* 13/2, 1991, 141–50.

Flower, *PE*
Flower, Joseph James Roswell. *PE* 217, 8.4, 1956, 3f.

Flynn, *Irish Experience*
Flynn, Thomas. *The Charismatic Renewal and the Irish Experience.* London: Hodder & Stoughton, 1974.

Föller, *Charisma und Unterscheidung*
Föller, Oskar. *Charisma und Unterscheidung, Systematische und pastorale Aspekte der Einordnung und Beurteilung enthusiastisch-charismatischer Frömmigkeit im katholischen und evangelischen Bereich.* Wuppertal/Zürich: Brockhaus Verlag, 1994.

Ford, John, "Findings"
Ford, John (ed.). "Ecumenical Findings," unpublished papers for the Commission on Faith and Order, National Council of Churches of Christ in the USA.

Ford, J. M., *Baptism*
Ford, J. M. *Baptism in the Spirit. Three Essays on the Pentecostal Experiences.* Techny, Ill.: Divine Word Publ., 1971.

Ford, J. M., "Catholicism"
_____. "Pentecostal Catholicism." *Concilium* 9/8, Nov. 1972, 85–90.

Ford, J. M., "Mary"
_____. "Mary and the Holy Spirit." *Dictionary,* 584f.

Ford, J. M., "Neo-Pentecostalism"
_____. "Neo-Pentecostalism Within the Roman Catholic Communion." *Dialog* 13/1, Winter 1974, 45–50.

Ford, J. M., *Person*
_____. *The Spirit and the Human Person. A Meditation.* Dayton, Ohio: Pflaum Press, 1970.

Ford, J. M., "Theology"
_____. "Toward a Theology of 'Speaking in Tongues.' " *Theological Studies* 32, 1971, 3–29.

Foster, *Black Women*
    Foster, Elaine. *Black Women: Their Contribution to the Growth and Development of Black-led Churches in Great Britain.* Unpublished Mphil.: University of Birmingham, 1990.
Freire, *Pedagogy*
    Freire, Paulo. *Pedagogy of the Oppressed.* New York: Herder, 1970.
Friedli, *Frieden*
    Friedli, Richard. *Frieden wagen. Ein Beitrag der Religionen zur Gewaltanalyse und zur Friedensarbeit.* Oekumenische Beihefte 14. Freiburg, Switzerland: Universitätsverlag, 1986.
Fritsche, "Heilung/Heilungen"
    Fritsche, U. "Heilung/Heilungen." II, *Theologische Realenzyklopädie* 14 (1985), 768–74.
Frodsham, *With Signs Following*
    Frodsham, Stanley Howard. *With Signs Following. The Story of the Pentecostal Revival in the Twentieth Century.* Springfield, Mo.: Gospel Publishing House; London: Assemblies of God Publishing House, 1926, 1945^2, 1946^3.
Fry, "Perspective"
    Fry, George. "Pentecostalism in Historical Perspective." *The Springfielder* 39 (March 1972).
Fuchs, *Horizons*
    Fuchs, Ernst. *The Two Horizons.* Grand Rapids: Eerdmans, 1980.
Fundamentals
    The Fundamentals: A Testimony to the Truth. 12 vols. Chicago: Testimony Publishing Co., 1910–15.
Gaëta, "Chili"
    Gaëta, Arturo. "Un cas d'adaptation: Les 'Pentecostales' au Chili." In R. P. Abd-el-Jali, D. Rops, R. P. Houang, O. Lacombe, P.-H. Simon, *L'Eglise, l'occident, le monde.* Paris, 1956, 142–49.
Gagg, *Kirche*
    Gagg, Robert. *Kirche im Feuer. Das Leben der südfranzösischen Hugenottenkirche nach dem Todesurteil durch Ludwig XIV.* Zurich: Zwingli Verlag, 1961.
Garibay, *Llave del Náhuatl*
    Garibay, K. Angel Maria. *Llave del Náhuatl.* Mexico: Editorial Porrua, 1970^3.
Gaxiola, "Poverty"
    Gaxiola, Adoniram. "Poverty as a Meeting and Parting Place: Similarities and Contrasts in the Experience of Latin American Pentecostalism and Ecclesial Base Communities." *Pneuma* 13/2, Fall 1991, 167–74.
Gaxiola-Gaxiola, "Inicios del Pentecostalism en Mexico"
    Gaxiola-Gaxiola, Manuel J. "Inicios del Pentecostalism en Mexico: Datos para la historia." *Spiritus. Estudios Sobre Pentecostalismo* 1/3, Sept.-Dec. 1985, 25–48.
Gaxiola-Gaxiola, "Latin American"
    _____. "Latin American Pentecostalism: A Mosaic Within a Mosaic." *Pneuma* 13/2, 1991, 107–29.
Gaxiola-Gaxiola, *Mexican*
    _____. *Mexican Protestantism: The Struggle for Identity and Relevance in a Pluralistic Society.* Unpubl. Ph.D. University of Birmingham, 1990.
Gaxiola-Gaxiola, "Pentecostal Ministry"
    _____. "Pentecostal Ministry." *Int. Review of Mission* 66, Jan. 1977, 57–63.
Gaxiola-Gaxiola, *The Serpent and the Dove*
    _____. *The Serpent and the Dove: The History of the Apostolic Church of the Faith in Christ Jesus in Mexico 1914–1968.* South Pasadena, Calif.: William Carey Library, 1969.
Gee, *All With One Accord*
    Gee, Donald. *All With One Accord.* Springfield, Mo.: Gospel Publishing Co. 1961.
Gee, "End"
    _____. "The End of Acts 2." *Pentecost* 14, 1950, 17.

Gee, *Flesh*
_____. *Upon All Flesh.* Springfield, Mo.: Gospel Publishing Co. and London: Assemblies of God Publishing House, 1934, 1947.
Gee, "Lead"
_____. "How to Lead a Meeting; the Breaking of Bread Service." *Study Hour* 5/2, 15.2.1946, 27–29.
Gee, "New Delhi"
_____. "Pentecostals at New Delhi." *Pentecost* 59, March-May, 1962.
Gee, *Pentecostal*
_____. *The Pentecostal Movement: A Short History and an Interpretation for British Readers* (1939; second and enlarged edition, 1941; third edition under the title *Wind and Flame*, incorporating the former book *The Pentecostal Movement* with additional chapters). London: Assemblies of God Publishing House, 1967.
Gee, "Possible"
_____. "Possible Pentecostal Unity." *Pentecost* 13, Sept. 1950.
Gee, *Trophimus*
_____. *Trophimus, I Left Sick. Our Problem of Divine Healing.* London: Elim Publishing Co.; Springfield, Mo.: Gospel Publishing House, 1952.
Gee, *Wind and Flame*
_____. *Wind and Flame.* London: Assemblies of God Publishing House, 1967.
Gelpi, "Ecumenical"
Gelpi, Donald E. "Ecumenical Problems and Possibilities." In Kilian McDonnell (ed.), *The Holy Spirit and Power: The Catholic Charismatic Renewal.* Garden City, N.Y.: Doubleday, 1975.
Gelpi, *Piety*
_____. *Pentecostal Piety.* New York: Paulist Press, 1972.
Gericke, *Christliche*
Gericke, P. *Christliche Vollkommenheit und Geisteserlebnisse.* Rietenau/Württ.: Gericke, 1950.
Gerlach, "Magische"
Gerlach, Hildegard. "Magische Heilkraft des Vertrauens. Von der Vernunft des Irrationalen in der Medizin." In G. K. Kaltenbrunner (ed.), *Die Pillenpest. Selbstvergiftung aus Angst vor dem Schmerz?* Herderbücherei Initiative 26, 1978.
Gerlach–Hine, "Factors"
Gerlach, Luther P. and Virginia H. Hine. "Five Factors Crucial to the Growth and Spread of a Modern Religious Movement." *Journal for the Scientific Study of Religion* 7, 1968, 23–40.
Gerlach–Hine, "Non-pathological"
_____. "Non-pathological Pentecostal Glossolalia: A Summary of Relevant Psychological Literature. A Report Prepared for Director of the Pentecostal Movement Research Committee, 1967, in Kilian McDonnell (ed.), *Presence, Power, Praise* I, 281.
Gerlach–Hine, *People, Power, Change*
_____. *People, Power, Change. Movements of Social Transformation.* Indianapolis and New York: Bobbs-Merrill Co. 1970.
Gerloff, "Afrikanische Diaspora"
Gerloff, Roswith I. H. "Der Heilige Geist und die afrikanische Diaspora. Spirituelle, kulturelle und soziale Wurzeln und Traditionen schwarzer Pfingstkirchen." *Pastoraltheologie,* 84/4, April 1995, 185–98; English: "The Holy Spirit and the African Diaspora. Spiritual, cultural and social roots of Black Pentecostal Churches." SPS and EPTA Conference, Mattersey, England, July 1995.
Gerloff, "Education"
_____. "Theological Education in Black and White: The Centre for Black and White Christian Partnership (1978–1985)." In Jongeneel, 1992, 41–60.
Gerloff, "Lebendige Bibel"
_____. "Lebendige Bibel. Afrikanische und afro-karibische Kirchen in Europa." *Evangelische Kommentare* 23/7, July 1995, 411–14.

Gerloff, *Plea*
_____. *A Plea for British Black Theologies. The Black Church Movement in Britain and its Transatlantic Cultural and Theological Interaction.* IC 77, 1992, 2 vols.
Gerloff, "Schwarze Kirchen"
_____. "Schwarze Kirchen 2. Afrikanische Diaspora." *Evangelisches Kirchenlexikon.* 4 (1995), 134–39.
Gerloff and van Beek, *Report*
Gerloff, Roswith, and Huibert van Beek (eds.). *Report of the Proceedings of the Consultation between the WCC and African and African-Caribbean Church Leaders in Britain, 30 November–2 December 1995.* Geneva: WCC, 1996.
Gerrard/Gerrard, *Scrabble Creek*
Gerrard, Nathan L., and Louise B. *Scrabble Creek Folk.* Multilithed manuscript. Report Dept. of Sociology, Morris Harvey College, Charlestown, West Virginia, 1966.
Giese, *Pastor*
Giese, Ernst. *Pastor Jonathan Paul, ein Knecht Jesu Christi. Leben und Werk.* Altdorf/Nbg.: Missionsbuchhandlung und Verlag, 1964.
Gilis, *Kimbangu, fondateur de l'église*
Gilis, Charles André. *Kimbangu, fondateur de l'église.* Brussels: La librairie encyclopédique, 1960.
Gill, *Contextualised*
Gill, Kenneth. *Towards a Contextualised Theology for the Third World: The Emergence of Jesus' Name Pentecostalism in Mexico.* IC 90, 1994.
Gill, "Oneness"
_____. "Oneness Doctrine as a Contextualized Doctrine for Mexico." In Jongeneel, 1992, 107–14.
Giraud, "Congo"
Giraud, J. "La Pentecôte au Congo." *Viens et Vois* 35/7–8, July/Aug. 1967, 22f.; 35/11, Nov. 1967, 24f.
Goba, "Role"
Goba, Bonganjalo. "The Role of the Black Church in the Process of Healing Human Brokenness." *Journal of Theology for Southern Africa*, no. 28, Sept. 1979, 7–13.
Godoy, "Ochenta"
Godoy, Daniel. "Ochenta años del Pentecostalismo chileno." *Pastoral popular* no. 194, Sept.-Oct. 1989, 25–28.
Goff, *Fields*
Goff, James R. Jr. *Fields White Unto Harvest. Charles F. Parham and the Missionary Origins of Pentecostalism.* Fayetteville, Ark. and London: University of Arkansas Press, 1988.
Goff, "History"
_____. "Charles Parham and the Problem of History in the Pentecostal Movement: A Response to Cecil M. Robeck." *Brighton*, 186–91.
Goff, "Parham"
_____. "Parham, Charles Fox (1873–1929)." *Dictionary*, 660–61.
Golder, *History of the Pentecostal Assemblies of the World*
Golder, Morris E. *History of the Pentecostal Assemblies of the World.* n. p., 1973.
Goodman, "Apostolics of Yucatan"
Goodman, Felicitas D. "Apostolics of Yucatan: A Case Study of a Religious Movement." In Erica Bourguignon (ed.), *Religion, Altered States of Consciousness and Social Change.* Columbus, Ohio: Ohio State University Press, 1973, 178–218.
Goodman, *Cross-Cultural*
_____. *Speaking in Tongues. A Cross-Cultural Study of Glossolalia.* Chicago and London: University of Chicago Press, 1972.
Goodman, "Shaman"
_____. "Shaman and Priest in Yucatan Pentecostalism." In Agehandanda Bharati (ed.), *Realm of Extra-Human: Agents and Audiences.* The Hague: Mouton; Chicago: Aldine, 1976, 159–65.

Graf, "Vrouw"
    Graf, Annemarie. "De Vrouw in het ambt." *Parakleet* (Holland) 8/28, Summer 1988,
    3–8.
Graham, Billy, "Lausanne"
    Graham, Billy. "Why Lausanne?" In J. D. Douglas (ed.), *Let the Earth Hear His Voice*,
    22–36.
Graham, Roy E., *White*
    Graham, Roy E. *Ellen G. White: Co-Founder of the Seventh-Day Adventist Church.*
    (American University Studies, series VII, vol. 12) New York: Lang, 1985.
Grayson, *Early Buddhism and Christianity in Korea*
    Grayson, James Huntley. *Early Buddhism and Christianity in Korea: A Study in the
    Emplantation of Religion.* Leiden: E. J. Brill, 1985.
Green, "Evangelism"
    Green, Michael. "Evangelism in the Early Church." In J. D. Douglas (ed.), *Let the
    Earth Hear His Voice*, 173–80.
Greenspahn, *Ethical Issues*
    Greenspahn, Frederick (ed.). *Contemporary Ethical Issues in the Jewish and Christian
    Tradition.* Hoboken, N.J.: Ktav, 1986.
Gringoire, "El hombre"
    Gringoire, Pedro. "El hombre que se enfrento a Hitler" Mexico, 1938.
Gros, "Confessing"
    Gros, Jeffrey, FSC. "Confessing the Apostolic Faith from the Perspective of the
    Pentecostal Churches." *Pneuma* 9/1, Spring 1987, 5–16.
Grundmann, "Heilung"
    Grundmann, Christopher. "Heilung und Heil vermitteln." *Zeitschrift für Mission* 17/1,
    1991, 8–18.
Guelich, "Warfare"
    Guelich, Robert A. "Spiritual Warfare: Jesus, Paul and Peretti." *Pneuma* 13/1, Spring
    1991, 33–64.
Guerrero, *Chicano*
    Guerrero, Andres. *A Chicano Theology.* New York: Orbis Books, 1987.
Haenchen, *Acts*
    Haenchen, Ernst. *The Acts of the Apostles.* Philadelphia: Westminster, 1971.
Haire, "Animism"
    Haire, I. James. "Animism in Indonesia and Christian Pneumatology." In Jongeneel,
    1992, 177–88.
Haire, *Character*
    _____. *The Character and Theological Struggle of the Church in Halmahera, Indonesia,
    1941–1979*, IC 26, 1981.
Hall, J. L. "Oneness"
    Hall, J. L. "A Oneness Looks at Initial Evidence." In G. B. McGee (ed.), *Initial
    Evidence*, Peabody, Mass.: Hendrickson, 1991.
Hall, Mary, *Quest*
    Hall, Mary. *A Quest for the Liberated Christian. Examined on the Basis of a Mission, a
    Man and a Movement as Agents of Liberation.* IC 19, 1978.
Handbook
    Ans van der Bent (ed.). *The Handbook of Member Churches, WCC.* Geneva, WCC, 1985,
    revised.
Handbuch
    See Hollenweger, *Handbuch*.
Hanft, "Theologie"
    Hanft, Walter. "Theologie und schwarze Kunst." *Musik und Kirche* (Basel), 28/4,
    July/Aug. 1958, 160–68.
Harder, "Expanding"
    Harder, Kathleen. "The Expanding Politicization of the World Pentecostal
    Movement." SPS 1992, T.

Harnack, *Lehrbuch*
    Harnack, Adolf von. *Lehrbuch der Dogmengeschichte* I, 5th edition, 1931.

Harper, "Dialogue"
    Harper, Michael. "Dialogue Between Pentecostals and Vatican Officials." *Renewal* 37, Feb./March 1972, 7–9.

Harper, "Question"
    _____. "Question of Colour." *Renewal* no. 15, June/July 1968, 2f.

Harrell, *Oral Roberts*
    Harrell, David E. Jr. *Oral Roberts: An American Life.* Bloomington: Indiana University Press, 1985.

Hasted, *Metal-Benders*
    Hasted, John. *The Metal-Benders.* London: Routledge & Kegan Paul, 1981.

Hastings, *History of African Christianity*
    Hastings, Adrian. *A History of African Christianity 1950–1975* (African Studies Series 26). London: Cambridge University Press, 1979.

Hastings, "Ministry"
    _____. "The Ministry of the Catholic Church in Africa, 1960–1975." In Fasholé-Luke, *Christianity in Independent Africa,* 26–43.

Hayes, *Black Charismatic Anglicans*
    Hayes, Stephen. *Black Charismatic Anglicans: The Iviyo loFakazi baka Kristu and its relations with other renewal movements.* Pretoria: University of South Africa, 1990.

Heber, *Jeremy Taylor*
    Heber, Reginald (ed.). *The Whole Works of Jeremy Taylor.* London, 1847–54, vol. IV (also in German).

Heimer, "Kimbanguists"
    Heimer, H. E. "Kimbanguists in the Congo." *World Call* (Indianapolis) March 1970, 16f.

Heine, *Women*
    Heine, Susanne. *Women and Early Christianity. Are the Feminist Scholars Right?* London: SCM, 1987.

Hempelmann, "Glaubens-Gemeinde"
    Hempelmann, Reinhard. "Die 'Biblische Glaubens-Gemeinde' (BGG). Geschichte—Aktivitäten—Beurteilung." *MD* 57/5 1.5.1994, 135–40.

Hempelmann, "German Protestantism"
    _____. "The Charismatic Movement in German Protestantism." *Pneuma* 16/2, 1994, 215–26.

Hempelmann, "Toronto"
    _____. "Der Segen von Toronto." *MD* 58/2, 1.2.1995, 33–43.

Hennecke–Schneemelcher, *Neutestamentliche Apokrypen*
    Hennecke, Edgar, and Wilhelm Schneemelcher. *Neutestamentliche Apokrypen in deutscher Uebersetzung,* vol. II: *Apostolisches, Apokalypsen und Verwandtes.* Tübingen: J. C. B. Mohr (Paul Siebeck), 1964.

Henry–Mooneyham, *One Task*
    Henry, C. F., and W. Stanley Mooneyham (eds.). *One Race, One Gospel, One Task. World Congress on Evangelism. Berlin 1966. Official Reference Volumes: Papers and Reports.* Minneapolis, Minn., 1967, 2 vols.

Hernández, "Hombres nuevos"
    Hernández, Venancio. "Hombres nuevos—sociedad sana." *Estudios ecuménicos* (Mexico), 1969/2, 1–10.

Herskovits, *Myth*
    Herskovits, Melville J. *The Myth of the Negro Past.* New York, 1941.

Heuberger, "Hollenweger als Dichter und Liturgiker"
    Heuberger, Marianne. "Hollenweger als Dichter und Liturgiker." In Jongeneel, 1992, 61–72.

Hidalgo, *Perú*
> Hidalgo, Ruben Zavalo. *Historia de las Asambleas de Dios del Perú.* Lima: Ediciones Dios
> es Amor, 1989.
Higher Christian Life
> 50 vols., facsimile reprints edited by Donald W. Dayton and others. New York and
> London: Garland Publ. Inc., 1985.
Hilgard–Hilgard, *Hypnotic*
> Hilgard, Ernest R., and Josephine R. *Hypnotic Susceptibility.* New York: Harcourt,
> Brace and World, 1965.
Hilton, "Future"
> Hilton, D. "The Future of Medical Mission." *Int. Review of Mission* 76/301, Jan. 1987,
> 78ff.
Hilton, *Mr. Chips*
> Hilton, James. *Goodbye, Mr. Chips.* Boston: Little Brown, 1934.
Historia del avivamiento
> *Historia del avivamiento. Origen y desarrollo de la Iglesia Evangélica Pentecostal.*
> Santiago, Chile: Corporación Iglesia Evangélica Pentecostal, 1977.
Hoaas–Tegnander, *Kvinnen*
> Hoaas, Ole-Georg and Oddvar Tegnander. *Kvinnen fir til tjenste?* Oslo:
> Filadelfia-forlaget, 1986.
Hobhouse, *Selected*
> Hobhouse, Stephen. *Selected Mystical Writings of William Law, edited with notes and 24*
> *studies in the mystical Theology of William Law and Jacob Boehme and an enquiry into the*
> *influence of Jacob Boehme on Isaac Newton.* London, 1938, 1949[4].
Hocken, "Berlin"
> Hocken, Peter. "Berlin Declaration." *Dictionary,* 55.
Hocken, "Charismatic"
> _____. "Charismatic Renewal in the Roman Catholic Church: Reception and
> Challenge." In Jongeneel, 1992, 301–9.
Hocken, "Charismatic Movement in the U.S."
> _____. "The Charismatic Movement in the United States." *Pneuma* 16/2, Fall 1994,
> 191–214.
Hocken, "Communities"
> _____. "Charismatic Communities." *Dictionary,* 127–30.
Hocken, "Dallière"
> _____. "Dallière, Louis (1897–1976)," *Dictionary,* 236.
Hocken, "Ecumenical Dialogue"
> _____. "Ecumenical Dialogue: The Importance of Dialogue with Evangelicals and
> Pentecostals." *One in Christ* 30, 1994, 101–23.
Hocken, "Extraordinary"
> _____. "Dialogue Extraordinary." *One in Christ* 24/2, 1988, 202–13.
Hocken, "Independent"
> _____. "A Survey of Independent Charismatic Churches." *Pneuma* 18/1, Spring 1996,
> 93–105.
Hocken, "Layman"
> _____. "Cecil Polhill—Pentecostal Layman." *Pneuma* 10/2, Fall 1988, 116–40.
Hocken, "Movement"
> _____. "Charismatic Movement," *Dictionary,* 130–60.
Hocken, "Mülheim"
> _____. "Mülheim Association." *Dictionary,* 630.
Hocken, *One Lord*
> _____. *One Lord, One Spirit, One Body: The Ecumenical Grace of the Charismatic*
> *Movement.* Exeter, Devon: The Paternoster Press; Washington: The Word Among Us,
> 1987.
Hocken, "Polhill"
> _____. "Polhill, Cecil H. (1860–1938)." *Dictionary,* 218.

Hocken, "Renewal"
_____. "The Pentecostal-Charismatic Movement as Revival and Renewal." *Pneuma* 3/1, Spring 1981, 31–47.
Hocken, "Scott"
_____. "Scott, Douglas R. (1900–1967)." *Dictionary,* 772.
Hocken, *Streams*
_____. *Streams of Renewal. The Origins and Early Development of the Charismatic Movement in Great Britain.* Exeter, Devon: The Paternoster Press; Washington: The Word Among Us, 1986.
Hocken, "Survey"
_____. "A Survey of the Worldwide Charismatic Movement." *Bossey,* 117–47.
Hocken, "Union"
_____. "Pentecostal Missionary Union." *Dictionary,* 706.
Hocken with Cartwright, "European"
_____. with D. W. Cartwright. "European Pentecostalism." *Dictionary,* 268–78.
Hodges, "Indigenous"
Hodges, Melvin. "Why Indigenous Church Principles?" Reprinted from Melvin Hodges, *The Indigenous Church* (Springfield, Mo.: Gospel Publishing House, 1953). In Charles H. Kraft/Tom N. Wisley (eds.), *Readings in Dynamic Indigeneity.* Pasadena, Calif.: William Carey Library, 1979.
Hodges, *Indigenous*
_____. *The Indigenous Church.* Springfield, Mo.: Gospel Publishing House, 1953.
Hodgson, *Out of the Darkness*
Hodgson, E. *Out of the Darkness. The Story of an Indigenous Church in the Belgian Congo.* London: Victory Press, 1946.
Hoerschelmann, *Christliche Gurus*
Hoerschelmann, Werner. *Christliche Gurus. Darstellung von Selbstverständnis und Funktion indigenen Christsein durch unabhängige, charismatisch geführte Gruppen in Südindien.* IC 12, 1977.
Hoerschelmann, "Machtfaktor"
_____. "Der Heilige Geist als Machtfaktor. Pfingstfrömmigkeit verändert die ökumenische Landschaft." *Lutherische Monatshefte,* Febr. 1990, 67–70.
Hoggart, *Uses*
Hoggart, Richard. *The Uses of Literacy.* Pelican Book A 431.
Hokkanen, *Oletko*
Hokkanen, Lauri. *Oletko uudestisyntynyt.* Helsinki, 1932.
Holdcroft, "Order"
Holdcroft, Thomas. "The New Order of the Latter Rain." *Pneuma* 2/2, Fall 1970, 46–58.
Holiness Tracts
Holiness Tracts Defending the Ministry of Women, ed. by Donald W. Dayton, 1853, 1891, 18??, 1905. Reprinted in *The Higher Christian Life,* vol. 11.
Hollander, *Council*
Hollander, Jet den. *The Council for World Mission. A Viable Model for Contemporary Mission?* Unpubl. Mphil. University of Birmingham, 1991.
Hollenweger, "After"
Hollenweger, Walter J. "After Twenty Years Research on Pentecostalism." *Theology* 87/720, Nov. 1984, 403–412; *Int. Review of Mission* 75/297, Jan. 1986, 3–12.
Hollenweger, "Ave Maria"
_____. "Ave Maria. The Reformers and the Protestants." *One in Christ,* 13/4, 1977, 285–90.
Hollenweger, *Black Pentecostal Concept*
_____. *Black Pentecostal Concept. Concept* 30. Geneva: WCC. June 1970.

Hollenweger, "Bonhoeffer"

———. "Dietrich Bonhoeffer and William J. Seymour. A Comparison Between Two Ecumenists." *Norsk Tidsskrift for Misjon* (Festschrift for Nils E. Bloch-Hoell) 39/3–4, 1985, 192–201.

Hollenweger, *Christen*

———. *Christen ohne Schriften. Fünf Fallstudien zur Sozialethik mündlicher Religion.* Erlangen: Verlag der Evangelisch-Lutherischen Mission, 1975.

Hollenweger, *Church for Others*

———. (ed.). *The Church for Others and The Church for the World. A Quest for Structures for Missionary Congregations.* Final Report of the Western European Working Group and the North American Working Group of the Department on Studies in Evangelism. Geneva: WCC, 1967 (also in German, Spanish and Portuguese).

Hollenweger, *Conflict*

———. *Conflict in Corinth/Memoirs of an Old Man.* New York: Paulist Press, 1982. (also German, French, Italian, Indonesian, etc.)

Hollenweger, "Content"

———. "The 'What' and the 'How': Content and Communication of the One Message. A Consideration of the Basis of Faith, as Formulated by the World Council of Churches." *Expository Times* 86/11, Aug. 1975, 324–28; 86/112, Sept. 1975, 365–9.

Hollenweger, "Creator"

———. "Creator Spiritus: The Challenge of Pentecostal Experience to Pentecostal Theology." *Theology* 81, Jan. 1978, 32–40.

Hollenweger, "Creatures"

———. "All Creatures Great and Small: Towards a Pneumatology of Life." In David Martin/Peter Mullen (eds.), *Strange Gifts? A Guide to Charismatic Renewal.* Oxford: Blackwell, 1984, 41–53.

Hollenweger, "Danced"

———. "Danced Documentaries. The Theological and Political Significance of Pentecostal Dancing." In J. G. Davies (ed.), *Worship and Dance.* Birmingham: Birmingham University, Dept. of Theology, 1975, 76–82.

Hollenweger, "Devotion"

———. "Zwingli's Devotion to Mary." *One in Christ* 16/1–2, 1980, 59–68.

Hollenweger, "Efficiency"

———. "Efficiency and Human Values. A Theological Action-Research-Report on Co-Decision in Industry." *Expository Times* 86/8, May 1975, 228–32.

Hollenweger, "Ein Forschungsbericht"

———. "Ein Forschungsbericht." In Hollenweger, *Die Pfingstkirchen,* 307–46.

Hollenweger, "Einfluss"

———. "Zwinglis Einfluss in England." In Heiko A. Obermann et al., *Reformiertes Erbe Festschrift für Gottfried W. Locher zu seinem 80. Geburtstag* (Zurich: TVZ, 1992/93, 2 vols, Zwingliana XIX/1–2), I, 171–86.

Hollenweger, *El Pentecostalismo*

———. *El Pentecostalismo. Historia y Doctrina.* Buenos Aires: La Aurora, 1976, 83–117.

Hollenweger, "Europe"

———. "Pentecostal Research in Europe: Problems, Promises, People." *EPTA Bulletin* 4/4, 1985, 124–53.

Hollenweger, *Evangelism*

———. *Evangelism Today: Good News or Bone of Contention?* Belfast: Christian Journals, 1976 (also in German).

Hollenweger, "Exegesis"

———. "The Other Exegesis." *Horizons in Biblical Theology. An International Dialogue* 3, 1981, 155–79.

Hollenweger, " 'Flowers and Songs' "

———. " 'Flowers and Songs.' A Mexican Contribution on Hermeneutics." *Int. Review of Mission* 60/238, April 1971, 232–44. In Spanish: *Spiritus* 1/1, 1985, 31–46.

Hollenweger, *Glaube*
_____. *Glaube, Geist und Geister. Professor Unrat zwischen Bangkok und Birmingham.*
Frankfurt: Otto Lembeck, 1975.
Hollenweger, "Goes to Bangkok"
_____. "Mr. Chips Goes to Bangkok." *Frontier* 16/2, Summer 1973, 93–100.
Hollenweger, *Handbuch*
_____. *Handbuch der Pfingstbewegung,* 10 vols. Available from Yale University, Divinity
School, New Haven.
Hollenweger, "Healing Through Prayer"
_____. "Healing Through Prayer: Superstition or Forgotten Christian Tradition."
Theology 97/747, May 1989, 166–74 (also Danish in *Praeste Foreningens Blad* 1990/33,
657–63).
Hollenweger, Heilt die Kranken"
_____. "Heilt die Kranken!" *Theologia practica* 1987, 44–62.
Hollenweger, "Interaction"
_____. "Interaction Between Black and White in Theological Education." *Theology*
90/737, Sept. 1987, 341–50.
Hollenweger, "Intercultural"
_____. "Towards an Intercultural History of Christianity." *Int. Review of Mission*
76/304, Oct. 1987, 526–56.
Hollenweger, *Jona*
_____. *Jona—eine Kind unserer Zeit.* Kindhausen, Switzerland: Metanoia Verlag, n.d.
Hollenweger, *Kirche*
_____. *Kirche, Benzin und Bohnensuppe. Auf den Spuren dynamischer Gemeinden.* Zurich:
TVZ, 1971.
Hollenweger, "Koinonia"
_____. "The Koinonia of the Establishment." *Pneuma* 12/2, 1990, 154–57.
Hollenweger, "Latinamerika"
_____. "Pingstvänner, katoliker och politik in Latinamerika." *Svensk Missionstidskrift*
60/2, 1972, 90–98 (also in German in *Reformation* 22/6, June, 1973, 334–41).
Hollenweger, *Latinoamericano*
_____. *Concepto Latinoamericano* III: "Flores y Cantos: Un Concepto Mexicano"
Concept, Special Issue 32, Oct. 1970. Geneva: WCC. Summary later in *Int. Review of
Mission* 60/238, April 1971, 232–44 and in *Pentecost Between Black and White.*
Hollenweger, "L'expérience"
_____. "L'expérience de l'Esprit dans l'église et hors de l'église." *Le Point théologique*
no. 44. Paris: Beauchesne, 1985, 195–209.
Hollenweger, "Liturgies"
_____. "Pentecostal Liturgies." and "Spirituals." In J. G. Davies (ed.), *Dictionary of
Liturgy and Worship* (London: SCM), 1973, 241; 1986[2], 311f; 1973, 340f.; 1986[2], 497f.
Hollenweger, *Marxist and Kimbanguist Mission*
_____. *Marxist and Kimbanguist Mission. A Comparison.* Birmingham: Birmingham
University, 1973.
Hollenweger, *Mirjam*
_____. *Mirjam, Mutter Jesu.* Kindhausen, Switzerland: Metanoia Verlag, n.d.
Hollenweger, "Mission"
_____. "The Future of Mission and the Mission of the Future." *Occasional Paper* no.
2, Selly Oak Colleges, Birmingham, UK, 1989; in a different form under the title "The
Discipline of Thought and Action in Mission." *Int. Review of Mission* 80/317, Jan.
1991, 89–104.
Hollenweger, "Music"
_____. "Music in the Service of Reconciliation." *Theology* 92/748, July 1989, 276–86;
also in *Hymnology Annual* (Berrien Springs, Mich.) 1, 1991, 149–60.
Hollenweger, "Narrative Exegese"
_____. "Theologie tanzen. Warum wir eine 'narrative Exegese' brauchen."
Evangelische Kommentare 28/7, July 1995, 403–4.

Hollenweger, *New Wine*

_____. *New Wine in Old Wineskin. Protestant and Catholic Neo-Pentecostalism.*
Gloucester, England: Fellowship Press, 1973.

Hollenweger, *Pentecost Between Black and White*

_____. *Pentecost Between Black and White. Five Case Studies on Pentecost and Politics.*
Belfast: Christian Journals, 1974 (also in German and Dutch).

Hollenweger, "Pentecostalism"

_____. "Pentecostalism and Academic Theology. From Confrontation to
Cooperation." *EPTA Bulletin* 10/1+2, 1992, 42–49.

Hollenweger, *Pfingstkirchen*

_____. (ed.). *Die Pfingstkirchen. Selbstdarstellungen, Dokumente, Kommentare.* (Die
Kirchen der Welt VII). Stuttgart: Evangelisches Verlagswerk, 1971.

Hollenweger, "Priorities"

_____. "Priorities in Pentecostal Research." In Jongeneel, 1991, 7–22.

Hollenweger, *Requiem*

_____. *Requiem für Bonhoeffer. Den Toten aller Völker.* Kindhausen, Switzerland:
Metanoia Verlag, n.d.

Hollenweger, "Reviews Bangkok"

_____. "Mr. Chips Reviews Bangkok." *Int. Review of Mission* 63/249, Jan. 1974,
132–36.

Hollenweger, "Saints"

_____. "Saints in Birmingham," *Bossey*, 87–99; *Theological Renewal* 17, Feb. 1981,
27–38; *Research Bulletin*, Dept. of Theology, University of Birmingham 1981, 102–13.

Hollenweger, "Salvation"

_____. "Salvation Today in Pentecostalism." In Rienk Lanooy (ed.), *For Us and Our
Salvation. Seven Perspectives on Christian Soteriology.* Utrecht-Leiden: Interuniversitair
Instituut voor Missiologie en Oecumenica, 1994, 1–13.

Hollenweger, "Significance"

_____. "The Social and Ecumenical Significance of Pentecostal Liturgy." *Studia
Liturgica* 8/4, 1971/72, 207–15.

Hollenweger, "Spiel"

_____. "Spiel als eine Form von Theologie; zum geplanten Dialog mit der
Pfingstbewegung" *Lutherische Monatshefte* 9/10, Oct. 1970, 532–34.

Hollenweger, "Spirituals"

_____. "Pentecostal Liturgies." and "Spirituals." In J. G. Davies (ed.), *Dictionary of
Liturgy and Worship* (London: SCM), 1973, 241; 1986^2, 311f; 1973, 340f.; 1986^2, 497f.

Hollenweger, "Theology"

_____. "Theology and the Church of the Future." In *Companion Encyclopedia of
Theology* (London), forthcoming.

Hollenweger, " 'Touching' "

_____. " 'Touching' and 'Thinking' the Spirit: Some Aspects of European
Charismatics." In Russell P. Spittler (ed.), *Perspectives on the New Pentecostalism.* Grand
Rapids, Mich.: Baker Book House, 1976, 44–56.

Hollenweger, "Verheissung"

_____. "Verheissung und Verhängnis der Pfingstbewegung." *Evangelische Theologie* 53,
1993, 265–88.

Hollenweger, *Wagnis*

_____. *Das Wagnis des Glaubens.* Kindhausen, Switzerland: Metanoia Verlag, n.d.

Hollenweger, *Wie*

_____. *Wie aus Grenzen Brücken werden. Ein theologisches Lesebuch.* Munich: Kaiser,
1980.

Hollenweger, "Zwingli"

_____. "Zwingli Writes the Gospel in His World's Agenda." *The Mennonite Quarterly
Review* 43/1, Jan. 1969, 70–94.

Holmes, *Pfingst-*
Holmes, Stephen Lloyd. *Die Pfingst- und Neopfingstbewegung in der US-Armee in Süddeutschland. Eine Ethnographie über Ritus und soziale Kontrolle.* Ph.D. Heidelberg, 1984.
Hood, *Mission*
Hood, George. *Mission Accomplished? The English Presbyterian Mission in Lingtun, South China.* IC 42, 1986.
Hoover, *Historia*
Hoover, W. C. *Historia del avivamiento pentecostal en Chile.* Valparaiso: Imprenta Excelsior, 1909, 1948.
Horgan, "Consultation"
Horgan, Thaddeus. "Consultation Summary: A Conciliar Perspective." *Pneuma* 9/1, Spring 1987, 99–102.
Horn, "Apostolic Leadership"
Horn, J. Nico. "Apostolic Leadership: Renewal of the Church or Pentecostal Heresy?" SPS 1991.
Horn, "Experience"
_____. "The Experience of the Spirit in Apartheid. The Possibilities of the Rediscovery of the Black Roots of Pentecostalism for South African Theology." In Jongeneel, 1991, 117–40.
Horn, "Response"
_____. "A Response to Karla Poewe-Hexham and Irving Hexham." *Brighton,* 84–90.
Horn, "South African Pentecostals and Apartheid"
_____. "South African Pentecostals and Apartheid." In Jongeneel, 1992, 157–68.
Horn–Louw, *Eén Kudde*
_____. and J. J. Louw. *Eén Kudde, Eén Herder,* Kuilsirver: Ekklesia, 1987.
Hoskyns, *Congo*
Hoskyns, C. *The Congo Since Independence, January 1960–December 1961.* Oxford University Press, 1965.
Huamán, *Primera*
Huamán, P. Santiago A. *La primera historia del movimento pentecostal del Perú.* n.p., n.d.
Huber, "Buchbesprechung"
Huber, Richard. "Buchbesprechung." In Kaltenbrunner, Gerd-Klaus (ed.), *Die Pillenpest,* 164–67.
Hudson–Warrington, "Cohabitation"
Hudson, Neil, and Keith Warrington. "Cohabitation and the Church." *EPTA Bulletin* 13, 1994, 63–73.
Hug, *Haben*
Hug, Ed. "Was haben wir am Heiligen Geist?" *SE* 28.5.1898, 172f.
Hummel, "Kopfermann"
Hummel, Reinhard. "Wolfram Kopfermann, Abschied von einer Illusion. Volkskirche ohne Zukunft." *MD* 53/8, 1.8.1990, 235–38.
Hunt, "Wimberites"
Hunt, Stephen. "The Anglican Wimberites." *Pneuma* 17/1, 1995, 105–18.
Hunter, "Spirit-Baptism"
Hunter, Harold. "Spirit-Baptism and the 1896 Revival in Cherokee County, North Carolina." *Pneuma* 5/2, 1983, 1–17.
Hurtado, "Spirit"
Hurtado, L. W. "Spirit in Scripture." *Dictionary,* 801–4.
Hutten, *Seher*
Hutten, Kurt. *Seher, Grübler, Enthusiasten. Sekten und religiöse Sondergemeinschaften.* 1950, 11th ed. 1968. Stuttgart: Quell Verlag.
Hymns of Glorious Praise
Hymns of Glorious Praise. Comp. and ed. by the Music Division. Springfield, Mo.: Gospel Publishing House, 1969.

Hywel-Davies, *Baptized*
    Hywel-Davies, Jack. *Baptized By Fire. The Story of Smith Wigglesworth*. London:
    Hodder & Stoughton, 1987.
IC
    Studies in the Intercultural History of Christianity, ca 100 vols. Frankfurt, Berne,
    Paris, New York: Lang, n.d.
Iglesia Metodista Pentecostal, *Himnos*
    Iglesia Metodista Pentecostal, *Himnos Evangélicos pare al uso de la Iglesia Metodista
    Pentecostal*. Santiago, 1940.
Illich, *Limits*
    Illich, Ivan. *Limits to Medicine. Medical Nemesis: The Expropriation of Health*. Penguin
    Books, 1976.
Introduction
    An Introduction to the Catholic Charismatic Renewal. Notre Dame, Ind.: Communication
    Center, n.d.
Irvin, "One Bond"
    Irvin, Dale T. " 'Drawing All Together in One Bond of Love': The Ecumenical Vision
    of William J. Seymour and the Azusa Street Revival." *Journal of Pentecostal Theology* 6,
    1995, 25–53.
Irvine, "Birth"
    Irvine, Cecilia. "The Birth of the Kimbanguist Movement in the Bas-Zaïre 1921."
    Journal of Religion in Africa 6/1, 1974, 23–76.
Israel, "Pentecostalism"
    Israel, Richard D. et al. "Pentecostalism and Hermeneutics: Texts, Rituals,
    Community." SPS 1990, A.
Italiaander, "Prophet"
    Italiaander, n.i. "Prophet und Märtyer im Kongo. Wirksamkeit und Leiden des Simon
    Kimbangu." *Evangelisches Missions-Jahrbuch* 1970. Hamburg: Missionshilfe Verlag,
    1970, 31–44.
ITh 1
    Walter J. Hollenweger. *Erfahrungen der Leibhaftigkeit. Interkulturelle Theologie* 1.
    Munich: Kaiser, 1979, 1990[2].
ITh 2
    Walter J. Hollenweger. *Umgang mit Mythen. Interkulturelle Theologie* 2. Munich: Kaiser,
    1982, 1992[2].
ITh 3
    Walter J. Hollenweger. *Geist und Materie. Interkulturelle Theologie* 3. Munich: Kaiser,
    1988.
Jackson, Eleanor M., *Tape*
    Jackson, Eleanor M. *Red Tape and the Gospel. The Ecumenical Struggle of Dr. William
    Paton 1886–1943*. Birmingham, UK: Selly Oak Colleges, 1981.
Jackson, G. P., "Spirituals"
    Jackson, George Pullen. "Spirituals." *Grove's Dictionary of Music and Musicians*, vol. 8.
    London and New York: Macmillan, 1954, 8–12.
Jacoby, *Handbuch*
    Jacoby, L. S. *Handbuch des Methodismus*, Bremen, 1855[2].
Jehu-Appiah, "Overview"
    Jehu-Appiah, Jerisdan H. "An Overview of Indigenous African Churches in Britain: An
    Approach Through the Historical Survey of African Pentecostalism." In Gerloff and
    van Beek, *Report*, 49–65.
Jennings, "Glossolalia"
    Jennings, George J. "An Ethnological Study of Glossolalia." *Journal of the American
    Scientific Association*, March 1968, 5–16.

John Paul II, "Address"
    John Paul II in Santo Domingo: "Opening Address for Fourth General Conference of
    Latin American Episcopate." *Origins, CNS Documentary Service* 22/19, 22 October
    1992, 322–26.
Johns/Bridges-Johns, "Yielding"
    Johns, Jackie David, and Cheryl Bridges-Johns. "Yielding to the Spirit: A Pentecostal
    Approach to Group Bible Study." *Journal of Pentecostal Theology* 1, Oct. 1992, 109–34.
Johnson, *Books of American Negro Spirituals*
    Johnson, James Weldon. *The Books of American Negro Spirituals*. New York: The Viking
    Press, 1956, 2 vols. in one.
Johnston, "Hermeneutics"
    Johnston, Robert K. "Pentecostalism and Theological Hermeneutics: Evangelical
    Options." *Pneuma* 6/1, Spring 1984, 51–66.
Jones, C. E., *Black Holiness*
    Jones, Charles Edwin. *Black Holiness. A Guide to the Study of Black Participation in
    Wesleyan, Perfectionist and Glossolalic Pentecostal Movements*. ATLA Bibliography
    Series, no. 18. Metuchen, N.J.: The Scarecrow Press and The American Theological
    Library Association, 1987.
Jones, C. E., "Church of God in Christ"
    _____. "Church of God in Christ." *Dictionary*, 204f.
Jones, C. E., *Holiness*
    _____. *A Guide to the Study of the Holiness Movement*. ATLA Bibliography Series, no.
    1. Metuchen, N.J.: The Scarecrow Press and the American Theological Library
    Association, 1974.
Jones, C. E., "Hoover"
    _____. "Hoover, Willis Collins (1856–1936)." *Dictionary*, 445.
Jones, C. E., "Living God"
    _____. "Church of the Living God. . . ." *Dictionary*, 211.
Jones, C. E., *Pentecostal*
    _____. *A Guide to the Study of the Pentecostal Movement*, 2 vols. ATLA Bibliography
    Series, no. 6. Metuchen, N.J.: The Scarecrow Press and the American Theological
    Library Association, 1979.
Jones, C. E., *Perfectionist*
    _____. *Perfectionist Persuasion. The Holiness Movement and American Methodism,
    1867–1936*. ATLA Monograph Series, no. 5, Metuchen, N.J.: The Scarecrow Press and
    The American Theological Library Association, 1974.
Jones, C. E., "Welsh"
    _____. "Welsh Revival." *Dictionary*, 881f.
Jones, O. T. "Crisis"
    Jones, O. T. "Our Pentecostal Opportunity in This Hour of Religious Crisis." In
    Donald Gee (ed.), *Fifth World Pentecostal Conference, Toronto*. Toronto: Testimony
    Press, 1958, 149–60.
Jongeneel, 1991
    Jongeneel, Jan A.B. (ed.). *Experiences of the Spirit. Conference on Pentecostal and
    Charismatic Research in Europe at Utrecht University*, 1989. IC 68, 1991.
Jongeneel, 1992
    Jongeneel, Jan A.B., et al. (eds.). *Pentecost, Mission and Ecumenism. Essays on
    Intercultural Theology. Festschrift in Honor of Professor Walter J. Hollenweger*. IC 75,
    1992.
Judd, "Political Action"
    Judd, W. H. "Political Action Should Be by Christians, not by Churches." *Church of
    God Evangel* 53/24, 19.8.1963, 23.
Jung, "Psychotherapie"
    Jung, Carl Gustav. "Ueber die Beziehung der Psychotherapie zur Seelsorge.
    Psychoanalyse und Seelsorge (1932/48)." *Gesammelte Werke* 9. Zurich and Stuttgart,
    1963, 355–83.

Juster, "Messianic"
    Juster, D. C. "Messianic Judaism." *Dictionary*, 602–04.
Juster, "Union"
    _____. "Union of Messianic Jewish Congregations." *Dictionary*, 856.
Juul, Kåre (ed.), *Norsk*
    Juul, Kåre (ed.). *Til jordens ender. Norsk pinsemisjon gjenommen 50 år.* Oslo:
    Filadelfia-forlaget, 1960.
Kairos Document
    The Kairos Document: Challenge to the Church. Grand Rapids, Mich.: Eerdmans, 1986.
Kalilombe, "Local Churches"
    Kalilombe, Patrick A. "The African Local Churches and the World-Wide Roman
    Catholic Communion: Modification of Relationships, as Exemplified by Likongwe
    Diocese." In Fasholé-Luke et al. (eds.), *Christianity in Independent Africa*, 75–95.
Kaltenbrunner, *Pillenpest*
    Kaltenbrunner, Gerd-Klaus (ed.). *Die Pillenpest. Selbstvergiftung aus Angst vor dem
    Schmerz?* Herderbücherei Initiative 26, 1978.
Kampf
    Der Kampf um die Pfingstbewegung. Sonderabdruck aus den *Pfingstgrüssen.*
    Mülheim/Ruhr: Verlag der Gesellschaft für Mission, Diakonie und Kolportage, n.d.
Kamphausen, *Anfänge*
    Kamphausen, Erhard. *Anfänge der kirchlichen Unabhängigkeitsbewegung in Südafrika.
    Geschichte und Theologie der Aethiopischen Bewegung 1872–1912.* IC 6, 1976.
Kamu, *Samoan*
    Kamu, Lalomilo. *The Samoan Culture and the Christian Gospel.* Unpubl. Ph.D.
    University of Birmingham, 1989.
Kay, "Boddy"
    Kay, William K. "Alexander Boddy and the Outpouring of the Holy Spirit in
    Sunderland." *EPTA Bulletin* 5/2, 1986, 44–56.
Kay, "Characteristics"
    _____. "Characteristics of Pentecostal (Assemblies of God) Ministers in Britain." SPS
    and EPTA Conference at Mattersey, England July, 1995.
Kay, *Inside*
    _____. *Inside Story. A History of the British Assemblies of God.* Stourport-on-Severn,
    Worcs.: Assemblies of God Bible College, 1990.
Kay, "Interactions"
    _____. "Pentecostal/Non-Pentecostal Interactions: Questions and Perspectives."
    EPTA Bulletin 9/2, 3, 1990, 63–70.
Kay, "1930s"
    _____. "British Assemblies of God in the 1930s." *EPTA Bulletin* 7/1, 1988, 4–11.
Kay, "War Years"
    _____. "British Assemblies of God: The War Years." *Pneuma* 11/1, Fall 1989, 51–58.
Kaye, "Challenge"
    Kaye, Bruce. "Congress Challenge to World Council." *Church of England Newspaper*
    26.7.1974.
Kaye, "Tomorrow"
    _____. "Theology Comes Tomorrow." *The Churchman* 88/4, Oct.-Nov. 1974, 277–87.
Keller, "La Biblia"
    Keller, Helen. "La Biblia tien un mensaje para todos los tiempos." *Mensajero Pentecostés*
    3/10, Aug-Sept. 1964, 13f.
Kelsey, *Tongue Speaking*
    Kelsey, Morton. *Tongue Speaking. An Experiment in Spiritual Experience.* Garden City,
    N.Y.: Doubleday, 1964.
Kendall, "Missionary Factor"
    Kendall, R. Elliott. "The Missionary Factor in Africa." In Fasholé-Luke, *Christianity
    in Independent Africa*, 16–25.

Kendrick, *Promise Fulfilled*
  Kendrick, Klaude. *The Promise Fulfilled. A History of the Modern Pentecostal Movement.* Springfield, Mo.: Gospel Publishing House, 1961.
Kennedy, *Dream*
  Kennedy, N. L. *Dream Your Way to Success.* 1980.
Kern, "Jazz"
  Kern, Adolf. "Zur 'Theologie des Jazz.' " *Musik und Kirche* (Basel), July/Aug. 1958, 169–71.
Kerr, *Power to Love*
  Kerr, Cecil. *Power to Love. Christian Renewal and Reconciliation.* Belfast: Christian Journals, 1976.
Kessler, *Study*
  Kessler, Jr., Jean Baptiste August. *A Study of the Older Protestant Missions and Churches in Peru and Chile. With Special Reference to the Problems of Divisions, Nationalism and Native Ministry.* Goes, Holland: Oosterbaan and Le Cointre, 1967.
Kildahl, *Psychology*
  Kildahl, John P. *The Psychology of Speaking in Tongues.* New York: Harper & Row, 1972.
Kim, "Korean"
  Kim, Byong-Suh. "The Explosive Growth of the Korean Church Today: A Sociological Analysis." *Int. Review of Mission* 74/293, 1985, 61–74.
Kinnamon, *Signs*
  Kinnamon, Michael (ed.). *Signs of the Spirit. Official Report Seventh Assembly.* Geneva: WCC and Grand Rapids, Mich.: Eerdmans, 1991.
Kinne, *People's*
  Kinne, Warren H. *A People's Church? The Mindanao-Sulu Church Debacle.* IC 64, 1990.
Kirchenordnung
  Kirchenordnung der Methodistenkirche, gekürzte deutsche Ausgabe. Zurich, 1938.
Kirchner/Planer-Friedrich/Sens/Ziemer, *Charismatische*
  Kirchner, Hubert, Götz Planer-Friedrich, Matthias Sens, and Christoph Ziemer (eds.). *Charismatische Erneuerung und Kirche. Im Auftrag der Theologischen Studienabteilung beim Bund der Evangelischen Kirchen in der DDR.* Neukirchen-Vluyn: Neukirchner Verlag, 1984.
Kirkpatrick, *Struggle of Life*
  Kirkpatrick, Dow (ed). *Faith Born in the Struggle of Life.* Grand Rapids, Mich.: Eerdmans, 1988.
Klaiber, "Aus Glauben"
  Klaiber, Walter. "Aus Glauben, damit aus Gnaden. Der Grundsatz paulinischer Soteriologie und die Gnadenlehre von John Wesley." *Zeitschrift für Theologie und Kirche* 88/3, Sept. 1991, 313–38.
Klaus–Triplett, "National"
  Klaus, Byron D. and Loren O. Triplett. "National Leadership in Pentecostal Mission." *Called,* 225–41.
Klauser, *Western Liturgy*
  Klauser, Theodor. *A Short History of the Western Liturgy.* Oxford University Press, 1969.
Klöcker, *Gesundheit*
  Klöcker, Michael, Udo Tworuschka, Hans-Jürgen Becken. (eds.). *Gesundheit.* Ethik der Religionen, vol. 3. Munich and Göttingen, 1985.
Koch, "Variationen"
  Koch, Joh. H. E. "Variationen über Musik des Protests. Zur Psychologie des Jazz." *Hausmusik* (Kassel) 22/3, May/June 1958, 77f.
Korthaus, "Sprechende Bibel"
  Korthaus, Estella F. "Sprechende Bibel. Wie die Bibel in Kopf und Herz dringt." *Evangelische Kommentare* 28/7, July 1995, 404–11.

Korzybski, *Science*
  Korzybski, Alfred. *Science and Sanity*. Lakeville: International Non-Aristotelian Library Publishing Company, 1958, second ed.
Kovaleski, "Charismen"
  Kovaleski, Eugraph. "Die Charismen in der Geschichte der Orthodoxen Kirche." In R. F. Edel (ed.), *Kirche und Charisma. Die Gaben des Heiligen Geistes im Neuen Testament, in der Kirchengeschichte und in der Gegenwart*. Marburg a.d.L.: Edel, 1966.
Kraft, *Culture*
  Kraft, Charles H. *Christianity in Culture. A Study in Dynamic Biblical Theologizing in Cross-Cultural Perspective*. Maryknoll, New York: Orbis Books, 1979.
Kraft/Wisley, *Readings*
  Kraft, Charles H., and Tom N. Wisley (eds.). *Readings in Dynamic Indigeneity*. Pasadena, Calif.: William Carey Library, 1979.
Krehbiel, *Afro-American Folk Songs*
  Krehbiel, H. E. *Afro-American Folk Songs*. New York, n. p., 1914.
Krige, *Paar*
  Krige, A. V. *'n Paar Grondwaarhede in die volkaakte Verlossingsplan en 'n Getuinis. Die Spade Reën Boodskaper* 3, 1930; off-print: Benoni, South Africa, P.O.B. 416, 1951.
Krüger, "Ein"
  Krüger, C. "Ein heiliges Leben." *Glaube, Liebe, Hoffnung* 15/11, Nov. 1962, 1f.
Krusche, *Wirken*
  Krusche, Werner. *Das Wirken des Heiligen Geistes nach Calvin*. Göttingen, 1957.
Krust, "Churches"
  Krust, Christian. "Pentecostal Churches and the Ecumenical Movement." In *The Uppsala Report, 1968. Official Report of the Fourth Assembly of the WCC Uppsala July 4–20, 1968*, ed. N. Goodall, Geneva: WCC, 1968, 340ff.
Krust, *Fünfzig*
  ———. *Fünfzig Jahre deutsche Pfingstbewegung Mülheimer Richtung*. Altdorf/Nbg.: Missionsbuchhandlung und Verlag, 1963.
Krust, "Geistesbewegung"
  ———. "Geistesbewegung oder Zungenbewegung." *Heilszeugnisse* 52, Febr. 1967, 24ff.: 52, March 1967, 38ff.
Krust, *Glauben*
  ———. *Was wir glauben, lehren und bekennen*. Altdorf/Nbg.: Missionsbuchhandlung und Verlag, 1963.
Krust, "Heilige Geist"
  ———. "Der Heilige Geist und die Katholizität der Kirche. Bericht der Sektion I an die Vierte Vollversammlung des OeRK in Uppsala, Juli 1968." *Heilszeugnisse* 53 (December 1, 1968), 180–85.
Krust, "Kimbanguistenkirche"
  ———. "Die Kimbanguistenkirche im Kongo." *Heilszeugnisse* 55/10, 1.10.1970, 147f.
Krust, "Mülheimer"
  ———. "Bericht vom Mülheimer Hauptbrüdertag (3.-6. April 1967)." *Heilszeugnisse* 52, July 1, 1967, 98–102.
Krust, "Mülheim-Ruhr"
  ———. "Bericht vom Hauptbrüdertag in Mülheim-Ruhr (23.-25. April 1968), *Heilszeugnisse* 53, August 1, 1968, 114f.
Krust, "Ökumenische"
  ———. "Die ökumenische Bewegung." *Heilszeugnisse* 52, Aug. 1, 1967, 116–18.
Krust, "Pfingstbewegung"
  ———. "Wie sich die Pfingstbewegung im Lichte des Neuen Testaments als Kirche versteht." *Heilszeugnisse* 52, Sept. 1, 1967, 131–36.
Krust, "Uppsala"
  ———. "Die Vierte Vollversammlung des OeRK in Uppsala." *Heilszeugnisse* 53 (Oct. 1, 1968), 146–59; 53, Nov. 1, 1968, 163–66, 171–74.

Kuhn, *The Structure of Scientific Revolutions*
 Kuhn, Thomas S. *The Structure of Scientific Revolutions* Chicago, 1962, 1970[2].
Kuzmič, "Respond"
 Kuzmič, Peter. "Pentecostals Respond to Marxism." *Called,* 143–64; also in *EPTA Bulletin* 9/1, 1990, 4–32.
Kuzmič, *Vuk-Danicicevo*
 ———. *Vuk-Danicicevo Sveto Pismo I Biblijska Drustva* (Analecta Croatica Christiana 17). Zagreb: Krscanska Sadsnjost, 1984.
Kuzmič, "War-Time Reading"
 ———. "A Croatian War-Time Reading." *Journal of Pentecostal Theology* 4, April 1994, 17–24.
Kydd, "Canada"
 Kydd, R. A. N. "Pentecostal Assemblies of Canada." *Dictionary,* 695–99.
LaBerge, *What*
 LaBerge, Agnes N. O. *What God Hath Wrought,* n.d., reprint in *The Higher Christian Life,* vol. 24.
Lähnemann, *Kolosserbrief*
 Lähnemann, Johannes. *Der Kolosserbrief. Komposition, Situation und Analyse.* Gütersloh: Gütersloher Verlagshaus Gerd Mohn, 1971 (Studien zum Neuen Testament 3).
Lalive d'Epinay, "Chile"
 Lalive d'Epinay, Christian. "The Pentecostal 'Conquista' in Chile." *Ecumenical Review* 20/1, Jan. 1968, 16–32.
Lalive d'Epinay, *Haven of the Masses*
 ———. *Haven of the Masses. A Study of the Pentecostal Movement* (World Studies of Churches in Mission). London: Lutterworth Press, 1969.
Lambert, *Bibliographique*
 Lambert, n.i. *Essai bibliographique de langue française.* Brussels: Bureau de documentation pastoral, *Bulletin trimestriel* 6, Jan. 1973.
Lang, "Scopuli"
 Lang, H. "Scopuli." *Lexikon für Theologie und Kirche* 4 (1937), 389.
Lange, *Predigen*
 Lange, Ernst. *Predigen als Beruf. Aufsätze.* Stuttgart/Berlin: Kreuz-Verlag, 1976.
Lanternari, *Movimenti*
 Lanternari, Vittorio. *Movimenti religiosi di libertà e di salvezza.* G. Feltrinelli, 1960.
Lapoorta, "African"
 Lapoorta, Japie. "An African Response." *Journal of Pentecostal Theology* 4, April 1994, 51–58.
Lapoorta, "South Africa"
 ———. "The Necessity for a Relevant Pentecostal Witness in South Africa." *EPTA Bulletin* 10/1, 1991, 25–33.
Lapsley–Simpson, "Song of the Self"
 Lapsley, James N., and John H. Simpson. "Speaking in Tongues: Infantile Babble or Song of the Self?" *Pastoral Psychology* 15, Sept. 1964, 16–24.
Lapsley–Simpson, "Token"
 ———. "Speaking in Tongues: Token of Group Acceptance and Divine Approval." *Pastoral Psychology* 15, May 1964, 48–55.
Lartey, *Pastoral Counseling*
 Lartey, Emmanuel Yartekwei. *Pastoral Counseling in Inter-Cultural Perspective. A Study of Some African (Ghanaian) and Anglo-American Views of Human Existence and Counseling.* IC 43, 1987.
Láscari, "Josefina Láscari"
 Láscari, B. Guadelupe. "Josefina Láscari." *Mensajero Pentecostés* 3/9, June-July 1964, 13f.
Las Casas, *Opúsculos*
 Las Casas, Fray de Bartolome. *Opúsculos, cartas y memoriales,* ed. J. Pérez de Tudela Bueso. Biblioteca de Autores Españoles 110. Madrid, 1958.

Lasserre, "L'eglise"
  Lasserre, Jean. "L'eglise Kimbanguiste du Congo." In *Le monde non-chrétien,* no. 79–80, July–Dec. 1966, 45–52.
Läuchli, "Negro Spirituals"
  Läuchli, Samuel. "Negro Spirituals als christliche Verkündigung." *Theologische Zeitschrift* 12, 1956, 446ff.
Law, *A Serious Call*
  Law, William. *A Serious Call to a Devout and Holy Life. Adapted to the State and Condition of All Orders of Christians.* 2d edition corrected. London, 1732.
Law, *Treatise*
  _____. *Practical Treatise on Christian Perfection. Not as Though I Had Already, Either Were Already Perfect, Phil. 3.12.* 4th edition, London, 1737.
Law, *Works*
  _____. J. H. Overton (ed.). *Works of the Rev. William Law in 9 volumes,* vol. III contains "A Serious Call . . .". London, 1898.
Lawless, *Peculiar*
  Lawless, Elaine J. *God's Peculiar People. Women's Voices and Folk Tradition in a Pentecostal Church.* Lexington, Kentucky: The University Press of Kentucky, 1988.
Lederle, " 'Initial Evidence' "
  Lederle, Henry I. " 'Initial Evidence' and the Charismatic Movement: an Ecumenical Appraisal or Distinguishing Between the Pearl and the Oyster." Pentecostal Research Conference at Kappel, Switzerland, 1991. Published in McGee, *Initial Evidence,* 131–41.
Lederle, *Treasures*
  _____. *Treasures Old and New. Interpretations of "Spirit Baptism" in the Charismatic Renewal Movement.* Peabody, Mass.: Hendrickson, 1988.
Lee, Jae Bum, *Korean*
  Lee, Jae Bum. *Pentecostal Type Distinctives and Korean Protestant Church Growth.* Ph.D. dissertation School of World Mission, Fuller Theological Seminary, Pasadena, California, 1986.
Lee, Jae Bum, *History*
  _____. *A History of Pentecostal Movement* (Korean). Seoul: Voice Publishing Company, n.d.
Lee, Ki Ban, *Validity*
  Lee, Ki Ban. *The Validity of Ricci's Intercultural Mission in China and His Position Within the Context of Contemporary Missiological and Theological Proposals.* Ph.D. Birmingham, 1989.
Lee, Paul D., *Ecclesiology*
  Lee, Paul D. *Pneumatological Ecclesiology in the Roman Catholic-Pentecostal Dialogue: A Catholic Reading of the Third Quinquennium (1985–1989).* Theol. Diss. Pontifical University, Rome, 1994.
Lehmann, *Sterbende Götter*
  Lehmann, Walter. *Sterbende Götter und christliche Heilsbotschaft. Wechselreden indianischer Vornehmer und spanischer Glaubensapostel in Mexico.* Spanischer und mexikanischer Text mit deutscher Uebersetzung. Stuttgart: W. Kohlhammer, 1949.
Leinberger/Hollenweger/Bubmann, *Getanztes Leben*
  Leinberger, Bodo, W. J. Hollenweger, and Peter Bubmann. *Getanztes Leben. Heilende Liturgie.* Hammersbach: Wort im Bild, 1993.
Leinemann-Perrin, *Relevant*
  Leinemann-Perrin, Christiane. *Training for Relevant Ministry.* Madras: Christian Literature Society, 1981.
Lemke, "Begegnung"
  Lemke, Ch. "Ein Tag der Begegnung." *Der Leuchter* 21, Febr. 1970, 5f.
León-Portilla, *La filosofía náhuatl*
  León-Portilla, M. *La filosofía náhuatl, estudiada en sus fuentes.* Mexico: Universidad Nacional, 1963; English: *Aztec Thought and Culture. A Study of the Ancient Nahuatl*

Mind. Oklahoma City: University of Oklahoma Press, 1963 (not exactly corresponding to the Spanish original).

le Roux, "Die Gees"
le Roux, P. "Die Gees van die Tyd en die Gess van God." *Trooster*, Febr. 1939, 6f.

Lerrigo, "Prophet Movement in the Congo"
Lerrigo, P. H. J. "The Prophet Movement in the Congo." *Int. Review of Mission* 11/42, April 1922, 270–77.

Lettau, "Briefmappe"
L[ettau], R. "Aus meiner Briefmappe." *Pfingstgrüsse* 2/23, Jan. 1910, 7.

Lewis, *Moravian*
Lewis, A. Kingsley O'R. *The Moravian Mission in Barbados 1816-1886. A Study of the Historical Context and Theological Significance of a Minority Among an Oppressed People*. IC 37, 1985.

Ley, *Spirituals*
Ley, Margrit. *Spirituals. Ein Beitrag zur Analyse der religiösen Liedschöpfung bei den nordamerikanischen Negren in der Zeit der Sklaverei*. Unpublished Ph.D. University of Munich, n.d.

Liebe, *Erfüllte Prophetie*
Liebe, Roger. *Erfüllte Prophetie. Messianische Prophetie—ihre Erfüllung und historische Echtheit*. Berneck (Switzerland): Schwengler Verlag, 1983.

Lienhard, *Aspect*
Lienhard, Jean Paul. *Un aspect de l'oecuménisme: le dialogue entre églises de multitudes issues de la réforme et communautés de professants dites 'évangéliques' nées du réveil. Recherche sociologique sur quelques tentatives de rapprochement à différents niveaux entre 'oecuméniques' et 'évangéliques' dites 'conservateurs' dans la France actuelle. La quête difficile de l'unité du protestantisme*. Unpubl. Thesis, University of Strasbourg, 1967.

Lincoln, C. E., "Preface"
Lincoln, C. E. "Preface." In Washington, J. R., *Black Sects and Cults*.

Lincoln–Mamiya, *Black Church*
Lincoln, C. Eric, and Lawrence H. Mamiya. *The Black Church in the African American Experience*. Durham, N.C.: Duke University Press, 1990.

Lindberg, "Swedish"
Lindberg, Alf. "The Swedish Pentecostal Movement: Some Ideological Features." *EPTA Bulletin* 6/2, 1987, 40–46.

Linden, "Rwanda"
Linden, Ian. "The Roman Catholic Church in Social Crisis: The Case of Rwanda." In Fasholé-Luke, *Christianity in Independent Africa*, 242–54.

Lindsay, *Apostle to Africa*
Lindsay, Gordon. *John G. Lake, Apostle to Africa*, 1981.

Lindsay, *John Lake*
_____. (ed.). *Sketches from The Life and Ministry of John Lake* (1922).

Lochman, *Encountering Marx*
Lochman, Jan Milic. *Encountering Marx: Bonds and Barriers Between Christians and Marxists*. Philadelphia: Fortress Press, 1977.

Lohmann, "Wie?"
Lohmann, E. "Wie kommt es?" *Auf der Warte* 2/43, 22.10.1905, 3f.

"Gregor Lopez."
"Gregor Lopez." *Enciclopedia universal ilustrada europeo-americano* XXXI, 113, Barcelona, n.d.

Lovell, *Black Song*
Lovell, John. *Black Song: The Forge and the Flame. The Story of How the Afro-American Spiritual Was Hammered Out*. New York/London: Collier-Macmillan, 1972.

Lovell, "Social Implications"
_____. "The Social Implications of the Negro Spirituals." *Journal of Negro Education*, 8 Oct. 1939, 634–43.

Lovett, "Black Holiness-Pentecostals"

    Lovett, Leonard. "Black Holiness-Pentecostals: Implications for Ethics and Social Transformation." Emory University, Ph.D. diss. 1979.

Lovett, "Black Origins"

    _____. "Black Origins of the Pentecostal Movement." In Vinson Synan (ed.), *Aspects of Pentecostal-Charismatic Origins*. Plainfield, N.J.: Logos International, 1975, 123–42.

Lovett, "Black Theology"

    _____. "Black Theology." *Dictionary*, 84–86.

Lovett, "Holiness Pentecostalism"

    _____. "Black Holiness Pentecostalism." *Dictionary*, 76–84.

Lovett, "Liberation"

    _____. "Liberation: A Dual-Edged Sword." *Pneuma* 9/2, Fall 1987, 155–71.

Lovett, "Perspectives"

    _____. "Perspectives on Black Pentecostalism." Unpubl. paper, 1972.

Lovett, "Positive"

    _____. "Positive Confession Theology." *Dictionary*, 718–20.

Lovett, "Response"

    _____. "Response to Perspectives on Koinonia." *Pneuma* 12/2, Fall 1990, 166–69.

Lovsky, *Louis Dallière*

    Lovsky, F. *La pensée théologique du pasteur Louis Dallière* (*Etudes Théologiques et Religieuses*, vol. 53). Montpellier, France, 1978/2.

Lozano, "Crossroads"

    Lozano, Felipe Emmanuel Agredano. "The Apostolic Assembly at the Crossroads: The Politics of Gender." SPS 1994.

Lucas, *Browning*

    Lucas, Isidro. *The Browning of America*. Chicago: Fides/Claretian, 1981.

Lucente, *Movimento*

    Lucente, Giulio. *Il movimento pentecostale del Crotonese*. Ph.D. University of Bari, 1967, unpubl.

Lundgren, "Das neue Pfingsterwachen"

    Lundgren, Ivar. "Das neue Pfingsterwachen." *Wort und Geist* 3/10, Oct. 1971, 4; 3/12, Dec. 1971, 6–8.

Lundgren, "Dialog"

    _____. "Vår dialog med pinstvannerna berikar hela ecumeniken," *Svenska Journalen*, No. 33, 1980, 7, 37.

Lundgren, *Ny pingst*

    _____. *Ny pingst. Rapport fran en nutida väckelse I gamla kyrkor.* Oslo: Den kristna bokringen, 1970.

Luntadila, *L'Essor*

    Luntadila, Lucien. "Abandonnez les lances empoisonnées." *L'Essor* (La Chaux-de-Fonds, Switzerland) 61/13, 29.9.1966, 1f.

Luzolo, *Mvand'avelela*

    Luzolo, K. P. *Mvand'avelela mu Ntumwa Yisu*. N'Kamba; EJCSK, 1959 (dupl.).

Lyon, *Karl Marx*

    Lyon, David. *Karl Marx: A Christian Appreciation of His Life and Thought*. London: Lion Publishing and Inter-Varsity Press, 1979.

Lys, *"Rûach"*

    Lys, Daniel. *"Rûach." le souffle dans l'Ancien Testament*. (Etudes d'histoire et de Philosophie religieuse). Paris: Presse Universitaires de France, 1972.

Lyttleton, "Knowledge"

    Lyttleton, R. A. "The Nature of Knowledge." In Ronald Duncan/Miranda Western-Smith, *The Encyclopedia of Ignorance, Everything you ever wanted to know about the unknown*. Oxford: Pergamos Press, 1977, 1978, 9–17.

Macchia, "Confused Situation"
> Macchia, Frank. "God Present in a Confused Situation. The Mixed Influence of the Charismatic Movement on Classical Pentecostalism." *Pneuma* 18/1, Spring 1996, 33–54.

Macchia, "Response"
> _____. "A North American Response." *Journal of Pentecostal Theology* 4, April 1994, 25–33.

Macchia, "Sighs too Deep for Words"
> _____. "Sighs too Deep for Words: Toward a Theology of Glossolalia." *Journal of Pentecostal Theology* 1/1, Oct. 1992, 47–73.

Macchia, "Tongues"
> _____. "Tongues as a Sign: Towards a Sacramental Understanding of the Pentecostal Experience." *Pneuma* 15/1, 1993, 61–76.

Macchia, "Waiting and Hurrying"
> _____. "Waiting and Hurrying for the Healing of Creation: Implications in the Message of the Blumhardts for a Pentecostal Theology of Divine Healing." SPS and EPTA Conference, Mattersey, England, July 1995.

MacDonald, "Cross"
> MacDonald, W. "The Cross Versus Personal Kingdom." *Pneuma* 3/2, Fall 1982, 26–37.

MacGaffey, "Beloved City"
> MacGaffey, W. "The Beloved City: Commentary on a Kimbanguist Text." *Journal of Religion in Africa* 2/2, 1969, 129–47.

Machoveč, *Marxist*
> Machoveč, Milan. *A Marxist Looks at Jesus*. London: Darton, Longman & Todd, 1976.

Mackay, *Ecumenics*
> Mackay, John A. *Ecumenics. The Science of the Church Universal*. Englewood Cliffs, N.J.: Prentice Hall, Inc. 1964.

MacNutt, "Solution"
> MacNutt, Francis. "A Proposed Solution to the Re-Baptism Dilemma." *Ministries* 3, Spring 1985, 58–61.

MacRobert, *Black Pentecostalism*
> MacRobert, Iain. *Black Pentecostalism: Its origins, functions and theology with special reference to a Midland borough*. Edinburgh: St. Andrews Press, 1993.

MacRobert, "Black Roots"
> _____. "The Black Roots of Pentecostalism." In Jongeneel, 1992, 73–84.

MacRobert, *Racism*
> _____. *The Black Roots and White Racism of Early Pentecostalism in the USA*. London: Macmillan, 1988.

Maempa, "Interracial"
> Maempa, John T. "Interracial Conference Unites Major Pentecostal Denominations." *PE* 4205, 11.12.1994, 24–26.

Mahan, *Out*
> Mahan, Asa. *Out of Darkness Into Light*, 1877, reprint in *The Higher Christian Life*, vol. 28.

Maldonado, "Mexicanos"
> Maldonado, Oscar. "Mexicanos marginados." *Apostol, Revista del Seminario de Guadalajara* 1/2, March/April 1970, 20–25.

Mann, "Polygamy"
> Mann, Pamela S. "Towards a Biblical Understanding of Polygamy." *Missiology* 17, Jan. 1989, 11–26.

Manriquez, "Religion of the People and Evangelism"
> Manriquez, Samuel Palma. "Religion of the People and Evangelism: A Pentecostal Perspective." *Int. Review of Mission* 82/327, July/Oct. 1993, 365–374.

Marcel, "W. E. Hocking"
> Marcel, Gabriel. "W. E. Hocking et la dialectique de l'instinct." *Revue philosophique de France et de l'étranger* 88, 1919, 19–54.

Marcom, "Fire"
    Marcom, John. "The Fire Down South." *Forbes*, Oct. 15, 1990, 56–71.
Maríz, *Coping*
    Maríz, Cecilia Loreta. *Religion and Coping With Poverty in Brazil*, Unpubl. Ph.D.
    dissertation University of Boston, 1989. Published as: *Coping With Poverty: Pentecostals
    and Christian Base Communities in Brazil*. Philadelphia: Temple University Press, 1994.
Martin, David, *Tongues*
    Martin, David. *Tongues of Fire: The Explosion of Protestantism in Latin America*.
    Oxford: Blackwell, 1990.
Martin, M.-L., "Afrikanische Gestalt"
    Martin, M.-L. "Afrikanische Gestalt des christlichen Glaubens: Die Kirche Jesu
    Christi auf Erden durch den Propheten Simon Kimbangu." *Evangelische
    Missionszeitschrift* 28/1, Jan. 1971, 16–29.
Martin, M.-L., "Congolese Church Celebrates"
    _____. "Congolese Church Celebrates." *Pro Veritate* (Braamfontein, Transwaal) 10,
    15.6.1971, 4f.
Martin, M.-L., *Kirche ohne Weisse*
    _____. *Kirche ohne Weisse. Simon Kimbangu und seine Millionenkirche im Kongo*. Basel:
    Friedrich Reinhardt Verlag, 1971; English: *Kimbangu, an African Prophet and His
    Church*. Oxford: Blackwell, 1975.
Martin, M.-L., *Prophetic Christianity in the Congo*
    _____. *Prophetic Christianity in the Congo. The Church of Christ on Earth Through the
    Prophet Simon Kimbangu*. Braamfontein/Johannesburg, n.d.
Martin, M.-L., "Prophetism in the Congo"
    _____. "Prophetism in the Congo. Origin and Development of an Independent African
    Church." *Ministry* 8/4, Oct. 1968, 154–63.
Martin, R., "Vision"
    Martin, R. "David Wilkerson's Vision." *New Covenant* 3/6, Jan. 1974, 11f.
Martin, R. Francis, "Apocalypse"
    Martin, R. Francis. "Apocalypse, Book of." *Dictionary*, 11–13.
Martin, W. C., *Hymns*
    Martin, W. C. "My Anchor Holds." In *Hymns of Glorious Praise*, Springfield: Gospel
    Publishing House, 1969, no. 297.
Masembo, *Le Prophétisme kongo*
    Masembo, I. *Le Prophétisme kongo*. Strasbourg: thèse de licence en théologie, 1966,
    (unpubl).
Masters, *Colección*
    Masters, Carlos. *Colección Circulos Biblicos*. Petropolis, Brazil: Editores Vozes, 1973.
Massey, *Another Springtime*
    Massey, Richard D. *Another Springtime. Donald Gee, Pentecostal Pioneer. A Biography*.
    Guildford, Surrey: Highland Books, 1992.
Massey, "Flirtation With Elim"
    _____. "Flirtation With Elim. Donald Gee's Negotiations to Join the Elim Pentecostal
    Alliance in 1923." *EPTA Bulletin* 8/1, 1989, 4–13.
Massey, *Sound*
    _____. *A Sound and Scriptural Union. An Examination of the Origins of the Assemblies of
    God of Great Britain and Ireland During the Years 1920–1925*. Unpubl. Ph.D.
    Birmingham, 1987.
Masson, "Chants kimbanguistes"
    Masson, J. "Simples réflexions sur les chants kimbanguistes." In *Devant les sectes
    non-chrétiennes. Rapports et compte rendu de la XXXième semaine de missiologie*. Louvain,
    1961, 82–90.
Mathai, "Whatever"
    Mathai, Samuel. "Whatever Happened to the Pearly Gates?" SPS 1990, H.
Maurer, "Pentecôtisme"
    Maurer, D. "Pentecôtisme et nous." *Réforme* 3/115, 31.5.1947, 2.

Mazibuko, *Education*
　　Mazibuko, Bongani. *Education in Mission—Mission in Education. A Critical Comparative Study of Selected Approaches.* IC 47, 1987.
Mbiti, "Impotence"
　　Mbiti, John. "Theological Impotence and the Universality of the Church." *Lutheran World* 21/3, 1974, reprinted in *Mission Trends* no. 3: Third World Theologies, 1976, 6–18.
McAll, *Healing the Family Tree*
　　McAll, Kenneth. *Healing the Family Tree.* London: Sheldon Press, 1982.
McCarthy, *Significance*
　　McCarthy, Jerome. *The Significance of Neo-Pentecostalism for Ecumenism.* Phil. Diss. University of Hull, 1973.
McCarthy, "Charismatic Renewal"
　　_____. "The Charismatic Renewal and Reconciliation in Northern Ireland," *One in Christ* 10/1, Jan 1974, 31–43.
McClung, *Azusa*
　　McClung, Grant, Jr. (ed.). *Azusa Street and Beyond. Pentecostal Missions and Church Growth in the Twentieth Century.* South Plainfield, N.J.: Bridge Publications, 1986.
McClung, "Interdependence"
　　_____. "Interdependence in Global Pentecostalism." *World Pentecost* 28, Spring 1991, 18–22.
McClung, "Missiology"
　　_____. "Missiology." *Dictionary,* 607–09.
McConnell, *Different*
　　McConnell, D. R. *A Different Gospel: A Historical and Biblical Analysis of the Modern Faith Movements.* Peabody, Mass.: Hendrickson, 1988.
McDonnell, "Catholic Charismatics"
　　McDonnell, Kilian. "Catholic Charismatics. The Rediscovery of a Hunger for God and the Sense of his Presence." *Commonweal* 96/9, 1972, 207–11.
McDonnell, "Catholic Pentecostalism"
　　_____. "Catholic Pentecostalism: Problems in Evaluation." *Dialog,* Winter 1970, 35–54; reprint: Watchung, N.J.: Charisma Books, 1971.
McDonnell, *Charismatic Renewal*
　　_____. *Charismatic Renewal and the Churches.* New York: The Seabury Press, 1976.
McDonnell, "Death"
　　_____. "The Death of Mythologies: The Classical Pentecostal/Roman Catholic Dialogue." *America* 172, March 25, 1995, 14–19.
McDonnell, "Distinguishing Characteristics"
　　_____. "The Distinguishing Characteristics of the Charismatic-Pentecostal Spirituality." *One in Christ* 10/2, 1974, 117–28.
McDonnell, "Ecumenical Significance"
　　_____. "The Ecumenical Significance of the Pentecostal Movement." *Worship* 40/10, Dec. 1966, 608–29.
McDonnell, *Ecumenism*
　　_____. *The Charismatic Renewal and Ecumenism.* New York: Paulist Press, 1978.
McDonnell, "Experience"
　　_____. "I Believe That I Might Experience." *Continuum,* Winter 1967/68, 637–85.
McDonnell, "Experiential and the Social"
　　_____. "The Experiential and the Social: New Models from Pentecostal/Roman Catholic Dialogue." *One in Christ* 9/1, 1972, 43–58.
McDonnell, "Five Defining Issues"
　　_____. "Five Defining Issues: The International Pentecostal/Roman Catholic Dialogue." *One in Christ* 31/2, 1995, 110–21.
McDonnell, "Holy Spirit and Pentecostalism"
　　_____. "Holy Spirit and Pentecostalism." *Commonweal* 89/6, 8.11.1968, 198–204; reprint Watchung, N.J.: Charisma Books, 1971.

McDonnell, "Ideology"

———. "The Ideology of Pentecostal Conversion." *Journal of Ecumenical Studies,* Winter 1968, 105–26.

McDonnell, "Improbable Conversations"

———. "Improbable Conversations: The Classical Pentecostal/Roman Catholic International Dialogue." *One in Christ* 31/1, 1995, 20–31.

McDonnell, *Open*

———. (ed). *Open the Windows. The Popes and the Charismatic Renewal.* South Bend, Ind: Greenlawn Press, 1989.

McDonnell, "Pentecostals"

———. "Pentecostals and the Holy Spirit Today." *Sisters Today* 40, May 1969, 496–506.

McDonnell, *Power*

———. (ed). *The Holy Spirit and Power. The Catholic Charismatic Renewal.* New York, Garden City: Doubleday & Co., 1975.

McDonnell, *Presence*

———. *Presence, Power, Praise. Documents on the Charismatic Renewal.* Collegeville, Minn.: The Liturgical Press, 1980, 3 vols.

McDonnell, "Protestants"

———. "Protestants, Pentecostals and Mary." *New Covenant* 6/6, March 1977, 27–29.

McDonnell, "Reactions"

———. "Church Reactions to the Charismatic Renewal." *Bossey,* 147–74.

McDonnell (with Bittlinger), *Problem*

———. (with Arnold Bittlinger). *The Baptism in the Holy Spirit as an Ecumenical Problem. Two Essays Relating the Baptism in the Holy Spirit to Sacramental Life.* South Bend, Ind.: (Charismatic Renewal Series), 1972.

McDonnell with Montague, *Initiation*

———. (with George T. Montague). *Christian Initiation and Baptism in the Holy Spirit. Evidence from the First Eight Centuries.* Collegeville, Minn.: The Liturgical Press, 1991.

McGee, "Abrams"

McGee, Gary. "Abrams, Minnie (1859–1912)." *Dictionary,* 7.

McGee, "Early Pentecostal Hermeneutics"

———. "Early Pentecostal Hermeneutics. Tongues as Evidence in the Book of Acts." Pages 96–118. In McGee, *Initial Evidence.*

McGee, *Gospel*

———. *This Gospel Shall Be Preached. History of the Assemblies of God Foreign Missions to 1959.* Springfield, Mo.: Gospel Publishing House, 1986.

McGee, "Hodges"

———. "Hodges, Melvin Lyle (1909–1988)." *Dictionary,* 403f.

McGee, *Initial Evidence*

———. (ed.). *Initial Evidence: Historical and Biblical Perspectives on the Pentecostal Doctrine of Spirit Baptism.* Peabody, Mass.: Hendrickson Publishers, 1991.

McGee, "Maranatha"

———. "Maranatha Campus Ministries, International." *Dictionary,* 573.

McGee, "Missions"

———. "Missions, Overseas (North American)." *Dictionary,* 610–25.

McGilvray, *Gesundheit*

McGilvray, James. *Die verlorene Gesundheit. Das verheissene Heil.* Stuttgart, 1982.

McGilvray, "Verwaltung"

———. "Die Verwaltung von Gesundheit und Krankheit und die Kommerzialisierung von Medizing als globales Problem." In: *Auf der Suche,* 51–58.

McLean, "Gap"

McLean, Mark. "The Gap." SPS 1990, D.

McLean, "Hermeneutic"

"———. Toward a Pentecostal Hermeneutic." *Pneuma* 6/2, Fall 1984, 35–56.

McLeod, "Renew"

McLeod, George. "He Will Renew the Earth." *New Covenant* 2/12, June 1973, 10–12.

McNutt, "Solution"
McNutt, Francis. "A Proposed Solution to the Re-Baptism Dilemma." *Ministries* 3, Spring 1985, 58–61.

McPherson, *This*
McPherson, Aimee Semple. *This is That: Personal Experiences, Sermons, Writings,* 1919. Reprint in *The Higher Christian Life,* vol. 27.

McPherson (comp.), *Declaration of Faith*
———. (comp.), *Declaration of Faith compiled by A. S. McPherson for the International Church of the Foursquare Gospel.* Los Angeles, n.d.

MD
Materialdienst der Evangelischen Zentralstelle für Weltanschauungsfragen. Stuttgart, n.d.

Melton, *Bibliography*
Melton, J. Merton. *A Bibliography of the Catholic Pentecostal Movement.* Garrett Bibliographical Lectures, no. 3, Evanston, Ill.: Garrett Theological Seminary Library, 1971.

Mensajero Pentecostés, 2/51
Mensajero Pentecostés, 2/51, Aug. 1961, 5–7 (on special women's meetings).

Mensajero Pentecostés, 2/62
Mensajero Pentecostés 2/62, March 1961, 20 (on persecution of Pentecostals).

Mensajero Pentecostés, 2/63
———.2/63, May 1961, 25: El Cardenal José 'Efrain' Garibi Rivera (quoted from *Rototemas,* 6.12.1958).

Menzies, *Anointed to Serve*
Menzies, William M. *Anointed to Serve. The Story of the Assemblies of God.* Springfield, Mo.: Gospel Publishing House, 1971.

Mercier, "Scopuli"
Mercier, J. "Lorenzo Scopuli." *Dictionnaire de Théologie Catholique* XIV, Paris, 1941, 1745.

Merwe Burger, *Die Geloofsgeskiedenis*
Merwe Burger, I. van der. *Die Geloofsgeskiedenis van die Apostoliese Geloofsending van Suid-Afrika (1908–1958).* Johannesburg: Evangelie Uitgewers, 1988.

Merz, "Toronto"
Merz, Andreas. "Der 'Segen von Toronto' oder Wie der Heilige Geist die Gläubigen reihenweise umkippen lässt." *Sonntagszeitung* (Zurich), 12.2.1995, 92.

Meyer, "Brasilien"
Meyer, Harding. "Die Pfingstbewegung in Brasilien." *Jahrbuch Die evangelische Diaspora* 39, 1968, 9–50.

Meyers Handbuch über Literatur
Meyers Handbuch über Literatur, herausgegeben und bearbeitet von den Fachredaktoren des Bibliographischen Institutes Mannheim. Mannheim: Bibliographisches Institut, 1964.

Mills, *Charismatic*
Mills, Watson E. *Charismatic Religion in Modern Research. A Bibliography.* Bibliographic series 1, National Association of Baptist Professors of Religion (Macon, Ga.: Mercer University Press, 1985).

Mills, *Glossalalia*
———. *Glossalalia. A Bibliography* (Studies in the Bible and Early Christianity, vol. 6). New York and Toronto: The Edwin Mellen Press, 1985.

Minutes of the 182nd General Assembly
Minutes of the 182nd General Assembly of the United Presbyterian Church in the USA. Philadelphia: Office of the General Assembly, 1970.

Miranda, "A Response"
Miranda, Jesse. "A Response to the Report on the Dialogue Between Classical Pentecostals and Roman Catholics." In *Pneuma* 12/2, Fall 1990, 169–72.

Mitchell, "Towards the Sociology of Religious Independency"
Mitchell, R. C. "Towards the Sociology of Religious Independency." *Journal of Religion in Africa* 3/1, 1970, 2–21.

Mitchell–Turner, *Bibliography*
———. (and H. W. Turner). *A Bibliography of Modern African Movements.* Northwestern University Press, 1966. Follow-up in *Journal of Religion in Africa* 1, 1968, 173–210.

Mitscherlich, *Die Unfähigkeit*
Mitscherlich, A. and M. *Die Unfähigkeit zu trauern. Grundlagen kollektiven Verhaltens.* Munich: Piper & Co. 1970.

Mojzes, *Varieties of Christian-Marxist Dialogue*
Mojzes, Paul (ed.). *Varieties of Christian-Marxist Dialogue.* Philadelphia: Ecumenical Press, 1978.

Möller, *Church and Politics*
Möller, F. P. *Church and Politics. A Pentecostal View of the South African Situation.* Braamfontein: Gospel Publishers, 1988.

Möller, *Diskussie oor die Charismata*
———. *Diskussie oor die Charismata* Johannesburg: Evangelie Uitgewers, 1980.

Moltmann, *Creation*
Moltmann, Jürgen. *Gott in der Schöpfung. Oekologische Schöpfungslehre.* Munich: Kaiser, 1985. English: *God in Creation: A New Theology of Creation and the Spirit of God.* (The Gifford Lectures, 1984–1985). San Francisco: Harper & Row, 1985.

Moltmann, "Life"
———. "The Spirit Gives Life: Spirituality and Vitality." *Brighton,* 22–37.

Moltmann, "Response"
———. "A Response to My Pentecostal Dialogue Partners." *Journal of Pentecostal Theology* 4, April 1994, 59–70.

Moore, Everett LeRoy, *Handbook*
Moore, Everett LeRoy. *Handbook of Pentecostal Denominations in the United States.* M.A. Thesis, Graduate Studies in Religion, Pasadena College, 1954 (unpublished).

Moore, Rich D., "Approach"
Moore, Rich D. "Pentecostal Approach to Scripture." *The Seminary Viewpoint* 8/1, 1987, 4.

Moore, Rich D., "Canon"
———. "Canon and Charisma in the Book of Deuteronomy." *Journal for Pentecostal Theology* 1, Oct. 1992, 75–92.

Moorhead, *Congo Forest*
Moorhead, M. W. *Missionary Pioneering in Congo Forest. A Narrative of the Labours of William F. P. Burton and His Companions in the Native Villages of Luba-Land, compiled from Letters, Diaries and Articles.* n.p., n.d.

Morse, *Koyama*
Morse, Merril P. *Kosuke Koyama: A Model for Intercultural Theology,* IC 71, 1991.

Moscato, "Alcuni"
Moscato, Antonio. "Alcuni aspetti della diffusione del protestantesimo nell'Italia post-unitaria." *Sociologia religiosa* 15–16/1967, 105–23.

Moser, "Dialog"
Moser, Tilbert. "Der römisch-katholisch/pfingstliche Dialog." *Schweizerische Kirchenzeitung* 148/10, 6 March 1980, 144–49.

Mosimann, *Das Zungenreden*
Mosimann, Eddison. *Das Zungenreden, geschichtlich und psychologisch untersucht.* Tübingen: J. C. B. Mohr (Paul Siebeck), 1911.

Moskalenko, *Piatidesiatniki*
Moskalenko, Aleksei Trofimovich. *Piatidesiatniki* (=The Pentecostals), Moscow: Publishing House for Political Literature, 1966.

Mostert, "Men"
  Mostert, J. P. "Men of 'The Spirit'—or of 'Spirit.' " In G. C. Oosthuizen, *Religion Alive*, 82–89.
Mouw, "Life"
  Mouw, Richard J. "Life in the Spirit in an Unjust World." *Pneuma* 9/2, Fall 1987, 109–28.
Mukuan, "Dupl. minutes"
  Mukuan, Martin-Joseph. Dupl. minutes of "Resolution du 6ième Congrès National de l'Union de la Jeunesse Protestante" 21.2.1971, Kinshasa/Nganda.
Müller, "Mexiko"
  Müller, Reinhard. "Mexiko." *Theologische Realenzypklopädie* 22 Berlin/New York: Walter de Gruyter, 1992, 685–95.
Müller-Bohn, "Zungenreden-Weissagung"
  Müller-Bohn, Jost. "Zungenreden-Weissagung." *Wort und Geist* 1/10, Oct. 1972, 12–13.
Mullins, "Empire"
  Mullins, Mark R. "The Empire Strikes Back: Korean Pentecostal Mission to Japan." In Karla Poewe (ed.), *Charismatic Christianity as a Global Culture*, 87–102.
Mullins, "History"
  _____. "The History, Spread and Internationalism of Pentecostal and Charismatic Christianity in South Korea and Japan." Paper given at the conference on Global Culture: Pentecostal and Charismatic Movements Worldwide, May 9–11, 1991, Calgary University, Canada.
Mulrain, *Theology*
  Mulrain, George M. *Theology in Folk Culture: A Study of the Theological Significance of Haitian Folk Religion.* IC 33, 1984.
Munden, "Encountering"
  Munden, Alan. "Encountering the House Church Movement: 'A Different Kind of Christianity.' " *Anvil* 1/3, 1985, 201–17.
Murillo, "Un ángel mexicano"
  Murillo, Gerardo (pseudonym Dr. Atl). "Un ángel mexicano." In *"El galano arte de leer."* Antologia didactica. Literatura Castellana. Mexico 1963.
Muschg, "Arzt"
  Muschg, Adolf. "Der Arzt als Medizinmann." *Tagesanzeiger Magazin* (Zurich) 1.3.1986, 14–19.
Mushete, "Authenticity and Christianity in Zaïre"
  Mushete, Ngindu. "Authenticity and Christianity in Zaïre." In Fasholé-Luke, *Christianity in Independent Africa*, 228–41.
M'Vuendy, *Kimbanguisme*
  M'Vuendy, F. *Le Kimbanguisme de la clandestinité à la tolérance 1921–1959.* Paris, Diplôme E.P.H.E. 1969, unpublished.
Mwene-Batende, *Etude sociologique*
  Mwene-Batende, G. *Etude sociologique des conflits entre les Eglises congolaises. Cas particulier des quelques Eglises de souche kimbanguiste.* Kinshasa, Université Lovanium, Mémoire de licence en sociologie, 1970 (unpublished).
Naegeli–Osjord, *Besessenheit;* English: *Possession*
  Naegeli–Osjord, Hans. *Besessenheit und Exorzismus.* Remagen, Otto Reichl Verlag, 1983. English: *Possession and Exorcism.* Gerards Cross, Bucks. England: Colin Smythe Ltd., 1988.
Naegeli–Osjord, *Logurgie*
  _____. *Die Logurgie in den Philippinen.* In *Imago Mundi*, vol. 4: Der kosmische Mensch. Paderborn, 1973.
Nederlands Hervormde Kerk, *De Kerk*
  Nederlands Hervormde Kerk. *De Kerk en de Pinkstergroepen. Herderlijk Schrijven, van de Generale Synode der Nederlandse Hervormde Kerk*, (1960), n.p., 1961[3].

Nelson, *For Such a Time as This*
 Nelson, Douglas. *For Such a Time as This. The Story of Bishop William J. Seymour and the Azusa Street Revival. A Study of Pentecostal Charismatic Roots.* Birmingham, Ph.D., 1981.

Nelson–Gerloff, "Seymour"
 ———. (with Roswith Gerloff). "Seymour, William Joseph."
 Biographisch-Bibliographisches Kirchenlexikon 9. Herzberg: Traugott Bautz, 1995, 905–8.

Nelson, J. Robert, "Unity of the Church"
 Nelson, J. Robert. "The Unity of the Church and the Unity of Mankind." In R. Groscurth (ed.), *What Unity Implies. Six Essays After Uppsala.* (WCC Studies 7). Geneva: WCC, 1969, 101–14.

Nelson, P. C., *Doctrines*
 Nelson, P. C. *Bible Doctrines, a Handbook of Pentecostal Theology Based on Scriptures and Following the Lines of the Statement of Fundamental Truths as Adopted by the General Council of The Assemblies of God.* Enid, Okla.: Southwestern Press, 1934; revised and enlarged: Enid, Okla.: Southwestern Press, 1936[2]; Springfield, Mo.: Gospel Publishing House, 1940; revised: Springfield, Mo.: Gospel Publishing House, and London: Assemblies of God Publishing House, 1962.

Das Neue Testament in der Sprache der Gegenwart
 Das Neue Testament in der Sprache der Gegenwart. Neue Mülheimer Ausgabe mit Anmerkungen und Wörterverzeichnis. Mülheim/Ruhr: Verlag der Gesellschaft für Mission, Diakonie und Koportage m.b.H., 1914; Altdorf/Nbg.: Missionsbuchhandlung und Verlag, 1968[7].

Newell, *Health*
 Newell, Kenneth W. (ed.). *Health By the People.* Geneva: World Health Organization, 1975.

Nfinanangani–Nzungu, "Kimbangu"
 Nfinanangani and Nzungu. "Histoire de Simon Kimbangu. Prophète (1921)." French: *Archives de Sociologie des Religions* 16/31, 1971, 15–42.

Ngindu, "Colloque"
 Ngindu, "Colloque sur le Kimbanguisme." (1972) *Revue du Clergé Africain* 27/6, Nov. 1972, 631–45.

Niederberger, "Kimbangu-Kirche"
 Niederberger, O. "Die Kimbangu-Kirche im Weltrat der Kirchen." *Neue Zeitschrift für Missionswissenschaft* 27/3, 1971, 215–19.

Niemöller, "Nochebuena"
 Niemöller, Martin. "Nochebuena." *Mensajero Pentecostés* 3/6 [2], Jan. 1964, 3–5.

Nikoloff, "Awakening"
 Nikoloff, Nicholas. "New Awakening in Germany." *PE,* April 24, 1960, 4f.

Novaes, *Os*
 Novaes, Regina. *Os escolhidos de Deus. Pentecostais, travalhodores & cidadancia.* Rio de Janeiro: Instituto de Estudos de Religião, Cuadernos de ISER no. 19, 1985.

Ntontolo, *Mouvements prophétiques*
 Ntontolo, B. *Les mouvements prophétiques et les réveils spirituels dans le Bas-Congo.* Brussels: Faculté libre de théologie protestante, 1968 (unpubl.).

Nuelsen, *Fletcher*
 Nuelsen, John L. *John William Fletcher, der erste schweizerische Methodist. Ein Gedenkblatt zu seinem 200. Geburtstag 12.9.1729.* Zurich 1929.

Nxumalo, "Pastoral"
 Nxumalo, J. A. "Pastoral Ministry and African Worldview." *The Journal of Theology for Southern Africa,* no. 28, Sept. 1979, 27–36.

O'Connor, *Laying on of Hands*
 O'Connor, Edward D. *The Laying on of Hands.* Pecos, New Mexico: Dove Publications, 1969 and Watchung, N.J.: Charisma Books, 1971.

O'Connor, *Pentecostal Movement*
_____. *The Pentecostal Movement in the Catholic Church*. Notre Dame, Ind.: Ave Maria Press, 1971.
O'Connor, *Pentecost in the Catholic Church*
_____. *Pentecost in the Catholic Church*. Pecos, New Mexico: Dove Publications, 1970 and Watchung, N.J.: Charisma Books, 1971.
O'Connor, *Pentecost in the Modern World*
_____. *Pentecost in the Modern World. The Charismatic Renewal Compared With Other Trends in the Church and the World Today*. Notre Dame, Ind.: Ave Maria Press, 1972.
O'Docharty, "Tried"
O'Docharty, L. "I Tried to Be a Good Catholic . . ." *Testimony* 4/1, First Quarter, 1965, 8.
Odum, "Religious Folk Songs"
Odum, Howard W. "Religious Folk Songs and the Southern Negro." *American Journal of Religious Psychology and Education* 3, July 1909, 265–365.
O'Mahony, *Question*
O'Mahony, Patrick J. *A Question of Life: Its Origin and Transmission. An Analysis of the Marxist Utilitarian Approaches*. London: Sheed and Ward, 1990.
O'Mahony, *Swords*
_____. *Swords and Ploughshares. Can Man Live and Progress with a Technology of Death?* London: Sheed and Ward, 1986.
Omenyo, "Ghana"
Omenyo, Cephas. "Charismatic Renewal in the Mainline Churches in Ghana: The Case of the Bible Study and Prayer Group of the Presbyterian Church of Ghana." SPS and EPTA Conference in Mattersey, England, July 1995.
Omoyajowo, "Aladura Churches"
Omoyajowo, Akin. "The Aladura Churches in Nigeria Since Independence." In Fasholé-Luke, *Christianity in Independent Africa*, 96–110.
One in Christ, "Dialogue"
One in Christ 9/1, 1973, 73f.: "Roman Catholic/Pentecostal Dialogue."
Oosthuizen, *Religion Alive*
Oosthuizen, G. C. *Religion Alive. Studies in the New Movements and Indigenous Churches in Southern Africa*. Johannesburg: Hodder & Stoughton, 1986.
Oosthuizen, *Theology*
_____. *The Theology of a South African Messiah. An Analysis of the Hymnal of "The Church of the Nazarites."* Leiden/Cologne, 1967.
Orchard, *Witness in Six Continents*
Orchard, R. K. (ed.). *Witness in Six Continents: Records of the Commission of World Mission and Evangelism of the WCC Held in Mexico City, 1963*, London, 1964.
Orlien, "Sykehuset i nya Kaziba"
Orlien, Osvald. "Sykehuset i nya Kaziba." In Juul (ed.), *Til jordens ender*, 169–75.
Ornelas, "Libertad"
Ornelas, Andrés. "Libertad y patriotismo!" *Mesajero Pentecostés* 2/80, Sept. 1962, 5f.
Oropeza, *Laugh*
Oropeza, B. J. *A Time to Laugh: The Holy Laughter Phenomenon Examined*. Peabody, Mass.: Hendrickson Publishers, 1995.
Osborn, T. L., "Hoy"
Osborn, T. L. "Hoy la escritura puede ser cumplida," *Mensajero Pentecostés*, 3/9, June/July 1964, 3–7.
Osborn, T. L., "Preguntas"
_____. "Preguntas y respuestas," *Mensajero Pentecostés*, 3/8, April/May 1964, 6–8.
Oshun, "Perspective"
Oshun, C. O. "The Pentecostal Perspective of the Christ Apostolic Church." *Orita. Ibadan Journal of Religious Studies* 15/2, Dec. 1981, 105–14; *EPTA Bulletin* 4/2, 1985, 73f.

Osobo, "Fascinating"
  Osobo, S. O. "Fascinating But Largely Speculative." *Orita. Ibadan Journal of Religious Studies* 4/1, June 1970, 64–69.
Ossa, *Espiritualidad popular*
  Ossa, Manuel. *Espiritualidad popular y acción política. El Pastor Victor Mora y la Misión Wesleyana Nacional. 40 años de historia religiosa y social (1928–1969).* Medellín: Ediciones Rehue, Centro ecuménico de Medellín, ca. 1990.
Ossa, *Lo ajeno*
  _____. *Lo ajeno y lo propio. Identidad Pentecostal y Trabajo.* Medellín: Ediciones Rehue. Centro ecuménico de Medellín, 1991.
O'Sullivan, "Ichthus Fellowship"
  O'Sullivan, Anthony. "Roger Forster and the Ichthus Christian Fellowship: The Development of a Charismatic Missiology." *Pneuma* 16/2, Fall 1994, 247–63.
Overbeck, "Taylor"
  Overbeck, Joseph. "Jeremy Taylor." *Realenzyklopädie für protestantische Theologie und Kirche,* third edition 1896–1913, XIV, n.p., n.d., 463–67.
Oyarzún, *Reminiscencias*
  Oyarzún, Arturo. *Reminiscencias históricas de la obre evangélica en Chile.* Valdivia: Imp. Alianza, 1921.
Padilla, "Evangelism"
  Padilla, René. "Evangelism and the World." In Douglas, *Earth,* 134–46.
Padilla, *Mission*
  _____. *Mission Between the Times.* Grand Rapids, Mich.: Eerdmans, 1985.
Palma, Irma, *En tierra extraña*
  Palma, Irma (ed.). *En tierra extraña. Itinerario del pueblo Pentecostal Chileno.* Santiago: Editorial Amerina, 1968.
Palma, Marta, "Conciliar Movement"
  Palma, Marta. "A Pentecostal Church in the Conciliar Movement." *The Ecumenical Review* 37/2, April 1985, 223–29.
Palma–Villela, "Volksreligion"
  Palma, Samuel, and Hugo Villela. "Die Pfingstbewegung als Volksreligion." *Zeitschrift für Mission* 16/1, 1990, 24–32.
Panikkar, "Secularization"
  Panikkar, Raymundo. "Secularization and Worship." In Vos, *Worship,* 28–31.
Parham, Charles F., *Sermons*
  Parham, Charles F. *The Sermons of Charles F. Parham,* 1902, 1911. Reprint in *The Higher Christian Life,* vol. 36.
Parham, Charles F., *Voice*
  _____. *Kol Kare Bomidbar: A Voice Crying in the Wilderness.* Kansas City, Missouri: By the author, 1902; reprints: Baxter Springs, Kansas: Apostolic Faith Bible College, 1910; Joplin, Missouri: Joplin Printing Co., 1944.
Parham, Charles F./Parham, Sarah E., *Selected Sermons*
  _____. and Sarah E. Parham. *Selected Sermons of the Late Charles F. Parham and Sarah E. Parham.* Compiled by Robert L. Parham. Baxter Springs, Kansas: By the compiler, 1941.
Parham, Sarah E., *Life*
  Parham, Sarah E. *The Life of Charles F. Parham, Founder of the Apostolic Faith Movement,* Joplin, Missouri: Tri–State Printing Co. 1930; reprint: Birmingham, Alabama: Commercial Printing Co. 1977; reprint in *The Higher Christian Life,* vol. 35.
Parrat, *Reader in African Christian Theology*
  Parrat, John (ed.). *A Reader in African Christian Theology.* London: SPCK, 1987.
Parsons, *Healing*
  Parsons, Stephen. *The Challenge of Christian Healing.* London: SPCK, 1986.
Pascal, *Pensées*
  Pascal, Blaise. *Pensées.* Texte de l'édition Brunschvicg. Introduction par Ch.-Marc Granges. Paris: Garnier Frères, n.d.

Pate, "Pentecostal Missions from the Two-Thirds World"
 Pate, Larry D. "Pentecostal Missions from the Two-Thirds World." *Called,* 242–58.
Patterson, *Holy Convocation*
 Patterson, J. O. (ed.). *Holy Convocation Church of God in Christ 1969.* Memphis, Tenn.:
 Church of God in Christ Publ., 1969.
Pattison, "Behavioral"
 Pattison, E. Mansell. "Behavioral Science Research on the Nature of Glossolalia."
 Journal of the American Scientific Affiliation 20, 1968, 73–86.
Pattison, "Effects"
 ———. "The Effects of a Religious Culture's Values on Personality Psychodynamics."
 Read to Section H, Anthropology, American Association for the Advancement of
 Science, December 1965.
Pattison, "Speaking"
 ———. "Speaking in Tongues and About Tongues." *Christian Standard* 99, Feb. 15,
 1964, 3–5.
Paul, "Antwort"
 Paul, Jonathan. "Antwort an Pastor Thimme." *Pfingstgrüsse* 6 (March 1, 1914), 168ff.
Paul, "Beantwortung"
 ———. "Beantwortung von Fragen." *Pfingstgrüsse* 2, Oct. 1909, 8; 2, July 24, 1910, 151.
Paul, *Die Taufe*
 ———. *Die Taufe in ihrem Vollsinn.* Mülheim: Verlag der Gesellschaft für Mission,
 Diakonie und Kolportage m.b.H. 1930.
Paul, "Herz"
 ———. "Das reine Herz." *Die Heiligung* 139 (April 1910).
Paul, *Kraft*
 ———. *Ihr werdet die Kraft des Heiligen Geistes empfangen.* Altdorf/Nbg.: Pranz, 1896,
 1956[3].
Paul, "Krone"
 ———. "Um eine unvergängliche Krone." *Heilszeugnisse* 23 (June 23, 1931), 165.
Paul, "Sollen"
 ———. "Was sollen und wollen die Pfingstgrüsse." *Pfingstgrüsse* 1, Febr. 1909, 2.
Paul, *Taufe*
 ———. *Taufe und Geistestaufe: Ein Beitrag zur Lösung einer ungemein wichtigen Frage,
 besonders auch für solche, welche in Gewissensbedenken sich befinden.* Berlin: Deutsche
 Evangelische Buch- und Tractat-Gesellschaft, 1894, 1896, 1898.
Paul, "Verhältnis"
 ———. "Das Verhältnis von natürlicher Begabung und Geistesgaben." *Pfingstgrüsse* 8,
 (March 26, 1916), 201–3; 8 (April 2, 1916), 209–11.
Pauwels/Bergier, *Aufbruch*
 Pauwels, L., and J. Bergier. *Aufbruch ins dritte Jahrtausend.* Bern/Munich, 1970[5].
PE
 Pentecostal Evangel
Pejsti, *Zasady*
 Pejsti, N. I. (ed.). *Zasady wiary Kościoła Chrześcijan Wiary. Ewangeliczney w Polsce.*
 Ketrszyn, woj. Olsztyńskie, skrz. poczt. N-4 (Poland), 1948.
Pemberton, *A Study of Caribbean Religions*
 Pemberton, Eric E. *A Study of Caribbean Religions.* M.phil. Birmingham, 1988.
Peñafiel, *Cantares Mexicanos*
 Peñafiel, Antonio. *Cantares Mexicanos.* Ms de la Biblioteca Nacional, Copia fotográfica.
 Mexico 1904.
Pentecostal Assemblies of the World, *1963 Minute Book*
 Pentecostal Assemblies of the World. *1963 Minute Book of the Pentecostal Assemblies of
 the World.* n. p., 1963.
The Pentecostals
 English editions: Walter J. Hollenweger. *The Pentecostals.* London: SCM, 1972, 1976[2]

American editions: Walter J. Hollenweger. *The Pentecostal and Charismatic Movements.* Minneapolis, Minn.: Augsburg Publ. House, 1972, 1976[2]. *The Pentecostals.* Peabody, Mass.: Hendrickson, 1988[3] (revised). Latin American edition: Walter J. Hollenweger. *El Pentecostalismo. Historia y Doctrina.* Buenos Aires: La Aurora, 1976. German edition: Walter J. Hollenweger. *Enthusiastisches Christentum. Die Pfingstbewegung in Geschichte und Gegenwart,* Zurich: Zwingli Verlag; Wuppertal: Theologischer Verlag Rolf Brockhaus, 1969. The different editions do not exactly correspond.

Pentecostal Tracts
Three Early Pentecostal Tracts. Ed. by Donald W. Dayton, 1910, ca. 1907, 1916. Reprint in *The Higher Christian Life,* vol. 14.

Pérez-Torrez, *Puerto Rico*
Pérez-Torrez, Rubén. *Classical Pentecostalism in Puerto Rico. History, Catholic Roots and Its Theological Significance.* Unpubl. Th.D. diss., University of Fribourg, Switzerland.

Peter, *Geschichte*
Peter, L. *Geschichte der Bischöflichen Methodistenkirche in der Schweiz.* Bremen and Zurich, 1893.

Petersen, "Kingdom"
Petersen, Douglas. "The Kingdom of God and the Hermeneutical Circle: Pentecostal Praxis in the Third World." *Called,* 44–58.

Pfingstjubel
Pfingstjubel. Altdorf/Nbg.: Missionsbuchhandlung und Verlag, 1956.

Pfister, "Culture"
Pfister, Raymond. "Culture and Change: Pentecostalism in the Making in Alsace, France." SPS 1990 E.

Pfister, *Soixante*
_____. *Soixante ans de Pentecôtisme en Alsace (1930–1990). Une approche socio-historique.* IC 93, 1995.

Pfleiderer–Bichman, *Krankheit*
Pfleiderer, Beatrix and Wolfgang Bichman. *Krankheit und Kultur. Eine Einführung in Ethnomedizin.* Berlin, 1985.

Pickthorn, *Manual*
Pickthorn, W. E. (ed.). *Minister's Manual.* Springfield, Mo.: Gospel Publishing House, 1965, 3 vols.

Piepkorn, *Religious Bodies*
Piepkorn, A. C. *Profiles in Belief. The Religious Bodies of the United States and Canada.* Vol. III: *Holiness and Pentecostal.* San Francisco and London: Harper & Row, 1979.

Pinnock, "Evangelism"
Pinnock, Clark H. "Evangelism and Other Living Faiths: An Evangelical Charismatic Perspective." *Brighton,* 208–14.

Plüss, "European"
Plüss, Jean-Daniel. "European Pentecostal Reactions to Totalitarianism: A Study of Ethical Commitment in the 1930s." *EPTA Bulletin* 4/2, 1985, 40–55; 4/3, 1985, 88–100.

Plüss, *Narratives*
_____. *Therapeutic and Prophetic Narratives in Worship. A Hermeneutic Study of Testimonies and Visions. Their Potential Significance for Christian Worship and Secular Society.* IC 54, 1988.

Plüss, "Public"
_____. "How Public Are Public Testimonies? A Short Reflection on a Liturgical Practice." *EPTA Bulletin* 6/1, 1987, 4–12.

Pneuma
The Journal of the Society for Pentecostal Studies, P.O. Box 2671, Gaithersburg, Md., 20886, USA.

Pobee, *Exploring Afro-Christology*
Pobee, John Samuel (ed.). *Exploring Afro-Christology*. IC 79, 1992.
Poewe, "Introduction"
Poewe, Karla. "Introduction. The Nature, Globality and History of Charismatic Christianity." In Karla Poewe (ed.), *Charismatic Christianity as a Global Culture*, 1–29.
Poewe, "Links and Parallels"
_____. "Links and Parallels Between Black and White Charismatic Churches in South Africa and the States." *Pneuma* 10/2, 1988, 141–58.
Poewe, "Theologies of Black South Africans"
_____. "Theologies of Black South Africans and the Rhetoric of Peace *versus* Violence." *Canadian Journal of African Studies* 27/1, 1993, 43–65.
Poewe-Hexham/Hexham, "Apartheid"
Poewe-Hexham, Karla and Irving Hexham. "Charismatic Churches and Apartheid in South Africa." *Brighton*, 73–83.
Poloma, "Charisma"
Poloma, Margaret M. "Charisma and Institution: The Assemblies of God." *Christian Century* 107/29, 17.10.1990, 932–34.
Poloma, *Crossroads*
_____. *The Assemblies of God at the Crossroads. Charisma and Institutional Dilemma.* n.p., 1990.
Poloma, "Empirical"
_____. "An Empirical Study of Perceptions of Healing Among the Assemblies of God Members." *Pneuma* 7/1, Spring 1985, 61–82.
Pomerville, *Third*
Pomerville, Paul A. *The Third Force in Missions. A Pentecostal Contribution to Mission Theology.* Peabody, Mass.: Hendrickson, 1985.
Pope, *Millhands*
Pope, Liston. *Millhands and Preachers. A Study of Gastonia.* New Haven: Yale University Press, 1942, 1958[4].
Potter, "Charismatic Renewal"
Potter, Philip. "Charismatic Renewal and the World Council of Churches." *Bossey*, 73–87.
Potter, *Das Heil*
_____. (ed.). *Das Heil der Welt heute. Ende oder Beginn der Weltmission? Dokumente der Weltmissionskonferenz Bangkok.* Stuttgart: Kreuz Verlag, 1973.
Potter, "Zur sogenannten Grundlagenkrise der Mission"
_____. Interview "Zur sogenannten Grundlagenkrise der Mission." *Evangelischer Pressedienst, Dokumentation* (Frankfurt) 35/70, 7.9.1970, 7–12; also in *Das Wort in der Welt. Allgemeine Missionsnachrichten* no. 5, Oct. 1970, 146–48.
Poujol, *Cévenne*
Poujol, Pierre. *La Cévenne protestante*, 5 vols. Paris: Published by the author, 29, rue Bonaparte, 1963–67.
Pratt, "Dialogue"
Pratt, Thomas. "The Need to Dialogue: A Review of the Debate on the Controversy of Signs, Wonders, Miracles and Spiritual Warfare Raised in the Literature of the Third Wave Movement." *Pneuma* 13/1, Spring 1991, 7–32.
Prior, *Indonesian*
Prior, John Mansford. *Church and Marriage in an Indonesian Village. A Study of Customary and Church Marriage among the Ata Lio of Central Flores, Indonesia, as a Paradigm of the Ecclesial Interrelationship Between Village and Institutional Catholicism.* IC 55, 1988.
Puharich, *Arigo*
Puharich, A. *The Work of the Brazilian Healer Arigo.* Los Altos, Calif.: Academy of Parapsychology and Medicine, 1971.

Pyun, *Diary*
     Pyun, Chon-ho (ed.). *Minister Yi Yong-do's Diary* (Korean). Seoul: Sinsaengkwan, 1966.
Quebedeaux, *The New Charismatics*
     Quebedeaux, Richard. *The New Charismatics* II. San Francisco: Harper & Row, 1983.
Quy, "Nuns"
     Quy, Douglas. "Pentecostal Nuns." *Redemption Tidings* 54/41, 12.10.1978, 7, 15.
Raiser, "Interview"
     Raiser, Konrad. "Interview." *Der Saemann* (Bern) 109/8, Aug. 1993, 5.
Raj, *Christian Folk Religion*
     Raj, P. Solomon. *Christian Folk Religion in India. A Study of the Small Church Movements in Andhra Pradesh, South India, with a Special Reference to the Bible Mission and the Theological Ideas of its Founder, Father Devadas, and Their Significance to the Mainline Churches in India.* IC 40, 1986.
Ramírez, *Bodas de Oro*
     Ramírez, Raymundo. *Bodas de Oro. Movimiento de la Iglesia Cristiana Independiente Pentecostés.* Pachuco, Hgo: Iglesia Cristiana Independiente Pentecostés, 1972.
Ramírez, "Hilario Aragón"
     _____. "El pastor evangélico Hilario Aragón brutalmente asesinado." *Mensajeres Pentecostés*, quoted from *Pensamiento liberal*, 15.11.1961.
Ramírez-Ramírez, "I Could Have Danced"; German: "Ich hätte"
     Ramírez-Ramírez, Alfredo. "I Could Have Danced . . ." *Monthly Letter About Evangelism.* Geneva: WCC, Oct. 1969. In German: "Ich hätte tanzen mögen . . ." In Hollenweger, *Kirche*, 115–21.
Ranaghan, *Catholic Pentecostals*
     Ranaghan, Kevin and Dorothy. *Catholic Pentecostals.* New York: Paulist Press, 1969.
Ranaghan, *Spirit*
     _____. (eds.). *As the Spirit Leads Us.* New York: Paulist Press, 1971.
Randall, "Importance"
     Randall, Claire. "The Importance of the Pentecostal and Holiness Churches in the Ecumenical Movement." *Pneuma* 9/1, Spring 1987, 50–60.
Ranger, "Medical"
     Ranger, Terence. "Medical Science and Pentecost: The Dilemma of Anglicanism in Africa." In W. J. Sheils (ed.), *The Church and Healing.* 1982, 333–66. (Papers Read at the Twentieth Summer Meeting and the Twenty-First Winter Meeting of the Ecclesiastical Historical Society Oxford, 1982).
Rappleye, "Medicine"
     Rappleye, W. C. "Medicine in New Dimensions." In: *Science, Man's Master or Servant.* New York: Academy of Medicine, Lectures to the Laity, series 24, 1958/59.
Rausch, *Messianic*
     Rausch, David A. *Messianic Judaism: Its History, Theology, and Polity* (Texts and Studies in Religion, vol. 14). New York: Edwin Mellen Press, 1982.
Raymaekers, "Kimbanguisme"
     Raymaekers, Paul. "D'un évangile à une église. Note sur le Kimbanguisme et la diversité de ses images." *Archives de sociologie des religions* 16/31, 1971, 7–14.
Raymaekers, *Zaïre*
     _____. "L'Eglise de Jésus-Christ sur la terre par le prophète Simon Kimbangu: contribution à l'étude des mouvements messianiques dans le Bas-Kongo." *Zaïre* 13/7, 1959, 675–756.
Record
     Record of the Convention for the Promotion of Scriptural Holiness Held at Brighton, May 29th to June 7th, 1875. Reprint in *The Higher Christian Life*, vol. 39.
Reddy, *New Covenant*
     Reddy, Sr. Mary. *New Covenant* 1/9, March 1972, 10–13, 21.
Reed, "Assemblies"
     Reed, David A. "Pentecostal Assemblies of the World." *Dictionary*, 700f.

Reed, "Oneness"
_____. "Oneness Pentecostalism." *Dictionary*, 644–51.
Regehly, "Sehend"
Regehly, P. "Sehend." *Auf der Warte* 3/31, 29.7.1906, 4f.
Reimer, H.-D., *Wenn der Geist in der Kirche wirken*
Reimer, Hans-Diether. *Wenn der Geist in der Kirche wirken will. Ein Vierteljahrhundert charismatische Bewegung*. Stuttgart: Quell Verlag, 1987.
Reimer, I., "Neue Gemeindebildungen"
Reimer, Ingrid. "Neue Gemeindebildungen." *MD* 54/8, 1.8.1991, 245–52.
Relevant Pentecostal Witness
A Relevant Pentecostal Witness. Chatsglen, South Africa: Relevant Pentecostal Witness, n.d.
Renewal, "Dialogue"
Renewal 36, Dec. 1971/Jan. 1972, 10f.: "Dialogue Between Roman Catholics and Charismatics Starts in 1972."
Renewal, "Orthodox"
_____. 45, June/July 1973, 25f.: "The Orthodox Church."
Rhine, "Introduction"
Rhine, J. B. "How to Cope with a Mystery: Introduction." In Cavendish, *Encyclopedia*, 11–18.
Rice, *Actas*
Rice, n.i. *Actas de la conferencia metodista*. Valparaiso 4–11 de febrero 1910, n.p., n.d.
Richardson, *Miracle*
Richardson, A. *The Miracle Stories of the Gospel*. London, 1941.
Riss, "Durham"
Riss, Richard. "Durham, William H. (1873–1912)," *Dictionary*, 255f.
Riss, "1948"
_____. "The Latter Rain Movement of 1948." *Pneuma* 3/1, Spring 1981, 32–45.
Riss, "Women"
_____. "Women, Role of." *Dictionary*, 893–99.
The Road to Damascus
The Road to Damascus: Kairos and Conversion. Johannesburg: Skotaville Publ., 1989.
Robeck, "Apostolicity"
Robeck, Cecil M. Jr. "A Pentecostal Perspective on Apostolicity." Faith and Order NCCUSA, "American Born Churches." March 1992, unpubl.
Robeck, "Authority"
_____. "Written Prophecies: A Question of Authority." *Pneuma* 2/2, Fall 1981, 26–45.
Robeck, "Azusa"
_____. "Azusa Street Revival." *Dictionary*, 31–36.
Robeck, "Bartleman"
_____. "Bartleman, Frank (1871–1953)." *Dictionary*, 50f.
Robeck, "Canberra", 1992
_____. "A Pentecostal Reflects on Canberra." unpubl. paper ca. 1992.
Robeck, "Canberra", 1993
_____. "A Pentecostal Reflects on Canberra." In Bruce J. Nicholls and Bong Rin Ro (eds.), *Beyond Canberra. Evangelical Responses to Contemporary Ecumenical Issues*. Oxford: Regnum Books, 1993, 108–20.
Robeck, "Canon"
_____. "Canon, *Regula Fidei*, and continuing revelation in the Early Church." In James E. Bradley and Richard A. Muller (eds.), *Church, Word and Spirit. Historical and Theological Essays in Honor of Geoffrey W. Bromiley*. Grand Rapids, Mich.: 1987, 65–92.
Robeck, "Carothers"
_____. "Carothers, Warren Fay (1872–1953)." *Dictionary*, 108f.
Robeck, "Catholics"
_____. "What Should Roman Catholics Know About Pentecostals?" *The Catholic World*, Nov.–Dec. 1995.

Robeck, Conversation
_____. Conversation, July 1993.
Robeck, "Du Plessis"
_____. "David Du Plessis and the Challenge of Dialogue." *Pneuma* 9/1, 1987, 1–4.
Robeck, "Ecclesiology"
_____. "The Ecclesiology of Koinonia and Baptism." *Journal of Ecumenical Studies* 27/3, Summer 1990, 504–34 (with Jerry L. Sandidge).
Robeck, "Ecumenical Cooperation"
_____. "The Assemblies of God and Ecumenical Cooperation: 1920–1965." In Wonsuk Ma and Robert Menzies (eds.), *Pentecostalism in Context: Essays in Honor of William W. Menzies.* (Journal of Pentecostal Theology Suppl. series). Sheffield Academic Press, 1996, 107–50.
Robeck, "Ethics"
_____. "Pentecostals and Social Ethics" *Pneuma* 5/2, Fall 1987, 103–7.
Robeck, "Frank Bartleman"
_____. "The Writings and Thought of Frank Bartleman." Introduction to reprints vol. 5 (*Witness to Pentecost,* vii–xxvii) in *The Higher Christian Life,* vol. 5.
Robeck, "Growing"
_____. "Growing Up Pentecostal." *Theology News and Notes* (Fuller Theological Seminary) 35/1, March 1988, 4–7, 26.
Robeck, "Haywood"
_____. "Haywood, Garfield Thomas (1880–1931)." *Dictionary,* 349f.
Robeck, "Implications"
_____. "Pentecostals and the Apostolic Faith: Implications for Ecumenism." *Pneuma* 9/1, Spring 1987, 61–84.
Robeck, "McDonnell"
_____. "McDonnell, Kilian (1921–)." *Dictionary,* 566f.
Robeck, "McPherson"
_____. "McPherson, Aimee Semple." *Dictionary,* 568–71.
Robeck, "Memphis"
_____. "The Memphis Miracle." *Ministries Today* 13/1, Jan./Feb. 1995, 36–73.
Robeck, "Mission"
_____. "Mission and the Issue of Proselytism." *Int. Bulletin of Missionary Research,* 20/1, Jan. 1996, 1–8.
Robeck, "National"
_____. "National Association of Evangelicals." *Dictionary,* 634–36.
Robeck, "Origins"
_____. "Pentecostal Origins in Global Perspective." *Brighton,* 166–80.
Robeck, "Pentecostals and Ecumenism"
_____. "Pentecostals and Ecumenism. An Expanding Frontier." paper given at the Pentecostal Research Conference, Kappel, Switzerland, 1991.
Robeck, "Perspectives"
_____. "Pentecostal Perspectives and the Ecumenical Challenge." dupl. typescript, unpubl. n.d., available from the author.
Robeck, "Pike"
_____. "Pike, John Martin (1840–1932)." *Dictionary,* 715.
Robeck, "Pope"
_____. "What the Pope Said." *Commonweal* 18, December 1992, 30f.
Robeck, *Prophecy*
_____. *Prophecy in Carthage. Perpetua, Tertullian and Cyprian.* Cleveland, Ohio: The Pilgrim Press, 1992.
Robeck, "Seymour"
_____. "William J. Seymour and 'The Bible Evidence.' " In McGee, *Initial Evidence,* 72–95.
Robeck, "Signs"
_____. "Signs, Wonders and Witness." *Pneuma* 3/2, Fall 1982, 1–5.

Robeck, "Social Concern"
_____. "The Social Concern of Early American Pentecostalism." In Jongeneel, 1992, 97–106.
Robeck, "Society"
_____. "The Society for Pentecostal Studies." *Ecumenical Trends* (Graymoor Ecumenical Institute, Garrison, New York) 14/2, Feb. 1985, 28–30.
Robeck, "Southern"
_____. "Southern Religion With a Latin Accent." *Pneuma,* 13/2, 1991, 101–6.
Robeck, "Specks"
_____. "Specks and Logs. Catholics and Pentecostals." *Pneuma* 12/2, 1990, 77–83.
Robeck, "Taking Stock"
_____. "Taking Stock of Pentecostalism: The Personal Reflections of a Retiring Editor." *Pneuma* 15/1, 1993, 35–60.
Robeck, "Unity"
_____. "Revisioning the Unity We Seek: The Calling of Faith and Order." *Ecumenical Trends* (forthcoming).
Robeck, "Where?"
_____. "Where Do We Go From Here?" *Pneuma* 7/1, 1985, 1–5.
Robeck, "Williams"
_____. "Williams, Ernest Swing (1885–1981)." *Dictionary,* 886f.
Robeck, *Witness*
_____. (ed.). *Witness to Pentecost: The Life of Frank Bartleman,* 1925, ca. 1926. Reprint *The Higher Christian Life,* vol. 5.
Robeck, "World Council"
_____. "A Pentecostal Looks at the World Council of Churches." *Ecumenical Review* 47/1, Jan. 1995, 60–69.
Robeck, "Yeomans"
_____. "Yeomans, Lilian Barbary (1861–1942)." *Dictionary,* 907.
Robeck, "Yoakum"
_____. "Yoakum, Finis Ewing (1851–1920)." *Dictionary,* 907f.
Robeck, Patsy, "Ecumenical Ministry in the Hospital"
Robeck, Patsy. "Ecumenical Ministry in the Hospital." *Occasional Papers* of the Institute for Ecumenical and Cultural Research, Collegeville, Minnesota, May 1991, 7–11.
Robert, "Dallière"
Robert, Daniel. "Dallière, Louis." In *Dictionnaire du monde religieux dans la France contemporaine,* 5: *Les Protestants.* Paris: Beauchesne, 1993, 160f.
Roberts, Mark E., "Weakness"
Roberts, Mark E. "Weakness and Power. The Contribution of 2 Corinthians 10–13 to a Pentecostal Charismatic Spirituality." SPS 1992, N.
Roberts, Oral, *The Call*
Roberts, Oral. *The Call. An Autobiography.* London: Hodder & Stoughton, 1971.
Roberts, Oral. "Fe contra"
_____. "Fe contra las tormentas de la vida," *Mensajero Pentecostés,* 3/8, April/May 1964, 9–11.
Robin, "Chronology"
Robin, Roger. "A Chronology of Peace. Attitudes Toward War and Peace in the Assemblies of God 1914–18." *Pneuma* 6/1, Spring 1984, 3–26.
Robinson, *Oral*
Robinson, Wayne A. *Oral. The Warm, Intimate, Unauthorized Portrait of a Man of God.* Los Angeles, California: Acton House Inc. 1976.
Robinson, *Spoke*
_____. *I Once Spoke in Tongues.* Wheaton, Ill.: Tyndale House Publishers, 1973.

Robinson, *Clergymen*
    Robinson, Martin. *Two Anglican Pentecostal Clergymen—a Comparison Between the Life and Work of Alexander A. Boddy and Michael C. Harper.* Unpubl. M.Litt. University of Birmingham, 1976.
Robinson, "David Du Plessis"
    ———. "David Du Plessis—A Promise Fulfilled." In Jongeneel, 1992, 143–56.
Robinson, *To the Ends of the Earth*
    ———. *To the Ends of the Earth. The Pilgrimage of an Ecumenical Pentecostal, David J. Du Plessis.* Ph.D. University of Birmingham, 1987.
Rochat, *Regime*
    Rochat, Giorgio. *Regime fascista e chiese evangeliche.* Collana della Società di Studi Valdesi 12. Torino: Claudiana, 1990.
Röckle, "Biblische"
    Röckle, Christian. "Die biblische und die geistige Entrückungslehre." *Philadelphiabrief* 15/165–66, March-April 1963, 2–13.
Roebuck, "Brothers"
    Roebuck, David G. "Go and Tell My Brothers: The Waning of Women's Voices in American Pentecostalism." SPS 1990, F.
Rolim, *Pentecostais*
    Rolim, Francisco Cartaxo. *Pentecostais no Brasil. Uma interpretacão sócio-religiosa.* Petrópolis: Vozes, 1985.
Rosas, "Música"
    Rosas, Carlos. "La Música al Servicio del Reino." *Apuntes: Reflexiones teológicas desde el Margen Hispano* 6, Spring 1986, 3–6.
Rose, *Sent*
    Rose, William Ernest. *Sent from Coventry. A Mission of International Reconciliation.* London: Oswald Wolff, 1980.
Ross, *Gee*
    Ross, R. M. *Donald Gee: In Search of a Church. A Sectarian in Transition.* Th.D. thesis, Knox College, Toronto, 1974.
Ross, "Sectarian"
    ———. "Donald Gee: Sectarian in Search of a Church." *Evangelical Quarterly* 50, 1978, 94–103.
Rottmann, "Mülheim-Ruhr"
    Rottmann, H. "Bericht vom Hauptbrüdertag in Mülheim-Ruhr vom 8.-10.10.1968." *Heilszeugnisse* 53, Dec. 1, 1968, 179f.
Roux, *Désunion*
    Roux, Hébert. *De la désunion vers la communion. Un itinéraire pastoral et oecuménique.* Paris: Le Centurion, 1978.
Runyon, *Sanctification and Liberation*
    Runyon, Theodore (ed.). *Sanctification and Liberation.* Nashville: Abingdon, 1981.
Rusch, "Theology"
    Rusch, William G. "The Theology of the Holy Spirit and the Pentecostal Churches in Ecumenical Movement." *Pneuma* 9/1, Spring 1987, 17–30.
Rutenborn, "Theologie"
    Rutenborn, Günter. "Beitrage zur Theologie des Jazz." *Musik und Kirche* 28/2, March/April 1958, 65–69.
Ryckmans, *Les mouvements prophétiques du kongo*
    Ryckmans, A. (ed.). *Les mouvements prophétiques du kongo en 1958. Contribution à l'étude de l'histoire du Congo.* Kinshasa: Bureau d'Organisation des Programmes Ruraux, 1970 (reprinted from *N'Konge-Kongo,* 1964, no. 7).
Saayman, "Some Reflections"
    Saayman, Willem. "Some Reflections on the Development of the Pentecostal Model in South Africa." *Missionalia* 21/1, April 1993, 40–56.

Sai, "Planning"
Sai, F. T. "Planning for the Health Needs of the People." *Ghana Medical Journal,* Sept. 1965, 108–12.

Samarin, *Tongues*
Samarin, William J. *Tongues of Men and Angels. The Religious Language of Pentecostalism.* New York and London: Collier-Macmillan, 1970.

Sampedro, *Pentecostalismo*
Sampedro, N. Francisco, c. m. (ed.). *Pentecostalismo, sectas y pastoral.* Santiago: Comisión Nacional de Ecumenismo, 1989.

Sampson, *The Neglected Ethics*
Sampson, Chris. *The Neglected Ethics.* London: n.p., 1982.

Sandeen, *Roots*
Sandeen, Ernest R. *The Roots of Fundamentalism: British and American Millenarianism 1800–1930.* Chicago: University of Chicago Press, 1970.

Sandidge, "Consultation Summary"
Sandidge, Jerry L. "Consultation Summary: A Pentecostal Perspective." *Pneuma* 9/1, Spring 1987, 96–98.

Sandidge, "Dialogue"
———. "Roman Catholic/Pentecostal Dialogue: A Contribution to Christian Unity." *Pneuma* 7/1, Spring 1985, 41–60.

Sandidge, *Dialogue (1977–1982)*
———. *Roman Catholic/Pentecostal Dialogue (1977–1982). A Study in Developing Ecumenism.* IC 44, 1987, 2 vols.

Sandidge, "Kuzmič"
———. "Kuzmič, Peter (1946–)." *Dictionary,* 530.

Sandru, *Doctrinele*
Sandru, Trandafir. *Doctrinele Biblice ale Bisericii.* Bukarest: Editura Cultului Pentecostal Biserica lui Dumnezeu Apostolica din Republica Socialista Romania, 1989.

Sandru, "Rumänien"
———. "Rumänien." In Hollenweger, *Pfingstkirchen,* 82–90.

Saracco, *Argentine*
Saracco, José Norberto. *Argentine Pentecostalism. Its History and Theology.* Ph.D. Birmingham, 1990.

Schaefer, *Medizin*
Schaefer, Hans. *Die Medizin in unserer Zeit. Theorie, Forschung, Lehre.* Munich 1963[2].

Schaeffer, *Portofino*
Schaeffer, Frank. *Portofino. A Novel.* New York: Macmillan, 1992.

Schaerer–Richemond, *Retour*
Schaerer, Henri, and René de Richemond. *Retour historique sur les origines de l'Union de Prière.* Speeches given August 24, 1969, in the Reformed Church of Charmes, mimeographed.

Schäfer, "Dualistische"
Schäfer, Heinrich. "Dualistische Religion aus gesellschaftlichen Gegensätzen. Gesellschaftliche Krise und Nachfrage im Protestantismus Mittelamerikas." *Wege zum Menschen* 41/2, Febr./March 1989, 52–70.

Schäfer, " . . .und erlöse uns von dem Bösen"
———. " . . .und erlöse uns von dem Bösen. Zur politischen Funktion des Fundamentalismus in Mittelamerika." In Uwe Birnstein (ed.), *"Gottes einzige Antwort . . ." Christlicher Fundamentalismus als Herausforderung an Kirche und Gesellschaft.* Wuppertal: Peter Hammer, 1990, 118–39.

Schäfer, "Wo der Geist des Herrn ist"
———. "Wo der Geist des Herrn ist, da ist Freiheit" (2. Kor. 3.17). Oekumenische Ueberlegungen zur charismatischen Bewegung. Eine Einladung zum Gespräch. November 1992, privately printed, available from Heinrich Schäfer, University of Bochum, Germany.

Schäfer, *Zentralamerika*
_____. *Protestantismus in Zentralamerika. Christliches Zeugnis im Spannungsfeld von US-amerikanischem Fundamentalismus, Unterdrückung und Wiederbelebung "indianischer" Kultur.* IC 84, 1992.

Scheel, *Dokumente*
Scheel, Otto (ed.). *Dokumente zu Luthers Entwicklung.* Tübingen, 1929.

Schiavone, *I Pentecostali*
Schiavone, Saverio. *I Pentecostali di Accadia e del Suappenino.* Ph.D. University of Bari, 1968/69, unpubl.

Schick–Talbert, *La Iglesia Metodista Pentecostal*
Schick, Alice Rasmussen and Dean Helland Talbert. *La Iglesia Metodista Pentecostal. Ayer y hoy.* Santiago: Iglesia Metodista Pentecostal de Chile, 1987.

Schippers, "Julio"
Schippers, n. i. "Julio de Santa Ana: Economie is zoiets als religioe." *Trouw,* 20th January, 1988.

Schlosser, *Eingeborenenkirchen*
Schlosser, Katesa. *Eingeborenenkirchen in Süd- und Südwestafrika, ihre Geschichte und Sozialstruktur. Ergebnisse einer völkerkundlichen Studien-Studienreise.* Mühlau: Walter, 1953.

Schmid, "Christliches"
Schmid, Otto. "Christliches Zentrum Trimmis GR." *Informationsblatt* 31/2, June 1994, 20–21.

Schmid, "Die Dritte Welle"
_____. "Die Dritte Welle." *Informationsblatt* 31/2, June 1994, 16–20; 31/3, Aug. 1994, 30–33.

Schmidt, Martin, *John Wesley*
Schmidt, Martin. *John Wesley. A Theological Biography.* London: Epworth Press, I, 1962 (translated from the German).

Schmidt, Wolfgang, *Finnland*
Schmidt, Wolfgang. *Die Pfingstbewegung in Finnland.* Helsinki: Kirchengeschichtliche Gesellschaft Finnlands, 1935.

Schmithals, *Lukas*
Schmithals, Walter. *Das Evangelium nach Lukas.* Zürcher Bibelkommentare NT 3.1. Zurich: TVZ, 1980.

Schmieder, *Geisttaufe*
Schmieder, Lucida. OSB, *Geisttaufe. Ein Beitrag zur neueren Glaubensgeschichte* Paderborn: Schöningh, 1982.

Schulgen, "Heaven"
Schulgen, F. J. "I Knew That Heaven Begins on Earth." *Testimony,* 4/1 First Quarter 1965, 1–7.

Schulz, *Die Bedeutung*
Schulz, Walter. *Die Bedeutung der vom angelsächsischen Meethodismus beeinflussten Liederdichtung für unsere deutschen Kirchengesänge illustriert an den Liedern von Ernst Gebhard. Ein Beitrag zur Geschichte der Frömmigkeit.* Greifswald, 1934.

Schwab, "Charismes"
Schwab, Jean-Claude. "Charismes et médiations. Ou Comment le Saint-Esprit intervient dans la vie des hommes." *Hokhma, Revue de réflexion théologique* (Switzerland) no. 43, 1990, 11–24.

Schwarz, *Die Dritte Reformation*
Schwarz, Christian A. *Die Dritte Reformation. Paradigmenwechsel in der Kirche.* Neukirchen-Vluyn: Aussaat Verlag, 1993.

Schweizer, *Kolosser*
Schweizer, Ed. *Der Brief an die Kolosser* (Evangelisch-Katholischer Kommentar). Zurich/Neukirchen-Vluyn: Neukirchner Verlag, 1976.

Schweizer, *Matthäus;* English: *Matthew*
_____. *Das Evangelium nach Matthäus* (NTD 2). Göttingen: Vandenhoeck & Ruprecht, 1973. English: *The Good News According to Matthew.* London: SPCK, 1979.
Schweizer, *Order*
_____. *Church Order in the New Testament.* London: SCM, 1961.
Schweizer, "pneuma"
_____. "pneuma." *Theological Dictionary of the New Testament* (1968), 6.396–451.
Schweizer, "Spirit"
_____. "Spirit of God." In G. Kittel (ed.), *Bible Key Words.* London: A. & C. Black, vol. 9, 1960, and New York: Harper & Row, III/1, 1961.
Scopuli, *Il combattimento spirituale*
Scopuli, Lorenzo. *Il combattimento spirituale.* English: Juan de Castañiza, *The Christian Pilgrim in His Spiritual Conflict and Conquest* (in two parts, Paris 1652 and further editions). Latin: *Pugna spiritualis sive de perfectione vitae Christianae.* Tractatus aureos: A. R. P. Ionne Castanzia, Ord. S. Benedicti, Editio novissima ad exemplar Hispanicum. Herbipoli (Würzburg): author, 1641, Dillingen, 1640, Cologne 1663, 1666, Lyon 1643. German: G. Wettstein, 1934.
Scott, "Fletcher"
Scott, P. "Fletcher, John William (1729–85)." *Religion in Geschichte und Gegenwart* II (1958), 977.
Scougal, *Life*
Scougal, Henry. *The Life of God in the Soul of Man: or the Nature and Excellency of the Christian Religion. With the Methods of Attaining the Happiness which it Proposes. As an Account of the Beginnings and Advance of a Spiritual Life. With a preface by Bilbert Burnet, late Lord of Sarum.* London, 1733[6], 1770 (abridged).
Scougal, *Henry Scougal*
_____. *Henry Scougal. The Life of God in the Soul of Man.* 1733; 4th ed. 1944 by W. S. Hudson. Philadelphia: n.p., 1944.
SE
Schweizer Evangelist
Sengupta, *Pandita Ramabai*
Sengupta, Padmini. *Pandita Ramabai Saraswati. Her Life and Work.* London, Bombay, etc.: Asia Publ. House, 1970.
Sepúlveda, "Liberation"
Sepúlveda, Juan. "Pentecostalism and Liberation Theology: Two Manifestations of the Work of the Holy Spirit for the Renewal of the Church." *Brighton,* 51–64.
Sepúlveda, "Pentecostalism"
_____. "Pentecostalism and Popular Religiosity." *Int. Review of Mission* 78, Jan. 1989, 80–88.
Sepúlveda, "Perspective"
_____. "The Perspective of Chilean Pentecostalism." *Journal of Pentecostal Theology* 4, April 1994, 41–49.
Sepúlveda, "Reflections"
_____. Reflections on the Pentecostal Contribution to the Mission of the Church in Latin America, unpubl. paper Buenos Aires, April 1989.
Sepúlveda, "Struggle"
_____. "Pentecostal Theology in the Context of the Struggle of Life." In Dow Kirkpatrick (ed.), *Faith Born in the Struggle of Life.* Grand Rapids, Mich.: Eerdmans, 1988, 298–318.
Sepúlveda, "3a Asamblea"
_____. "3a Asamblea del Consejo Latinoamericano de Iglesias Concepción Chile." *Evangelio y Sociedad* no. 18, July-Sept. 1993, 21–25.
Setiloane, "Traditional"
Setiloane, Gabriel. "How the Traditional World View Persists in the Christianity of the Sotho-Twsana." In Fasholé-Luke, *Christianity in Independent Africa,* 402–412.

Sheppard, "Dispensationalism"
    Sheppard, Gerald T. "Pentecostals and the Hermeneutics of Dispensationalism: The
    Anatomy of an Uneasy Relationship." *Pneuma* 6/2, Fall 1984, 5–33.
Sheppard, "Nicene"
    _____. "The Nicene Creed, *Filioque,* and the Pentecostal Movements in the United
    States." Ecumenical Perspectives on the Holy Spirit." *The Greek Orthodox Theological
    Review,* 31, 3–4, 1986.
Sheppard, "Tradition"
    _____. "Word and Spirit: Scripture in the Pentecostal Tradition." *Agora* 1/4, Spring
    1978, 4–5, 17–22; 2/1, Summer 1978, 14–19.
Shepperd, "Worship"
    Shepperd, J. W. "Worship." *Dictionary,* 903–05.
Sherman, *Wonderhealers*
    Sherman, M. *Wonderhealers of the Philippines.* Los Angeles: n.p., 1967.
Sherrill, *Tongues*
    Sherrill, John L. *They Speak With Other Tongues.* Westwood, N.J.: Spire Books, 1965.
Shorter, *Jesus*
    Shorter, Aylward. *Jesus and the Witchdoctors.* London/New York: n.p., 1985.
Shuman, "Patriotism"
    Shuman, Joel. "Pentecost and the End of Patriotism. A Call for the Restoration of
    Pacifism Among Pentecostal Christians." *Journal of Pentecostal Theology* 9, 1996, 70–96.
Si ahora vivimos
    Si ahora vivimos per el espiritu dejemos también que el espiritu nos guíe *(Si ahora
    vivimos per el espiritu dejemos también que el espiritu nos guíe).* Unpubl. Buenos Aires
    1989.
Simmonds, *"A Portrayal of Identity"*
    Simmonds, Martin H. *"A Portrayal of Identity."* A Study of the Life and Worship of the
    First United Church of Jesus Christ (Apostolic) U.K.* M.Phil. University of Birmingham,
    1988.
Simpfendörfer, *Offene Kirche*
    Simpfendörfer, Werner. *Offene Kirche, kritische Kirche.* Stuttgart: Kreuz-Verlag, 1969.
Sinclair, "Solidarity"
    Sinclair, John H. "A New Pentecostal: Hope in Solidarity." *The Christian Century* 106:3
    (25 January 1989).
Sinda, *Le messianisme congolais*
    Sinda, Martial. *Le messianisme congolais et ses incidences politiques. Kimbanguisme
    matrsouanisme, autres mouvements.* Paris: Payot, 1972.
Singleton, "Direction"
    Singleton, Michael. "Spirit and 'Spiritual Direction': the Pastoral Counseling of the
    Possessed." In Fasholé-Luke, *Christianity in Independent Africa,* 471–78.
Sjögreen, "Pingsrörelsens organisationsformer"
    Sjögreen, Holger. "Pingsrörelsens organisationsformer." *Dagen* 27.2.1974.
Slootweg, "Mujeres"
    Slootweg, Hanneke. "Mujeres pentecostales chilenos. Un caso en Iquique." In Barbara
    Boudewinse, André Droogers and Frans Kamsteeg (eds.), *Algo más que opio. Una lectura
    antropológica del pentecostalismo latinoamericano y caribeño.* San José, Costa Rica:
    Departamento Ecuménico de Investigaciones, Sabanilla, 1991, 77–94.
Smedes, *Ministry*
    Smedes, Lewis B. (ed.). *Ministry and the Miraculous. A Case Study at Fuller Theological
    Seminary.* Pasadena, California: Fuller Theological Seminary, 1987.
Smeeton, "Missiology"
    Smeeton, Donald D. "Toward a Pentecostal Missiology. A Review Article." *EPTA
    Bulletin* 5/4, 1986, 128–36.
Smith, Dennis, "Coming"
    Smith, Dennis. "Coming of Age: A Reflection on Pentecostals, Politics and Popular
    Religion in Guatemala." *Pneuma* 13/2, Fall 1991, 131–39.

Smith, Denis and Gwen, *River*
    Smith, Denis and Gwen. *A River Is Flowing*. St. Agnes, South Australia: Assemblies of God in Australia, 1987.
Smith, Hannah Whitall, *Unselfishness*
    Smith, Hannah Whitall. *The Unselfishness of God and How I Discovered It*. 1903. Reprint in *The Higher Christian Life*, vol. 44.
Smith, Oswald J., "Then Jesus Came"
    Smith, Oswald J. "Then Jesus Came." In N. J. Clayton (ed.), *Melodies of Life*. Malverne, N.Y.: Gospel Songs Inc., 1946.
Smith, Robert Pearsall and Hannah Whitall, *Devotional*
    Smith, Robert Pearsall and Hannah Whitall. *The Devotional Writings of Robert Pearsall Smith and Hannah Whitall Smith*. Ed. Donald W. Dayton, 1870, 1885. Reprint in *The Higher Christian Life*, vol. 43.
Smith, Timothy, *Revivalism*
    Smith, Timothy. *Revivalism and Social Reform*. New York, 1957.
Snell, "Beyond the Individual"
    Snell, Jeffrey T. "Beyond the Individual and Into the World: A Call to Participation in the Larger Purposes of the Spirit on the Basis of Pentecostal Theology." *Pneuma* 14/1, Spring 1992, 43–57.
Solivan, "Cultural Glossolalia"
    Solivan, Samuel. "Cultural Glossolalia in Acts 2: A Theological Reassessment of the Importance of Culture and Language." SPS 1994.
Solomon, *Living*
    Solomon, Robert M. *Living in Two Worlds. Pastoral Response to Possession in Singapore*. Ph.D. University of Edinburgh, 1992, publication planned in IC.
Soustelle, *La vie quotidienne*
    Soustelle, Jacques. *La vie quotidienne des Aztèques à la veille de la conquête espagnole*. Paris: Hachette, 1955.
Spencer, *Protest and Praise*
    Spencer, Jon Michael. *Protest and Praise. Sacred Music of Black Religion*. Minneapolis: Fortress Press, 1990.
"Spiritual Life" committee, "Being"
    "Spiritual Life" committee of the Assemblies of God, "Being the People God Called." In *Parish Evangel*, 29.9.1991.
Spittler, "Du Plessis"
    Spittler, R. P. "Du Plessis, David Johannes." *Dictionary*, 250–54.
Spittler, "Fundamentalists"
    _____. "Are Pentecostals and Charismatics Fundamentalists? A Review of American Uses of These Categories." In Karla Poewe (ed.), *Charismatic Christianity as a Global Culture*, 103–16.
Spittler, "Glossolaia"
    _____. "Glossolalia." *Dictionary*, 335–41.
Spittler, "How"
    _____. "How Are Pentecostalism and Fundamentalism Related? In What Way Are Pentecostals Fundamentalists?" Paper given at the conference on "Global Culture: Pentecostal/Charismatic Worldwide," May 9–11, 1991, University of Calgary, Canada.
Spittler, "Implicit"
    _____. "Implicit Values in Pentecostal Mission." *Missiology* 10, April 1988, 421–22.
Spittler, "Menzies"
    _____. "Menzies, William Watson (1931–)." *Dictionary*, 602.
Spittler, "Suggested"
    _____. "Suggested Areas for Further Research in Pentecostal Studies." *Pneuma* 5/2, Fall 1983, 39–57.
SPS
    Society for Pentecostal Studies, papers of the annual conferences, available from *Pneuma*.

Stampe, "Pinsebevegelsen"
Stampe, Laurids. "Pinsebevegelsen." *Illustreret Religionsleksikon* III Copenhagen, 1950, 125–28.
Steady, "Role of Women"
Steady, Filomena Chioma. "The Role of Women in the Churches in Freetown, Sierra Leone." In Fasholé-Luke, *Christianity in Independent Africa,* 151–63.
Steele, "Burdens"
Steele, Minnie A. "My Burdens Rolled Away." *Hymns of Glorious Praise.* Springfield: Gospel Publishing House, 1969, no. 452.
Steiner, B. "Untersuchungen"
Steiner, B. "Historisch-kritische Untersuchungen über den Verfasser des 'Geistlichen Kampfes.' " *Studien und Mitteilungen* 17, 1896, 444–62.
Steiner, L., "Healing"
Steiner, L. "Divine Healing in God's Redemption." In Donald Gee (ed.), *Fifth World Pentecostal Conference. Pentecostal World Conference Messages, preached at the Fifth Triennial World Conference,* held in the Coliseum Arena, Exhibition Ground, Toronto, Canada, from September 14–21, 1958, published by the Advisory Committee for the Conference. Toronto: Testimony Press, 1958, 137–48.
Steiner, L., "Kimbanguistenkirche"
————. "Die Kimbanguistenkirche im Kongo." *Wort und Geist* 2/7, July 1970, n.p.
Steiner, L., *Mit folgenden Zeichen*
————. *Mit folgenden Zeichen. Eine Darstellung der Pfingstbewegung.* Basel: Mission für das volle Evangelium, 1954.
Steiner, L., "Oekumenische"
————. "Oekumenische Konsultation in Gunten." *Heilszeugnisse* 52 (Jan. 1, 1967), 3f.
Stelter, *Psi–Heilung*
Stelter, Alfred. *Psi–Heilung.* Munich, 1977.
Stenholm, "Svenska"
Stenholm, Gustav. "Svenska pinstvännernas skola i Kongo under eget tak efter tio år verskamhet." *Dagen* 8.2.1956, quoted by Axel Blomquist (ed.), *Svenska pingstväckelsen femtio år. En krönika i ord och bild.* Stockholm: Förlaget Filadelfia, 1957, 264.
Stibbe, "Appraisal"
Stibbe, Mark W. G. "A British Appraisal." *Journal of Pentecostal Theology* 4, April 1994, 5–16.
Stiglmeyer, "Medizinmann"
Stiglmeyer, E. "Medizinmann." *Die Religion in Geschichte und Gegenwart,* 3rd ed. VI (1962), 826–28.
Stockmayer, *Gnade*
Stockmayer, Otto. *Gnade und Sünde. Ein Wort an Kinder Gottes.* Basel, 1924[6]. English: *Grace and Sin.* Parthridge: Paternoster Row 9, London, n.d.
Stockwell, "Pentecostal Consultation"
Stockwell, Eugene. "Pentecostal Consultation: Salvador, Brazil: 6–9 January 1988." Unpubl. internal paper of the WCC.
Stone, "Orthodox"
Stone, Derek. "From An Orthodox in Australia." *Aion. Biannual Journal of St. Symeon's Fellowship,* July 1972, 10.
Stott, "Twenty Years"
Stott, John R. W. "Twenty Years After Lausanne: Some Personal Reflections." *International Bulletin of Missionary Research* 19/2, April 1995, 50–55.
Stotts, *Pentecôtisme*
Stotts, G. R. *Pentecôtisme au pays de Voltaire.* F 69290 Craponne (France): Viens et Vois, 1978.
Stout, "Fire-Baptized"
Stout, B. Maurice. "Pentecostal Fire-Baptized Holiness Church." *Dictionary,* 701.
Stout, "Forbes"
————. "Forbes, James Alexander (1935–)." *Dictionary,* 314.

Stout, "Swaggart"
_____. "Swaggart, Jimmy Lee (1935–)." *Dictionary*, 837.

Strachan, *Pentecostal Theology*
Strachan, C. Gordon. *The Pentecostal Theology of Edward Irving*. London: Darton, Longman & Todd, 1973.

Strand/Strøm/Ski, *Urkristendommen*
Strand, Egil, Erling Strøm, Martin Ski (eds.). *Fram til urkristendommen. Pinsevekkelsen, gjenonom 50 år*. Oslo: Filadelfiaforlaget, 1956–59, 3 vols.

Ströbele-Gregor, "Indios"
Ströbele-Gregor, Juliana. "Wir sind die Indios mit der weissen Haut." *Wege zum Menschen* 41/2, Febr./March 1989, 70–87.

Stronstad, "Diversity"
Stronstad, Roger. "Presidential Address. Affirming Diversity: God's People as a Community of Prophets." SPS 1994.

Stronstad, "Experiential"
_____. "Pentecostalism, Experiential Presuppositions and Hermeneutics." SPS 1990.

Stronstad, *Luke*
_____. *The Charismatic Theology of St. Luke*. Peabody, Mass.: Hendrickson, 1984.

Stronstad, "Trends"
_____. "Trends in Pentecostal Hermeneutics" *Paraclete* 22/3, Summer 1988, 1–12.

Stroup, *Promise*
Stroup, George W. *The Promise of Narrative Theology. Recovering the Gospel for the Church*. Atlanta: John Knox Press, 1981.

Struble, *Samfundsfria*
Struble, Rohde. *Den samfundsfria församlingen och die karismatiska gåvorna och tjänsterna. Den Svenska Pingströrelsens församlingssyn 1907–1947*. (Bibliotheca Historico-Ecclesiastica Lundensis 11) Stockholm: Almqvist & Wiksell International, 1982.

Stuhlmacher, *Neuen Testaments*
Stuhlmacher, Peter. *Vom Verstehen des Neuen Testaments. Eine Hermeneutik*. (NTD Erg. 6). Göttingen: Vandenhoeck & Ruprecht, 1979.

Sturm, "Stadtmission"
Sturm, Klaus. "Die 'Tübinger Offensive Stadmission' (TOS)." *MD* 57/6, 1.6.1994, 176–79.

Sudbrack, "Im Spiegel der Zeit"
Sudbrack, Josef. "Im Spiegel der Zeit. Streiflichter des nordamerikanischen Christentums." *Geist und Leben* 43/5, Nov. 1970, 369–87.

Suh, "Forty Years of Korean Protestant Churches: 1945–1985"
Suh, David Kwang. "Forty Years of Korean Protestant Churches: 1945–1985." *Korea and World Affairs: A Quarterly Review* 9/4, 1985.

Sundkler, *Zulu Zion*
Sundkler, Bengt. *Zulu Zion and Some Swazi Zionists*. (Studia Missionalia Upsaliensia XXIV). Oxford: University Press, 1976.

Sundstedt, *Pingstväckelsen*
Sundstedt, Arthur. *Pingstväckelsen—des uppkomst och första utvecklingsskede*. Stockholm: Normans Förlag, 1969ff. 5 vols.

Suurmond, "Christ King"
Suurmond, Jean-Jacques. "Christ King: A Charismatic Appeal for Ecological Lifestyle." *Pneuma* 10/1, 1988, 26–35.

Suurmond, *Ethical*
_____. *The Ethical Influence of the Spirit of God: An Exegetical and Theological Study With Special Reference to I Corinthians, Romans 7:14–8:30 and the Johannine Literature*. Ann Arbor: University Microfilm Int. 1983 (Fuller Theological Seminary, Pasadena, Calif. Ph.D.)

Suurmond, *Word and Spirit at Play*
_____. *Word and Spirit at Play: Towards a Charismatic Theology.* Trans. by John Bowden. Grand Rapids, Mich.: Eerdmans, 1995.

Swantz, "Changing Role"
Swantz, Marja-Liisa. "Church and the Changing Role of Women in Tanzania." In Fasholé-Luke, *Christianity in Independent Africa,* 136–50.

Synan, "Boundaries"
Synan, Harold Vinson. "Theological Boundaries: The Arminian Tradition." *Pneuma* 3/2, 1982, 38–53.

Synan, "Evangelicalism"
_____. "Evangelicalism," *Dictionary,* 281–84.

Synan, *Explosion*
_____. *The Twentieth Century Pentecostal Explosion. The Exciting Growth of Pentecostal Churches and the Charismatic Renewal Movement.* Altamonte Springs, Fla.: Creation House, 1987.

Synan, "Fire-Baptized"
_____. "Fire-Baptized Holiness Church." *Dictionary,* 309.

Synan, "Fundamentalism"
_____. "Fundamentalism" *Dictionary,* 324–27.

Synan, *Holiness-Pentecostal*
_____. *The Holiness-Pentecostal Movement in the United States.* Grand Rapids, Mich.: Eerdmans, 1971.

Synan, "Miracle"
_____. "The Miracle of Memphis. Racial Reconciliation. North American Service Committee." *AD 2000 Time Lines,* Fall 1994, n. p.

Synan, "Pentecostalism"
_____. "Pentecostalism: Varieties and Contributions," *Pneuma* 9/1, 1987, 31–49.

Synan, "Seymour"
_____. "Seymour, William Joseph (1870–1922)." *Dictionary,* 778–81.

Tamez, *Contratoda*
Tamez, Elsa. *Contratoda condena. La justificación por la fé desde los excluidos.* San José: DEI-Sebila, 1991.

Tamez, "Mujer"
_____. "Que la mujer no calle en la congregación." *Evangelio y Sociedad* no. 18, July/Sept. 1993, 28–32.

Tarr, "Preaching"
Tarr, Del. "Preaching the Word in the Power of the Spirit: A Cross-Cultural Analysis." *Called,* 120–36.

Tasie–Gray, "Introduction"
Tasie, Godwin and Richard Gray. "Introduction." In E. Fasholé-Luke, *Christianity in Independent Africa,* 3–15.

"Taylor"
"Jeremy Taylor." *The Dictionary of National Biography,* 1885ff. UK, LV, 422–29.

Taylor, *Discourse*
Taylor, Jeremy. *Discourse of the Liberty of Prophesying.* London, 1648.

Taylor, *Holy Living*
_____. *The Rule and Experience of Holy Living*; in which are described the means and instruments of obtaining every virtue, and the remedies against every vice, and considerations serving to the resisting of all temptations. Together with prayers containing the whole duty of a Christian. London, 1710[21]; New York, 1875; also in Reginald Heber (ed.), *The Whole Works of Jeremy Taylor,* London 1847–54, vol. IV (also in German).

Taylor, *The Rule . . . . Dying*
_____. *The Rule . . . Dying*; in which . . . instruments of preparing our selves and others respectively for a blessed death; and the remedies against the evils and temptations proper to the state of sickness; together with prayers and acts of virtue to

be used by sick and dying persons . . . to which are added rules for the visitation of the sick. London, 1710[21]; New York, 1876; also in Reginald Heber (ed.), *The Whole Works of Jeremy Taylor*. London, 1847–54, vol. IV (also in German).

TEF
Theological Education Fund (WCC).

Tennekes, *El movimiento*
Tennekes, Hans. *El movimiento pentecostal en la sociedad chilena*. Publicaciones occasionales, no. 1. Iquique, Chile: Centro de Investigación de la Realidad del Norte, 1985.

Tennekes, "Mouvement Pentecôtiste"
———. "Mouvement Pentecôtiste Chilien et la politique." *Social Compass: International Review of Socio-Religious Studies* 25/1, 1978, 55–88.

"Tenth Annual Convention"
"Report of the Tenth Annual Convention of the World's Christian Fundamentalist Association: Chicago, 13–20 May," 1928. In *Christian Fundamentalist* 12, 1.6.1928, 3–10.

ter Haar, "Strangers"
ter Haar, Gerrie. "Strangers in the Promised Land. African Christians in Europe." *Exchange* 24/1, 1995, 1–31.

Theissen, *Urchristliche*; English: *Miracle*
Theissen, Gerd. *Urchristliche Wundergeschichten. Ein Beitrag zur formgeschichtlichen Erforschung der synoptischen Evangelien.* (Studien zum Neuen Testament 8). Gütersloh: Gerd Mohn, 1974. English: *Miracle Stories of the Early Christians*. Edinburgh: Clark, 1983. Atlanta, Georgia: John Knox Press, 1975.

Thomas, "An Angel From Satan"
Thomas, John Christopher. " 'An Angel From Satan': Paul's Thorn in the Flesh (2 Cor. 12.7–10)," *Journal of Pentecostal Theology* 9, 1996, 39–53.

Thomas, "Deliverance"
———. "The Devil, Disease and Deliverance: The Pauline Literature." SPS 1992, M.

Thompson, "Popular Religiosity in Britain"
Thompson, T. Jack. "Some Reflections on Popular Religiosity in Britain". *Int. Review of Mission* 82/327, July/Oct. 1993, 375–381.

Thoorens, *L'Union*
Thoorens, Jean. *L'Union de Prière de Charmes s/Rhône.* Mémoire de l'Institut Catholique de Paris, n.d.

Thurman, *New*
Thurman, Joyce. *New Wineskins. A Study of the House Church Movement.* IC 30, 1982.

Tiérsot, "La musique"
Tiérsot, J. "La musique chez les peuples indigène de l'Amérique du Nord." Sammelbände der Internationalen Musikgesellschaft 1909/10. Leipzig: n.p., 1910, 141–231.

Tillich, "Marx"
Tillich, Paul. "How Much Truth is There in Karl Marx?" *The Christian Century* 8.9.1949.

Tinney, "Blackness"
Tinney, James. "The Blackness of Pentecostalism." *Spirit: A Journal of Issues Incident to Black Pentecostalism* 3/2, 1979, 27–36.

Tinney, "Seymour"
———. "William J. Seymour (1855?–1920?): Father of Modern Day Pentecostalism." *The Journal of the Interdenominational Theological Center* 4, Fall 1976, 33–44. Also published under the same title in *The Journal of Religious Thought* 4/1, 1976, 33–44 and in James S. Tinney and Stephen N. Short, *In the Tradition of William J. Seymour: Essays Commemorating the Dedication of Seymour House at Howard University.* Washington, D.C.: Spirit Press, 1978, 10–20.

Tippett, *Child*
Tippett, Michael. *A Child of Our Time. Oratorio.* London: Schott & Co. 1944.

Tomlin, *Black Preaching Style*
    Tomlin, Carol. *Black Preaching Style*. M.Phil. University of Birmingham, 1988.
Tomlinson, *Conflict*
    Tomlinson, A. J. *The Last Great Conflict*, 1913. Reprint in *The Higher Christian Life*, vol. 46.
Tonks, *Decision-Making*
    Tonks, Harold. *Faith, Hope and Decision-Making. The Kingdom of God and Social Policy Making. The Work of Arthur Rich of Zurich*. IC 35, 1984.
Torkelson, "Filled"
    Torkelson, Willmar. "They're Filled With the Spirit," *This Month* (WCC) no. 21, Aug. 1972, 3–4.
Tortorelli, *I Pentecostali*
    Tortorelli, Doménico Gentile. *I Pentecostali nella provincia di Matera*. Ph.D. University of Bari, 1966/67, unpubl.
Traettino, *Pentecostale*
    Traettino, Giovanni. *Il movimento pentecostale in Italia (1908–1959)*. Ph.D. University of Naples, 1970/71, unpubl.
Tschuy, "Lateinamerika"
    Tschuy, Theo. "Lateinamerika im Umbruch." *Der Wanderer von Land zu Land* 37/1, 1963, 1–4.
Tugwell, *Catholic Pentecostalism*
    Tugwell, Simon. *Catholic Pentecostalism. An Evaluation*. London: Catholic Truth Society, 1973.
Tugwell, "Gift"
    ———. "The Gift of Tongues in the New Testament." *Expository Times* 84/5, Feb. 1973, 137–40.
Tugwell, *Receive*
    ———. *Did You Receive the Spirit?* London: Darton, Longman & Todd, 1972.
Tugwell, "Reflections"
    ———. "Reflections on the Pentecostal Doctrine of the 'Baptism in the Holy Spirit.' " *Heythrop Journal* 13/3, July 1972, 268–81; 13/4, Oct. 1972, 402–414.
Tugwell, "The Speech-Giving Spirit"
    ———. "The Speech-Giving Spirit." In Simon Tugwell, Peter Hocken, George Every, John Orme Mills, *New Heaven? New Earth? An Encounter with Pentecostalism*. London: Darton, Longman & Todd, 1976, 119–60.
Turner, *Independent Church*
    Turner, Harold W. *An African Independent Church. The Life and Faith of the Church of the Lord (Aladura)*. Oxford: University Press, 1967, 2 vols.
Turner, "Nigeria"
    ———. "Pentecostal Movements in Nigeria," *Orita* 6/1, 1972, 39–47.
Turner, "Patterns"
    ———. "Patterns of Ministry and Structures Within Independent Churches." In Fasholé-Luke, *Christianity in Independent Africa*, 44–59.
Tutu, "Whither African Theology?"
    Tutu, Desmond M. "Whither African Theology?" In Fasholé-Luke, *Christianity in Independent Africa*, 364–69.
Twelftree, *Christ Triumphant*
    Twelftree, G. *Christ Triumphant. Exorcism Then and Now*. London: Hodder & Stoughton, 1985.
"Unity"
    "The Unity of the Church and the Unity of Mankind." *Study Encounter* 5/4, 1969, 163–81 (WCC).
Upham, "Congress"
    Upham, Thomas C. "Essay on a Congress of Nations." In American Peace Society, *Prize Essays on a Congress of Nations*, 1840.

Upham, *Life*
_____. *The Life of Faith*. 1845. Reprint in *The Higher Christian Life*, vol. 47.
Upham, *Manual*
_____. *The Manual of Peace*. Brunswick, 1836.
Ustorf, *Afrikanische Initiative*
Ustorf, Werner. *Afrikanische Initiative. Das aktive Leiden des Propheten Simon Kimbangu*. IC 5, 1975.
Valencia, *En tierra extraña*
Valencia, Eduardo et al. *En tierra extraña: itinerario del pueblo pentecostal chileno*. Santiago: Editorial Amerinda, 1988.
Valle, "Psicologia"
Valle, Edenio, svd. "Psicologia Social e Catolicismo Popular." *Revista Eclesiástica Brasileira* 36/141, March 1972.
van der Laan, C., "Holland"
van der Laan, Cornelis. "The Pentecostal Movement in Holland, Its Origins and Its International Position." *Pneuma* 5/1, Fall 1983, 30–38.
van der Laan, C., "Proceedings"
_____. "The Proceedings of the Leaders' Meetings (1908–1911) and of the International Pentecostal Council (1912–14)." *EPTA Bulletin* 6/2, 1987, 36–49.
van der Laan, C., "Portret"
_____. "Portret van Alexander Alfred Boddy (1854–1930)." *Parakleet* (Holland) 11/39, 1991, 11–14.
van der Laan, C., *Sectarian Against His Will*
_____. *Sectarian Against His Will: Gerrit Roelof Polman and the Birth of Pentecostalism in the Netherlands* (Studies in Evangelicalism 11). Metuchen, N.J. and London: Scarecrow Press, 1991.
van der Laan, C. "Seymour"
_____. "Portret van William Joseph Seymour (1870–1922)," *Parakleet* 11/38, 1991, 7–11.
van der Laan, C., "Theology"
_____. "The Theology of Gerrit Polman: Dutch Pentecostal Pioneer." *EPTA Bulletin* 8/1, 1989, 13–33.
van der Laan, C. and P., *Pinksteren*
_____. and Paul van der Laan. *Pinksteren in beweging: Vijfenzwentig jaar pinkstergeschiedenis in Nederland en Vlaanderen*. n.p., n.d.
van der Laan, P., "Dynamics"
van der Laan, Paul. "Dynamics in Pentecostal Mission: A Dutch Perspective." *Int. Review of Mission* 75/297, Jan. 1986, 47–50.
van der Laan, P., "Hollenweger"
_____. "Walter J. Hollenweger: A Pluriform Life." In Jongeneel 1992, 5–14.
van der Laan, P., *Question*
_____. *The Question of Spiritual Unity: The Dutch Pentecostal Movement in Ecumenical Perspective*. Ph.D. University of Birmingham, 1988.
Vanelderen, "Conference"
Vanelderen, Marlin. "Pentecostal World Conference." *Dictionary of the Ecumenical Movement*. Geneva: WCC, 1991, 792.
Vanelderen, "WCC"
_____. "WCC, Membership of." *Dictionary of the Ecumenical Movement*. Geneva: WCC, 1991, 1098–1100.
van Gijs, *Het*
van Gijs, Jan. *Het feest gat door*. Gorinchem: Kracht van Omhoog, 1962.
van Wing, "Kimbanguisme"
van Wing, J. "Le Kimbanguisme (sic) vu par un témoin." *Zaïre* 12/6, 1958, 563–618.
Veenhof, "Charisma"
Veenhof, J. "Charisma—bovennatuurlijk of natuurlijk?" In *Ervaren waarheid. Festschrift voor Prof. Dr. H. Jonke*, Nijkerk, 1984, 130–33.

Vergara, "Avance"
      Vergara, Ignacio. "Avance de los 'Evangélicos' en Chile." *Mensaje* 3/41, Aug. 1955, 257–62.
Vergara, *Protestantismo*
      _____. *El protestantismo en Chile.* Santiago: Editorial del Pacifico, 1962.
Vernaud, "Congo"
      Vernaud, J. "Congo." *Viens et Vois* 37/6, June 1969, 23f.; 37/7–8, July–Aug. 1969, 20f.; 36/10, Oct. 1968, 21f.
Vezzosi, *Scrittori*
      Vezzosi, A. F. *Scrittori dei Chierici Regorali.* Rome, 1780.
Vidal, M. and Ana, *El pentecostal*
      Vidal, M. and Ana. *El pentecostal y "su actitud socio-politica en el Chile hoy."* (Estudio socio-religioso 1). Concepción, Chile: Cemuir, 1986.
Villafañe, *The Liberating Spirit*
      Villafañe, Eldin. *The Liberating Spirit. Toward an Hispanic American Pentecostal Social Ethic.* Grand Rapids, Mich.: Eerdmans, 1993.
Villafañe, "Call"
      _____. "A Pentecostal Call to Social Spirituality." Society for Pentecostal Studies, 1990.
Vischer, *Spirit*
      Vischer, Lukas (ed.). *Spirit of God, Spirit of Christ. Ecumenical Reflections on the Filioque Controversy.* London: SPCK; Geneva: WCC, 1981.
Vivier, *Glossolalia*
      Vivier, van Eetveldt L. M. *Glossolalia.* Med.Diss. University of Witwatersrand, South Africa, 1960.
Vivier, "Glossolalic"
      _____. "The Glossolalic and His Personality." In Th. Spoerri (ed.), *Beiträge zur Ekstase.* Basel and New York: S. Karger, 1968, 153–75.
Vogt, *Bibelarbeit*
      Vogt, Theophil. *Bibelarbeit. Grundlegung und Praxismodelle einer biblisch orientierten Erwachsenenbildung.* Stuttgart: W. Kohlhammer, 1985.
Volf, "Exclusion and Embrace"
      Volf, Miroslav. "Exclusion and Embrace: Theological Reflections in the Wake of 'Ethnic Cleansing.' " *Journal of Ecumenical Studies* 29/2, Spring 1992, 230–46.
Volf, "Human Work"
      _____. "Human Work, Divine Spirit, and New Creation: Toward a Pneumatological Understanding of Work." *Pneuma,* 9/2, Fall 1987, 173–93.
Volf, "Kirche"
      _____. "Kirche als Gemeinschaft. Ekklesiologische Ueberlegungen aus freikirchlicher Perspektive." *Evangelische Theologie* 49/1, 1989, 52–76.
Volf, "Materiality"
      _____. "Materiality of Salvation: An Investigation in the Soteriologies of Liberation and Pentecostal Theologies." *Journal of Ecumenical Studies* 26/3, Spring 1989, 447–67.
Volf, "Rhythm"
      _____. "A Rhythm of the Spirit and the Variety of Charisms: A Response to Jürgen Moltmann." *Brighton,* 38–45.
Volf, "Vision"
      _____. "A Vision of Embrace: Theological Perspectives on Cultural Identity and Conflict." *Ecumenical Review* 47/2, April 1995, 195–205.
Volf, *Zukunft*
      _____. *Zukunft der Arbeit—Arbeit der Zukunft. Das Marxsche Verständnis der Arbeit und seine theologische Wertung.* Munich/Mainz: Chr. Kaiser/Matthias Grünewald, 1987. English: *Work in the Spirit. Toward a Theology of Work.* Oxford: University Press, 1991.
von Allmen, *El Culto*
      von Allmen, Jean-Jacques. *El Culto Cristiano.* Salamanca, Spain: Ediciones Sígueme, 1986.

Vongbock, *Minjung Theology*
    Vongbock, Kim (ed.). *Minjung Theology: People as the Subjects of History.* Zed Press, 1983.
von Hornbostel, "American Negro Music"
    von Hornbostel, Erich M. "American Negro Music." *Africa* 1/1, 1928, 30–62.
von Hornbostel, "American Negro Songs"
    _____. "American Negro Songs." *Int. Review of Mission* 15/60, Oct. 1926, 748–53.
Vos, *Worship*
    Vos, Wiebe (ed.). *Worship and Secularization.* Bussum, Holland: Paul Brand, 1970.
WA
    Luther, Martin. *Werke. Kritische Gesamtausgabe* ("Weimarer Ausgabe").
Wächterstimmen
    Wächterstimmen: "Kirchliche Rundschau," Jan. 1910, 25.
Wacker, "Bibliography"
    Wacker, Grant. "Bibliography and Historiography on Pentecostalism (U.S.)." *Dictionary,* 65–76.
Wagner, "Vineyard"
    Wagner, C. Peter. "Vineyard Christian Fellowship." *Dictionary,* 871f.
Wagner, "Wimber"
    _____. "Wimber, John (1934–)." *Dictionary,* 889.
Wainwright, "Reflections"
    Wainwright, Geoffrey. "Theological Reflections on 'The Catechism Concerning the Prophet Simon Kimbangu' of 1970." *Orita. Ibadan Journal of Religious Studies* 6/1, June 1971, 18–35.
Walker, Andrew, *Restoring*
    Walker, Andrew. *Restoring the Kingdom. The Radical Christianity of the House Church Movement.* London: Hodder & Stoughton, 1985.
Walker, B., "Physical"
    Walker, B. "Physical Power." In Cavendish, *Encyclopedia,* 193–96.
Wardlaw, *Preaching*
    Wardlaw, Don M. (ed.). *Preaching Biblically: Creating Sermons in the Shape of Scripture.* Philadelphia: Westminster, 1983.
Warner, "Bell"
    Warner, Wayne E. "Bell, Eudorus N. (1866–1923)." *Dictionary,* 53.
Warner, "Frodsham"
    _____. "Frodsham, Stanley Howard (1882–1947)." *Dictionary,* 317.
Warner, "Hezmalhalch"
    _____. "Hezmalhalch, Thomas." *Dictionary,* 389.
Warner, "Pentecostal Fellowship"
    _____. "Pentecostal Fellowship of North America." *Dictionary,* 703f.
Warner, "Wigglesworth"
    _____. "Wigglesworth, Smith (1859–1947)." *Dictionary,* 883f.
Warrington, "Observations"
    Warrington, Keith. "Some Observations on James 5.13–18." *EPTA Bulletin* 8/4, 1989, 160–77.
Warrington, "Weakness in James 5:13–18"
    _____. "The Identity of Weakness in James 5:13–18." SPS 1992, N.
Washington, Booker T., *The Story of the Negro*
    Washington, Booker T. *The Story of the Negro: The Rise of the Race from Slavery.* London: Fisher & Unwin, 1909.
Washington, J. R., *Black Sects and Cults*
    Washington, Joseph R. Jr. *Black Sects and Cults.* New York, Garden City (Anchor Books): Doubleday, 1972.
Watt, *From Africa's Soil*
    Watt, Peter. *From Africa's Soil. The Story of the Assemblies of God in Southern Africa.* Cape Town: Struik Christian Books, 1992.

WCC
  World Council of Churches, Geneva.
WCC, *Consultation*
  WCC (ed.). *Consultation with Pentecostal Churches.* Lima, Peru, 14–19 Nov. 1994.
  Geneva: WCC, 1996.
WCC/Kimbanguists
  WCC/Kimbanguists. "The Kimbanguist Church in the Congo." *Ecumenical Review*
  19/1, Jan. 1967, 29–36.
WChH
  Coxhill, H. Wakelin, and Sir Kenneth Grubb (eds.). *World Christian Handbook.*
  London, Lutterworth, 1962, 1968.
Wead, *Charismatics*
  Wead, R. Douglas. *Catholic Charismatics. Are They For Real?* Carol Stream, Ill.:
  Creation House, 1973.
Weaver, *Branham*
  Weaver, C. Douglas. *The Healer-Prophet William Marrion Branham: A Study of the
  Prophetic in American Pentecostalism.* Macon, Ga.: Mercer University Press, 1987.
Weber, Emil, *Friedrich Dürrenmatt*
  Weber, Emil. *Friedrich Dürrenmatt und die Frage nach Gott. Zur theologischen Relevanz
  der frühen Prosa eines merkwürdigen Protestanten.* Zurich: TVZ, 1980.
Weber, H.-R., "Bibel"
  Weber, H.-R. "Die Bibel im Babel von Bangkok." In Philip Potter (ed.), *Das Heil der
  Welt heute. Ende oder Beginn der Weltmission? Dokumente der Weltmissionskonferenz
  Bangkok 1973.* Stuttgart: Kreuz-Verlag, 1973, 97–107.
Weber, H.-R., *Experiments*
  _____. *Experiments with Bible Study.* Geneva: WCC, 1981.
Weber, Karl, "Amerika"
  Weber, Karl. "Katholische Pfingstbewegung in Amerika." *Orientierung* 36/7, 15.4.1972,
  84–86.
Werin–Elovson, "Lidman"
  Werin, Algot and Harold Elovson. "Carl Hendrik Sven Rudolphsson Lidman." *Svensk
  Uppslagsbok,* XVIII (1956), 50f.
Wesley, *Journal*
  Wesley, John. *The Journal of John Wesley.* Standard Edition. Ed. N. Curnock. London:
  Epworth Press, 1938. In German: Wesley, John. *Johannes Wesleys Tagebuch.* In Auswahl
  übersetzt von Paulus Scharpff. Frankfurt, 1954. (The German edition was used in this
  book.)
Wesley, *Letters*
  _____. *The Letters of John Wesley.* Standard Edition. Ed. J. Telford. London: Epworth
  Press, 1931.
Wesley, "Plain Account"
  _____. "A Plain Account of Christian Perfection, as believed and taught by the Rev.
  Mr. John Wesley, from the year 1725 to the year 1755." *WW* XI, 366–466.
Wesley, "Short Account"
  _____. "A Short Account of the Life and Death of the Rev. John Fletcher." *WW* XI,
  273–365.
Wesley, *Works of John Wesley*
  _____. *Works of John Wesley.* Ed. Frank Baker. Nashville: Abingdon (in process of
  publication).
WW
  The Works of John Wesley, Grand Rapids, Mich.: Zondervan. Reprint from *The Works of
  John Wesley.* London, England: Wesleyan Conference Office, 1872.
Wessels, "Distinguished"
  Wessels, Roland H. "How is the Baptism in the Holy Spirit to Be Distinguished from
  Receiving the Spirit at Conversion?" SPS 1990, I.

Westmeier, *Reconciling*
> Westmeier, Karl-Wilhelm. *Reconciling Heaven and Earth. The Transcendental Enthusiasm and Growth of an Urban Protestant Community, Bogota, Colombia.* IC 41, 1986.

de Wet, *Apostolic Faith Mission in South Africa*
> de Wet, Christiaan Rudolph. *The Apostolic Faith Mission in South Africa: 1908–88. A Case Study in Church Growth in a Segregated Society.* Ph.D. Cape Town University, 1989, unpubl.

Whitefield, *Works*
> Whitefield, George. *The Works of the Rev. George Whitefield, M.A.* London, 1771.

Widmer, *Kampf*
> Widmer, Johannes. *Im Kampf gegen Satans Reich,* vol. II. 2nd ed. Berne: Gemeinde für Urchristentum, 1949.

Wieser, *Planning for Mission*
> Wieser, Thomas (ed.). *Planning for Mission. Working Papers on the New Quest for Missionary Communities.* London: Epworth Press; New York: WCC, 1966.

Wikisi–Yowani–Luntadila–Diata, *Mise au point*
> Wikisi, Raymond, Albert Yowani, Lucien Luntadila, Norbert Diata. *Mise au point sur le kimbanguisme,* Brussels: C.R.I.S.P. no. 47, 8.1.1960, 18–20.

Wilkerson, *Switchblade*
> Wilkerson, David R. *The Cross and the Switchblade.* New York: B. Geis Ass., 1963.

Wilkerson, *Vision*
> _____. *The Vision.* Old Tappan, N.J.: Fleming H. Revell Co. Spire Books; New York: Pyramid Books, 1974.

Wilkinson, *Church in Black and White*
> Wilkinson, John. *The Black Christian Tradition in "Mainstream" Churches: A White Response and Testimony.* M. Litt. University of Birmingham, 1992. Published under the title *Church in Black and White* Edinburgh: St. Andrews Press, 1993.

Willems, *New Faith*
> Willems, Emilio. *Followers of the New Faith. Culture Change and the Rise of Protestantism in Brazil and Chile.* Vanderbilt University Press, 1967.

"William Law."
> "William Law." *Dictionary of National Biography,* 1885ff. UK, XXXII, 236–40.

Williams, Cyril, *Tongues*
> Williams, Cyril. *Tongues of the Spirit: A Study of Pentecostal Glossolalia and Related Phenomena.* Cardiff: University of Wales Press, 1981.

Williams, Ernest S. "Your Questions"
> Williams, Ernest S. "Your Questions." *PE* 2443, 5.3.1961, 11; *PE* 2692, 9.1.1966, 17.

Williams, Rodman J., "Baptism"
> Williams, Rodman J. "Baptism in the Holy Spirit." *Dictionary,* 40–48.

Williams, Rodman J., "Breakthrough"
> _____. "Ecumenical Breakthrough." *New Covenant* 2/101, April 1973, 5.

Willis, *Kingdom*
> Willis, Wendell (ed.). *The Kingdom of God in 20th-Century Interpretation.* Peabody, Mass.: Hendrickson, 1987.

Wilson, Bryan, *Sects*
> Wilson, Bryan. *Sects and Society. The Sociology of Three Religious Groups in Britain.* London: Heinemann, 1961.

Wilson, D. J., "Branham"
> Wilson, Dwight J. "Branham, William Marrion." *Dictionary,* 95–97.

Wilson, D. J. "Brumback"
> _____. "Brumback, Carl (1917–87)." *Dictionary,* 100.

Wilson, D. J. "Cho"
> _____. "Cho, Paul Yonggi." *Dictionary,* 161f.

Wilson, E. A. G., *Making Many Rich*
Wilson, Elizabeth A. Galley. *Making Many Rich*. Springfield, Mo.: Gospel Publishing House, 1955.
Wilson, E. A., "Harris"
Wilson, Everett A. "Harris, Thoro, 1874–1955." *Dictionary*, 347f.
Wilson, E. A., "Passion and Power"
_____. "Passion and Power: A Profile of Emergent Latin American Pentecostalism." *Called*, 67–97.
Wilson, E. A., "Potential"
_____. "Latin American Pentecostals: Their Potential for Ecumenical Dialogue." *Pneuma* 9/1, Spring 1987, 85–95.
Wilson, Michael, *Hospital*
Wilson, Michael. *The Hospital—a Place of Truth. A Study of the Role of the Hospital Chaplain*. Birmingham Dept. of Theology, University of Birmingham, 1971.
Wilson, Michael, "Materialism"
_____. "The Winter of Materialism." *Journal of Theology for Southern Africa*, no. 28, Sept. 1979, 3–6.
Wimber, *Power*
Wimber, John. *Power Evangelism*. San Francisco, Calif.: Harper & Row, 1986.
Wink, *Bible in Human Transformation*
Wink, Walter. *The Bible in Human Transformation. Toward a New Paradigm for Biblical Study*. Philadelphia: Fortress Press, 1973.
Wink, *Engaging*
_____. *Engaging the Powers. Discernment and Resistance in a World of Domination*. Minneapolis: Fortress Press, 1989.
Wogen, *Jesus*
Wogen, Norris L. *Jesus, Where Are You Taking Us? Messages From the First International Lutheran Conference on the Holy Spirit*. Carol Stream, Ill.: n.p., 1973.
Wood, *Culture*
Wood, William W. *Culture and Personality. Aspects of the Pentecostal Holiness Religion*. The Hague: Mouton, 1965.
World Pentecost, "Zimmerman"
World Pentecost 28, Spring 1991, 6f.: "Thomas F. Zimmerman, a Pentecostal Statesman par excellence."
Worsfold, *Great Britain*
Worsfold, James E. *The Origins of the Apostolic Church in Great Britain and a Breviate of its Early Missionary Endeavours*. Thorndon, Wellington, New Zealand: Julian Literature Trust, 1991.
Worsfold, *New Zealand*
_____. *A History of the Charismatic Movements in New Zealand including a Pentecostal Perspective and a Breviate of the Catholic Apostolic Church in Great Britain*. Bradford, England: Puritan Press Ltd. and Julian Literature Trust, 1974.
Wumkes, "De Pinksterbeweging," 1916
Wumkes, G. A. "De Pinksterbeweging voornamelijk in Nederland." *Stemmen des Tijds* 5/11, Sept. 1916.
Wumkes, *Pinksterbeweging*, 1917
_____. *De Pinksterbeweging voornamelijk in Nederland*. Amsterdam: G. R. Polman, 1917.
Wyatt, *Birth*
Wyatt, Thomas. *The Birth and Growth of a World-Wide Ministry*. Los Angeles: Wings of Healing, n.d.
Ximénez, *Historia*
Ximénez, F. *Historia de la Provincia de San Vincente de Chiapa y Guatemala Ordinis Praedicatorum*. Ms of 1720, printed in 3 vols. Guatemala: Biblioteca Goathemalca, Sociedad de Geografia y Historia, 1–2, 1929/31.
Yoo, *Korean Pentecostalism*
Yoo, Boo-Woong. *Korean Pentecostalism: Its History and Theology*. IC 52, 1988.

Yoo, "Response to Korean Shamanism"
_____. "Response to Korean Shamanism by the Pentecostal Church." *Int. Review of Mission* 75/297, Jan. 1986, 70–75.

Zanuso, *Iglesias*
Zanuso, Hermenegildo. *Iglesias y Sectas en América Latina*. Mexico, D.F.: Libreria Parroquial de Clavería, 1986.

Zeegers, "R. K. Kerk"
Zeegers, J. "Het volle Evangelie in den R. K. Kerk." *Pinksterboodschap* 3/4, April 1962, 13.

Zeegwaart, "Apocalyptic"
Zeegwaart, Huibert. "Apocalyptic Eschatology and Pentecostalism: The Relevance of John's Millennium for Today." *Pneuma* 10/1, 1988, 3–25.

Zeegwaart, " 'Myth' "
_____. "The Concept of 'Myth.' An Attempt to Philosophically Clarify the Concept of 'Myth.' " Paper read at the European Pentecostal Research Conference, University of Birmingham, 1984.

Zeigler, "Lake"
Zeigler, James R. "Lake, John Graham." *Dictionary*, 531.

Zenetti, *Heisse*
Zenetti, Lothar. *Heisse (W)Eisen. Jazz, Spirituals, Beatsongs, Schlager in der Kirche*. Munich: J. Pfeiffer, 1966.

Ziegler, *Zwingli*
Ziegler, Albert. *Zwingli, katholisch gesehen, ökumenisch befragt*. Zurich: NZN Buchverlag, 1984.

Zopfi, "Answer"
Zopfi, Jakob. "Answer to a Call for Cooperation." *World Pentecost* 9, March 1986, 9.

Zopfi, "Candid Thoughts"
_____. "Candid Thoughts on Perspectives," *Pneuma* 12/2, Fall 1990, 182f.

Zopfi, "Now What?"
_____. "1906–1985, Now What?" *World Pentecost* 6, July 1985, 3.

Zopfi, "Sind"
_____. "Sind die 'Heiden' wirklich verloren?" *Wort und Geist* 70/8, Aug. 1991, 3–6.

Zwink, "Oberlin"
Zwink, Eberhard. "Oberlin, Johann Friedrich." *Theologische Realenzyklopädie* 24 (1994), 720–723.

Index of Authors and Subjects